AA

Atlas of the World

1st Edition July 2007 for the Automobile Association

Publisher's notes:
Published by Automobile Association Developments Limited
whose registered office is Fanum House, Basing View,
Basingstoke RG21 4EA, UK. Registered number 1878835.

Hardback edition with slipcase
ISBN-13: 978 0 7495 5306 7
ISBN-10: 0 7495 5306 5

Hardback edition (without slipcase)
ISBN-13: 978 0 7495 5095 0
ISBN-10: 0 7495 55095 3

A CIP catalogue record of this atlas is available from The British Library.

Printer
Printed in U.A.E. by Oriental Press, Dubai.

Front cover photographs:
AA World Travel Library:
tl C Sawyer; tc A Kouprianoff; tr K Paterson; cl N Sumner;
c C Sawyer; cr B Davies; bl D Corrance; bc G Marks; br P Kenward.

Photographs:
p11 L Cook/Science Photo Library
p13 R Royer/Science Photo Library
p15 R Edmaier/Science Photo Library
p17 K Svenson/Science Photo Library

AA

Atlas of the World

Contents

Key map 6
An Introduction to our World 8-23
Our star and our neighbours 10
The Earth and the Moon 12
A world in motion 14
Shaping the Earth 16
Contrasting conditions 18
Peopling the Globe 20
The Population Explosion 22
Country facts and flags 24
Key to map symbols 40
World political 42

Europe

Europe *physical* 44
Europe *political* 46
Scandinavia 48
Central Europe 50
Germany 52
Benelux 54
British Isles 56
France 58
Spain and Portugal 60
The Alpine States 62
Italy 64
The Balkans 66
Greece and Western Turkey 68
European Russia 70

Asia

Asia *physical* 72
Asia *political* 74
Northwest Asia 76
Northeast Asia 78
Eastern China 80
Japan and Korea 82
Southeast Asia 84
Malaysia and Indonesia 86
Southern Asia 88
The Middle East 90
Turkey 92
Israel and the Gulf States 94

Africa

Africa *physical* 96
Africa *political* 98
Northeast Africa 100
Northwest Africa 102
West Africa 104
Central Africa 106
Southern Africa 108

Oceania

Oceania *physical* 110
Oceania *political* 112
Australia 114
New Zealand 116

North America

North America *physical* 118
North America *political* 120
Canada 122
United States 124
Northwest United States 126
Northeast United States 128
Southeast United States 130
Southwest United States 132
Central America and the Caribbean 134

South America

South America *physical* 136
South America *political* 138
Northern South America 140
Southern South America 142
Polar Regions 144

Index to country maps 145
Glossary 146
Index 147-192

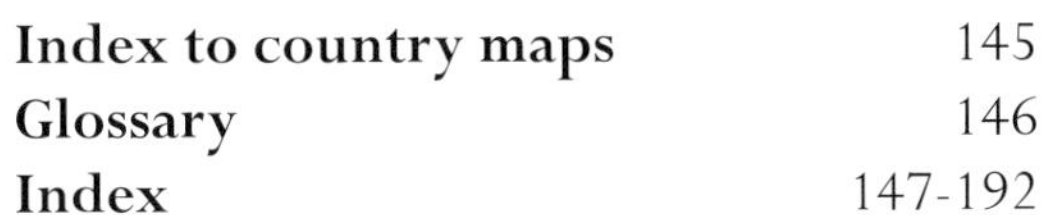

Key Map

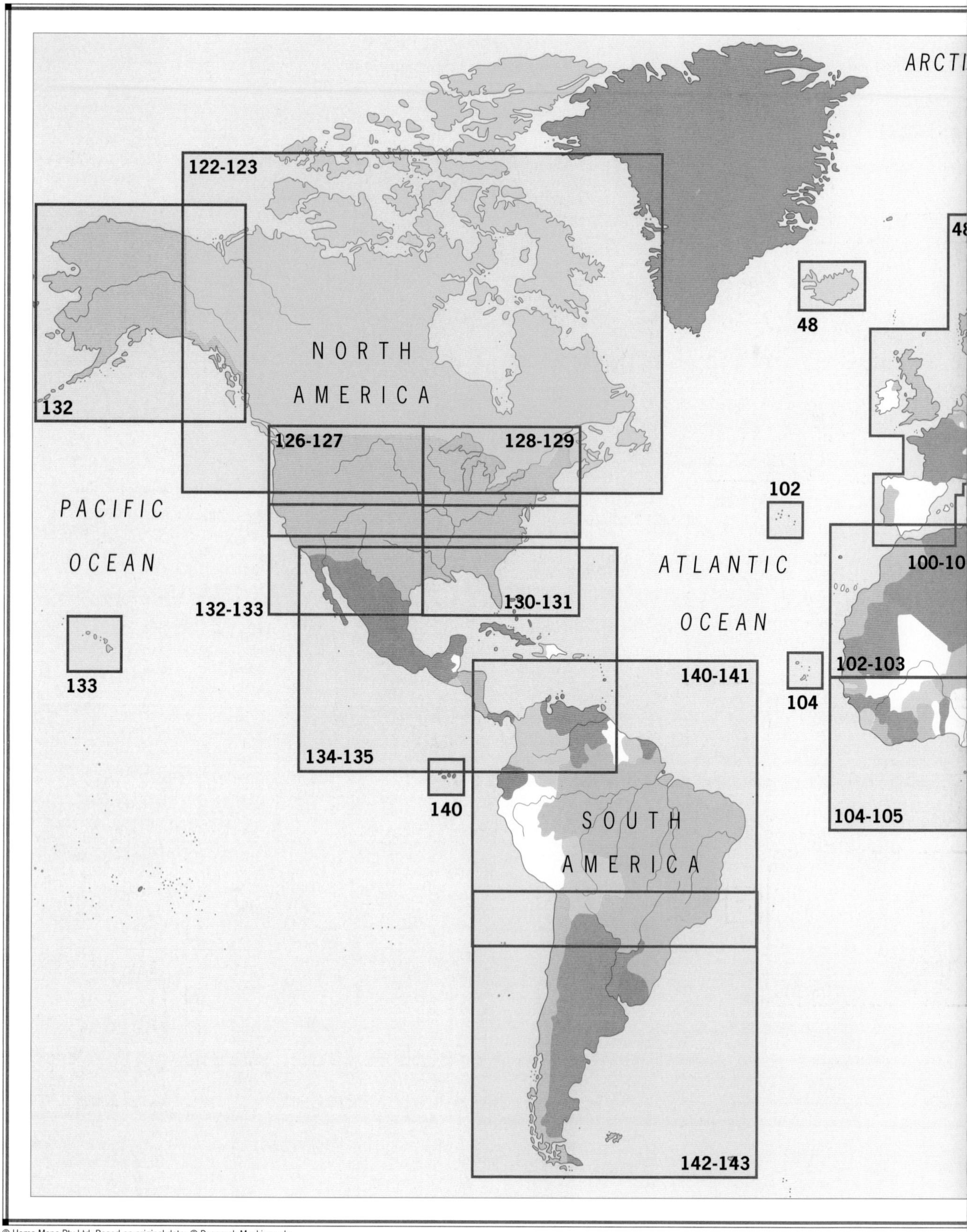

KEY TO CONTINENTAL RECORD SYMBOLS

- Highest point
- Lowest point
- Lowest average annual rainfall
- Highest average annual rainfall
- Longest river
- Largest lake

Europe	44-47	Africa	96-99	North America	118-121	Polar	144
Asia	72-75	Oceania	110-113	South America	136-139	Index	145-192

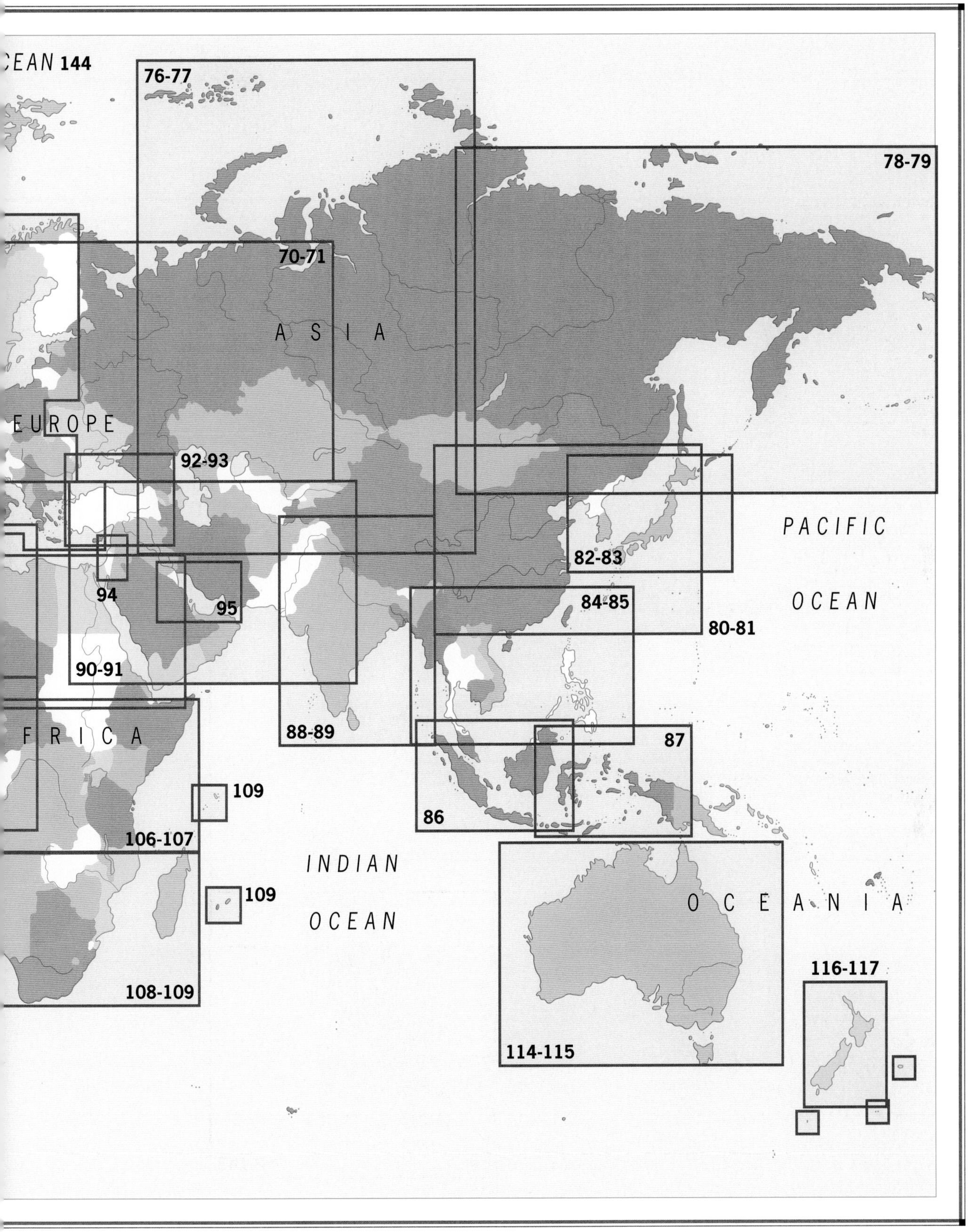

The first eight symbols show the most extreme value of the feature described, as well as its location. If that description is in ***bold****, it is not only the continental record, but also the World record.*

Coldest place

Hottest place

Estimated population

Population density

Land area

Number of countries (including dependencies)

An introduction to our

World

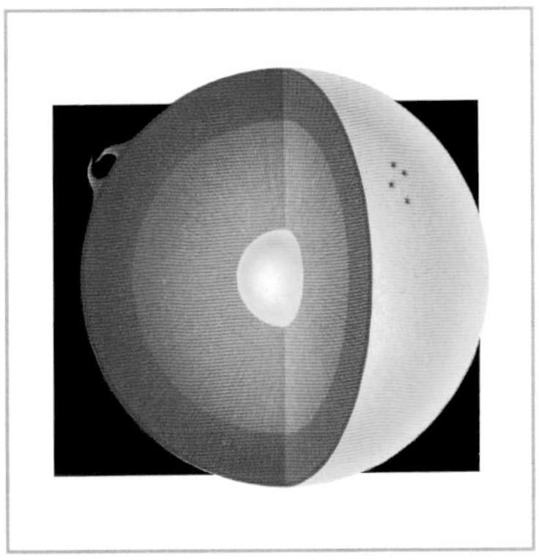

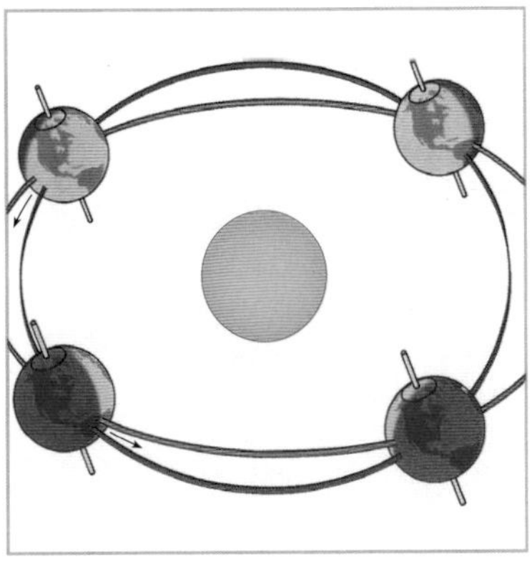

Our Star and our Neighbours

The Earth is one member of a Solar System of nine planets orbiting our local star – the Sun. All these bodies formed from a single cloud of gas and dust around 4.5 billion years ago as it was compressed, possibly by shockwaves from a giant supernova explosion. The centre of the cloud collapsed most rapidly, becoming denser and attracting more material until eventually it reached a point so hot and dense that nuclear reactions began inside it. These reactions continue today and are the source of the sunlight that heats our planet and sustains life. The Sun is critical to the regulation of our climate and environment – fine alterations in Earth's orbit are thought to cause periodic ice ages, so we are fortunate that the Sun is not likely to change drastically for another 5 billion years.

On a shorter scale, the Sun's output does have slight fluctuations. A cycle of sunspot formation (comparatively cool regions of the Sun's surface caused by magnetic activity), reaches a maximum every 11 years. From 1645–1705 almost no sunspots were seen, a dip in solar activity which coincided with a 'mini-Ice Age' of unusually low temperatures on Earth.

Once the Sun had formed, a disk of material would have been left outside the newly-formed star, which condensed to form the planets. Particles in the gas and dust cloud collided and stuck together, becoming increasingly larger bodies. Eventually these 'proto-planets' were pulled into a spherical shape by their increasing gravity.

The Solar System we see today reflects the composition of that gas and dust cloud, and divides into two regions. The inner portion contains the four terrestrial (Earth-like) planets – from Mercury orbiting close to the Sun, through Venus and Earth, to Mars. Beyond the orbit of Mars lies the asteroid belt, a ring of rocky debris, outside which are the gas giants, enormous planets created where the cloud bulged with huge quantities of gas.

The inner rocky worlds

The terrestrial planets are all very different. Mercury is a small, baking world, quite similar to our own Moon, and covered in craters. Venus is shrouded in a thick atmosphere of carbon dioxide and toxic molecules, with a surface pressure 95 times that of Earth's atmosphere, and temperatures of 470°C.

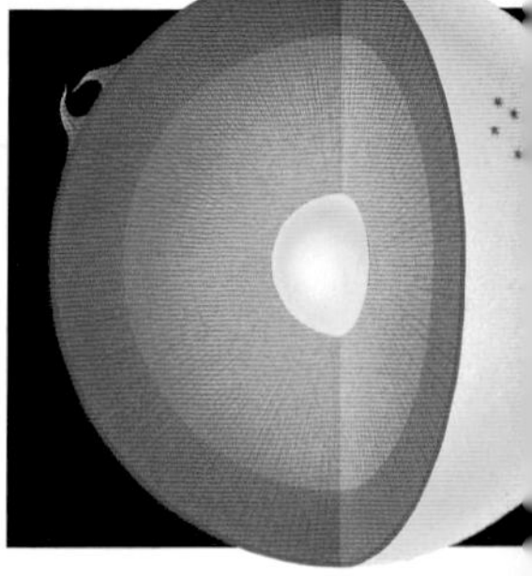

▶ THE SUN
The Sun is a massive ball of hydrogen gas **[B]**, *1.39 million km across. Energy is generated at its heart, where temperatures exceed 15 million°C, by nuclear fusion – the joining together through a chain reaction of two hydrogen atoms to form one helium. In the process, a large amount of excess energy is released, carried to the surface of the Sun in giant convection cells, and then radiated across the Solar System from the top of the 'photosphere' – the visible disk of the Sun, with a temperature of 5500°C.*

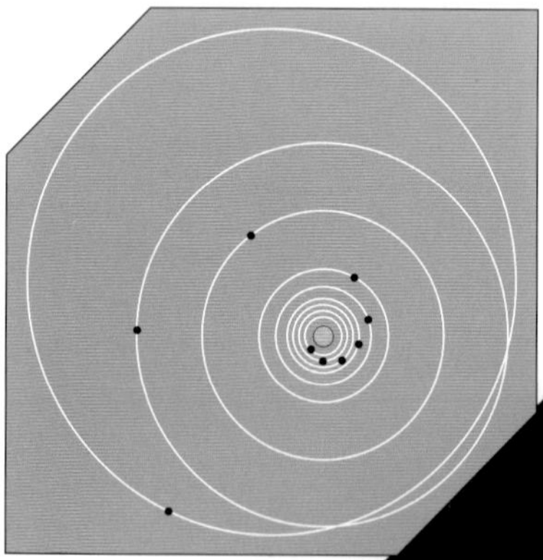

◀ THE SOLAR SYSTEM
The solar system consists of 9 planets **[A]**: *Pluto [1], the smallest, is the furthest away from the Sun, though once in every 248.6 years its orbit crosses inside Neptune's path. Neptune [2], the outermost of the gas giants, has a diameter of 49,400km, and orbits every 164.8 years.*

Uranus [3] is similar in size to Neptune and orbits every 84 years. All the gas giants have ring systems, but Uranus's are second only to Saturn's. The planet is tilted at over 98° to the plane of the Solar System, so it seems to roll around its orbit.

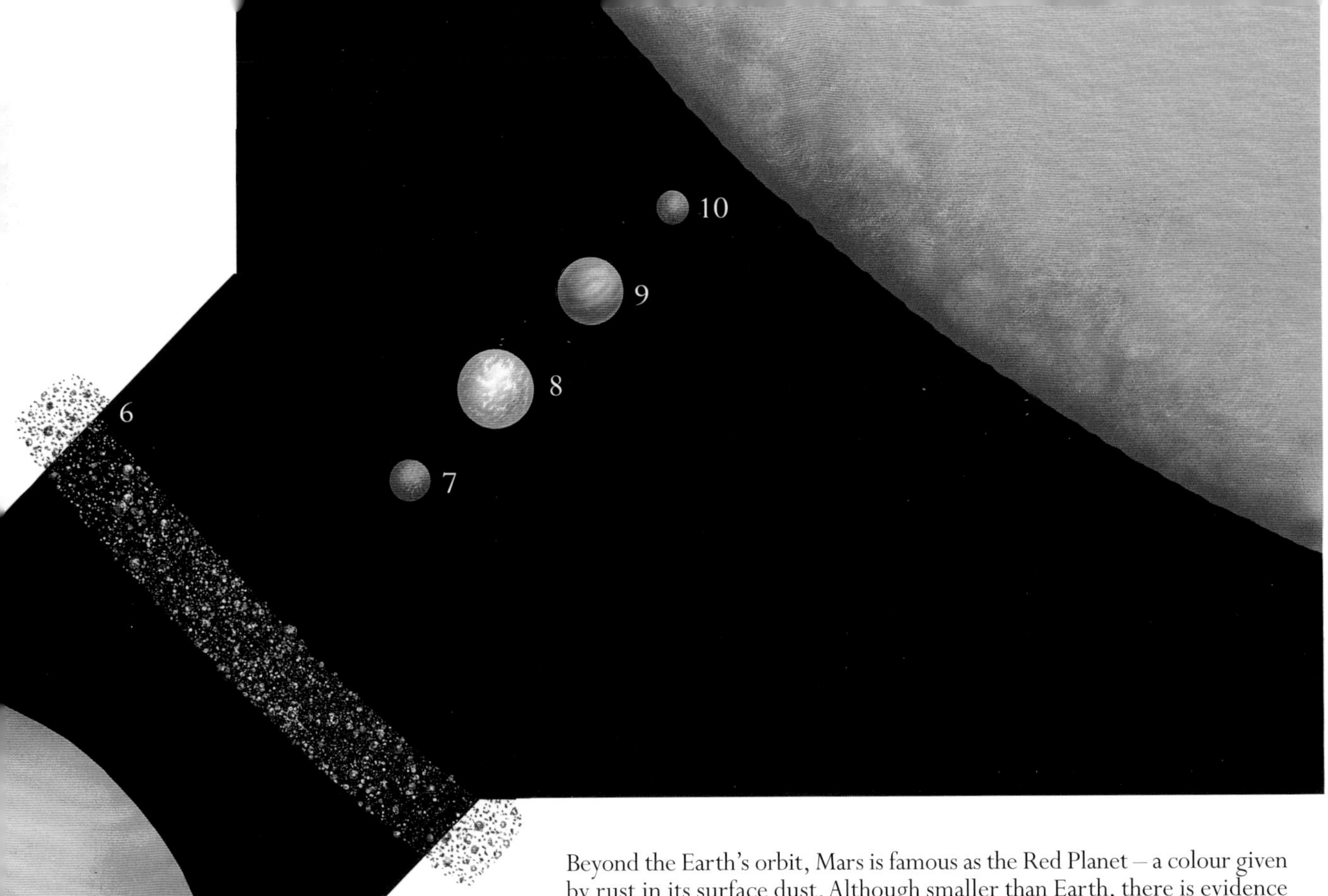

Saturn [4] is noted for its spectacular ring system – the planet has a diameter of 105,000km, while the rings stretch out to 300,000km. It orbits the Sun every 29.5 years, and has a huge family of satellites.

Jupiter [5] orbits the Sun every 11.9 years. With a diameter of 137,400km it is the largest planet in the Solar System. It has complex weather systems, including the Great Red Spot, a storm with a diameter larger than the Earth's.

Between Jupiter and Mars is the asteroid belt [6], rocky debris left over from the Solar System's formation. Inside it lie the terrestrial planets. Mars [7], the red planet, circles the Sun in 1.9 years, and has a diameter of 6790km. Its surface is scoured by massive dust storms, and it shows evidence of running water on the surface in its past. Next in towards the Sun is our own blue planet, the Earth [8], with a diameter of 12,700km. Within the orbit of the Earth lies its near twin Venus [9], circling the Sun in 225 days, and with a diameter of 12,100km. The atmosphere of Venus, however, is a poisonous mixture of carbon dioxide and other gases, with clouds of sulphuric acid. Mercury [10] is the second smallest planet with a diameter of only 4,880km, and a solar orbit that lasts 88 days. Its proximity to the Sun (58 million km) makes it a scorched world with no atmosphere, and a cratered surface similar to that of the Moon. It orbits the Sun once every 88 days.

Beyond the Earth's orbit, Mars is famous as the Red Planet – a colour given by rust in its surface dust. Although smaller than Earth, there is evidence that Mars once had a thick atmosphere, and that water ran on its surface – although now it is frozen into polar ice-caps.

The gas giants

The outer Solar System contains worlds quite different from those nearer the Sun – the gas giants. Largest of these is Jupiter, more massive than all the other planets in the Solar System put together, with churning weather systems that include the Great Red Spot, a storm large enough to engulf Earth. Beyond Jupiter lies Saturn, with its spectacular ring system of icy particles, and then the smaller giants Uranus and Neptune. Space probes have shown that Jupiter, Uranus and Neptune also have thin ring systems, although these are nothing to match Saturn's spectacle.

All four of these worlds have large families of moons orbiting round them. Jupiter has a vast family of moons, including Io, the most volcanic body in the Solar System, whose eruptions launch yellow plumes of sulphur into space, scarring its surface with streaks. The most interesting member of Uranus's satellite system is Miranda – a small, deeply-cratered world which displays so many variations in terrain that it must have suffered some great cataclysm in the past. Neptune's giant satellite Triton has active geysers shooting water, ammonia and methane 8km above its surface.

◀ *The Sun is just one of over 200 billion stars in the vast spiral of the Milky Way galaxy, like every other star that we see with the naked eye in the night sky. It lies roughly two-thirds of the way towards the edge of the galactic disc, orbiting the centre at a speed of 250 kilometres per second, taking 200 million years to complete each revolution. This view is what the galaxy would look like to an observer outside. But because of our position in the plane, we see the dense star clouds as a pale band across the sky.*

The Earth and the Moon

The Earth's satellite, the Moon, is so large by comparison with our own world (at 3746km, it is over one-quarter the Earth's diameter) that astronomers consider the two together as a 'double planet'. This massive size and proximity means that the Moon has a great influence on the Earth itself, for example through the tides.

The origins of the Moon are open to debate – some believe that the Moon is a chunk of debris flung off when the still-molten Earth collided with another body the size of Mars, in the early days of the Solar System. Since then, the two bodies have had very different histories. The Moon's small size meant that it cooled more quickly and its low gravity made it unable to hold onto an atmosphere – the factor which has been crucial in shaping our own planet's terrain. In fact, the Moon has altered so little that it provides valuable information about the history of the early Solar System. The lack of an atmosphere also means that, unlike Earth, the Moon is not shielded from the extremes of heat from the Sun. Temperatures at noon climb to 150°C, while at night they can plummet to -200°C. These acute differences can even cause moon-quakes as the surface stretches and contracts.

A familiar face

The Moon's surface divides into two distinct types of terrain, which can be easily distinguished with the naked eye from Earth. The bright highlands are highly cratered areas created more than 4 billion years ago during an era of bombardment by rock particles from space. The numbers of these particles dwindled until only a few massive chunks were left, which created enormous impact basins as they crashed into the Moon's surface. The gnarled highlands contrast sharply with the smoother, darker Maria (from the Latin for seas).

After the cratering had died away, the Moon seems to have undergone a brief period of intense volcanic activity. Red-hot fissures opened up across its surface, out of which huge volumes of lava poured, flooding low-lying areas. These lava lakes solidified to form the Maria, marked by only a few, very small craters.

Lunar attraction

The changing direction of the Sun and Moon from Earth cause our monthly cycle of tides. Twice a month, at full and new moon, the high Spring Tides occur, with Moon and Sun lined up, or directly opposed, so the tidal effect is at its strongest. Such tidal effects have influenced the Earth-Moon system as a whole. Over millions of years, the friction of the oceans' movement has slowed the lunar 'day', so it now lasts exactly as long as the time the Moon takes to orbit Earth, with the result that it always keeps the same face turned towards us.

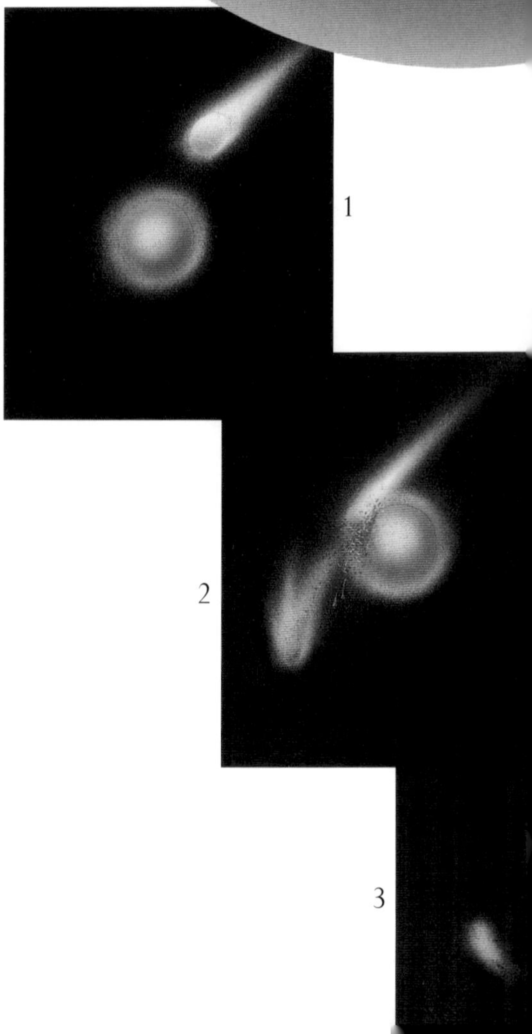

▶ *STRUCTURE OF THE MOON*
The Earth's satellite, the Moon **[B]**, *has a structure that reflects its different size, and possibly origin. Because it is a much smaller body – around one-twentieth the volume of the Earth – it has a higher surface area to volume ratio. It cooled down more rapidly early in the history of the Solar System, and is now inactive. The lunar crust [1] is actually thicker than Earth's – an average of 70km, though it is thinner on the Earth-facing side, possibly due to the tidal effects of the Earth's gravity. This could be a possible explanation of why the smooth 'seas' are found far more on this side, formed from eruptions of lava through the thin crust. Beneath this lie layers of solidified, cold rock, which decrease in rigidity. At the centre there may be a cold core [2], although its existence is still debated.*

B

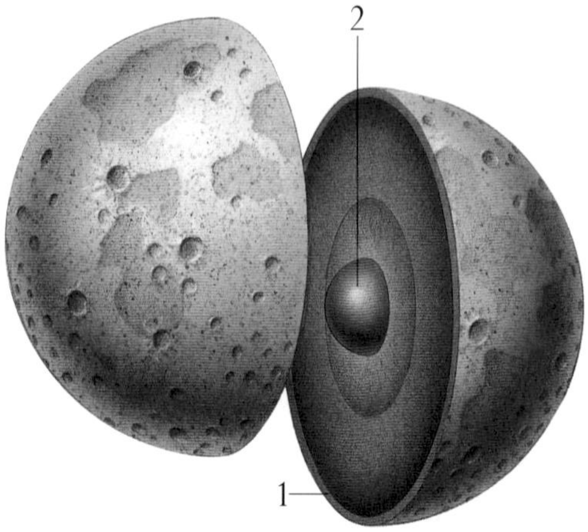

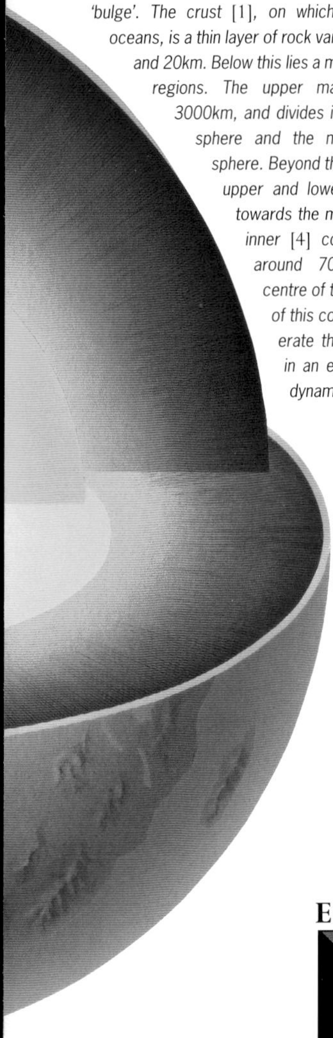

◀ THE STRUCTURE OF THE EARTH

The Earth has the shape of a squashed ball or a spheroid [A]. It has a diameter at the poles of 12,703km, but is wider at the Equator, thrown outward by the rapid daily spin which causes a 'bulge'. The crust [1], on which lie the continents and oceans, is a thin layer of rock varying in depth between 10 and 20km. Below this lies a mantle [2], divided into two regions. The upper mantle extends down to 3000km, and divides into the mainly solid lithosphere and the mostly molten aesthenosphere. Beyond this, the molten rock of the upper and lower mantle extends down towards the molten outer [3] and solid inner [4] cores of iron and nickel, around 7000km across, at the centre of the Earth. It is the rotation of this core that is believed to generate the Earth's magnetic field, in an effect similar to that of a dynamo.

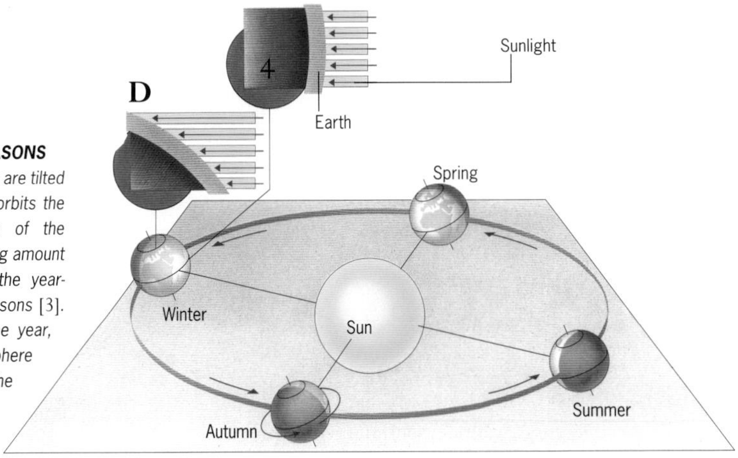

▶ THE EARTH'S SEASONS

The Poles of the Earth are tilted at 23.5° [D]. As it orbits the Sun, different parts of the globe receive a varying amount of sunlight through the year-long cycle of the seasons [3]. For six months of the year, the Northern Hemisphere is tilted towards the Sun, which therefore appears higher in the sky, giving warmer temperatures and longer days [1]. Six months later, when the Northern Hemisphere is tilted in the other direction, the days are shorter and the Sun stays closer to the horizon [2]. The situation is reversed in the Southern Hemisphere. The Tropics of Cancer and Capricorn are lines around the globe at the lines of latitude +/- 23.5°. They mark the northernmost and southernmost points where the Sun appears directly overhead.

Fossil records show that there were once 400 days in each Earth year, so the same effect must also be slowing its rotation as well. Hence in the distant future, the spin of the Earth could be so slow that its day and year are equal, so that one scorched side of the planet will permanently face the Sun.

Complete coverage

Very occasionally, as the Moon orbits around the Earth and it in turn moves around the Sun, all three bodies – Sun, Earth and Moon – line up exactly and an eclipse is seen. If the Earth blocks out the Sun shining onto the full Moon, a rather unspectacular lunar eclipse happens. Far more spectacular are solar eclipses, when the new Moon passes right across the face of the Sun. By chance the Moon and Sun have discs in the sky that are almost the same size. This means that total solar eclipses can only be seen for short periods of time from tiny regions of the Earth. The effect is breathtaking as the Moon covers the bright central disk of the Sun, and reveals the wispy white corona of gas streaming out from the Sun's surface.

◀ HOW THE MOON BEGAN

The Moon orbits too far from the Earth to be a captured asteroid. Instead, it is thought to have been formed when a body the size of Mars collided with the still-molten Earth during the formation of the Solar System, some 5 billion years ago [1]. The collision resulted in a stream of debris being thrown off into orbit round the Earth [2], and this eventually condensed to form the Moon [3]. The iron-rich cores of the two original bodies combined and remained within the Earth, becoming its very dense central region, whilst the Moon formed from the two lighter outer sections. This may explain why the Earth is thought to have a more complicated structure than the Moon, and also the lack of iron in Moon rock.

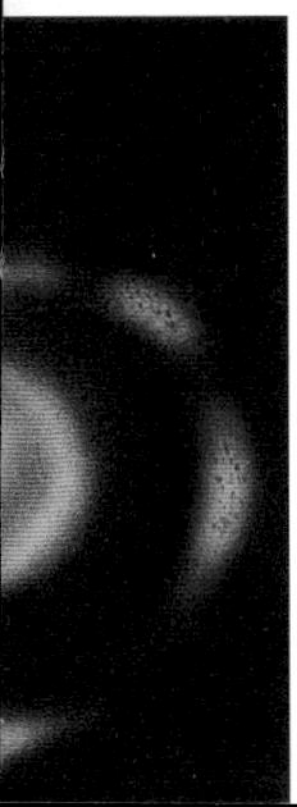

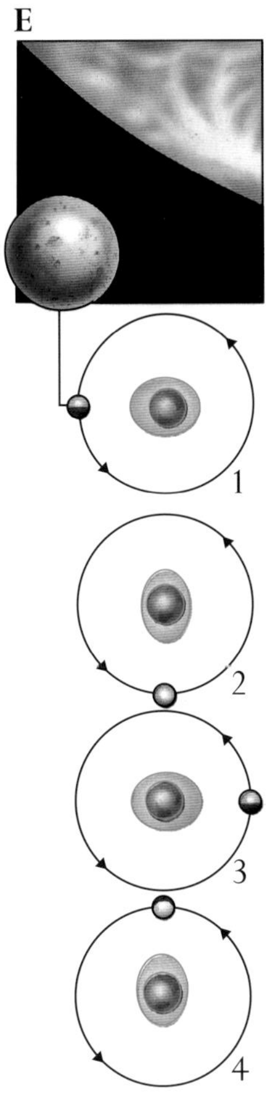

◀ HOW THE MOON AFFECTS THE EARTH'S TIDES

The proximity of the Moon to the Earth, coupled with its size, causes strong gravitational forces between the two worlds, which is shown in the tides [E].

As the Moon exerts a gravitational pull on the Earth, it draws the seas towards it, and creates a bulge in the seawater on one side of the planet. At the same time, the Earth itself is attracted towards the Moon, pulling it away from the sea on the opposite side of the globe and creating a smaller tidal bulge on the opposite side. Because the Moon is relatively slow-moving, the tidal bulges in the sea remain in almost the same place, while the Earth rotates under them [1,2,3,4]. As each bulge passes a point on the Earth roughly once each day, seashores experience two high and two low tides each day (although the shape of an inlet can alter their spacing). As the Moon circles the Earth once a month, the tides occur at different times each day.

▼ During the brief minutes of the eclipse, the corona of the Sun can be seen. Normally this is an invisible halo, made up of two distinct regions of gas which overlap, the K-corona and the F-corona. The latter reaches out many millions of kilometres from the Suns surface while the K-corona extends for a mere 75,000km.

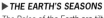

A World in motion

We think of the ground as being steady and immovable: in fact the surface of the Earth is in a constant state of movement, propelled by the intense heat of the interior. Although our planet is 12,700km wide, the crust on which the continents and oceans lie is only a few tens of kilometres thick at its deepest. This thin crust is broken into slabs or plates, which float on top of an inner molten layer, the mantle. Where these plates collide with each other or slowly draw apart are areas of violent activity, subject to earthquakes and studded with volcanoes. This drama is not restricted to dry land: satellite photography has shown that the two-thirds of Earth's surface under the ocean is just as fascinating, with features such as chains of volcanic mountains that stretch for 60,000km around the globe.

The idea that the continents are slowly moving was first put forward to explain how the coastlines of different continents appear to fit together like pieces of a jigsaw puzzle. For example, the eastern coast of South America nestles snugly into the western coast of Africa. Such continental drifts can be traced back to a point around 250 million years ago, when all the land masses on Earth were joined into a supercontinent called Pangaea (from the Greek for all earth), surrounded by a single vast sea, the Tethys Ocean. This supercontinent slowly disintegrated into the major land masses we know today.

Geologists call their model for the movements of the Earth's crust plate tectonics. This describes the surface, both continents and ocean floor, as being split into plates whose movements are driven by the churning of the molten rock in the inner mantle. The largest plates are as wide as the Pacific Ocean, while others are much smaller. Their thickness varies from around 10km beneath the oceans, to 30km under major land masses, and up to 60km where a plate has to support the weight of a mountain range. In general, ocean floor plates are made of dense basaltic rocks, while the continents are formed from less dense granite.

Earthquakes

Most of the areas where plates are separating are hidden beneath the ocean. At the fault between the plates molten rock wells up through a fissure and solidifies, creating new ocean floor. Only in a few places can this process be seen on dry land, notably in the volcanoes of Iceland, which sits on a fault called the Mid-Atlantic Ridge.

Plates can meet in a number of ways. At earthquake zones they grind past each other in opposite directions, being compressed so that they store huge amounts of energy. This is released in calamitous movements of the ground – earthquakes. The most famous earthquake zone of all, the San Andreas Fault in California, is a region where the North American and Pacific Plates are moving past each other. Earthquake prediction hinges on the theory that major quakes are preceded by 'quiet' periods during which the plates lock together, and store up the energy. Not all the plate boundaries are earthquake or volcano zones – the Himalayas are the result of a head-on collision between the relatively fast-moving Indo-Australian Plate, and the Eurasian Plate. These two continental plates buckled upwards, forming the mountain range, and halting the Indo-Australian plate's movement. Conversely, not all volcanoes are at plate boundaries. The volcanic Hawaiian Islands, for instance, lie in the middle of the Pacific Plate.

▼PANGAEA

The continents of the world have not always looked as they do today **[A]**. *The process of plate tectonics means that that they have migrated across the surface of the Earth. 200 million years ago, in the Jurassic era, all the land masses were joined in a single supercontinent, Pangaea* [1]. *Eventually, 120 million years ago, Pangaea split in two, the northern Laurasia made up of present-day North America and Eurasia, and the southern Gondwana, comprising South America, Africa, Australia and India* [2].

By 40 million years ago the world had taken on a familiar look, although India had yet to collide with Eurasia (and create the Himalayas in the process) and Australia was still located very close to Antarctica [3].

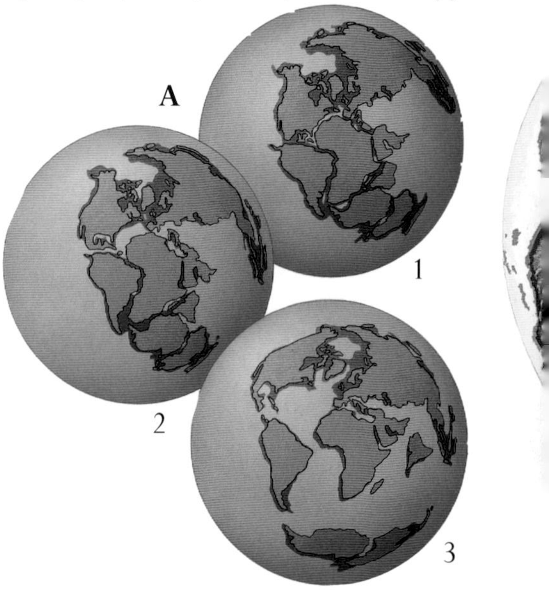

▼PLATE TECTONICS

The processes of plate tectonics can be seen most clearly on a section of ocean floor **[B]**. *At a subduction zone* [1], *an oceanic plate meets a much thicker continental plate and is forced down into the Earth's upper mantle. The heat in this zone melts the upper basalt layer of the oceanic plate, forming liquid magma which then rises to the surface and is vented through volcanoes.*

At a mid-oceanic ridge [2] *new crust is constantly being generated where two plates are separating. Magma rises up from the Earth's mantle, forcing its way through cracks in the crust, and solidifying. As the cracks expand, a striated ocean floor is formed. When the new crust solidifies, traces of iron in it align with the Earth's magnetic field and so preserve a record of the various reversals in the field over millions of years.*

A hot spot volcano [3] *forms where the crust thins above a hot plume rising from the inner mantle. It is only the latest in a string of volcanoes that form as the oceanic plate moves over the stationary plume. The earlier volcanoes become extinct, subsiding to volcanic islands with coral fringes, and eventually become atolls, where only the ring of coral remains above the surface of the ocean.*

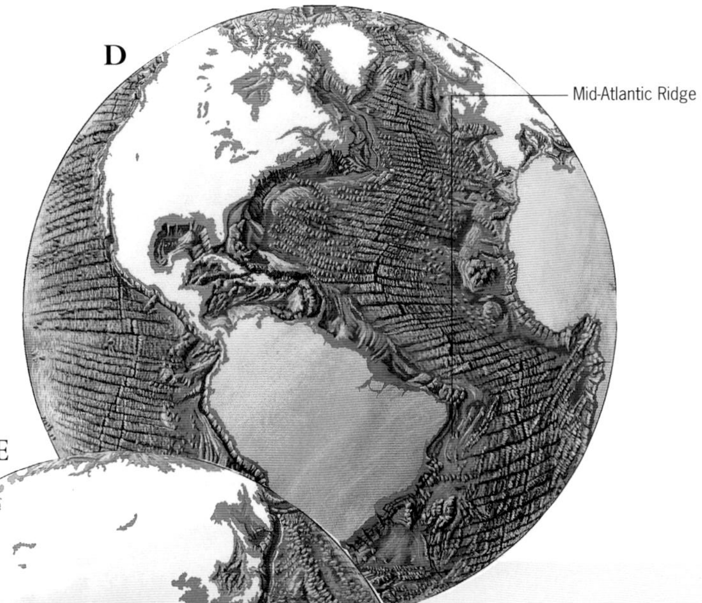

◀ ***THE ATLANTIC AND THE PACIFIC***

The floors of the two largest oceans reveal important differences in their structures.

The Atlantic Ocean **[D]** *is divided by the Mid-Atlantic Ridge that runs for its entire length, from Greenland down to the Antarctic Plate. This is a region where the Earth's crust is stretching, new floor being pumped out so that the Atlantic is gradually widening. As the rock is pulled apart, large slabs sink, creating the series of rifts that run parallel to the ridge along its length. Only in a few places does the ridge emerge above the sea, most spectacularly in Iceland, the shape of which is constantly being redefined by volcanic activity.*

In contrast, the floor of the Pacific Ocean **[E]** *shows signs of many different seismic activities. It is surrounded by the so-called 'ring of fire' – volcanic zones where the oceanic plates dive below continental ones and create volcanoes. At other places, oceanic plates converge, creating trenches where one plate dives below the other, such as the Marianas Trench, the deepest place on Earth.*

THE SEVEN SEAS

The phrase 'the seven seas' dates back to the seas known to Muslim voyagers before the fifteenth century. Nowadays, the waters of the world are divided into seven oceans – the North Pacific, the South Pacific, the North Atlantic, the South Atlantic, the Indian, the Arctic and the Antarctic. But divisions such as these are in reality arbitrary, as all these waters can just as easily be considered as parts of one continuous global ocean.

The Pacific Ocean	***The Atlantic Ocean***	***The Indian Ocean***
Water Area:	Water Area:	Water Area:
180,000,000 square kilometres	*106,000,000 square kilometres*	*75,000,000 square kilometres*
Volume:	Volume:	Volume:
724,000,000 cubic kilometres	*355,000,000 cubic kilometres*	*292,000,000 cubic kilometres*
Average Depth: *3940 metres*	Average Depth:*3310 metres*	Average Depth: *3840 metres*

▼***SEA CHANGE***

A coastal region **[C]** *is shaped by the forces of longshore drift. Sand is pushed along the shore by ocean currents to build up spits* [1]*, bars* [2] *and sometimes enclosing bays to form lagoons.*

A river carries vast amounts of sediment out to sea, which is deposited to form a delta [3]*. Under the sea, the accumulation of sediment forms the continental shelf* [4]*, a region that slopes gently out from the coastline for about 75km, to depths of 100-200m. In places it is cut through by submarine gorges, formed either by rivers when the sea level was lower or by the undercutting effect of river currents flowing out to sea. The shelf gives way to the steep continental slope, which dives to depths of several kilometres. From the base of the slope, the continental rise extends up to 1000km from the coast into the ocean.*

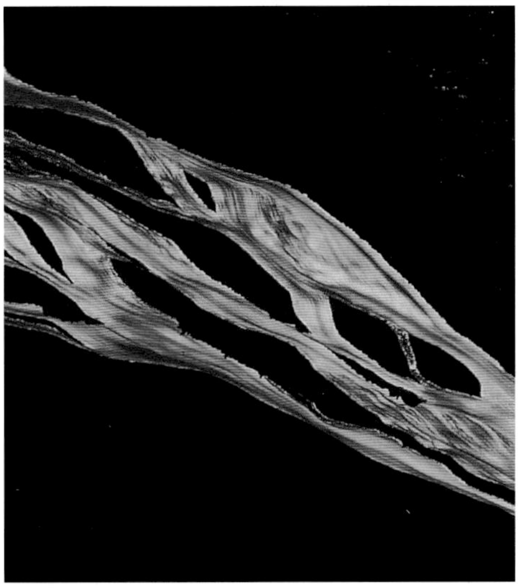

◀ *Lava which erupts from the earth's surface can take on a number of forms Aa, or block lava, is runny, and quickly forms a hard pastry-like crust when it cools. Pahoehoe lava has a sheen to it like satin and often consolidates in rope-like forms. When this kind of lava comes into contact with the sea it takes on the form of a jumbled heap of pillows, hence its name pillow lava.*

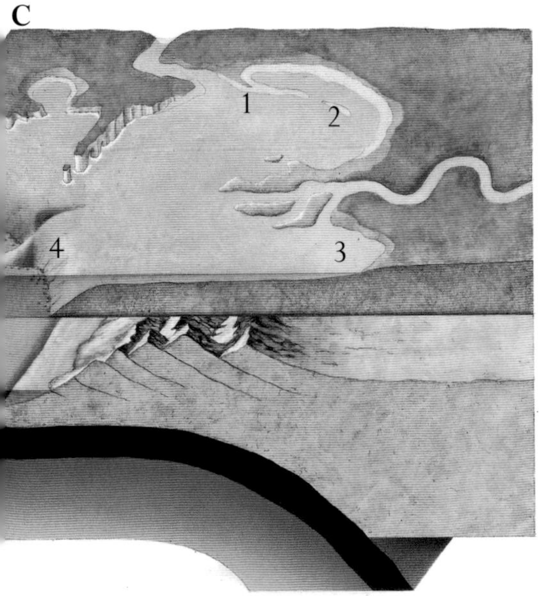

This chain of volcanic mountains is caused by a semi-permanent 'hot spot' where molten magma rises from the depths of the mantle through the crust, and spews out of a volcano. Although the hot spot in the mantle is stationary, the Pacific Plate, and with it the volcano, is continually moving. Hawaii itself is only the most recent in a chain of 107 volcanic vents formed by the plume. As the plate moves on, each volcano becomes extinct, and a new one forms further along the chain. Many thousands of these 'hot spot' volcanoes are known – mostly beneath the ocean surface – so there must be hundreds of hot plumes in the mantle to have created them all.

While plates are being destroyed in the subduction zones where they collide, new plate material is being produced all the time deep beneath the ocean surface. The sea floor is just as geologically fascinating as the continental land surface, and is still awaiting full exploration.

Occasionally, the volcanic activity of the mid-oceanic ridges reaches the surface, and forms islands. At other places, hot gases venting from the depths of the Earth create pools of warmth on the ocean floor, where life can flourish.

Shaping the World

Over billions of years, the harsh landscape created by geological activity such as plate tectonics and volcanism has been softened and sculpted by the eroding forces of ice, water and air. Glaciers have ground out valleys, and rivers have carved huge gorges, including America's Grand Canyon. At the same time the steady pounding of the seas and oceans eats away and remodels coastlines.

Studies of the changing climate in the past show that the Earth has gone through periodic 'ice ages' when the ice-caps pushed into temperate regions closer to the Equator. These periods were critical in shaping the landscape that we see today – during the last Ice Age, which ended 10,000 years ago, an ice sheet covered most of Northern Europe, Asia and North America. The ice ages can be dated by drilling out an ice core from a polar cap. Each year a layer of new ice is laid down, which in colder years – during ice ages – is thicker. These records surprisingly reveal that over the last 4 million years, successive ice ages have gripped Earth for longer than the warmer periods in between.

Variations in the Earth's climate are thought to be the result of cyclical changes in its orbit, which becomes more, then less, elongated. According to these models the Earth's average temperature should currently be on the increase – which means that the measured increases in temperature cited as evidence of global warming and the greenhouse effect may have a natural cause.

Getting in shape

During the ice ages, massive glaciers formed across the globe. As these vast, slow-moving rivers of ice rolled forward, the sheer weight of ice ground down rocks in their paths, leaving a softened, altered landscape once they had retreated. These forces are still at work today: on Greenland and in Antarctica there are many glaciers which eventually find their way to the sea, where they break up into icebergs.

Although glaciers are the most dramatic form of erosion, there are others: over longer periods, rivers and seas can cut through rock and carve out valleys. Even rain has a profound cumulative effect on rock. Raindrops dissolve gases from the atmosphere and become dilute acid, chemically attacking igneous rocks formed from volcanic lava. In time, the particles broken off build up to great depths and are converted by pressure and heat into sedimentary rocks such as limestone. When these are subjected to the intense heat of the Earth's crust they become metamorphic rocks, such as marble and slate.

▼ ***A WOBBLING WORLD***
The climate of the Earth is not constant but gradually varies over time in cycles of thousands of years **[B]**. *The shape of the Earth's orbit around the Sun can vary between an almost perfect circle* [1] *and a pronounced ellipse* [2] *over a cycle of around 100,000 years. When the orbit is more elliptical, the climate of the Earth is more extreme. At the same time, another cycle changes the angle of tilt of the planet between a minimum 21.8° and a maximum 24.4°* **[C]**. *At the maximum inclination, every 22,000 years, the climate is most extreme, and the seasons are especially marked, with the Poles pointing further away from the Sun during winter. When the effects of these cycles are combined, they lead to ice ages of varying severity, the last of which ended around 10,000 years ago.*

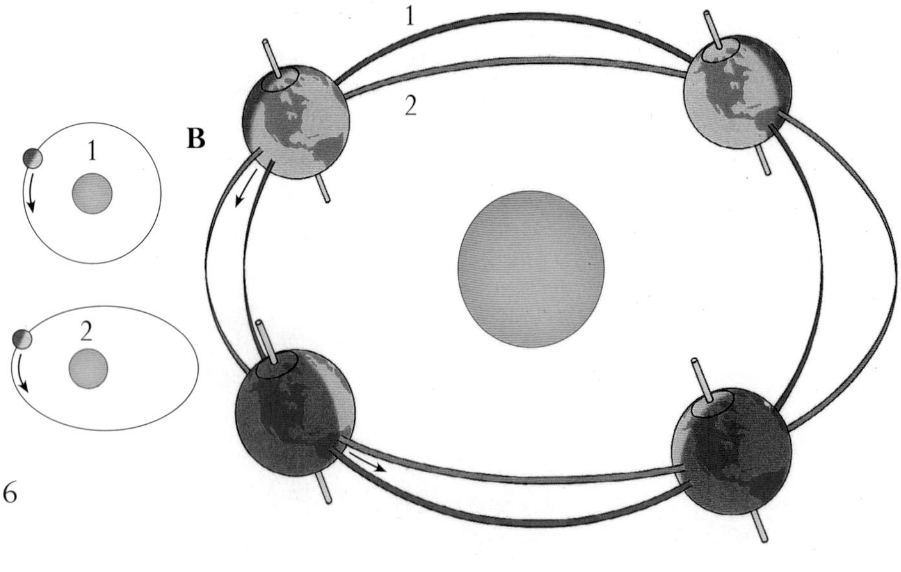

▶ ***EARTH SCRAPER***
Glaciers **[A]** *are dramatic rivers of ice slowly creeping down valleys and carving mountain ranges into a series of sharp peaks. They usually originate where ice or hard-packed snow builds up in a cirque* [1], *a basin near a mountain top. After a sufficient mass has built up, it will start to move under its own gravity, wearing down rocks by pressure, scraping and frost action, to form glacial spoil called 'moraines'. The boulders of moraine underneath the glacier act as abrasives, scouring the landscape.*
Lateral moraines [2] *are rocks cut away and pulled along at the sides of the glacier. Where two ice-rivers meet, the lateral moraines can join to form a medial moraine* [3] *– a stripe of rubble down the centre of the glacier. As the glacier grinds along over rocks and boulders, the stresses induced can open up deep and jagged splits called crevasses* [4]. *A glacier terminates at a snout* [5] *which may empty into the sea, or a great lake. On dry land the shape of the snout depends on the climatic conditions, and especially the rate at which the snout melts compared with the rate at which the glacier advances. If the the two rates are exactly balanced, the snout remains in the same place, but*

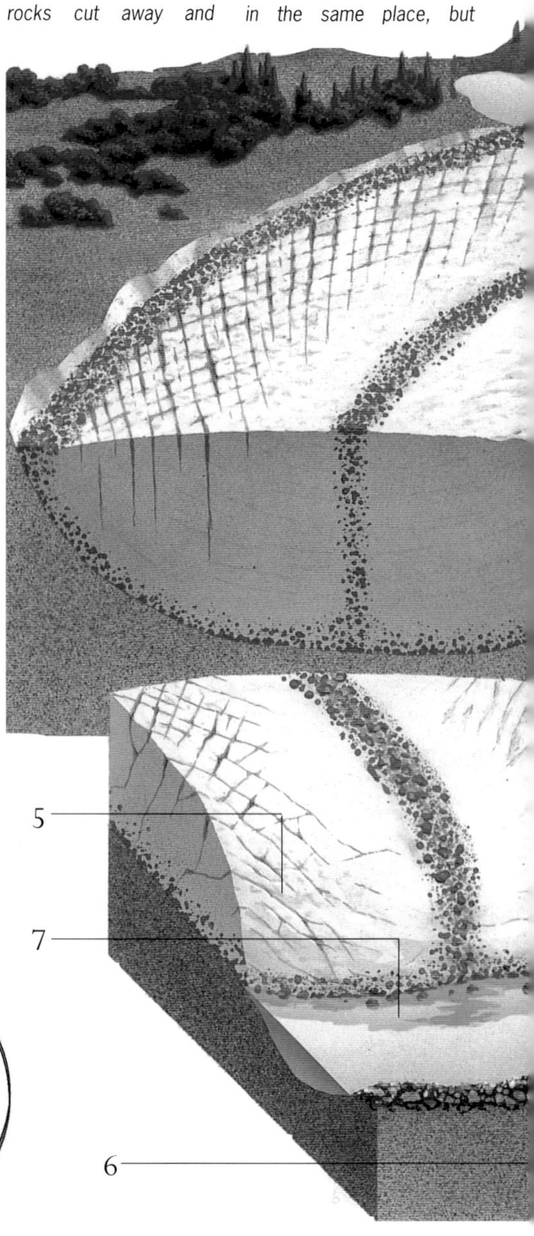

slowly deposits a growing pile of spoil.

If the rate of melting is faster than the advance the glacier slowly retreats up the valley. A terminal moraine [6] forms at the point of the glacier's greatest extent, and this pile of rubble acts as a dam which holds back meltwater in a ribbon lake [7]. Often streams emerge from beneath the cliff-like terminus of the glacier and these can excavate caves through the solid ice.

The retreating glacier will also leave tell-tale signs of its presence, such as hummocks of rock which are ground by the ice into a distinctive shape. The uphill part is worn smooth and grooved, while the downhill parts become jagged as they are split apart by melting and refreezing ice.

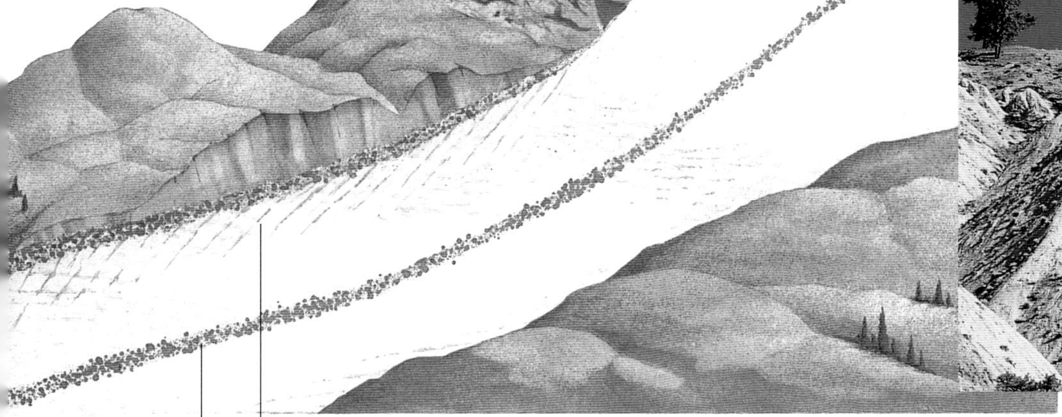

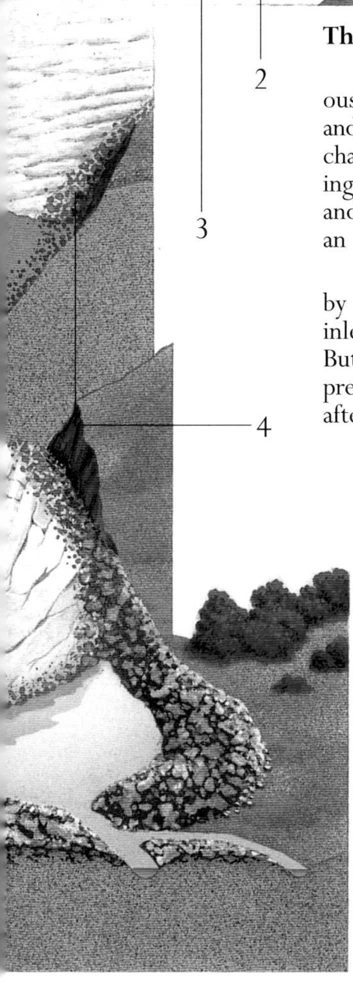

The relentless ocean

The forces of erosion can be seen on the seashore, where continuous battering by the elements destroys cliffs, carves out headlands, and creates beaches. Headlands can emerge from the sea due to sea-level changes or geological shifts. They are gradually eroded by the unceasing waves which attack them from all sides, creating caves, overhangs, and even arches under the cliffs. Often the cliff is undermined to such an extent that parts of it collapse in rockfalls.

The sand or pebbles created by this process are driven along the coast by 'longshore drift'. They form beaches, sandbanks and spits in the inlets between headlands, and eventually create a smooth coastline. But not all coastlines have reached this state: the sea only rose to its present level after the last Ice Age, and many areas are still springing back after being crushed under the weight of glacial ice.

▲ The exposed rock walls of this canyon have been caused by a process called freeze-thawing. Water enters cracks in the rock wall, it freezes and expands breaking off fragments of rock and deepening the cracks. After melting, the water trickles into other cracks and re-freezes, repeating the process. This rock surface is then further eroded by wind and rain action.

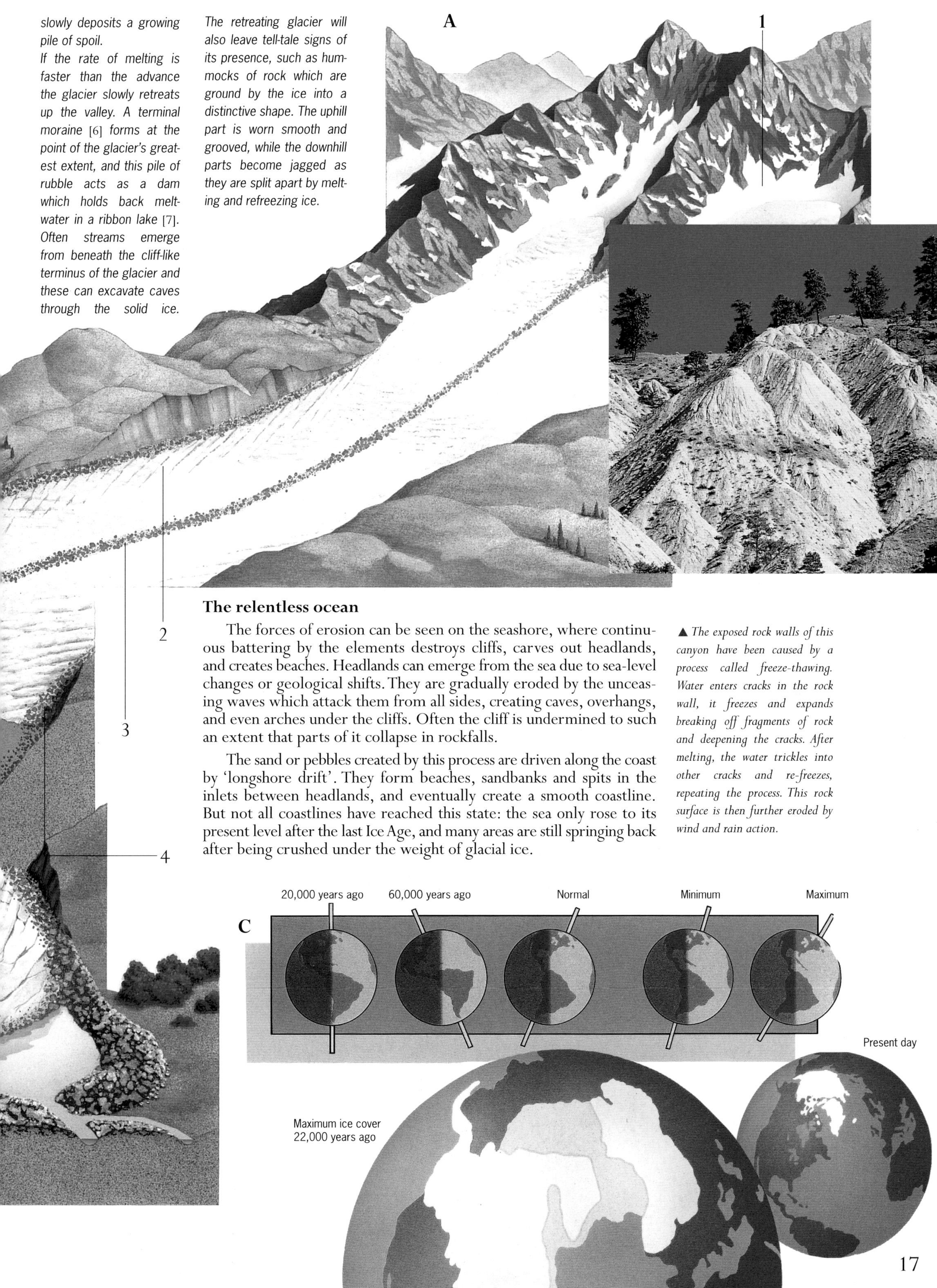

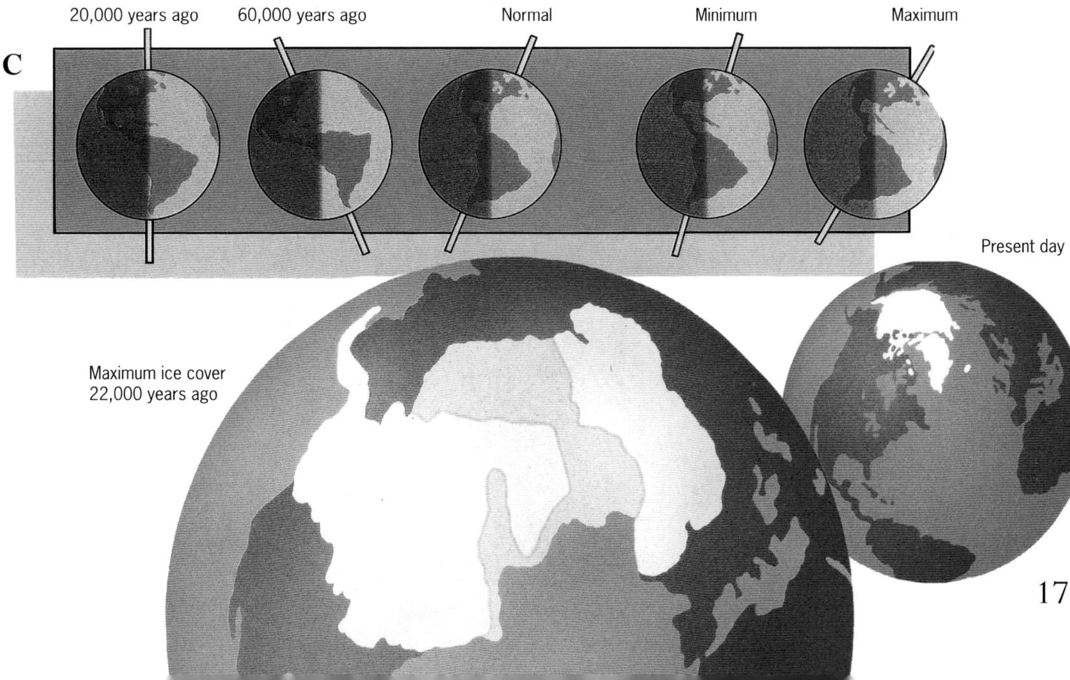

Contrasting conditions

We talk so much about the weather because of its infinite changeability. As the Sun's radiation heats up the Equatorial zones of the planet much more than the Polar regions, it creates wide temperature contrasts. The hottest places on Earth can be a blistering 50°C in the shade, while in the depths of an Antarctic winter, levels as low as -70°C have been recorded. This variable heat produces hot air at the Equator, which rises, while cooler air further north and south sinks under it, producing wind patterns that stretch across the globe. These in turn create swirling eddies of air that can absorb water vapour over the sea, forming clouds, and deposit it as rain over land. Such air currents couple with the variable heat of the Sun to produce the wide variety of climates found on Earth, ranging from hot, rainless deserts to cool, wet, temperate coastal regions.

The atmosphere of the Earth just after it formed was an unbreatheable mixture of hydrogen and helium. In time this was replaced by an equally unbreatheable mixture belched out from volcanoes, which in turn has been modified by lifeforms to the air we breathe today. This is made up of 78 per cent nitrogen, 21 per cent oxygen, and a small proportion of carbon dioxide, which plants then recycle into oxygen. The remainder of the atmosphere is water vapour and small traces of other gases. The balance is a delicate one, perfectly suited to life as it has evolved, and the entire planet – both living things and minerals – is needed to maintain it.

The outer limits of the atmosphere stretch 2400 km above the surface, but the lower 15km, the troposphere, is the densest, holding nearly all the atmosphere's water vapour – which condenses under different conditions to create clouds. Beyond this region, up to 40 km high, lies the stratosphere, which contains a thin ozone layer that blocks out harmful ultraviolet radiation.

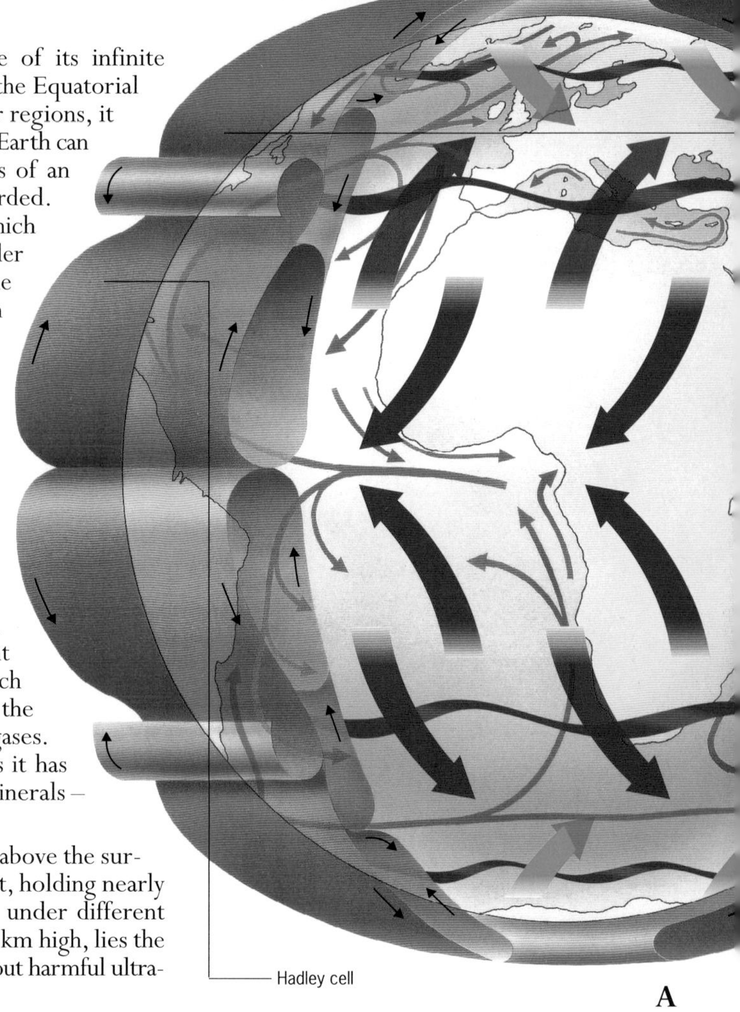

▲ ***CREATING WINDS***

The amount of heat absorbed at the Equator is much greater than at the Poles. The temperature difference creates giant circulation cells which transfer heat from the Equator to the Poles **[A]**. *The Hadley cell is driven by hot air rising from the Equator which cools and returns to the surface at 30° latitude. Some of this returning air is drawn back towards the Equator, creating the trade winds. The Ferrel cell guides warm air towards the Poles, creating winds which the Earth's rotation skews to become the Westerlies. Where these winds meet cold air blowing directly from the Pole, frontal depressions form giving unsettled weather. At the cell boundaries jet streams form – channels of high winds which encircle the planet. This circulation from the Equator to the Poles is complicated by the Earth's rotation, creating the Coriolis force which bends winds to the right in the Northern Hemisphere, and to the left in the Southern Hemisphere.*

Climate types

Land near the Equator has weather patterns typified by those of southern Asia. For six months of the year cold dry winds blow from the land out to sea, giving arid conditions and little rain. In the summer the wind reverses direction and starts to blow warm air off the ocean. This air is heavy with water vapour and triggers torrential rainstorms over land.

Weather in the temperate latitudes of northern Europe is dominated by the jet stream, a band of high winds at altitudes of about 12km. It forms where warm air from the tropics meets cold Polar air, creating a jet of air travelling at speeds around 200kmh in summer, 400kmh in winter. The jet stream's direction develops in a similar way to a slowly flowing river, meandering and forming eddies. These are seen as high-pressure anticyclones, wind systems that create clear, dry weather, or low pressure depressions with associated clouds and weather fronts.

The circulation patterns of the oceans are just as important in regulating climate. In general, the oceans circulate in large eddies, clockwise in the Northern Hemisphere, anticlockwise in the Southern.

▶ *Deserts can be created in many ways, and they may be hot or cold. The Antarctic, being one of the driest places in the world, is classed as a cold desert. The Sahara and the Arabian Deserts are classic examples of hot deserts. The photograph shows a sand dune in the Simpson Desert in Australia.*
Winds blowing over the land constantly shift dunes in ever changing patterns.

▶ *A tornado can form during a very severe thunderstorm* **[C]**. *Hot air evaporating off land or sea rises rapidly through the atmosphere, condensing to form clouds. As surface air rushes inward the low pressure at the centre of the storm, the spin of the Earth makes the whole complex spin, producing a typhoon or hurricane (right). Tornadoes occur when the fast-rising thermals, which create a storm, begin to spin even more quickly, perhaps in response to the local geography. As the thermal winds up on itself, it draws a funnel of cloud down from the bottom of the storm towards the ground, where the winds often exceed 200kmh. The extreme low pressure sucks up material from the ground, flinging it out at the top of the tornado, sometimes to land several kilometres away. Waterspouts are similar vortices that form over water.*

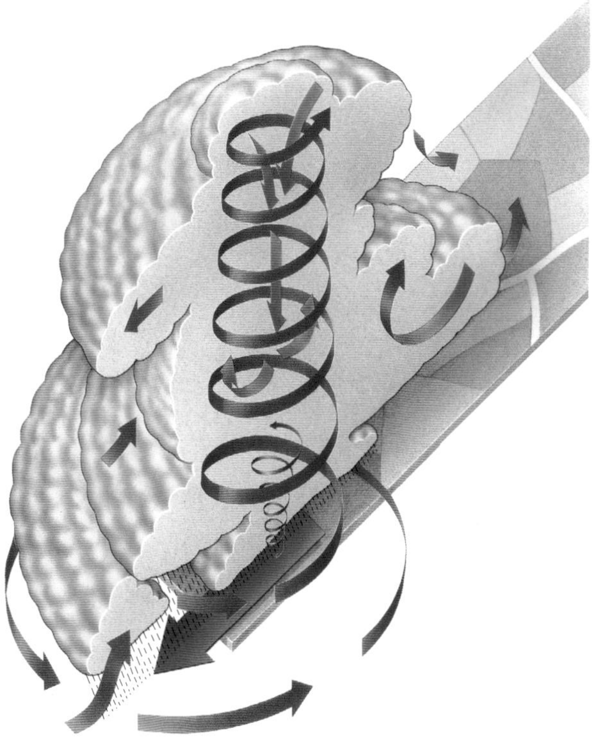

C

▶ ***VARIETY OF CLIMATE***

The patterns of rainfall and temperature around the world divide the Earth into different regions of vegetation **[B]**. *Seven cities around the world illustrate the wide variety of weather these produce.*

New York has an east coast continental climate, with cold winters, hot summers and steady rainfall all year round. London's climate is marine west coast, similarly wet to New York's but with less variation between summer and winter temperatures. Omsk has typical steppe climate, with low rainfall and very cold winters followed by hot summers. Singapore's tropical climate gives almost constant hot and very wet weather. Manaus in Brazil's region of tropical savanna has constant high temperatures, with very dry summer months. A desert climate like that of Alice Springs has very high average temperatures (with a slight dip during the southern winter months), but almost no rain throughout the year.

The Nigerian capital, Lagos, has a constantly hot tropical rainforest climate, characterised by its extremely wet summer months.

B

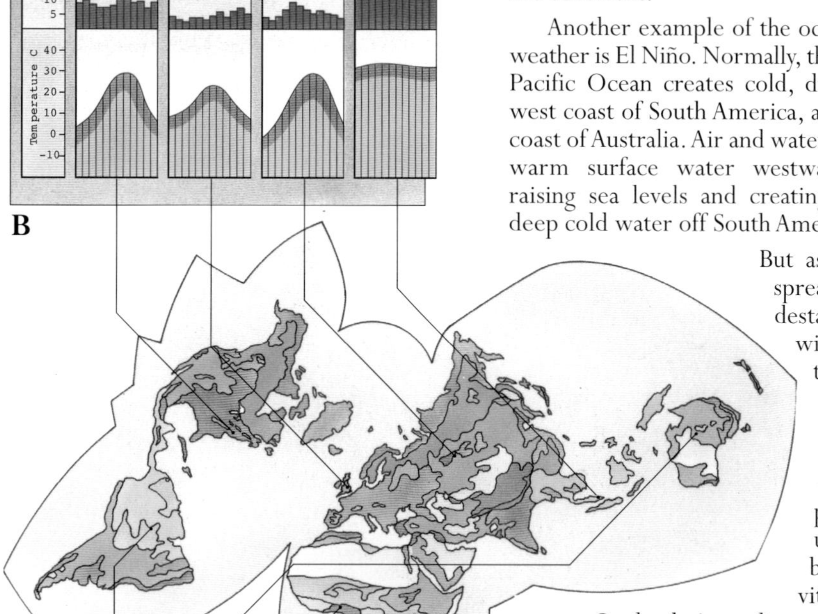

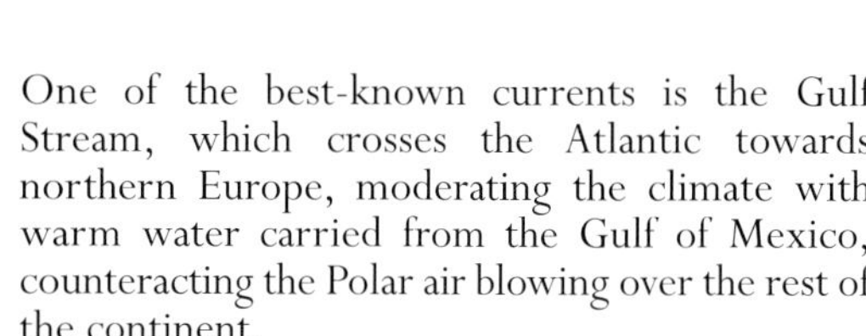

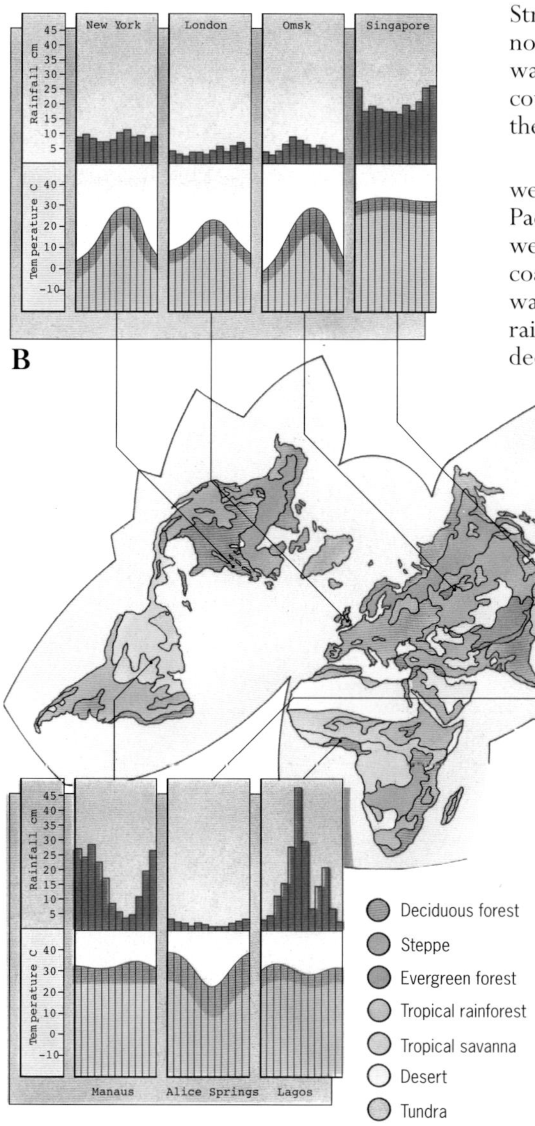

One of the best-known currents is the Gulf Stream, which crosses the Atlantic towards northern Europe, moderating the climate with warm water carried from the Gulf of Mexico, counteracting the Polar air blowing over the rest of the continent.

Another example of the oceanic effect on the weather is El Niño. Normally, the circulation of the Pacific Ocean creates cold, dry weather on the west coast of South America, and rain on the east coast of Australia. Air and water currents circulate warm surface water westwards to Australia, raising sea levels and creating an upwelling of deep cold water off South America.

But as the warm water spreads eastwards it destabilises the trade winds, which reverse their direction. The ocean circulation reverses as well, with warm water off South America preventing the cold upwelling which brings up nutrients vital to fish stocks. On land, Australia experiences drought, and South America suffers torrential rain. Such drastic climatic changes show how delicate the balance is between climate and the environment.

Major volcanic eruptions can also affect the climate, throwing dust particles high into the upper atmosphere, where they block out sunlight. Sudden climate changes are believed to have caused mass extinction of life on Earth in the past, and as yet there is little humanity can do to counter, or even predict, these changes.

Peopling the Globe

The origins of humankind are very hard to determine. The fossil record of our ancestors is very patchy, and thus the story involves large amounts of guesswork. Archaeologists believe that between 7 and 10 million years ago, a human ancestor, called Ramapithecus, developed from the same stock as chimpanzees and gorillas. The route from these creatures to modern man can be traced in terms of changing skeletons. Bipedal motion required a sturdy pelvis, while the increasing intelligence of these progenitors can be followed through increasing brain capacities. Ramapithecus was succeeded by Australopithecus, whose later form is named Homo habilis, the handy man, because fossil evidence shows that it used simple tools.

Homo erectus appeared in Africa 1.7 million years ago and spread to the rest of the world roughly 1 million years ago. They were almost as tall as modern humans, with skull capacities twice as large as Homo habilis. This species lived longer in Asia than in Africa – it includes Peking Man, who lived 250,000 years ago. It was gradually succeeded by our species, Homo sapiens, which appeared in Africa more than 500,000 years ago. The expansion was a slow drift as bands of hunter-gatherers followed prey animals. There can have been no population pressure: 10,000 years ago the world population was between 5 and 10 million, about the population of New York City today. As people settled in various places, climate and food sources led them to evolve differently. For example, those in very hot Equatorial countries kept a dark skin to protect them from ultraviolet sunlight; those in colder climates developed lighter skins to maximise the effect of a weaker sun – vitamin D, essential to bone growth, is gained from sunlight.

At first only Africa, Asia and the warmer parts of Europe were colonised: America and Australia remained empty for thousands of years. Movement between continental land masses was made possible by climate changes. During the last Ice Age, much of the world's water was locked into the ice caps. Sea levels dropped dramatically, what is now the Bering Strait became a land passage, and vast stretches of ocean became navigable by small boats.

Hunters to farmers

For two million years, human ancestors lived as hunter-gatherers, following a nomadic pattern of life, with a diet of animals and seasonal fruits.

▼THE ICE AGE

In the Ice Age, parts of Europe were covered in glacial sheets and the North Sea was a great plain **[A]**. *The climate and terrain were very like Alaska today, and herds of reindeer roamed the area. These were a main food source for groups of hunter-gatherers, traces of whom have been found in Europe, mostly in the warmer areas (southern Spain, south-west France and along main rivers). These people followed the deer herds on their grazing migrations, augmenting their diet with small game as well as vegetables, berries and grains. As the climate became warmer various groups settled near coasts to become fisher-gatherers.*

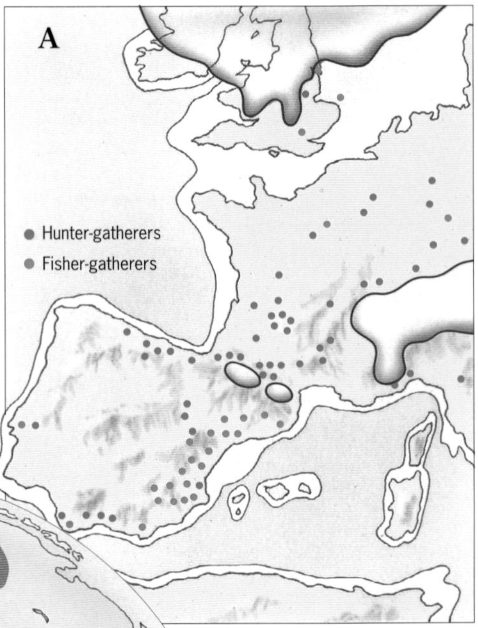

◀ HOMO SAPIENS

From central and southern Africa Homo sapiens spread out to populate the whole world **[B]**. *The first migration spread from Africa eastwards across to Asia. Routes branched off to northern Africa and southern Europe. A second wave occurred 15,000 years ago, when glaciation provided a land bridge across the Bering Strait, allowing movement from northern Asia to the Americas.*

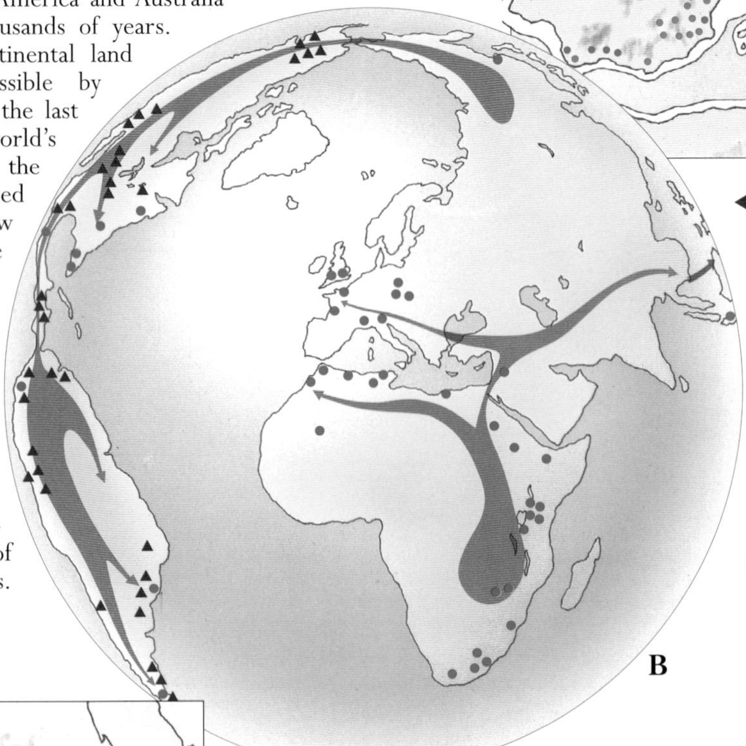

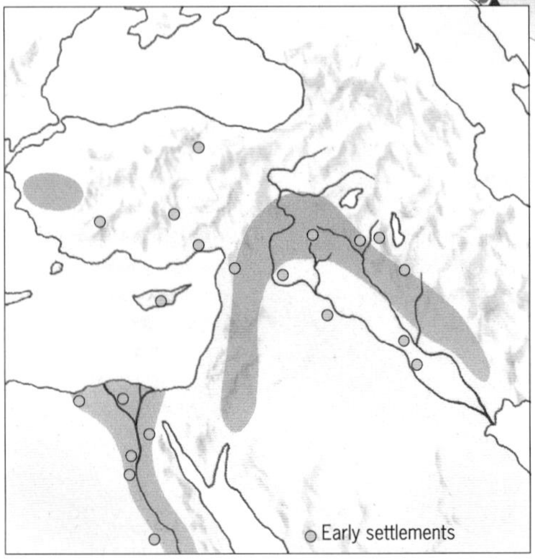

◀THE FIRST FARMERS

The first farming settlements, which developed into the first cities, were probably founded around 10,000 years ago in the 'Fertile Crescent' **[C]**, *a band of land stretching from the Mediterranean to the rivers Tigris and Euphrates, in modern Jordan, Lebanon, Syria, Turkey and Iraq. Civilisation also flowered along the banks of the river Nile, similarly suited to agriculture. From simple farmsteads grew villages, towns, cities and eventually whole civilisations.*

▲ *This skull of* Australopithicus africanus *is over 2 million years old.* Africanus *was the first hominid to leave the forest for the open plain.*

This changed between 20,000 and 10,000 years ago with the development of agriculture. About 15,000 years ago, as temperatures rose, primitive farming practices began to appear wherever the climate allowed it. The most important of these were Mesopotamia, the crescent between the rivers Tigris and Euphrates in modern Iraq, south-eastern Turkey and eastern Syria, the Nile valley, Central America and north-east China. Once wandering groups settled down the population soared, increasing from 5 to 300 million in 8000 years.

Small farming settlements developed into villages, then towns, then cities. Social and political organisations developed to control large groups of people. Gradually, the great civilisations grew, in the fertile fields of these first settlements. Along the Nile Valley, the Egyptians started to build a sophisticated culture around 3000BC, at the same time as the Sumerians were developing a system of city states in Mesopotamia. Similar civilisations appeared in China and Central America. Influences from these civilisations rippled outwards, laying down the pattern for the shape of the modern world.

▶ ***OUT OF AFRICA***

It is now considered that the ancestors of humankind first appeared in Africa **[D]**. *As well as indications of early Homo sapiens, the evidence for Africa's claims to be the cradle of humanity comes from fossils of Australopithecus and Homo erectus found in South Africa, Olduvai Gorge in Kenya, and Ethiopia. These are older than any others so far discovered in the world and so it seems likely that the human beings who evolved in Africa gradually spread out to other parts of the world. This is corroborated by fossils of a later date found in India, Java and China which indicate the direction of migration out of Africa. Early Homo sapiens fossils have also been found in China, southern Europe, North and South America and the Middle East. In Europe, the fossils found so far are confined to early forms of Homo sapiens and Neanderthal man, whose traces have been found in Germany, Hungary, France, Belgium, Greece, Czechoslovakia, Russia and the Middle East.*

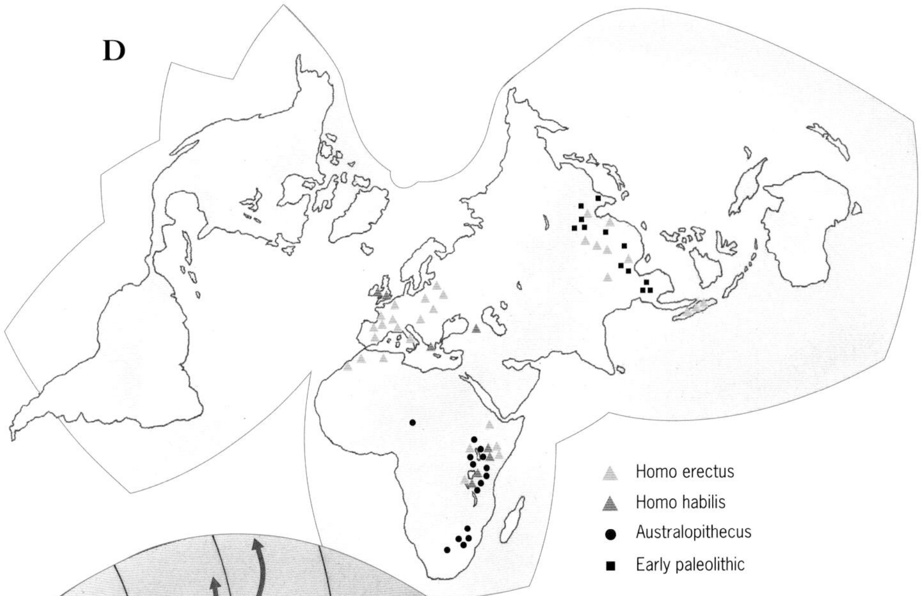

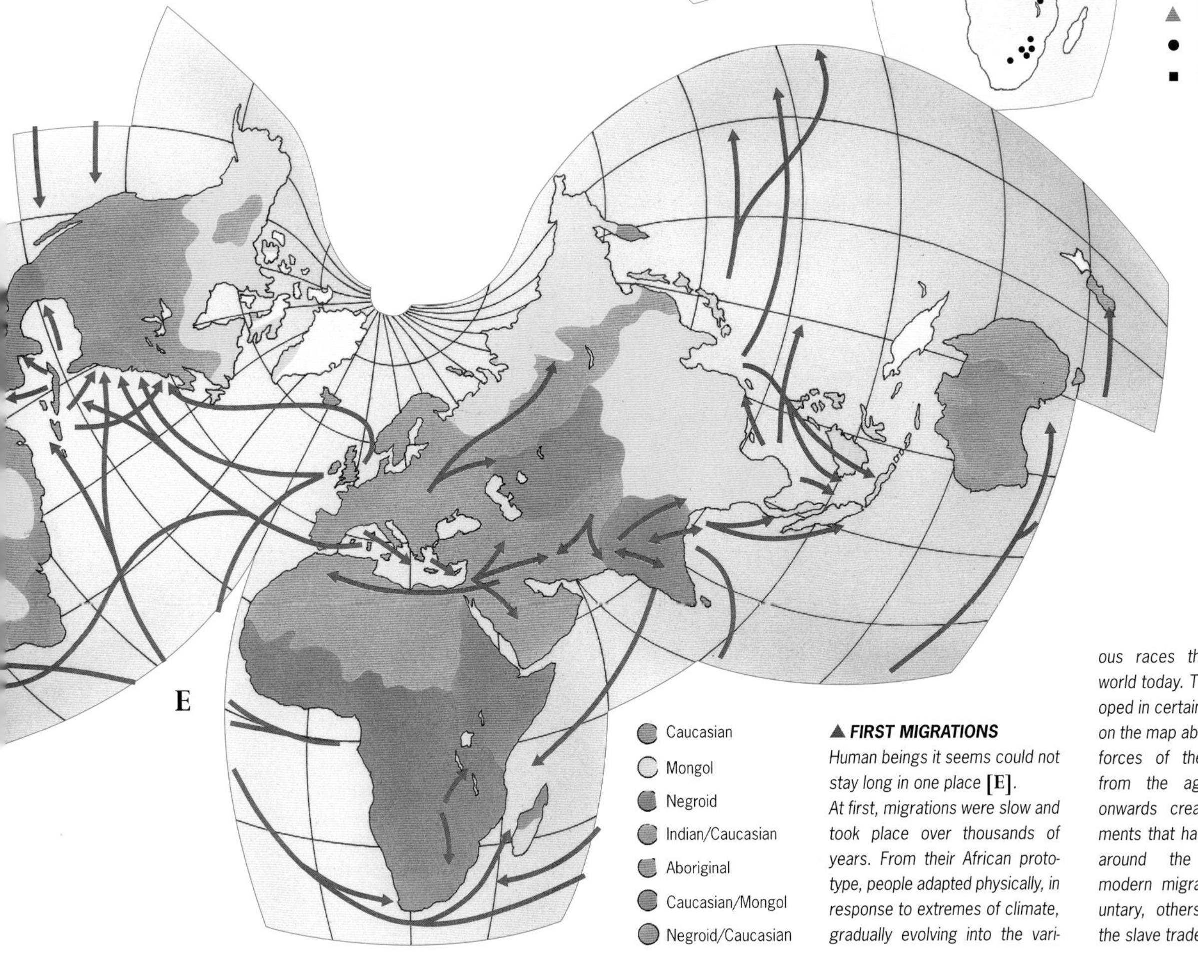

▲ ***FIRST MIGRATIONS***

Human beings it seems could not stay long in one place **[E]**.
At first, migrations were slow and took place over thousands of years. From their African prototype, people adapted physically, in response to extremes of climate, gradually evolving into the various races that populate the world today. These races developed in certain areas, as shown on the map above, however, the forces of the modern world from the age of discovery onwards created later movements that have spread people around the world. These modern migrations, some voluntary, others enforced as in the slave trade, are also shown.

The population explosion

There are more than 6 billion people in the world today. This figure is rising at a rate of 140 million each year, an increase of more than the population of Japan. But until comparatively recently, the rate of increase of the world population was low. Two thousand years ago, there were an estimated 300 million people on Earth; by 1650 this had increased to a mere 500 million. Then in only 200 years this number had doubled, and in the 150 years since then it has increased five-fold. In spite of recurrent famine and war, the world population seems set on an inexorable upward curve, doubling every 39 years.

This population explosion is a result of social developments since the Industrial Revolution. Proportionally there are the same number of births each year – or perhaps fewer. But the advances of improved sanitation and nutrition made possible by the industrial and scientific advances of the 18th and 19th centuries meant that fewer babies died at birth and that people lived longer.

At first these changes were confined to the countries of the developed world, in Europe and America, but as they have spread around the world, the population has ballooned. Now in most European countries the population remains stable, mainly because of the availability of reliable contraception. Indeed, in some countries the birth rate has fallen below the number needed to maintain stability; this will result in a top-heavy 'age pyramid', with too many grandparents and not enough grandchildren to support them. Some countries, such as France and Sweden, have tried to encourage people to have more babies through maternity payments and tax discounts for large families.

In the developing world the situation is different. There are many cultural and religious objections to the use of contraception. In a traditional agricultural community, too, a large family was desirable. As well as ensuring that the parents would have surviving children to look after them, many children provided a workforce to farm the land. But fewer people now live on the land, as farming becomes mechanised; and a large family in an urban industrialised setting just creates more mouths to feed. China, the most populated country in the world, has solved the problem, rationing families to one child each.

The rush to the cities

All over the world, more people live in cities than in the country, because it is no longer possible to make a living working on the land.

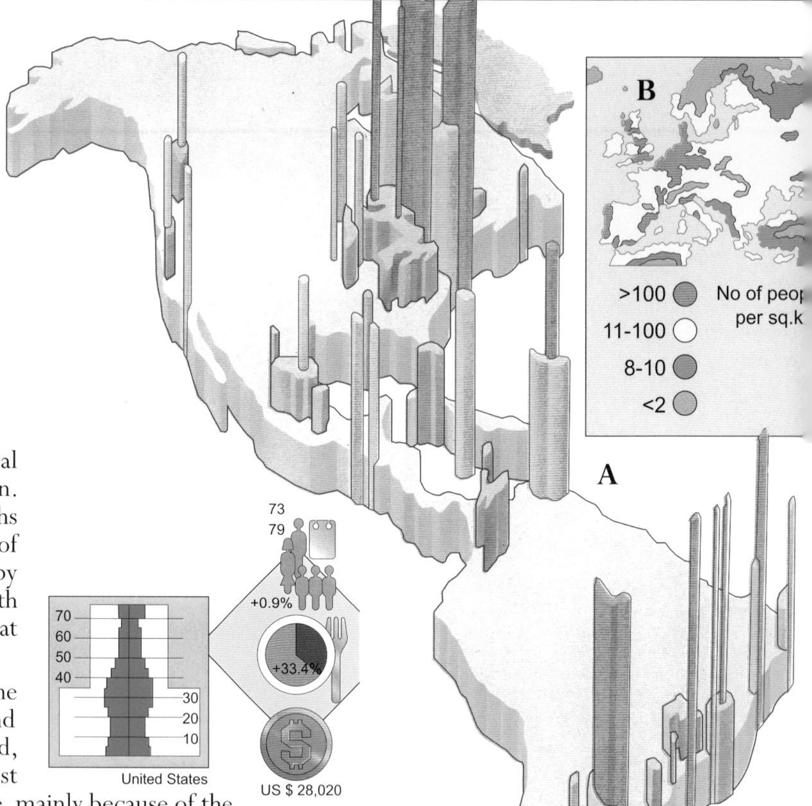

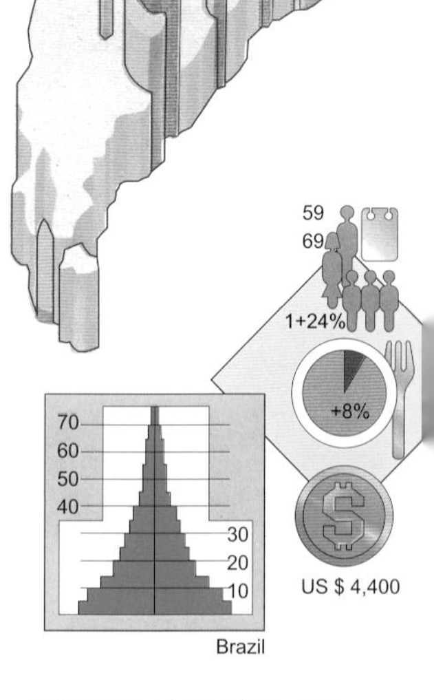

▲ ***GLOBAL POPULATION***
The global population is distributed in clumps and clusters around the world. In hotter countries, most people live on a narrow ribbon along the coast, leaving vast arid inner tracts of land underpopulated. In cooler countries, the population is able to spread itself more evenly about the landmass. The map makes clear the huge numbers of people living all across China and India, in contrast with the comparatively sparse population of much of the United States. The graphics around illustration **[A]** *show for each continent the rate of population growth, the average longevity of men and women, the gross national product per capita (a measure of wealth), and the calorific intake per head as a percentage of an adult's average daily requirement. These illustrate the gap in health and wealth between the developed world and the developing nations.*

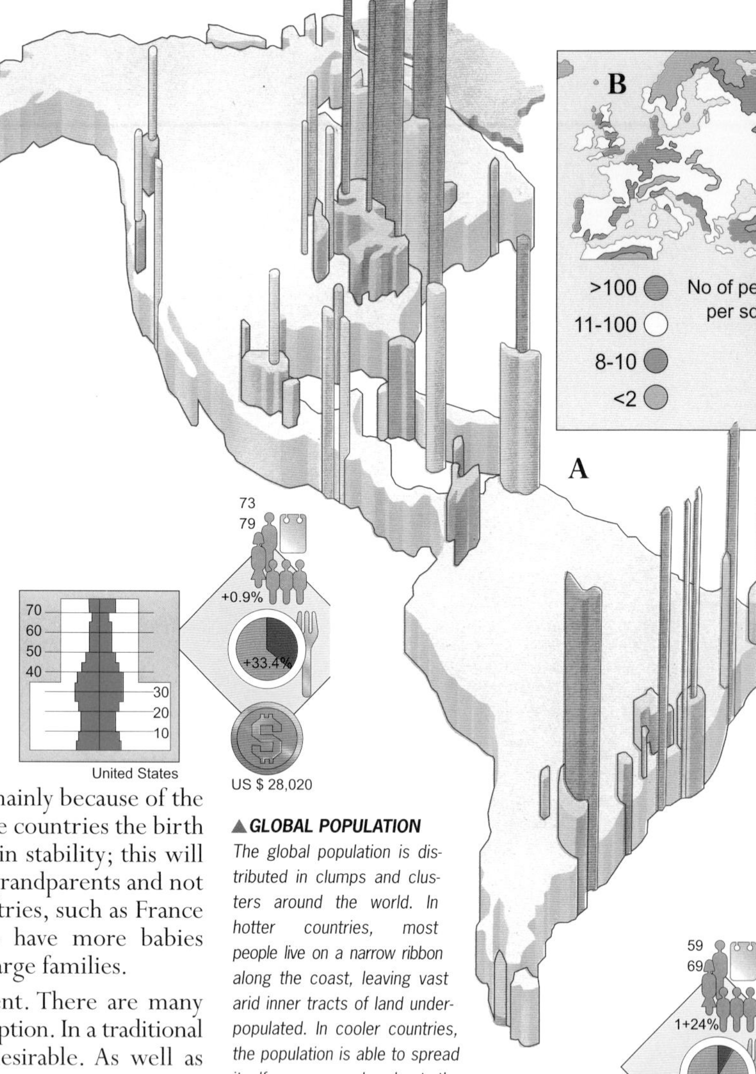

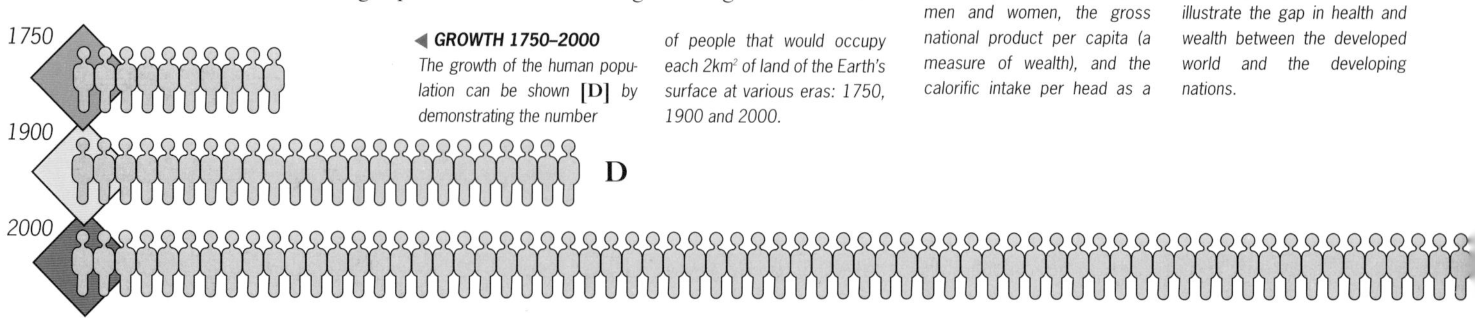

◀ ***GROWTH 1750–2000***
The growth of the human population can be shown **[D]** *by demonstrating the number of people that would occupy each 2km² of land of the Earth's surface at various eras: 1750, 1900 and 2000.*

▶ ***POPULATION GROWTH***
The Earth's population has swollen from a mere 250 million 1000 years ago (roughly the present-day population of the United States) to 6 billion today.

For most of the intervening period growth was very slow, and there were even slight declines caused by plagues such as the Black Death. However, from about the time of the Industrial Revolution the rate of growth increased, accelerating further with each improvement in hygiene and healthcare.

A graph of world population growth over the past 300 years **[C]** *can be split to show how the relative increases in each continent have been staggered. Throughout recorded history, the population of Asia has been greater than that of all the other continents combined. However, during the 19th century the population of Europe grew at twice the rate of Asia's, thanks mainly to the improvements in living conditions brought about by scientific advances and the Industrial Revolution. This rate of growth has slowed in Europe this century, whereas that of Asia has accelerated spectacularly – its population seems likely to have tripled in the fifty years from 1950. Over the last two centuries the populations of North and South America have been increasing just as fast. In the 19th century this was due to immigration, whereas this century's gains can be attributed to better health and hygiene, improvements which have gradually spread to the developing world.*

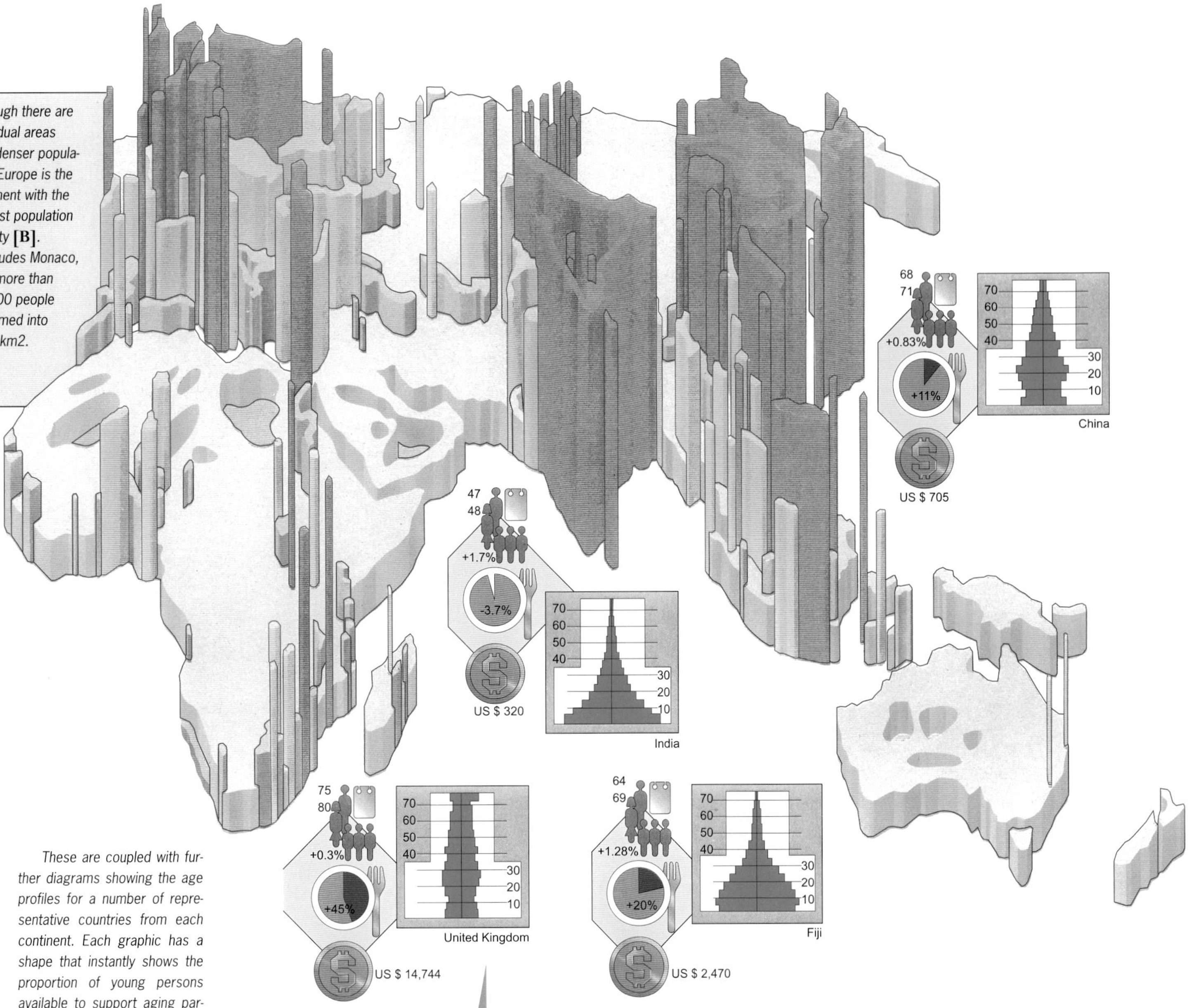

Although there are individual areas with denser population, Europe is the continent with the highest population density **[B]**. *It includes Monaco, with more than 15,000 people crammed into each km2.*

These are coupled with further diagrams showing the age profiles for a number of representative countries from each continent. Each graphic has a shape that instantly shows the proportion of young persons available to support aging parents and grandparents. In Brazil and Kenya, the pronounced pyramid shape indicates a high birth rate providing large numbers of young people supporting a dwindling older population. For the UK and USA, the shape is dramatically different – more a column than a pyramid, with the birth rate barely keeping up with the long-living older generation.

The diagram for the USA shows a bulge of middle-aged people, the product of the 'baby boom', a period of high birth-rate after World War 2. In China, a rigorous family planning regime has resulted in a taper at the young end of its curve, beginning to have an effect on the shape of the pyramid.

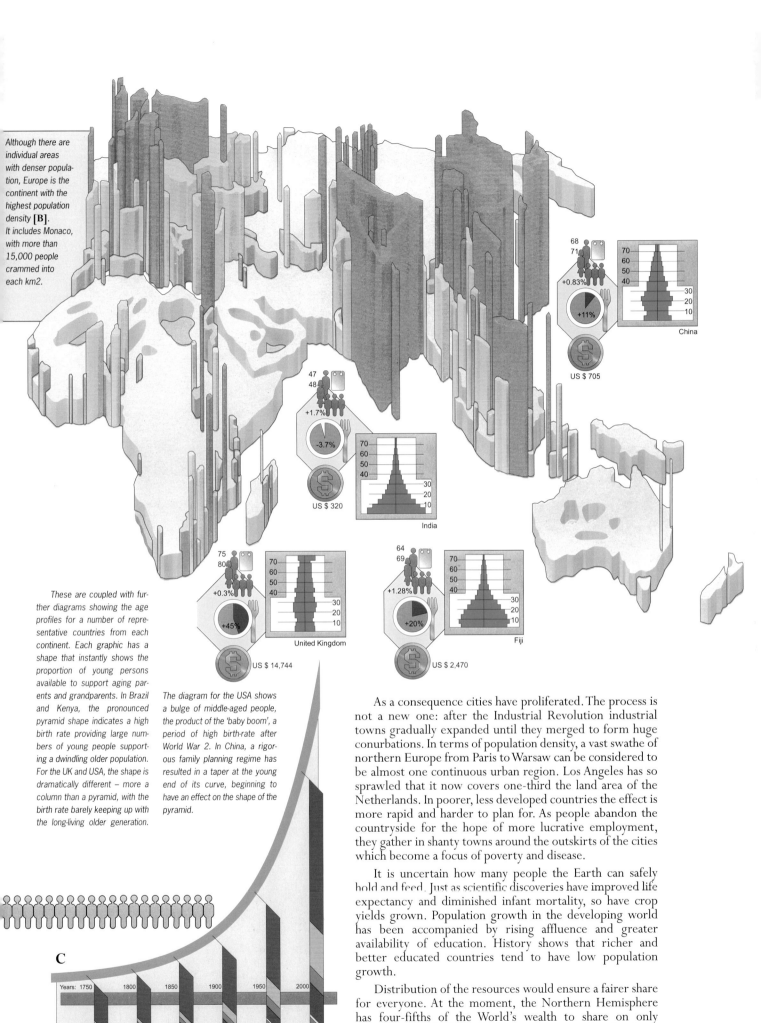

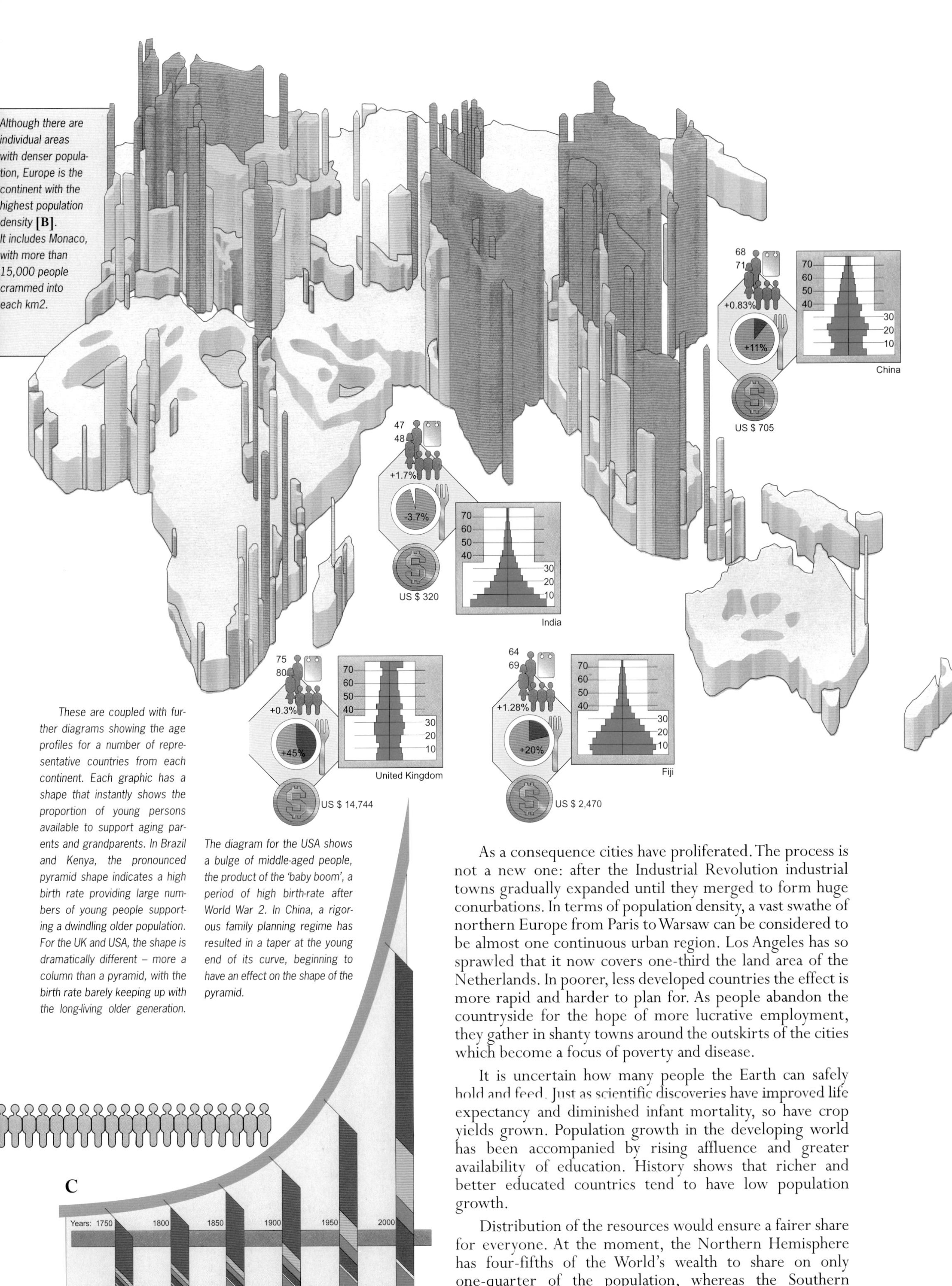

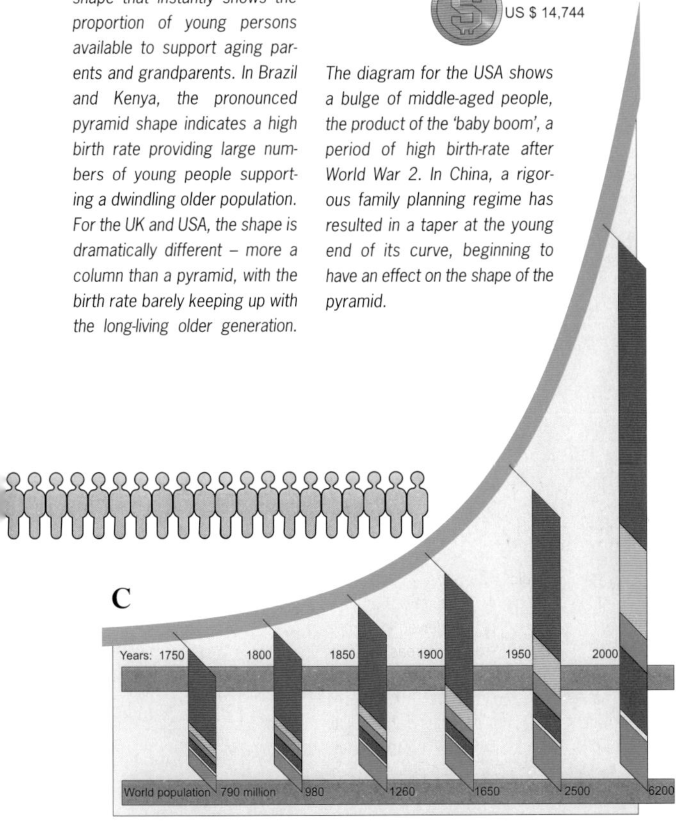

As a consequence cities have proliferated. The process is not a new one: after the Industrial Revolution industrial towns gradually expanded until they merged to form huge conurbations. In terms of population density, a vast swathe of northern Europe from Paris to Warsaw can be considered to be almost one continuous urban region. Los Angeles has so sprawled that it now covers one-third the land area of the Netherlands. In poorer, less developed countries the effect is more rapid and harder to plan for. As people abandon the countryside for the hope of more lucrative employment, they gather in shanty towns around the outskirts of the cities which become a focus of poverty and disease.

It is uncertain how many people the Earth can safely hold and feed. Just as scientific discoveries have improved life expectancy and diminished infant mortality, so have crop yields grown. Population growth in the developing world has been accompanied by rising affluence and greater availability of education. History shows that richer and better educated countries tend to have low population growth.

Distribution of the resources would ensure a fairer share for everyone. At the moment, the Northern Hemisphere has four-fifths of the World's wealth to share on only one-quarter of the population, whereas the Southern Hemisphere, with the majority of the population to sustain, has to make do with one-fifth of the World's resources.

COUNTRY FACTS & FLAGS

AFGHANISTAN

Capital: Kabul
Area: 647,500 km²
Population: 31,056,997
Currency: Afghani (AFA)
Main Religions: Sunni Muslim 80%, Shi'a Muslim 19%, other 1%
Main Languages: Pashtu 35%, Afghan Persian (Dari) 50%, Turkic languages 11%, 30 minor languages 4%
Int Dial Code: 93
Map Page: 91

ALBANIA

Capital: Tirana
Area: 28,748 km²
Population: 3,581,655
Currency: Lek (ALL)
Main Religions: Muslim 70%, Albanian Orthodox 20%, Roman Catholic 10%
Main Languages: Albanian (Tosk is the official dialect), Greek
Int Dial Code: 355
Map Page: 68

ALGERIA

Capital: Algiers
Area: 2,381,740 km²
Population: 32,930,091
Currency: Algerian dinar (DZD)
Main Religions: Sunni Muslim 99%, Christian and Jewish 1%
Languages: Arabic (official), French, Berber dialects
Int Dial Code: 213
Map Page: 103

ANDORRA

Capital: Andorra la Vella
Area: 468 km²
Population: 71,201
Currency: Euro (EUR)
Main Religions: Roman Catholic
Main Languages: Catalan (official), French, Castilian
Int Dial Code: 376
Map Page: 61

ANGOLA

Capital: Luanda
Area: 1,246,700 km²
Population: 12,127,071
Currency: Kwanza (AOA)
Main Religions: Indigenous beliefs 47%, Roman Catholic 38%, Protestant 15%
Main Languages: Portuguese (official), Bantu and other African languages
Int Dial Code: 244
Map Page: 98

ANTIGUA AND BARBUDA

Capital: Saint John's
Area: 442.6 km² (Antigua 281 km²; Barbuda 161 km²)
Population: 67,000
Currency: East Caribbean dollar (XCD)
Main Religions: Anglican (predominant), Protestant, Roman Catholic
Main Languages: English (official), local dialects
Int Dial Code: 1 + 268
Map Page: 135

ARGENTINA

Capital: Buenos Aires
Area: 2,766,890 km²
Population: 39,921,833
Currency: Argentine Peso (ARS)
Main Religions: Roman Catholic 92%, Protestant 2%, Jewish 2%, other 4%
Main Languages: Spanish (official), English, Italian, German, French
Int Dial Code: 54
Map Page: 142

ARMENIA

Capital: Yerevan
Area: 29,800 km²
Population: 2,976,372
Currency: Dram (AMD)
Main Religions: Armenian Orthodox 94%
Main Languages: Armenian 96%, Russian 2%, other 2%
Int Dial Code: 374
Map Page: 93

AUSTRALIA

Capital: Canberra
Area: 7,686,850 km²
Population: 20,264,082
Currency: Australian dollar (AUD)
Main Religions: Anglican 26.1%, Roman Catholic 26%, other Christian 24.3%, non-Christian 11%
Main Languages: English, native languages
Int Dial Code: 61
Map Page: 114

AUSTRIA

Capital: Vienna
Area: 83,870 km²
Population: 8,192,880
Currency: Euro (EUR)
Main Religions: Roman Catholic 74%, Protestant 5%, Muslim and other 21%
Main Languages: German
Int Dial Code: 43
Map Page: 63

AZERBAIJAN

Capital: Baku
Area: 86,600 km²
Population: 7,961,619
Currency: Azerbaijani manat (AZM)
Main Religions: Muslim 93.4%, Russian Orthodox 2.5%, Armenian Orthodox 2.3%, other 1.8%
Main Languages: Azerbaijani (Azeri) 89%, Russian 3%, Armenian 2%
Int Dial Code: 994
Map Page: 93

BAHAMAS, THE

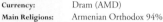

Capital: Nassau
Area: 13,940 km²
Population: 303,770
Currency: Bahamian dollar (BSD)
Main Religions: Baptist 35%, Anglican 15%, Roman Catholic 13%, Pentecostal 8%, Methodist 4%, Church of God 5%
Main Languages: English, Creole
Int Dial Code: 1 + 242
Map Page: 135

BAHRAIN

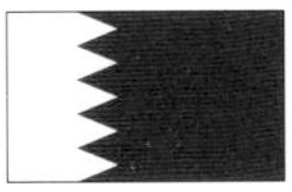

Capital:	Manama
Area:	665 km²
Population:	698,585
Currency:	Bahraini dinar (BHD)
Main Religions:	Muslim 81% (Shi'a & Sunni), Christian 9%
Main Languages:	Arabic, English, Farsi, Urdu
Int Dial Code:	973
Map Page:	95

BANGLADESH

Capital:	Dhaka
Area:	144,000 km²
Population:	147,365,352
Currency:	Taka (BDT)
Main Religions:	Muslim 83%, Hindu 16%, other 1%
Main Languages:	Bangla (official, also known as Bengali), English
Int Dial Code:	880
Map Page:	88

BARBADOS

Capital:	Bridgetown
Area:	431 km²
Population:	279,912
Currency:	Barbadian dollar (BBD)
Main Religions:	Protestant 67% (Anglican 40%, Pentecostal 8%, Methodist 7%, other 12%), Roman Catholic 4%
Main Languages:	English
Int Dial Code:	1 + 246
Map Page:	135

BELARUS

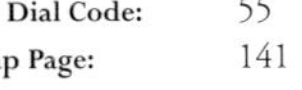

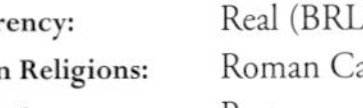

Capital:	Minsk
Area:	207,600 km²
Population:	10,293,011
Currency:	Belarusian ruble (BYB/BYR)
Main Religions:	Eastern Orthodox 80%, other (including Roman Catholic, Protestant, Jewish, and Muslim) 20%
Main Languages:	Belarusian, Russian
Int Dial Code:	375
Map Page:	70

BELGIUM

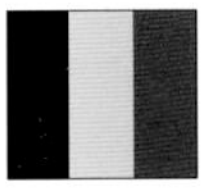

Capital:	Brussels
Area:	30,528 km²
Population:	10,379,067
Currency:	Euro (EUR)
Main Religions:	Roman Catholic 75%, Protestant or other 25%
Main Languages:	Dutch 60%, French 40% legally bilingual (Dutch and French)
Int Dial Code:	32
Map Page:	55

BELIZE

Capital:	Belmopan
Area:	22,966 km²
Population:	287,730
Currency:	Belizean dollar (BZD)
Main Religions:	Roman Catholic 50%, Protestant 27%
Main Languages:	English (official), Spanish, Mayan, Garifuna , Creole
Int Dial Code:	501
Map Page:	134

BENIN

Capital:	Porto-Novo
Area:	112,620 km²
Population:	7,862,944
Currency:	Communaute Financiere Africaine franc (XOF)
Main Religions:	Indigenous beliefs 50%, Christian 30%, Muslim 20%
Main Languages:	French (official), Fon and Yoruba, tribal languages
Int Dial Code:	229
Map Page:	105

BHUTAN

Capital:	Thimphu
Area:	47,000 km²
Population:	2,279,723
Currency:	Ngultrum (BTN); Indian rupee (INR)
Main Religions:	Lamaistic Buddhist 75%, Hinduism 25%
Main Languages:	Dzongkha (official), Bhotes speak various Tibetan dialects, Nepalese dialects
Int Dial Code:	975
Map Page:	88

BOLIVIA

Capital:	La Paz (seat of government); Sucre (legal capital and seat of judiciary)
Area:	1,098,580 km²
Population:	8,989,046
Currency:	Boliviano (BOB)
Main Religions:	Roman Catholic 95%, Protestant 5%
Main Languages:	Spanish (official), Quechua (official), Aymara
Int Dial Code:	591
Map Page:	140

BOSNIA AND HERZEGOVINA

Capital:	Sarajevo
Area:	51,129 km²
Population:	4,498,976
Currency:	Marka (BAM)
Main Religions:	Muslim 40%, Orthodox 31%, Roman Catholic 15%, Protestant 4%, other 14%
Main Languages:	Croatian, Serbian, Bosnian
Int Dial Code:	387
Map Page:	66

BOTSWANA

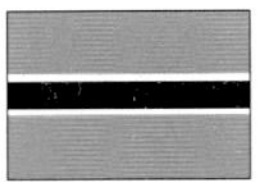

Capital:	Gaborone
Area:	600,370 km²
Population:	1,639,833
Currency:	Pula (BWP)
Main Religions:	Christian 72%, Badimo 6%
Main Languages:	Setswana, Kalanga, Sekgalagadi, English
Int Dial Code:	267
Map Page:	108

BRAZIL

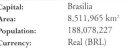

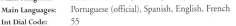

Capital:	Brasilia
Area:	8,511,965 km²
Population:	188,078,227
Currency:	Real (BRL)
Main Religions:	Roman Catholic (nominal) 74%, Protestant 15%
Main Languages:	Portuguese (official), Spanish, English, French
Int Dial Code:	55
Map Page:	141

BRUNEI

Capital: Bandar Seri Begawan
Area: 5,770 km²
Population: 379,444
Currency: Bruneian dollar (BND)
Main Religions: Muslim (official) 67%, Buddhist 13%, Christian 10%, indigenous beliefs and other 10%
Main Languages: Malay (official), English, Chinese
Int Dial Code: 673
Map Page: 86

BULGARIA

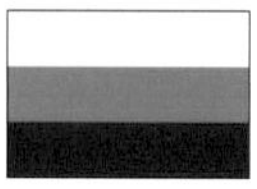

Capital: Sofia
Area: 110,910 km²
Population: 7,385,367
Currency: Lev (BGL)
Main Religions: Bulgarian Orthodox 82.6%, Muslim 13%, Roman Catholic 1.5%, Uniate Catholic 0.2%, Jewish 0.8%
Main Languages: Bulgarian, Turkish
Int Dial Code: 359
Map Page: 67

BURKINA

Capital: Ouagadougou
Area: 274,200 km²
Population: 13,902,972
Currency: Communaute Financiere Africaine franc (XOF)
Main Religions: Indigenous beliefs 40%, Muslim 50%, Christian 10%
Main Languages: French (official), native African languages belonging to Sudanic family spoken by 90% of the population
Int Dial Code: 226
Map Page: 104

BURUNDI

Capital: Bujumbura
Area: 27,830 km²
Population: 8,090,068
Currency: Burundi franc (BIF)
Main Religions: Christian 67% (Roman Catholic 62%, Protestant 5%), indigenous beliefs 23%, Muslim 10%
Main Languages: Kirundi (official), French (official), Swahili
Int Dial Code: 257
Map Page: 106

CAMBODIA

Capital: Phnom Penh
Area: 181,040 km²
Population: 13,881,427
Currency: Riel (KHR)
Main Religions: Theravada Buddhist 95%, other 5%
Main Languages: Khmer (official) 95%, French, English
Int Dial Code: 855
Map Page: 84

CAMEROON

Capital: Yaounde
Area: 475,440 km²
Population: 17,340,702
Currency: Communaute Financiere Africaine franc (XAF)
Main Religions: Indigenous beliefs 40%, Christian 40%, Muslim 20%
Main Languages: 24 major African language groups, English (official), French (official)
Int Dial Code: 237
Map Page: 105

CANADA

Capital: Ottawa
Area: 9,984,670 km²
Population: 33,098,932
Currency: Canadian dollar (CAD)
Main Religions: Roman Catholic 42%, Protestant 23%, other 18%
Main Languages: English 59.3% (official), French 23.2% (official), other 17.5%
Int Dial Code: 1
Map Page: 122

CAPE VERDE

Capital: Praia
Area: 4,033 km²
Population: 420,979
Currency: Cape Verdean escudo (CVE)
Main Religions: Roman Catholic, Protestant
Main Languages: Portuguese, Crioulo
Int Dial Code: 238
Map Page: 104

CENTRAL AFRICAN REPUBLIC

Capital: Bangui
Area: 622,984 km²
Population: 4,303,356
Currency: Communaute Financiere Africaine franc (XAF)
Main Religions: Indigenous beliefs 35%, Protestant 25%, Roman Catholic 25%, Muslim 15%
Main Languages: French (official), Sangho , Arabic, Hunsa, Swahili
Int Dial Code: 236
Map Page: 106

CHAD

Capital: N'Djamena
Area: 1.284 million km²
Population: 9,944,201
Currency: Communaute Financiere Africaine franc (XAF)
Main Religions: Muslim 50%, Christian 35%
Main Languages: French (official), Arabic (official), Sara and Sango, over 100 different languages and dialects
Int Dial Code: 235
Map Page: 100

CHILE

Capital: Santiago
Area: 756,950 km²
Population: 16,134,219
Currency: Chilean peso (CLP)
Main Religions: Roman Catholic 89%, Protestant 11%
Main Languages: Spanish
Int Dial Code: 56
Map Page: 142

CHINA

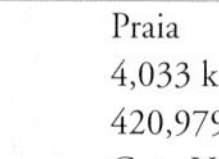

Capital: Beijing
Area: 9,596,960 km²
Population: 1,313,973,713
Currency: Yuan (CNY)
Main Religions: Daoist (Taoist), Buddhist, Christian 3-4%, Muslim 1-2%
Main Languages: Standard Chinese or Mandarin (Putonghua), Yue (Cantonese), Wu (Shanghaiese), Minbei (Fuzhou), Minnan (Hokkien-Taiwanese), Xiang, Gan, Hakka
Int Dial Code: 86
Map Page: 80

COLOMBIA

Capital: Bogota
Area: 1,138,910 km^2
Population: 43,593,035
Currency: Colombian peso (COP)
Main Religions: Roman Catholic 90%
Main Languages: Spanish
Int Dial Code: 57
Map Page: 140

COMOROS

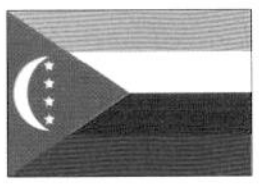

Capital: Moroni
Area: 2,170 km^2
Population: 690,948
Currency: Comoran franc (KMF)
Main Religions: Sunni Muslim 98%, Roman Catholic 2%
Main Languages: Arabic (official), French (official), Comoran
Int Dial Code: 269
Map Page: 109

CONGO

Capital: Brazzaville
Area: 342,000 km^2
Population: 3,702,314
Currency: Communaute Financiere Africaine franc (XAF)
Main Religions: Christian 50%, Animist 48%, Muslim 2%
Main Languages: French (official), Lingala and Monokutuba
Int Dial Code: 242
Map Page: 105

CONGO, DEM. REP. OF THE

Capital: Kinshasa
Area: 2,345,410 km^2
Population: 62,660,551
Currency: Congolese franc (CDF)
Main Religions: Roman Catholic 50%, Protestant 20%, Kimbanguist 10%, Muslim 10%, other 10%
Main Languages: French (official), Lingala, Kingwana, Kikongo, Tshiluba
Int Dial Code: 243
Map Page: 106

COSTA RICA

Capital: San José
Area: 51,100 km^2
Population: 4,075,261
Currency: Costa Rican colon (CRC)
Main Religions: Roman Catholic 76.3%, Evangelical 13.7%, other Protestant 0.7%, Jehovah's Witnesses 1.3%,
Main Languages: Spanish (official), English spoken around Puerto Limon
Int Dial Code: 506
Map Page: 135

COTE D'IVOIRE

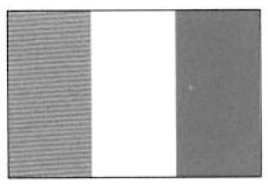

Capital: Yamoussoukro - capital since 1983, Abidjan is the administrative center
Area: 322,460 km^2
Population: 17,654,843
Currency: Communaute Financiere Africaine franc (XOF)
Main Religions: Muslim 35%, Indigenous 25%, Christian 20%
Main Languages: French (official), 60 native dialects
Int Dial Code: 225
Map Page: 104

CROATIA

Capital: Zagreb
Area: 56,542 km^2
Population: 4,494,749
Currency: Kuna (HRK)
Main Religions: Roman Catholic 87.8%, Orthodox 4.4%,
Main Languages: Croatian 96%, other 4% (Italian, Hungarian, Czech)
Int Dial Code: 385
Map Page: 66

CUBA

Capital: Havana
Area: 110,860 km^2
Population: 11,382,820
Currency: Cuban peso (CUP) and convertible Peso (CUC)
Main Religions: Roman Catholic 85% , Protestants, Jehovah's Witnesses, Jews
Main Languages: Spanish
Int Dial Code: 53
Map Page: 135

CYPRUS

Capital: Nicosia
Area: 9,250 km^2 (3,355 km^2 in the Turkish Cypriot area)
Population: 784,301
Currency: Cypriot pound (CYP); Turkish new lira (YTL)
Main Religions: Greek Orthodox 78%, Muslim 18%,
Main Languages: Greek, Turkish, English
Int Dial Code: 357
Map Page: 92

CZECH REPUBLIC

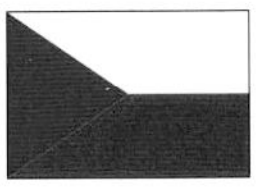

Capital: Prague
Area: 78,866 km^2
Population: 10,235,455
Currency: Czech koruna (CZK)
Main Religions: Roman Catholic 26.8%, Protestant 2.1%, Orthodox 3%
Main Languages: Czech
Int Dial Code: 420
Map Page: 51

DENMARK

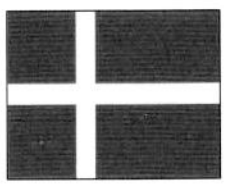

Capital: Copenhagen
Area: 43,094 km^2
Population: 5,450,661
Currency: Danish krone (DKK)
Main Religions: Evangelical Lutheran 95%, other Protestant and Roman Catholic 3%, Muslims 2%
Main Languages: Danish, Faroese, Greenlandic, German, English
Int Dial Code: 45
Map Page: 49

DJIBOUTI

Capital: Djibouti
Area: 23,000 km^2
Population: 486,530
Currency: Djiboutian franc (DJF)
Main Religions: Muslim 94%, Christian 6%
Main Languages: French (official), Arabic (official), Somali, Afar
Int Dial Code: 253
Map Page: 101

DOMINICA

Capital: Roseau
Area: 754 km²
Population: 68,910
Currency: East Caribbean dollar (XCD)
Main Religions: Roman Catholic 77%, Protestant 15% (Methodist 5%, Pentecostal 3%, Seventh-Day Adventist 3%, Baptist 2%, other 2%), none 2%, other 6%
Main Languages: English (official), French patois
Int Dial Code: 1 + 767
Map Page: 135

DOMINICAN REPUBLIC

Capital: Santo Domingo
Area: 48,730 km²
Population: 9,183,984
Currency: Dominican peso (DOP)
Main Religions: Roman Catholic 95%
Main Languages: Spanish
Int Dial Code: 1 + 809
Map Page: 135

EAST TIMOR

Capital: Dili
Area: 15,007 km²
Population: 1,062,777
Currency: US dollar
Main Religions: Roman Catholic, Muslim
Main Languages: Tetum, Portugese, Indonesian, English
Int Dial Code: 670
Map Page: 87

ECUADOR

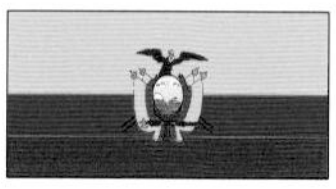

Capital: Quito
Area: 283,560 km²
Population: 13,547,510
Currency: US dollar (USD)
Main Religions: Roman Catholic 95%
Main Languages: Spanish (official), Amerindian languages (especially Quechua)
Int Dial Code: 593
Map Page: 140

EGYPT

Capital: Cairo
Area: 1,001,450 km²
Population: 78,887,007
Currency: Egyptian pound (EGP)
Main Religions: Muslim (mostly Sunni) 90%, Coptic Christian and other 6%
Main Languages: Arabic (official), English and French
Int Dial Code: 20
Map Page: 100

EL SALVADOR

Capital: San Salvador
Area: 21,040 km²
Population: 6,822,378
Currency: Salvadoran colon (SVC); US dollar (USD)
Main Religions: Roman Catholic 83%
Main Languages: Spanish, Nahua
Int Dial Code: 503
Map Page: 134

EQUATORIAL GUINEA

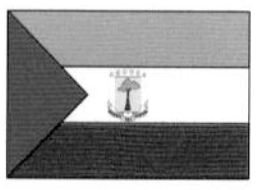

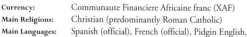

Capital: Malabo
Area: 28,051 km²
Population: 540,109
Currency: Communaute Financiere Africaine franc (XAF)
Main Religions: Christian (predominantly Roman Catholic)
Main Languages: Spanish (official), French (official), Pidgin English, Fang, Bubi, Ibo
Int Dial Code: 240
Map Page: 105

ERITREA

Capital: Asmara
Area: 121,320 km²
Population: 4,786,994
Currency: Nakfa (ERN)
Main Religions: Muslim, Coptic Christian, Roman Catholic, Protestant
Main Languages: Afar, Amharic, Arabic, Tigre and Kunama, Tigrinya, other Cushitic languages
Int Dial Code: 291
Map Page: 101

ESTONIA

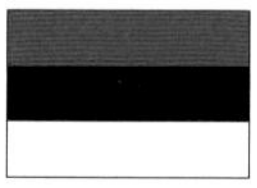

Capital: Tallinn
Area: 45,226 km²
Population: 1,324,333
Currency: Estonian kroon (EEK)
Main Religions: Evangelical Lutheran, Russian Orthodox, Estonian Orthodox, Baptist, Methodist, Seventh-Day Adventist
Main Languages: Estonian (official), Russian, Ukrainian, English, Finnish
Int Dial Code: 372
Map Page: 49

ETHIOPIA

Capital: Addis Ababa
Area: 1,127,127 km2
Population: 74,777,981
Currency: Birr (ETB)
Main Religions: Muslim 45%-50%, Ethiopian Orthodox 35%-40%, animist 12%, other 3%-8%
Main Languages: Amharic, Tigrinya, Oromigna, Guaragigna, Somali, Arabic, English
Int Dial Code: 251
Map Page: 107

FIJI

Capital: Suva
Area: 18,270 km²
Population: 905,949
Currency: Fijian dollar (FJD)
Main Religions: Christian 52% (Methodist 37%, Roman Catholic 9%), Hindu 38%, Muslim 8%, other 2%
Main Languages: English (official), Fijian, Hindustani
Int Dial Code: 679
Map Page: 112

FINLAND

Capital: Helsinki
Area: 338,145 km²
Population: 5,231,372
Currency: Euro (EUR)
Main Religions: Evangelical Lutheran 89%, Greek Orthodox 1%, none 9%, other 1%
Main Languages: Finnish 93.4% (official), Swedish 5.9% (official), small Lapp- and Russian-speaking minorities
Int Dial Code: 358
Map Page: 48

FRANCE

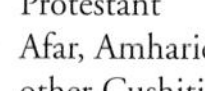

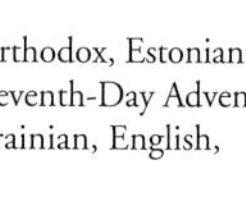

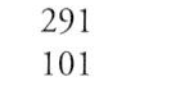

Capital: Paris
Area: 547,030 km²
Population: 60,876,136
Currency: Euro (EUR)
Main Religions: Roman Catholic 90%, Protestant 2%, Jewish 1%, Muslim 3%, unaffiliated 4%
Main Languages: French 100%, Provencal, Breton, Alsatian, Corsican, Catalan, Basque, Flemish
Int Dial Code: 33
Map Page: 58

GABON

Capital: Libreville
Area: 267,667 km^2
Population: 1,424,906
Currency: Communaute Financiere Africaine franc (XAF)
Main Religions: Christian 55%-75%, Animist, Muslim less than 1%
Main Languages: French (official), Fang, Myene, Bapounou/Eschira, Bandjabi
Int Dial Code: 241
Map Page: 105

GAMBIA, THE

Capital: Banjul
Area: 11,300 km^2
Population: 1,641,564
Currency: Dalasi (GMD)
Main Religions: Muslim 90%, Christian 9%, Indigenous beliefs 1%
Main Languages: English (official), Mandinka, Wolof, Fula
Int Dial Code: 220
Map Page: 104

GEORGIA

Capital: T'bilisi
Area: 69,700 km^2
Population: 4,661,473
Currency: Lari (GEL)
Main Religions: Georgian Orthodox 65%, Muslim 11%, Russian Orthodox 10%, Armenian Apostolic 8%
Main Languages: Georgian 71% (official), Russian 9%, Armenian 7%,
Int Dial Code: 995
Map Page: 93

GERMANY

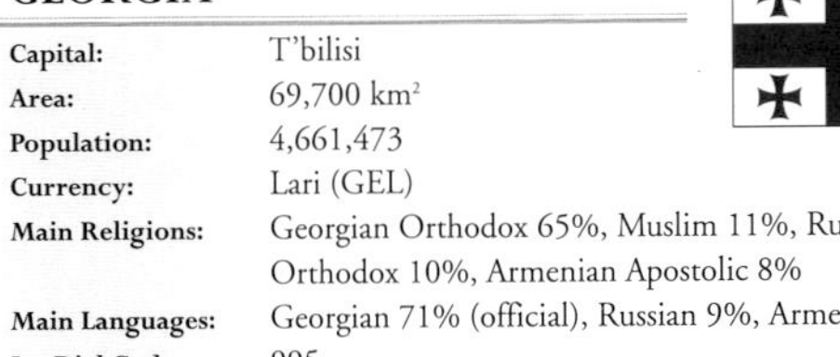

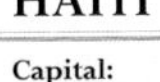

Capital: Berlin
Area: 357,021 km^2
Population: 82,422,299
Currency: Euro (EUR)
Main Religions: Protestant 34%, Roman Catholic 34%, Muslim 3.7%, unaffiliated or other 28.3%
Main Languages: German
Int Dial Code: 49
Map Page: 52

GHANA

Capital: Accra
Area: 239,460 km^2
Population: 22,409,572
Currency: Cedi (GHC)
Main Religions: Indigenous beliefs 38%, Muslim 30%, Christian 24%, other 8%
Main Languages: English (official), African languages (Akan, Moshi-Dagomba, Ewe, and Ga)
Int Dial Code: 233
Map Page: 104

GREECE

Capital: Athens
Area: 131,940 km^2
Population: 10,688,058
Currency: Euro (EUR)
Main Religions: Greek Orthodox 98%, Muslim 1.3%, other 0.7%
Main Languages: Greek 99% (official), English, French
Int Dial Code: 30
Map Page: 68

GRENADA

Capital: Saint George's
Area: 344 km^2
Population: 89,703
Currency: East Caribbean dollar (XCD)
Main Religions: Roman Catholic 53%, Anglican 13.8%, other Protestant 33.2%
Main Languages: English (official), French patois
Int Dial Code: 1 + 473
Map Page: 135

GUATEMALA

Capital: Guatemala
Area: 108,890 km^2
Population: 12,293,545
Currency: Quetzal (GTQ), US dollar (USD), others allowed
Main Religions: Roman Catholic, Protestant, Indigenous Mayan beliefs
Main Languages: Spanish 60%, Amerindian languages 40%
Int Dial Code: 502
Map Page: 134

GUINEA

Capital: Conakry
Area: 245,857 km^2
Population: 9,690,222
Currency: Guinean franc (GNF)
Main Religions: Muslim 85%, Christian 8%, Indigenous beliefs 7%
Main Languages: French (official), each ethnic group has its own language
Int Dial Code: 224
Map Page: 104

GUINEA-BISSAU

Capital: Bissau
Area: 36,120 km^2
Population: 1,442,029
Currency: Communaute Financiere Africaine franc (XOF)
Main Religions: Indigenous beliefs 50%, Muslim 45%, Christian 5%
Main Languages: Portuguese (official), Crioulo, African languages
Int Dial Code: 245
Map Page: 104

GUYANA

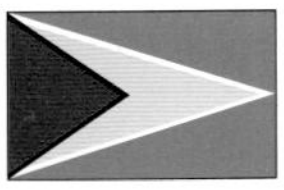

Capital: Georgetown
Area: 214,970 km^2
Population: 767,245
Currency: Guyanese dollar (GYD)
Main Religions: Christian 50%, Hindu 35%, Muslim 10%, other 5%
Main Languages: English, Amerindian dialects, Creole, Hindi, Urdu
Int Dial Code: 592
Map Page: 141

HAITI

Capital: Port-au-Prince
Area: 27,750 km^2
Population: 8,308,504
Currency: Gourde (HTG)
Main Religions: Roman Catholic 80%, Protestant 16% (Baptist 10%, Pentecostal 4%, Adventist 1%, other 1%)
Main Languages: French (official), Creole (official)
Int Dial Code: 509
Map Page: 135

HONDURAS

Capital: Tegucigalpa
Area: 112,090 km^2
Population: 7,326,496
Currency: Lempira (HNL)
Main Religions: Roman Catholic 97%, Protestant
Main Languages: Spanish, Amerindian dialects
Int Dial Code: 504
Map Page: 134

HUNGARY

Capital: Budapest
Area: 93,030 km^2
Population: 9,981,334
Currency: Forint (HUF)
Main Languages: Hungarian 98.2%, other 1.8%
Int Dial Code: 36
Map Page: 66

ICELAND

Capital: Reykjavik
Area: 103,000 km^2
Population: 299,388
Currency: Icelandic krona (ISK)
Main Languages: Icelandic
Int Dial Code: 354
Map Page: 48

INDIA

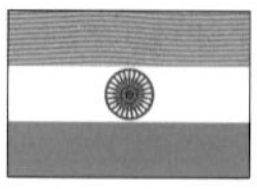

Capital: New Delhi
Area: 3,287,590 km^2
Population: 1,095,351,995
Currency: Indian rupee (INR)
Main Religions: Hindu 80.5%, Muslim 13.4%, Christian 2.3%, Sikh 1.9%,Buddhist, Jain, Parsi 2.5%
Main Languages: English, Hindi 30%, Bengali, Telugu, Marathi, Tamil, Urdu, Gujarati, Malayalam, Kannada, Oriya, Punjabi
Int Dial Code: 91
Map Page: 88

INDONESIA

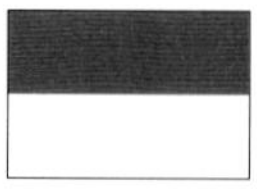

Capital: Jakarta
Area: 1,919,440 km^2
Population: 245,452,739
Currency: Indonesian rupiah (IDR)
Main Religions: Muslim 88%, Protestant 5%, Roman Catholic 3%, Hindu 2%, Buddhist 1%, other 1%
Main Languages: Bahasa Indonesia (official), English, Dutch, local dialects
Int Dial Code: 62
Map Page: 86

IRAN

Capital: Tehran
Area: 1.648 million km^2
Population: 68,688,433
Currency: Iranian rial (IRR)
Main Religions: Shi'a Muslim 89%, Sunni Muslim 10%, Zoroastrian, Jewish, Christian, Baha'i 1%
Main Languages: Persian and Persian dialects 58%, Turkic and Turkic dialects 26%, Kurdish 9%, Luri 2%, Balochi 1%
Int Dial Code: 98
Map Page: 90

IRAQ

Capital: Baghdad
Area: 437,072 km^2
Population: 26,783,383
Currency: New Iraqi dinar (NID)
Main Religions: Muslim 97% (Shi'a 60%-65%, Sunni 32%-37%), Christian or other 3%
Main Languages: Arabic, Kurdish, Assyrian, Armenian
Int Dial Code: 964
Map Page: 90

IRELAND

Capital: Dublin
Area: 70,280 km^2
Population: 4,062,235
Currency: Euro (EUR)
Main Religions: Roman Catholic 88.4%, Church of Ireland 3%
Main Languages: English, Irish (Gaelic)
Int Dial Code: 353
Map Page: 57

ISRAEL

Capital: Jerusalem
Area: 20,770 km^2
Population: 6,352,117
Currency: New Israeli shekel (ILS or NIS)
Main Religions: Jewish 76.5%, Muslim 15.9%, Arab Christian 1.7%
Main Languages: Hebrew (official), Arabic, English
Int Dial Code: 972
Map Page: 94

ITALY

Capital: Rome
Area: 301,230 km^2
Population: 58,133,509
Currency: Euro (EUR)
Main Religions: predominately Roman Catholic, Protestant, Jewish and Muslim
Main Languages: Italian (official), German, French, Slovene
Int Dial Code: 39
Map Page: 64

JAMAICA

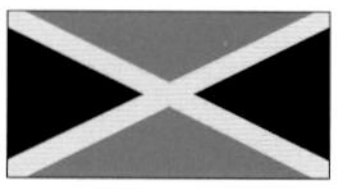

Capital: Kingston
Area: 10,990 km^2
Population: 2,758,124
Currency: Jamaican dollar (JMD)
Main Religions: Protestant 61.3%, Roman Catholic 4%, other 34.7%
Main Languages: English, Creole
Int Dial Code: 1 + 876
Map Page: 135

JAPAN

Capital: Tokyo
Area: 377,835 km^2
Population: 127,463,611
Currency: Yen (JPY)
Main Religions: Shinto and Buddhist 84%, other 16% (including Christian 0.7%)
Main Languages: Japanese
Int Dial Code: 81
Map Page: 83

JORDAN

Capital: Amman
Area: 92,300 km^2
Population: 5,906,760
Currency: Jordanian dinar (JOD)
Main Religions: Sunni Muslim 92%, Christian 6% (majority Greek Orthodox), other 2%
Main Languages: Arabic (official), English
Int Dial Code: 962
Map Page: 94

KAZAKHSTAN

Capital: Astana
Area: 2,717,300 km^2
Population: 15,233,244
Currency: Tenge (KZT)
Main Religions: Muslim 47%, Russian Orthodox 44%, Protestant 2%, other 7%
Main Languages: Kazakh (Qazaq, state language), Russian (official)
Int Dial Code: 7
Map Page: 77

KENYA

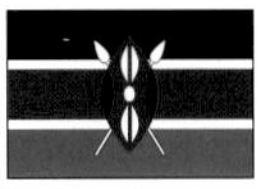

Capital: Nairobi
Area: 582,650 km^2
Population: 34,707,817
Currency: Kenyan shilling (KES)
Main Religions: Protestant 45%, Roman Catholic 33%, indigenous beliefs 10%, Muslim 10%
Main Languages: English (official), Kiswahili (official)
Int Dial Code: 254
Map Page: 107

KIRIBATI

Capital: Tarawa
Area: 811 km^2
Population: 105,432
Currency: Australian dollar (AUD)
Main Religions: Roman Catholic 54%, Protestant (Congregational) 30%, Seventh-Day Adventist, Baha'i, Latter-day Saints and Church of God
Main Languages: English (official), I-Kiribati
Int Dial Code: 686
Map Page: 113

KUWAIT

Capital: Kuwait
Area: 17,820 km^2
Population: 2,418,393
Currency: Kuwaiti dinar (KD)
Main Religions: Muslim 85% (Sunni 70%, Shi'a 30%), Christian, Hindu, Parsi, and other 15%
Main Languages: Arabic (official), English
Int Dial Code: 965
Map Page: 95

KYRGYZSTAN

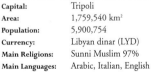

Capital: Bishkek
Area: 198,500 km^2
Population: 5,213,898
Currency: Kyrgyzstani som (KGS)
Main Religions: Muslim 75%, Russian Orthodox 20%, other 5%
Main Languages: Kirghiz (Kyrgyz) - official, Russian (official)
Int Dial Code: 996
Map Page: 77

LAOS

Capital: Vientiane
Area: 236,800 km^2
Population: 6,368,481
Currency: Kip (LAK)
Main Religions: Buddhist 60%, Animist and other 40%
Main Languages: Lao (official), French, English
Int Dial Code: 856
Map Page: 84

LATVIA

Capital: Riga
Area: 64,589 km^2
Population: 2,274,735
Currency: Latvian lat (LVL)
Main Religions: Lutheran, Roman Catholic, Russian Orthodox
Main Languages: Latvian or Lettish (official), Lithuanian, Russian
Int Dial Code: 371
Map Page: 49

LEBANON

Capital: Beirut
Area: 10,400 km^2
Population: 3,874,050
Currency: Lebanese pound (LBP)
Main Religions: Muslim 59.7% (including Shi'a, Sunni, Druze, Isma'ilite, Alawite or Nusayri), Christian 39% (including Orthodox Christian, Catholic, Protestant)
Main Languages: Arabic (official), French, English, Armenian
Int Dial Code: 961
Map Page: 94

LESOTHO

Capital: Maseru
Area: 30,355 km^2
Population: 2,022,331
Currency: Loti (LSL); South African Rand (ZAR)
Main Religions: Christian 80%, Indigenous beliefs 20%
Main Languages: Sesotho (southern Sotho), English (official), Zulu, Xhosa
Int Dial Code: 266
Map Page: 108

LIBERIA

Capital: Monrovia
Area: 111,370 km^2
Population: 3,042,004
Currency: Liberian dollar (LRD)
Main Religions: Indigenous beliefs 40%, Christian 40%, Muslim 20%
Main Languages: English 20% (official), ethnic group languages
Int Dial Code: 231
Map Page: 104

LIBYA

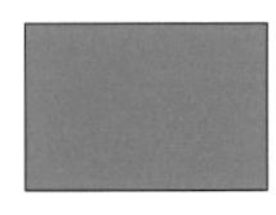

Capital: Tripoli
Area: 1,759,540 km^2
Population: 5,900,754
Currency: Libyan dinar (LYD)
Main Religions: Sunni Muslim 97%
Main Languages: Arabic, Italian, English
Int Dial Code: 218
Map Page: 100

LIECHTENSTEIN

Capital:	Vaduz
Area:	160 km^2
Population:	33,987
Currency:	Swiss franc (CHF)
Main Religions:	Roman Catholic 80%, Protestant 7.4%, unknown 7.7%, other 4.9%
Main Languages:	German (official), Alemannic dialect
Int Dial Code:	423
Map Page:	62

LITHUANIA

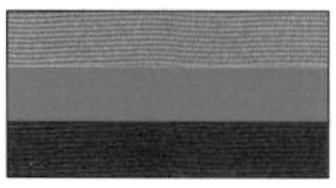

Capital:	Vilnius
Area:	65,200 km^2
Population:	3,585,906
Currency:	Litas (LTL)
Main Religions:	Roman Catholic (primarily), Lutheran, Russian Orthodox, Protestant, Evangelical Christian Baptist, Muslim, Jewish
Main Languages:	Lithuanian (official), Polish, Russian
Int Dial Code:	370
Map Page:	49

LUXEMBOURG

Capital:	Luxembourg
Area:	2,586 km^2
Population:	474,413
Currency:	Euro (EUR)
Main Religions:	Roman Catholic with Protestants, Jews, and Muslims
Main Languages:	Luxembourgish (national language), German (administrative language), French
Int Dial Code:	352
Map Page:	55

MACEDONIA

Capital:	Skopje
Area:	25,333 km^2
Population:	2,050,554
Currency:	Macedonian denar (MKD)
Main Religions:	Macedonian Orthodox 67%, Muslim 30%, other 3%
Main Languages:	Macedonian 70%, Albanian 21%, Turkish 3%, Serbo-Croatian 3%, other 3%
Int Dial Code:	389
Map Page:	68

MADAGASCAR

Capital:	Antananarivo
Area:	587,040 km^2
Population:	18,595,469
Currency:	Madagascar Ariary (MGA)
Main Religions:	Indigenous beliefs 52%, Christian 41%, Muslim 7%
Main Languages:	French (official), Malagasy (official)
Int Dial Code:	261
Map Page:	109

MALAWI

Capital:	Lilongwe
Area:	118,480 km^2
Population:	13,013,926
Currency:	Malawian kwacha (MWK)
Main Religions:	Christian 79.9%, Muslim 12.8%
Main Languages:	English (official), Chichewa (official)
Int Dial Code:	265
Map Page:	109

MALAYSIA

Capital:	Kuala Lumpur; Putrajaya is the federal government administration centre
Area:	329,750 km^2
Population:	24,385,858
Currency:	Ringgit (MYR)
Main Religions:	Muslim, Budhist, Duoist, Hindu, Christian, Sikh, Shamanism
Main Languages:	Bahasa Melayu (official), English, Chinese dialects (Cantonese, Mandarin, Hokkien, Hakka, Hainan, Foochow), Tamil, Telugu, Malayalam, Panjabi, Thai
Int Dial Code:	60
Map Page:	86

MALDIVES

Capital:	Male
Area:	300 km^2
Population:	359,008
Currency:	Rufiyaa (MVR)
Main Religions:	Sunni Muslim
Main Languages:	Maldivian Dhivehi (dialect of Sinhala, script derived from Arabic), English
Int Dial Code:	960
Map Page:	89

MALI

Capital:	Bamako
Area:	1.24 million km^2
Population:	11,716,829
Currency:	Communaute Financiere Africaine franc (XOF)
Main Religions:	Muslim 90%, Indigenous beliefs 9%, Christian 1%
Main Languages:	French (official), Bambara 80%, numerous African languages
Int Dial Code:	223
Map Page:	102

MALTA

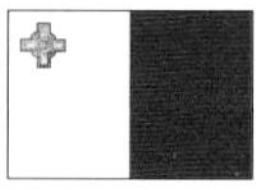

Capital:	Valletta
Area:	316 km^2
Population:	400,214
Currency:	Maltese lira (MTL)
Main Religions:	Roman Catholic 98%
Main Languages:	Maltese (official), English (official)
Int Dial Code:	356
Map Page:	65

MARSHALL ISLANDS

Capital:	Majuro
Area:	181 km^2
Population:	60,422
Currency:	US dollar (USD)
Main Religions:	Christian (mostly Protestant)
Main Languages:	English (official), two major Marshallese dialects from the Malayo-Polynesian family, Japanese
Int Dial Code:	692
Map Page:	112

MAURITANIA

Capital:	Nouakchott
Area:	1,030,700 km^2
Population:	3,177,388
Currency:	Ouguiya (MRO)
Main Religions:	Muslim 100%
Main Languages:	Hasaniya Arabic (official), Pulaar, Soninke, Wolof, French
Int Dial Code:	222
Map Page:	102

MAURITIUS

Capital: Port Louis
Area: 2,040 km²
Population: 1,240,827
Currency: Mauritian rupee (MUR)
Main Religions: Hindu 48%, Roman Catholic 23.6%, Muslim 16.6%, other christian 8.6%
Main Languages: English (official), Creole, French, Hindi, Urdu, Hakka, Bojpoori
Int Dial Code: 230
Map Page: 109

MEXICO

Capital: Mexico
Area: 1,972,550 km²
Population: 107,449,525
Currency: Mexican peso (MXN):
Main Religions: Nominally Roman Catholic 89%, Protestant 6%, other 5%
Main Languages: Spanish, Mayan, Nahuatl
Int Dial Code: 52
Map Page: 134

MICRONESIA, FED. STATES OF

Capital: Palikir
Area: 702 km²
Population: 108,004
Currency: US dollar (USD)
Main Religions: Roman Catholic 50%, Protestant 47%, other 3%
Main Languages: English (official), Trukese, Pohnpeian, Yapese, Kosrean
Int Dial Code: 691
Map Page: 112

MOLDOVA

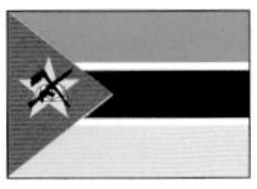

Capital: Chisinau
Area: 33,843 km²
Population: 4,466,706
Currency: Moldovan leu (MDL)
Main Religions: Eastern Orthodox 98.5%, Jewish 1.5%, Baptist
Main Languages: Moldovan (official), Russian, Gagauz (a Turkish dialect)
Int Dial Code: 373
Map Page: 67

MONACO

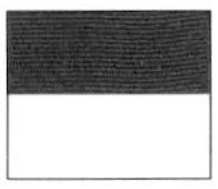

Capital: Monaco
Area: 1.95 km²
Population: 32,543
Currency: Euro (EUR)
Main Religions: Roman Catholic 90%
Main Languages: French (official), English, Italian, Monegasque
Int Dial Code: 377
Map Page: 62

MONGOLIA

Capital: Ulaanbaatar
Area: 1.565 million km²
Population: 2,832,224
Currency: Togrog/tugrik (MNT)
Main Religions: Buddhist Lamaism 50%, Muslim, Shamanism, and Christian
Main Languages: Khalkha Mongol 90%, Turkic, Russian
Int Dial Code: 976
Map Page: 75

MONTENEGRO

Capital: Podgorica
Area: 14,026 km²
Population: 630,548
Currency: Euro (EUR)
Main Religions: Orthodox, Muslim, Roman Catholic
Main Languages: Serbian, Montenegrin
Int Dial Code: 381 (shared with Serbia - new code expected)
Map Page: 66

MOROCCO

Capital: Rabat
Area: 446,550 km²
Population: 33,241,259
Currency: Moroccan dirham (MAD)
Main Religions: Muslim 98.7%, Christian 1.1%, Jewish 0.2%
Main Languages: Arabic (official), Berber dialects, French
Int Dial Code: 212
Map Page: 102

MOZAMBIQUE

Capital: Maputo
Area: 801,590 km²
Population: 19,686,505
Currency: Metical (MZM)
Main Religions: Catholic 23.8%, Muslim 17.8%, Zionist Christian 17.5%
Main Languages: Portuguese (official), indigenous dialects
Int Dial Code: 258
Map Page: 109

MYANMAR (BURMA)

Capital: Naypyidaw
Area: 678,500 km²
Population: 47,382,633
Currency: Kyat (MMK)
Main Religions: Buddhist 89%, Christian 4% (Baptist 3%, Roman Catholic 1%), Muslim 4%, Animist 1%, other 2%
Main Languages: Burmese
Int Dial Code: 95
Map Page: 84

NAMIBIA

Capital: Windhoek
Area: 825,418 km²
Population: 2,044,147
Currency: Namibian dollar (NAD); South African rand (ZAR)
Main Religions: Christian 80% - 90% (Lutheran 50%), Indigenous beliefs 10%-20%
Main Languages: English 7% (official), Afrikaans, German 32%, indigenous languages: Oshivambo, Herero, Nama
Int Dial Code: 264
Map Page: 108

NAURU

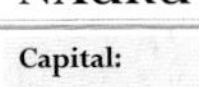

Capital: no official capital; government offices in Yaren District
Area: 21 km²
Population: 13,287
Currency: Australian dollar (AUD)
Main Religions: Christian (66% Protestant, 33% Roman Catholic)
Main Languages: Nauruan (official), English
Int Dial Code: 674
Map Page: 112

NEPAL

Capital: Kathmandu
Area: 147,181 km²
Population: 28,287,147
Currency: Nepalese rupee (NPR)
Main Religions: Hinduism 80.6%, Buddhism 10.7%, Muslim 4.2%
Main Languages: Nepali (official; spoken by 90% of the population), 30 major dialects, English
Int Dial Code: 977
Map Page: 88

NETHERLANDS

Capital: Amsterdam; The Hague is the seat of government
Area: 41,526 km²
Population: 16,491,461
Currency: Euro (EUR)
Main Religions: Roman Catholic 31%, Protestant 21%, Muslim 4.4%, other 3.6%, unaffiliated 40%
Main Languages: Dutch
Int Dial Code: 31
Map Page: 55

NEW ZEALAND

Capital: Wellington
Area: 268,680 km²
Population: 4,076,140
Currency: New Zealand dollar (NZD)
Main Religions: Anglican 14.9%, Roman Catholic 12.4%, Presbyterian 10.9%, Methodist 2.9%,
Main Languages: English (official), Maori (official)
Int Dial Code: 64
Map Page: 116

NICARAGUA

Capital: Managua
Area: 129,494 km²
Population: 5,570,129
Currency: Gold cordoba (NIO)
Main Religions: Roman Catholic 72.9%, Evangelical 15.1%
Main Languages: Spanish (official)
Int Dial Code: 505
Map Page: 135

NIGER

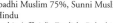

Capital: Niamey
Area: 1.267 million km²
Population: 12,525,094
Currency: Communaute Financiere Africaine franc (XOF)
Main Religions: Muslim 80%, Indigenous beliefs and Christians
Main Languages: French (official), Hausa, Djerma
Int Dial Code: 227
Map Page: 103

NIGERIA

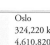

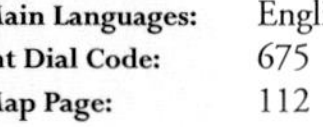

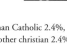

Capital: Abuja
Area: 923,768 km²
Population: 131,859,731
Currency: Naira (NGN)
Main Religions: Muslim 50%, Christian 40%, Indigenous beliefs 10%
Main Languages: English (official), Hausa, Yoruba, Igbo (Ibo), Fulani
Int Dial Code: 234
Map Page: 105

NORTH KOREA

Capital: P'yongyang
Area: 120,540 km²
Population: 23,113,019
Currency: North Korean won (KPW)
Main Religions: Buddhist and Confucianist, some Christian and syncretic Chondogyo (Religion of the Heavenly Way)
Main Languages: Korean
Int Dial Code: 850
Map Page: 82

NORWAY

Capital: Oslo
Area: 324,220 km²
Population: 4,610,820
Currency: Norwegian krone (NOK)
Main Religions: Church of Norway 85.7%, Roman Catholic 2.4%, Muslim 1.8%, Pentecostal 1%, other christian 2.4%
Main Languages: Norwegian (official)
Int Dial Code: 47
Map Page: 48

OMAN

Capital: Muscat
Area: 212,460 km²
Population: 3,102,229
Currency: Omani rial (OMR)
Main Religions: Ibadhi Muslim 75%, Sunni Muslim, Shi'a Muslim, Hindu
Main Languages: Arabic (official), English, Baluchi, Urdu, Indian dialects
Int Dial Code: 968
Map Page: 91

PAKISTAN

Capital: Islamabad
Area: 803,940 km²
Population: 165,803,560
Currency: Pakistani rupee (PKR)
Main Religions: Muslim 97% (Sunni 77%, Shi'a 20%)
Main Languages: Punjabi 48%, Sindhi 12%, Siraiki 10%, Pashtu 8%, Urdu 8%, Balochi 3%, Hindko 2%, Brahui 1%
Int Dial Code: 92
Map Page: 91

PALAU

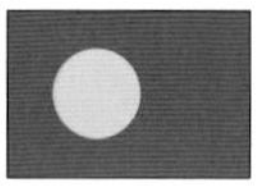

Capital: Koror
Area: 458 km²
Population: 20,579
Currency: US dollar (USD)
Main Religions: Christian (Catholics, Seventh-Day Adventists, Jehovah's Witnesses, Assembly of God, the Liebenzell Mission, and Latter-Day Saints), Modekngei 33%
Main Languages: English and Palauan, Tobi and Angaur
Int Dial Code: 680
Map Page: 112

PANAMA

Capital: Panama
Area: 78,200 km²
Population: 3,191,319
Currency: Balboa (PAB); US dollar (USD)
Main Religions: Roman Catholic 85%, Protestant 15%
Main Languages: Spanish (official), English 14%
Int Dial Code: 507
Map Page: 135

PAPUA NEW GUINEA

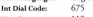

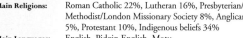

Capital: Port Moresby
Area: 462,840 km²
Population: 5,670,544
Currency: Kina (PGK)
Main Religions: Roman Catholic 22%, Lutheran 16%, Presbyterian/Methodist/London Missionary Society 8%, Anglican 5%, Protestant 10%, Indigenous beliefs 34%
Main Languages: English, Pidgin English, Motu
Int Dial Code: 675
Map Page: 112

PARAGUAY

Capital: Asuncion
Area: 406,750 km^2
Population: 6,506,464
Currency: Guarani (PYG)
Main Religions: Roman Catholic 90%, Mennonite, and other Protestant
Main Languages: Spanish (official), Guarani (official)
Int Dial Code: 595
Map Page: 142

PERU

Capital: Lima
Area: 1,285,220 km^2
Population: 28,302,603
Currency: Nuevo sol (PEN)
Main Religions: Roman Catholic 90%
Main Languages: Spanish (official), Quechua (official), Aymara
Int Dial Code: 51
Map Page: 140

PHILIPPINES

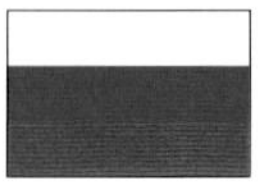

Capital: Manila
Area: 300,000 km^2
Population: 89,468,677
Currency: Philippine peso (PHP)
Main Religions: Roman Catholic 83%, Protestant 9%, Muslim 5%
Main Languages: Filipino, English, eight major dialects including Tagalog, Cebuano, Ilocan, Hiligaynon or Ilonggo and Bicol
Int Dial Code: 63
Map Page: 85

POLAND

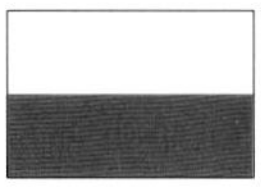

Capital: Warsaw
Area: 312,685 km^2
Population: 38,536,869
Currency: Zloty (PLN)
Main Religions: Roman Catholic 95%, Eastern Orthodox, Protestant, and other 5%
Main Languages: Polish
Int Dial Code: 48
Map Page: 50

PORTUGAL

Capital: Lisbon
Area: 92,391 km^2
Population: 10,605,870
Currency: Euro (EUR)
Main Religions: Roman Catholic 94%, Protestant
Main Languages: Portuguese, Mirandese
Int Dial Code: 351
Map Page: 60

QATAR

Capital: Doha
Area: 11,437 km^2
Population: 885,359
Currency: Qatari rial (QAR)
Main Religions: Muslim 95%
Main Languages: Arabic (official), English
Int Dial Code: 974
Map Page: 95

ROMANIA

Capital: Bucharest
Area: 237,500 km^2
Population: 22,303,552
Currency: Leu (RON)
Main Religions: Eastern Orthodox 86.8%, Protestant 7.5%, Roman Catholic 4.7%
Main Languages: Romanian, Hungarian, German
Int Dial Code: 40
Map Page: 67

RUSSIAN FEDERATION

Capital: Moscow
Area: 17,075,200 km^2
Population: 142,893,540
Currency: Russian ruble (RUR)
Main Religions: Russian Orthodox, Muslim
Main Languages: Russian
Int Dial Code: 7
Map Page: 74

RWANDA

Capital: Kigali
Area: 26,338 km^2
Population: 8,648,248
Currency: Rwandan franc (RWF):
Main Religions: Roman Catholic 52.7%, Protestant 24%, Adventist 10.4%, Muslim 1.9%, Indigenous beliefs 6.5%
Main Languages: Kinyarwanda, Bantu vernacular, French, English
Int Dial Code: 250
Map Page: 106

SAINT KITTS AND NEVIS

Capital: Basseterre
Area: 261 km^2 (Saint Kitts 168 km^2; Nevis 93 km^2)
Population: 39,129
Currency: East Caribbean dollar (XCD)
Main Religions: Anglican, other Protestant, Roman Catholic
Main Languages: English
Int Dial Code: 1 + 869
Map Page: 135

SAINT LUCIA

Capital: Castries
Area: 616 km^2
Population: 168,458
Currency: East Caribbean dollar (XCD)
Main Religions: Roman Catholic 67.5%, Seventh Day Adventist 8.5%, Pentecostal 5.7%, Anglican 2%, Evangelical 2%
Main Languages: English (official), French patois
Int Dial Code: 1 + 758
Map Page: 135

SAINT VINCENT & THE GRENADINES

Capital: Kingstown
Area: 389 km^2 (Saint Vincent 344 km^2)
Population: 117,848
Currency: East Caribbean dollar (XCD)
Main Religions: Anglican 47%, Methodist 28%, Roman Catholic 13%,Seventh-Day Adventist, Hindu, other Protestant
Main Languages: English, French patois
Int Dial Code: 1 + 784
Map Page: 135

SAMOA

Capital: Apia
Area: 2,944 km²
Population: 176,908
Currency: Tala (SAT)
Main Religions: Christian 99.7% (London Missionary Society; includes Congregational, Roman Catholic, Methodist, Latter-Day Saints, Seventh-Day Adventist)
Main Languages: Samoan (Polynesian), English
Int Dial Code: 685
Map Page: 113

SAN MARINO

Capital: San Marino
Area: 61.2 km²
Population: 29,251
Currency: Euro (EUR)
Main Religions: Roman Catholic
Main Languages: Italian
Int Dial Code: 378
Map Page: 63

SÃO TOMÉ AND PRÍNCIPE

Capital: São Tomé
Area: 1,001 km²
Population: 193,413
Currency: Dobra (STD)
Main Religions: Christian 80% (Roman Catholic, Evangelical Protestant, Seventh-Day Adventist)
Main Languages: Portuguese (official)
Int Dial Code: 239
Map Page: 105

SAUDI ARABIA

Capital: Riyadh
Area: 1,960,582 km²
Population: 27,019,731
Currency: Saudi riyal (SAR)
Main Religions: Muslim 100%
Main Languages: Arabic
Int Dial Code: 966
Map Page: 90

SENEGAL

Capital: Dakar
Area: 196,190 km²
Population: 11,987,121
Currency: Communaute Financiere Africaine franc (XOF)
Main Religions: Muslim 92%, Indigenous beliefs 6%, Christian 2% (mostly Roman Catholic)
Main Languages: French (official), Wolof, Pulaar, Jola, Mandinka
Int Dial Code: 221
Map Page: 104

SERBIA

Capital: Belgrade
Area: 88,361 km²
Population: 9,396,411
Currency: New Yugoslav dinar (YUM)
Main Religions: Serbian Orthodox, Muslim, Roman Catholic, Protestant
Main Languages: Serbian (official), Romanian, Hungarian, Slovak, Croatian, Albania
Int Dial Code: 381
Map Page: 66

SEYCHELLES

Capital Victoria
Area: 455 km²

Population: 81,541

Currency: Seychelles rupee (SCR)
Main Religions: Roman Catholic 90%, Anglican 8%, other 2%
Main Languages: English (official), French (official), Creole
Int Dial Code: 248
Map Page: 109

SIERRA LEONE

Capital: Freetown
Area: 71,740 km²
Population: 6,005,250
Currency: Leone (SLL)
Main Religions: Muslim 60%, indigenous beliefs 30%, Christian 10%
Main Languages: English (official), Mende, Temne, Krio (English-based Creole)
Int Dial Code: 232
Map Page: 104

SINGAPORE

Capital: Singapore
Area: 692.7 km²
Population: 4,492,150
Currency: Singapore dollar (SGD)
Main Religions: Buddhist (Chinese), Muslim (Malays), Christian, Hindu, Sikh, Taoist, Confucianist
Main Languages: Chinese (official), Malay (official and national), Tamil (official), English (official)
Int Dial Code: 65
Map Page: 86

SLOVAKIA

Capital: Bratislava
Area: 48,845 km²
Population: 5,439,448
Currency: Slovak koruna (SKK)
Main Religions: Roman Catholic 60.3%, Atheist 9.7%, Protestant 8.4%, Orthodox 4.1%, other 17.5%
Main Languages: Slovak (official), Hungarian
Int Dial Code: 421
Map Page: 51

SLOVENIA

Capital: Ljubljana
Area: 20,273 km²
Population: 2,010,347
Currency: Tolar (SIT)
Main Religions: Catholic 57.8%, Muslim 2.4%, Orthodox 2.3%, other christian 0.9%
Main Languages: Slovenian 91%, Serbo-Croatian 6%, other 3%
Int Dial Code: 386
Map Page: 63

SOLOMON ISLANDS

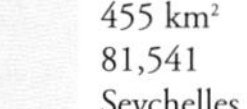

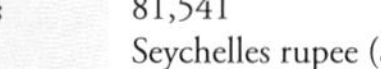

Capital: Honiara
Area: 28,450 km²
Population: 552,438
Currency: Solomon Islands dollar (SBD)
Main Religions: Church of Melanesia 32.8%, Roman Catholic 19%, South Sea Evangelical 17%, Seventh Day Adventist 11.2%, United Church 10.3%, Christian Fellowship Church 2.4%, other christian 4.4%
Int Dial Code: 677
Map Page: 112

SOMALIA

Capital: Mogadishu
Area: 637,657 km^2
Population: 8,863,338
Currency: Somali shilling (SOS)
Main Religions: Sunni Muslim
Main Languages: Somali (official), Arabic, Italian, English
Int Dial Code: 252
Map Page: 107

SOUTH AFRICA, REPUBLIC OF

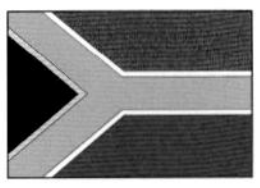

Capital: Pretoria (executive); Bloemfontein (judicial); Cape Town (legislative)
Area: 1,219,912 km^2
Population: 44,187,637
Currency: Rand (ZAR)
Main Religions: Christian 68%, Muslim 2%, Hindu 1.5%, Indigenous beliefs and Animist 28.5%
Main Languages: IsiZulu, IsiXhosa, Afrikaans, Sepedi, English, Setswana, Sesotho, Xitsonga
Int Dial Code: 27
Map Page: 108

SOUTH KOREA

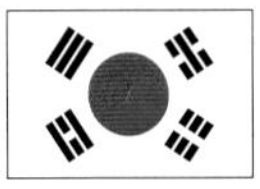

Capital: Seoul
Area: 98,480 km^2
Population: 48,846,823
Currency: South Korean Won (KRW)
Main Religions: Christian 26%, Buddhist 26%, Confucianist 1%
Main Languages: Korean, English
Int Dial Code: 82
Map Page: 82

SPAIN

Capital: Madrid
Area: 504,782 km^2
Population: 40,397,842
Currency: Euro (EUR)
Main Religions: Roman Catholic 94%, other 6%
Main Languages: Castilian Spanish (official) 74%, Catalan 17%, Galician 7%, Basque 2%
Int Dial Code: 34
Map Page: 60

SRI LANKA

Capital: Sri Jayewardenepura Kotte
Area: 65,610 km^2
Population: 20,222,240
Currency: Sri Lankan rupee (LKR)
Main Religions: Buddhist 70%, Hindu 15%, Christian 8%, Muslim 7%
Main Languages: Sinhala 74%, Tamil 18%, other 8%
Int Dial Code: 94
Map Page: 89

SUDAN

Capital: Khartoum
Area: 2,505,810 km^2
Population: 41,236,378
Currency: Sudanese dinar (SDD)
Main Religions: Sunni Muslim 70%, indigenous beliefs 25%, Christian 5%
Main Languages: Arabic, Nubian, Ta Bedawie, diverse dialects of Nilotic, Nilo-Hamitic, Sudanic languages, English
Int Dial Code: 249
Map Page: 100

SURINAME

Capital: Paramaribo
Area: 163,270 km^2
Population: 439,117
Currency: Surinamese guilder (SRG)
Main Religions: Hindu 27.4%, Muslim 19.6%, Roman Catholic 22.8%, Protestant 25.2%, Indigenous beliefs 5%
Main Languages: Dutch (official), English, Sranang Tongo, Hindustani, Javanese
Int Dial Code: 597
Map Page: 141

SWAZILAND

Capital: Mbabane; Lobamba is the royal and legislative capital
Area: 17,363 km^2
Population: 1,136,334
Currency: Lilangeni (SZL)
Main Religions: Zionist 40%, Roman Catholic 20%, Muslim 10%, Anglican, Bahai, Methodist, Mormon, Jewish
Main Languages: English (official), Swati (official)
Int Dial Code: 268
Map Page: 109

SWEDEN

Capital: Stockholm
Area: 449,964 km^2
Population: 9,016,596
Currency: Swedish krona (SEK)
Main Religions: Lutheran 87%, Roman Catholic, Orthodox, Baptist, Muslim, Jewish, Buddhist
Main Languages: Swedish
Int Dial Code: 46
Map Page: 48

SWITZERLAND

Capital: Bern
Area: 41,290 km^2
Population: 7,523,934
Currency: Swiss franc (CHF)
Main Religions: Roman Catholic 41.8%, Protestant 35.3%
Main Languages: German (official) 63.7%, French (official) 19.2%, Italian (official) 7.6%, Romansch (official) 0.6%, other 8.9%
Int Dial Code: 41
Map Page: 62

SYRIA

Capital: Damascus
Area: 185,180 km^2
Population: 18,881,361
Currency: Syrian pound (SYP)
Main Religions: Sunni Muslim 74%, Alawite, Druze, and other Muslim sects 16%, Christian 10%, Jewish
Main Languages: Arabic (official); Kurdish, Armenian, Aramaic, Circassian, French, English
Int Dial Code: 963
Map Page: 90

TAIWAN

Capital: Taipei
Area: 35,980 km^2
Population: 23,036,087
Currency: Taiwan dollar (TWD)
Main Religions: Buddhist, Confucian, and Taoist 93%, Christian 4.5%, other 2.5%
Main Languages: Mandarin Chinese (official), Taiwanese (Min), Hakka dialects
Int Dial Code: 886
Map Page: 85

TAJIKISTAN

Capital:	Dushanbe
Area:	143,100 km^2
Population:	7,320,815
Currency:	Somoni (SM)
Main Religions:	Sunni Muslim 85%, Shi'a Muslim 5%
Main Languages:	Tajik (official), Russian
Int Dial Code:	992
Map Page:	91

TANZANIA

Capital:	Dodoma
Area:	945,087 km^2
Population:	37,445,392
Currency:	Tanzanian shilling (TZS)
Main Religions:	Christian 45%, Muslim 35%, indigenous beliefs 20%; Zanzibar - more than 99% Muslim
Main Languages:	Kiswahili or Swahili, Kiunguju, English, Arabic
Int Dial Code:	255
Map Page:	107

THAILAND

Capital:	Bangkok
Area:	514,000 km^2
Population:	64,631,595
Currency:	Baht (THB)
Main Religions:	Buddhism 95%, Muslim 3.8%, Christianity 0.5%, Hinduism 0.1%, other 0.6%
Main Languages:	Thai, English, ethnic and regional dialects
Int Dial Code:	66
Map Page:	84

TOGO

Capital:	Lome
Area:	56,785 km^2
Population:	5,548,702
Currency:	Communaute Financiere Africaine franc (XOF)
Main Religions:	Indigenous beliefs 59%, Christian 29%, Muslim 12%
Main Languages:	French (official), Ewe and Mina, Kabye and Dagomba
Int Dial Code:	228
Map Page:	104

TONGA

Capital:	Nuku'alofa
Area:	748 km^2
Population:	114,689
Currency:	Pa'anga (TOP)
Main Religions:	Christian (Free Wesleyan Church claims over 30,000 adherents)
Main Languages:	Tongan, English
Int Dial Code:	676
Map Page:	113

TRINIDAD AND TOBAGO

Capital:	Port-of-Spain
Area:	5,128 km^2
Population:	1,065,842
Currency:	Trinidad and Tobago dollar (TTD)
Main Religions:	Roman Catholic 29.4%, Hindu 23.8%, Anglican 10.9%, Muslim 5.8%, Presbyterian 3.4%, other 26.7%
Main Languages:	English (official), Hindi, French, Spanish, Chinese
Int Dial Code:	1 + 868
Map Page:	135

TUNISIA

Capital:	Tunis
Area:	163,610 km^2
Population:	10,175,014
Currency:	Tunisian dinar (TND)
Main Religions:	Muslim 98%, Christian 1%, Jewish and other 1%
Main Languages:	Arabic (official), French (commerce)
Int Dial Code:	216
Map Page:	103

TURKEY

Capital:	Ankara
Area:	780,580 km^2
Population:	70,413,958
Currency:	Turkish lira (YTL)
Main Religions:	Muslim 99.8% (mostly Sunni), other 0.2% (Christian and Jews)
Main Languages:	Turkish (official), Kurdish, Arabic, Armenian, Greek
Int Dial Code:	90
Map Page:	92

TURKMENISTAN

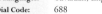

Capital:	Ashgabat
Area:	488,100 km^2
Population:	5,042,920
Currency:	Turkmen manat (TMM)
Main Religions:	Muslim 89%, Eastern Orthodox 9%, unknown 2%
Main Languages:	Turkmen 72%, Russian 12%, Uzbek 9%, other 7%
Int Dial Code:	993
Map Page:	91

TUVALU

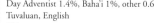

Capital:	Funafuti
Area:	26 km^2
Population:	11,810
Currency:	Australian dollar (AUD); also a Tuvaluan dollar
Main Religions:	Church of Tuvalu (Congregationalist) 97%, Seventh-Day Adventist 1.4%, Baha'i 1%, other 0.6%
Main Languages:	Tuvaluan, English
Int Dial Code:	688
Map Page:	112

UGANDA

Capital:	Kampala
Area:	236,040 km^2
Population:	28,195,754
Currency:	Ugandan shilling (UGX)
Main Religions:	Roman Catholic 33%, Protestant 33%, Muslim 16%, Indigenous beliefs 18%
Main Languages:	English, Ganda or Luganda, other Niger-Congo languages, Nilo-Saharan languages, Swahili, Arabic
Int Dial Code:	256
Map Page:	106

UKRAINE

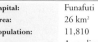

Capital:	Kiev (Kyiv)
Area:	603,700 km^2
Population:	46,710,816
Currency:	Hryvnia (UAH)
Main Religions:	Ukrainian Orthodox - Moscow Patriarchate, Ukrainian Orthodox Kiev Patriarchate
Main Languages:	Ukrainian, Russian, Romanian, Polish, Hungarian
Int Dial Code:	380
Map Page:	70

UNITED ARAB EMIRATES

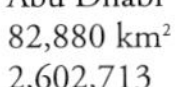

Capital: Abu Dhabi
Area: 82,880 km²
Population: 2,602,713
Currency: Emirati dirham (AED)
Main Religions: Muslim 96% (Shi'a 16%), Christian, Hindu, and other 4%
Main Languages: Arabic (official), Persian, English, Hindi, Urdu
Int Dial Code: 971
Map Page: 90

UNITED KINGDOM

Capital: London
Area: 244,820 km²
Population: 60,609,153
Currency: British pound (GBP)
Main Religions: Christian 71.6%, Muslim 2.7%, Hindu 1%
Main Languages: English, Welsh, Scottish form of Gaelic
Int Dial Code: 44
Map Page: 56

UNITED STATES

Capital: Washington, D.C.
Area: 9,631,420 km²
Population: 298,444,215
Currency: US dollar (USD)
Main Religions: Protestant 52%, Roman Catholic 24%, Jewish 1%, Muslim 1%
Main Languages: English, Spanish
Int Dial Code: 1
Map Page: 124

URUGUAY

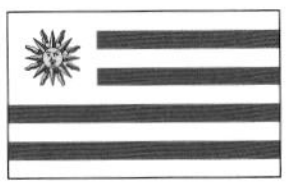

Capital: Montevideo
Area: 176,220 km²
Population: 3,431,932
Currency: Uruguayan peso (UYU)
Main Religions: Roman Catholic 66%, Protestant 2%, Jewish 1%, nonprofessing or other 31%
Main Languages: Spanish, Portunol, or Brazilero
Int Dial Code: 598
Map Page: 143

UZBEKISTAN

Capital: Toshkent (Tashkent)
Area: 447,400 km²
Population: 27,307,134
Currency: Uzbekistani sum (UZS)
Main Religions: Muslim 88% (mostly Sunnis), Eastern Orthodox 9%, other 3%
Main Languages: Uzbek 74.3%, Russian 14.2%, Tajik 4.4%, other 7.1%
Int Dial Code: 998
Map Page: 77

VANUATU

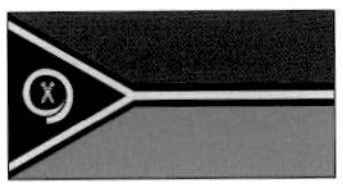

Capital: Port-Vila
Area: 12,200 km²
Population: 208,869
Currency: Vatu (VUV)
Main Religions: Presbyterian 31.4%, Anglican 13.4%, Roman Catholic 13.1%, indigenous beliefs 5.6%
Main Languages: English, French, Pidgin
Int Dial Code: 678
Map Page: 112

VATICAN CITY

Capital: Vatican City
Area: 0.44 km²
Population: 932
Currency: Euro (EUR)
Main Religions: Roman Catholic
Main Languages: Italian, Latin, French
Int Dial Code: 39
Map Page: 64

VENEZUELA

Capital: Caracas
Area: 912,050 km²
Population: 25,730,435
Currency: Bolivar (VEB)
Main Religions: Roman Catholic 96%, Protestant 2%, other 2%
Main Languages: Spanish (official), numerous indigenous dialects
Int Dial Code: 58
Map Page: 140

VIETNAM

Capital: Hanoi
Area: 329,560 km²
Population: 84,402,966
Currency: Dong (VND)
Main Religions: Buddhist, Hoa Hao, Cao Dai, Christian (Roman Catholic, some Protestant), Indigenous beliefs, Muslim
Main Languages: Vietnamese, English, French, Chinese, and Khmer
Int Dial Code: 84
Map Page: 84

YEMEN

Capital: Sanaa
Area: 527,970 km²
Population: 21,456,188
Currency: Yemeni rial (YER)
Main Religions: Muslim including Shaf'i (Sunni) and Zaydi (Shi'a), Jewish, Christian, and Hindu
Main Languages: Arabic
Int Dial Code: 967
Map Page: 90

ZAMBIA

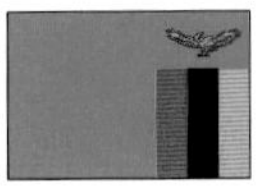

Capital: Lusaka
Area: 752,614 km²
Population: 11,502,010
Currency: Zambian kwacha (ZMK)
Main Religions: Christian 50%-75%, Muslim and Hindu 24%-49%, Indigenous beliefs 1%
Main Languages: English (official), Bemba, Kaonda, Lozi, Lunda, Luvale, Nyanja, Tonga, 70 other indigenous languages
Int Dial Code: 260
Map Page: 108

ZIMBABWE

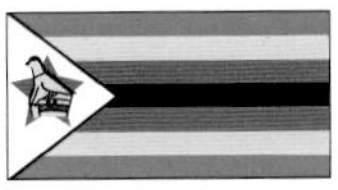

Capital: Harare
Area: 390,580 km²
Population: 12,236,805
Currency: Zimbabwean dollar (ZWD)
Main Religions: Syncretic (part Christian, part indigenous beliefs) 50%, Christian 25%, indigenous beliefs 24%, Muslim and other 1%
Main Languages: English (official), Shona, Sindebele, tribal dialects
Int Dial Code: 263
Map Page: 108

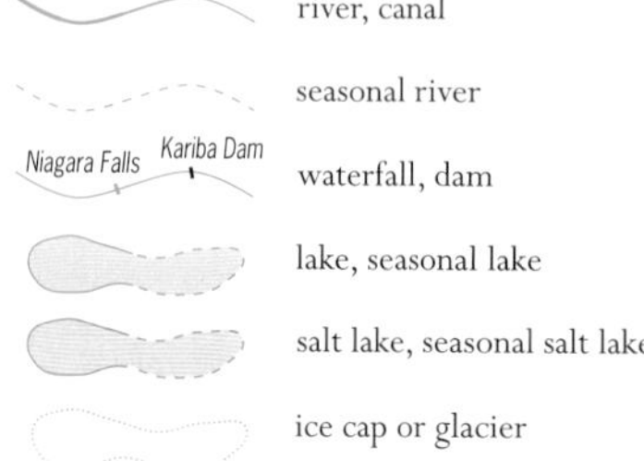

Key to map symbols

KEY TO MAP SYMBOLS

Political Regions

CANADA	country
ONTARIO	state or province
	international boundary
	state or province boundary
	undefined/disputed boundary or ceasefire/demarcation line

Communications

	motorway
	main road
	other road or track
	railway
	international airport

Hydrographic Features

	river, canal
	seasonal river
Niagara Falls Kariba Dam	waterfall, dam
	lake, seasonal lake
	salt lake, seasonal salt lake
	ice cap or glacier

Cities, Towns & Capitals

CHICAGO	over 3 million
HAMBURG	1 – 3 million
Bulawayo	250 000 – 1 million
Antofogasta	100 000 – 250 000
Ajaccio	25 000 – 100 000
Indian Springs	under 25 000
LONDON	country capital
Columbia	state or province capital
	urban area

Cultural Features

Persepolis	ancient site or ruin
	ancient wall

Topographic Features

Mount Ziel 1510	elevation above sea level (in metres)
133	elevation of land below sea level (in metres)
Khyber Pass 1080	mountain pass (height in metres)

Each page also features a guide to relief colours

The World in Maps

Political

Physical

Equatorial Scale 1 : 112 000 000

0 1000 2000 3000 4000 km

0 1000 2000 miles

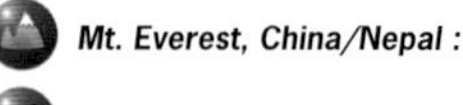

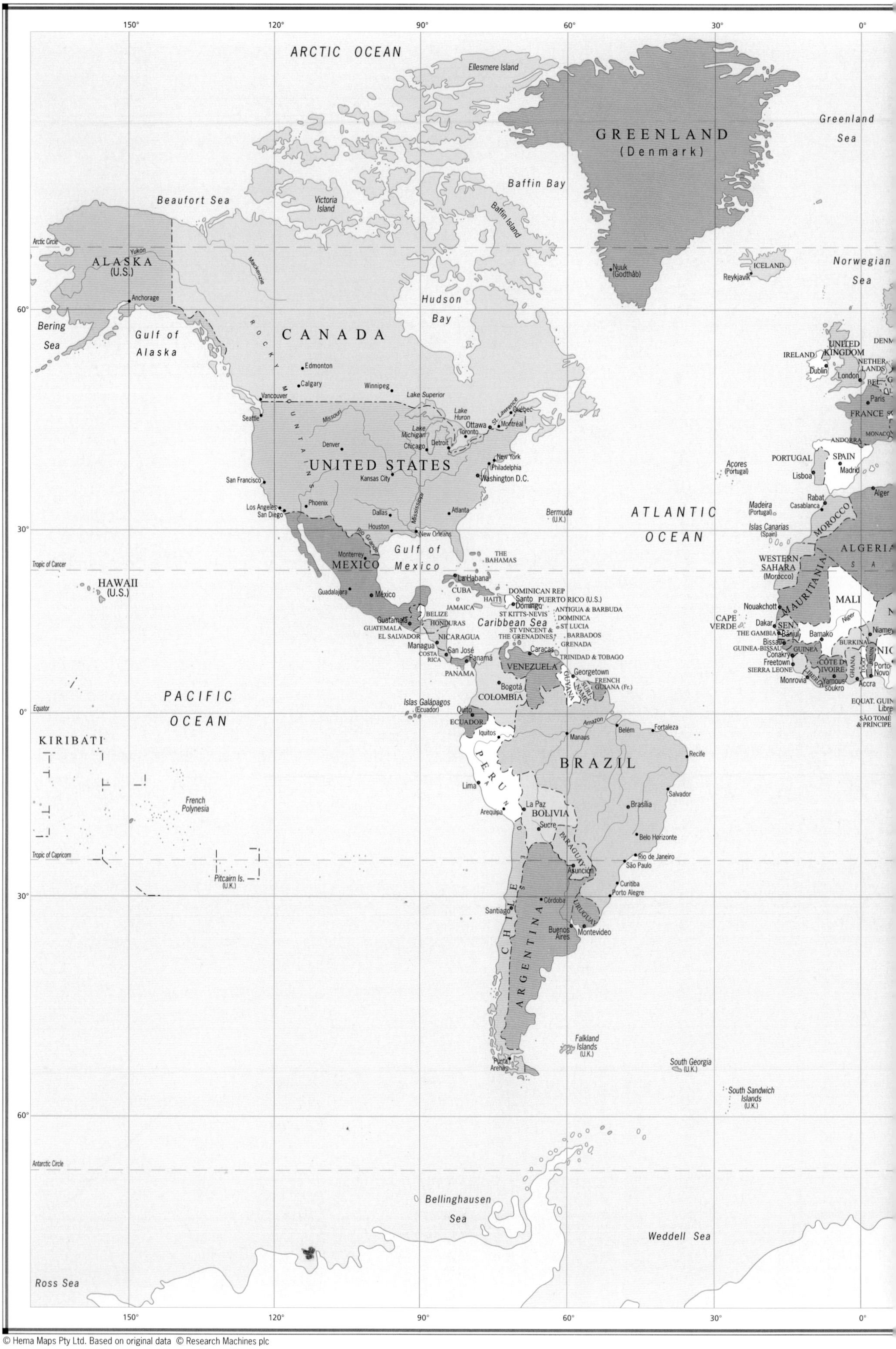

© Hema Maps Pty Ltd. Based on original data © Research Machines plc

Mt. Everest, China/Nepal : 8,848 m or 29,029 ft

Dead Sea, Israel/Jordan : 400 m or 1312 ft

Arica, Chile : 0.08 cm or 0.03 in

Mawsynram, India : 1187.2 cm or 467.4 in

Nile, Egypt : 6,690 km or 4,160 mi

Caspian Sea : 371,000 km² or 143,240 sq mi

World: Political

ARCTIC OCEAN
Zemlya Frantsa-Iosifa
Severnaya Zemlya
Novaya Zemlya
Svalbard (Norway)
Barents Sea

FINLAND
Helsinki
Tallinn EST.
Stockholm
Riga LAT.
Vilnius LITH.
Minsk
POLAND BELARUS
Warszawa
UKRAINE Kharkiv
Kyiv
MOLDOVA
ROMANIA
Bucuresti
BULGARIA
Sofiya
Istanbul
Ankara
TURKEY
GREECE
Athina
CYPRUS
Mediterranean Sea
SYRIA Dimashq Baghdad
LEB. ISRAEL
JORDAN
El Qahira
LIBYA
EGYPT
IRAQ
IRAN
KUWAIT
BAHRAIN
SAUDI ARABIA
Ar Riyad QATAR Abu Zabi
Makkah
OMAN
YEMEN
Sana
CHAD
El Khartum Asmara ERITREA
SUDAN
Ndjamena
CENTRAL AFRICAN REP.
Bangui
ETHIOPIA
Adis Abeba
DJIBOUTI
Adan
SOMALIA
UGANDA
KENYA
Nairobi
DEMOCRATIC REP. OF THE CONGO
Brazzaville
Kisangani
RWANDA
Kananga
TANZANIA
Dodoma
Dar es Salaam
Lake Victoria
ZAMBIA
Lusaka
Lilongwe
Harare
ZIMB.
ANGOLA
NAMIBIA
BOTSWANA
Gaborone
Pretoria (Tshwane)
SOUTH AFRICA
Durban
Cape Town
SWAZILAND
LESOTHO
Maputo
MOZAMBIQUE
MADAGASCAR
Antananarivo
COMOROS
Moroni
Reunion (France)
Port Louis MAURITIUS
SEYCHELLES

RUSSIA
Arkhangel'sk
Nizhny Novgorod
Moskva
Sankt-Peterburg
Yekaterinburg
Omsk
Samara
Volgograd
GEORGIA
ARMENIA AZER.
Baki
TURKMENISTAN
Ashgabat
KAZAKHSTAN
Astana
Aral Sea
Caspian Sea
Black Sea
UZBEKISTAN
Tashkent
Bishkek KYRGYZSTAN
Almaty
TAJIKISTAN
Dushanbe
AFGHANISTAN
Kabul
Tehran
PAKISTAN
Islamabad
Karachi
New Delhi
INDIA
Mumbai
Hyderabad
Chennai
Kolkata (Calcutta)
Ganges
NEPAL
Kathmandu
BHUTAN
BANG.
Dhaka
MYANMAR (BURMA)
Naypyidaw
Yangon
SRI LANKA
Colombo
Sri Jayewardenepura Kotte
MALDIVES

Irtysh
MONGOLIA
Ulaanbaatar
GOBI DESERT
Urumqi
CHINA
Lanzhou
Beijing
Shenyang
Harbin
Vladivostok
Yakutsk
Anadyr'
Arctic Circle
Bering Sea
Petropavlovsk-Kamchatskiy
Sea of Okhotsk
Sapporo
NORTH KOREA
Pyongyang
SOUTH KOREA
Seoul
Sea of Japan (East Sea)
JAPAN
Tokyo
Osaka
PACIFIC OCEAN
Qingdao
Huang He
Chang Jiang
Wuhan
Shanghai
Chongqing
East China Sea
T'ai-pei
TAIWAN
Hong Kong
South China Sea
LAOS
Viangchan
THAILAND
Krung Thep
CAMB.
Phnum Penh
Ha Noi
VIETNAM
PHILIPPINES
Manila
Cebu
Davao
PALAU
Northern Mariana Islands (U.S.)
MARSHALL ISLANDS
FEDERATED STATES OF MICRONESIA
NAURU
KIRIBATI
TUVALU
Equator
BRUNEI
Bandar Seri Begawan
MALAYSIA
Kuala Lumpur
Putrajaya
SINGAPORE
Singapore
INDONESIA
Jakarta
Surabaya
Banjarmasin
Dili
E TIMOR
PAPUA NEW GUINEA
Port Moresby
SOLOMON ISLANDS
Honiara
VANUATU
FIJI
Suva
INDIAN OCEAN
Iles Kerguelen (France)
AUSTRALIA
Perth
Adelaide
Melbourne
Sydney
Canberra
Brisbane
Tasman Sea
Tasmania
NEW ZEALAND
Auckland
Wellington
Christchurch
Chatham Island (N.Z.)
Tropic of Cancer
Tropic of Capricorn
SOUTHERN OCEAN
Antarctic Circle
ANTARCTICA
London Selected capital cities
Brisbane Other cities

Country Abbreviations

ALB.	ALBANIA	LUX.	LUXEMBOURG
AZER.	AZERBAIJAN	MAC.	MACEDONIA
BANG.	BANGLADESH	MAL.	MALAWI
BEL.	BELGIUM	MON.	MONTENEGRO
BHT.	BHUTAN	RUS.	RUSSIA
BOS.	BOSNIA AND HERZEGOVINA	RW.	RWANDA
BUR.	BURUNDI	SEN.	SENEGAL
CAMB.	CAMBODIA	SER.	SERBIA
CRO.	CROATIA	SL.	SLOVENIA
EST.	ESTONIA	SLOVAK.	SLOVAKIA
HUNG.	HUNGARY	SWITZ.	SWITZERLAND
LAT.	LATVIA	U.A.E.	UNITED ARAB EMIRATES
LEB.	LEBANON	ZIMB.	ZIMBABWE
LITH.	LITHUANIA

Verkhoyansk & Oymyakon, Russia : -68˚C or -90˚F

Al Aziziyah, Libya : 58˚C or 136˚F

5,900,825,000

43 per km² or 112 per sq mi

136,268,000 km² or 52,614,000 sq mi

192

Scale 1 : 20 200 000

0 250 500 750 1000 km

0 100 200 300 400 500 miles

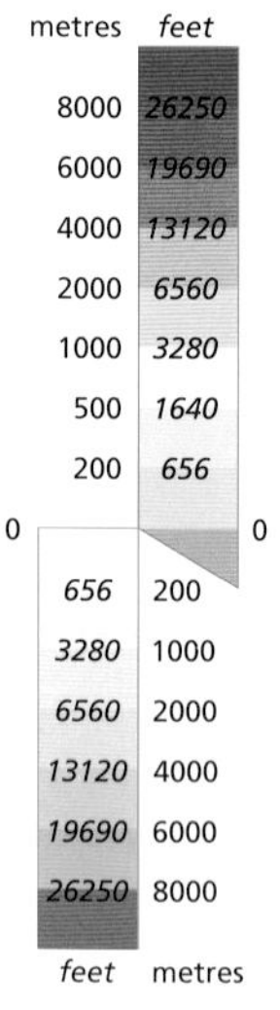

Elbrus, Russia : 5,642 m or 18,510 ft

Caspian Sea : 29 m or 84 ft

Astrakhan, Russia : 16.3 cm or 6.4 in

Crkvica, Bosnia-Herzegovina : 465 cm or 183 in

Volga, Russia : 3,531 km or 2,194 mi

Caspian Sea : 371,000 km² or 143,240 sq mi

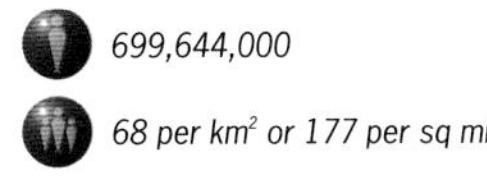

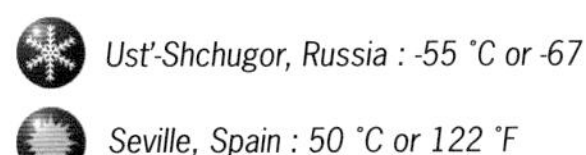

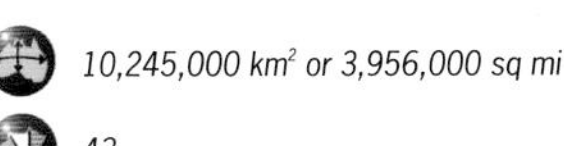

Ust'-Shchugor, Russia : -55 °C or -67 °F

Seville, Spain : 50 °C or 122 °F

699,644,000

68 per km² or 177 per sq mi

10,245,000 km² or 3,956,000 sq mi

43

Scale 1 : 20 200 000

0 250 500 750 1000 km

0 100 200 300 400 500 miles

Elbrus, Russia : 5,642 m or 18,510 ft

Caspian Sea : 29 m or 84 ft

Astrakhan, Russia : 16.3 cm or 6.4 in

Crkvica, Bosnia-Herzegovina : 465 cm or 183 in

Volga, Russia : 3,531 km or 2,194 mi

Caspian Sea : 371,000 km² or 143,240 sq mi

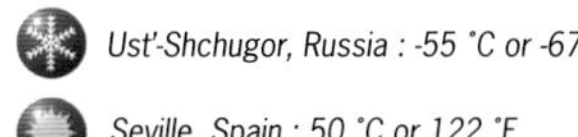

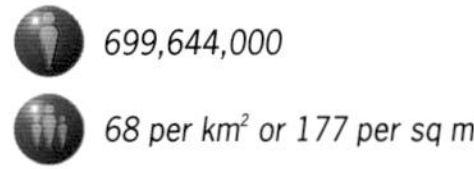

30° | H | 40° | J | 50° | K | 60° | 70° | L | 70° | | M | 1 | 80° E | | N | 60°

Barents Sea

Vorkuta

O. Kolguyev

Vadsø

Murmansk

Surgut

NOVOSIBIRSK Ob'

2

White Sea

Ob'

Arkhangel'sk

Irtysh

80°

OMSK

Severnaya Dvina

Onezhskoye Ozero
(Lake Onega)

50°

Ladozhskoye Ozero
(Lake Ladoga)

Vologda

Kirov

PERM'

YEKATERINBURG

Astana

Kama

R U S S I A

CHELYABINSK

**SANKT-PETERBURG
(ST. PETERSBURG)**

Ural'skiy Khrebet (Ural Mountains)

Pechora

Rybinskoye Vdkhr.

KAZAN'

UFA

Volga

**NIZHNIY
NOVGOROD**

Dvina

**MOSKVA
(MOSCOW)**

SAMARA

3

70°

nius

MINSK

Volga

Don

Khoper

Ural

Aral Sea

ELARUS

Prypyats'

**KYYIV
(KIEV)**

VOLGOGRAD

KHARKIV

Donets

40°

U K R A I N E

Don

Astrakhan'

Volga

DNIPROPETROVS'K

DONETS'K

ROSTOV-NA-DONU

MOLDOVA

Chişinău

Dnipro

Aktau

**ODESA
(ODESSA)**

Sea of Azov

Stavropol'

C a s p i a n S e a

NIA

Krym'

**Ashgabat
(Ashkhabad)**

**BUCUREŞTI
(BUCHAREST)**

Elbrus
5642

Groznyy

Sevastopol'

C a u c a s u s

ARIA

B l a c k S e a

**BAKI
(BAKU)**

MASHHAD

Burgas

Samsun

T'BILISI

İSTANBUL

YEREVAN

Bursa

ANKARA

**TEHRĀN
(TEHERAN)**

60°

İZMIR

A S I A

30°

Gaziantep

Antalya

*Rodos
(Rhodes)
(Greece)*

BAGHDĀD

eio
klion)

**Lefkosia
(Nicosia)**

5

**BEYROUTH
(BEIRUT)**

**DIMASHQ
(DAMASCUS)**

AMMĀN

**Al Kuwayt
(Kuwait)**

**Yerushalayim
(Jerusalem)**

P e r s i a n G u l f

**EL QÂHIRA
(CAIRO)**

Nile

30° | H | 40° | J | 50° | K

Ust'-Shchugor, Russia : -55 °C or -67 °F

Seville, Spain : 50 °C or 122 °F

699,644,000

68 per km² or 177 per sq mi

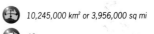

10,245,000 km² or 3,956,000 sq mi

43

Scale 1 : 5 800 000

0 100 200 300 km

0 50 100 150 miles

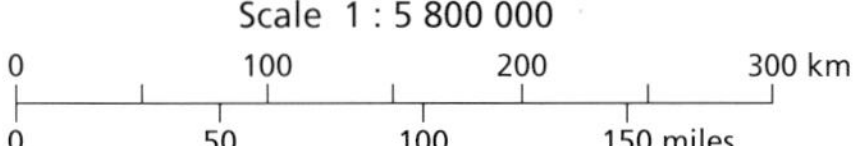

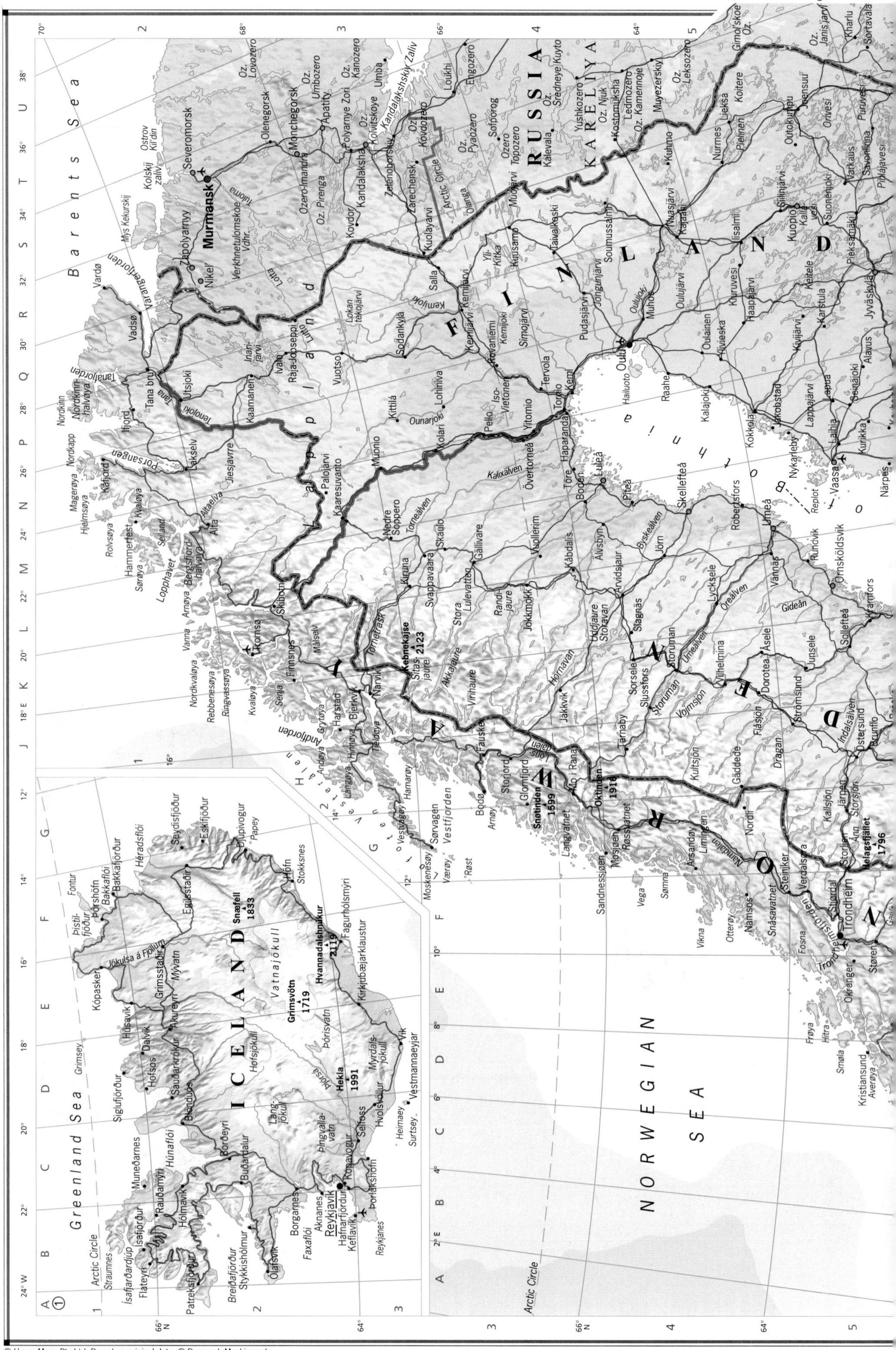

metres	feet
8000	26250
6000	19690
4000	13120
2000	6560
1000	3280
500	1640
200	656
0	0
656	200
3280	1000
6560	2000
13120	4000
19690	6000
26250	8000
feet	metres

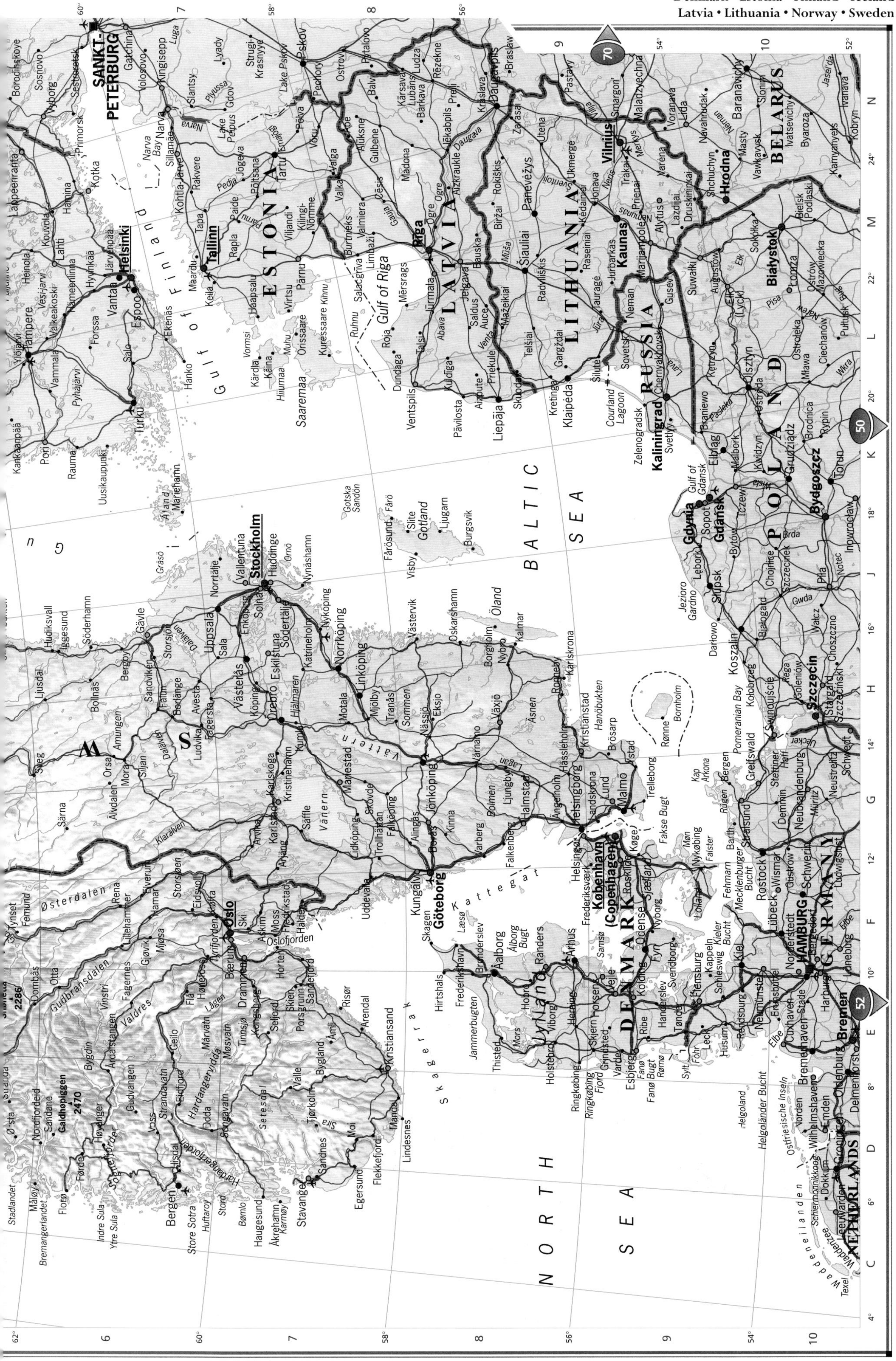

■ over 3 million
■ 1 – 3 million
● 250 000 – 1 million
● 100 000 – 250 000
● 25 000 – 100 000
• under 25 000
country capital underline

Scale 1 : 3 450 000

0 50 100 150 km

0 25 50 75 miles

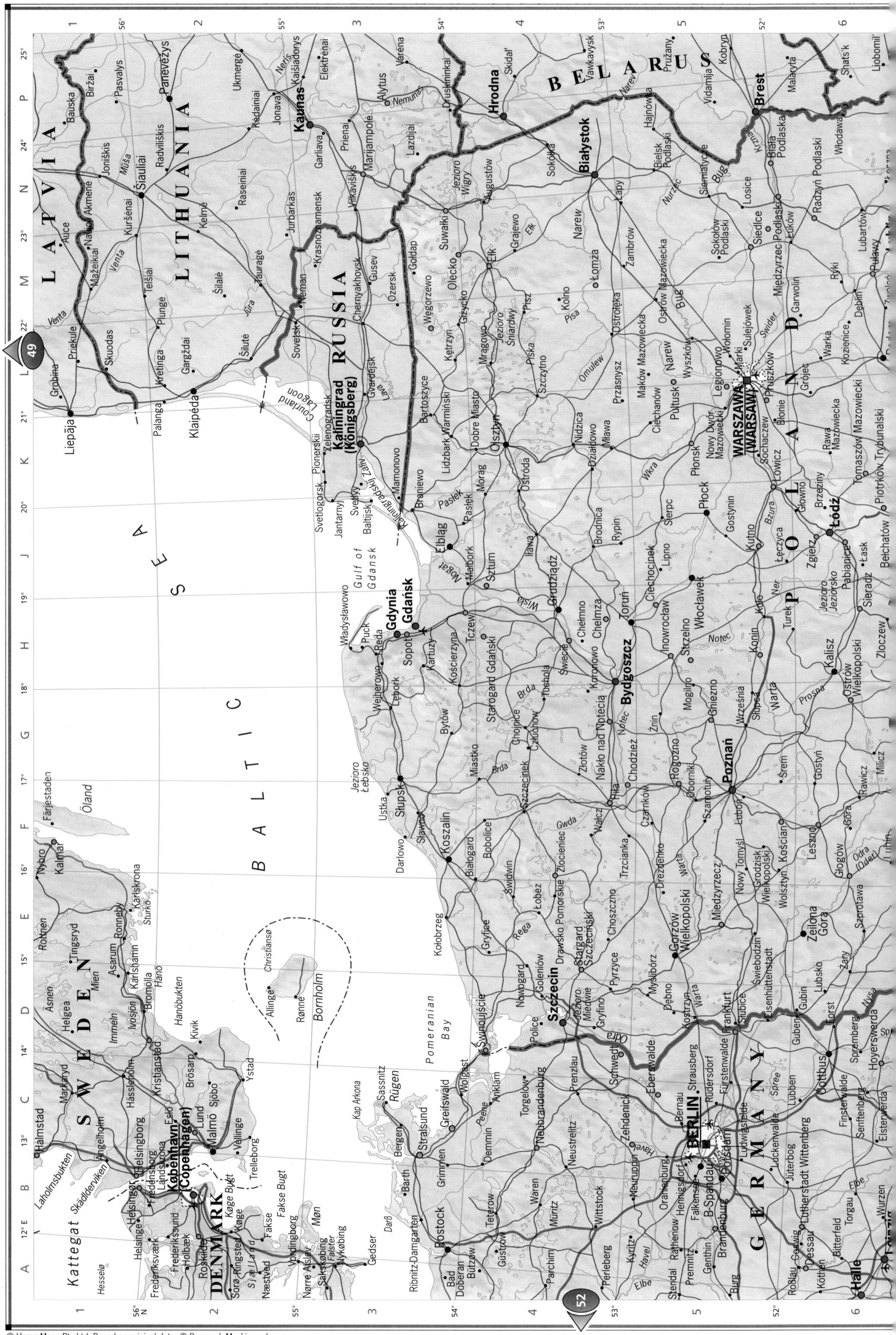

metres	feet
8000	26250
6000	19690
4000	13120
2000	6560
1000	3280
500	1640
200	656
0	0
656	200
3280	1000
6560	2000
13120	4000
19690	6000
26250	8000
feet	metres

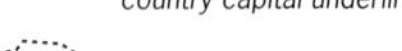

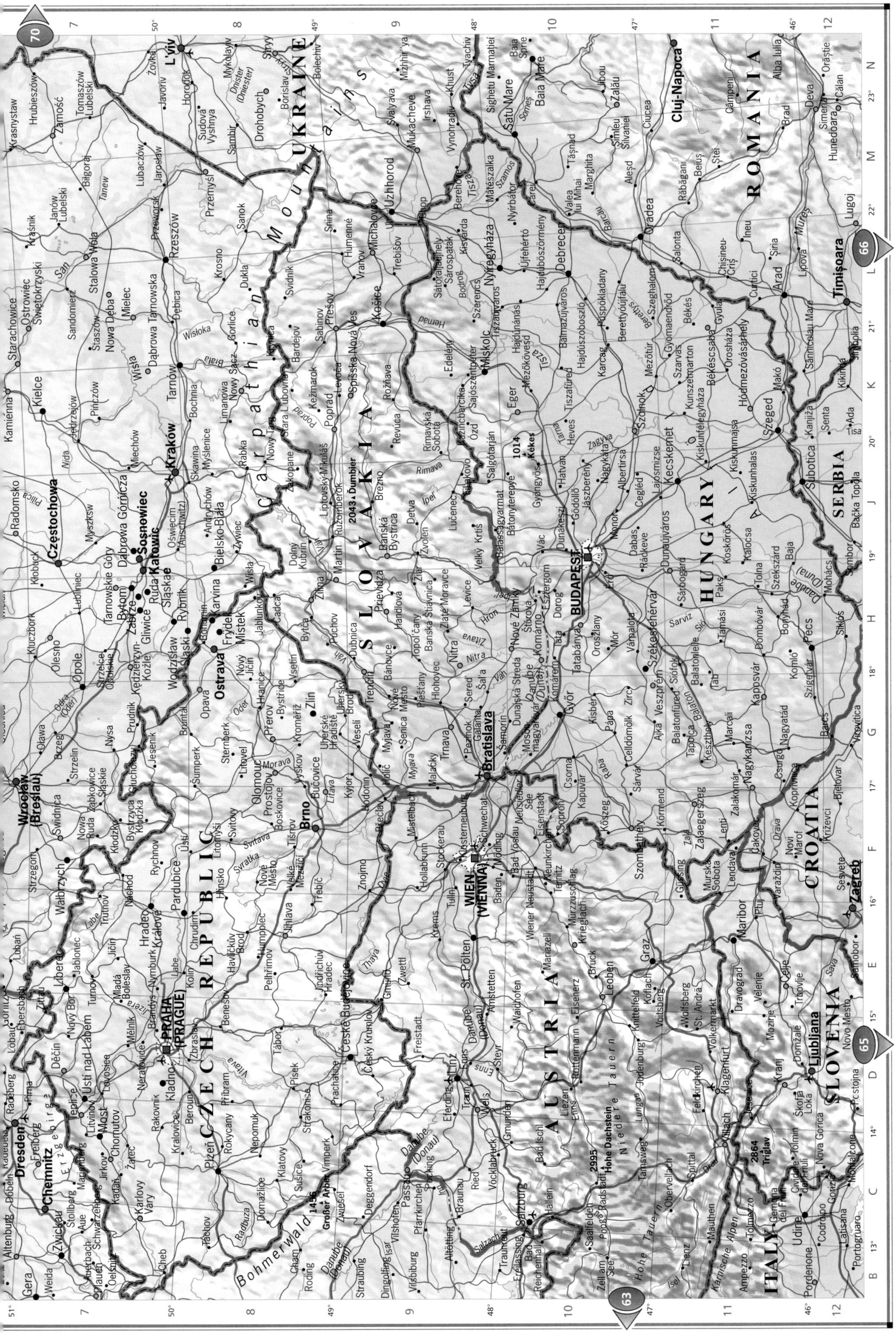

■ over 3 million
■ 1 – 3 million
● 250 000 – 1 million
• 100 000 – 250 000
◦ 25 000 – 100 000
• under 25 000
country capital underline
urban area

Scale 1 : 2 600 000

0 50 100 150 km

0 25 50 75 miles

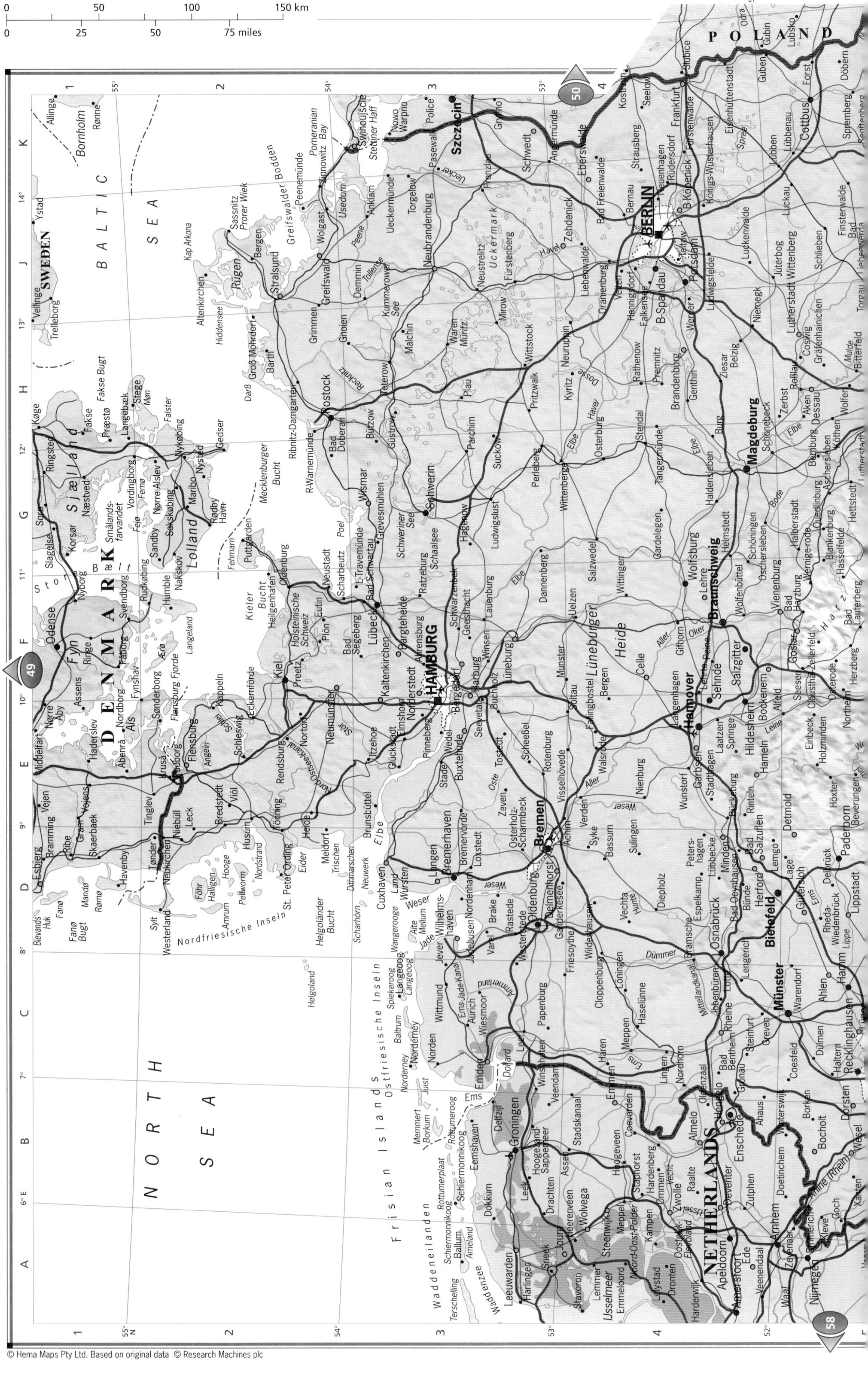

metres	feet
8000	26250
6000	19690
4000	13120
2000	6560
1000	3280
500	1640
200	656
0	0
656	200
3280	1000
6560	2000
13120	4000
19690	6000
26250	8000
feet	metres

Germany

Germany • Luxembourg

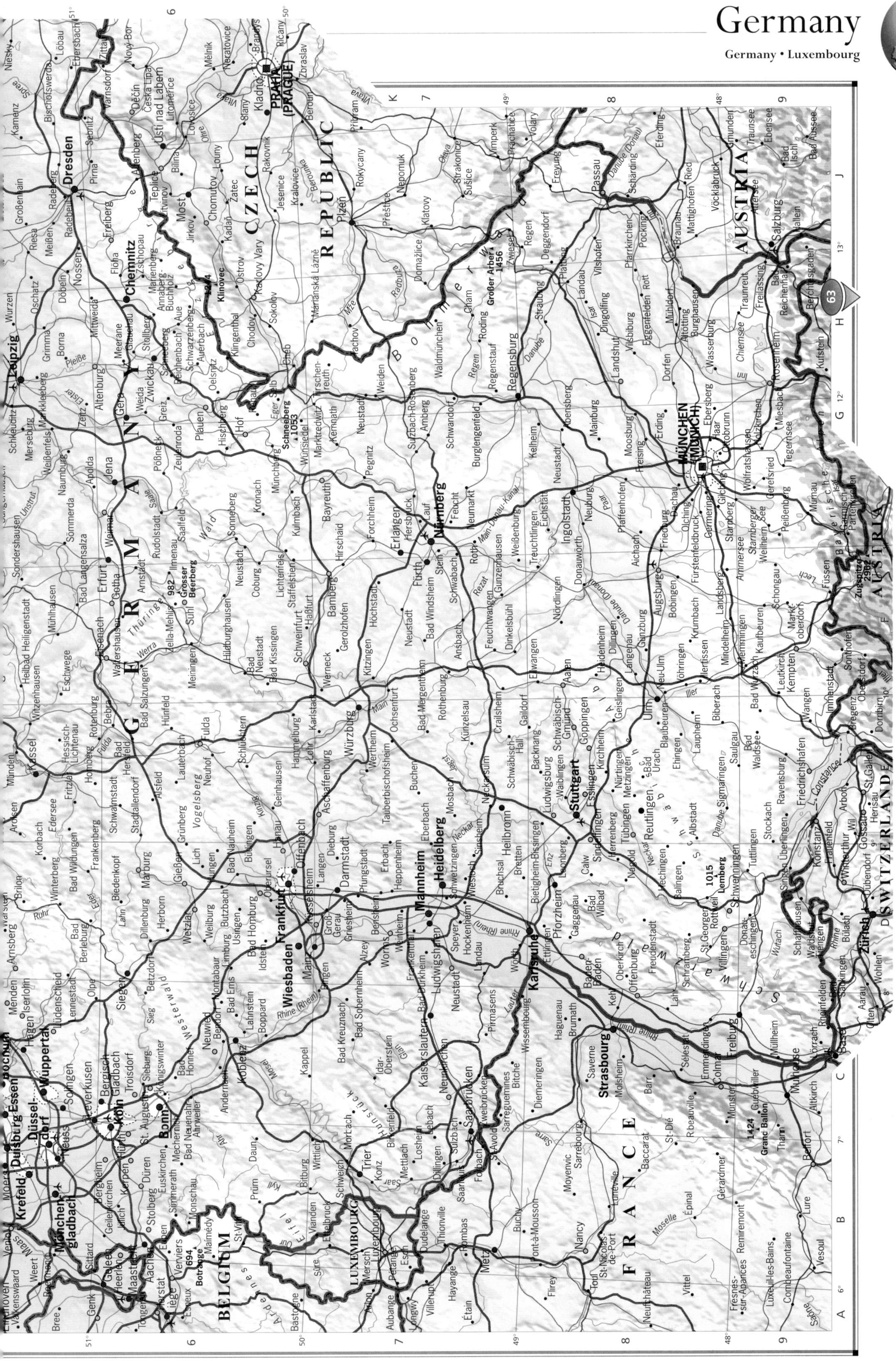

■ over 3 million
■ 1 – 3 million
● 250 000 – 1 million
● 100 000 – 250 000
○ 25 000 – 100 000
• under 25 000
country capital underline
urban area

Scale 1 : 2 300 000

0 50 100 150 km

0 25 50 75 miles

UNITED

KINGDOM

Buxton
Worksop
East Retford
Louth
Mablethorpe
Chesterfield
Bolsover
Matlock
Mansfield
Lincoln
Horncastle
Leek
Alfreton
Newark-on-Trent
Sleaford
Skegness
Derby
Nottingham
Grantham
Boston
The Wash
Hunstanton
Cromer
Long Eaton
Burton upon Trent
Loughborough
Spalding
King's Lynn
The Broads
Great Yarmouth
Leicester
Melton Mowbray
Oakham
Stamford
Wisbech
East Dereham
Norwich
Lowestoft
Cannock
Tamworth
Nuneaton
Peterborough
March
Yare
Walsall
BIRMINGHAM
Bedworth
Market Harborough
Corby
The Fens
Ely
Great Ouse
Southwold
Coventry
Rugby
Kettering
Nene
Huntingdon
Thetford
Little Ouse
Diss
Redditch
Warwick
Royal Leamington Spa
Wellingborough
Newmarket
Bury St. Edmunds
Stowmarket
Aldeburgh
Avon
Stratford-upon-Avon
Daventry
Northampton
Cambridge
Stour
Sudbury
Woodbridge
Orford Ness
Evesham
Towcester
Bedford
Ipswich
Banbury
Milton Keynes
Bicester
Letchworth
Royston
Braintree
Felixstowe
Harwich
Chipping Norton
Leighton Buzzard
Stevenage
Bishop's Stortford
Colchester
The Naze
Woodstock
Aylesbury
Luton
Welwyn Garden City
Harlow
Clacton-on-Sea
Witney
Oxford
Hemel Hempstead
St. Albans
Chelmsford
Thames
Abingdon
High Wycombe
Watford
Enfield
Cheshunt
Brentwood
Foulness
Didcot
Swindon
Maidenhead
Slough
LONDON
Basildon
Southend-on-Sea
Hungerford
Reading
Windsor
Grays
Thames
Walcheren
Newbury
Bracknell
Staines
Kingston upon Thames
Gravesend
Rochester
Herne Bay
Margate
Knokke-Heist
Basingstoke
Camberley
Woking
Epsom
Gillingham
Whitstable
North Foreland
Zeebrugge
Blankenberge
Oostbu
Andover
Farnborough
Guildford
Faversham
Canterbury
Ramsgate
Deal
Oostende
Middelkerke
Brugg
Salisbury
Aldershot
Reigate
Sevenoaks
Maidstone
Nieuwpoort
De Panne
Veurne
Winchester
Alton
Haslemere
Crawley
Ashford
Dover
Diksmuide
Roeselare
Tielt
zegern
Romsey
Petersfield
Horsham
East Grinstead
Royal Tunbridge Wells
Folkestone
Calais
Gravelines
Dunkerque
Poperinge
Ieper
Menen
Kortrijk
Wareg
Leie
Southampton
Eastleigh
South Downs
The Weald
Rye
Dungeness
Cap Gris-Nez
St-Omer
Hazebrouck
Bailleul
Armentières
Tourcoing
Roubaix
Fareham
Havant
Worthing
Brighton
Lewes
Bexhill
Hastings
Boulogne-sur-Mer
Desvres
Lille
Tourn
Portsmouth
Gosport
Chichester
Shoreham-by-Sea
Newhaven
Eastbourne
Beachy Head
Etaples
Fruges
Béthune
Lens
Avion
Denain
Lymington
Cowes
Newport
Ryde
Bognor Regis
The Solent
Berck
Montreul
Hesdin
Hénin-Beaumont
Douai
Isle of Wight
Rue
St-Pol-sur-Ternoise
Arras
Cambra
Caud
Doullens
Bapaume
Péronne

N O R T H

S E A

E n g l i s h C h a n n e l

Baie de la Somme
Le Crotoy
St-Valéry-sur-Somme
Abbeville
Albert
St-Quen
Fauville-en-Caux
Dieppe
Blangy-sur-Bresle
Somme
Amiens
Fécamp
Cap d'Antifer
Étretat
Tôtes
Neufchâtel-en-Bray
Forges-les-Eaux
Marseille-en-Beauvaisis
Breteuil
Montdidier
Roye
Tergnier
Chauny
Bolbec
Yvetôt
Barentin
Gournay-en-Bray
Beauvais
Noyon
Le Havre
Gonfreville-Orcher
Lillebonne
Seine
Rouen
Clermont
Aisne
Soissons
Baie de la Seine
Honfleur
St-Étienne-du-Rouvray
Méru
Creil
Compiègne
Carentan
La Haye-du-Puits
Isigny-sur-Mer
Bayeux
Oustreham
Elbeuf
Louviers
Les Andelys
Chambly
Senlis
Villers-Cotterêts
Crépy-en-Valois
Cherbourg
Valognes
Périers
Hérouville-St-Clair
Caen
Lisieux
Vernon
Pontoise
Chantilly
F
Coutances
St-Lô
Villers-Bocage
Orbec
Bernay
Evreux
Mantes-la-Jolie
St-Germain-en-Laye
Hertlay
St-Denis
Bobigny
Meaux
Château-Thierr
Granville
Julliouville
Vire
Villedieu-les-Poêles
Tinchebray
Condé-sur-Noireau
Flers
Vimoutiers
Gacé
Conches-en-Ouche
Eure
Houdan
Versailles
PARIS
Créteil
Orly
Marne-la-Vallée
Coulommiers
Pontorson
Avranches
Mortain
Rânes
Argentan
Falaise
L'Aigle
Verneuil
Dreux
Trappes
Orsay
Courtacon

53° N
52°
51°
50°
49°

2° W
A
1°
B
0°
C
1°
D
2°
E
3°

ENGLAND

Isle of Wight

57

58

metres	feet
8000	26250
6000	19690
4000	13120
2000	6560
1000	3280
500	1640
200	656
0	0
656	200
3280	1000
6560	2000
13120	4000
19690	6000
26250	8000
feet	metres

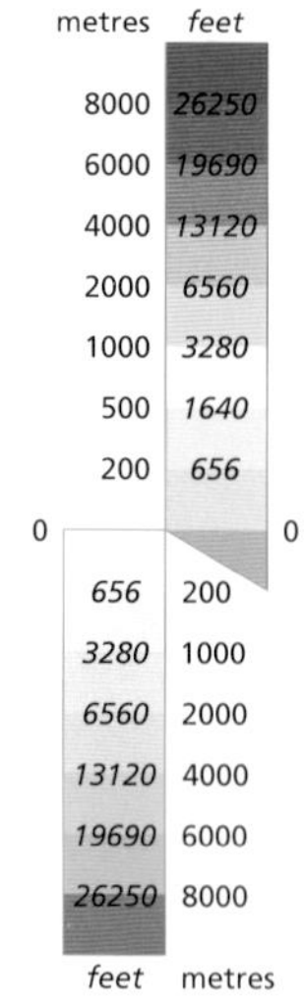

Benelux

Belgium • Luxembourg • Netherlands

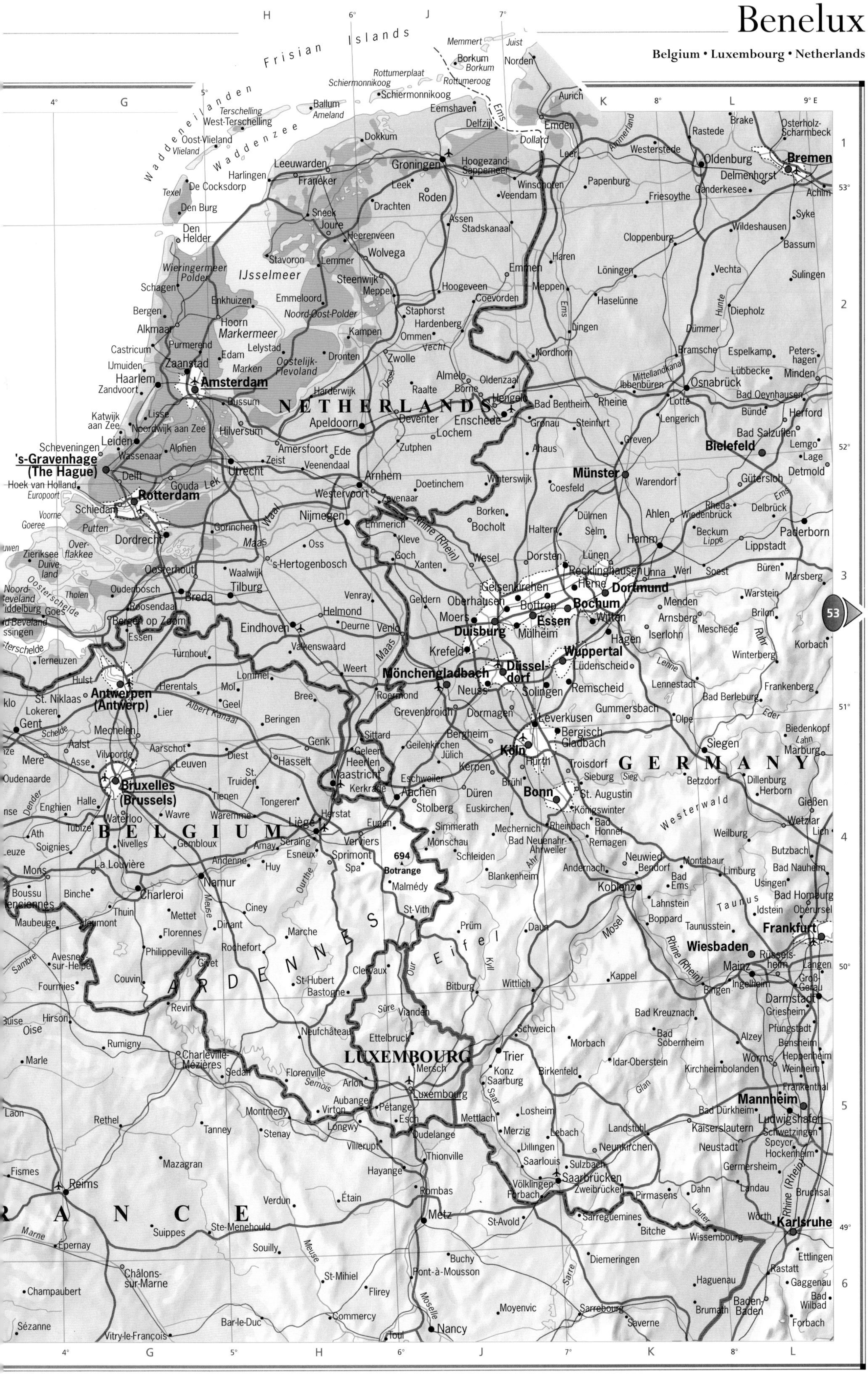

■ over 3 million	● 100 000 – 250 000	country capital underline
■ 1 – 3 million	○ 25 000 – 100 000	urban area
● 250 000 – 1 million	• under 25 000	

Scale 1 : 3 450 000

0 50 100 150 km

0 25 50 75 miles

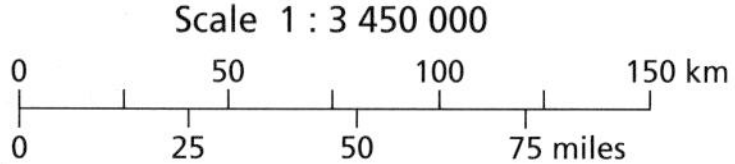

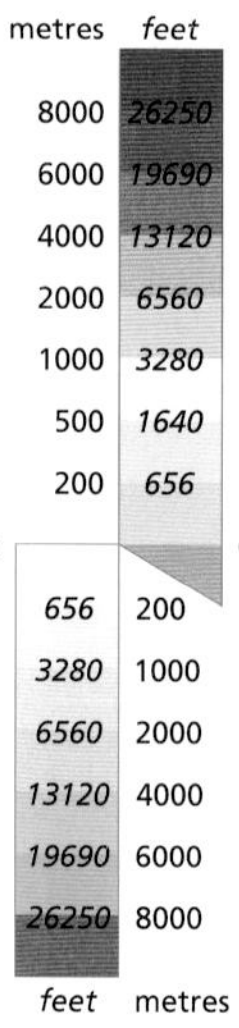

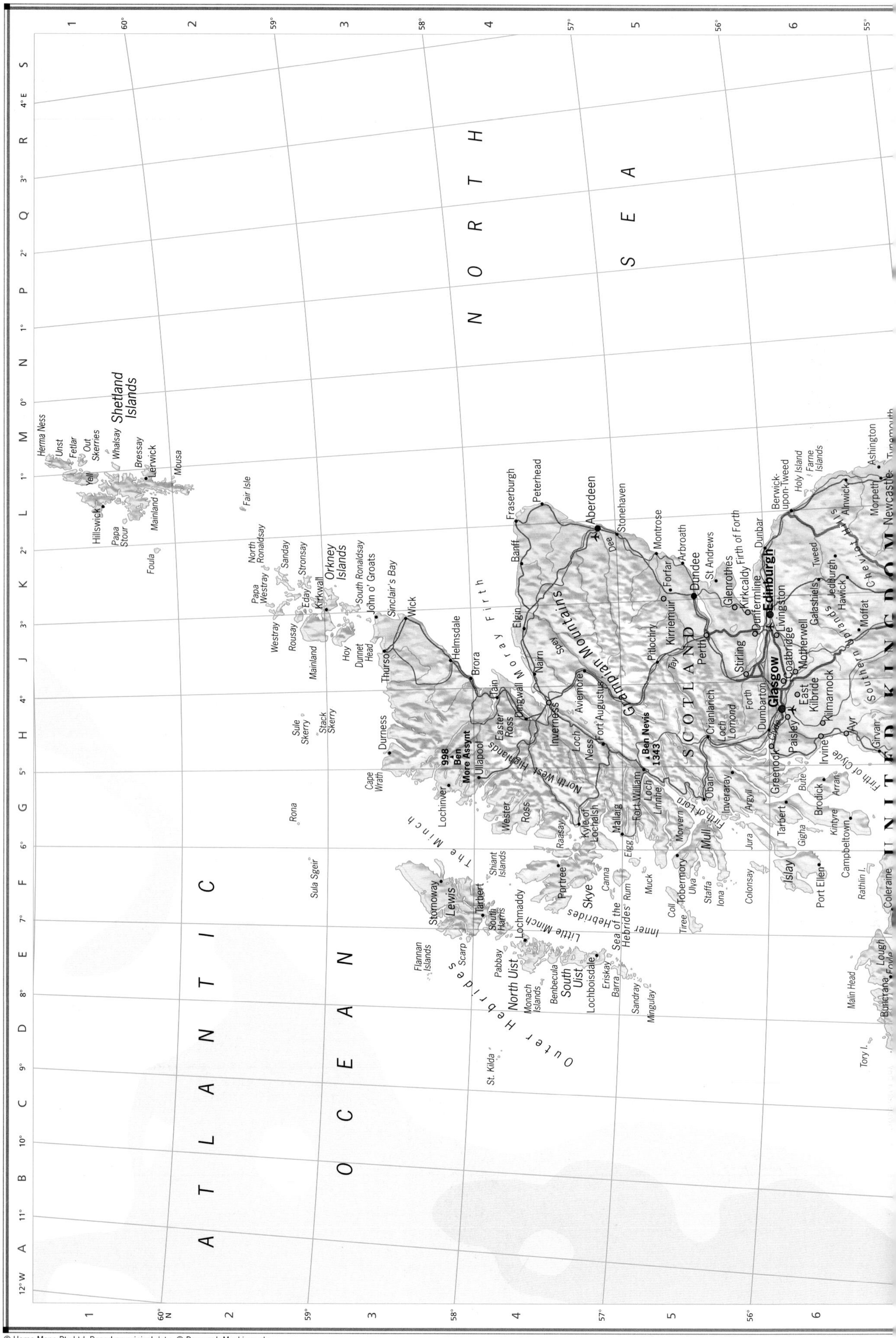

© Hema Maps Pty Ltd. Based on original data © Research Machines plc

British Isles

Republic of Ireland • United Kingdom

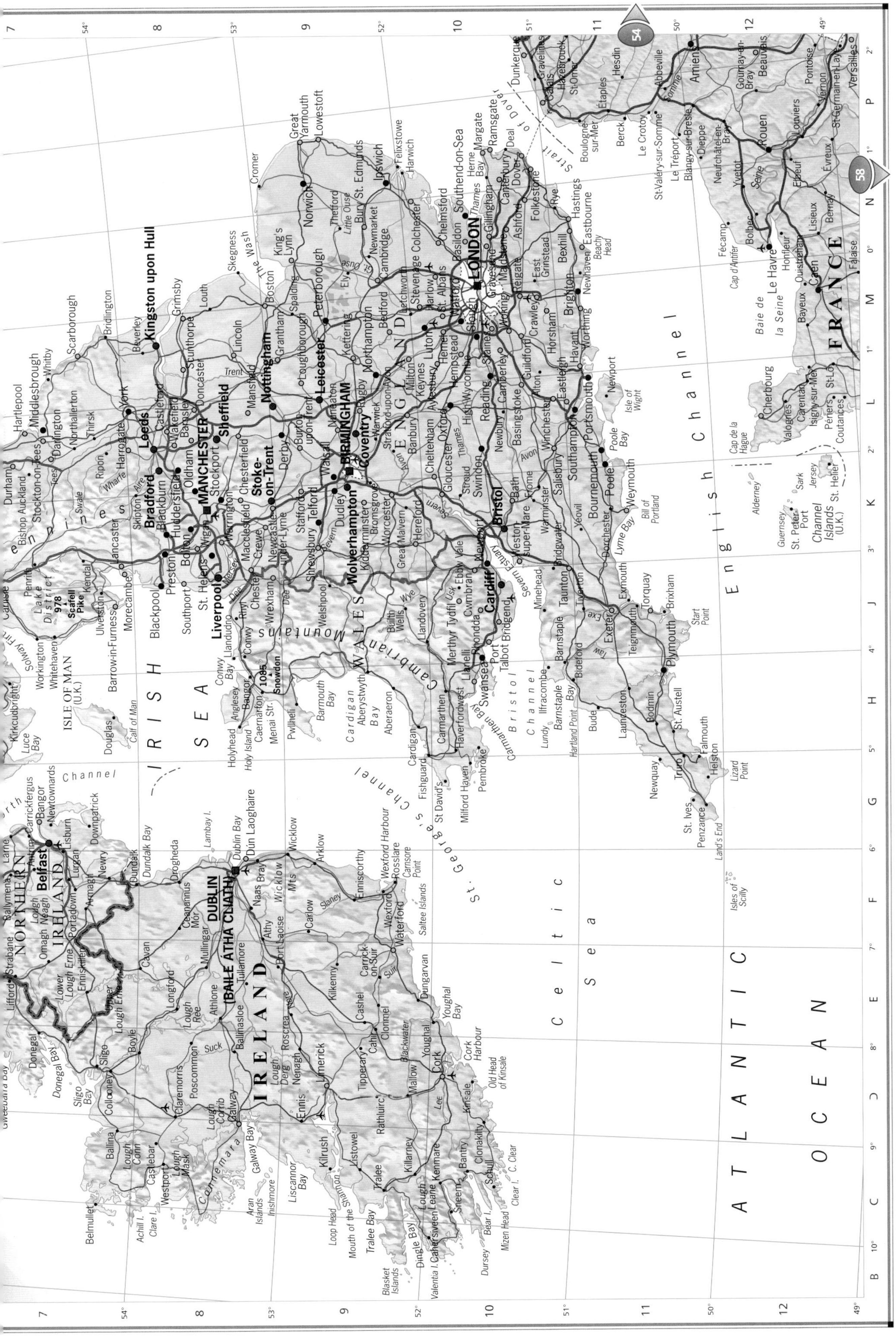

■ over 3 million
■ 1 – 3 million
● 250 000 – 1 million
• 100 000 – 250 000
○ 25 000 – 100 000
• under 25 000
country capital underline
state or province capital underline
urban area

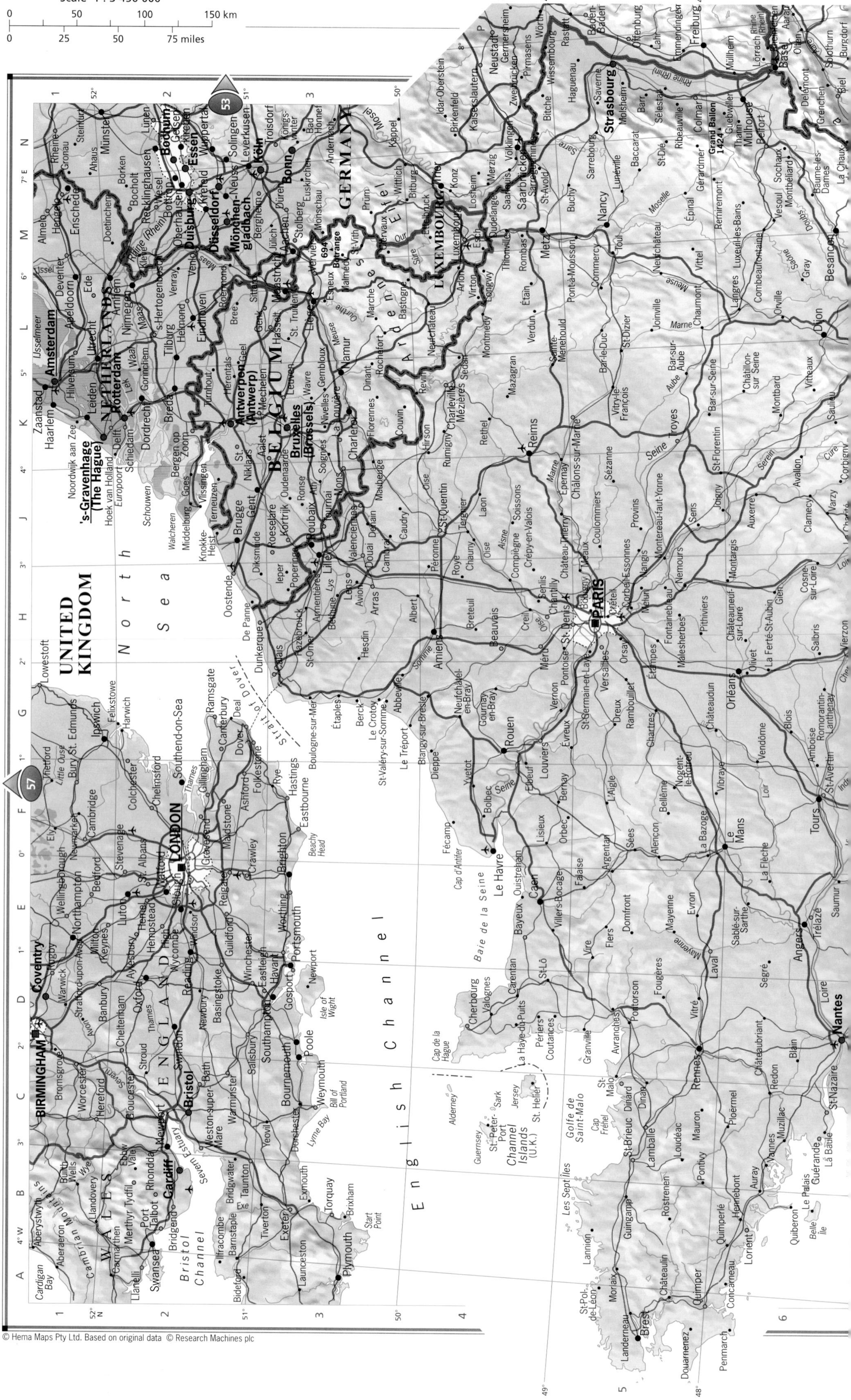

metres	feet
8000	26250
6000	19690
4000	13120
2000	6560
1000	3280
500	1640
200	656
0	0
656	200
3280	1000
6560	2000
13120	4000
19690	6000
26250	8000
feet	metres

Scale 1 : 3 450 000

0 50 100 150 km

0 25 50 75 miles

France

Andorra • Channel Islands • France • Monaco

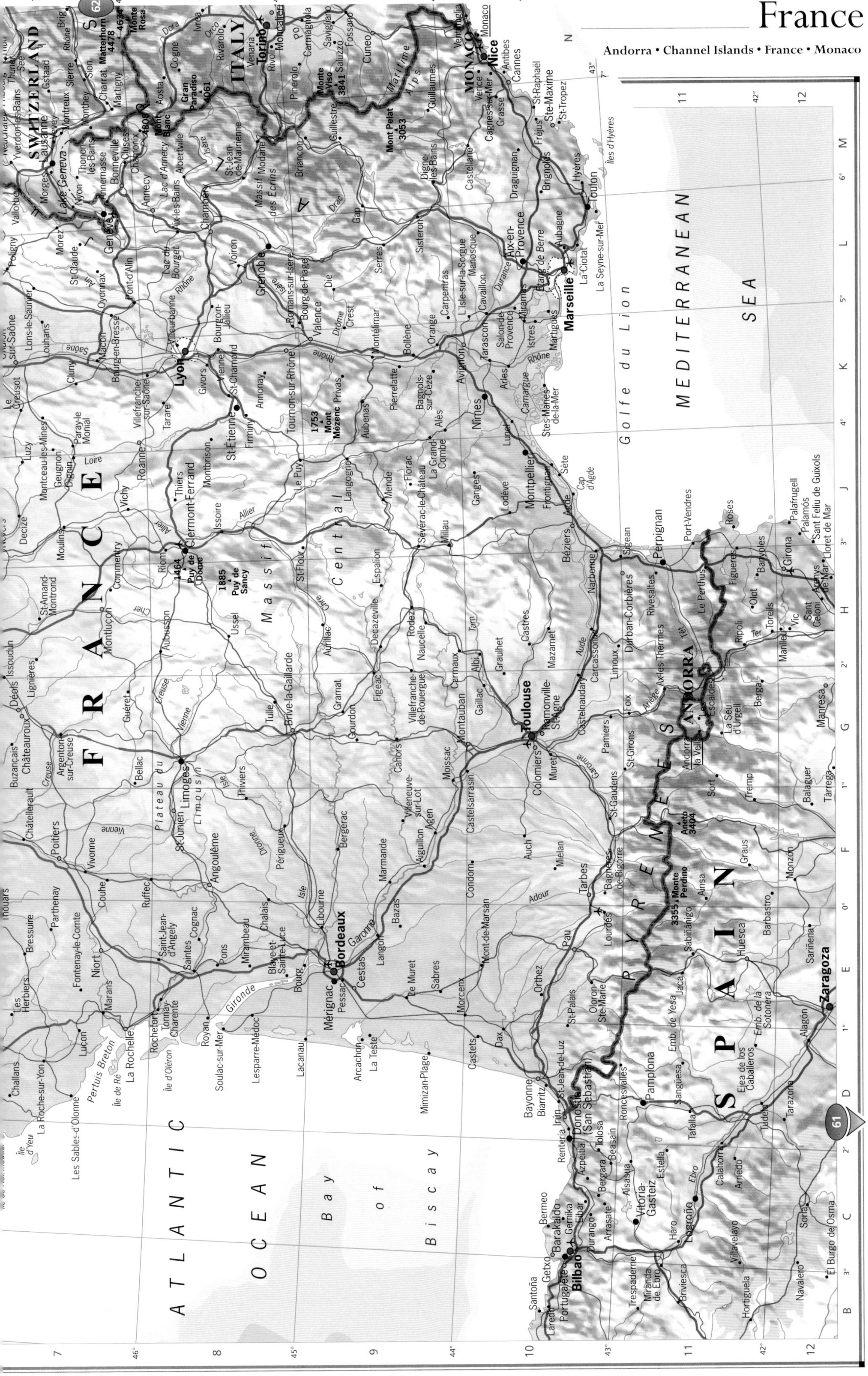

over 3 million	100 000 – 250 000	country capital underline
1 – 3 million	25 000 – 100 000	state or province capital underline
250 000 – 1 million	under 25 000	urban area

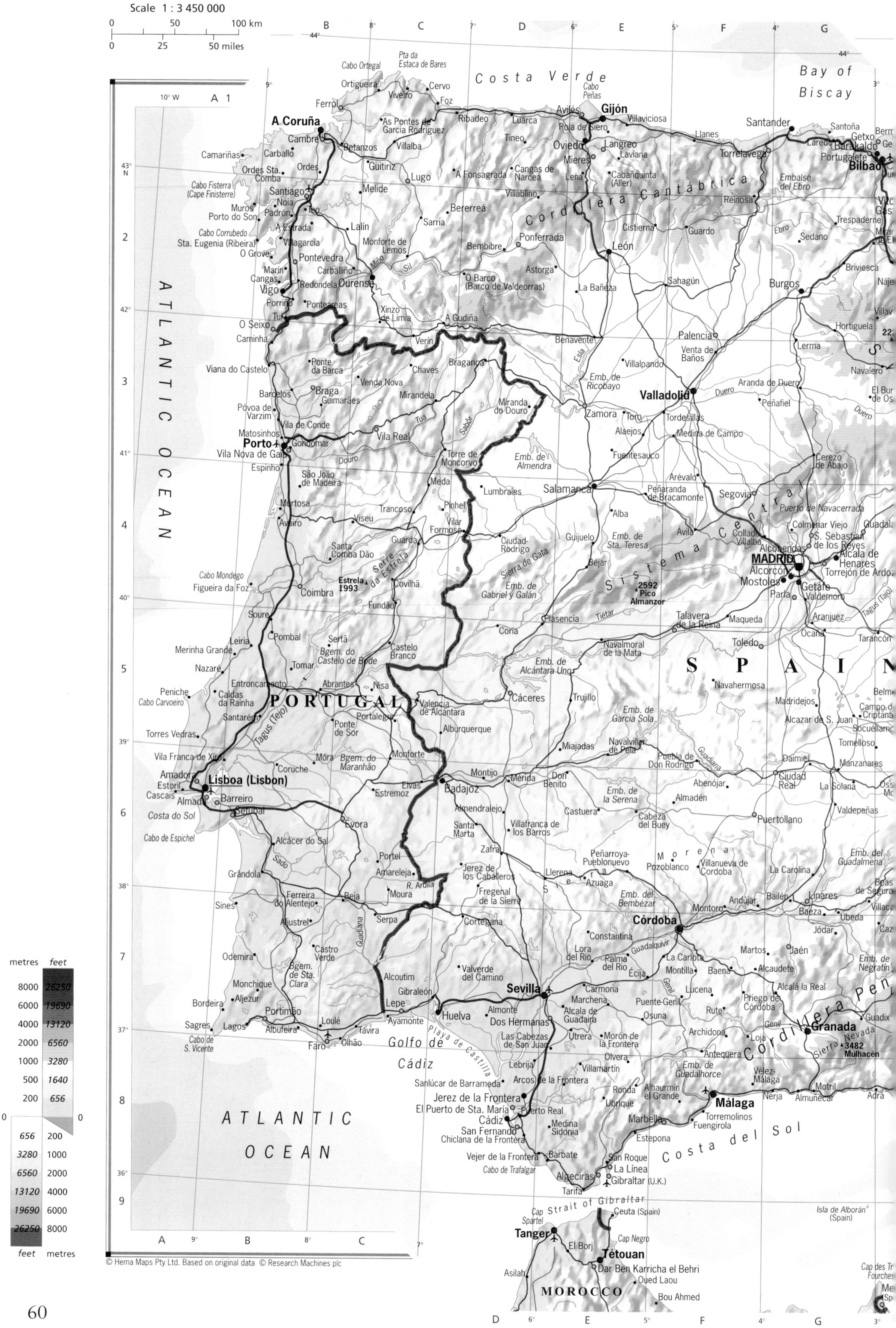
Scale 1 : 3 450 000
0 50 100 km
0 25 50 miles
ATLANTIC OCEAN
Bay of Biscay
Costa Verde
Cabo Ortegal
Pta da Estaca de Bares
Ortigueira
Cervo
Ferrol
Viveiro
Foz
A Coruña
Cambre
Betanzos
As Pontes de Garcia Rodriguez
Ribadeo
Luarca
Cabo Peñas
Avilés
Gijón
Villaviciosa
Camariñas
Carballo
Ordes Sta. Comba
Ordes
Villalba
Guitiriz
Lugo
A Fonsagrada
Tineo
Cangas de Narcea
Oviedo
Pola de Siero
Langreo
Laviana
Mieres
Llanes
Santander
Santoña
Laredo
Barakaldo
Getxo
Portugalete
Bilbao
Torrelavega
Embalse del Ebro
Reinosa
Cabo Fisterra (Cape Finisterre)
Santiago
Noia
Muros
Porto do Son
Padrón
Melide
Lena
Cabañaquinta (Aller)
Villablino
Cordillera Cantábrica
Bererreá
Sarria
Cabo Corrubedo
Sta. Eugenia (Ribeira)
A Estrada
Lalín
Vilagarcia
O Grove
Pontevedra
Monforte de Lemos
Bembibre
Ponferrada
Cistierna
Guardo
León
Trespaderne
Sedano
Ebro
Marín
Cangas
Carballiño
Miño
Sil
Astorga
Vigo
Redondela
Ourense
O Barco (Barco de Valdeorras)
La Bañeza
Sahagún
Burgos
Briviesca
Porriño
Ponteareas
Xinzo de Limia
A Gudiña
Tui
O Seixo
Caminha
Verín
Benavente
Palencia
Hortiguela
Lerma
Esla
Venta de Baños
Viana do Castelo
Ponte da Barca
Chaves
Bragança
Villalpando
Emb. de Ricobayo
Valladolid
Aranda de Duero
Duero
Peñafiel
Navalero
Barcelos
Braga
Guimarães
Venda Nova
Mirandela
Miranda do Douro
Póvoa de Varzim
Vila de Conde
Tua
Sabor
Zamora
Toro
Tordesillas
Alaejos
Medina de Campo
Matosinhos
Porto
Gondomar
Vila Real
Vila Nova de Gaia
Espinho
Douro
Torre de Moncorvo
Emb. de Almendra
Fuentesauco
Cerezo de Abajo
São João de Madeira
Meda
Lumbrales
Salamanca
Arévalo
Peñaranda de Bracamonte
Segovia
Ovar
Murtosa
Trancoso
Pinhel
Alba
Sistema Central
Puerto de Navacerrada
Aveiro
Viseu
Vilar Formoso
Guijuelo
Emb. de Sta. Teresa
Ávila
Collado Villalba
Colmenar Viejo
S. Sebastián de los Reyes
Alcobendas
Santa Comba Dão
Guarda
Serra da Estrela
Ciudad-Rodrigo
Sierra de Gata
MADRID
Alcalá de Henares
Torrejón de Ardoz
Alcorcón
Mostoles
Getafe
Parla
Valdemoro
Cabo Mondego
Figueira da Foz
Estrela 1993
Covilhã
Béjar
2592 Pico Almanzor
Coimbra
Emb. de Gabriel y Galán
Fundão
Soure
Plasencia
Tiétar
Talavera de la Reina
Maqueda
Aranjuez
Tagus (Tajo)
Tarancón
Leiria
Pombal
Sertã
Coria
Navalmoral de la Mata
Toledo
Ocaña
Merinha Grande
Bgem. do Castelo de Bode
Castelo Branco
Emb. de Alcántara Uno
Nazaré
Tomar
SPAIN
Navahermosa
Entroncamento
Abrantes
Nisa
Peniche
Cabo Carvoeiro
Caldas da Rainha
PORTUGAL
Valencia de Alcántara
Cáceres
Trujillo
Emb. de García Sola
Madridejos
Alcazar de S. Juan
Santarém
Ponte de Sor
Portalegre
Alburquerque
Torres Vedras
Miajadas
Navalvillar de Pela
Puebla de Don Rodrigo
Guadiana
Daimiel
Tomelloso
Manzanares
Vila Franca de Xira
Mora
Bgem. do Maranhão
Coruche
Monforte
Montijo
Mérida
Don Benito
Ciudad Real
Amadora
Lisboa (Lisbon)
Estoril
Cascais
Almada
Barreiro
Elvas
Badajoz
Estremoz
Emb. de la Serena
Abenójar
Almadén
La Solana
Setúbal
Costa do Sol
Almendralejo
Castuera
Cabeza del Buey
Puertollano
Valdepeñas
Évora
Santa Marta
Villafranca de los Barros
Cabo de Espichel
Alcácer do Sal
Sado
Portel
Zafra
Peñarroya-Pueblonuevo
Sierra Morena
Villanueva de Córdoba
Pozoblanco
Emb. del Guadalmena
Amareleja
Jerez de los Caballeros
Llerena
Azuaga
La Carolina
Grândola
R. Ardila
Fregenal de la Sierra
Emb. del Bembézar
Linares
Sines
Ferreira do Alentejo
Beja
Moura
Serpa
Montoro
Andújar
Bailén
Baeza
Úbeda
Aljustrel
Cortegana
Córdoba
Jódar
Guadiana
Constantina
Castro Verde
Lora del Río
Guadalquivir
La Carlota
Martos
Jaén
Odemira
Palma del Río
Écija
Montilla
Baena
Alcaudete
Emb. de Negratín
Bgem. de Sta. Clara
Alcoutim
Valverde del Camino
Monchique
Aljezur
Sevilla
Carmona
Genil
Alcalá la Real
Gibraleón
Almonte
Marchena
Lucena
Priego de Córdoba
Cordillera Penibética
Bordeira
Portimão
Lepe
Huelva
Dos Hermanas
Alcalá de Guadaíra
Puente-Genil
Rute
Sagres
Lagos
Albufeira
Loulé
Ayamonte
Tavira
Osuna
Granada
Guadix
Cabo de S. Vicente
Faro
Olhão
Golfo de Cádiz
Playa de Castilla
Las Cabezas de San Juan
Utrera
Morón de la Frontera
Archidona
Loja
Sierra Nevada
3482 Mulhacén
Antequera
Lebrija
Olvera
Villamartín
Sanlúcar de Barrameda
Arcos de la Frontera
Ronda
Alhaurín el Grande
Vélez-Málaga
Motril
Almuñécar
Adra
Nerja
Jerez de la Frontera
El Puerto de Sta. María
Puerto Real
Cádiz
Ubrique
Málaga
Torremolinos
Fuengirola
San Fernando
Chiclana de la Frontera
Medina Sidonia
Marbella
Estepona
Costa del Sol
Vejer de la Frontera
Barbate
Cabo de Trafalgar
San Roque
La Línea
Gibraltar (U.K.)
Algeciras
Tarifa
Strait of Gibraltar
Cap Spartel
Ceuta (Spain)
Isla de Alborán (Spain)
Tanger
Cap Negro
El Borj
Tétouan
Dar Ben Karricha el Behri
Asilah
Oued Laou
MOROCCO
Bou Ahmed
Cap des Trois Fourches
metres feet
8000 26250
6000 19690
4000 13120
2000 6560
1000 3280
500 1640
200 656
0 0
656 200
3280 1000
6560 2000
13120 4000
19690 6000
26250 8000
feet metres

■ over 3 million
■ 1 – 3 million
● 250 000 – 1 million
● 100 000 – 250 000
○ 25 000 – 100 000
• under 25 000
country capital underline
urban area

Scale 1 : 2 600 000

0 50 100 150 km

0 25 50 75 miles

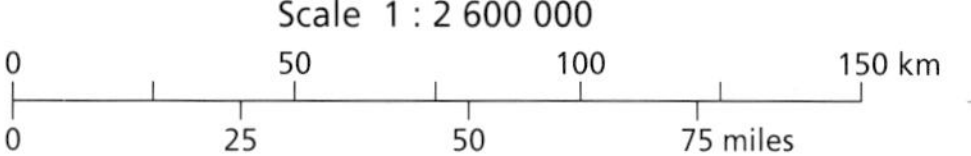

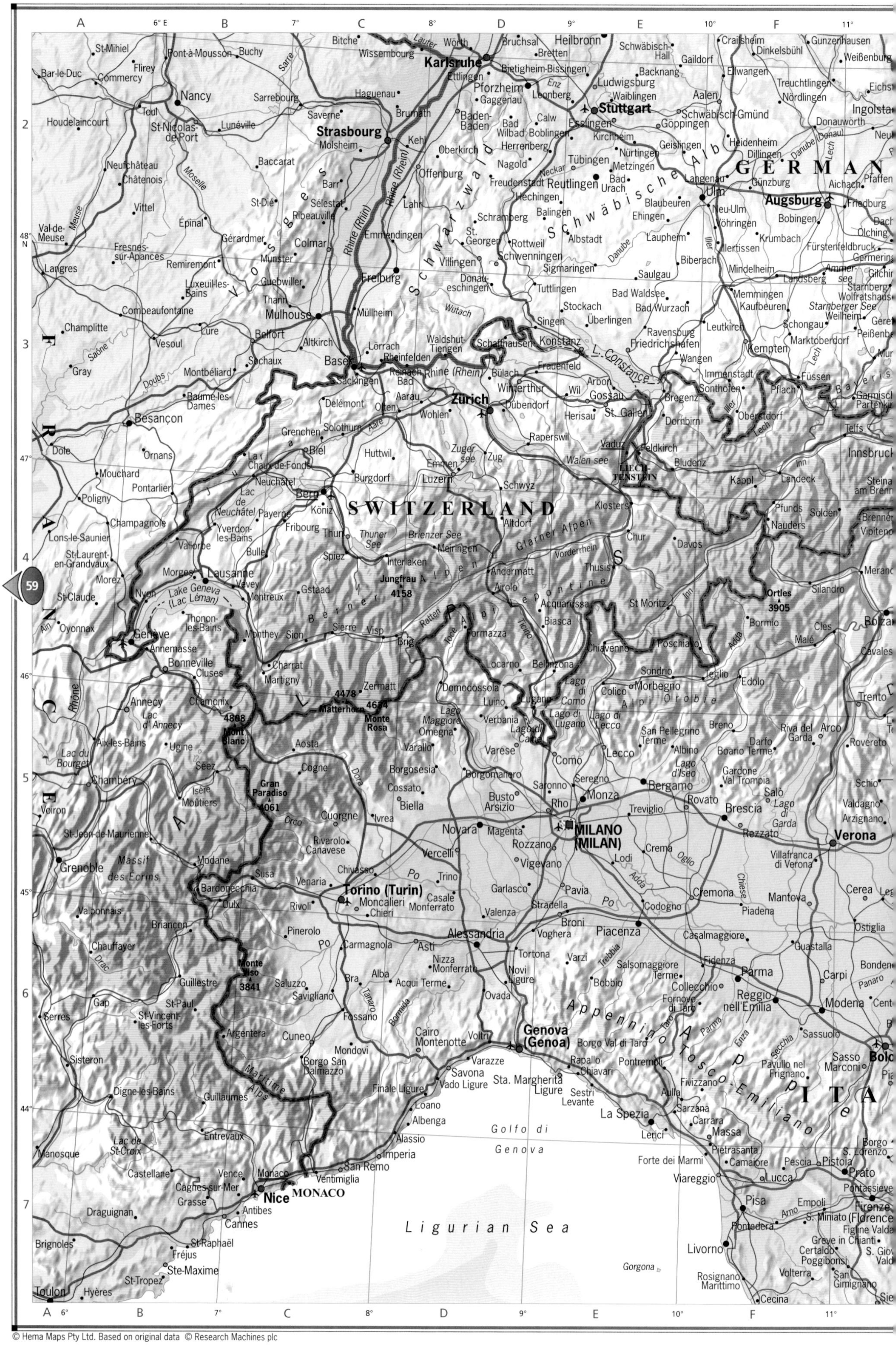

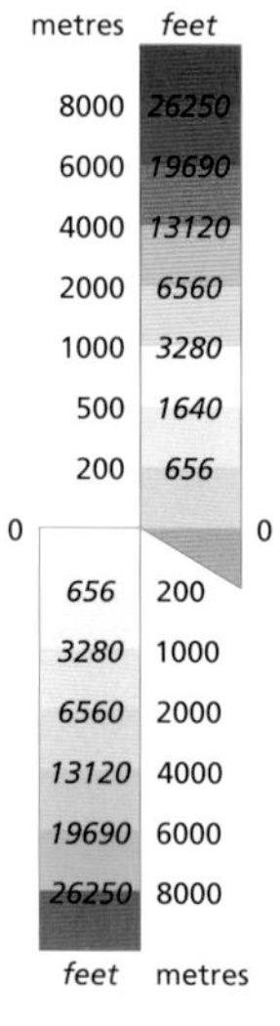

The Alpine States

Austria • Liechtenstein • Slovenia • Switzerland

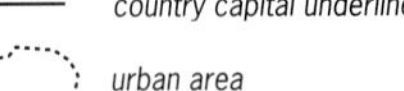

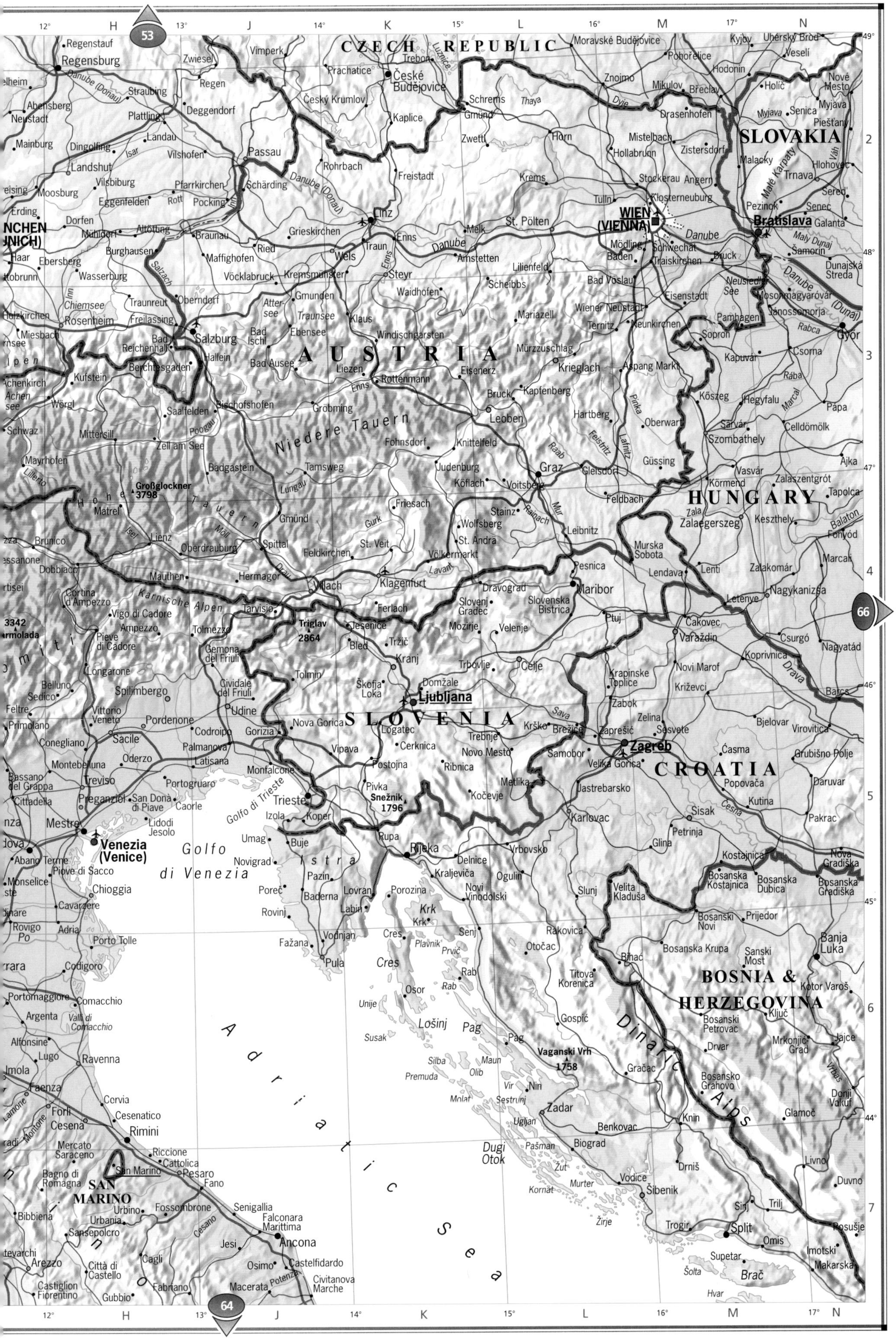

■ over 3 million
■ 1 – 3 million
● 250 000 – 1 million
● 100 000 – 250 000
● 25 000 – 100 000
• under 25 000
country capital underline
urban area

Scale 1 : 3 450 000

0 50 100 150 km

0 25 50 75 miles

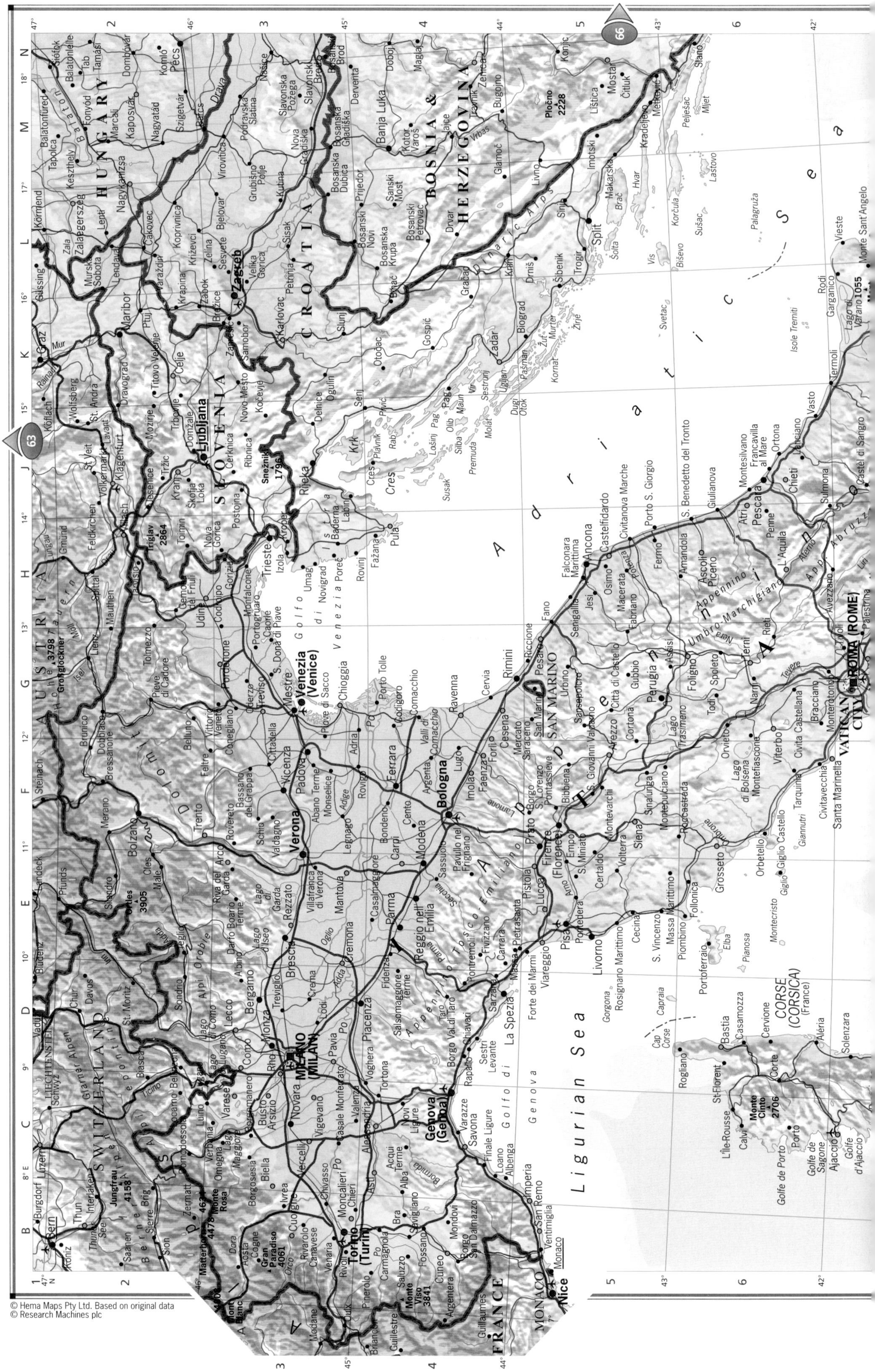

metres | feet
8000 26250
6000 19690
4000 13120
2000 6560
1000 3280
500 1640
200 656
0 0
656 200
3280 1000
6560 2000
13120 4000
19690 6000
26250 8000
feet | metres

Italy

Corsica • Malta • San Marino • Vatican City

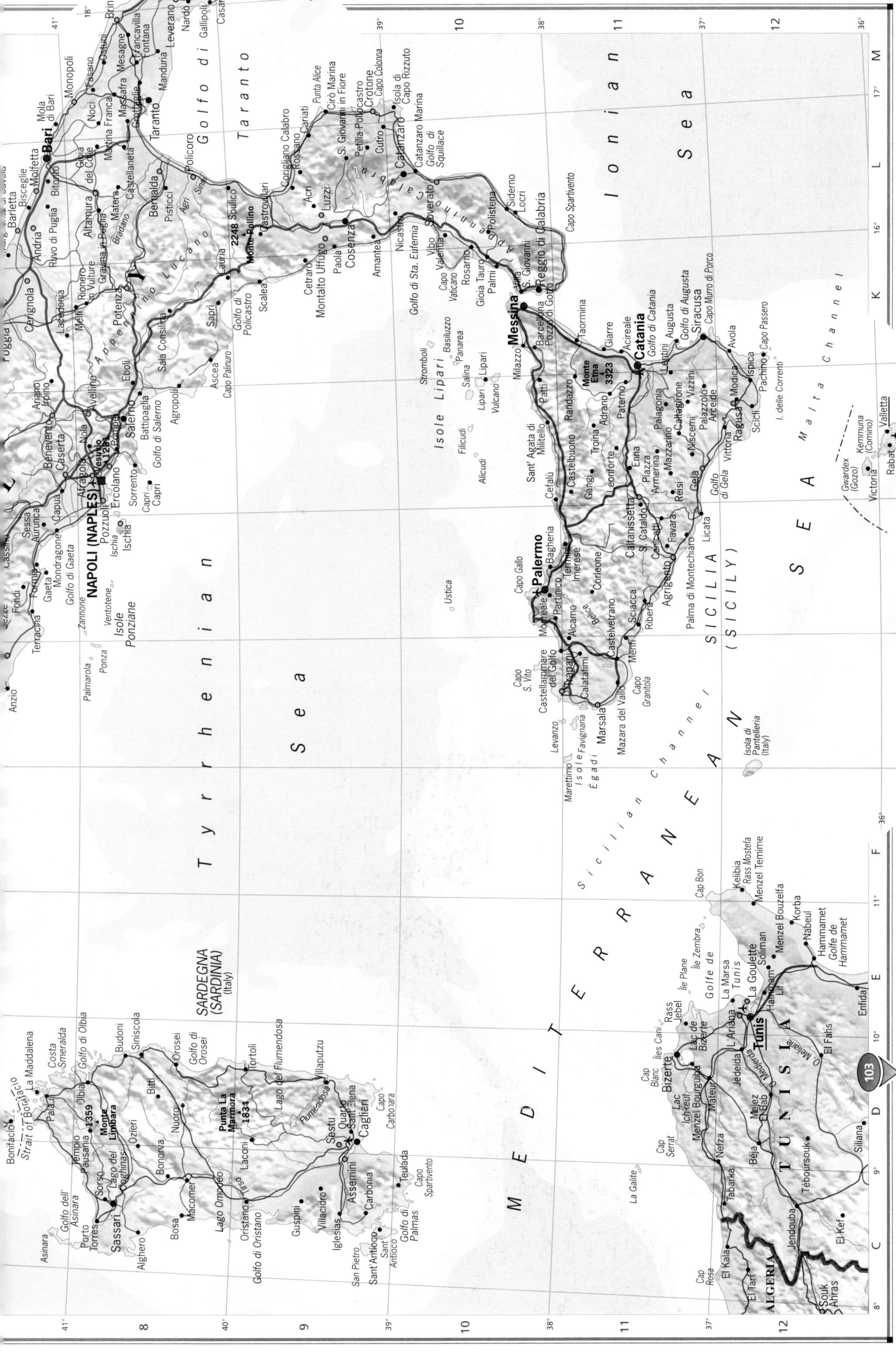

■ over 3 million
■ 1 – 3 million
● 250 000 – 1 million
• 100 000 – 250 000
○ 25 000 – 100 000
• under 25 000
country capital underline
urban area

Scale 1 : 3 450 000
0 50 100 150 km
0 25 50 75 miles
51
63
68
SLOVAKIA
AUSTRIA
HUNGARY
SLOVENIA
CROATIA
BOSNIA &
HERZEGOVINA
MONTENEGRO
SERBIA
KOSOVO
ALBANIA
ITALY
MACE
VOJVODINA
ADRIATIC SEA
WIEN
(VIENNA)
Bratislava
BUDAPEST
Ljubljana
Zagreb
BEOGRAD
(BELGRADE)
Sarajevo
Podgorica
Tiranë
(Tirana)
Skopje
Priština
Graz
Maribor
Klagenfurt
Villach
Trieste
Rijeka
Pula
Zadar
Split
Dubrovnik
Mostar
Banja Luka
Osijek
Novi Sad
Subotica
Szeged
Pécs
Győr
Debrecen
Miskolc
Košice
Timișoara
Arad
Kragujevac
Niš
Bari
Foggia
Shkodër
Durrës
Elbasan
Triglav
2864
Durmitor
2522
Kékes
1014
Monte Calvo
1055
Danube
Drava
Sava
Tisza
Balaton
metres feet
8000 26250
6000 19690
4000 13120
2000 6560
1000 3280
500 1640
200 656
0 0
656 200
3280 1000
6560 2000
13120 4000
19690 6000
26250 8000
feet metres

The Balkans

Bosnia-Herzegovina • Bulgaria • Croatia • Moldova • Romania • Serbia • Montenegro

UKRAINE

MOLDOVA

ROMANIA

BULGARIA

TURKEY

GREECE

BLACK SEA

■ *over 3 million*	● *100 000 – 250 000*	*country capital underline*
■ *1 – 3 million*	○ *25 000 – 100 000*	*state or province capital underline*
● *250 000 – 1 million*	• *under 25 000*	*urban area*

Scale 1 : 3 450 000

0 50 100 150 km

0 25 50 75 miles

metres	feet
8000	26250
6000	19690
4000	13120
2000	6560
1000	3280
500	1640
200	656
0	0
656	200
3280	1000
6560	2000
13120	4000
19690	6000
26250	8000
feet	metres

- over 3 million
- 1 – 3 million
- 250 000 – 1 million
- 100 000 – 250 000
- 25 000 – 100 000
- under 25 000
- country capital underline
- state or province capital underline
- urban area

Scale 1 : 10 400 000

0 200 400 600 km

0 100 200 300 miles

metres	feet
8000	26250
6000	19690
4000	13120
2000	6560
1000	3280
500	1640
200	656
0	0
656	200
3280	1000
6560	2000
13120	4000
19690	6000
26250	8000
feet	metres

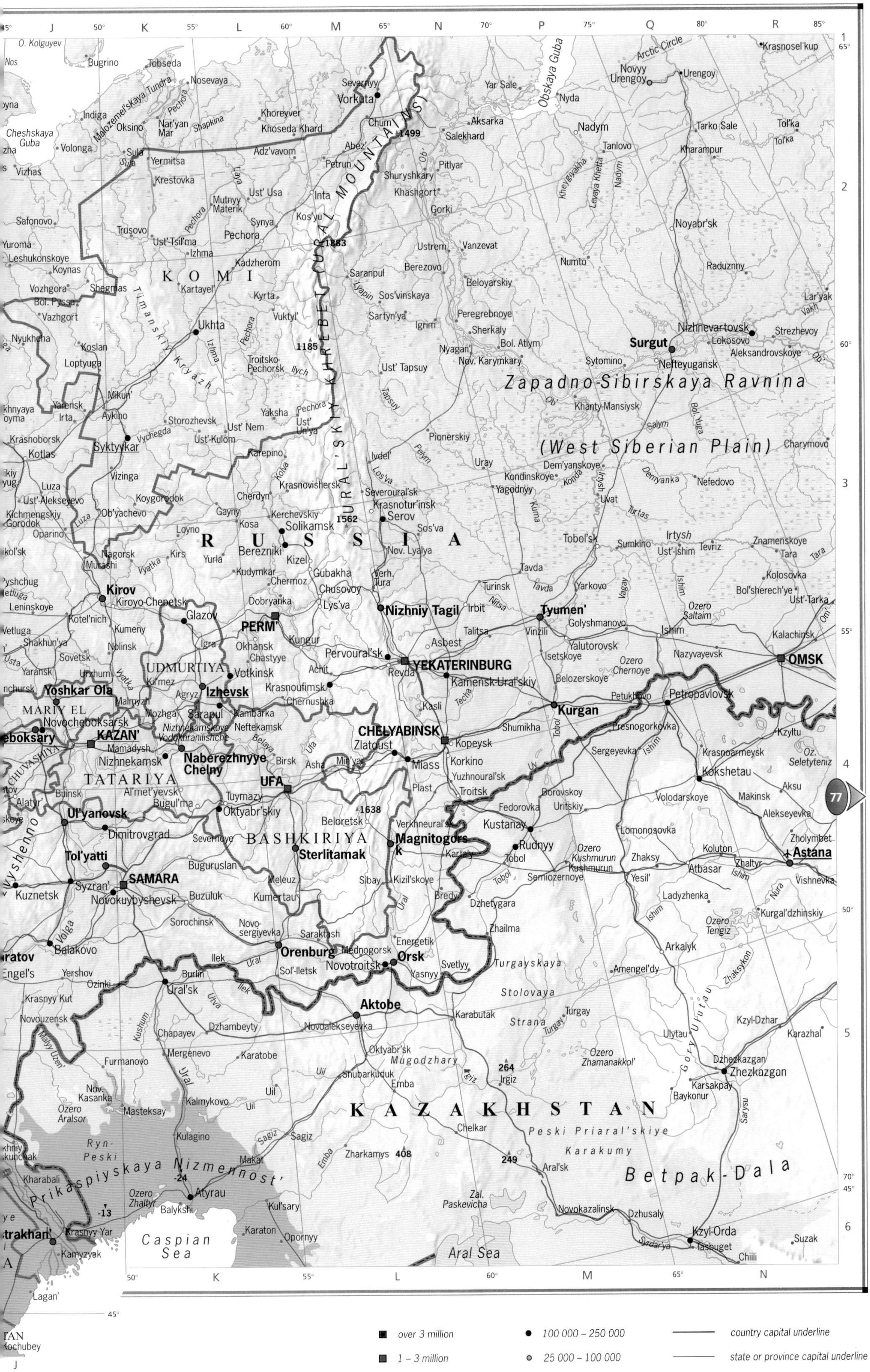

■ over 3 million
■ 1 – 3 million
● 250 000 – 1 million
● 100 000 – 250 000
○ 25 000 – 100 000
• under 25 000
country capital underline
state or province capital underline

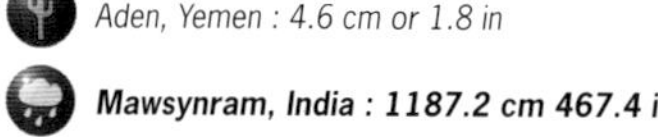

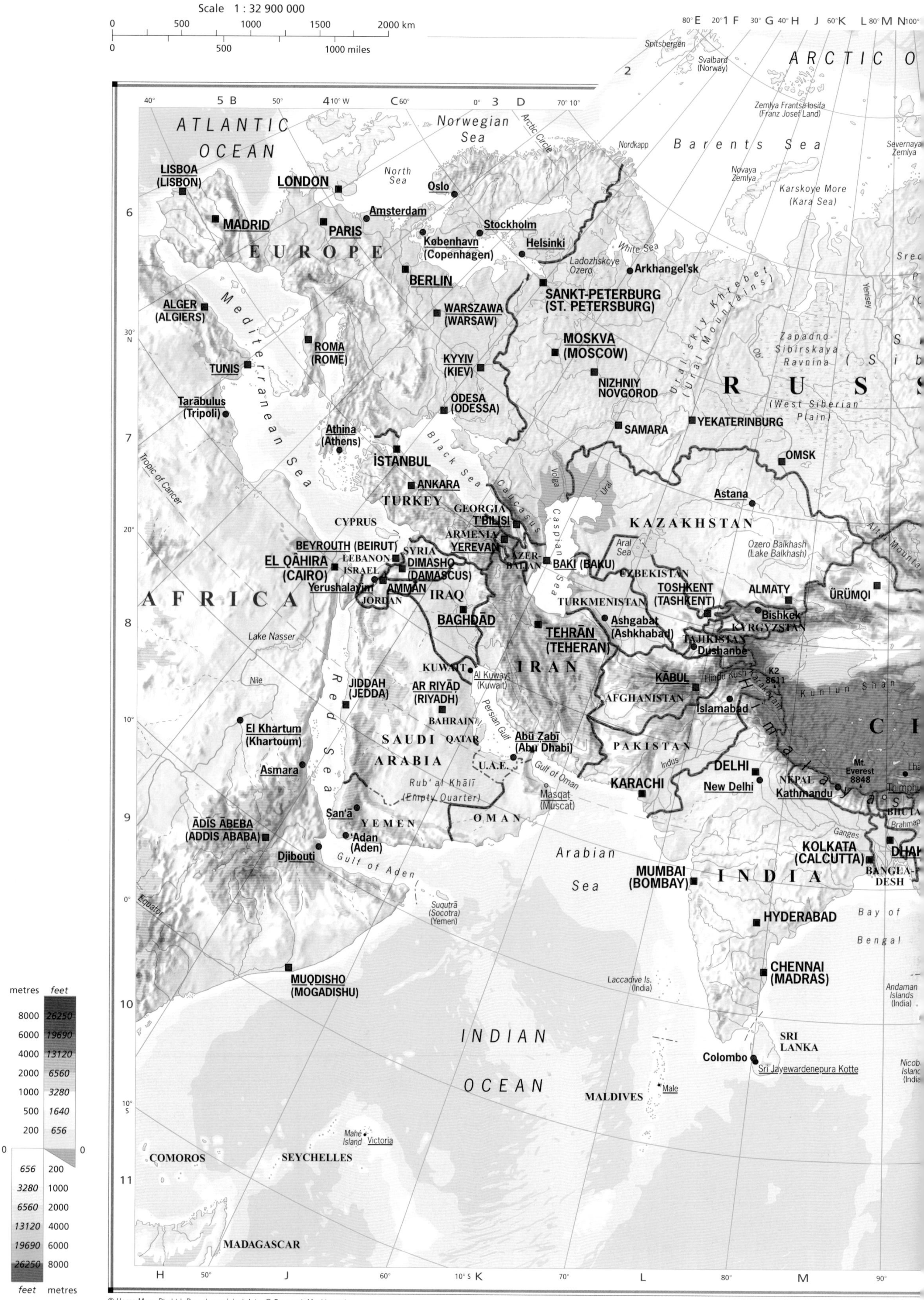
Scale 1 : 32 900 000
0 500 1000 1500 2000 km
0 500 1000 miles
ATLANTIC OCEAN
Norwegian Sea
North Sea
Arctic Circle
Barents Sea
ARCTIC O
Spitsbergen
Svalbard (Norway)
Zemlya Frantsa-Iosifa (Franz Josef Land)
Severnaya Zemlya
Nordkapp
Novaya Zemlya
Karskoye More (Kara Sea)
LISBOA (LISBON)
LONDON
Oslo
MADRID
Amsterdam
PARIS
Stockholm
København (Copenhagen)
Helsinki
EUROPE
White Sea
Ladozhskoye Ozero
Arkhangel'sk
BERLIN
SANKT-PETERBURG (ST. PETERSBURG)
ALGER (ALGIERS)
Mediterranean Sea
WARSZAWA (WARSAW)
MOSKVA (MOSCOW)
Ural'skiy Khrebet (Ural Mountains)
Zapadno-Sibirskaya Ravnina (West Siberian Plain)
Yenisey
Ob
ROMA (ROME)
TUNIS
KYYIV (KIEV)
NIZHNIY NOVGOROD
RUS
Tarābulus (Tripoli)
ODESA (ODESSA)
SAMARA
YEKATERINBURG
Athina (Athens)
İSTANBUL
Black Sea
OMSK
Tropic of Cancer
ANKARA
TURKEY
Caucasus
Volga
Ural
Astana
CYPRUS
GEORGIA
T'BILISI
ARMENIA
YEREVAN
Caspian Sea
KAZAKHSTAN
Aral Sea
Ozero Balkhash (Lake Balkhash)
BEYROUTH (BEIRUT)
SYRIA
LEBANON
DIMASHQ (DAMASCUS)
ISRAEL
AZERBAIJAN
BAKI (BAKU)
UZBEKISTAN
EL QÂHIRA (CAIRO)
Yerushalayim
AMMAN
JORDAN
IRAQ
TOSHKENT (TASHKENT)
ALMATY
ÜRÜMQI
AFRICA
TURKMENISTAN
BAGHDĀD
Ashgabat (Ashkhabad)
Bishkek
KYRGYZSTAN
Lake Nasser
TEHRĀN (TEHERAN)
TAJIKISTAN
Dushanbe
Nile
KUWAIT
Al Kuwayt (Kuwait)
IRAN
Red Sea
JIDDAH (JEDDA)
AR RIYĀD (RIYADH)
KĀBUL
Hindu Kush
Karakoram
K2 8611
Kunlun Shan
AFGHANISTAN
Islamabad
Persian Gulf
BAHRAIN
El Khartum (Khartoum)
SAUDI ARABIA
QATAR
Abū Zabī (Abu Dhabi)
PAKISTAN
Himalaya
U.A.E.
Gulf of Oman
Indus
DELHI
Asmara
Rub' al Khālī (Empty Quarter)
Masqat (Muscat)
KARACHI
New Delhi
NEPAL
Kathmandu
Mt. Everest 8848
San'ā
YEMEN
OMAN
ĀDĪS ĀBEBA (ADDIS ABABA)
'Adan (Aden)
Djibouti
Gulf of Aden
Arabian Sea
Ganges
KOLKATA (CALCUTTA)
BANGLADESH
MUMBAI (BOMBAY)
INDIA
Equator
Suquţrā (Socotra) (Yemen)
HYDERABAD
Bay of Bengal
MUQDISHO (MOGADISHU)
Laccadive Is. (India)
CHENNAI (MADRAS)
Andaman Islands (India)
INDIAN OCEAN
SRI LANKA
Colombo
Sri Jayewardenepura Kotte
MALDIVES
Male
Mahé Island
Victoria
COMOROS
SEYCHELLES
MADAGASCAR
metres feet
8000 26250
6000 19690
4000 13120
2000 6560
1000 3280
500 1640
200 656
0 0
656 200
3280 1000
6560 2000
13120 4000
19690 6000
26250 8000
feet metres

Mt. Everest, China/Nepal : 8,848 m or 29,029 ft

Dead Sea, Israel/Jordan : 400 m or 1312 ft

Aden, Yemen : 4.6 cm or 1.8 in

Mawsynram, India : 1187.2 cm 467.4 in

Yangtze, China : 5,980 km or 3,720 mi

Aral Sea, Kazakhstan : 62,000 km² or 23,940 sq mi

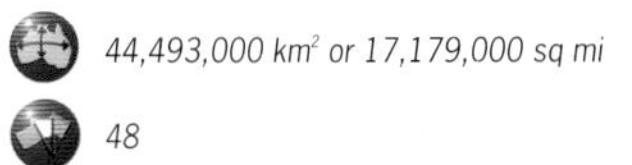

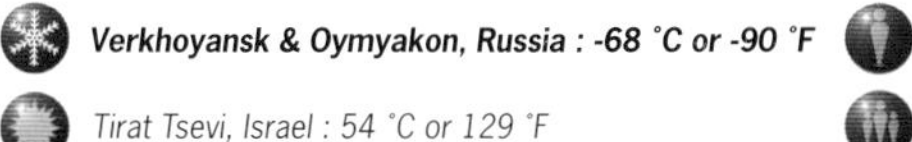

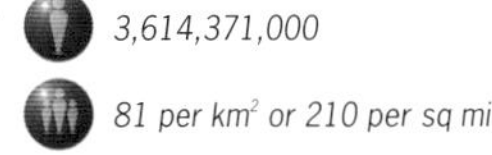

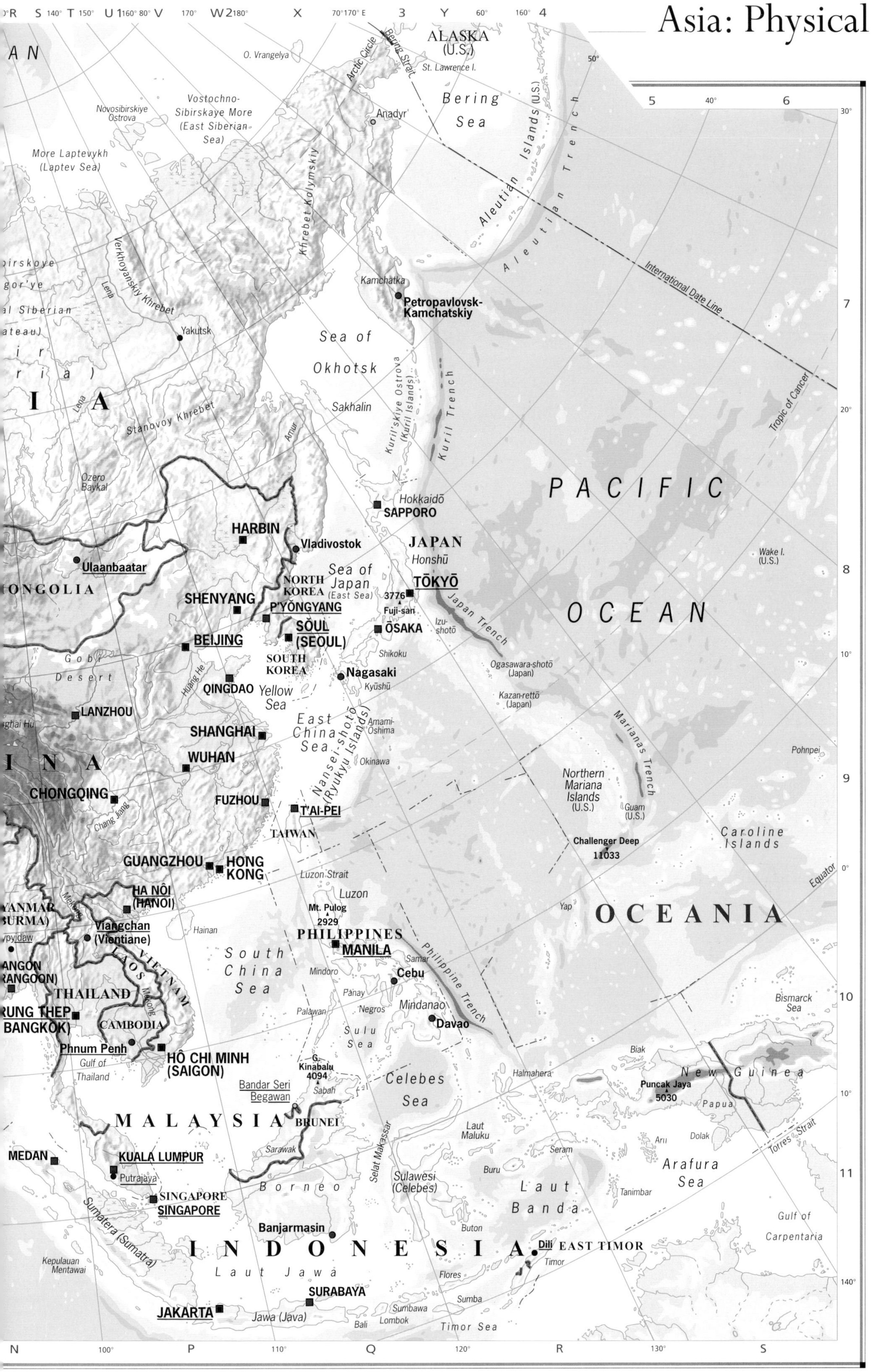
ALASKA (U.S.)
Bering Strait
Arctic Circle
St. Lawrence I.
O. Vrangelya
Novosibirskiye Ostrova
Vostochno-Sibirskaye More (East Siberian Sea)
More Laptevykh (Laptev Sea)
Anadyr'
Bering Sea
Aleutian Islands (U.S.)
Aleutian Trench
International Date Line
Khrebet Kolymskiy
Verkhoyanskiy Khrebet
Lena
Yakutsk
Kamchatka
Petropavlovsk-Kamchatskiy
Sea of Okhotsk
Sakhalin
Kuril'skiye Ostrova (Kuril Islands)
Kuril Trench
Stanovoy Khrebet
Amur
Tropic of Cancer
Ozero Baykal
PACIFIC OCEAN
Hokkaidō
SAPPORO
HARBIN
Vladivostok
JAPAN
Honshū
Ulaanbaatar
MONGOLIA
Sea of Japan (East Sea)
NORTH KOREA
TŌKYŌ
3776
Fuji-san
SHENYANG
P'YŎNGYANG
SŎUL (SEOUL)
ŌSAKA
Izu-shotō
Japan Trench
BEIJING
Gobi Desert
SOUTH KOREA
Shikoku
Nagasaki
Kyūshū
Ogasawara-shotō (Japan)
Kazan-rettō (Japan)
Wake I. (U.S.)
Huang He
QINGDAO
Yellow Sea
LANZHOU
SHANGHAI
East China Sea
Amami-Ōshima
Nansei-shotō (Ryukyu Islands)
Okinawa
Marianas Trench
Pohnpei
WUHAN
CHONGQING
FUZHOU
T'AI-PEI
TAIWAN
Chang Jiang
Northern Mariana Islands (U.S.)
Guam (U.S.)
Challenger Deep
11033
Caroline Islands
GUANGZHOU
HONG KONG
Luzon Strait
Luzon
Equator
HA NÔI (HANOI)
Mekong
Mt. Pulog
2929
Yap
OCEANIA
Hainan
Viangchan (Vientiane)
LAOS
VIETNAM
PHILIPPINES
MANILA
Samar
Philippine Trench
South China Sea
Mindoro
Cebu
THAILAND
Panay
Mindanao
Negros
Palawan
Davao
Bismarck Sea
CAMBODIA
Phnum Penh
HÔ CHI MINH (SAIGON)
Sulu Sea
Gulf of Thailand
G. Kinabalu
4094
Sabah
Celebes Sea
Halmahera
Biak
New Guinea
Puncak Jaya
5030
Papua
Bandar Seri Begawan
MALAYSIA
BRUNEI
Sarawak
Selat Makassar
Laut Maluku
Seram
Aru
Dolak
Torres Strait
MEDAN
KUALA LUMPUR
Putrajaya
Buru
Arafura Sea
SINGAPORE
Borneo
Sulawesi (Celebes)
Laut Banda
Tanimbar
Gulf of Carpentaria
Sumatera (Sumatra)
Banjarmasin
Buton
INDONESIA
Dili
EAST TIMOR
Timor
Kepulauan Mentawai
Laut Jawa
Flores
SURABAYA
Sumba
JAKARTA
Jawa (Java)
Sumbawa
Bali
Lombok
Timor Sea
N
P
Q
R
S
100°
110°
120°
130°
140°
5
6
7
8
9
10
11

Verkhoyansk & Oymyakon, Russia : -68 °C or -90 °F

Tirat Tsevi, Israel : 54 °C or 129 °F

3,614,371,000

81 per km² or 210 per sq mi

44,493,000 km² or 17,179,000 sq mi

48

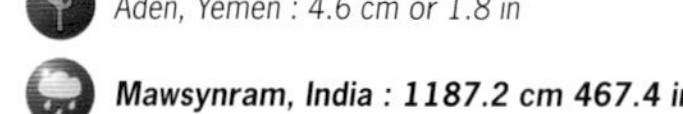

Scale 1 : 32 900 000
0 500 1000 1500 2000 km
0 500 1000 miles
ATLANTIC OCEAN
Norwegian Sea
North Sea
Arctic Circle
Barents Sea
ARCTIC O
Spitsbergen
Svalbard (Norway)
Zemlya Frantsa-Iosifa (Franz Josef Land)
Severnaya Zemlya
Nordkapp
Novaya Zemlya
Karskoye More (Kara Sea)
LISBOA (LISBON)
LONDON
Oslo
MADRID
PARIS
Amsterdam
Stockholm
København (Copenhagen)
Helsinki
EUROPE
BERLIN
White Sea
Ladozhskoye Ozero
Arkhangel'sk
SANKT-PETERBURG (ST. PETERSBURG)
Ural'skiy Khrebet (Ural Mountains)
ALGER (ALGIERS)
Mediterranean Sea
WARSZAWA (WARSAW)
ROMA (ROME)
MOSKVA (MOSCOW)
Zapadno-Sibirskaya Ravnina (West Siberian Plain)
TUNIS
KYYIV (KIEV)
NIZHNIY NOVGOROD
RUSS
Tarābulus (Tripoli)
ODESA (ODESSA)
SAMARA
YEKATERINBURG
Athina (Athens)
İSTANBUL
Black Sea
OMSK
Tropic of Cancer
ANKARA
Caucasus
Volga
Ural
Astana
TURKEY
GEORGIA
T'BILISI
KAZAKHSTAN
CYPRUS
ARMENIA
YEREVAN
Caspian Sea
Aral Sea
Ozero Balkhash (Lake Balkhash)
BEYROUTH (BEIRUT)
SYRIA
LEBANON
DIMASHQ (DAMASCUS)
EL QÂHIRA (CAIRO)
ISRAEL
AZERBAIJAN
BAKI (BAKU)
UZBEKISTAN
Yerushalayim
AMMAN
JORDAN
IRAQ
TURKMENISTAN
TOSHKENT (TASHKENT)
ALMATY
ÜRÜMQI
AFRICA
BAGHDĀD
Ashgabat (Ashkhabad)
Bishkek
KYRGYZSTAN
Lake Nasser
TEHRĀN (TEHERAN)
TAJIKISTAN
Dushanbe
KUWAIT
Al Kuwayt (Kuwait)
IRAN
Nile
Red Sea
JIDDAH (JEDDA)
AR RIYĀD (RIYADH)
KĀBUL
Hindu Kush
K2 8611
Kunlun Shan
AFGHANISTAN
Islamabad
Karakoram
Himalaya
BAHRAIN
Persian Gulf
El Khartum (Khartoum)
SAUDI ARABIA
QATAR
Abū Zabī (Abu Dhabi)
PAKISTAN
Indus
DELHI
New Delhi
Asmara
U.A.E.
Gulf of Oman
Rub' al Khālī (Empty Quarter)
KARACHI
Masqat (Muscat)
NEPAL
Kathmandu
Mt. Everest 8848
Thimphu
BHUTAN
Brahmaputra
Ganges
San'ā
YEMEN
OMAN
ĀDĪS ĀBEBA (ADDIS ABABA)
'Adan (Aden)
Djibouti
Gulf of Aden
Arabian Sea
KOLKATA (CALCUTTA)
DHAKA
BANGLADESH
MUMBAI (BOMBAY)
INDIA
Equator
Suquṭrā (Socotra) (Yemen)
HYDERABAD
Bay of Bengal
CHENNAI (MADRAS)
MUQDISHO (MOGADISHU)
Laccadive Is. (India)
Andaman Islands (India)
INDIAN OCEAN
SRI LANKA
Colombo
Sri Jayewardenepura Kotte
Nicobar Islands (India)
MALDIVES
Male
Mahé Island
Victoria
COMOROS
SEYCHELLES
MADAGASCAR

Mt. Everest, China/Nepal : 8,848 m or 29,029 ft

Aden, Yemen : 4.6 cm or 1.8 in

Yangtze, China : 5,980 km or 3,720 mi

Dead Sea, Israel/Jordan : 400 m or 1312 ft

Mawsynram, India : 1187.2 cm 467.4 in

Aral Sea, Kazakhstan : 62,000 km² or 23,940 sq mi

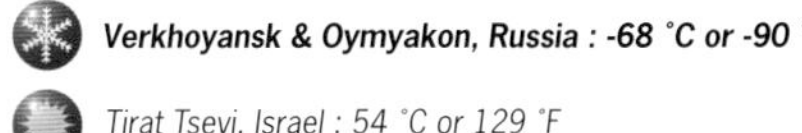

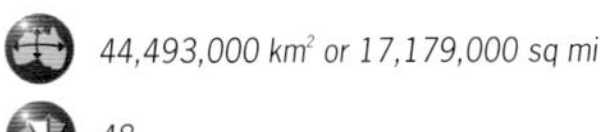

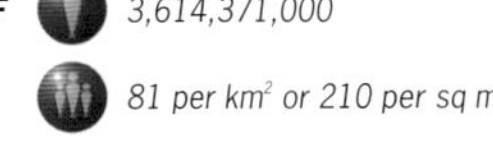

ALASKA (U.S.)
O. Vrangelya
Bering Strait
Arctic Circle
St. Lawrence I.
Novosibirskiye Ostrova
Vostochno-Sibirskaye More (East Siberian Sea)
Anadyr'
Bering Sea
Aleutian Islands (U.S.)
Aleutian Trench
More Laptevykh (Laptev Sea)
Khrebet Kolymskiy
Verkhoyanskiy Khrebet
Lena
International Date Line
Kamchatka
Petropavlovsk-Kamchatskiy
Yakutsk
Sea of Okhotsk
Kuril'skiye Ostrova (Kuril Islands)
Kuril Trench
Tropic of Cancer
Sakhalin
Stanovoy Khrebet
Amur
Ozero Baykal
PACIFIC OCEAN
Hokkaidō
SAPPORO
HARBIN
Vladivostok
JAPAN
Honshū
Wake I. (U.S.)
Ulaanbaatar
MONGOLIA
Sea of Japan (East Sea)
NORTH KOREA
TŌKYŌ
3776 Fuji-san
SHENYANG
P'YŎNGYANG
Japan Trench
SŎUL (SEOUL)
ŌSAKA
Izu-shotō
BEIJING
SOUTH KOREA
Shikoku
Gobi Desert
Huang He
Nagasaki
Kyūshū
Ogasawara-shotō (Japan)
QINGDAO
Yellow Sea
Kazan-rettō (Japan)
LANZHOU
East China Sea
Amami-Ōshima
Nansei-shotō (Ryukyu Islands)
Okinawa
Marianas Trench
SHANGHAI
WUHAN
Pohnpei
CHONGQING
Northern Mariana Islands (U.S.)
FUZHOU
T'AI-PEI
Guam (U.S.)
Chang Jiang
TAIWAN
Challenger Deep 11033
Caroline Islands
GUANGZHOU
HONG KONG
Luzon Strait
Equator
HA NÔI (HANOI)
Luzon
Mt. Pulog 2929
Yap
OCEANIA
Mekong
Hainan
PHILIPPINES
MANILA
Viangchan (Vientiane)
LAOS
VIETNAM
South China Sea
Samar
Philippine Trench
Mindoro
Cebu
THAILAND
Panay
Bismarck Sea
KRUNG THEP (BANGKOK)
Palawan
Negros
Mindanao
Davao
CAMBODIA
Sulu Sea
Phnum Penh
HÔ CHI MINH (SAIGON)
Biak
Gulf of Thailand
G. Kinabalu 4094
Celebes Sea
Halmahera
New Guinea
Puncak Jaya 5030
Sabah
Bandar Seri Begawan
Papua
MALAYSIA
BRUNEI
Laut Maluku
Aru
Dolak
Torres Strait
Sarawak
Selat Makassar
Seram
MEDAN
KUALA LUMPUR
Arafura Sea
Putrajaya
Buru
Sulawesi (Celebes)
Laut Banda
Borneo
SINGAPORE
Tanimbar
Gulf of Carpentaria
Sumatera (Sumatra)
Banjarmasin
Buton
INDONESIA
Dili
EAST TIMOR
Timor
Kepulauan Mentawai
Laut Jawa
Flores
SURABAYA
Sumba
JAKARTA
Sumbawa
Jawa (Java)
Bali
Lombok
Timor Sea

Verkhoyansk & Oymyakon, Russia : -68 °C or -90 °F

Tirat Tsevi, Israel : 54 °C or 129 °F

3,614,371,000

81 per km² or 210 per sq mi

44,493,000 km² or 17,179,000 sq mi

48

Scale 1 : 13 800 000

0 200 400 600 km

0 100 200 300 miles

metres | feet

metres	feet
8000	26250
6000	19690
4000	13120
2000	6560
1000	3280
500	1640
200	656
0	0

feet	metres
656	200
3280	1000
6560	2000
13120	4000
19690	6000
26250	8000

- ■ *over 3 million*
- ■ *1 – 3 million*
- ● *250 000 – 1 million*
- ● *100 000 – 250 000*
- ● *25 000 – 100 000*
- • *under 25 000*
- *country capital underline*
- *state or province capital underline*

Northwest Asia

Kazakhstan • Kyrgyzstan • Central Russia
Tajikistan • Turkmenistan • Uzbekistan

Scale 1 : 13 800 000

0 200 400 600 km

0 100 200 300 miles

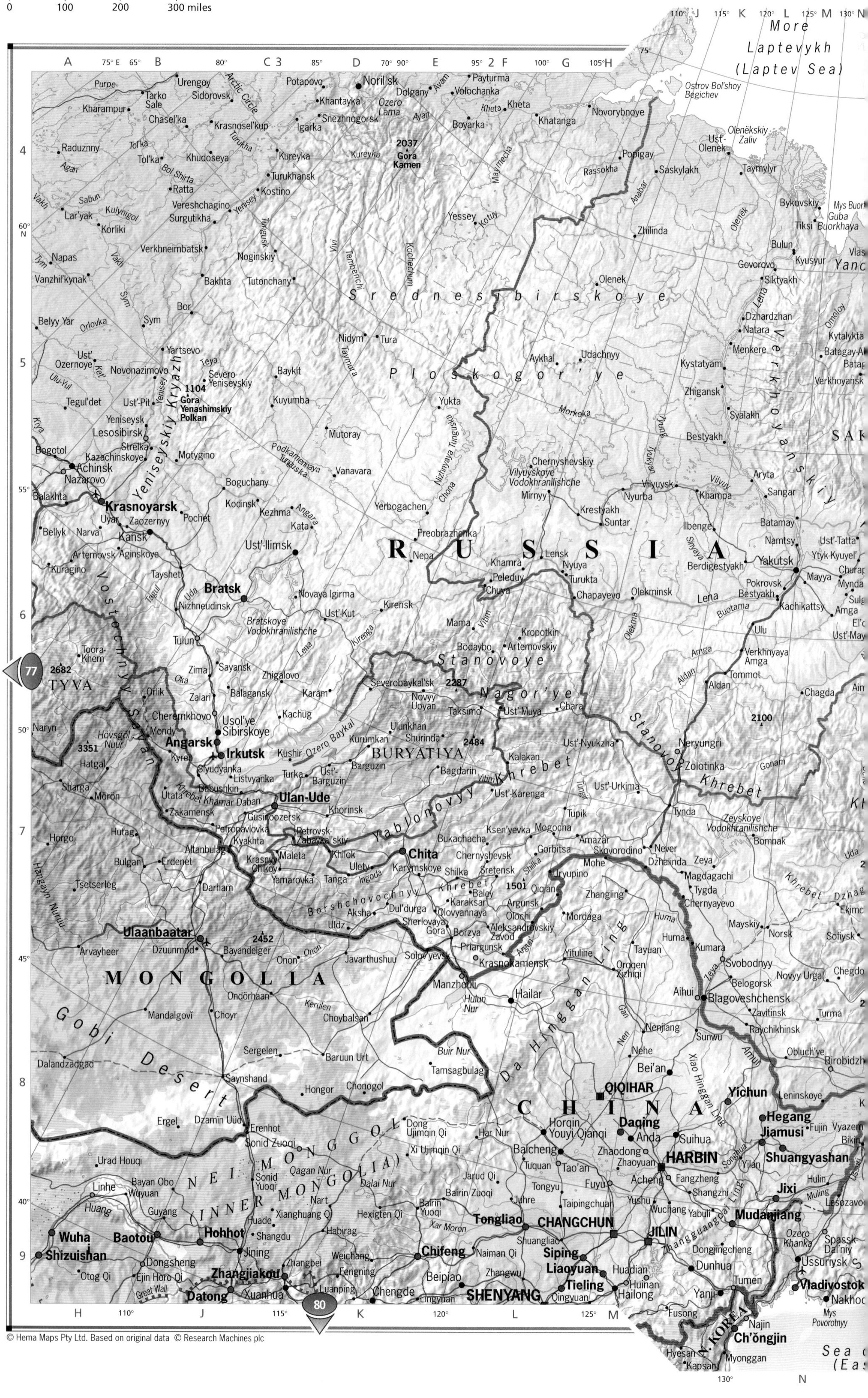

© Hema Maps Pty Ltd. Based on original data © Research Machines plc

metres	feet
8000	26250
6000	19690
4000	13120
2000	6560
1000	3280
500	1640
200	656
0	0
656	200
3280	1000
6560	2000
13120	4000
19690	6000
26250	8000
feet	metres

■ over 3 million
■ 1 – 3 million
● 250 000 – 1 million
● 100 000 – 250 000
◉ 25 000 – 100 000
• under 25 000
country capital underline
state or province capital underline

Scale 1 : 11 600 000

0 200 400 600 km

0 100 200 300 miles

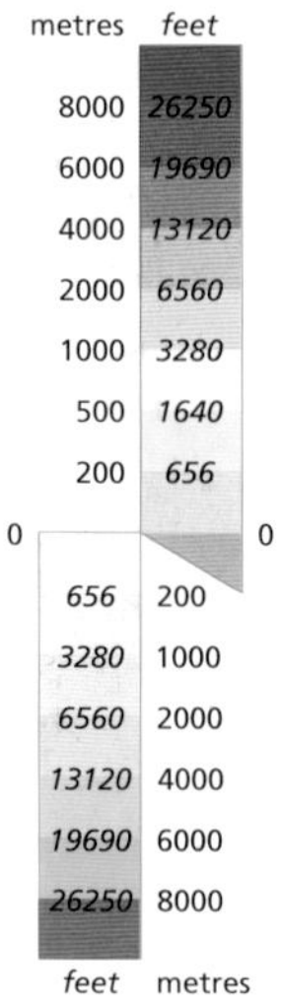

Eastern China

Eastern China • Japan
North Korea • South Korea • Taiwan

■ over 3 million
■ 1 – 3 million
● 250 000 – 1 million
● 100 000 – 250 000
○ 25 000 – 100 000
• under 25 000
—— country capital underline

Scale 1 : 5 800 000

0 100 200 300 km

0 50 100 150 miles

A 122° E B 124° C 126° D 128° E 130° F 132° G 134° H

Golin
Baixing 78
Fuyu Shangzhi Linkou Muling Lesozavodsk
Tongyu Sanchahe Wuchang Turiy Rog Jixi Ussuri
Taipingchuan Nong'an Yushu Yabuli Kamen' Ozero
Jurhe Zhangguangcal Ling Rybolov Khanka
Shulan Ning'an Suifenhe Grodekovo
44° Nong'an Spassk-Dal'niy
N Tongliao CHANGCHUN JILIN Naizishan Dongjingcheng Poltavka RUSSIA
Shuangliao Songhua Mudanjiang Dongning
C H I N A Hu Jinapo Ussuriysk
Siping Hu Dunhua Tianqiaoling Razdol'noye
42° Kangping Liaoyuan Yanji Tumen Artem Rudnaya
Zhangwu Faku Huadian Laotougou Hunchun Trudovoye Pristan'
Xinmin Hailong Fusong Helong Onsong Vladivostok Partizansk
SHENYANG Tieling Qingyuan Huanren Antu Hoeryong Nakhodka
Benxi Linjiang Paekdu San 2541 Najin Mys Povorotnyy
Liaoyang FUSHUN Hunjiang Dalizi 2750 Kambo Ho
Dawa ANSHAN Tianshifu Tonghua Huch'ang Ch'ongjin
Yingkou Haicheng Kuandian Ch'osan Hyesan Myonggan
Gai Xian Fengcheng Pyoktong Kanggye Mt.Tuun Kapsan Kilchu
40° Dandong Uiju Sakchu 2487 P'ungsan
Wafangdian Donggou Sinuiju Huich'on 2310 Kimch'aek
Zhuanghe Chongju Pakch'on Tanch'on
Korea Sinanju Pukch'ong
Bay NORTH Hamhung
81 KOREA Hungnam
Namp'o P'YONGYANG Yangdok Ch'ongp'yong SEA O
Songnim Yonghung
38° Sariwon Hoeyang Wonsan JAPA
Haeju P'yonggang Kosong
Ongjin Kaesong Sokch'o (E a s t S
1708
Chengshan Jiao Tongduch'on Ch'unch'on Kangnung
Rongcheng SOUL (SEOUL) Ulleung do
Puch'on Tonghae
INCH'ON Songnam Wonju 1321
Suwon Anyang Ch'ungju
Sosan Ch'onan Ulchin
36° Ch'ongju SOUTH
Yellow Taech'on Andong
TAEJON KOREA P'ohang Oki-shoto Dogo
Kunsan Ch'onju Kyongju Saigo
Sea Chongup Koch'ang TAEGU Fu
KWANGJU Namwon Masan Ulsan Matsue Tottori Toyooka Tsuru
Mokp'o Naju Sunch'on Chinju PUSAN Yonago Fukuchiyama Obama
Chin Haenam Posong Yosu Samch'onp'o Oda Izumo Tsuyama KYOTO
34° do Wando Kamitsushima Korea Strait Hamada Miyoshi Tojo Himeji OSAKA
Tsushima Masuda Yamaguchi Kurashiki Akashi Ko
Izuhara HIROSHIMA Hofu Huchi- Fukuyama Harima- Wakayar
Cheju Higashi-suido Shimonoseki Kure nada Takamatsu nada Awaji-
KITA-KYUSHU Ube Imabari Tokushima shima
Iki Suo-nada Tokuyama Matsuyama Anan Gobo
FUKUOKA Nakatsu Iyo-nada Shikoku-sanchi Tanabe Shing
Karatsu Usa Kochi Nankoku
Goto-retto Saga Kurume Oita Tosa-wan Muroto Kushimoto
Saseho Omuta Usuki Uwajima SHIKOKU
Omura 1788 Saiki Nakamura Ashizuri-misaki mi
Fukue-jima Isahaya Kumamoto Nobeoka
Nagasaki Shimabara Kyushu- Hyuga
Fukue Nomo-saki Yatsushiro sanchi
Amakusa-Shimo- KYUSHU
shima
East China Akune Hitoyoshi
Shimo-Koshiki-jima Kushikino Miyazaki
Kagoshima Miyakonojo
Noma-misaki Kanoya Toi-misaki
Sea Makurazaki Osumi-kaikyo
Osumi-shoto Nishinoomote
Kamiyaku Tanega-shima 81
Yaku-shima Kukinaga

metres feet
8000 26250
6000 19690
4000 13120
2000 6560
1000 3280
500 1640
200 656
0 0
656 200
3280 1000
6560 2000
13120 4000
19690 6000
26250 8000
feet metres

© Hema Maps Pty Ltd. Based on original data © Research Machines plc

82

B 124° C 126° D 128° E 130° F 132° G 134° H

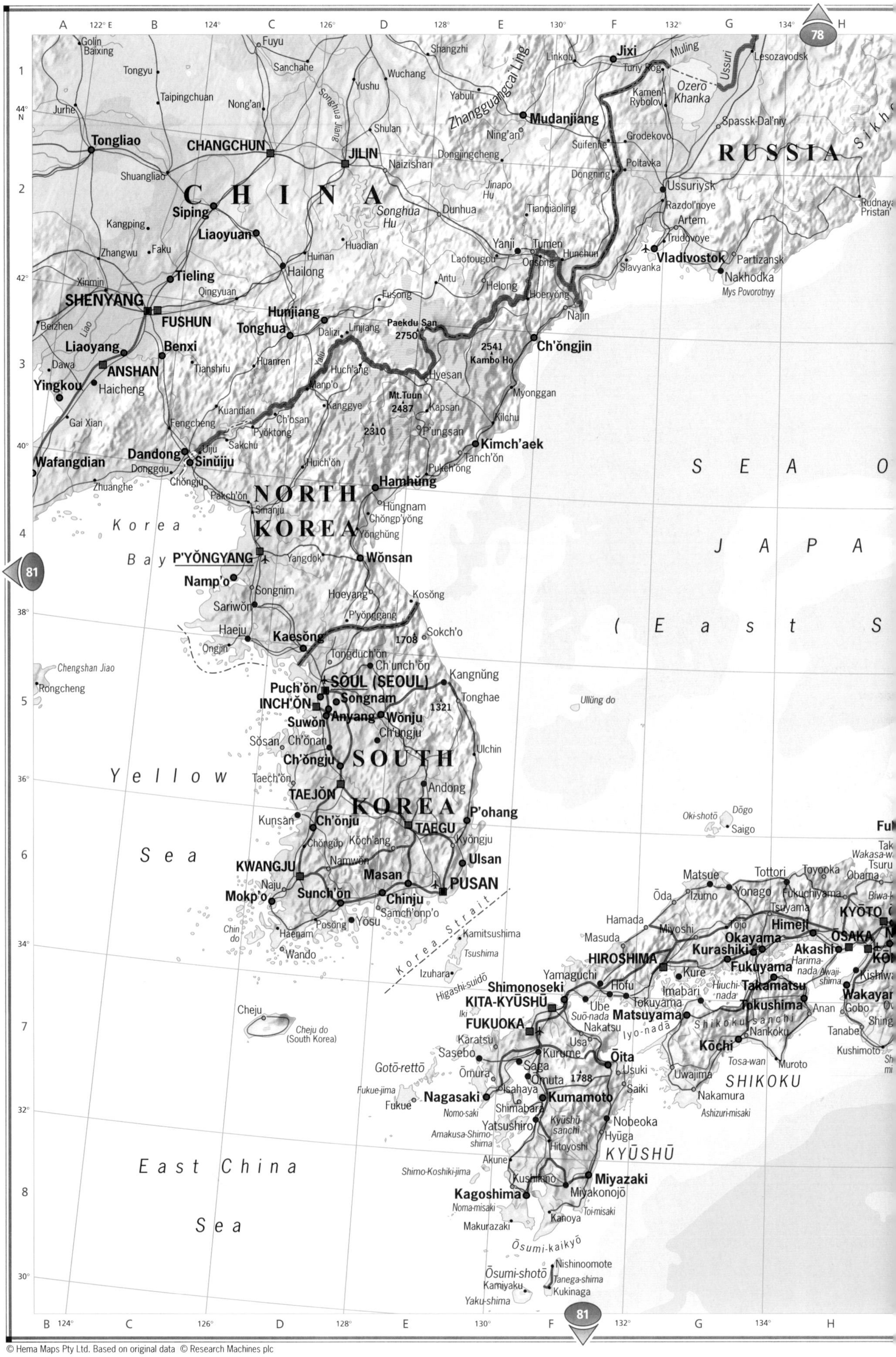

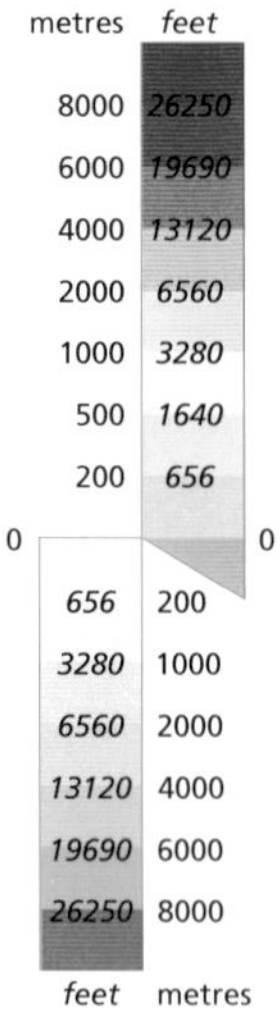

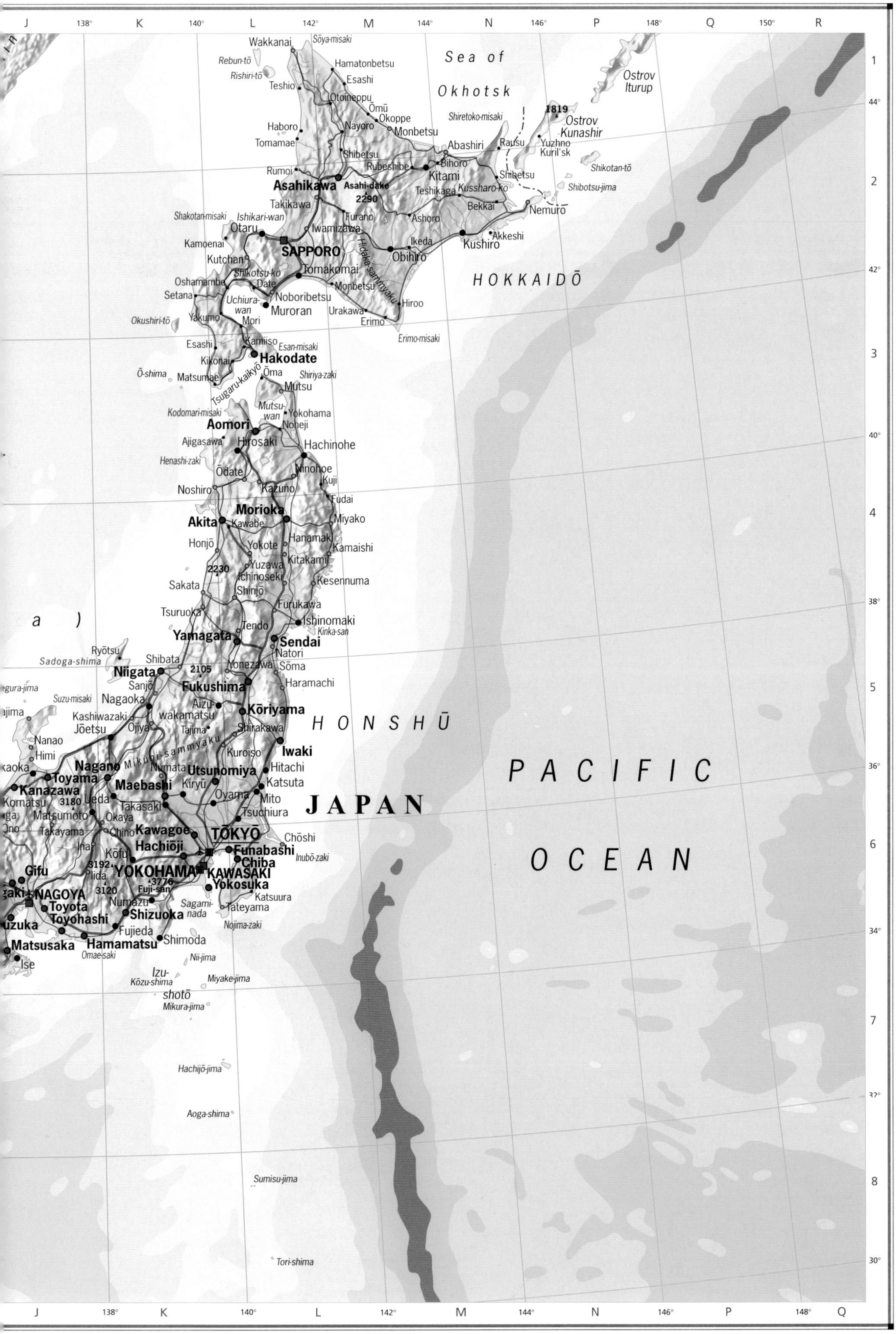

J 138° K 140° L 142° M 144° N 146° P 148° Q 150° R

Wakkanai
Sōya-misaki
Rebun-tō
Rishiri-tō Teshio Esashi
Hamatonbetsu

Sea of Okhotsk

Ostrov Iturup

Otoineppu
Ōmū
Nayoro Okoppe Monbetsu
Haboro *Shiretoko-misaki*
1819
Tomamae Shibetsu Rubeshibe Abashiri Rausu *Ostrov Kunashir*
Rumoi Bihoro Yuzhno-Kuril'sk
Asahikawa Takikawa Kitami Shibetsu *Shikotan-tō*
Asahi-dake 2290 Teshikaga *Shibotsu-jima*
Shakotan-misaki Ishikari-wan Furano Ashoro Bekkai
Kamoenai Iwamizawa Ikeda Kussharo-ko Nemuro
Kutchan **SAPPORO** Obihiro Akkeshi
Oshamambe *Shikotsu-ko* Tomakomai *Hidaka-sammyaku* Kushiro
Setana Date Noboribetsu **HOKKAIDŌ**
Uchiura-wan Muroran Urakawa Hiroo
Okushiri-tō Yakumo Mori Erimo
Mori *Erimo-misaki*

Esashi *Esan-misaki*
Kikonai Kamiso
Ō-shima **Hakodate** Ōma *Shiriya-zaki*
Matsumae Mutsu
Kodomari-misaki *Mutsu-wan* Yokohama
Tsugaru-kaikyō Noheji
Aomori
Ajigasawa Hirosaki Hachinohe
Henashi-zaki Ōdate Ninohe
Noshiro Kazuno Kuji
Fudai
Morioka Miyako
Akita Kawabe
Honjō Yokote Hanamaki Kamaishi
Kitakami
Sakata **2230** Yuzawa Kesennuma
Ichinoseki
Shinjō
Tsuruoka Furukawa
Tendo Ishinomaki
Yamagata *Kinka-san*
Sendai
Ryōtsu Shibata Natori
Sadoga-shima Yonezawa Sōma
Niigata **2105** Haramachi
Suzu-misaki Sanjō Aizu
gura-jima Nagaoka **Fukushima**
HONSHŪ
ajima Kashiwazaki wakamatsu **Kōriyama**
Jōetsu Ojiya Shirakawa
aoka **Nagano** Numata Kuroiso **Iwaki**
Toyama *Mikuni-sammyaku* **Utsunomiya** Hitachi
Kanazawa **Maebashi** Kiryū Katsuta
Komatsu **3180** Ueda Oyama Mito
iga Matsumoto Takasaki Tsuchiura **JAPAN**
Ono Takayama Okaya Chino
Inaz **Kawagoe** Chōshi
Takayama **Hachiōji** **TŌKYŌ** *Inubō-zaki*
Gifu **3192** Kōfu **Funabashi**
Iida **YOKOHAMA** **Chiba**
aki **NAGOYA** **3120** **KAWASAKI** Katsuura
Toyota *3776* **Yokosuka**
uzuka **Toyohashi** Numazu *Fuji-san* Tateyama
Shizuoka *Sagami-nada*
Matsusaka Fujieda *Nojima-zaki*
Ise **Hamamatsu** Shimoda
Omae-saki *Nii-jima*

Izu-Kōzu-shima
Miyake-jima
shotō
Mikura-jima

PACIFIC OCEAN

Hachijō-jima

Aoga-shima

Sumisu-jima

Tori-shima

J 138° K 140° L 142° M 144° N 146° P 148° Q

44°
1
42°
2
3
40°
4
38°
5
36°
6
34°
7
32°
8
30°

■ over 3 million
■ 1 – 3 million
● 250 000 – 1 million
● 100 000 – 250 000
● 25 000 – 100 000
• under 25 000
——— country capital underline

Scale 1 : 11 600 000

0 200 400 600 km

0 100 200 300 miles

95° E B 100° C 105° D 110°

BHUTAN
Tashigang
Hāpoli
Pangin
Zayü
Dêqên
Gongshan
Zhongdian
Xichang
Zunyi
Jishou
Huaihua
Wu

Barpeta
Itanagar
Dibrugarh
Tinsukia
Tazungdam
Putao
Weixi
Lijiang
Bijie
GUIYANG

Goalpara
Nagaon
Golaghat
Jorhat
Tabong
Maingkwan
Yongren
Dukou
Weining
Liupanshui
Anshun
Duyun
Kaili

I N D I A
Guwahati
Dimapur
Kohima
Myitkyina
Mogaung
Baoshan
Dali
Yuanmou
KUNMING
Qujing
Xingyi
Guanling
C H I

Shillong
Sylhet
Silchar
Imphal
Chindwin
Hopin
Chuxiong
Yanshan
Funing
Guilin

25° N
Bhairab Bazar
Agartala
Aizawl
Mawlaik
Bhamo
Katha
Wandingzhen
Mong Yu
Gengma
Cangyuan
Lancang
Simao
Lai Chau
Gejiu
Kaiyuan
Jingxi
Pingguo
Binyang
Nanning
Yangshuo
Ping
Liuzhou

Tropic of Cancer
Comilla
Feni
Karnafuli Reservoir
Saiha
Kalemyo
Kanbalu
Mabein
Hsweni
Lashio
Mong Yai
Kengtung
Phôngsali
Tuán Giao
Cao Bang
Tuyên Quang
Thai Nguyên
Wuxu
Pingxiang
Qinzhou
Hepu
Yu

Bose
Hechi
Heshan

CHITTAGONG
Rangamati
Haka
Chindwin
Monywa
Myingyan
Kyaukse
Amarapura
MANDALAY
Mongkung
Kunhing
Kengtung
Muang Sing
Louang Namtha
Muang Khoua
Son La
Lao Cai
Yuanjiang
Yuan
Qinzhou
Beihai
Zhanjiang

BANGLADESH
Cox's Bazar
Pakokku
Mt. Victoria
3053
Paletwa
Chauk
Meiktila
Taunggyi
MYANMAR (BURMA)
Taungdwingyi
Loikaw
Wan Hsala
Muang Xai
Viêt Tri
HA NÔI (HANOI)
Tien Yen
Hon Gai

Teknaf
Sittwe
Kyaukpyu
Ramree Island
Cheduba Island
Sinbaungwe
Minbu
Magwe
Lewe
Toungoo
Zigon
Salween
Mae Hong Sôn
Chiang Rai
Nan
Xiangkhoang
Ban Ban
Louangphrabang
Ninh Binh
Nam Dinh
HAI PHONG

20°
Bay of Bengal
Sandoway
Kyeintali
Henzada
Pegu
NAYPYIDAW
Pasawng
Chiang Mai
Lampang
Siri Kit Dam
Mekong
Muang Pakxan
Vinh
Ha Tinh
Dông Hoi
Gulf of Tongking
Dan Xian
Wenchar
Qionghai
Haikou
HAINAN
Tongshi
Sanya
Lings
Kyuawkyu

Pathein
Myaungmya
Bogale
Labutta
Insein
Thaton
Moulmein
Kawkareik
Mae Sariang
Uttaradit
Chiang Khan
Chum Phae
Sakhon Nakhon
Muang Khammouan
Muang Phin
Savannakhet
Quang Tri
Huê

YANGON (RANGOON)
Cape Negrais
Mouths of the Irawaddy
Gulf of Martaban
Ye
Tak
Nam Ping
Phitsanulok
Phichit
Loei
Udon Thani
Nong Khai
Viangchan (Vientiane)
Khon Kaen
Mukdahan
Ban Khémmarat
Pakxé
Da Nang
Hôi An

15°
Preparis North Channel
Preparis Island
Preparis South Channel
Coco Channel
Coco Island
Tavoy
Sangkhla Buri
Nakhon Sawan
Chaiyaphum
Lam Chi
Roi Et
Mae Nam Mun
Suwannaphum
Ubon Ratchathani
Surin
Attapu
Quang Ngai
Kon Tum

89
North Andaman
Andaman Islands (India)
Ritchie's Archipelago
Middle Andaman
South Andaman
Port Blair
Duncan Passage
Little Andaman
Palaw
Mergui
Nakhon Ratchasima
Chai Nat
THAILAND
Ayutthaya
Sara Buri
Det Udom
M. Khôngxédôn
Viröchey
Stoeng Trêng
Plây Cu
Qui Nhon

A n d a m a n
Mergui Archipelago
Rat Buri
Phet Buri
Samut Songkhram
KRUNG THEP (BANGKOK)
Aranyaprathet
Sisôphôn
Siêmréab
Bätdâmbâng
Phumi Sâmraông
M. Khong
Buôn Mê Thuôt
Tuy Hoa
Ninh Hoa

4°
S e a
Pattaya
Rayong
Bight of Bangkok
Chánthaburi
Ban Hua Hin
Ko Chang
Tônlé Sab
CAMBODIA
Da Lat
Nha Trang
Cam Ranh

Prachuap Khiri Khan
Kâmpông Chhnäng
Kampong Cham
Bao Lôc
Phan Rang

Bang Saphan Yai
Krông Kaôh Kong
Ta Khmau
Chon Thanh
Biên Hoa
Phan Thiêt

VIETNAM

10°
Ten Degree Channel
Gulf of Thailand
Chumphon
Kawthaung
Ranong
Ko Samui
Sihanoukville
Dao Phu Quôc
Kâmpôt
Long Xuyên
HÔ CHI MINH (SAIGON)
My Tho
Vung Tau

Car Nicobar
Takua Pa
Surat Thani
Rach Gia
Cân Tho
Bac Liêu
Mouths of the Mekong

Katchall
Nicobar Islands (India)
Little Nicobar
Great Nicobar
Krabi
Phuket
Nakhon Si Thammarat
Ca Mau
Nam Can
Côn Son

5°
Thung Song
Phatthalung
Trang
Thale Luang
Songkhla
Ban Hat Yai
Pattani

Sabang
Banda Aceh
Satun
Langkawi
Kangar
Narathiwat
Kota Bharu

metres feet
8000 26250
6000 19690
4000 13120
2000 6560
1000 3280
500 1640
200 656

Lhokseumawe
Alor Setar
Sungei Petani
George Town
Pinang
Yala
Ban Betong
Kuala Krai
Kuala Terengganu

5°
Bireun
Taiping
Gerik
M A L A Y

feet metres
656 200
3280 1000
6560 2000
13120 4000
19690 6000
26250 8000

Takengon
Langsa
Ipoh
G. Korbu
2182
Kuala Lipis
Dungun
Kemasik

I N D I A N
Meulaboh
SUMATERA (SUMATRA)
3145
Gunung Leuser
Bagun Datuk
MEDAN
Tebingtinggi
Bentung
Temerloh
Kuantan
Malay Peninsula
Natuna Besar
Panarik
Laut

6°
Sibigo
Danau Toba
Pematangsiantar
Kuala Lumpur
Putrajaya
Seremban
Segamat
Mersing
Kepulauan Natuna
Kepulauan Anambas (Indonesia)
Subi Besar

O C E A N
Simeuluë
Sinabang
Danau Toba
Singkilbaru
Balige
KUALA LUMPUR
Melaka
Muar
Keluang
Jemaja

Barus
Bagansiapiapi
Dumai
Batu Rahat
Sambas
Pemangkat

86
Sibolga
Gunungsitoli
Nias
Kotapinang
Duri
INDONESIA
Johor Bahru
SINGAPORE
SINGAPORE
Pemangkat
Kuchi
Tanjung Datu
Siluas

© Hema Maps Pty Ltd. Based on original data
© Research Machines plc

100° C 105° D 110°

84

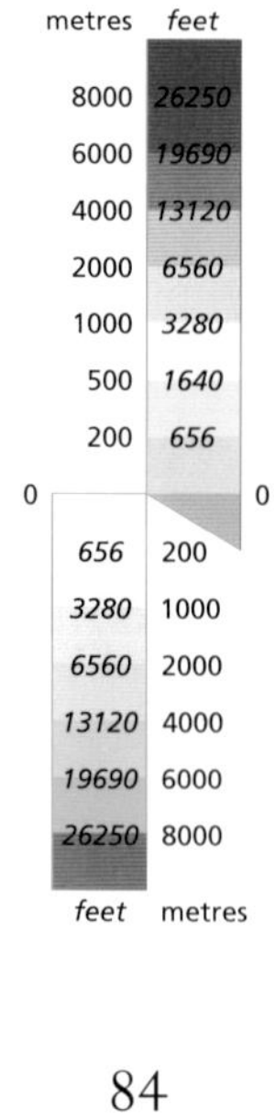

Southeast Asia

Cambodia • Laos • Myanmar (Burma)
Philippines • Thailand • Vietnam

EAST CHINA SEA

JAPAN

Nago Okinawa
Okinawa
Naha

Tropic of Cancer

Sakishima-shotō

PACIFIC

OCEAN

TAIWAN

T'ao-yuan Chi-lung
T'AI-PEI
Hsin-chu
3884 Hsueh-Shan
T'ai-chung
Chang-hua
Chia-i
3950 Yu Shan
T'ai-nan T'ai-tung
KAO-HSIUNG P'ing-tung
Oluan-pi

CHANGSHA
Xiangtan
Linchuan
Pingxiang
Lianyuan Xinyu
Lengshuijiang Yichun
Hengyang Ji'an Taihe
Leiyang Zixing Changting Yong'an
Chenzhou Ganzhou Jiangle
Lian Xian Shaoguan Longyan Quanzhou
He Xian Meizhou Zhangzhou Xiamen
Qingyuan
Wuzhou GUANGZHOU Huizhou Lufeng
Zhaoqing Dongguan Chaozhou
Jiangmen Foshan Shenzhen Shantou
Zhongshan Macau HONG KONG
Yangjiang

NA
Shangrao
Pucheng Wenzhou
Nanping Fuding
Ningde
FUZHOU
Putian
Matsu (Taiwan)
Chinmen (Taiwan)

Luzon Strait
Batan Islands
Basco
Balintang Channel
Babuyan Islands

Dongsha Qundao (Pratas) (China)

SOUTH

CHINA

SEA

Paracel Islands

Spratly Islands

Bangui Claveria San Vicente
Laoag Aparri
Kabugao Lal-lo
Vigan Bangued Tuguegarao
Santa Cruz Bontoc Ilagan Palanan
San Fernando Luzon
Baguio Mt. Pulog Santiago
2929 Casiguran
Alaminos Dagupan
Lingayen San Carlos Baler
Tarlac Cabanatuan
Angeles Gapan
Olongapo QUEZON CITY Polillo Is.
MANILA Calaguac Is.
Pasig San Pablo Daet Pandan
Nasugbu Calauag Naga Cantanduanes
Batangas Lucena Lopez Virac
Mamburao Boac Legaspi
Mindoro Calapan Pascual Sorsogon
2488 Pinamalayan Bulan Catarman
Mount Baco Masbate Allen Samar
San Pedro Masbate Calbayog
Calamian Nabas Catbalogan
Group Coron Placer Borongan
El Nido Kalibo Roxas Tacloban
Panay Ormoc
Roxas Iloilo Bacolod Bogo Leyte
San Jose de Bago Cebu Sogod Libjo
Buenavista Carcar Cebu Maasin Dinagat
Palawan Cauayan Talibon Surigao Dapa
Quezon Bais Bohol Tagbilaran Madrid
Puerto Princesa Negros Dumaguete Butuan Tandag
PHILIPPINES Dipolog Prosperidad
Brooke's Point Manukan 2560 Cagayan de Oro Bislig
Sulu Sea Liloy Iligan Malaybalay
Sibuco Pagadian Mindanao Tagum
Balabac Bugsuk Cotabato Davao
Balabac Strait Zamboanga Moro Mati
Kudat Isabela Gulf Tacurong 2954 Mt. Apo
Langkon 4094 Jolo Palimbang Polomoloc General Santos
G. Kinabalu Ranau Basilan Glan
Kota Kinabalu Sandakan Jolo Sarangani Is.
Beaufort SABAH Tawitawi Kepulauan
Lahad Datu Tungku Bongao Sulu Archipelago Nanusa
BRUNEI Semporna Kepulauan Karkaralong Beo
Bandar Seri Begawan Kalabakan Karkaralong Kepulauan Talaud
Seria Tawau Celebes INDONESIA
Gunung Mulu Sea Kepulauan Tahuna
2371 Sangir Morotai
Bintulu Belaga Tarakan Laut Maluku Daruba
SARAWAK 2499 Tanjungselor
Sibu Kapit Tanjungredeb
INDONESIA Sepinang
KALIMANTAN Sangkulirang
2988 Muarawahau

SIA

■ over 3 million	● 100 000 – 250 000	——— country capital underline
■ 1 – 3 million	○ 25 000 – 100 000	
● 250 000 – 1 million	• under 25 000	

Scale 1 : 11 600 000

0 200 400 600 km

0 100 200 300 miles

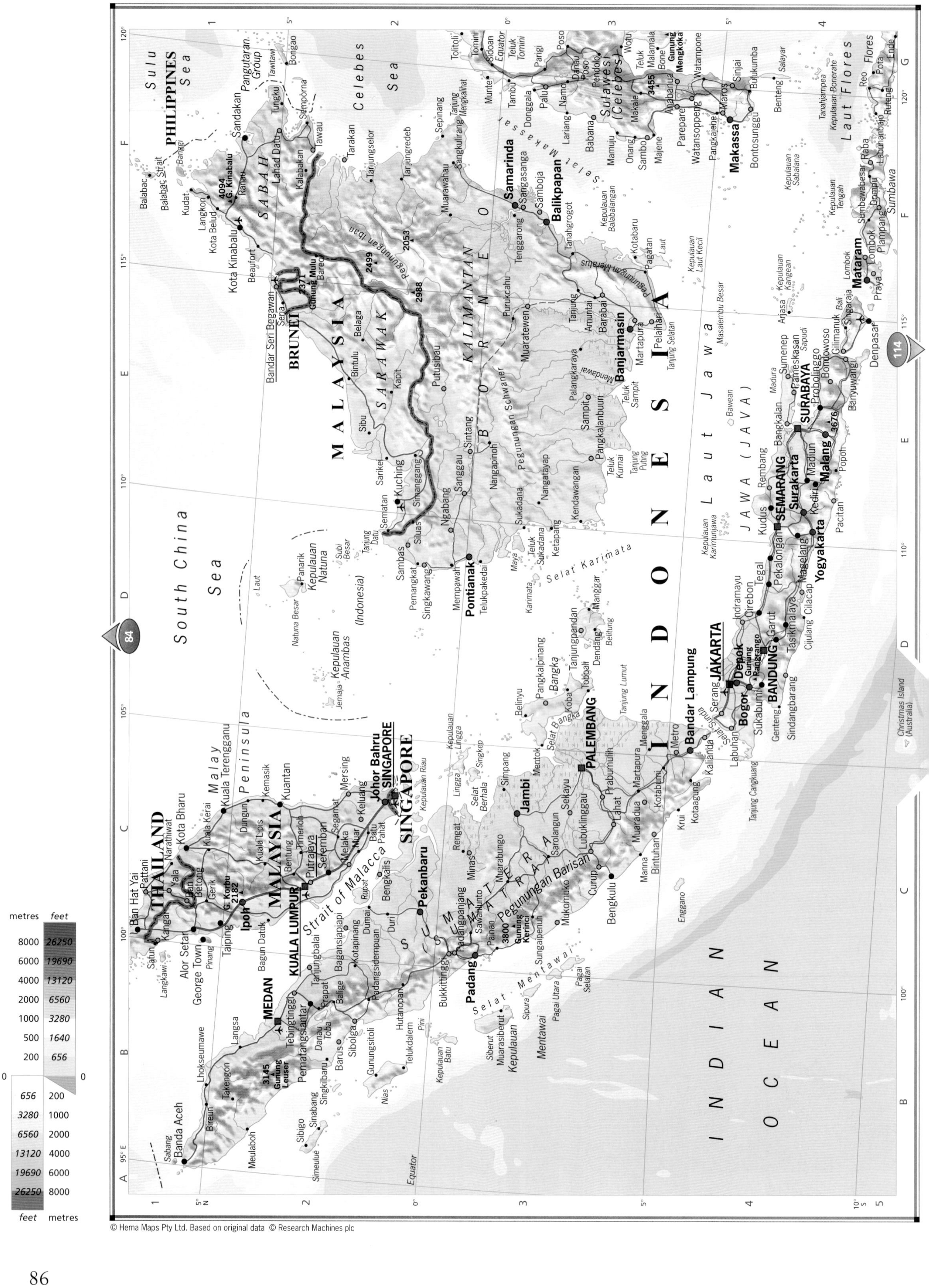

Malaysia and Indonesia

Brunei • Indonesia • Malaysia • Singapore

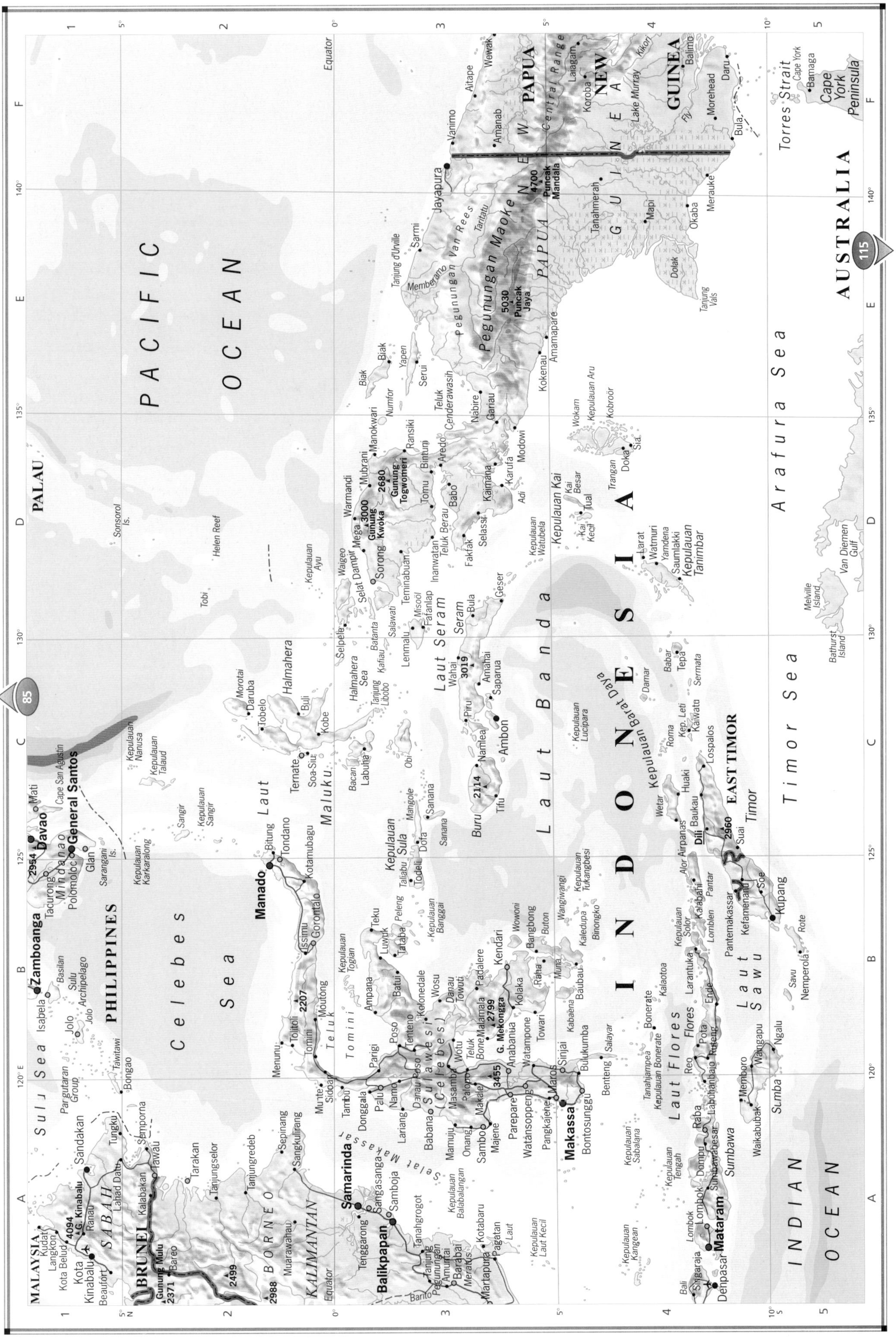

■ over 3 million

■ 1 – 3 million

● 250 000 – 1 million

• 100 000 – 250 000

○ 25 000 – 100 000

• under 25 000

—— country capital underline

Scale 1 : 11 600 000

0 200 400 600 km

0 100 200 300 miles

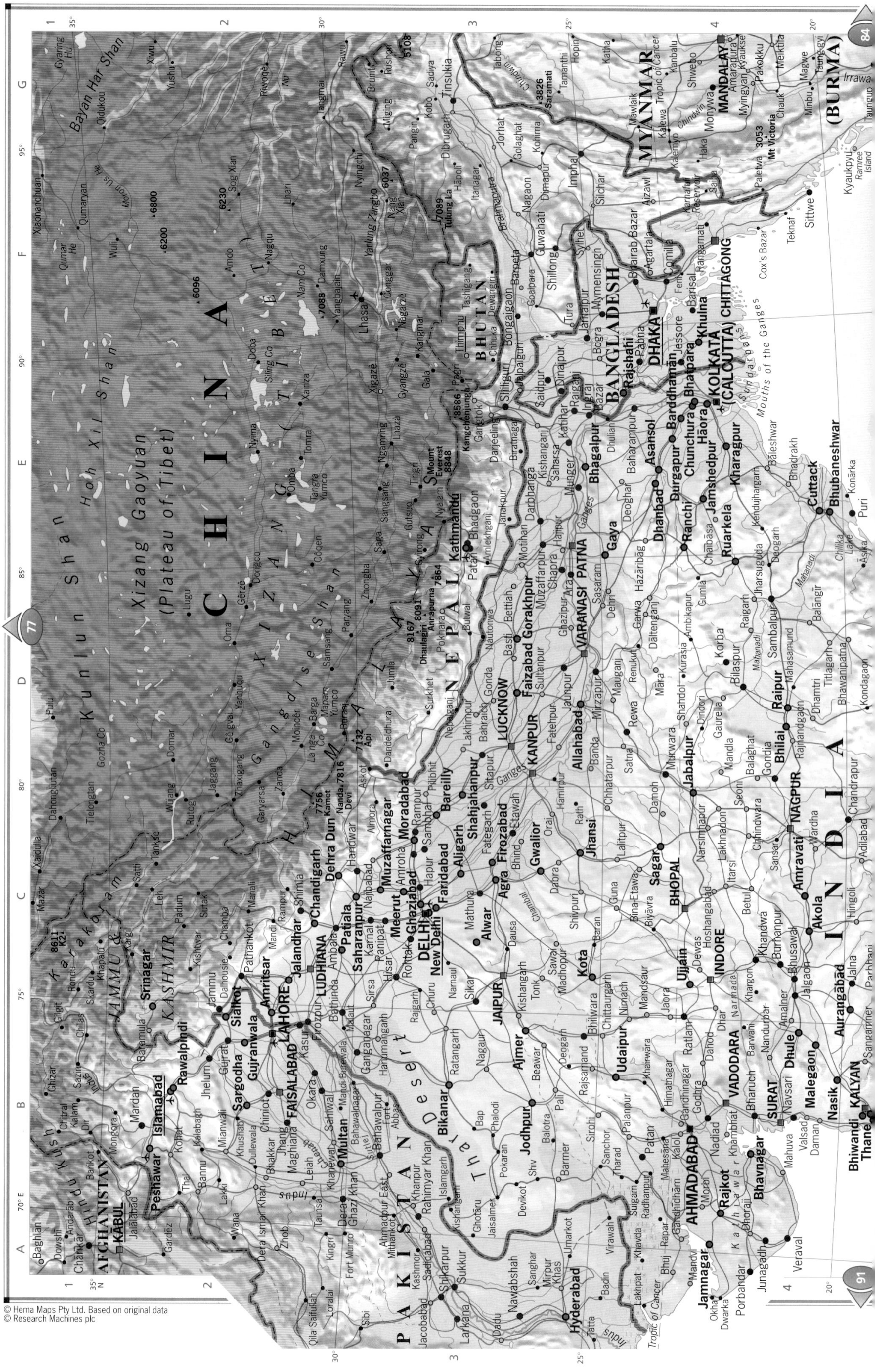

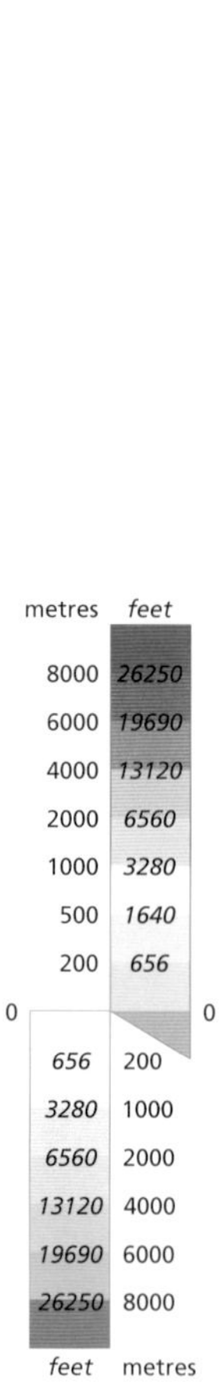

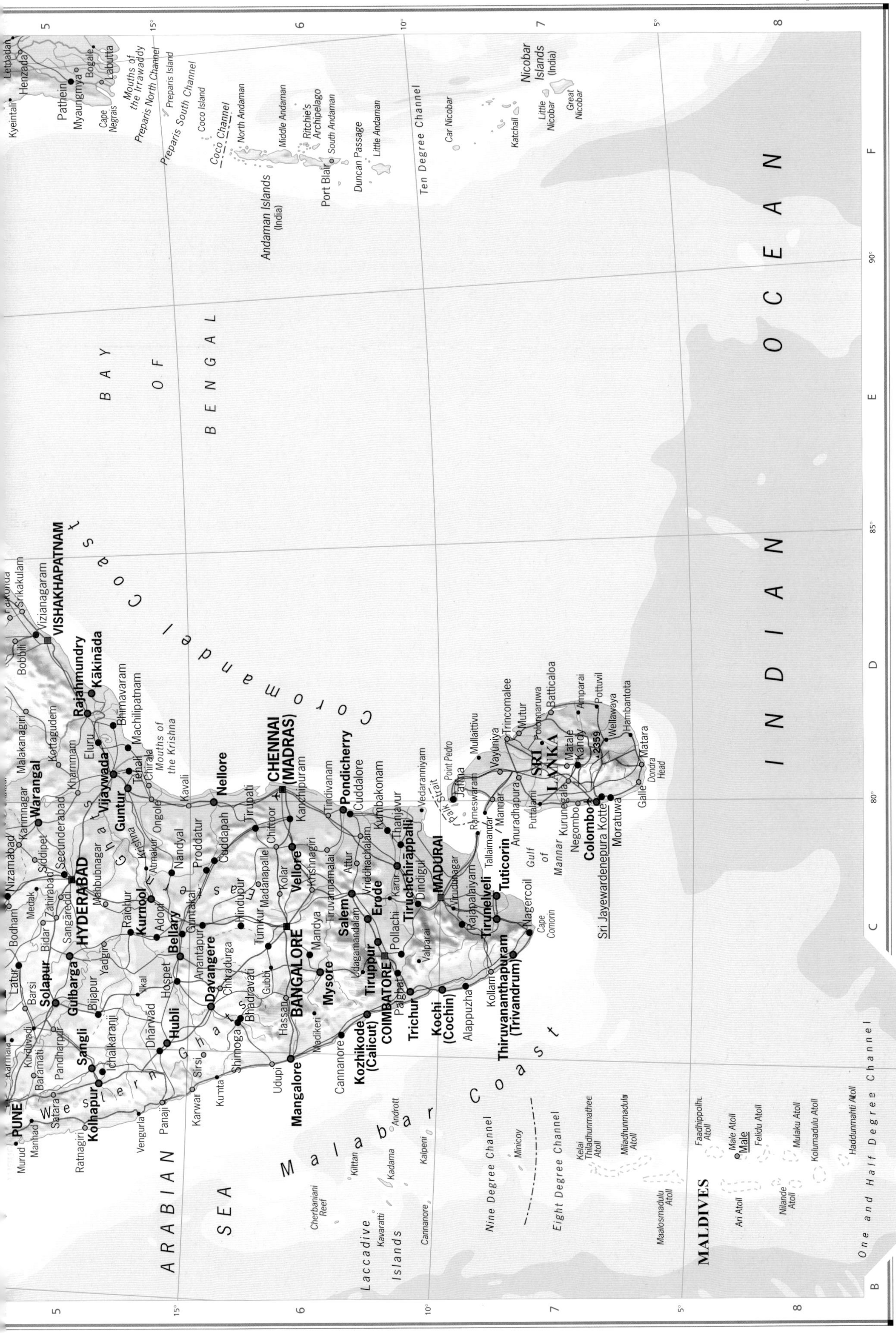

■ over 3 million	● 100 000 – 250 000	—— country capital underline
■ 1 – 3 million	○ 25 000 – 100 000	
● 250 000 – 1 million	• under 25 000	

Scale 1 : 12 700 000

0 200 400 600 km

0 100 200 300 miles

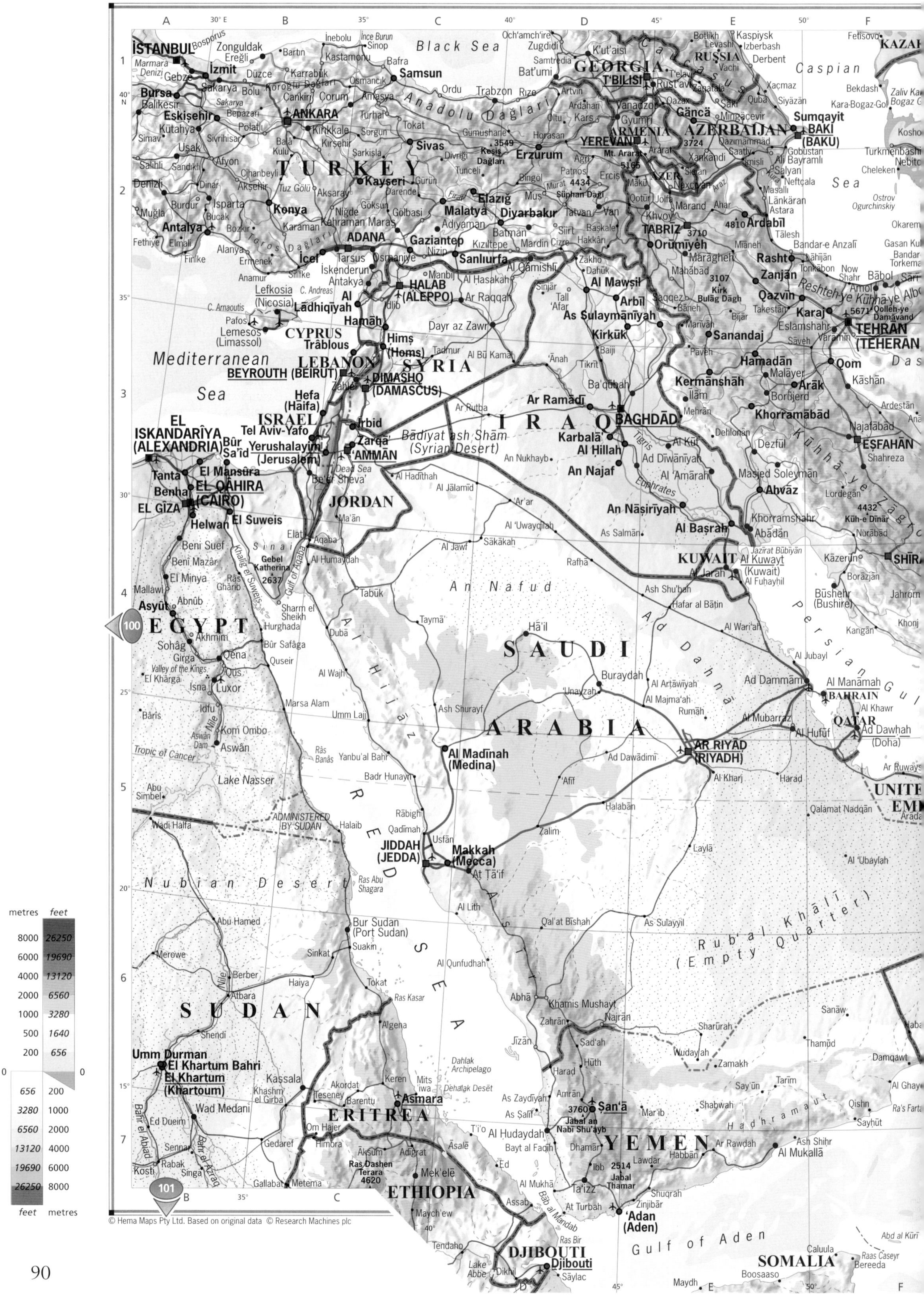

The Middle East

Afghanistan • Iran • Iraq • Oman
Pakistan • Saudi Arabia • Syria • Yemen

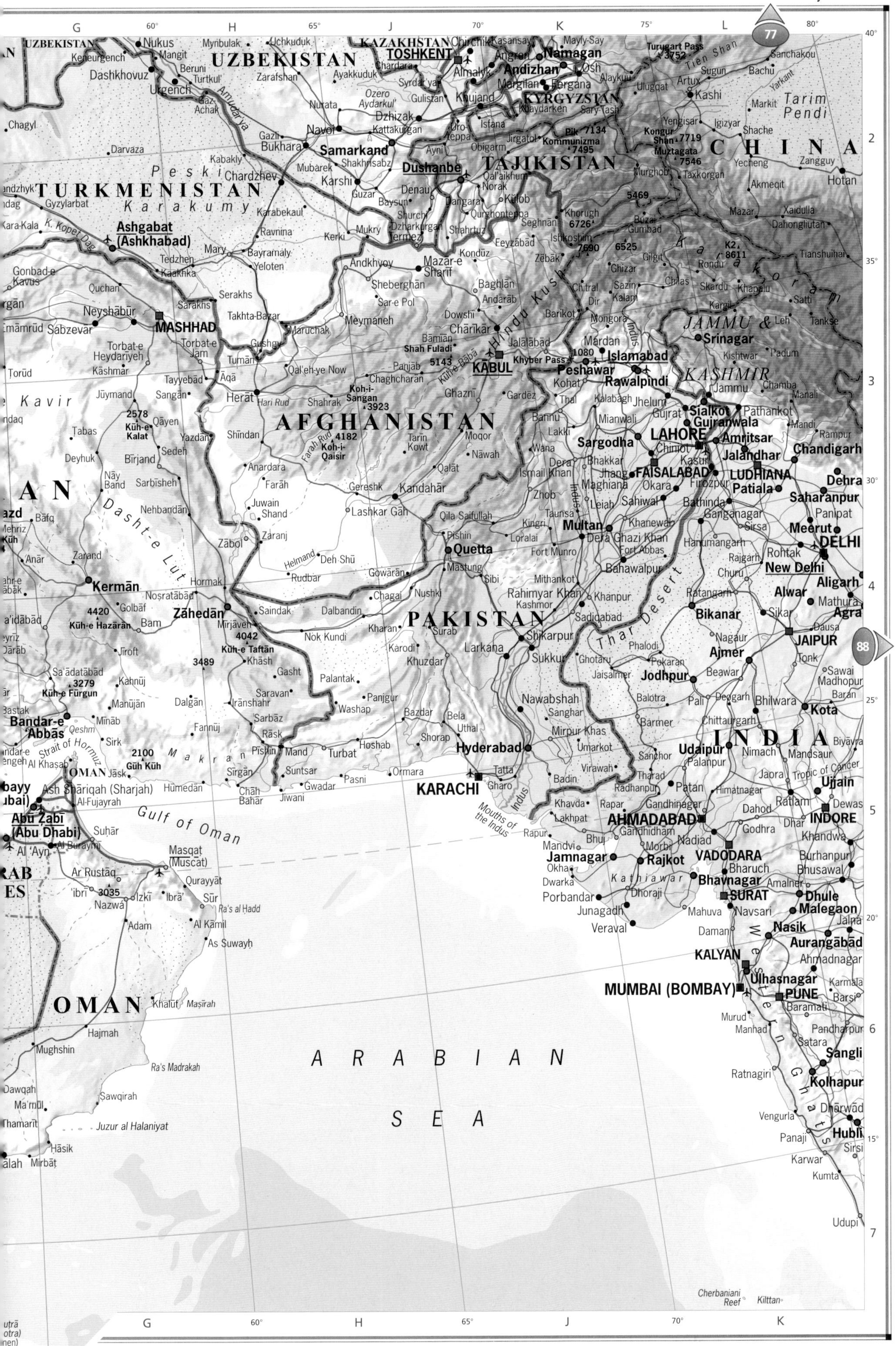

■ over 3 million
■ 1 – 3 million
● 250 000 – 1 million
• 100 000 – 250 000
○ 25 000 – 100 000
• under 25 000
—— country capital underline

Scale 1 : 5 800 000

0 100 200 300 km

0 50 100 150 km

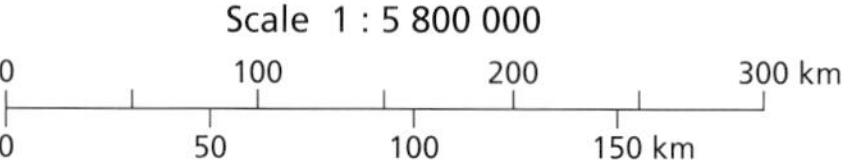

metres feet
8000 26250
6000 19690
4000 13120
2000 6560
1000 3280
500 1640
200 656
0 0
656 200
3280 1000
6560 2000
13120 4000
19690 6000
26250 8000
feet metres

■ over 3 million
■ 1 – 3 million
● 250 000 – 1 million
● 100 000 – 250 000
● 25 000 – 100 000
• under 25 000
country capital underline
state or province capital underline

Scale 1 : 2 850 000

0 50 100 150 km

0 25 50 75 miles

MEDITERRANEAN
SEA

CYPRUS

Lapithos
Keryneia
Akanthou
Lefkosia
(Nicosia)
Trikomon
C. Eleaia
Lefkonikon
Ammochostos Bay
Mesaoria Plain
Ammochostos (Famagusta)
Ceasefire line
Paralimni
Aya Napa
C. Greko
Dhekelia
Larnaka
Vasilikos
Lemesos
(Limassol)

LEBANON

Jablah
Bāniyās
1385
Al Qadmūs
Masyāf
Kafr
Buhum
Ṭarṭūs
Burj Ṣāfītā
Al Hamīdīyah
Tall Kalakh
Trâblous
(Tripoli)
Halba
2216
Zgharta
3087
Hermel
Qornet
es Saouda
Batroûn
Ba'albek
Jbail
Qartaba
Joûnié
2628
BEYROUTH
(BEIRUT)
Aley
Zahlé
Baqline
Az Zabadānī
Saïda
Jezzine
Marjayoûn
Mt. Hermon
2814
Soûr
Qiryat Shemona
Bent
Jbail
Enn Nâqoûra
Naharīyya
Zefat
'Akko
GOLAN
Qiryat Motzkin
Karmi'el
HEIGHTS
Ḥefa (Haifa)
Teverya
Qiryat Ata
Nazareth
'Afula
Zikhron Ya'aqov
Bet-She'an
Hadera
Jenin
Tubas
Netanya
Herzliyya
Tulkarm
Nablus
Tel Aviv-Yafo
Petah Tiqwa
Rishon le Ziyyon
Ramla
Rehovot
Ramallah
Yerushalayim
(Jerusalem)
Jericho
Ashdod
ISRAEL
Qiryat Gat
Ashqelon
Bethlehem
Gaza
GAZA
Sederot
Hebron
STRIP
Yatta
Khân Yûnis
Ofaqim
Yammit
Arad
Newe Zohar
Be'ér Sheva'
Sadût
Sedom
Rafah
Dimona
Revivim
El 'Arîsh
Safi
Sabkhet
el Bardawîl
El Mazâr
Negev
Abu Aweigila
Qezi'ot
Sede Boqer
'En Hazeva
El Quseima
G. Halâl
892
Bîr Hasana
Mizpe Ramon
Bîr Gifgâfa
1000
1094
1006
G. Yi'allaq
Har Saggi
Beer Menuha
EGYPT
1615
SINAI
Wâdi Mûsa
Jebel Mubrak
1727
Gharandal
El Kuntilla
Gebel el Tîh
Jebel el Batrâ
1555
Yotvata
El Quweira
Beer
J. Bâqir
Ora
1592
Ram
El Thamad
1030
J. Ram
1754
Nakhl
Bîr Tâba
Elat
1080
Aqaba
Râs el Nafas
Gulf of
Aqaba
1520

SYRIA

92
Khān Shaykhūn
Khirbat Isrīyah
As Sā'an
Hamāh
Salamīyah
Ar Rastan
Bahrat Ḥims
Ḥims
(Homs)
Furqlus
Al 'Qusayr
Tiyās
Hisyah
Ghunthūr
Al Qaryatayn
Al Burayj
Tal 'at Mūsá
Bīr Bazīrī
2659
An Nabk
Yabrūd
Jayrūd
Sab' Ābār
Az Zabadānī
Al Quṭayfah
Dumayr
Dūmā
DIMASHQ
(DAMASCUS)
Qaṭanā
Ghabāghib
Burāq
Aṣ Sanamayn
Al Qunayṭirah
Nawa
Izra'
Shahbā
Shaykh
Miskin
As Suwaydā'
1735
Irbid
Dar'a
Jabal ad Durūz
Husn
Ramtha
Busrā ash Shām
Ajlun
Tisīyah
Salkhad
•1247
Mafraq
Bādiyat ash Shām
Jarash
1234
(Syrian Desert)
Es Samrā
Salt
Zarqa'
Suweilih
Er Ruseifa
Na'ūr
AMMĀN
Sahāb
El Azraq
Qasr el
Azraq
Suweima
Mādabā
Qā 'Azamān
Dab'a
Qasr el
1010
Kharana
Dhībān
Khān az Zabīb
Dead
Mazra'
Sea
Qatrāna
Al Hadīthah
Kāf
Al Qarqar
An Nabk
Karak
Manzil
JORDAN
Mazār
Safi
'Ayn al Baida
Tafila
Bāyir
Ḥāsā
J. el Atā'ita
Jurf ed Darāwīsh
1641
1082
Shaubak
'Unayzah
Jebel Ithrīyah
Ma'ān
El Jafr
El Jafr
Naqb Ashtar
Ar Ramlah
Al Mudawwara
Aṭ Ṭubayq
SAUDI
1224
Ath Thāyat
ARABIA
Wādi as Sirḥān
101
90

metres	feet
8000	26250
6000	19690
4000	13120
2000	6560
1000	3280
500	1640
200	656
0	0
656	200
3280	1000
6560	2000
13120	4000
19690	6000
26250	8000
feet	metres

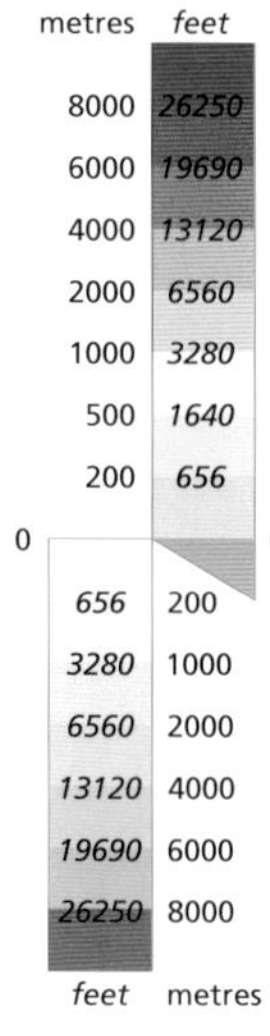

Scale 1 : 5 800 000

0 | 100 | 200 | 300 km

0 | 50 | 100 | 150 km

Israel and the Gulf States

Bahrain • Israel • Jordan • Kuwait
Lebanon • Qatar • United Arab Emirates

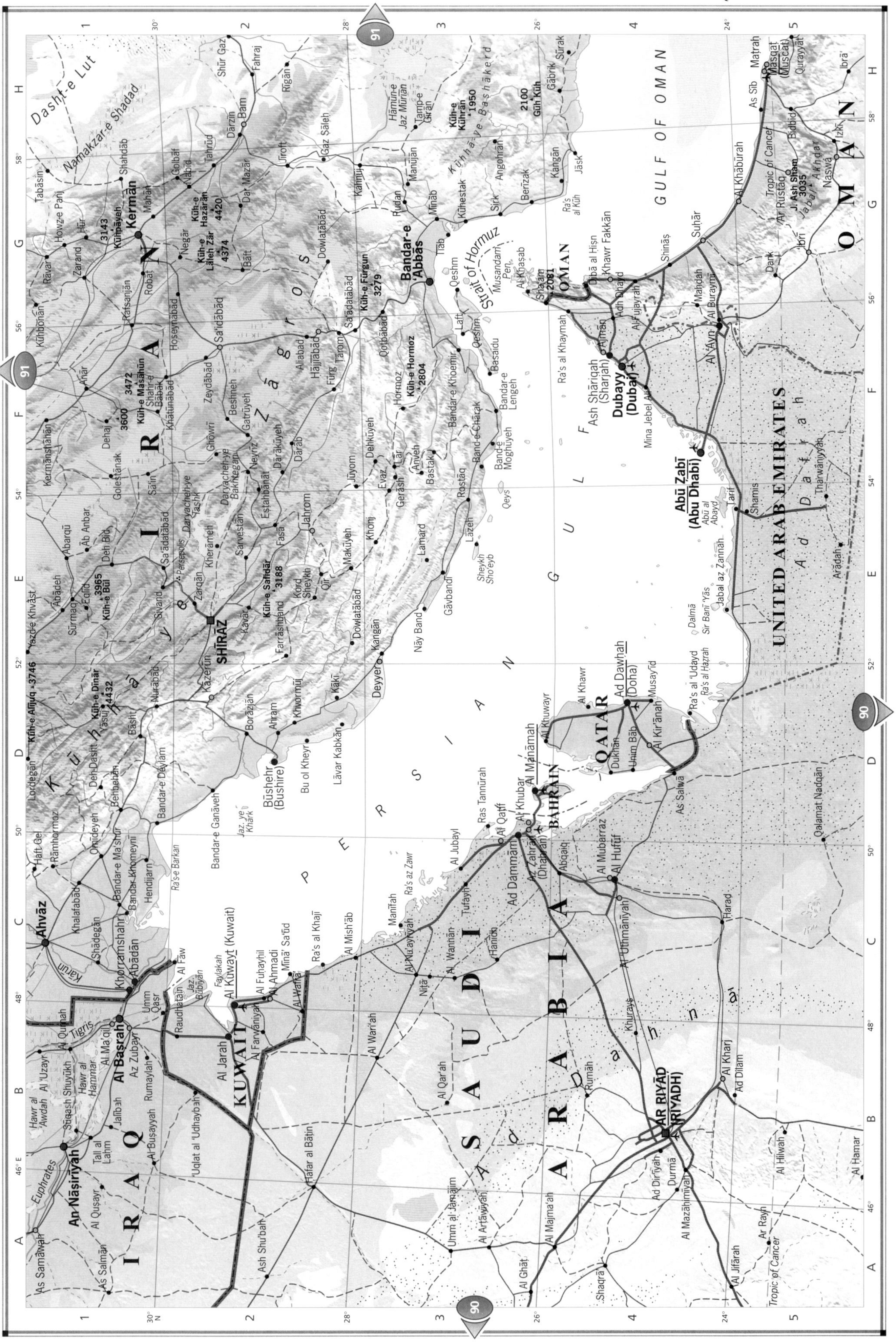

■ over 3 million	• 100 000 – 250 000	country capital underline
■ 1 – 3 million	○ 25 000 – 100 000	urban area
● 250 000 – 1 million	• under 25 000	

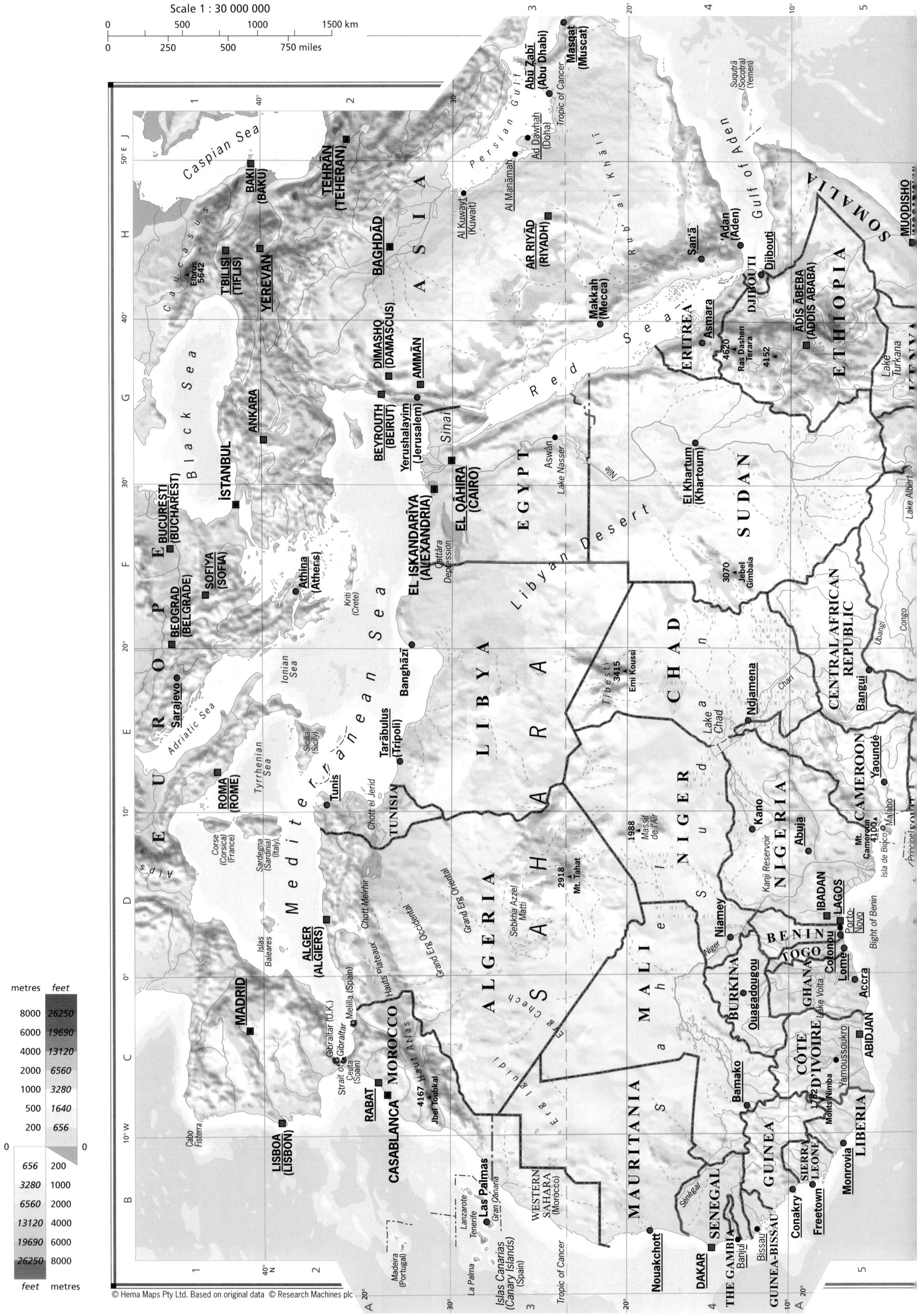

© Hema Maps Pty Ltd. Based on original data © Research Machines plc

Mt. Kilimanjaro, Tanzania : 5,895 m or 19,341 ft

Lake Assal, Djibouti : 156 m or 512 ft

Wadi Halfa, Sudan : less than 0.25 cm or 0.1 in

Debundscha, Cameroon : 1029 cm or 405 in

Nile, Egypt : 6,690 km or 4,160 mi

Lake Victoria, East Africa : 62,940 km² or 24,300 sq mi

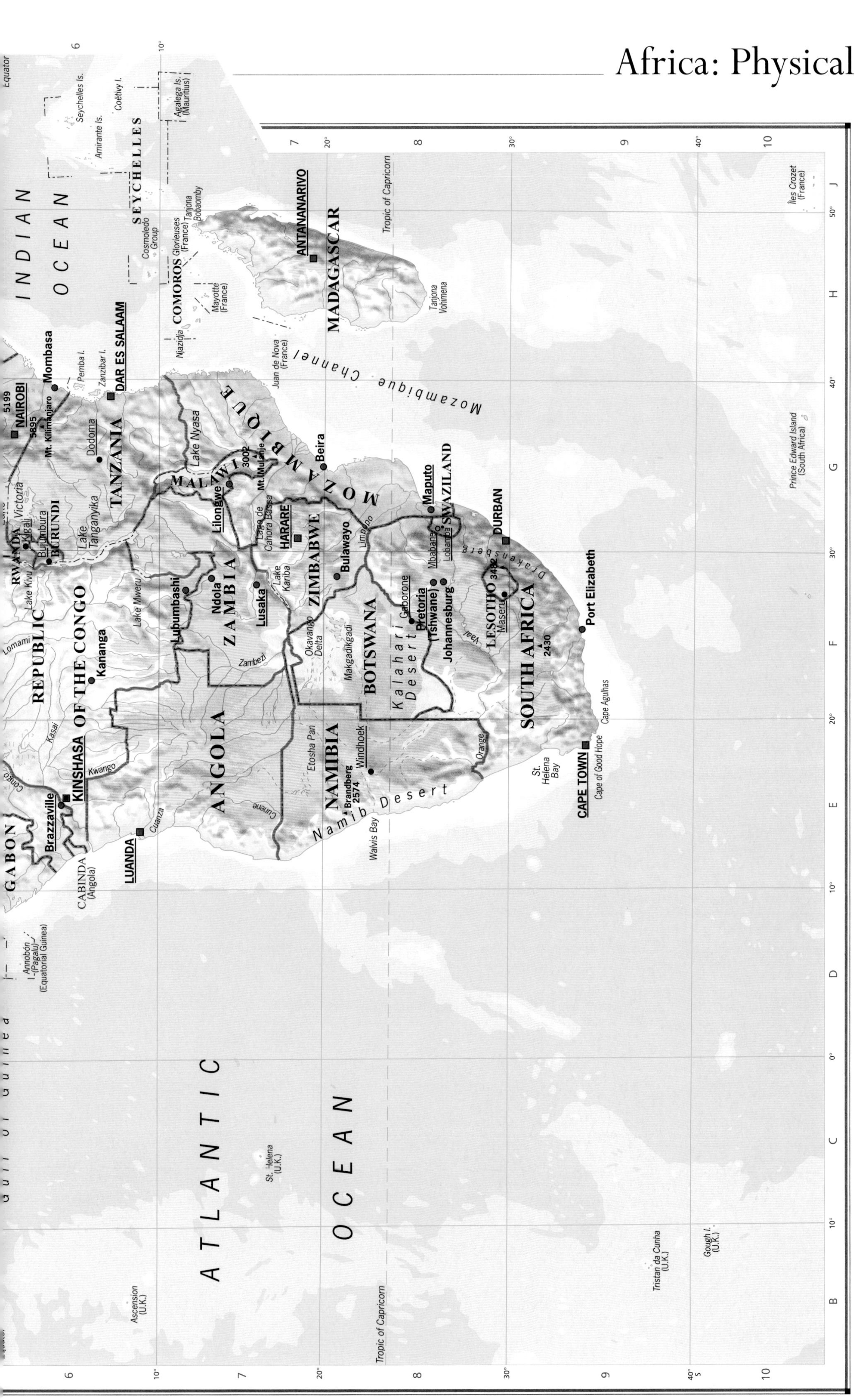
INDIAN OCEAN
ATLANTIC OCEAN
Mozambique Channel
Tropic of Capricorn
Equator
SEYCHELLES
Seychelles Is.
Amirante Is.
Coëtivy I.
Agalega Is. (Mauritius)
Cosmoledo Group
Glorieuses (France)
Tanjona Bobaomby
COMOROS
Mayotte (France)
Njazidja
Juan de Nova (France)
ANTANANARIVO
MADAGASCAR
Tanjona Vohimena
Îles Crozet (France)
Prince Edward Island (South Africa)
NAIROBI
5199
5895
Mt. Kilimanjaro
Mombasa
Pemba I.
Zanzibar I.
DAR ES SALAAM
Dodoma
TANZANIA
Lake Victoria
RWANDA
Kigali
Bujumbura
BURUNDI
Lake Kivu
Lake Tanganyika
Lake Mweru
Lake Nyasa
MALAWI
Lilongwe
3002
Mt. Mulanje
MOZAMBIQUE
Beira
Maputo
SWAZILAND
Mbabane
Lobamba
Lago de Cahora Bassa
HARARE
ZIMBABWE
Bulawayo
Limpopo
Lake Kariba
Lusaka
ZAMBIA
Ndola
Lubumbashi
Zambezi
REPUBLIC OF THE CONGO
Lomami
Kananga
Kasai
Kwango
Congo
KINSHASA
Brazzaville
GABON
CABINDA (Angola)
LUANDA
Cuanza
ANGOLA
Cunene
Okavango Delta
Makgadikgadi
BOTSWANA
Gaborone
Kalahari Desert
Pretoria (Tshwane)
Johannesburg
Vaal
LESOTHO
Maseru
3482
Drakensberg
DURBAN
SOUTH AFRICA
2430
Port Elizabeth
Cape Agulhas
Cape of Good Hope
CAPE TOWN
St. Helena Bay
Orange
Etosha Pan
NAMIBIA
Windhoek
Brandberg
2574
Namib Desert
Walvis Bay
Gulf of Guinea
Annobón (Pagalu) (Equatorial Guinea)
St. Helena (U.K.)
Ascension (U.K.)
Tristan da Cunha (U.K.)
Gough I. (U.K.)
B
C
D
E
F
G
H
J
6
7
8
9
10
0°
10°
20°
30°
40°
50°

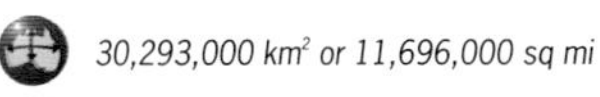

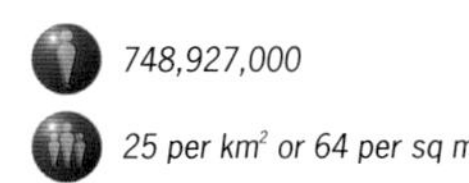

Ifrane, Morocco : -24 °C or -11 °F
Al Aziziyah, Libya : 58 °C or 136 °F
748,927,000
25 per km² or 64 per sq mi
30,293,000 km² or 11,696,000 sq mi
53

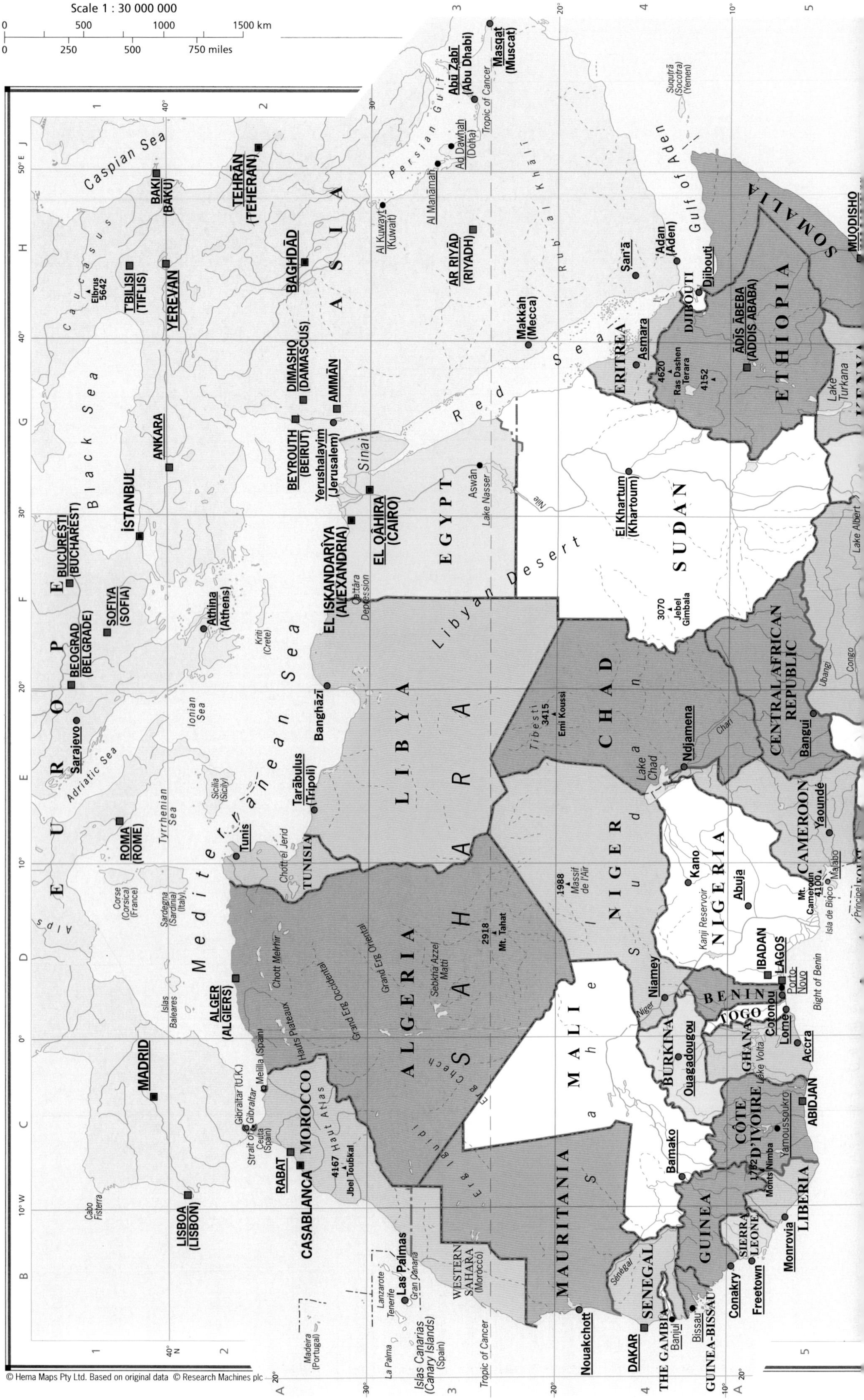
Scale 1 : 30 000 000
0 500 1000 1500 km
0 250 500 750 miles
E U R O P E
A S I A
Caspian Sea
Black Sea
Mediterranean Sea
Adriatic Sea
Tyrrhenian Sea
Ionian Sea
Persian Gulf
Gulf of Aden
Red Sea
Rub' al Khali
Libyan Desert
S A H A R A
S a h e l
Tropic of Cancer
LISBOA (LISBON)
MADRID
ROMA (ROME)
Sarajevo
BEOGRAD (BELGRADE)
SOFIYA (SOFIA)
BUCUREŞTI (BUCHAREST)
Athina (Athens)
İSTANBUL
ANKARA
T'BILISI (TIFLIS)
YEREVAN
BAKI (BAKU)
TEHRĀN (TEHERAN)
BAGHDĀD
DIMASHQ (DAMASCUS)
BEYROUTH (BEIRUT)
AMMĀN
Yerushalayim (Jerusalem)
Al Kuwayt (Kuwait)
Al Manāmah
Ad Dawhah (Doha)
Abū Zabī (Abu Dhabi)
Masqaţ (Muscat)
AR RIYĀD (RIYADH)
Makkah (Mecca)
Şan'ā
'Adan (Aden)
Suquţrā (Socotra) (Yemen)
Elbrus 5642
Corse (Corsica) (France)
Sardegna (Sardinia) (Italy)
Sicilia (Sicily)
Kriti (Crete)
Islas Baleares
Cabo Fisterra
Strait of Gibraltar
Gibraltar (U.K.)
Ceuta (Spain)
Melilla (Spain)
ALGER (ALGIERS)
Tunis
TUNISIA
Chott el Jerid
Tarābulus (Tripoli)
Banghāzī
EL ISKANDARĪYA (ALEXANDRIA)
EL QÂHIRA (CAIRO)
Qattâra Depression
Sinai
Aswân
Lake Nasser
Nile
EGYPT
LIBYA
ALGERIA
MOROCCO
RABAT
CASABLANCA
Haut Atlas
4167 Jbel Toubkal
Hauts Plateaux
Chott Melrhir
Grand Erg Occidental
Grand Erg Oriental
Sebkha Azzel Matti
2918 Mt. Tahat
Erg Chech
Erg Iguidi
WESTERN SAHARA (Morocco)
Islas Canarias (Canary Islands) (Spain)
Las Palmas
Gran Canaria
Lanzarote
Tenerife
La Palma
Madeira (Portugal)
MAURITANIA
Nouakchott
SENEGAL
DAKAR
Sénégal
THE GAMBIA
Banjul
GUINEA-BISSAU
Bissau
GUINEA
Conakry
SIERRA LEONE
Freetown
LIBERIA
Monrovia
1752 Monts Nimba
CÔTE D'IVOIRE
Yamoussoukro
ABIDJAN
MALI
Bamako
BURKINA
Ouagadougou
GHANA
Lake Volta
Accra
TOGO
Lomé
BENIN
Cotonou
Porto-Novo
LAGOS
IBADAN
Bight of Benin
NIGERIA
Abuja
Kano
Kanji Reservoir
Niger
NIGER
Niamey
1988 Massif de l'Aïr
CHAD
Ndjamena
Lake Chad
Chari
Tibesti
3415 Emi Koussi
SUDAN
El Khartum (Khartoum)
3070 Jebel Gimbala
CENTRAL AFRICAN REPUBLIC
Bangui
Ubangi
Congo
CAMEROON
Yaoundé
Mt. Cameroon 4100
Malabo
Isla de Bioco
Príncipe
ERITREA
Asmara
DJIBOUTI
Djibouti
ETHIOPIA
ĀDĪS ĀBEBA (ADDIS ABABA)
Ras Dashen Terara 4620
4152
Lake Turkana
Lake Albert
SOMALIA
MUQDISHO
Alps
Caucasus
© Hema Maps Pty Ltd. Based on original data © Research Machines plc

Mt. Kilimanjaro, Tanzania : 5,895 m or 19,341 ft

Lake Assal, Djibouti : 156 m or 512 ft

Wadi Halfa, Sudan : less than 0.25 cm or 0.1 in

Debundscha, Cameroon : 1029 cm or 405 in

Nile, Egypt : 6,690 km or 4,160 mi

Lake Victoria, East Africa : 62,940 km² or 24,300 sq mi

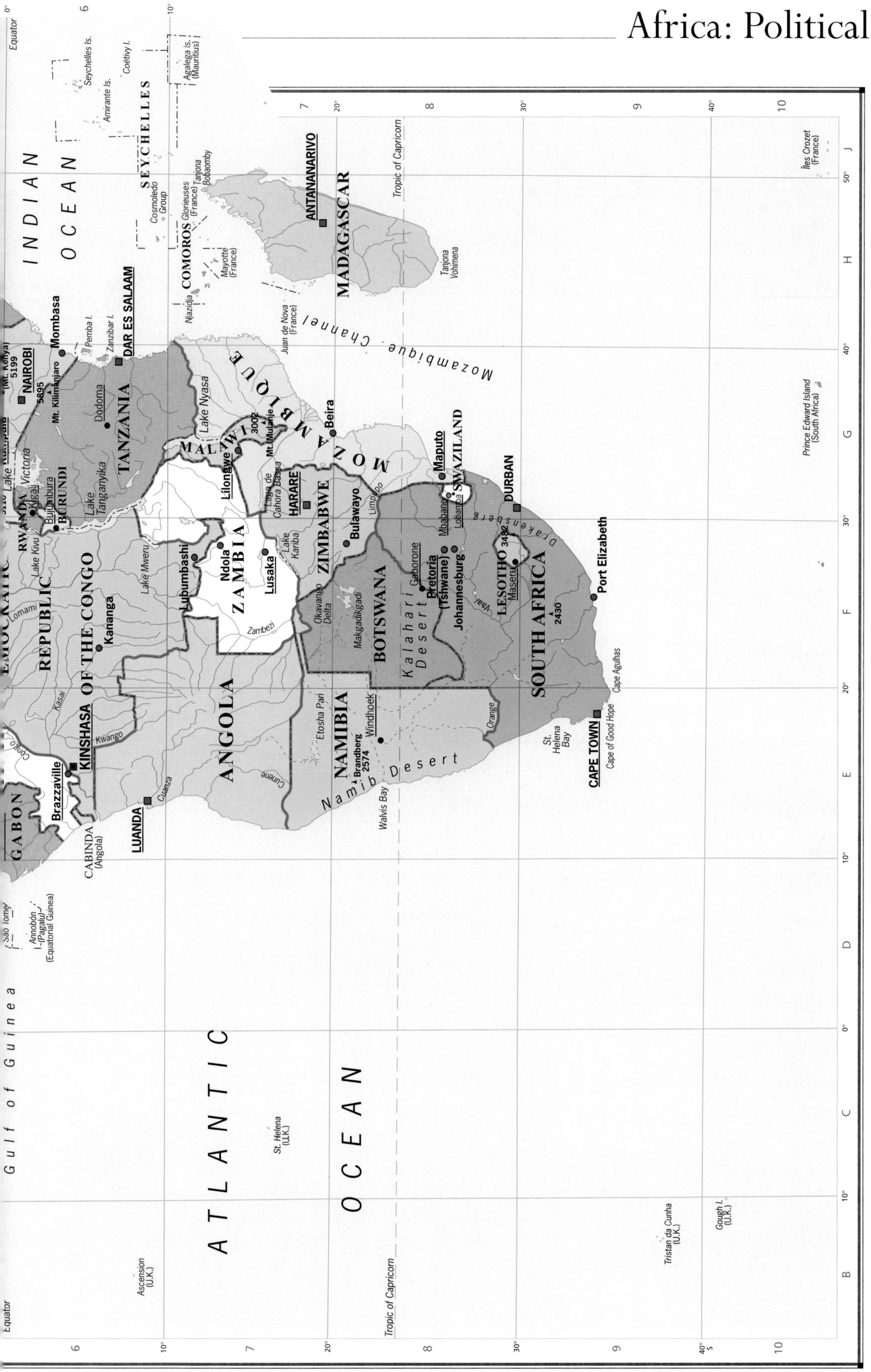

Ifrane, Morocco : -24 °C or -11 °F

Al Aziziyah, Libya : 58 °C or 136 °F

748,927,000

25 per km² or 64 per sq mi

30,293,000 km² or 11,696,000 sq mi

53

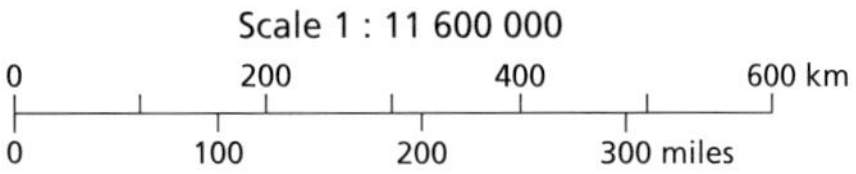
Scale 1 : 11 600 000
0
200
400
600 km
0
100
200
300 miles

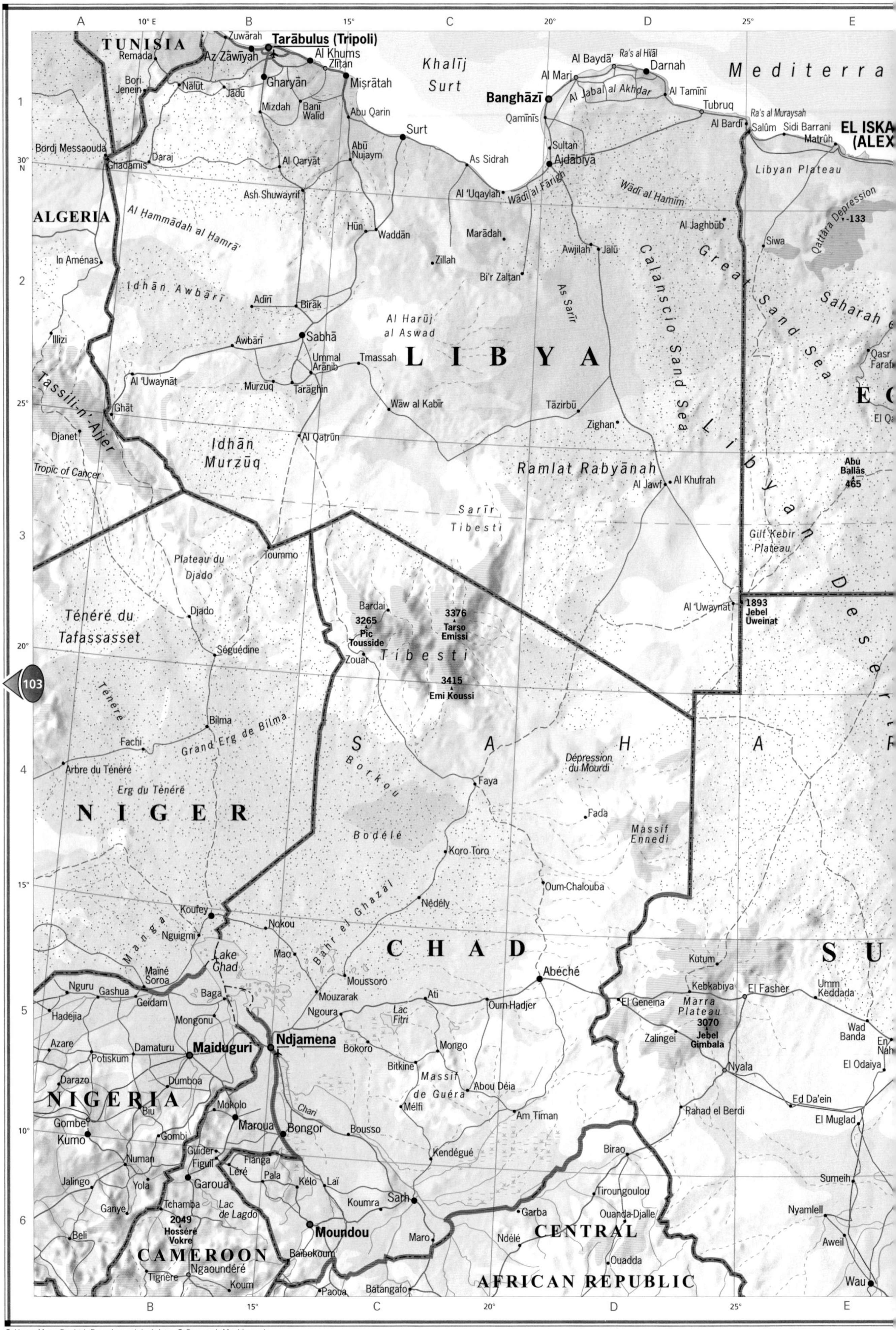
A
10° E
B
15°
C
20°
D
25°
E
1
2
3
4
5
6
30° N
25°
20°
15°
10°
103
TUNISIA
ALGERIA
LIBYA
NIGER
CHAD
NIGERIA
CAMEROON
CENTRAL
AFRICAN REPUBLIC
Zuwārah
Tarābulus (Tripoli)
Az Zāwīyah
Al Khums
Zlīṭan
Remada
Bori
Jenein
Nālūt
Jādū
Gharyān
Miṣrātah
Mizdah
Banī Walīd
Abu Qarin
Khalīj Surt
Surt
Banghāzī
Al Marj
Al Bayḍā'
Ra's al Hilāl
Darnah
Al Jabal al Akhḍar
Al Tamīmī
Tubruq
Qamīnis
Mediterra
Ra's al Muraysah
Al Bardī
Salûm
Sidi Barrani
Matrûh
EL ISKA
(ALEX
Bordj Messaouda
Ghadamis
Daraj
Al Qaryāt
Abū Nujaym
As Sidrah
Sultan
Ajdābiyā
Libyan Plateau
Ash Shuwayrif
Al 'Uqaylah
Wādī al Fārigh
Wādī al Ḥamīm
Qattara Depression
-133
Al Ḥammādah al Ḥamrā'
Hūn
Waddān
Marādah
Al Jaghbūb
Siwa
In Aménas
Zillah
Awjilah
Jālū
Great Sand Sea
Idhān Awbārī
Bi'r Zalṭan
As Sarīr
Calanscio Sand Sea
Adīrī
Birāk
Saharah
Illizi
Awbārī
Sabhā
Al Harūj al Aswad
Qasr Farafr
Ummal Arānib
Tmassah
Al 'Uwaynāt
Murzuq
Tarāghīn
Tassili-n'-Ajjer
Ghāt
Wāw al Kabīr
Tāzirbū
EG
Djanet
Idhān Murzūq
Al Qaṭrūn
Zighan
El Qa
Tropic of Cancer
Ramlat Rabyānah
Al Jawf
Al Khufrah
Libyan Desert
Abu Ballâs
465
Sarīr Tibesti
Gilf Kebir Plateau
Plateau du Djado
Toummo
Djado
Ténéré du Tafassasset
Bardai
3265
Pic Toussidé
3376
Tarso Emissi
Al 'Uwaynāt
1893
Jebel Uweinat
Séguédine
Zouar
Tibesti
3415
Emi Koussi
Ténéré
Bilma
Grand Erg de Bilma
Fachi
SAHARA
Arbre du Ténéré
Borkou
Dépression du Mourdi
Faya
Erg du Ténéré
Fada
Massif Ennedi
Bodélé
Koro Toro
Oum-Chalouba
Koufey
Nédéley
Bahr el Ghazal
Nokou
Nguigmi
Manga
Lake Chad
Mao
Kutum
SU
Mainé Soroa
Moussoro
Abéché
Nguru
Gashua
Baga
Geidam
Mouzarak
Ati
Kebkabiya
El Fasher
Umm Keddada
El Geneina
Marra Plateau
3070
Jebel Gimbala
Hadejia
Mongonu
Ngoura
Lac Fitri
Oum-Hadjer
Wad Banda
Azare
Potiskum
Damaturu
Maiduguri
Ndjamena
Bokoro
Mongo
Zalingei
Nyala
El Odaiya
Bitkine
Massif de Guéra
Abou Déia
Darazo
Dumboa
Mokolo
Chari
Biu
Mélfi
Am Timan
Ed Da'ein
Rahad el Berdi
El Muglad
Gombe
Maroua
Bongor
Bousso
Kumo
Gombi
Guider
Kendégué
Birao
Numan
Figuil
Flanga
Léré
Pala
Kélo
Laï
Jalingo
Garoua
Yola
Sumeih
Tiroungoulou
Ganye
Tchamba
Lac de Lagdo
Koumra
Sarh
2049
Hosséré Vokre
Garba
Ouanda-Djallé
Nyamlell
Beli
Moundou
Ndélé
Maro
Aweil
Baibokoum
Ouadda
Tignère
Ngaoundéré
Koum
Paoua
Batangafo
Wau

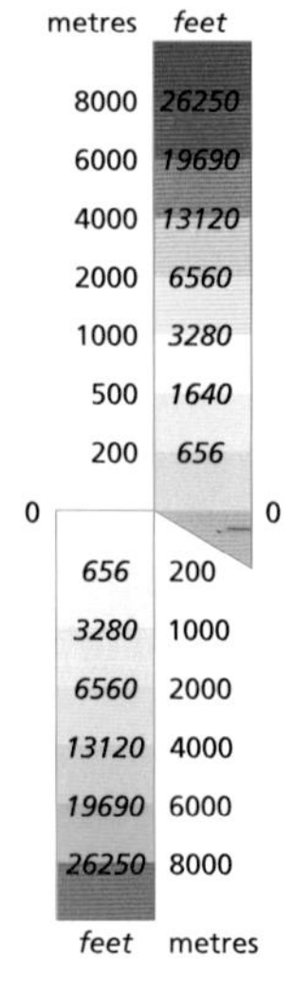
metres
feet
8000
26250
6000
19690
4000
13120
2000
6560
1000
3280
500
1640
200
656
0
0
656
200
3280
1000
6560
2000
13120
4000
19690
6000
26250
8000
feet
metres

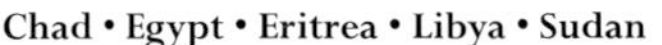

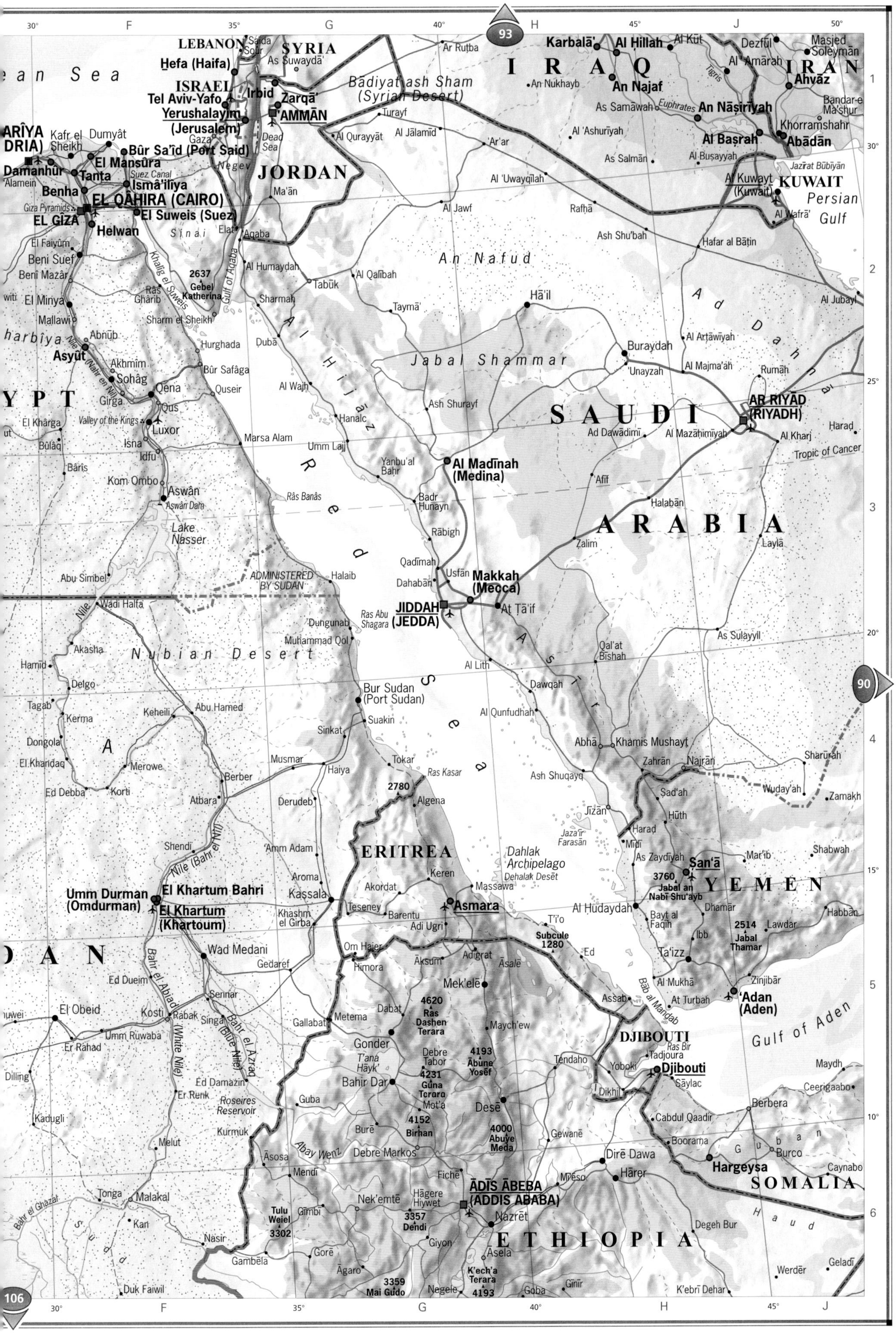

93
90
106
LEBANON
Saida
Sour
SYRIA
As Suwaydā'
Ḩefa (Haifa)
ISRAEL
Tel Aviv-Yafo
Irbid
Zarqā'
Yerushalayim (Jerusalem)
'AMMĀN
Gaza
Dead Sea
Negev
JORDAN
Ma'ān
Kafr el Sheikh
Dumyât
Bûr Sa'îd (Port Said)
Damanhûr
El Mansûra
Tanta
Suez Canal
Alamein
Benha
Ismâ'ilîya
EL QÂHIRA (CAIRO)
Giza Pyramids
EL GÎZA
El Suweis (Suez)
Helwan
Sinai
Elat
Aqaba
El Faiyûm
Beni Suef
Beni Mazâr
El Minya
Mallawi
Abnûb
Asyût
Akhmîm
Sohâg
Girga
Qena
Qus
El Khârga
Valley of the Kings
Luxor
Bûlâq
Isna
Idfu
Bârîs
Kom Ombo
Aswân
Aswân Dam
Lake Nasser
Abu Simbel
Wadi Halfa
Khalîg el Suweis
2637 Gebel Katherina
Ras Gharib
Gulf of Aqaba
Sharm el Sheikh
Hurghada
Bûr Safâga
Quseir
Marsa Alam
Râs Banâs
ADMINISTERED BY SUDAN
Halaib
Nile
Akasha
Hamid
Delgo
Nubian Desert
Tagab
Kerma
Keheili
Abu Hamed
Dongola
El Khandaq
Merowe
Ed Debba
Korti
Berber
Atbara
Musmar
Haiya
Derudeb
Shendi
Nile (Bahr el Nil)
'Amm Adam
Aroma
Kassala
Khashm el Girba
Umm Durman (Omdurman)
El Khartum Bahri
El Khartum (Khartoum)
Wad Medani
Gedaref
Ed Dueim
Bahr el Abiad
El Obeid
Kosti
Rabak
Sennar
Singa
Bahr el Azraq (Blue Nile)
(White Nile)
Umm Ruwaba
Er Rahad
Dilling
Ed Damazin
Er Renk
Roseires Reservoir
Kadugli
Kurmuk
Melut
Tonga
Malakal
Bahr el Ghazal
Sudd
Kan
Nasir
Gambela
Duk Faiwil
Dungunab
Muhammad Qol
Bur Sudan (Port Sudan)
Suakin
Sinkat
Tokar
Ras Kasar
2780
Algena
ERITREA
Keren
Akordat
Massawa
Teseney
Barentu
Asmara
Adi Ugri
Om Hajer
Himora
Aksum
Adigrat
Āsalē
Mek'elē
Dabat
Metema
Gallabat
4620 Ras Dashen Terara
Gonder
T'ana Hāyk'
Debre Tabor
4231 Guna Terara
Bahir Dar
4193 Ābune Yosēf
Maych'ew
Guba
Desē
Mot'a
4152 Birhan
Burē
4000 Abuye Meda
Abay Wenz
Debre Markos
Āsosa
Mendi
Fichē
Nek'emtē
Hāgere Hiywet
ĀDĪS ĀBEBA (ADDIS ABABA)
Tulu Weiel 3302
Gimbi
3357 Dendi
Nazrēt
Giyon
Gorē
Āgaro
Āsela
ETHIOPIA
3359 Mai Gudo
Negele
K'ech'a Terara 4193
Goba
Ginir
Ar Rutba
Bādiyat ash Sham (Syrian Desert)
Turayf
Al Qurayyāt
Al Jālamīd
'Ar'ar
Al 'Uwayqīlah
Al Jawf
Al Humaydah
Tabūk
Al Qalībah
An Nafud
Sharmah
Al Hijāz
Taymā'
Ḩā'il
Dubā
Jabal Shammar
Al Wajh
Ash Shurayf
Hanak
Umm Lajj
Yanbu'al Bahr
Al Madīnah (Medina)
Red Sea
Badr Ḩunayn
Rābigh
Qadīmah
Dahabān
Usfān
Makkah (Mecca)
JIDDAH (JEDDA)
Ras Abu Shagara
At Ṭā'if
'Asīr
Al Līth
Dawqah
Al Qunfudhah
Abhā
Khamīs Mushayṭ
Ash Shuqayq
Jīzān
Jaza'ir Farasān
Dahlak Archipelago
Dehalak Desēt
Subcule 1280
T'i'o
Ed
Karbalā'
Al Ḩillah
Al Kūt
IRAQ
An Nukhayb
An Najaf
As Samāwah
Euphrates
Tigris
An Nāṣirīyah
Al 'Amārah
Dezfūl
Masjed Soleymān
IRAN
Ahvāz
Bandar-e Ma'shur
Khorramshahr
Ābādān
Al Baṣrah
Al 'Ashurīyah
As Salmān
Al Buṣayyah
Jazīrat Būbīyān
Al Kuwayt (Kuwait)
KUWAIT
Persian Gulf
Al Wafrā'
Rafḩā
Ash Shu'bah
Ḩafar al Bāṭin
Ad Dahnā
Al Jubayl
Al Arṭāwiyah
Buraydah
'Unayzah
Al Majma'ah
Rumāh
SAUDI ARABIA
AR RIYĀD (RIYADH)
Ad Dawādimī
Al Mazāḩimīyah
Al Kharj
Ḩaraḑ
Tropic of Cancer
'Afīf
Ḩalabān
Zalim
Laylā
As Sulayyil
Qal'at Bīshah
Sharūrah
Zahrān
Najrān
Wuday'ah
Zamakh
Sad'ah
Ḩūth
Ḩaraḑ
Mīdī
As Zaydīyah
Şan'ā
Ma'rib
Shabwah
3760 Jabal an Nabī Shu'ayb
YEMEN
Al Ḩudaydah
Bayt al Faqīh
Dhamār
Ibb
2514 Jabal Thamar
Lawdar
Ḩabbān
Ta'izz
Al Mukhā
Zinjibār
At Turbah
'Adan (Aden)
Bāb al Mandab
Assab
DJIBOUTI
Ras Bir
Tadjoura
Tendaho
Yoboki
Djibouti
Dikhil
Saylac
Gulf of Aden
Maydh
Ceerigaabo
Berbera
Cabdul Qaadir
Gewanē
Dirē Dawa
Boorama
Guban
Burco
Hargeysa
Hārer
Mī'eso
Caynabo
SOMALIA
Haud
Degeh Bur
Werdēr
Geladī
K'ebrī Dehar
30°
35°
40°
45°
50°
F
G
H
J
1
2
3
4
5
6
30°
25°
20°
15°
10°

Scale 1 : 11 600 000

0 200 400 600 km

0 100 200 300 miles

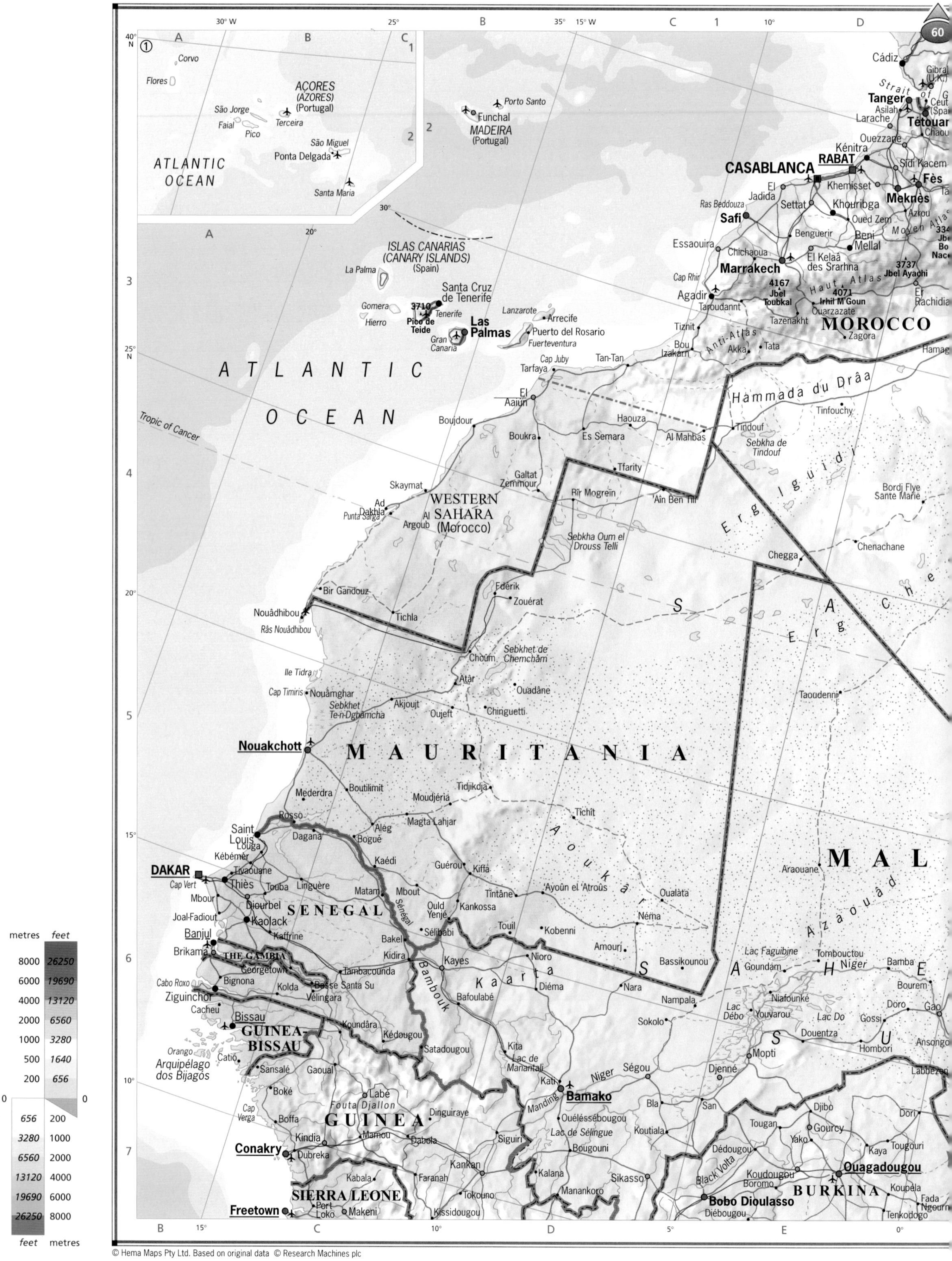

30° W · 25° · B · 35° · 15° W · C · 1 · 10° · D

40° N · A · B · C · 1

Corvo

Flores

AÇORES
(AZORES)
(Portugal)

São Jorge
Faial · Terceira
Pico

2 · 2

Porto Santo

Funchal
MADEIRA
(Portugal)

ATLANTIC
OCEAN

São Miguel
Ponta Delgada

Santa Maria

30° · A · 20° · 30°

ISLAS CANARIAS
(CANARY ISLANDS)
(Spain)

3 · La Palma

Gomera · 3710 · Santa Cruz
Hierro · Pico de · de Tenerife
Teide · Tenerife

Lanzarote
Arrecife

Las · Puerto del Rosario
Palmas · Fuerteventura
Gran
Canaria

Cádiz
Gibr.
(U.K.)
Ceut
(Spa
Tanger
Asilah · Tétouar
Larache · Chaou
Ouezzane
Kénitra
CASABLANCA · RABAT · Fès
Sidi Kacem · Meknès
El · Khemisset
Jadida · Ta
Settat · Khouribga · Azrou
Safi · Oued Zem · Moyen Atlas
Benguerir · Beni · Jbel
Essaouira · Mellal · Bo
Chichaoua · El Kelaâ · Nace
Ras Beddouza · des Srarhna · 3737
Cap Rhir · Marrakech · Jbel Ayachi · El
4167 · 4071 · Rachidia
Agadir · Jbel · Irhil M'Goun
Taroudannt · Toubkal · Ouarzazate
Tiznit · Tazenakht · MOROCCO
Anti-Atlas · Zagora
Akka · Tata · Hamag

Cap Juby · Tan-Tan · Bou
Tarfaya · Izakarn · Hammada du Drâa
El · Tinfouchy
Aaiún · Haouza
Boujdour · Tindouf
Boukra · Es Semara · Al Mahbàs · Sebkha de
Galtat · Tindouf · Bordj Flye
Zemmour · Tfarity · Sante Marie
4 · Skaymat · Rîr Mogrein
WESTERN · Aïn Ben Tili
Ad · SAHARA · Chenachane
Dakhla · Al · (Morocco) · Sebkha Oum el · Chegga
Punta Sarga · Argoub · Drouss Telli

25° N

ATLANTIC

OCEAN

Tropic of Cancer

Bir Gandouz · Fdérik
Nouâdhibou · Zouérat
Râs Nouâdhibou · Tichla · S · E · r · g
Ile Tidra · Sebkhet de · Chemchâm · Taoudenni
Cap Timiris · Nouâmghar · Choûm
Sebkhet · Atâr · Ouadâne
Te-n-Dghamcha · Akjoujt · Oujeft · Chinguetti
Nouakchott · M A U R I T A N I A
Mederdra · Boutilimit
Rosso · Moudjèria · Tidjikdja · Tichît
Saint · Aleg · Magta Lahjar · A · Araouane · M A L
Louis · Dagana · Bogué · o · u
Kébémèr · Kaédi · Guérou · Kiffa · Tintâne · k · Oualâta
DAKAR · Linguère · Matam · Mbout · Ayoûn el 'Atroûs · à · Néma
Cap Vert · Tivaouane · Ould · Kankossa · r · Tombouctou
Thiès · Touba · Yenjé · Touil · Kobenni · S · Bamba
Mbour · Diourbel · SENEGAL · Bakel · Sélibabi · Amourj · A · Lac Faguibine · Niger
Joal-Fadiout · Kaolack · Kidira · Nioro · Bassikounou · Goundam · H · Bourem
Banjul · Kaffrine · Kayes · Diéma · Nara · Nampala · Lac · Niafounké · Doro · Gao
Brikama · THE GAMBIA · Tambacounda · Kaarta · Débo · Gossi
Georgetown · Diéma · Sokolo · Lac Do · Ansongo
Cabo Roxo · Bignona · Bafoulabé · Youvarou · Hombori
Ziguinchor · Kolda · Bassé Santa Su · Douentza
Cacheu · Vélingara · Mopti
Bissau · Koundára · Kédougou · Kita · Djenné
GUINEA- · Satadougou · Lac de · Ségou · Djibo
BISSAU · Gaoual · Manantali · San
Orango · Sansalé · Kati · Niger · Bla · Dédougou · Gourcy
Arquipélago · Catió · Boké · Labé · BAMAKO · Koutiala · Yako · Kaya · Tougouri
dos Bijagós · Boffa · Fouta Djallon · Mandinga · Ouéléssébougou · Tougan · Ouagadougou
Cap · Dinguiraye · Boromo · Gourcy
Verga · Kindia · Mamou · Dabola · Siguiri · Lac de Sélingue · Sikasso · Koudougou · Fada
GUINEA · Bougouni · Koupèla · Ngourm
Conakry · Dubreka · Kankan · Kalana · Black Volta · BURKINA · Tenkodogo
Kabala · Faranah · Bobo Dioulasso
SIERRA LEONE · Tokouno · Mankono · Diébougou
Freetown · Port · Makeni · Kissidougou
Loko

3 · 20° · 4 · 15° · 5 · 10° · 6 · 5° · 7

metres	feet
8000	26250
6000	19690
4000	13120
2000	6560
1000	3280
500	1640
200	656
0	0
656	200
3280	1000
6560	2000
13120	4000
19690	6000
26250	8000

feet · metres

B · 15° · C · 10° · D · 5° · E · 0°

Northwest Africa

Algeria • Azores • Canary Islands • Madeira
Mali • Mauritania • Morocco • Niger • Tunisia

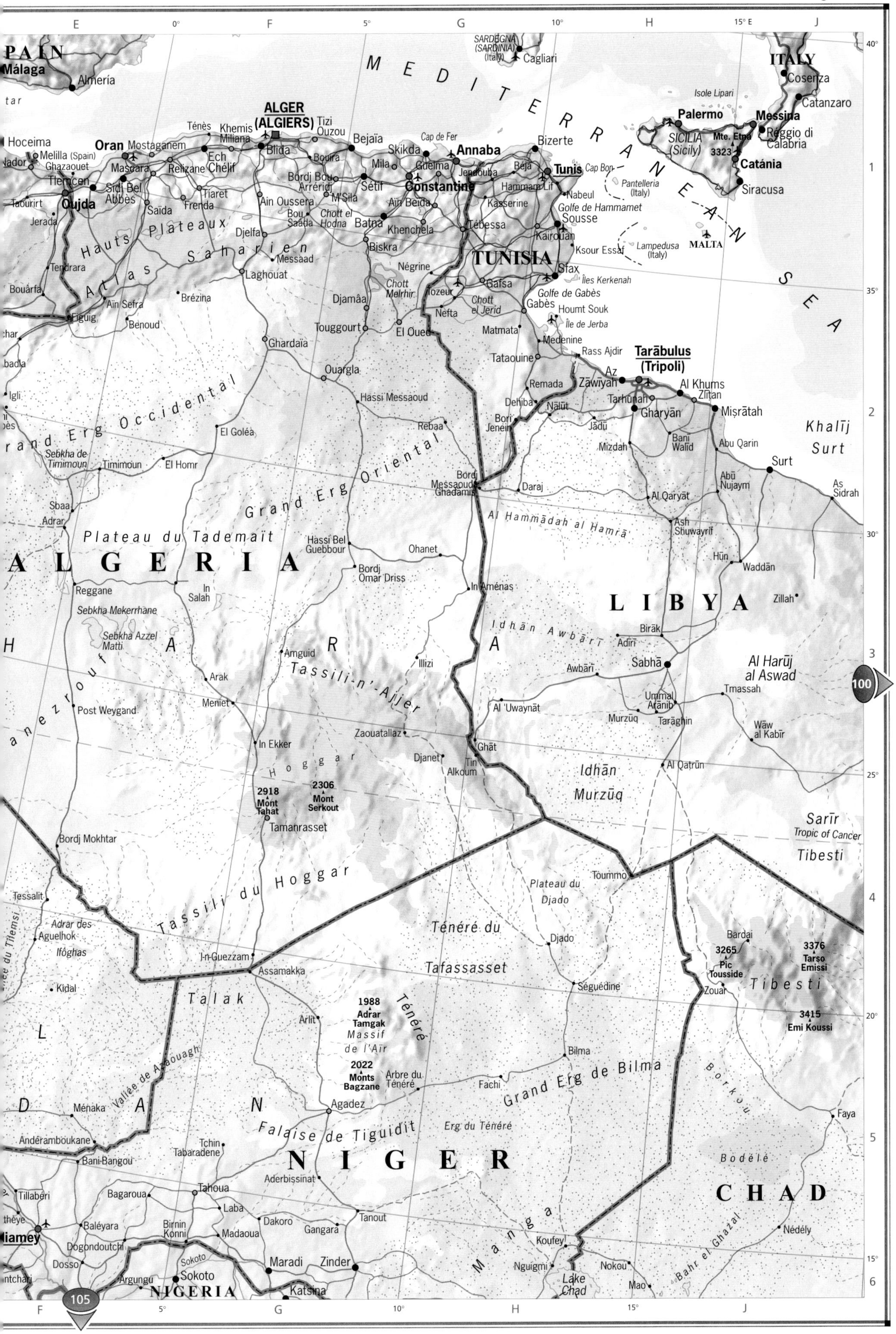

over 3 million	100 000 – 250 000	country capital underline
1 – 3 million	25 000 – 100 000	
250 000 – 1 million	under 25 000	

SPAIN
Málaga
Almería
Hoceima
Melilla (Spain)
Oran Mostaganem
Mascara Relizane
Sidi Bel Abbès
Tlemcen
Oujda
Jerada
Tendrara
Bouârfa
Figuig
Aïn Sefra
Bénoud
Igli
Adrar

MEDITERRANEAN SEA

SARDEGNA (SARDINIA) (Italy)
Cagliari
Isole Lipari
ITALY
Cosenza
Catanzaro
Palermo Messina
Mte. Etna Reggio di Calabria
SICILIA (Sicily) 3323 Catánia
Siracusa
Pantelleria (Italy)
MALTA
Lampedusa (Italy)

ALGER (ALGIERS) Tizi Ouzou
Khemis Miliana
Ténès
Blida Bejaïa
Bouira
Ech Chélif
Bordj Bou Arréridj
Mila Sétif
M'Sila
Aïn Oussera
Bou Saâda
Djelfa
Messaad
Laghouat
Biskra
Négrine
Djamâa
Touggourt
El Oued
Ghardaïa
Ouargla
Hassi Messaoud
Rebaa
El Goléa
El Homr
Timimoun

Cap de Fer
Skikda
Annaba
Guelma Jendouba
Constantine Beja
Hammam Lif
Kasserine
Aïn Beïda
Tébessa
Khenchela
Batna
TUNISIA
Gafsa
Tozeur
Nefta
Gabès
Matmata
Tataouine

Bizerte
Tunis Cap Bon
Nabeul
Golfe de Hammamet
Sousse
Kairouan
Ksour Essaf
Sfax
Îles Kerkenah
Golfe de Gabès
Houmt Souk
Île de Jerba
Medenine
Rass Ajdir
Remada
Dehiba
Bord Jenein
Daraj
Ghadamis

Tarābulus (Tripoli)
Az Zāwiyah Al Khums
Tarhūnah Zlītan
Nālūt Gharyān Mişrātah
Jādū
Bani Walid Abu Qarin
Mizdah
Surt
Abū Nujaym
Al Qaryāt As Sidrah
Ash Shuwayrif
Hūn
Waddān

Khalīj Surt

Hauts Plateaux
Saïda
Tiaret
Frenda
Chott el Hodna
Chott Melrhir
Chott el Jerid

Atlas Saharien
Brézina
Taourirt

Grand Erg Occidental
Sebkha de Timimoun

Plateau du Tademaït
Reggane
In Salah
Sebkha Mekerrhane
Sebkha Azzel Matti

ALGERIA

Hassi Bel Guebbour
Bordj Omar Driss
Ohanet
In Aménas

Grand Erg Oriental

Bordj Messaouda
Al Hammādah al Hamrā

LIBYA
Zillah

AHAGGAR

Tassili-n'-Ajjer
Amguid
Arak
Meniet
2918 Mont Tahat
2306 Mont Serkout
Tamanrasset
In Ekker
Illizi
Zaouatallaz
Djanet
Ghāt
Tin Alkoum

Idhān Awbārī
Birāk
Adiri
Awbārī Sabhā
Murzūq Tarāghin
Umm al Aranib
Al 'Uwaynāt

Al Harūj al Aswad
Tmassah
Wāw al Kabīr
Al Qatrūn

Idhān Murzūq

Sarīr
Tropic of Cancer
Tibesti

Tanezrouft

Tassili du Hoggar
Hoggar

Bordj Mokhtar

Tessalit
Adrar des Ifoghas
Aguelhok
Kidal

MALI

In-Guezzam
Assamakka
Talak
Arlit
1988 Adrar Tamgak
Massif de l'Aïr
2022 Monts Bagzane
Agadez
Falaise de Tiguidit

Plateau du Djado
Ténéré du Tafassasset
Djado
Séguédine
Ténéré
Bilma
Arbre du Ténéré
Fachi

Toummo
Bardai
3265 Pic Toussidé
Zouar
3376 Tarso Emissi
Tibesti
3415 Emi Koussi

Borkou

Grand Erg de Bilma
Erg du Ténéré
Faya

Vallée du Tilemsi
Vallée de l'Azaouagh
Ménaka
Andéramboukane
Bani-Bangou
Tillabéri
thèye
Niamey
Dogondoutchi
Dosso

Tchin Tabaradene
Tahoua
Aderbissinat
Laba
Tanout
Baléyara
Birnin Konni
Madaoua
Dakoro
Gangara
Tanout
Sokoto
Bagaroua
Argungu
Sokoto
Katsina
Maradi Zinder
NIGERIA

NIGER

Manga
Koufey
Nguigmi
Lake Chad
Bodélé
Nokou Nédély
Mao

CHAD

Bahr el Ghazal

Scale 1 : 11 600 000

0 200 400 600 km

0 100 200 300 miles

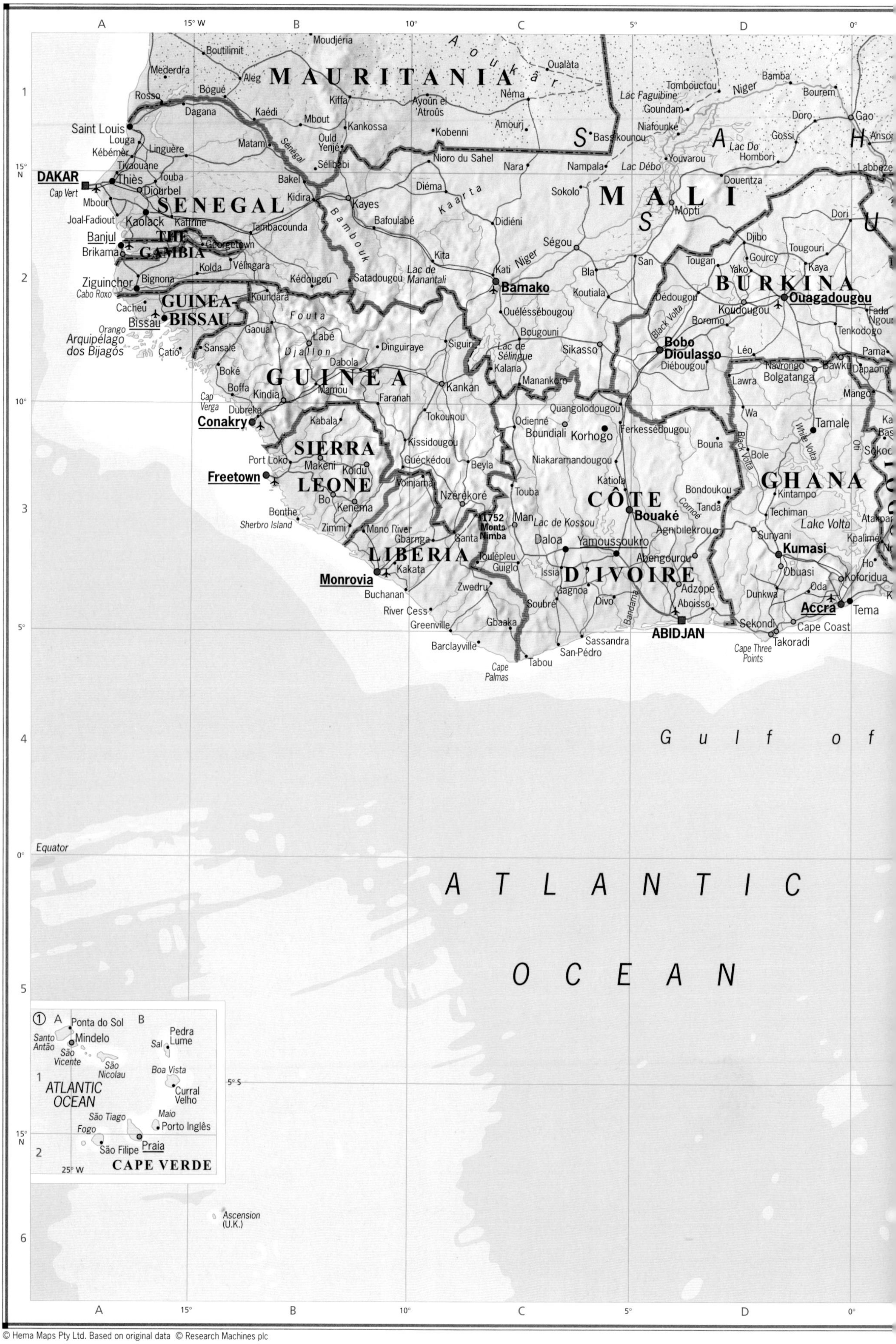

metres feet

metres	feet
8000	26250
6000	19690
4000	13120
2000	6560
1000	3280
500	1640
200	656
0	0
656	200
3280	1000
6560	2000
13120	4000
19690	6000
26250	8000

feet metres

Benin • Burkina • Cameroon • Cape Verde • Congo • Côte d'Ivoire • Equatorial Guinea • Gabon • The Gambia • Ghana • Guinea • Guinea-Bissau • Liberia • Nigeria • São Tomé & Príncipe • Senegal • Sierra Leone • Togo

- over 3 million
- 1 – 3 million
- 250 000 – 1 million
- 100 000 – 250 000
- 25 000 – 100 000
- under 25 000
- country capital underline
- state or province capital underline

Scale 1 : 11 600 000
0 200 400 600 km
0 100 200 300 miles

NIGERIA

Mokolo
Maroua Bongor
Guider
Fianga
Figuil Léré Pala
Lac Kélo Laï
de Koumra
Lagdo
Moundou
Doba
Goré
Baïbokoum
Ngaoundéré Paoua
Koum Bocaranga
Bozoum
Garoua Bouar
Boulaï Baoro
Bertoua Carnot Bossambélé
Berbérati Bossangoa
Gamboula
Yokadouma Nola

CHAD

Mélfi Massif
Abou Déïa du Guéra
Bousso
Kendégué Am Timan
Sarh
Garba
Maro
Ndélé

Birao
Tiroungoulou
Ouanda-
Djalié
Ouadda

Rahad el Berdi
Ed Da'ein Babanusa
El Muglad Kadugli

SUDAN

Sumeih
Nyamlell
Aweil Wau
Tonj
Rumbek

CENTRAL
AFRICAN REPUBLIC

Ippy Bria
Sibut Bambari
Damara Kouango Alindao
Bangui Zongo Bosobolo Mobaye Bangassou Rafaï Zémio
Mbaïki Libenge Yakoma Monga
Mobayi- Bondo
Mbongo
Gemena Businga Abumombazi
Kungu Akula Lisala Bumba
Dongo

Djéma

Obo Tambura
Doruma Yambio
Ango Maridi
Niangara Dungu Yei
Poko Watsa Faradje
Bambesa Isiro Mungbere
Bomili Wamba
Banalia Nia-Nia

Amadi Nimi
Lanya
Nebbi
Mahagi 2437
Aburo
Irumu Masisi
Mambasa Bunia Hoim

CAMEROON

Dja Sembé
Mékambo
Ouésso
Epéna Impfondo
Dongou
Bomossa
Makua
Equator Owando
Ewo Okoyo Obouya
Gamboma

CONGO

GABON

Pala Koum
Batangafo
Kaga Bandoro
Bozoum

Bomossa
Impfondo Makanza
Epéna
Bolomba
Mbandaka Busira Boende
Bokatola
Lac Tumba
Inongo Bokungu Anzi Opala
Monkoto Ikela

Congo
Bongandanga
Yohuma Basoko
Basankusu Djolu Yangambi Kisangani
Lindi
Bafwasende

Beni 5110
Butembo Mount
Stanley
Lubero Lake
Edward Masaka
Kamande Mbarara
Muhulu Lowa
Punia Mount
Karisimbi
4510 Goma Gisenyi Kigali
Lake Kivu RWANDA
Lubutu Bukavu Butare

DEMOCRATIC REPUBLIC
OF THE CONGO

Inongo
Lac Mai-Ndombe
Kutu
Bandundu
Kikwit
Kenge
Masi-Manimba
Mayamba
Idiofa
Luebo
Mweka
Ilebo
Bena Dibele
Dekese Kole
Lodja
Kombe
Lubefu
Lusambo
Lubao

Kama
Kibombo
Kasongo
Kongolo
Kabalo

Kindu
Kalima Shabunda
Kamituga
Uvira
Fizi
Kalemie

Ulindi
Bujumbura
Bururi Rutana
Makamba
Kigoma
Ujiji
Uvinza

BURUNDI
3303
Gitega
Muyinga
Ngozi
Kibondo
Nyanlel

Brazzaville
KINSHASA
Luozi
Mabanza-Ngungu
Inkisi-Kisantu
Boma Matadi Songololo
Banana
M'banza Congo
Maquela
do Zombo
Quimbele

Kwilu Kasai
Kasai
Popokabaka
Lukuni
Gungu
Kikwit
Kahemba
Chitato
Luremo

Kwango

Tshikapa
Kananga
Mwene-Ditu
Mbuji-Mayi
Gandajika
Luiza
Kaniama
Kapanga

Lusambo
Lubao Kongolo
Kabalo
Nyunzu
Manono
Kabongo

Kalemie
Moba
Mpanda

LUANDA
Caxito
Barra do
Cuanza
N'zeto
Porto Amboim
Lucala
Lucala Malanje
Sumbe Quibala
Musserde
Cacola
Dala
Muconda
Luau Dilolo
Caianda
Kolwezi
Likasi
Lubumbashi

Kamina
Kinda
Kilwa
Lubudi

Pweto
Lake
Mweru
Wantipa
Lac Mweru
Mporokoso
Kawambwa
Kasenga
Mwenda
Nsombo
Mansa
Lake
Bangweulu

Miloro
Mbala
Sumbawanga

Lobito Benguela
Cuio Cubal
Lucira Caluquembe Caconda
Huambo Kuito
Andulo Camacupa
Bailundo
Cuemba Sachanga
Lucusse
Lumbala
Kaquengue

Lac Nzilo
Tenke Goba
Minga
Lac de Retenue
de la Lufira

Chingola
Mufulira
Kitwe Ndola
Luanshya
Solwezi
Kasempa
Mukuku

ANGOLA

Cangamba Lutembo

ZAMBIA

Chavuma Zambezi
Manyinga Kabompo
Serenje

© Hema Maps Pty Ltd. Based on original data © Research Machines plc

106

metres feet
8000 26250
6000 19690
4000 13120
2000 6560
1000 3280
500 1640
200 656
0 0
656 200
3280 1000
6560 2000
13120 4000
19690 6000
26250 8000
feet metres

ATLANTIC OCEAN

105

Angola • Burundi • Central African Republic • The Democratic Republic of Congo
Djibouti • Ethiopia • Kenya • Rwanda • Somalia • Tanzania • Uganda

■ over 3 million
■ 1 – 3 million
● 250 000 – 1 million
• 100 000 – 250 000
○ 25 000 – 100 000
• under 25 000
—— country capital underline

Scale 1 : 11 600 000

0 200 400 600 km

0 100 200 300 miles

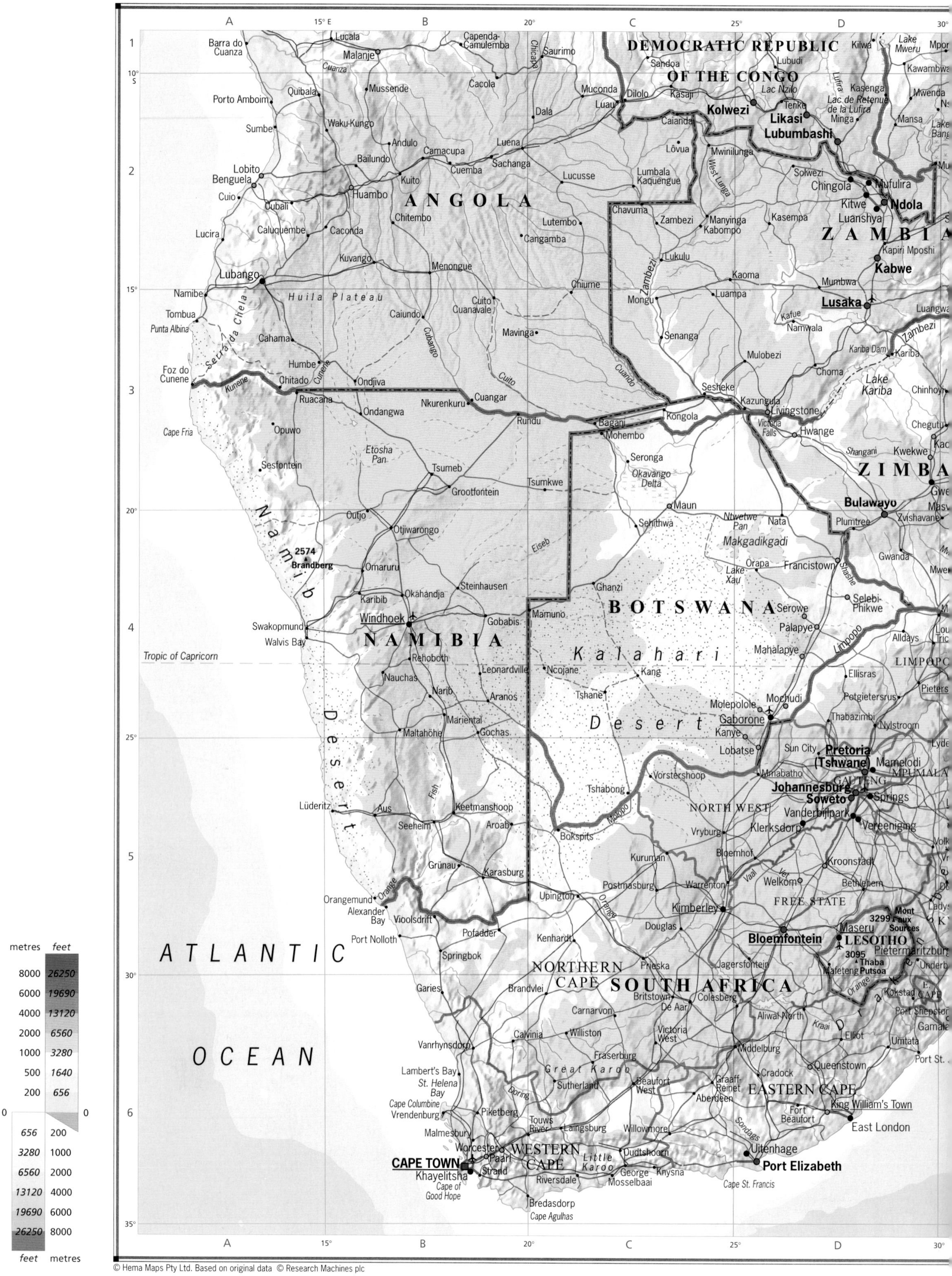

Southern Africa

Botswana • Comoros • Lesotho • Madagascar • Malawi • Mauritius
Mozambique • Namibia • Seychelles • South Africa • Swaziland • Zambia • Zimbabwe

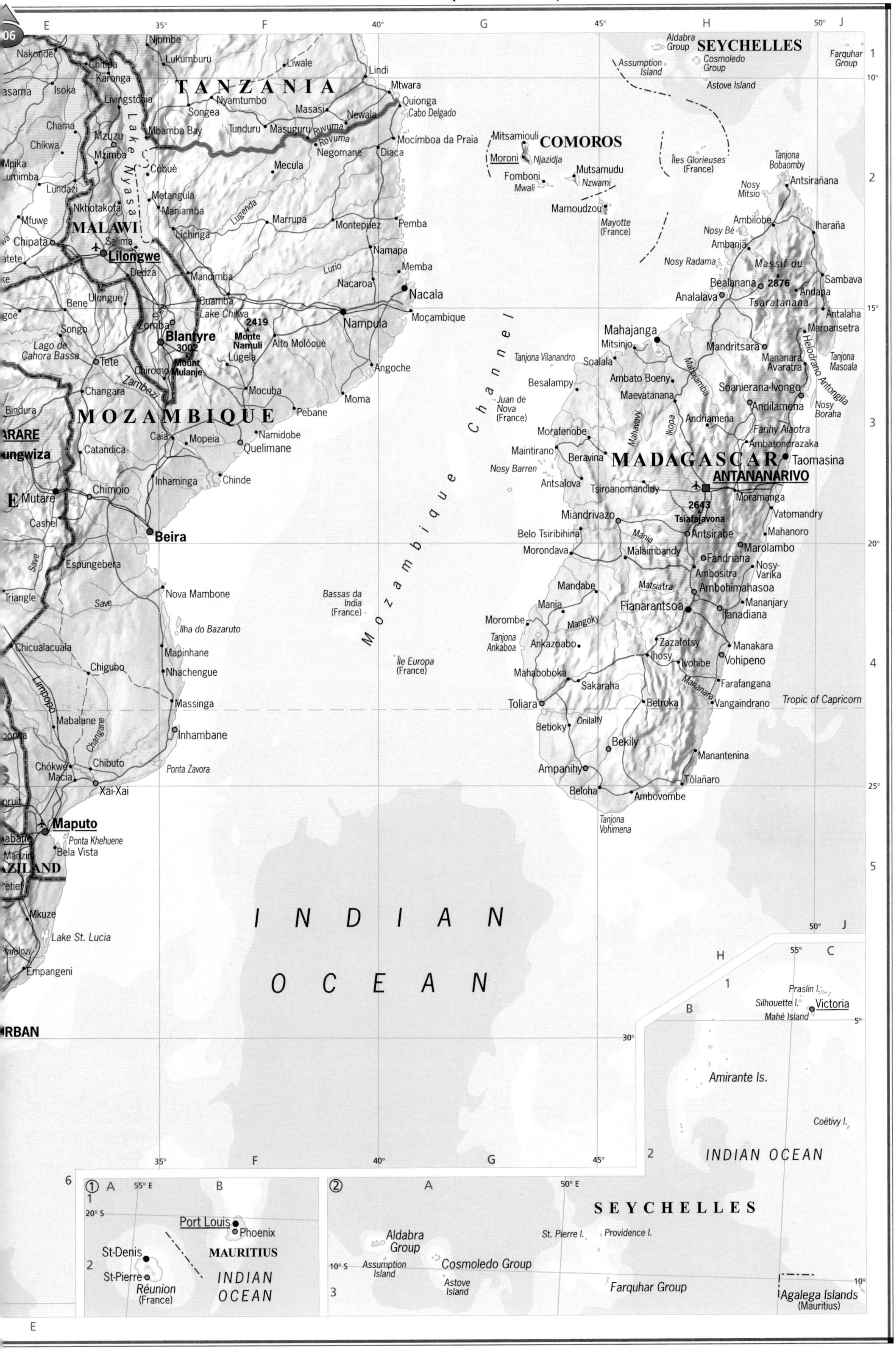

■ over 3 million	● 100 000 – 250 000	country capital underline
■ 1 – 3 million	● 25 000 – 100 000	state or province capital underline
● 250 000 – 1 million	• under 25 000	

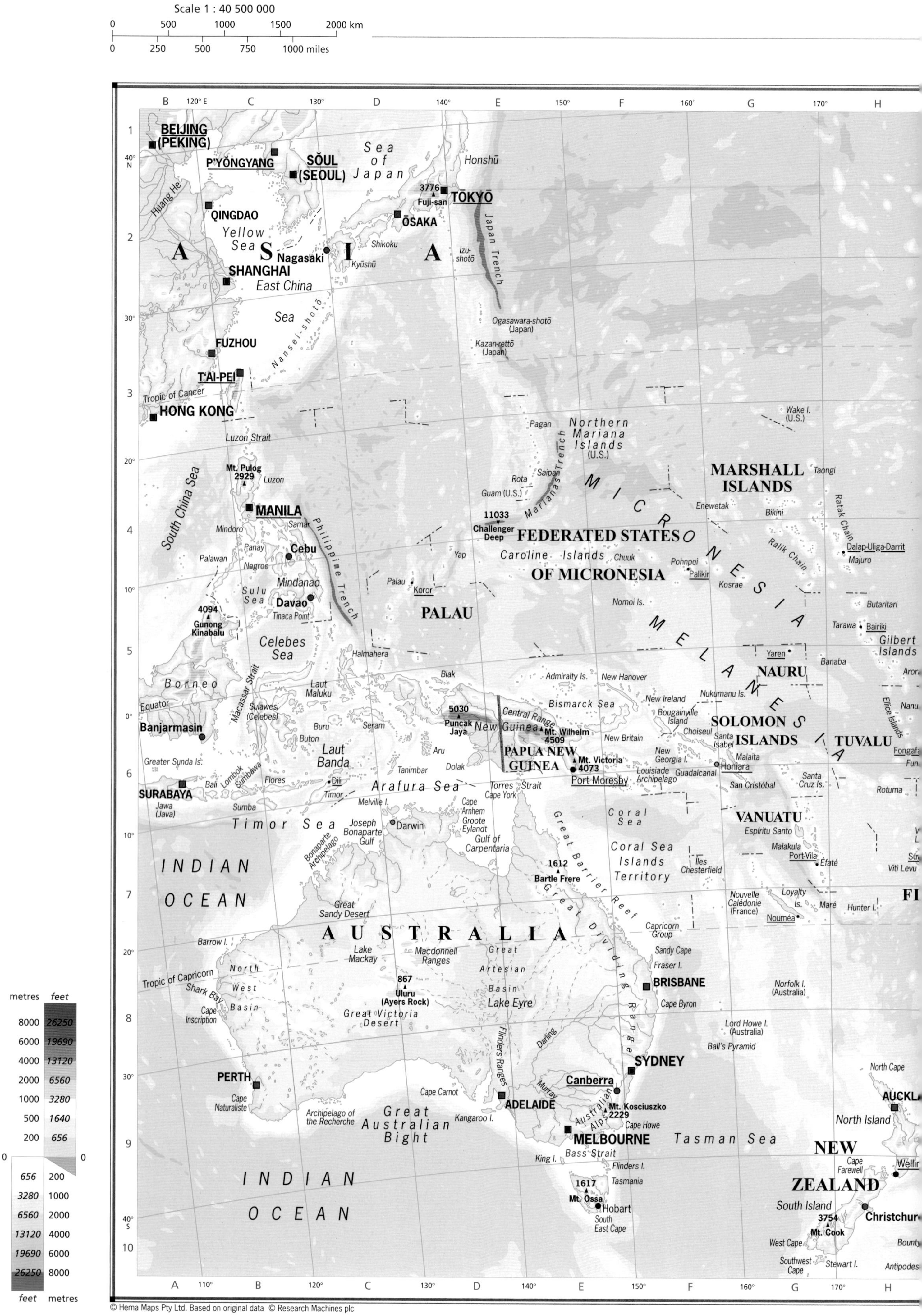

Mt. Wilhelm, Papua New Guinea : 4,509 m or 14,793 ft

Lake Eyre, Australia : 15 m or 49 ft

Mulka, Australia : 10.3 cm or 4.05 in

Mt. Waialeale, Hawaii : 1168 cm or 460 in

Murray-Darling, Australia : 3,750 km² or 2,330 sq mi

Lake Eyre, Australia : 8,800 km² or 3,400 sq mi

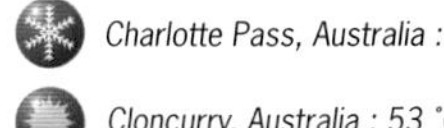

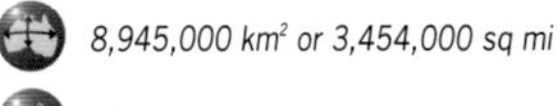

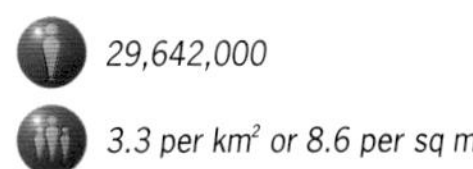

J | 170° | K | 160° | L | 150° | M | 140° | N | 130° | P | 120° W | Q

NORTH AMERICA

LOS ANGELES

SAN DIEGO

P A C I F I C

40°

30°

ure I.
vay Is.

Laysan I.

Necker I.

HAWAII
(U.S.)

Kauai
Oahu
Honolulu ● Maui
Hawaii

Guadalupe
(Mexico)

Tropic of Cancer

20°

Johnston I.
(U.S.)

N. W. Christmas Island Ridge

Is. Revillagigedo
(Mexico)

O C E A N

Palmyra I.
(U.S.)

Tabuaeran Kiritimati

Line Islands

10°

Howland (U.S.)
Baker (U.S.)

Jarvis
(U.S.)

Phoenix Islands

Birnie Rawaki
Orona Manra

KIRIBATI

Malden I.

Starbuck I.

Equator

0°

P O L Y N E S I A

Atafu
Nukunonu

Tokelau
(New Zealand)

Tongareva

Marquesas Islands

s et
una
nce)

Swains I.

Danger Is.
Nassau

Manihiki

Vostok I. Caroline I.

Nuku Hiva

Hiva Oa

SAMOA
Savaii Apia
oorn Is. Upolu
France) Tafahi
Tonga Islands

American
Samoa
Tutuila

Suvorov I.

Flint I.

Îles
Désappointement

Archipel des Tuamotu

Rose I.

Motu One

Îles Palliser

Pukapuka

Cook Islands

Raroia

10°

TONGA

Niue

(New Zealand)

Palmerston I.
(New Zealand)

Aitutaki

Arch.
de la Société Tahiti

Hao

Îles Duc de
Gloucester

Groupe Actéon

u'alofa
Ata

Rarotonga

Mangaia

French
Polynesia

Îles
Maria Rurutu

Rapa

Tubuai

Mururoa

Morane Gambier
Is.

va Horizon Depth
10882

Tonga Trench

Tubuai Islands

Raevavae

Mangareva

20°

Oeno

Henderson I.

Tropic of Capricorn

Rapa

Pitcairn Is.
(U.K.)

Ducie I.

Marotiri

Easter I.
(Chile)

rmadec Islands
New Zealand)

Kermadec Trench

South West

30°

Pacific

Basin

am Is.
Zealand)

40°

J | 170° | K | 160° | L | 150° | M | 140° | N | 130° | P | 120° | Q | 110° | R

Charlotte Pass, Australia : -23 °C or -9.4 °F

Cloncurry, Australia : 53 °C or 128 °F

29,642,000

3.3 per km² or 8.6 per sq mi

8,945,000 km² or 3,454,000 sq mi

14

Scale 1 : 40 500 000

0 500 1000 1500 2000 km

0 250 500 750 1000 miles

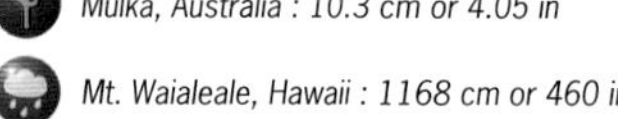

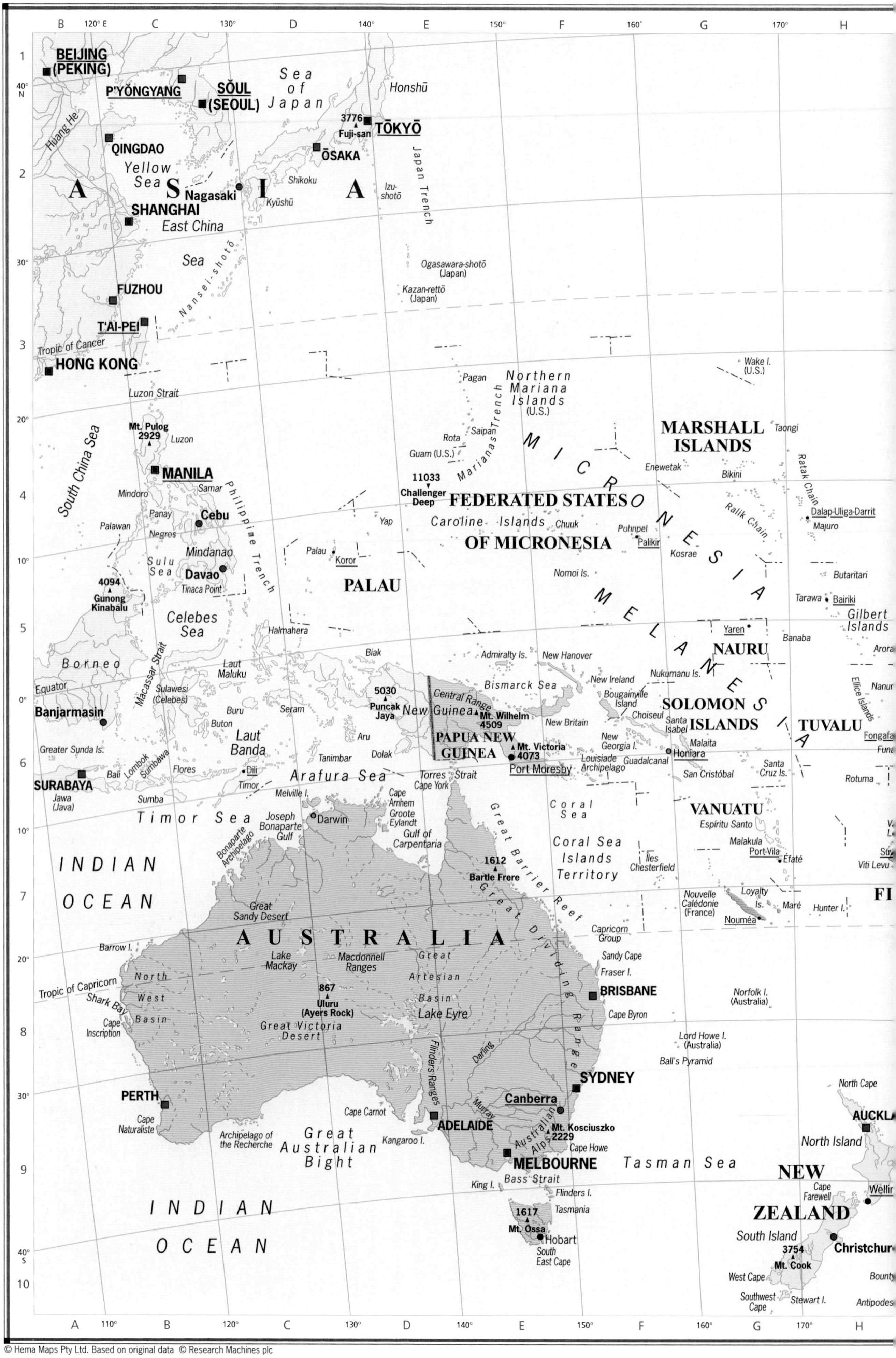

© Hema Maps Pty Ltd. Based on original data © Research Machines plc

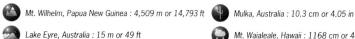

Mt. Wilhelm, Papua New Guinea : 4,509 m or 14,793 ft

Mulka, Australia : 10.3 cm or 4.05 in

Murray-Darling, Australia : 3,750 km^2 or 2,330 sq mi

Lake Eyre, Australia : 15 m or 49 ft

Mt. Waialeale, Hawaii : 1168 cm or 460 in

Lake Eyre, Australia : 8,800 km^2 or 3,400 sq mi

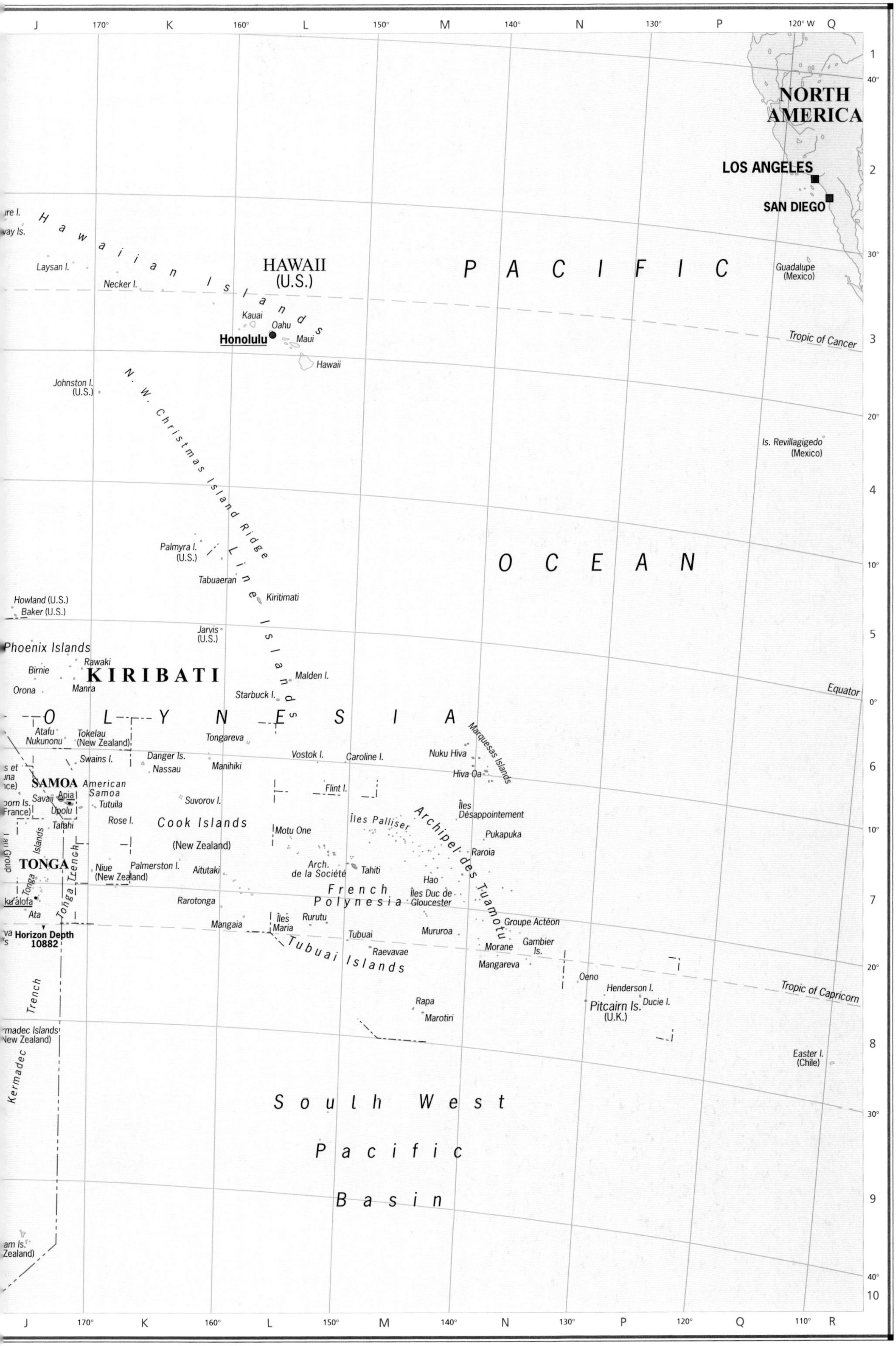
NORTH AMERICA
LOS ANGELES
SAN DIEGO
Guadalupe (Mexico)
Tropic of Cancer
PACIFIC
OCEAN
HAWAII (U.S.)
Hawaiian Islands
Laysan I.
Necker I.
Kauai
Oahu
Honolulu
Maui
Hawaii
Johnston I. (U.S.)
N. W. Christmas Island Ridge
Is. Revillagigedo (Mexico)
Palmyra I. (U.S.)
Tabuaeran
Line Islands
Kiritimati
Howland (U.S.)
Baker (U.S.)
Jarvis (U.S.)
Phoenix Islands
Rawaki
Birnie
KIRIBATI
Orona
Manra
Malden I.
Starbuck I.
Equator
POLYNESIA
Atafu
Nukunonu
Tokelau (New Zealand)
Tongareva
Swains I.
Danger Is.
Nassau
Manihiki
Vostok I.
Caroline I.
Nuku Hiva
Marquesas Islands
Hiva Oa
SAMOA
American Samoa
Apia
Savaii
Upolu
Tutuila
Flint I.
Suvorov I.
Îles Désappointement
Îles Palliser
Archipel des Tuamotu
Tafahi
Rose I.
Cook Islands (New Zealand)
Motu One
Pukapuka
Raroia
TONGA
Tonga Islands
Tonga Trench
Niue (New Zealand)
Palmerston I.
Aitutaki
Arch. de la Société
Tahiti
Hao
French Polynesia
Îles Duc de Gloucester
Nuku'alofa
Rarotonga
Ata
Horizon Depth 10882
Mangaia
Îles Maria
Rurutu
Tubuai
Mururoa
Groupe Actéon
Tubuai Islands
Raevavae
Morane
Gambier Is.
Mangareva
Oeno
Henderson I.
Ducie I.
Tropic of Capricorn
Pitcairn Is. (U.K.)
Rapa
Marotiri
Kermadec Trench
Easter I. (Chile)
South West Pacific Basin
40°
30°
20°
10°
0°
170°
160°
150°
140°
130°
120° W
110°

Charlotte Pass, Australia : -23 °C or -9.4 °F

Cloncurry, Australia : 53 °C or 128 °F

29,642,000

3.3 per km² or 8.6 per sq mi

8,945,000 km² or 3,454,000 sq mi

14

Scale 1 : 13 800 000

0 200 400 600 km

0 100 200 300 miles

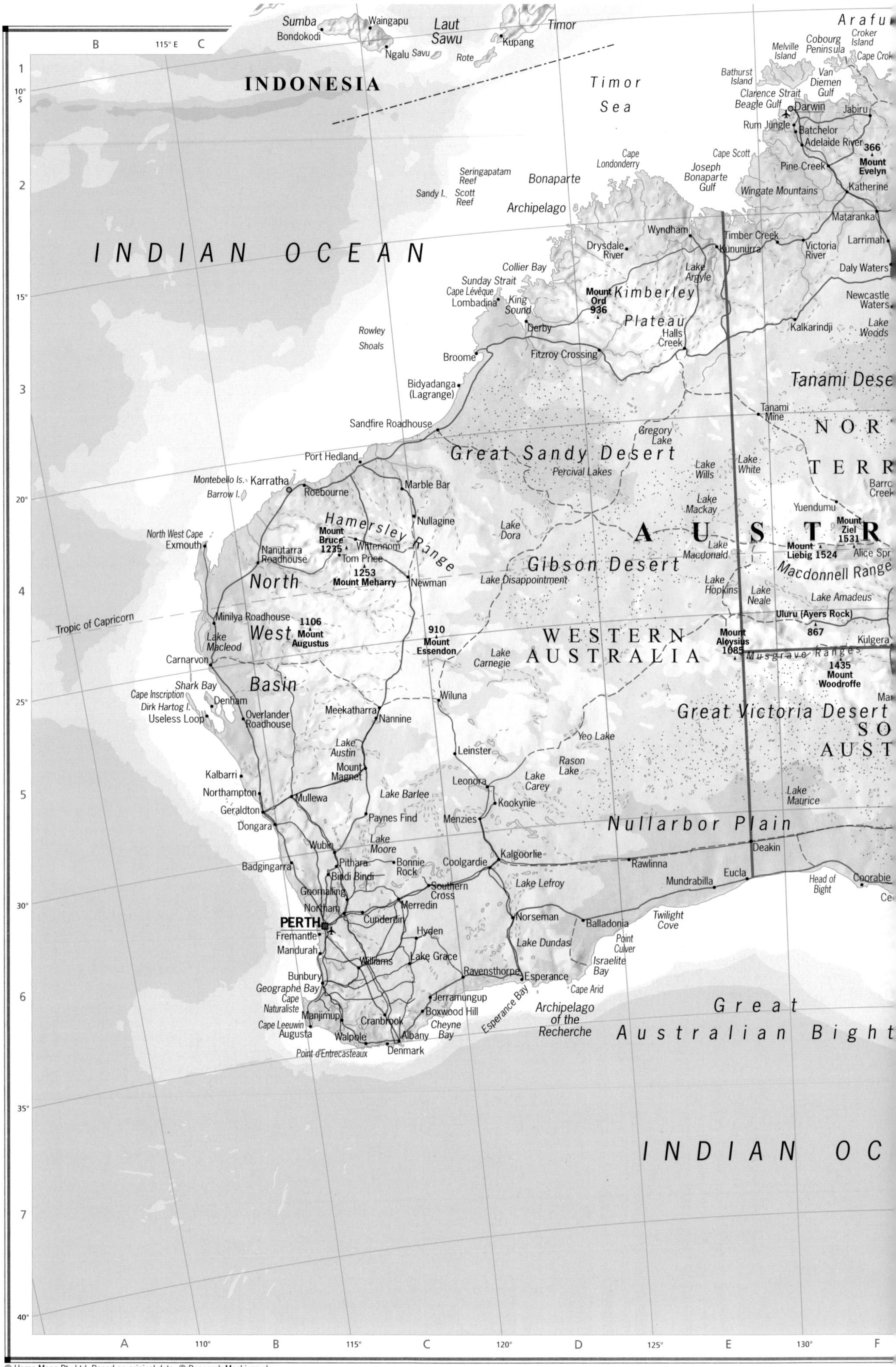

metres	feet
8000	26250
6000	19690
4000	13120
2000	6560
1000	3280
500	1640
200	656
0	0
656	200
3280	1000
6560	2000
13120	4000
19690	6000
26250	8000
feet	metres

- over 3 million
- 1 – 3 million
- 250 000 – 1 million
- 100 000 – 250 000
- 25 000 – 100 000
- under 25 000
- country capital underline
- state or province capital underline

87
116
135°
140°
145°
150°
155°
160°
10°
15°
20°
25°
30°
35°
40°
G
H
J
K
L
M
1
2
3
4
5
6
7
8
Port Moresby
PAPUA NEW GUINEA
Alotau
D'Entrecasteaux Islands
Louisiade Archipelago
Mulgrave I.
Moa (Banks Island)
Torres Strait
Prince of Wales Island
Cape York
Bamaga
Somerset
Cape Wessel
Wessel Islands
Cape Arnhem
Nangalala
Nhulunbuy
Cape Grenville
Duifken Point
Weipa
Albatross Bay
Aurukun
Cape York Peninsula
Cape Direction
Bickerton Island
Groote Eylandt
Gulf of Carpentaria
Numbulwar
Roper Bar
Coen
Princess Charlotte Bay
Cape Melville
Silver Plains
Sir Edward Pellew Group
Kowanyama
Laura
Cape Flattery
Cooktown
Borroloola
Wellesley Islands
Cape Crawford
Mornington I.
Bentinck I.
Port Douglas
Cairns
Mareeba
Karumba
Burketown
Normanton
1612 Mount Bartle Frere
Innisfail
Mount Garnet
Croydon
Georgetown
Forsayth
Barkly Tableland
Ingham
Halifax Bay
Greenvale
Mutarnee
Townsville
Camooweal
Ayr
Mount Isa
Cloncurry
Charters Towers
Bowen
The Whitsundays
Proserpine
Repulse Bay
Richmond
Hughenden
McKinlay
Dalrymple Lake
Mackay
Sarina
QUEENSLAND
Winton
Nebo
Broad Sound
Clairview
Boulia
Muttaburra
Clermont
Great Artesian Basin
Longreach
Barcaldine
Jericho
Emerald
Blackwater
Yeppoon
Rockhampton
Curtis I.
Capricorn Group
Simpson Desert
Blackall
Springsure
Gladstone
Jundah
Yaraka
Tambo
Banana
Biloela
Bundaberg
Sandy Cape
Birdsville
Betoota
Windorah
Lake Yamma Yamma
Augathella
Taroom
Eidsvold
Hervey Bay
Fraser I.
Maryborough
Lake Eyre Basin
Sturt Stony Desert
Charleville
Gayndah
Quilpie
Muckadilla
Roma
Gympie
Oodnadatta
Tirari Desert
Miles
Kingaroy
Caloundra
Lake Eyre North
Grey Range
Thargomindah
Glenmorgan
Moreton I.
St George
Moonie
Dalby
BRISBANE
Coober Pedy
Lake Eyre South
Cunnamulla
Toowoomba
North Stradbroke I.
Beenleigh
Hungerford
Dirranbandi
Bungunya
Goondiwindi
Mount Roberts 1387
Surfers Paradise
Gold Coast
Lake Blanche
Marree
Lake Callabonna
Tibooburra
Enngonia
Boggabilla
Casino
Cape Byron
Wanaaring
Moree
Tenterfield
Ballina
Leigh Creek
Lake Frome
Bourke
Brewarrina
Walgett
Glen Innes
Flinders Ranges
Glendambo
Lake Torrens
Pimba
White Cliffs
Darling
Louth
Narrabri
Round Mountain 1608
Grafton
Cobar
Coolabah
Gunnedah
Armidale
Coffs Harbour
Lake Gairdner
Broken Hill
Wilcannia
NEW SOUTH WALES
Coonabarabran
Tamworth
Black Sugarloaf 1494
Hawker
Gawler Ranges
Port Augusta
Menindee
Nyngan
Gilgandra
Quirindi
Port Macquarie
Whyalla
Orroroo
Dubbo
Kyancutta
Eyre Pen.
Port Pirie
Ivanhoe
Roto
Condobolin
Singleton
Taree
Cowell
Burra
Pooncarie
Murray River
1274
Orange
Cessnock
Newcastle
Spencer Gulf
Morgan
Murray
Marsden
Bathurst
Lithgow
Katoomba
1204
Mildura
Goolgowi
West Wyalong
Cowra
SYDNEY
ADELAIDE
Gawler
Renmark
Balranald
Hay
Cootamundra
Wollongong
Murray Bridge
Tailem Bend
Ouyen
Swan Hill
Narrandera
Wagga Wagga
Canberra
Nowra
Investigator Strait
Victor Harbor
Kingscote
Cape Borda
Kangaroo I.
Hopetoun
Deniliquin
Finley
Tumut
A.C.T.
Big Desert
VICTORIA
Albury
Bordertown
Lacepede Bay
Cape Jaffa
Robe
Little Desert
Bendigo
Shepparton
2229 Mount Kosciuszko
Cooma
Batemans Bay
Horsham
GREAT DIVIDING RANGE
Mount Bogong 1986
Omeo
Bombala
Hamilton
Ballarat
Yea
Eden
Mount Gambier
MELBOURNE
Geelong
Cape Howe
Portland
Cape Nelson
Warrnambool
Morwell
Bairnsdale
Sale
Korumburra
Apollo Bay
Walkerville
Port Albert
Wilson's Promontory
South East Point
King Island
Currie
Bass Strait
Flinders I.
Furneaux Group
Whitemark
Cape Barren I.
Cape Grim
Stanley
Burnie
George Town
Banks Strait
TASMANIA
Devonport
Launceston
1617 Mount Ossa
Queenstown
Swansea
Cape Forestier
Lake Gordon
Hobart
Port Arthur
South West Cape
Dover
South East Cape
Storm Bay
GREAT BARRIER REEF
CORAL SEA ISLANDS
CORAL SEA
TERRITORY (Australia)
Osprey Reef
Shark Reef
Bougainville Reef
Holmes Reefs
Diane Bank
Willis Group
Magdelaine Cays
Herald Cays
Diamond Islets
Flinders Reefs
Turtle I.
Tregosse Islets
Malay Reef
PACIFIC OCEAN
Swain Reefs
Townshend I.
Cato I.
Tropic of Capricorn
Lord Howe I.
Ball's Pyramid
TASMAN SEA
A.C.T. = Australian Capital Territory

Scale 1 : 4 650 000

0 100 200 km

0 50 100 miles

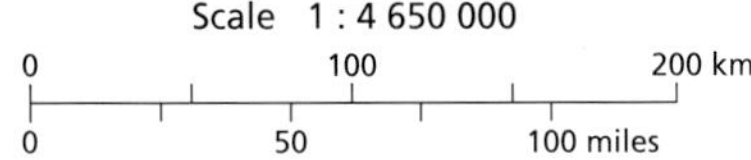

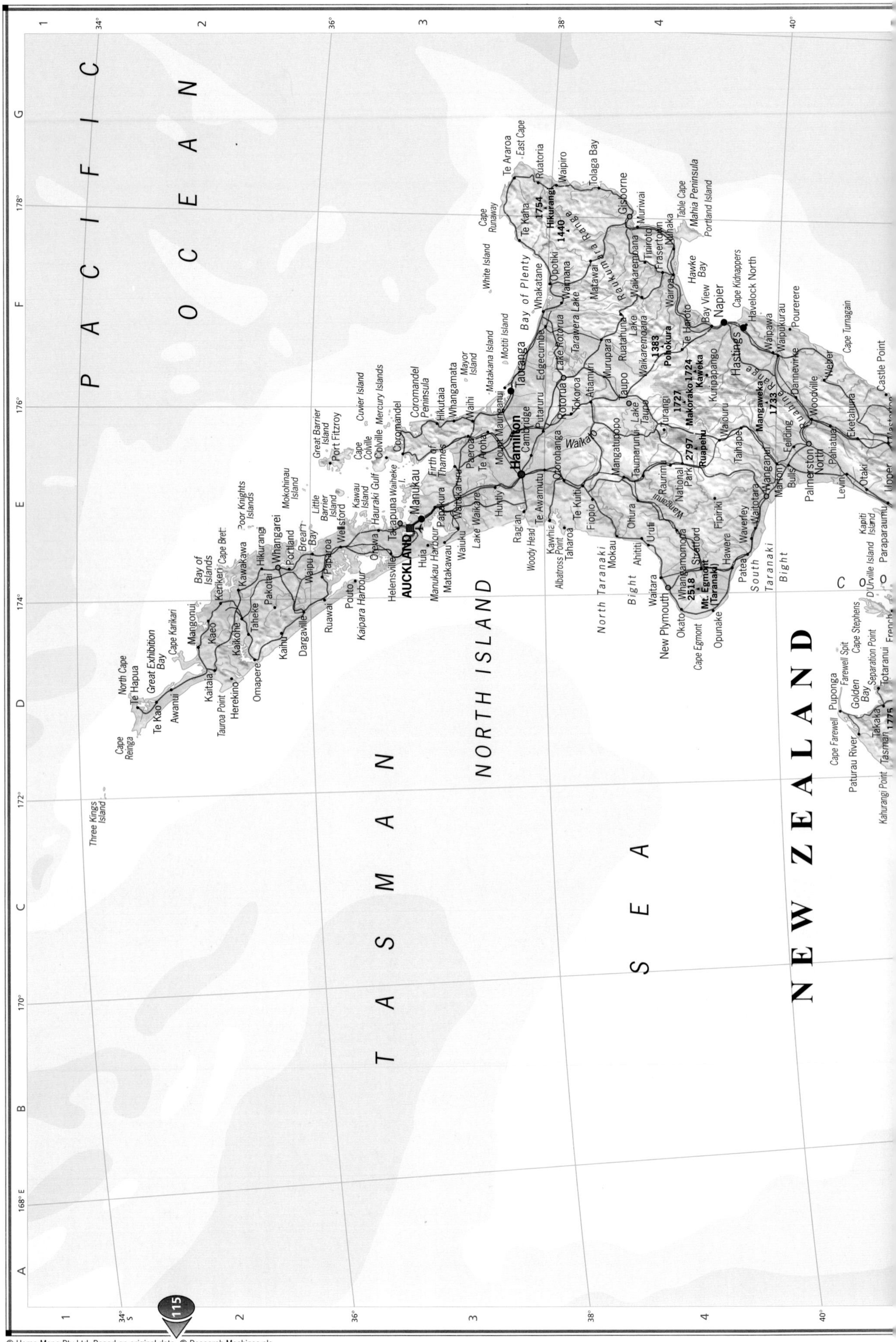

metres feet

metres	feet
8000	26250
6000	19690
4000	13120
2000	6560
1000	3280
500	1640
200	656
0	0
656	200
3280	1000
6560	2000
13120	4000
19690	6000
26250	8000
feet	metres

115

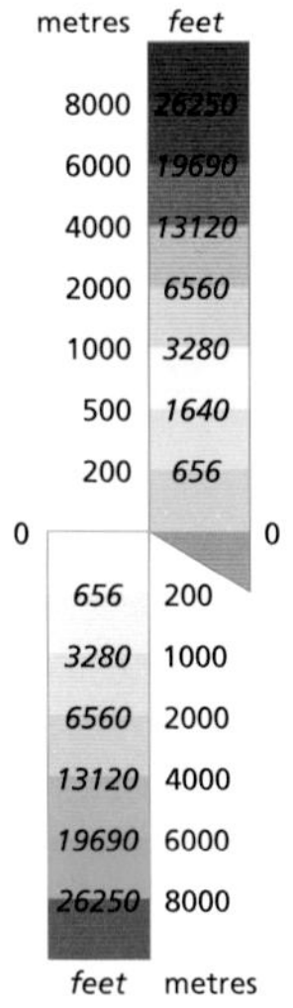

New Zealand

Antipodes Islands • Auckland Island
Campbell Island • Chatham Islands

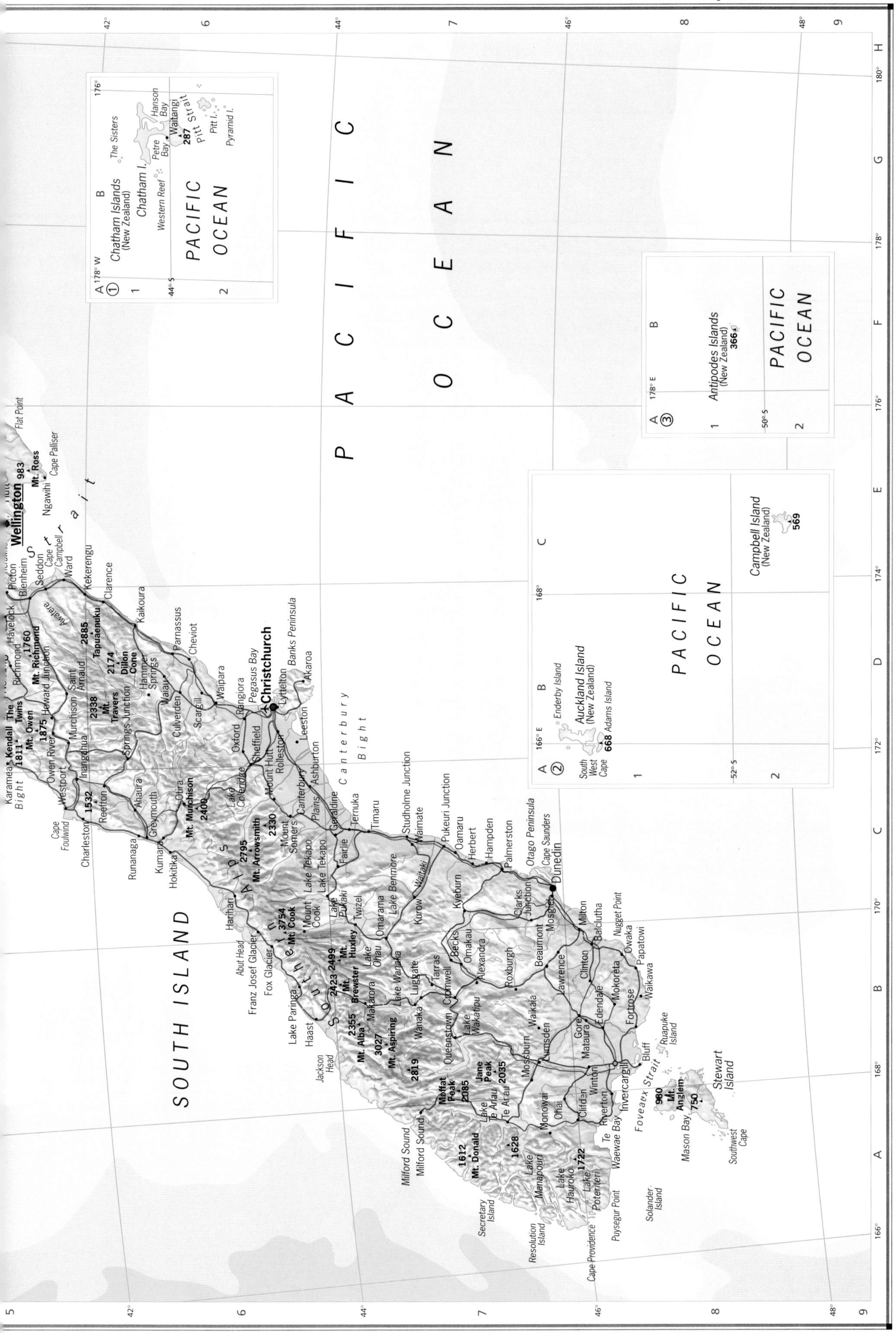

■ over 3 million	● 100 000 – 250 000	—— country capital underline
■ 1 – 3 million	◉ 25 000 – 100 000	
● 250 000 – 1 million	· under 25 000	

Scale 1 : 34 700 000

0 500 1000 1500 2000 km

0 500 1000 miles

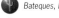

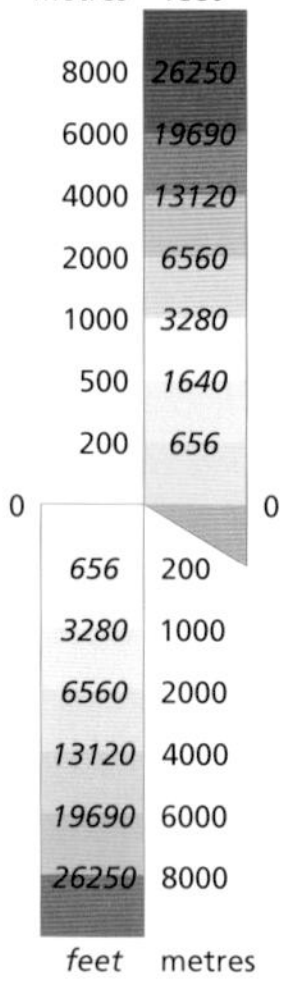

Mt. McKinley, Alaska : 6,194 m or 20,322 ft

Death Valley, USA : 86 m or 282 ft

Bateques, Mexico : 3.0 cm or 1.2 in

Henderson Lake, Canada : 650 cm or 256 in

Mississippi-Missouri, USA : 6,020 km or 3,740 mi

Lake Superior, USA/Canada : 82,260 km² or 31,760 sq mi

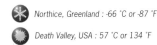

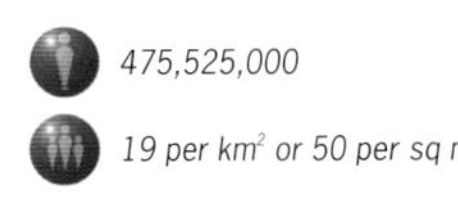

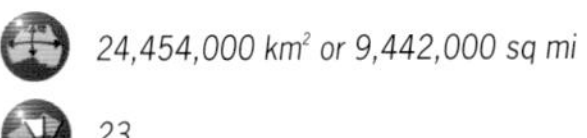

Northice, Greenland : -66 °C or -87 °F

Death Valley, USA : 57 °C or 134 °F

475,525,000

19 per km² or 50 per sq mi

24,454,000 km² or 9,442,000 sq mi

23

Scale 1 : 34 700 000

0 500 1000 1500 2000 km

0 500 1000 miles

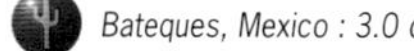

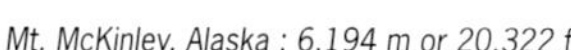

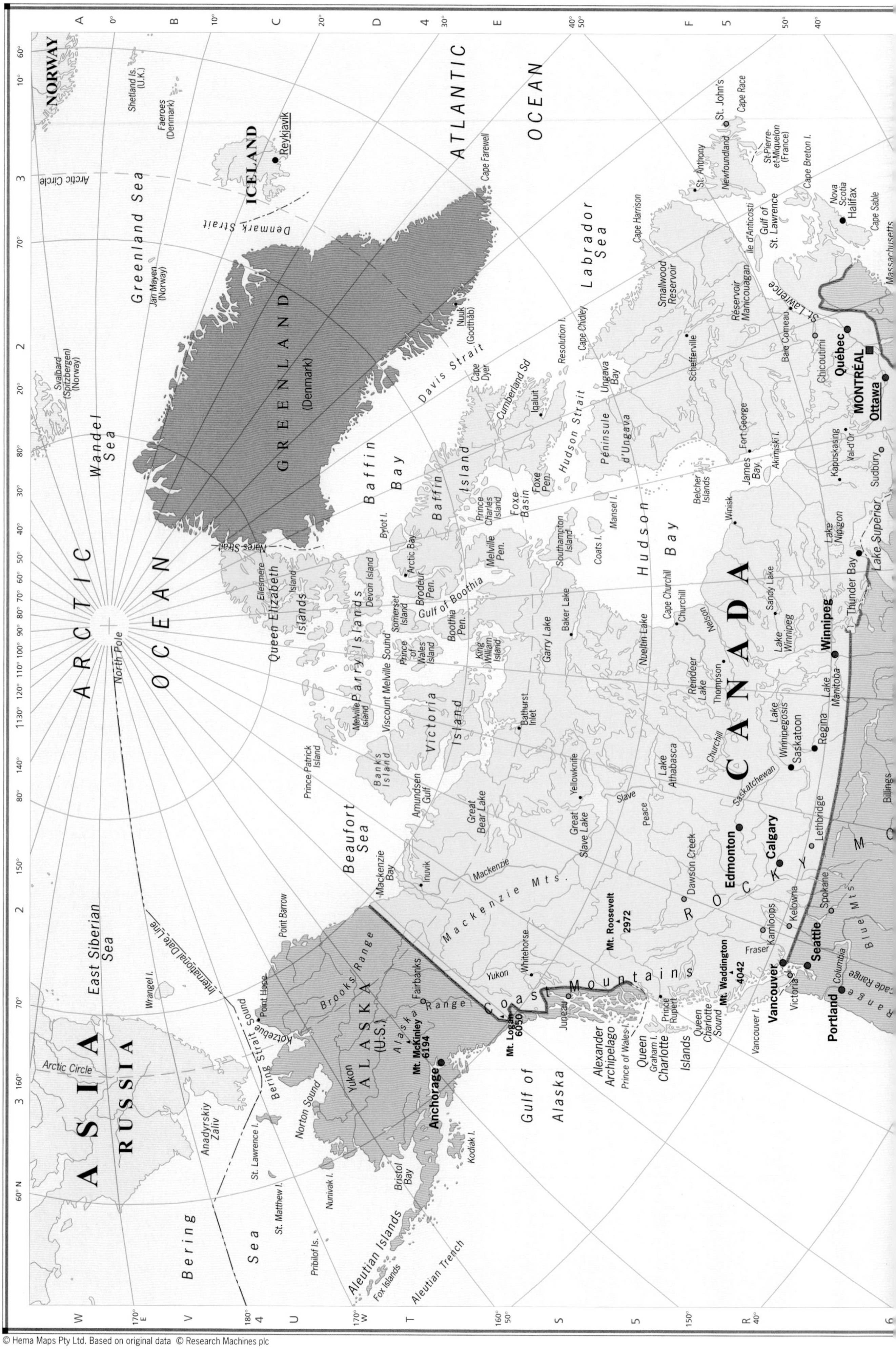

Mt. McKinley, Alaska : 6,194 m or 20,322 ft

Death Valley, USA : 86 m or 282 ft

Bateques, Mexico : 3.0 cm or 1.2 in

Henderson Lake, Canada : 650 cm or 256 in

Mississippi-Missouri, USA : 6,020 km or 3,740 mi

Lake Superior, USA/Canada : 82,260 km² or 31,760 sq mi

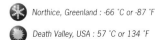

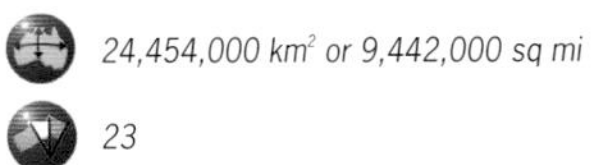

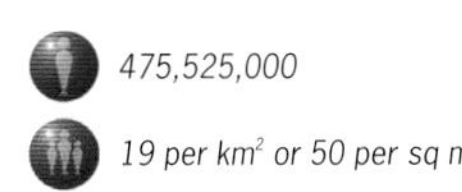

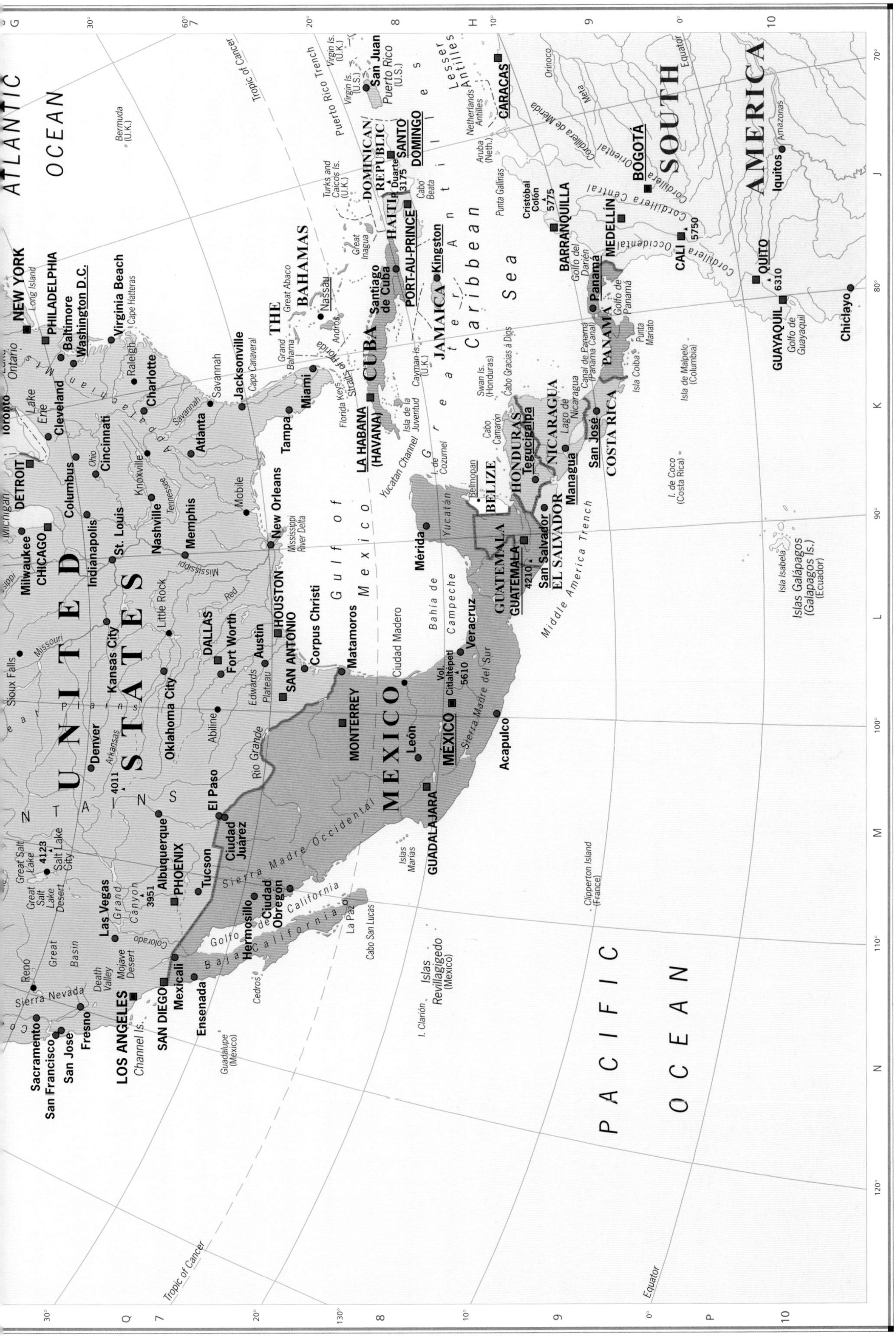

Northice, Greenland : -66 °C or -87 °F

Death Valley, USA : 57 °C or 134 °F

475,525,000

19 per km² or 50 per sq mi

24,454,000 km² or 9,442,000 sq mi

23

Scale 1 : 13 800 000

0 200 400 600 km

0 100 200 300 miles

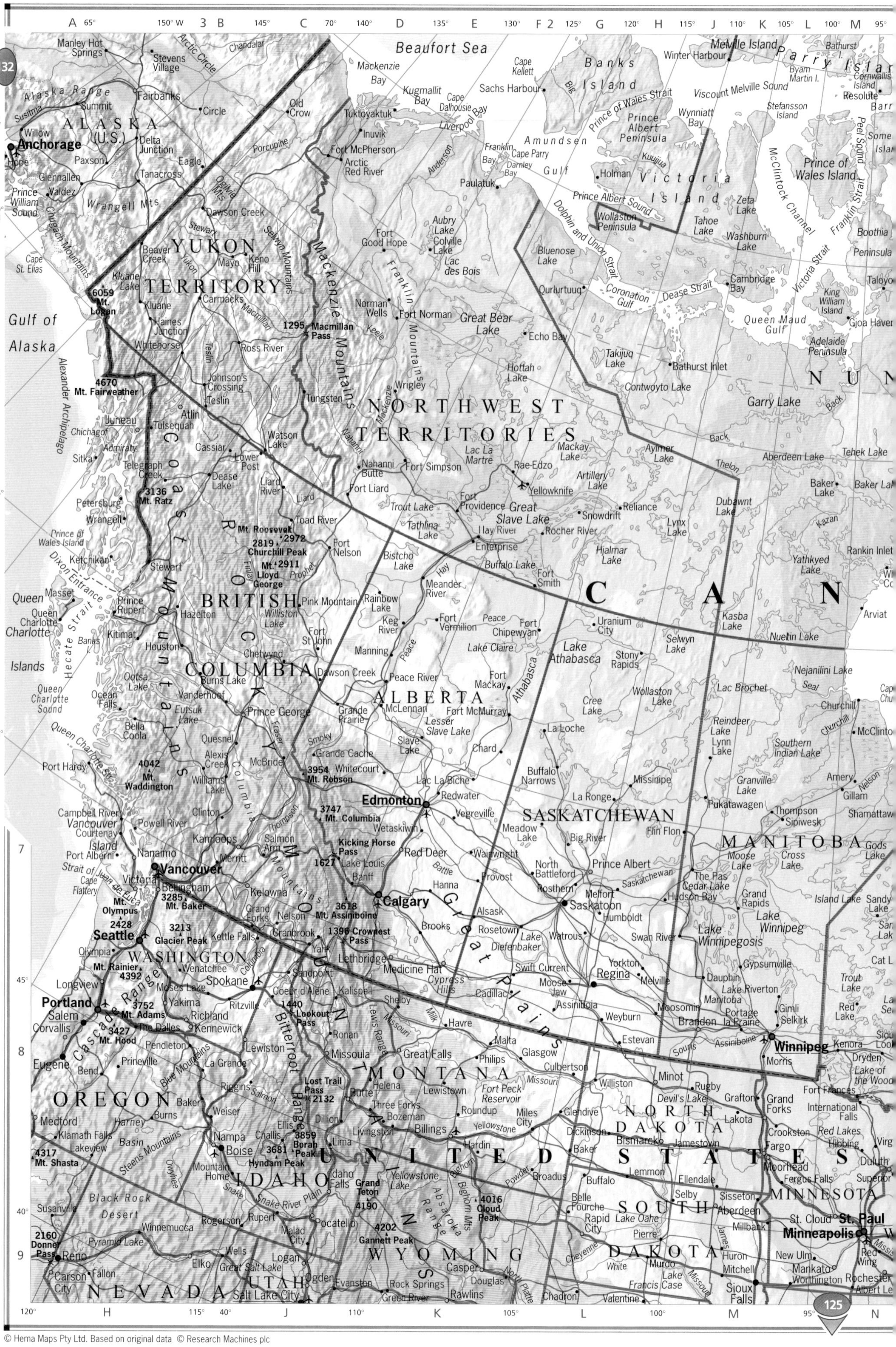

metres	feet
8000	26250
6000	19690
4000	13120
2000	6560
1000	3280
500	1640
200	656
0	0
656	200
3280	1000
6560	2000
13120	4000
19690	6000
26250	8000
feet	metres

132

125

- over 3 million
- 1 – 3 million
- 250 000 – 1 million
- 100 000 – 250 000
- 25 000 – 100 000
- under 25 000
- country capital underline
- state or province capital underline

GREENLAND
(Denmark)
Baffin Bay
Baffin Island
Davis Strait
LABRADOR SEA
ATLANTIC OCEAN
NEWFOUNDLAND AND LABRADOR
LABRADOR
QUÉBEC
ONTARIO
NEWFOUNDLAND
NOVA SCOTIA
NEW BRUNSWICK
PRINCE EDWARD ISLAND
MAINE
NEW HAMPSHIRE
VERMONT
MICHIGAN
NEW YORK
PENNSYLVANIA
RHODE ISLAND
HUDSON BAY
Foxe Basin
Hudson Strait
Ungava Bay
Péninsule d'Ungava
James Bay
Gulf of St. Lawrence
Lake Superior
Lake Huron
Lake Ontario
Lake Erie
Massachusetts Bay
Cabot Strait
Strait of Belle Isle
Bay of Fundy
Northumberland Strait
Arctic Circle
Kong Frederick VI Kyst
Devon Island
Jones Sound
Lancaster Sound
Bylot Island
Arctic Bay
Borden Peninsula
Brodeur Peninsula
Pond Inlet
Buchan Gulf
Scott Inlet
Cape Christian
Clyde River
Home Bay
Broughton Island
Cape Dyer
Igloolik
Rowley I.
Hall Beach
Melville Peninsula
Parry Bay
Prince Charles Island
Air Force I.
Nettilling Lake
Cumberland Peninsula
Pangnirtung
Cumberland Sound
Cape Mercy
Pelly Bay
Wales I.
Cape Dominion
Bowman Bay
Repulse Bay
Cape Dorchester
Amadjuak Lake
Hall Peninsula
Lemieux Islands
Wager Bay
Roes Welcome Sound
Foxe Peninsula
Foxe Channel
Iqaluit
Frobisher Bay
Loks Land
Southampton Island
Cape Dorset
Coral Harbour
Salisbury I.
Lake Harbour
Resolution Island
Nottingham I.
Cap de Nouvelle-France
Cape Chidley
Port Burwell
Chesterfield Inlet
Fisher Strait
Evans Strait
Coats Island
Mansel Island
Ivujivik
Salluit
Kangiqsujuaq
Quaqtaq
Akpatok Island
1729
Hebron
Cod Island
Nutak
Akulivik
Kangirsuk
Kangiqsualujjuaq
George
Nain
Puvurnituq
Ottawa Islands
Lac Payne
Kuujjuaq
Hopedale
Cape Harrison
Groswater Bay
Rigolet
Cartwright
Inukjuak
Lac Minto
Lake Melville
Port Hope Simpson
Battle Harbour
Belle Isle
Cape Bauld
St. Anthony
King George Is.
Sleeper Is.
Nastapoka Is.
Lac à l'Eau Claire
Schefferville
Smallwood Reservoir
Churchill
Churchill Falls
St-Augustin
Long Range Mts
Roddickton
White Bay
Fogo I.
Notre Dame Bay
Bonavista Bay
Gander
St. John's
Belcher Islands
Lac Bienville
Réservoir Caniapiscau
Labrador City
Wabush
Ashuanipi
Ashuanipi Lake
Petit Mécatina
Deer Lake
Grand Falls
Fort Severn
Kuujjuarapik
Long I.
Rés. de La Grande 4
Cape Henrietta Maria
Rés. de La Grande 2
Rés. de La Grande 3
Fort George
Réservoir Opinaca
Monts Otish
1021
Natashquan
Havre-St-Pierre
Stephenville
Harbour Breton
Fortune Bay
Grand Bank
Trepassey
Cape Race
Winisk
Severn
Big Trout Lake
Ekwan
Attawapiskat
Akimiski Island
Eastmain
Réservoir Manicouagan
Île d'Anticosti
Port-Menier
Cape Ray
Channel-Port aux Basques
St-Pierre-et-Miquelon (France)
Winisk Lake
Charlton I.
Rupert
Manouane Lake
Sept-Îles
Péninsule de Gaspé
Îles de la Madeleine
Moosonee
Fort Rupert
Albany
Baie du Poste
Chute des Passes
Manicouagan
Lac Evans
St. Lawrence
Matane
Sydney
Cape Breton Island
Lac St. Joseph
Fort Hope
Chibougamau
Mistassini
Réservoir Pipmuacan
Les Escoumins
Rimouski
Missinaibi
Harricanaw
Coral
Miquelon
Chicoutimi
Bathurst
Charlottetown
Port Hawkesbury
Lake Nipigon
Armstrong
Nakina
Hearst
Réservoir Gouin
Lac St-Jean
Jonquière
Edmundston
New Glasgow
Truro
Sable I.
Longlac
Geraldton
Kapuskasing
Cochrane
Amos
Senneterre
Baie St. Paul
Presque Isle
Moncton
Amherst
Nipigon
Timmins
Lake Abitibi
Val-d'Or
La Tuque
Montmagny
Houlton
Fredericton
Dartmouth
Halifax
Thunder Bay
Marathon
Foleyet
Rouyn
Québec
Lévis
St John
Kirkland Lake
Réservoir Cabonga
Jackman
Stephen
Bridgewater
Isle Royale
Chapleau
Wawa
Mont-Laurier
Trois Rivières
Liverpool
Copper Harbor
Keweenaw Pen.
Cobalt
Sorel
Sherbrooke
Yarmouth
Shelburne
Cape Sable
Apostle Is.
North Bay
Ottawa
MONTREAL
White Mts
Sault Ste. Marie
Sudbury
Pembroke
Cornwall
Granby
Mt. Washington 1917
Augusta
Ironwood
Marquette
Blind River
Manitoulin I.
Smiths Falls
Plattsburgh
Burlington
Lewiston
Manistique
Sault Ste Marie
Georgian Bay
Parry Sound
Huntsville
Ogdensburg
Montpelier
Portland
Rhinelander
Iron Mountain
Escanaba
Tobermory
Orillia
Kingston
1629
Alpena
Owen Sound
Barrie
Peterborough
Watertown
Portsmouth
Concord
Marinette
Wausau
Green Bay
Traverse City
Oshawa
Toronto
Brattleboro
Boston
Appleton
Oshkosh
Sheboygan
Lake Michigan
Mt. Pleasant
Bay City
Kitchener
Rochester
Utica
Albany
Syracuse
Worcester
Cape Cod
Providence
New Bedford
Springfield
Hartford
Grand Rapids
Saginaw
Flint
London
Hamilton
St. Catharines
Buffalo
Catskill Mts. 1295
Binghamton
New Haven
Bridgeport
Muskegon
Milwaukee
Lansing
Ann Arbor
DETROIT
Sarnia
Chatham
Windsor
Jamestown
Erie
Meadville
Scranton
Paterson
Newark
NEW YORK
Long I.
Upernavik
Kangersuatsiaq (Prøven)
Upernavik Kujalleq
Svartenhuk Halvø
Ukkusissat
Uummannaq Fjord
Nuussuaq
Qeqertarsuatsiaq (Disko)
Ilulissat (Jakobshavn)
Qeqertarsuup Tunua (Disko Bugt)
Kangaatsiaq
Tasiilaq (Angmagssalik)
Gyldenløues Fjord
Sisimiut (Holsteinsborg)
Maniitsoq (Sukkertoppen)
Napasoq
Kangeq (Kap Cort Adelaer)
Kangerluarsoruseq (Færingehavn)
Nuuk (Godthåb)
Qeqertarsuatsiaat (Fiskenæsset)
Paamiut (Frederikshåb)
Ivittuut
Nanortalik
Nunarsuit
Lindenow Fjord
Uummannarsuaq (Kap Farvel)

Scale 1 : 15 500 000

0 200 400 600 km

0 100 200 300 miles

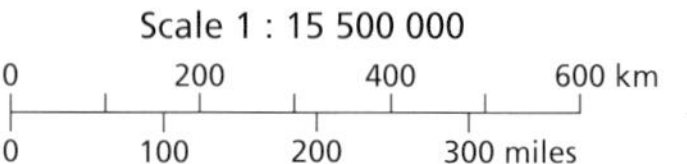

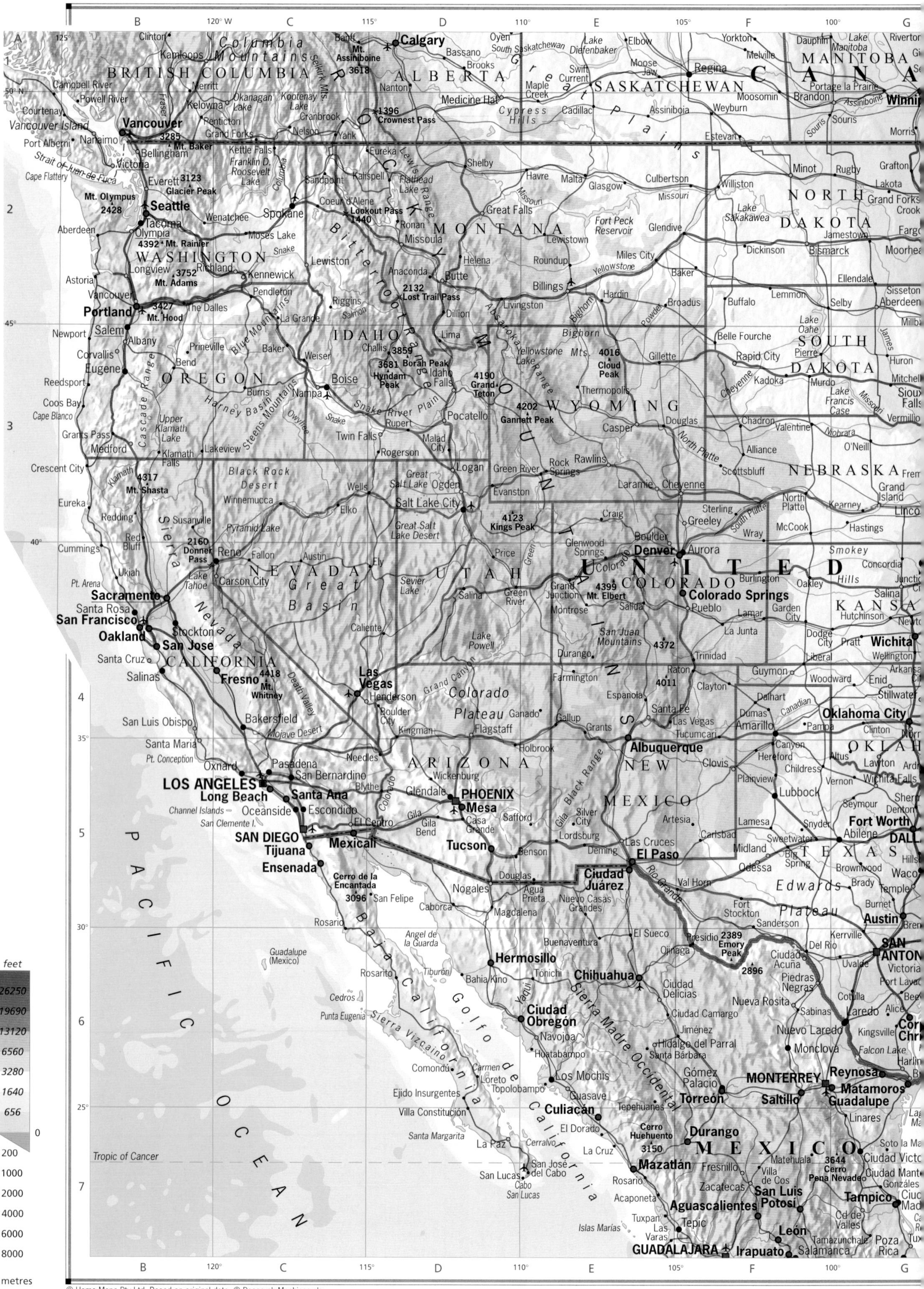

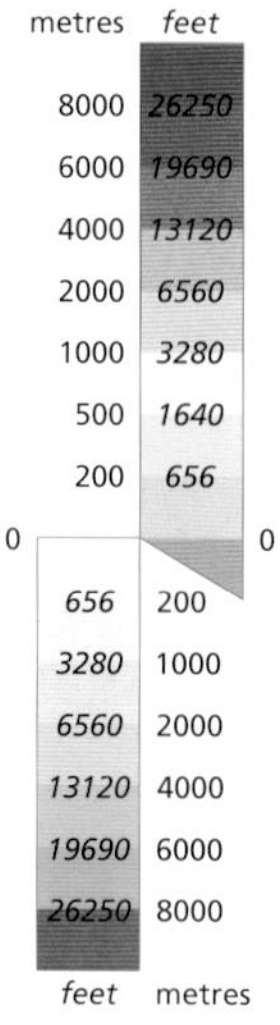

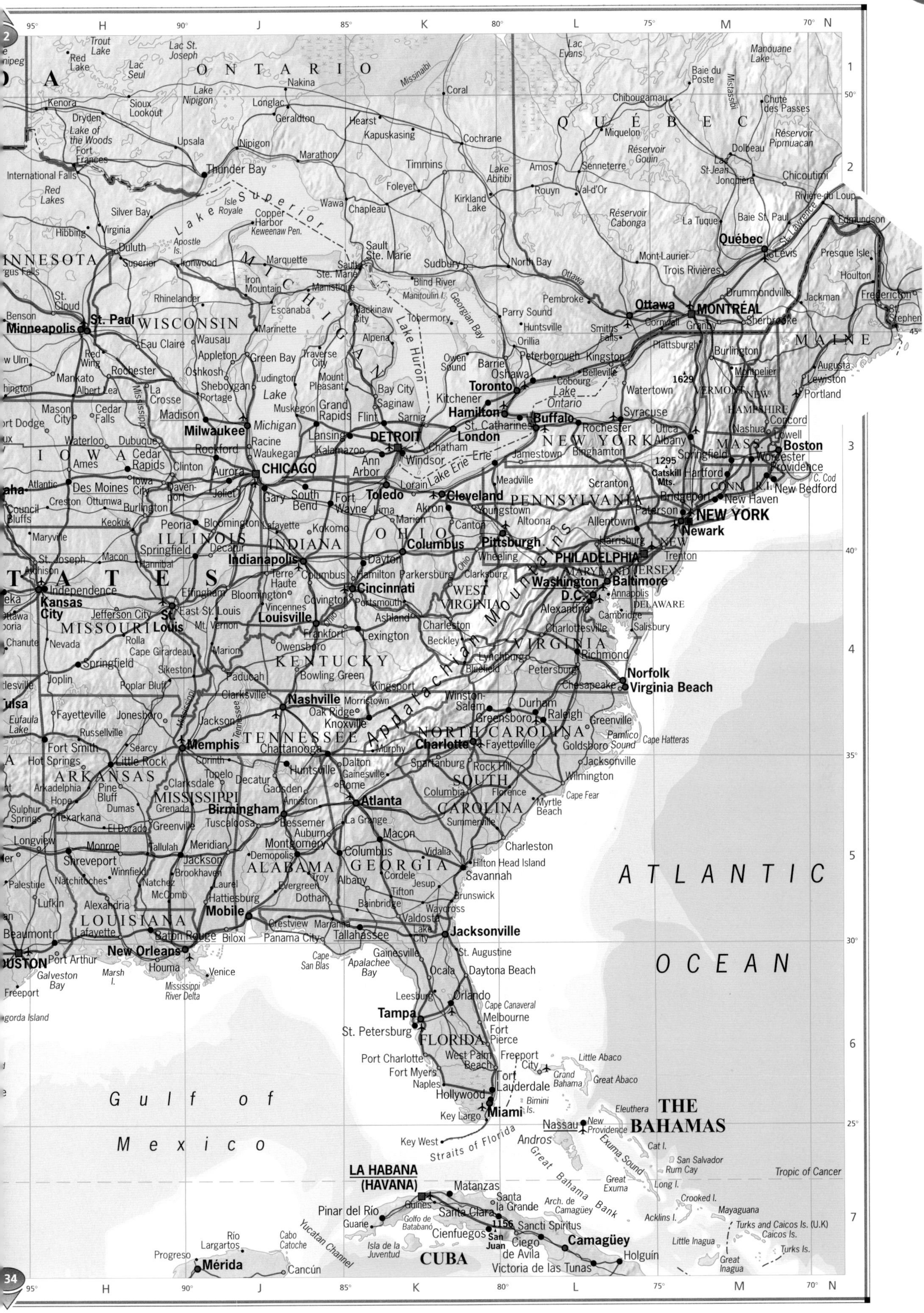

95° H 90° J 85° K 80° L 75° M 70° N
1 2 3 4 5 6 7
50° 45° 40° 35° 30° 25°
O N T A R I O
Q U É B E C
MINNESOTA
WISCONSIN
MICHIGAN
IOWA
ILLINOIS
INDIANA
OHIO
PENNSYLVANIA
NEW YORK
MAINE
VERMONT
NEW HAMPSHIRE
MASS.
CONN.
R.I.
NEW JERSEY
DELAWARE
MARYLAND
WEST VIRGINIA
VIRGINIA
KENTUCKY
TENNESSEE
NORTH CAROLINA
SOUTH CAROLINA
GEORGIA
ALABAMA
MISSISSIPPI
LOUISIANA
ARKANSAS
MISSOURI
FLORIDA
STATES
THE BAHAMAS
CUBA
LA HABANA
(HAVANA)
Lake Superior
Lake Michigan
Lake Huron
Lake Erie
Lake Ontario
Georgian Bay
Lake Nipigon
Lake of the Woods
Appalachian Mountains
ATLANTIC
OCEAN
Gulf of Mexico
Straits of Florida
Yucatan Channel
Great Bahama Bank
Exuma Sound
Tropic of Cancer
Cape Hatteras
Cape Fear
Cape Canaveral
C. Cod
Pamlico Sound
Apalachee Bay
Cape San Blas
Mississippi River Delta
Galveston Bay
Marsh I.
Réservoir Gouin
Réservoir Cabonga
Réservoir Pipmuacan
St. Lawrence
Ottawa
Mississippi
Ohio
Tennessee
Missinaibi
Mistassibi
1629
1295
Catskill Mts.
1156
Thunder Bay
Duluth
Minneapolis
St. Paul
Milwaukee
CHICAGO
DETROIT
Toledo
Cleveland
Buffalo
Toronto
Hamilton
London
Ottawa
MONTRÉAL
Québec
Pittsburgh
Columbus
Cincinnati
Indianapolis
Louisville
St. Louis
Kansas City
Nashville
Memphis
Birmingham
Atlanta
Charlotte
Norfolk
Virginia Beach
Washington D.C.
Baltimore
PHILADELPHIA
NEW YORK
Newark
Boston
Providence
Hartford
New Haven
Jacksonville
Tampa
Orlando
Miami
Mobile
New Orleans
Baton Rouge
HOUSTON
Nassau
Camagüey
Mérida
Cancún
Holguín
Santa Clara
Cienfuegos
Matanzas
Pinar del Río

over 3 million
1 – 3 million
250 000 – 1 million
100 000 – 250 000
25 000 – 100 000
under 25 000
country capital underline
state or province capital underline

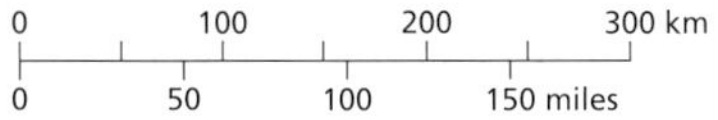
Scale 1 : 7 200 000
0
100
200
300 km
0
50
100
150 miles

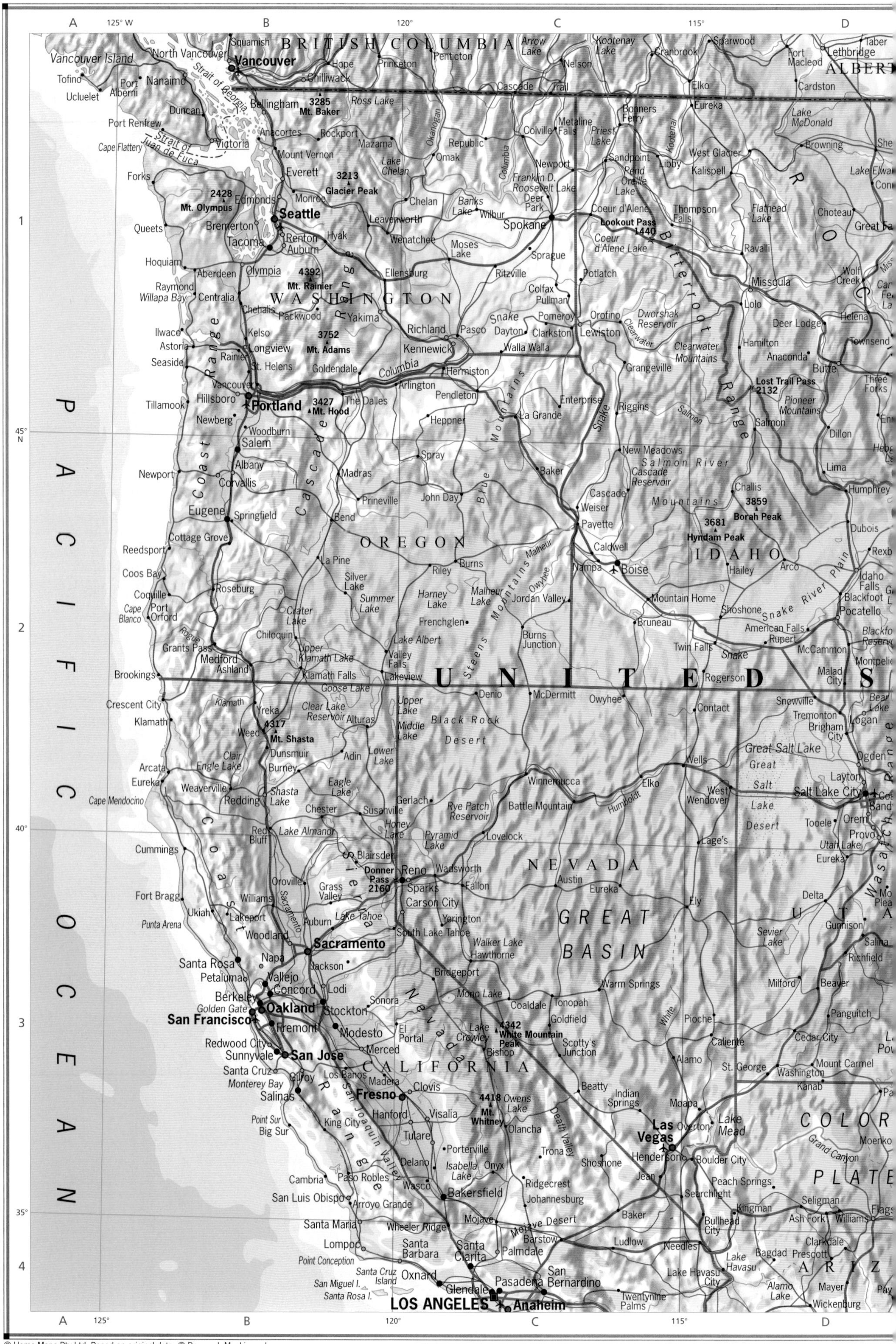
A
B
C
D
125° W
120°
115°
45° N
40°
35°
1
2
3
4
BRITISH COLUMBIA
ALBERTA
WASHINGTON
OREGON
IDAHO
NEVADA
CALIFORNIA
UNITED STATES
UTAH
ARIZONA
PACIFIC OCEAN
Vancouver Island
Vancouver
North Vancouver
Squamish
Nanaimo
Port Alberni
Tofino
Ucluelet
Duncan
Victoria
Port Renfrew
Cape Flattery
Strait of Georgia
Strait of Juan de Fuca
Hope
Chilliwack
Princeton
Penticton
Arrow Lake
Kootenay Lake
Nelson
Trail
Cascade
Cranbrook
Sparwood
Elko
Fort Macleod
Lethbridge
Taber
Cardston
Eureka
Bellingham
3285 Mt. Baker
Ross Lake
Anacortes
Rockport
Mount Vernon
Everett
3213 Glacier Peak
Mazama
Okanogan
Omak
Republic
Colville
Metaline Falls
Priest Lake
Bonners Ferry
Sandpoint
Pend Oreille Lake
Libby
West Glacier
Kalispell
Browning
Lake McDonald
Forks
2428 Mt. Olympus
Edmonds
Monroe
Seattle
Bremerton
Queets
Tacoma
Renton
Auburn
Hyak
Lake Chelan
Chelan
Leavenworth
Wenatchee
Banks Lake
Wilbur
Franklin D. Roosevelt Lake
Newport
Deer Park
Spokane
Coeur d'Alene
Coeur d'Alene Lake
Lookout Pass 1440
Thompson Falls
Flathead Lake
Choteau
Great Falls
Hoquiam
Aberdeen
Olympia
4392 Mt. Rainier
Ellensburg
Moses Lake
Ritzville
Sprague
Potlatch
Colfax
Pullman
Ravalli
Missoula
Lolo
Raymond
Willapa Bay
Centralia
Chehalis
Packwood
Yakima
Richland
Pasco
Kennewick
Snake
Dayton
Pomeroy
Clarkston
Lewiston
Orofino
Dworshak Reservoir
Clearwater
Clearwater Mountains
Deer Lodge
Helena
Ilwaco
Astoria
Seaside
Kelso
Longview
Rainier
St. Helens
3752 Mt. Adams
Goldendale
Walla Walla
Hermiston
Grangeville
Hamilton
Anaconda
Butte
Townsend
Vancouver
Hillsboro
Portland
3427 Mt. Hood
The Dalles
Columbia
Arlington
Pendleton
Enterprise
Riggins
Lost Trail Pass 2132
Pioneer Mountains
Three Forks
Tillamook
Newberg
Woodburn
Salem
Heppner
La Grande
Salmon
Dillon
Newport
Albany
Corvallis
Madras
Spray
Baker
New Meadows
Salmon River Mountains
Cascade Reservoir
Lima
Challis
3859 Borah Peak
Humphrey
Eugene
Springfield
Prineville
John Day
Blue Mountains
Cascade
Weiser
Payette
3681 Hyndam Peak
Dubois
Reedsport
Cottage Grove
Bend
Caldwell
Nampa
Boise
Hailey
Arco
Rexburg
Idaho Falls
Coos Bay
Coquille
Port Orford
Cape Blanco
Roseburg
La Pine
Silver Lake
Summer Lake
Riley
Burns
Harney Lake
Malheur Lake
Jordan Valley
Steens Mountains
Owyhee
Mountain Home
Snake River Plain
Blackfoot
Pocatello
Crater Lake
Frenchglen
Shoshone
American Falls
Rupert
Twin Falls
McCammon
Grants Pass
Rogue
Chiloquin
Upper Klamath Lake
Lake Albert
Valley Falls
Burns Junction
Bruneau
Medford
Ashland
Klamath Falls
Lakeview
Brookings
Goose Lake
Denio
McDermitt
Owyhee
Rogerson
Malad City
Crescent City
Klamath
Yreka
Clear Lake Reservoir
Alturas
Upper Lake
Middle Lake
Black Rock Desert
Contact
Snowville
Tremonton
Brigham City
Logan
Bear Lake
4317 Mt. Shasta
Weed
Dunsmuir
Adin
Lower Lake
Great Salt Lake
Ogden
Layton
Salt Lake City
Arcata
Eureka
Clair Engle Lake
Burney
Eagle Lake
Winnemucca
Elko
Wells
West Wendover
Great Salt Lake Desert
Weaverville
Redding
Shasta Lake
Cape Mendocino
Chester
Susanville
Gerlach
Rye Patch Reservoir
Battle Mountain
Humboldt
Tooele
Orem
Provo
Red Bluff
Lake Almanor
Honey Lake
Pyramid Lake
Lovelock
Lage's
Utah Lake
Cummings
Blairsden
Donner Pass 2160
Reno
Sparks
Wadsworth
Fallon
Eureka
Austin
Fort Bragg
Oroville
Grass Valley
Carson City
Yerington
Ely
Delta
Williams
Ukiah
Lakeport
Lake Tahoe
Auburn
Sacramento
GREAT BASIN
Punta Arena
Woodland
South Lake Tahoe
Walker Lake
Hawthorne
Sevier Lake
Gunnison
Salina
Richfield
Santa Rosa
Petaluma
Napa
Vallejo
Concord
Jackson
Bridgeport
Warm Springs
Milford
Beaver
Berkeley
Golden Gate
Oakland
San Francisco
Lodi
Stockton
Sonora
Mono Lake
Coaldale
Tonopah
Goldfield
Pioche
Panguitch
Fremont
Modesto
El Portal
Crowley Lake
4342 White Mountain Peak
Bishop
Scotty's Junction
Caliente
Cedar City
Redwood City
Sunnyvale
San Jose
Merced
Santa Cruz
Gilroy
Monterey Bay
Los Banos
Madera
Sierra Nevada
Alamo
St. George
Washington
Kanab
Mount Carmel
Salinas
Fresno
Clovis
4418 Mt. Whitney
Owens Lake
Death Valley
Beatty
Indian Springs
Moapa
Point Sur
Big Sur
King City
Hanford
Visalia
Olancha
Las Vegas
Overton
Lake Mead
COLORADO PLATEAU
Grand Canyon
Tulare
Porterville
Trona
Shoshone
Henderson
Boulder City
Moenkopi
San Joaquin Valley
Delano
Isabella Lake
Onyx
Jean
Cambria
Paso Robles
Wasco
Ridgecrest
Peach Springs
San Luis Obispo
Arroyo Grande
Bakersfield
Johannesburg
Searchlight
Kingman
Seligman
Santa Maria
Wheeler Ridge
Mojave
Mojave Desert
Baker
Bullhead City
Ash Fork
Williams
Lompoc
Santa Barbara
Santa Clarita
Barstow
Palmdale
Ludlow
Needles
Clarkdale
Prescott
Point Conception
Oxnard
Lake Havasu
Lake Havasu City
Bagdad
Santa Cruz Island
San Miguel I.
Santa Rosa I.
Glendale
Pasadena
San Bernardino
Twentynine Palms
Alamo Lake
Mayer
Wickenburg
LOS ANGELES
Anaheim

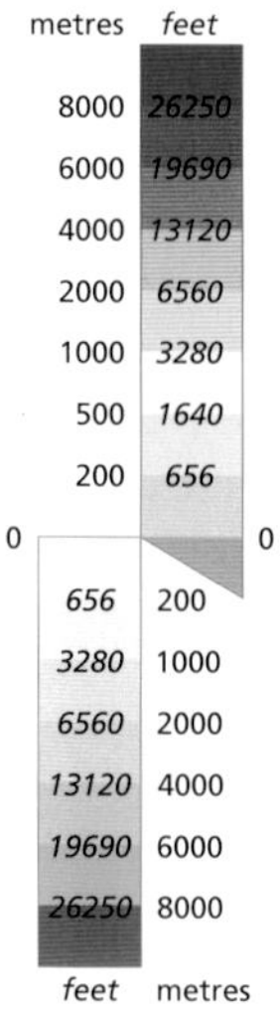
metres
feet
8000
26250
6000
19690
4000
13120
2000
6560
1000
3280
500
1640
200
656
0
0
656
200
3280
1000
6560
2000
13120
4000
19690
6000
26250
8000
feet
metres

Northwest United States

Colorado • Idaho • Montana • Nebraska • Nevada
North Dakota • Oregon • South Dakota • Utah • Washington • Wyoming

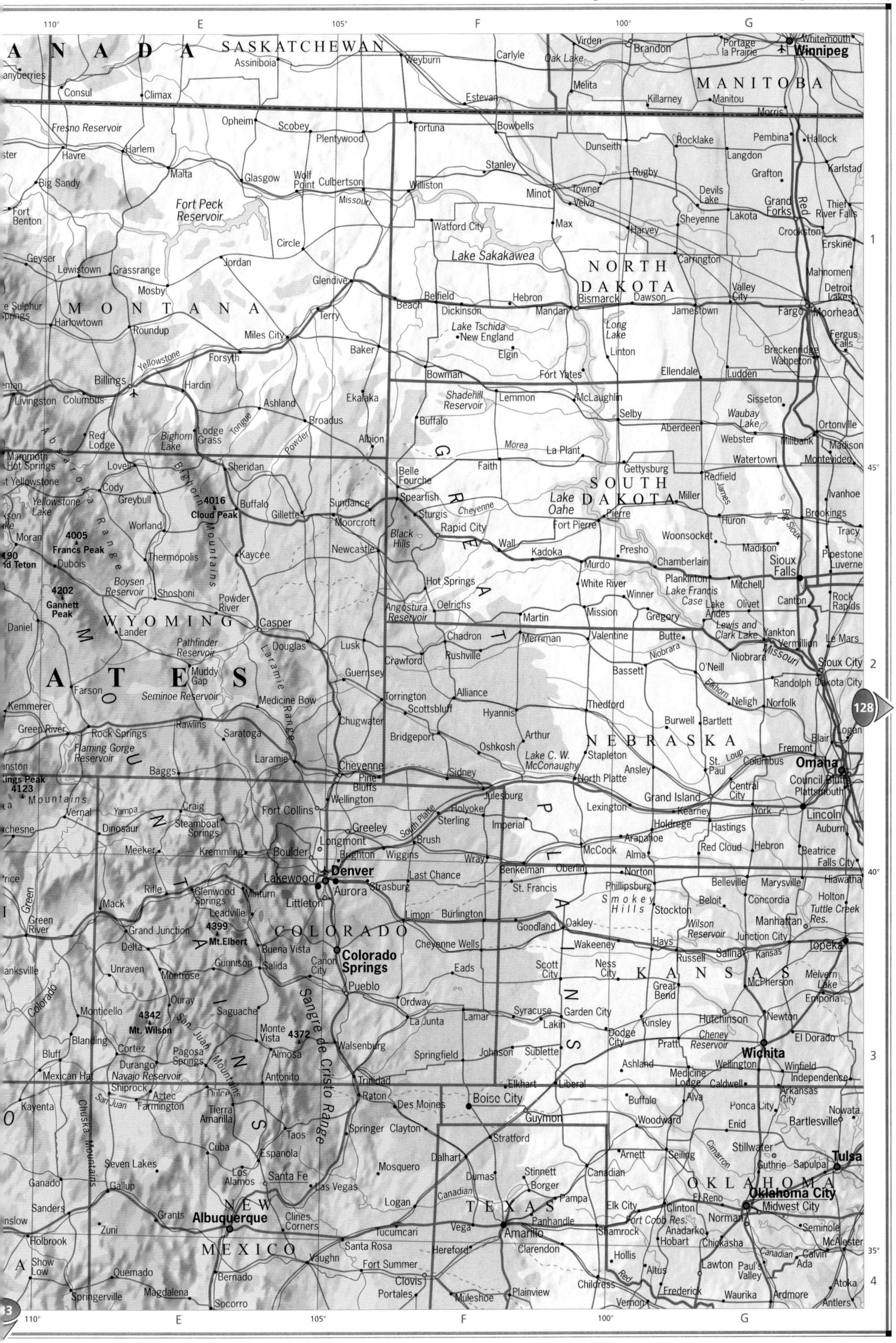

■ over 3 million
■ 1 – 3 million
● 250 000 – 1 million
● 100 000 – 250 000
○ 25 000 – 100 000
• under 25 000
country capital underline
state or province capital underline

Scale 1 : 7 200 000

0 100 200 300 km

0 50 100 150 miles

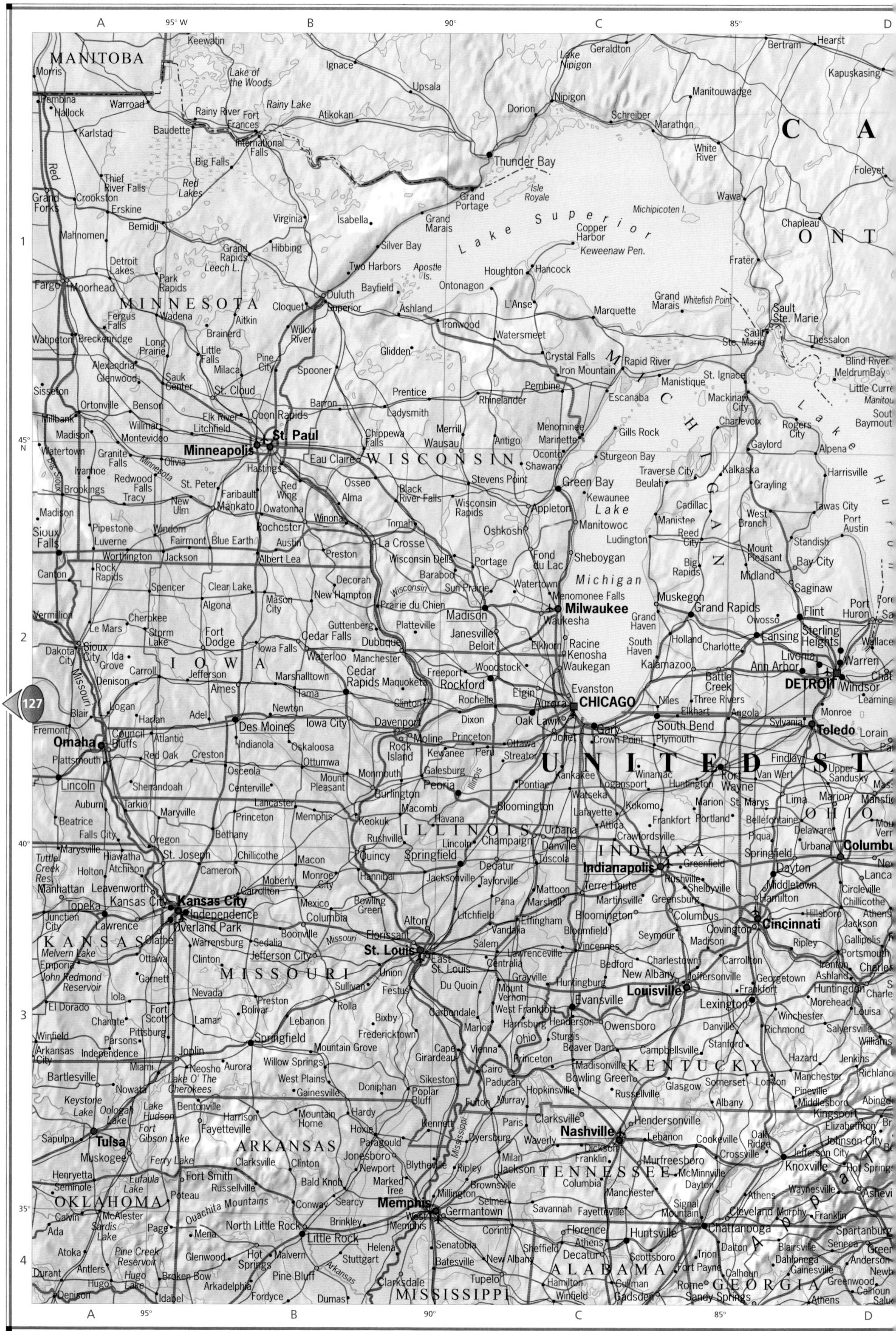

metres	feet
8000	26250
6000	19690
4000	13120
2000	6560
1000	3280
500	1640
200	656
0	0
656	200
3280	1000
6560	2000
13120	4000
19690	6000
26250	8000
feet	metres

Northeast United States

Connecticut • Delaware • District of Columbia • Illinois • Indiana • Iowa • Maine • Maryland • Massachusetts • Michigan
Minnesota • New Hampshire • New Jersey • New York • Ohio • Pennsylvania • Rhode Island • Vermont • West Virginia • Wisconsin

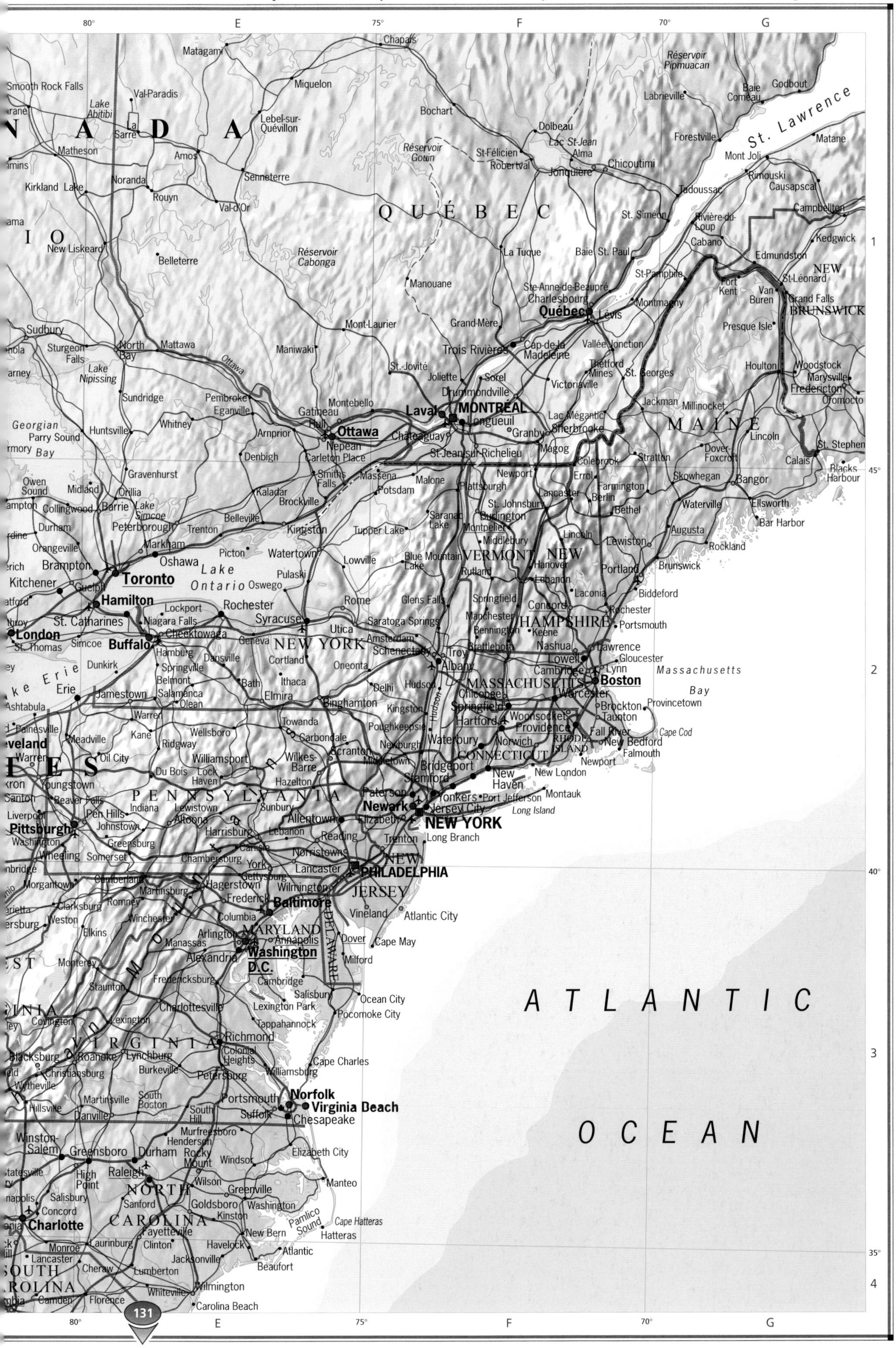

131

■ over 3 million	● 100 000 – 250 000	country capital underline
■ 1 – 3 million	◉ 25 000 – 100 000	state or province capital underline
● 250 000 – 1 million	• under 25 000	

Scale 1 : 7 200 000

0 100 200 300 km

0 50 100 150 miles

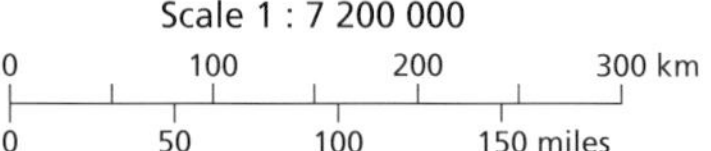

metres feet
8000 26250
6000 19690
4000 13120
2000 6560
1000 3280
500 1640
200 656
0 0
656 200
3280 1000
6560 2000
13120 4000
19690 6000
26250 8000
feet metres

Alabama • Arkansas • The Bahamas • Florida • Georgia • Kentucky • Louisiana
Mississippi • Missouri • North Carolina • South Carolina • Tennessee • Texas • Virginia

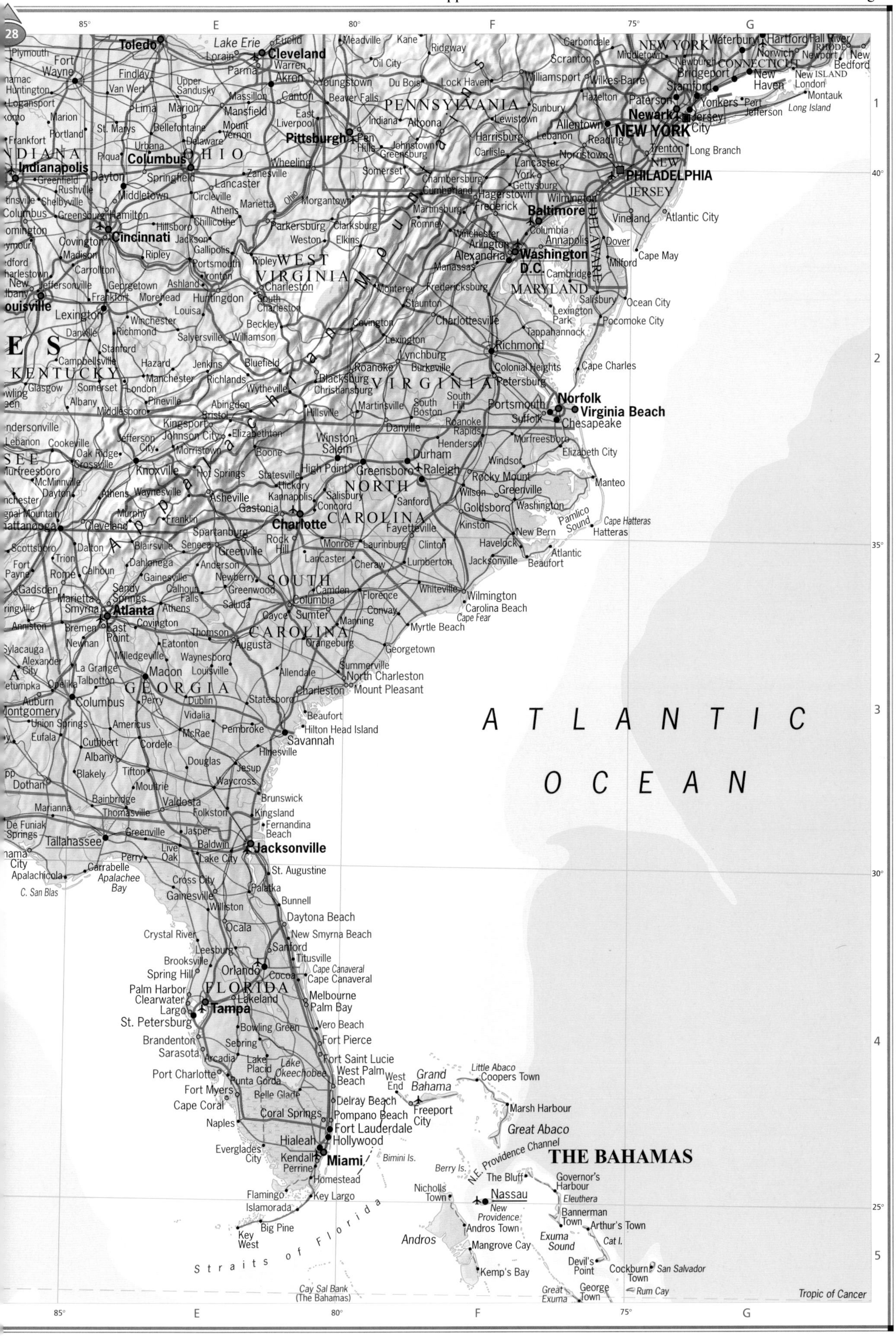

■ over 3 million
■ 1 – 3 million
● 250 000 – 1 million
● 100 000 – 250 000
● 25 000 – 100 000
• under 25 000
country capital underline
state or province capital underline

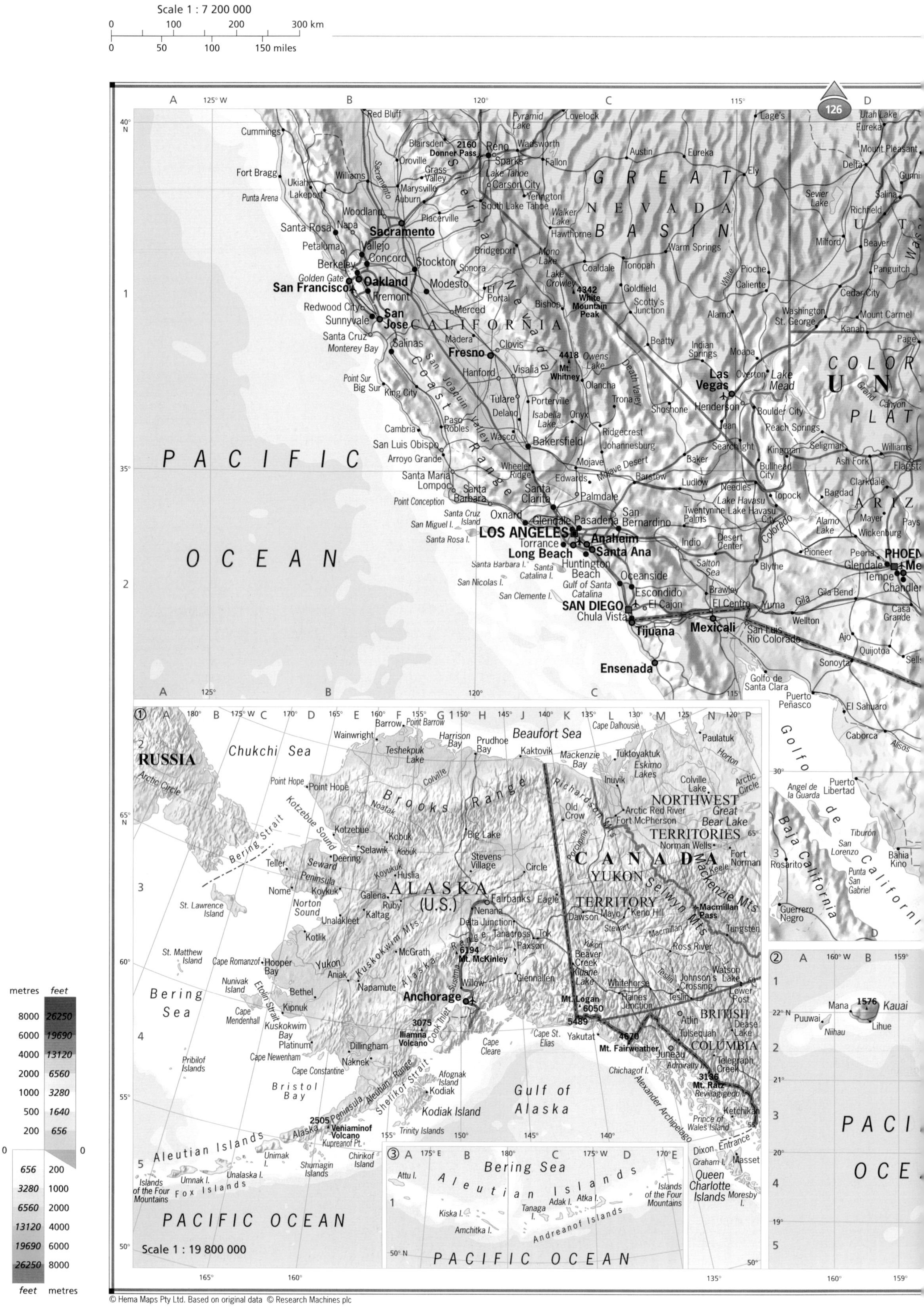

Scale 1 : 7 200 000
0
100
200
300 km
0
50
100
150 miles
A
B
C
D
125° W
120°
115°
126
40° N
35°
1
2
PACIFIC
OCEAN
Red Bluff
Pyramid Lake
Lovelock
Lage's
Utah Lake
Eureka
Cummings
Blairsden
2160
Donner Pass
Reno
Sparks
Wadsworth
Austin
Eureka
Mount Pleasant
Fort Bragg
Williams
Oroville
Grass Valley
Lake Tahoe
Carson City
Fallon
Ely
Delta
Gunni
Ukiah
Lakeport
Marysville
Auburn
Yerington
Sevier Lake
Salina
Punta Arena
Woodland
South Lake Tahoe
Walker Lake
Richfield
Placerville
GREAT
NEVADA
BASIN
Santa Rosa
Napa
Sacramento
Hawthorne
Milford
Beaver
Petaluma
Vallejo
Bridgeport
Mono Lake
Warm Springs
Concord
Berkeley
Stockton
Coaldale
Tonopah
Pioche
Panguitch
Golden Gate
Oakland
Sonora
Lake Crowley
Caliente
San Francisco
Modesto
4342
White Mountain Peak
Goldfield
Cedar City
Fremont
El Portal
Bishop
Scotty's Junction
Redwood City
Merced
Washington
St. George
Mount Carmel
Sunnyvale
San Jose
CALIFORNIA
Alamo
Kanab
Santa Cruz
Madera
Monterey Bay
Salinas
Clovis
Beatty
Page
Fresno
4418
Mt. Whitney
Owens Lake
Indian Springs
Moapa
COLOR
Point Sur
Big Sur
Hanford
Visalia
Las Vegas
Overton
Lake Mead
King City
Olancha
Death Valley
Grand Canyon
Tulare
Porterville
Trona
Henderson
Boulder City
Delano
Isabella Lake
Onyx
Shoshone
PLAT
Cambria
Paso Robles
Wasco
Ridgecrest
Jean
Peach Springs
San Luis Obispo
Bakersfield
Johannesburg
Searchlight
Seligman
Williams
Arroyo Grande
Mojave
Kingman
Ash Fork
Flagsta
Mojave Desert
Baker
Santa Maria
Wheeler Ridge
Edwards
Barstow
Bullhead City
Lompoc
Santa Barbara
Santa Clarita
Ludlow
Needles
Clarkdale
Palmdale
Topock
Bagdad
Point Conception
Lake Havasu
Lake Havasu City
Santa Cruz Island
Oxnard
San Bernardino
Twentynine Palms
San Miguel I.
Glendale
Pasadena
Alamo Lake
Mayer
Santa Rosa I.
LOS ANGELES
Colorado
Wickenburg
Torrance
Anaheim
Indio
Desert Center
Long Beach
Santa Ana
Pioneer
Peoria
PHOEN
Santa Barbara I.
Santa Catalina I.
Huntington Beach
Salton Sea
Blythe
Glendale
Tempe
San Nicolas I.
Oceanside
Chandler
Gulf of Santa Catalina
Escondido
Brawley
Gila Bend
San Clemente I.
SAN DIEGO
El Cajon
El Centro
Yuma
Gila
Casa Grande
Chula Vista
Wellton
Tijuana
Mexicali
San Luis Rio Colorado
Ajo
Quijotoa
Ensenada
Sonoyta
Sells
Golfo de Santa Clara
Puerto Peñasco
El Sahuaro
Caborca
Golfo de California
Puerto Libertad
Angel de la Guarda
Tiburón
San Lorenzo
Punta San Gabriel
Bahia Kino
Baja California
Rosarito
Guerrero Negro
30°
3
1
180°
175° W
170°
165°
160°
155°
150°
145°
140°
135°
130°
125°
120°
RUSSIA
Chukchi Sea
Arctic Circle
Barrow
Point Barrow
Wainwright
Harrison Bay
Prudhoe Bay
Beaufort Sea
Cape Dalhousie
Paulatuk
Teshekpuk Lake
Kaktovik
Mackenzie Bay
Tuktoyaktuk
Eskimo Lakes
Horton
Point Hope
Colville
Inuvik
Colville Lake
Arctic Circle
Brooks Range
Noatak
Old Crow
Arctic Red River
NORTHWEST
Great Bear Lake
Fort McPherson
TERRITORIES
Kotzebue Sound
Kotzebue
Bering Strait
Kobuk
Big Lake
Norman Wells
Fort Norman
Selawik
Teller
Seward Peninsula
Deering
Stevens Village
Circle
CANADA
YUKON
Mackenzie Mts.
Huslia
Nome
Koyukuk
ALASKA (U.S.)
Eagle
TERRITORY
Macmillan Pass
St. Lawrence Island
Norton Sound
Galena
Ruby
Fairbanks
Dawson
Mayo
Keno Hill
Selwyn Mts.
Kaltag
Nenana
Unalakleet
Delta Junction
Stewart
Tungsten
Kotlik
Tanacross
Tok
Ross River
St. Matthew Island
McGrath
6194
Mt. McKinley
Paxson
Beaver Creek
Kuskokwim Mts.
Cape Romanzof
Hooper Bay
Yukon
Aniak
Glennallen
Kluane Lake
Teslin
Johnson's Crossing
Watson Lake
Bering Sea
Nunivak Island
Napamute
Alaska Range
Whitehorse
Bethel
Anchorage
Mt. Logan
6050
Haines Junction
Teslin
Lower Post
Etolin Strait
Cape Mendenhall
Kipnuk
5489
Atlin
BRITISH
Kuskokwim Bay
3075
Iliamna Volcano
Cook Inlet
Cape St. Elias
Yakutat
4670
Mt. Fairweather
Tulsequah
Dease Lake
COLUMBIA
Platinum
Dillingham
Cape Cleare
Juneau
Admiralty I.
Telegraph Creek
Pribilof Islands
Cape Newenham
Naknek
Chichagof I.
Cape Constantine
Afognak Island
Gulf of Alaska
3136
Mt. Ratz
Revillagigedo I.
Bristol Bay
Kodiak
Alexander Archipelago
Shelikof Strait
Kodiak Island
Ketchikan
Aleutian Range
Alaska Peninsula
2505
Veniaminof Volcano
Prince of Wales Island
Trinity Islands
Aleutian Islands
Kupreanof Pt.
Dixon Entrance
Unimak I.
Shumagin Islands
Chirikof Island
Graham I.
Masset
Islands of the Four Mountains
Umnak I.
Unalaska I.
Fox Islands
Queen Charlotte Islands
Moresby I.
PACIFIC OCEAN
Scale 1 : 19 800 000
55°
60°
65° N
50°
175° E
Bering Sea
Attu I.
Aleutian Islands
Kiska I.
Tanaga I.
Adak I.
Atka I.
Islands of the Four Mountains
Amchitka I.
Andreanof Islands
50° N
PACIFIC OCEAN
2
160° W
159°
Mana
1576
Kauai
22° N
Puuwai
Lihue
Niihau
21°
20°
19°
PACI
OCE
metres
feet
8000
26250
6000
19690
4000
13120
2000
6560
1000
3280
500
1640
200
656
0
656
200
3280
1000
6560
2000
13120
4000
19690
6000
26250
8000
feet
metres

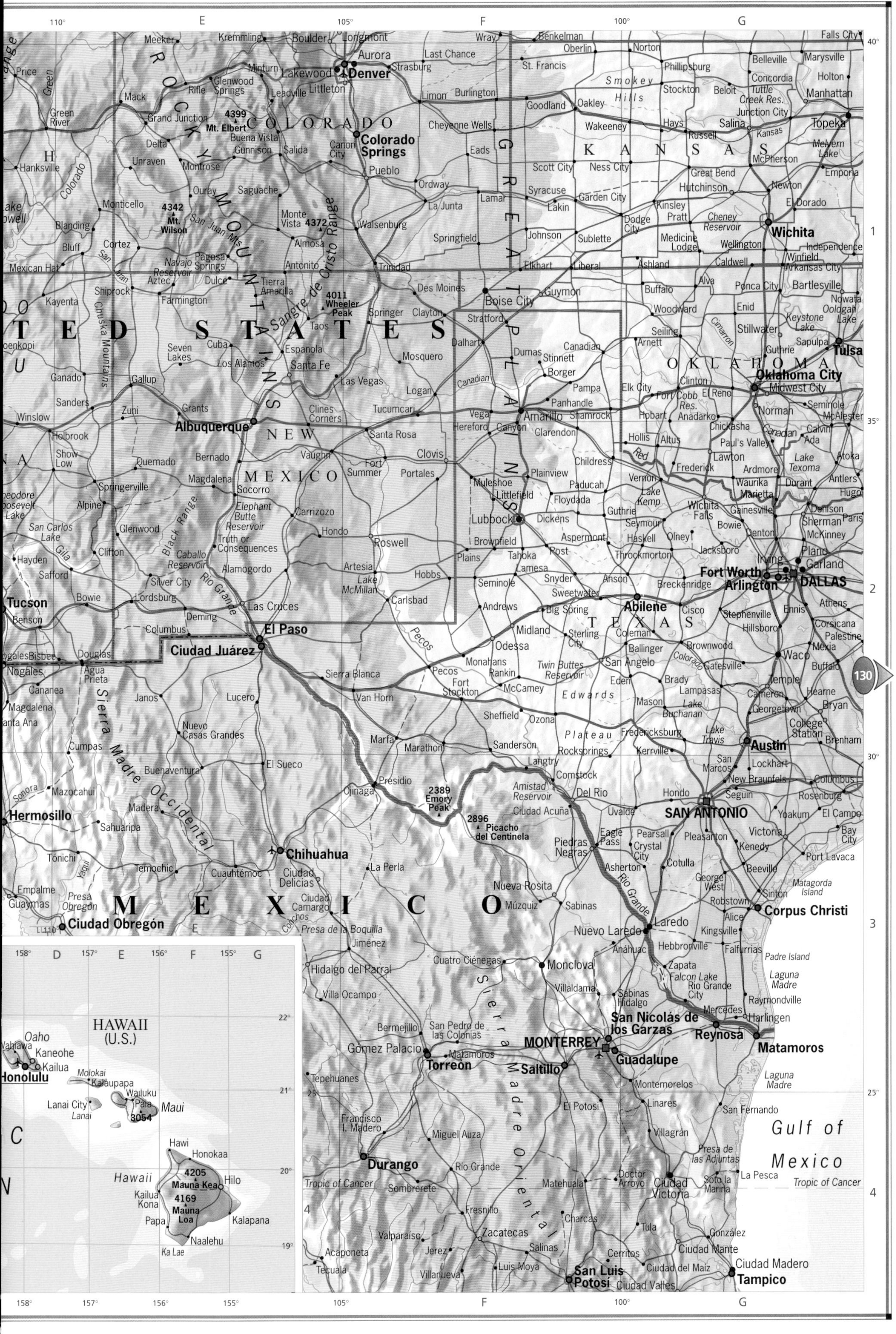

■ over 3 million
■ 1 – 3 million
● 250 000 – 1 million
● 100 000 – 250 000
○ 25 000 – 100 000
• under 25 000
country capital underline
state or province capital underline

Scale 1 : 16 100 000

0 200 400 600 km

0 100 200 300 miles

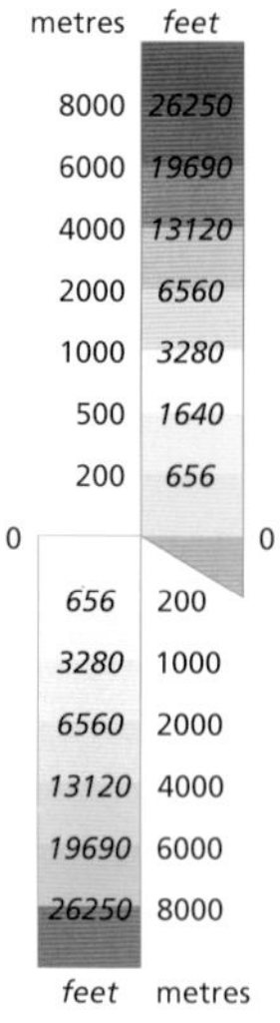

Central America and the Caribbean

Belize • Caribbean Islands • Costa Rica • El Salvador
Guatemala • Honduras • Nicaragua • Panama

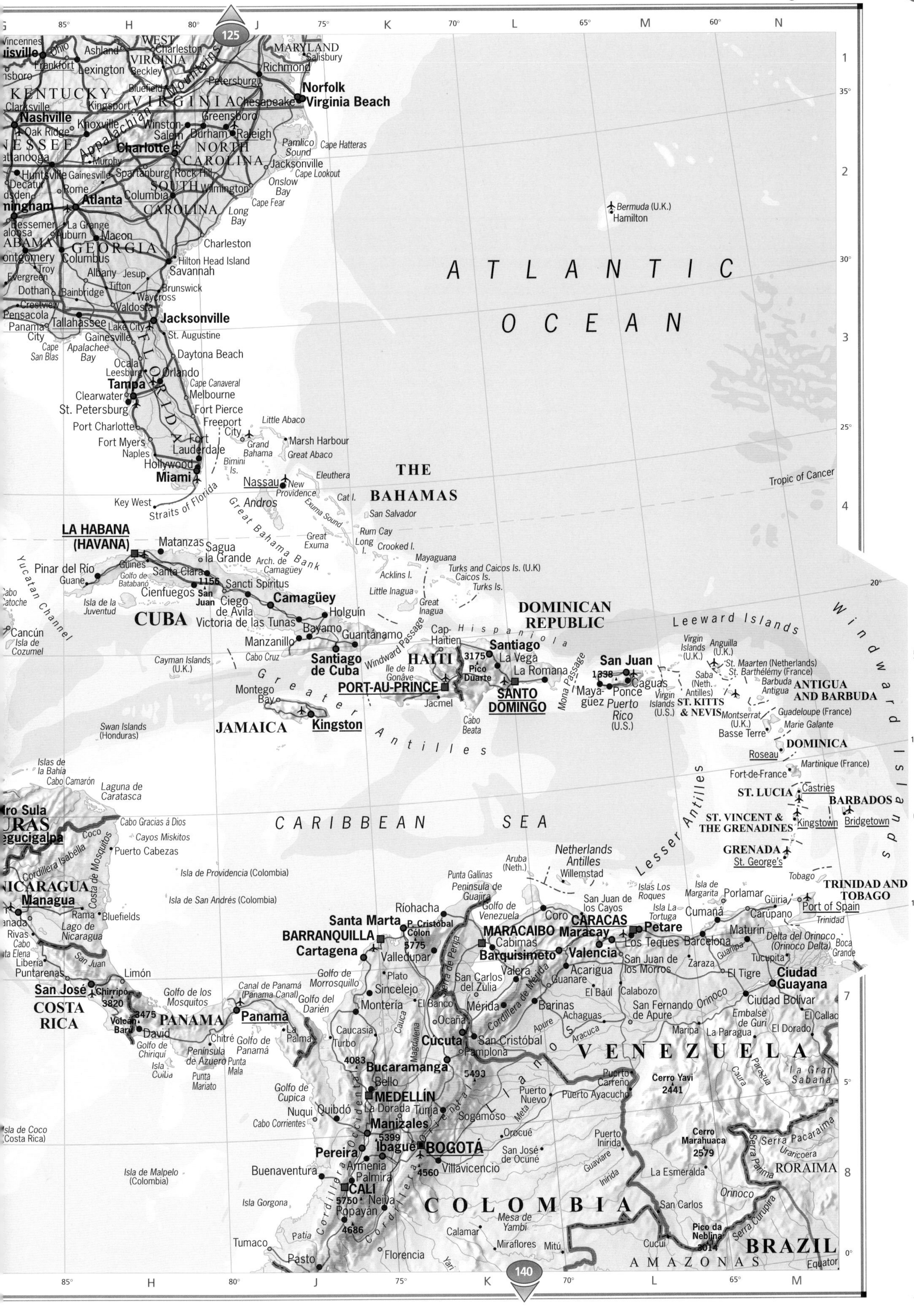

■ over 3 million
■ 1 – 3 million
● 250 000 – 1 million
• 100 000 – 250 000
○ 25 000 – 100 000
• under 25 000
country capital underline
state or province capital underline

Scale 1 : 28 000 000

0 500 1000 1500 km

0 250 500 750 miles

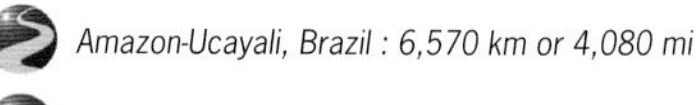

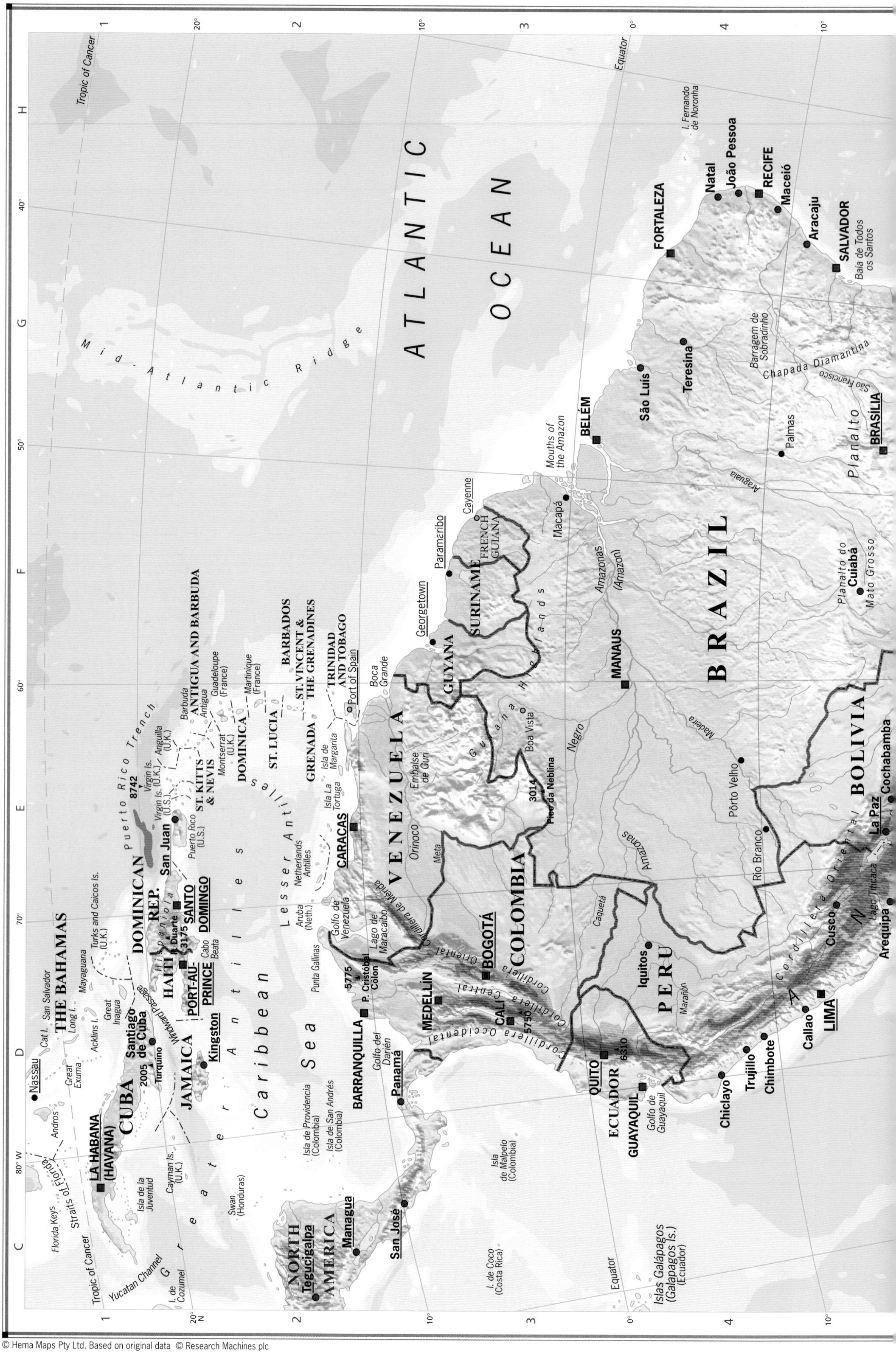

metres	feet
8000	26250
6000	19690
4000	13120
2000	6560
1000	3280
500	1640
200	656
0	0
200	656
1000	3280
2000	6560
4000	13120
6000	19690
8000	26250
metres	feet

Aconcagua, Argentina : 6,959 m or 22,835 ft

Península Valdés, Argentina : 40 m or 131 ft

Arica, Chile : 0.08 cm or 0.03 in

Quibdo, Colombia : 899 cm or 354 in

Amazon-Ucayali, Brazil : 6,570 km or 4,080 mi

Lake Maracaibo, Venezuela : 13,010 km² or 5,020 sq mi

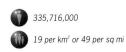

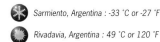

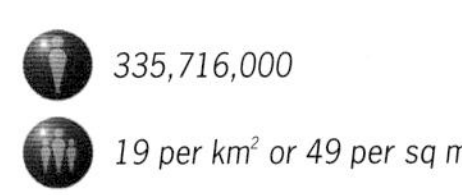

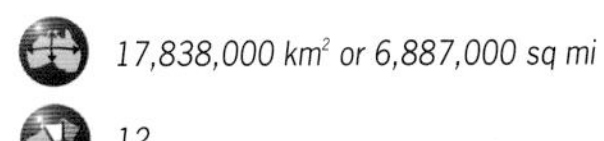

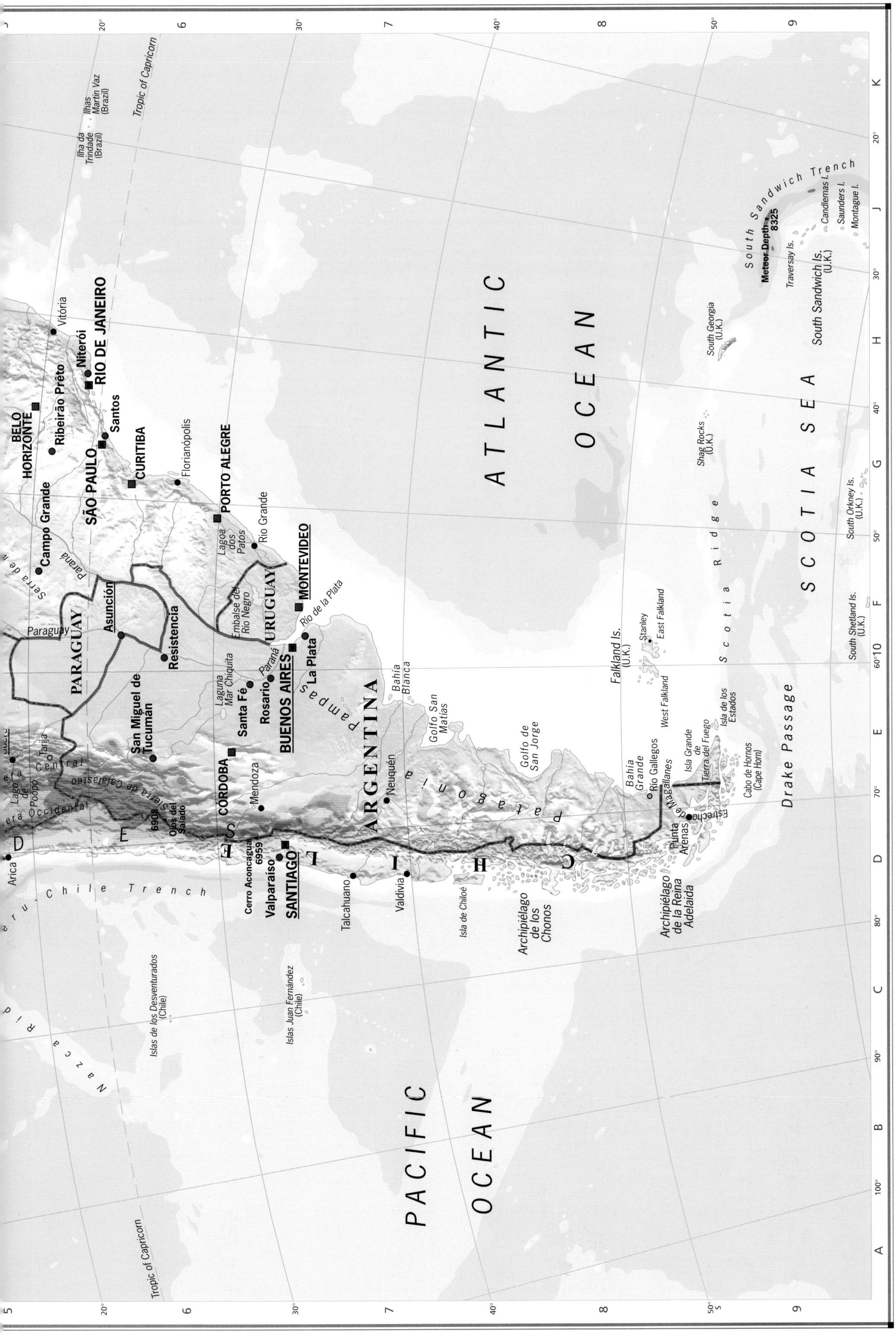
ATLANTIC OCEAN
PACIFIC OCEAN
SCOTIA SEA
Drake Passage
Scotia Ridge
South Sandwich Trench
Meteor Depth 8325
Chile Trench
Nazca Ridge
Tropic of Capricorn
ARGENTINA
PARAGUAY
URUGUAY
Pampas
Patagonia
BELO HORIZONTE
RIO DE JANEIRO
SÃO PAULO
CURITIBA
PORTO ALEGRE
MONTEVIDEO
BUENOS AIRES
SANTIAGO
CÓRDOBA
Asunción
Resistencia
San Miguel de Tucumán
Santa Fé
Rosario
La Plata
Mendoza
Valparaíso
Cerro Aconcagua 6959
Ojos del Salado 6908
Neuquén
Talcahuano
Valdivia
Bahía Blanca
Golfo San Matías
Golfo de San Jorge
Bahía Grande
Río Gallegos
Punta Arenas
Estrecho de Magallanes
Isla Grande de Tierra del Fuego
Isla de los Estados
Cabo de Hornos (Cape Horn)
Archipiélago de la Reina Adelaida
Archipiélago de los Chonos
Isla de Chiloé
Falkland Is. (U.K.)
Stanley
East Falkland
West Falkland
South Georgia (U.K.)
Shag Rocks (U.K.)
South Orkney Is. (U.K.)
South Shetland Is. (U.K.)
South Sandwich Is. (U.K.)
Traversay Is.
Candlemas I.
Saunders I.
Montague I.
Ilha da Trindade (Brazil)
Ilhas Martin Vaz (Brazil)
Islas de los Desventurados (Chile)
Islas Juan Fernández (Chile)
Campo Grande
Ribeirão Prêto
Vitória
Niterói
Santos
Florianópolis
Rio Grande
Lagoa dos Patos
Embalse del Río Negro
Laguna Mar Chiquita
Río de la Plata
Paraná
Paraguay
Sierra de Calalaste
Lago de Poopó
Tarija
Arica

Sarmiento, Argentina : -33 °C or -27 °F	Rivadavia, Argentina : 49 °C or 120 °F
335,716,000	19 per km² or 49 per sq mi
17,838,000 km² or 6,887,000 sq mi	12

Scale 1 : 28 000 000

0 500 1000 1500 km

0 250 500 750 miles

© Hema Maps Pty Ltd. Based on original data © Research Machines plc

Aconcagua, Argentina : 6,959 m or 22,835 ft

Península Valdés, Argentina : 40 m or 131 ft

Arica, Chile : 0.08 cm or 0.03 in

Quibdo, Colombia : 899 cm or 354 in

Amazon-Ucayali, Brazil : 6,570 km or 4,080 mi

Lake Maracaibo, Venezuela : 13,010 km² or 5,020 sq mi

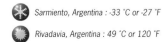

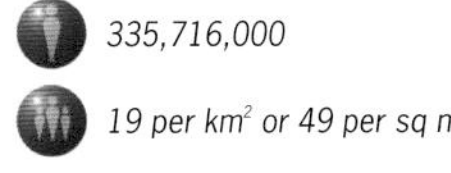

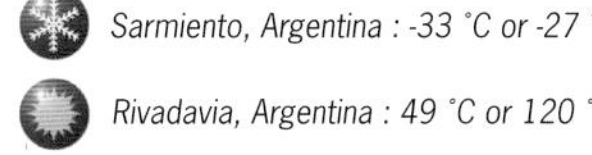

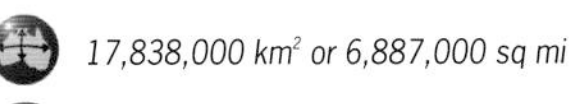

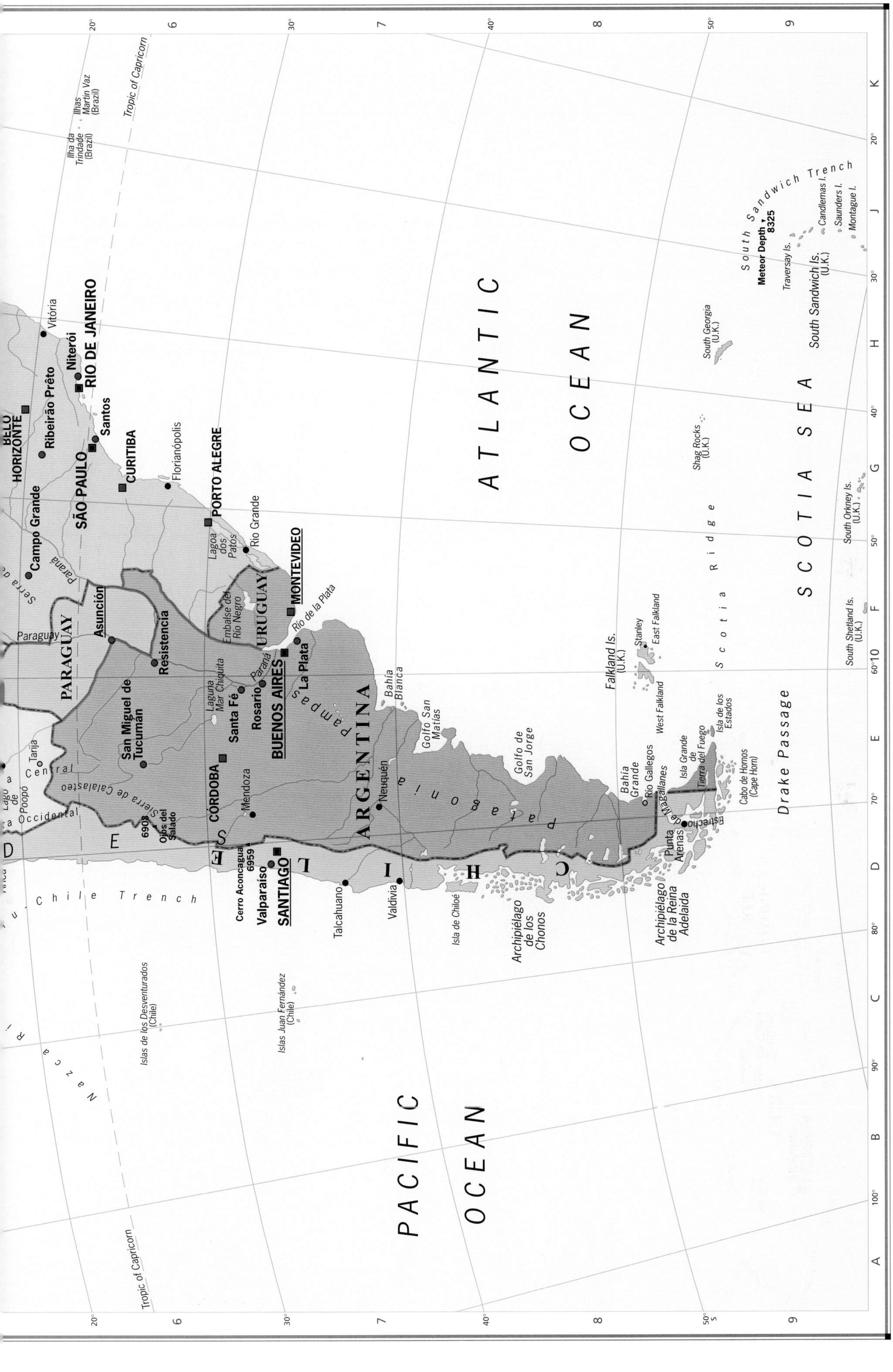
ATLANTIC OCEAN
PACIFIC OCEAN
SCOTIA SEA
Scotia Ridge
Drake Passage
South Sandwich Trench
Chile Trench
Nazca Ridge
Tropic of Capricorn
ARGENTINA
CHILE
PARAGUAY
URUGUAY
BUENOS AIRES
SANTIAGO
MONTEVIDEO
Asunción
RIO DE JANEIRO
SÃO PAULO
BELO HORIZONTE
CURITIBA
PORTO ALEGRE
Niterói
Santos
Vitória
Ribeirão Prêto
Campo Grande
Florianópolis
Rio Grande
Lagoa dos Patos
Embalse del Río Negro
Río de la Plata
La Plata
Resistencia
San Miguel de Tucumán
Laguna Mar Chiquita
Santa Fé
Rosario
Paraná
CÓRDOBA
Mendoza
Neuquén
Bahía Blanca
Golfo San Matías
Golfo de San Jorge
Bahía Grande
Río Gallegos
Estrecho de Magallanes
Punta Arenas
Isla Grande de Tierra del Fuego
Isla de los Estados
Cabo de Hornos (Cape Horn)
Archipiélago de la Reina Adelaida
Archipiélago de los Chonos
Isla de Chiloé
Valdivia
Talcahuano
Valparaíso
Cerro Aconcagua 6959
Ojos del Salado 6908
Sierra de Calalaste
Pampas
Patagonia
Tarija
Lago de Poopó
Cordillera Central
Cordillera Occidental
Serra de Maracaju
Islas Juan Fernández (Chile)
Islas de los Desventurados (Chile)
Ilha da Trindade (Brazil)
Ilhas Martin Vaz (Brazil)
Falkland Is. (U.K.)
Stanley
East Falkland
West Falkland
Shag Rocks (U.K.)
South Georgia (U.K.)
South Sandwich Is. (U.K.)
Traversay Is.
Candlemas I.
Saunders I.
Montague I.
Meteor Depth 8325
South Orkney Is. (U.K.)
South Shetland Is. (U.K.)

Sarmiento, Argentina : -33 °C or -27 °F

Rivadavia, Argentina : 49 °C or 120 °F

335,716,000

19 per km² or 49 per sq mi

17,838,000 km² or 6,887,000 sq mi

12

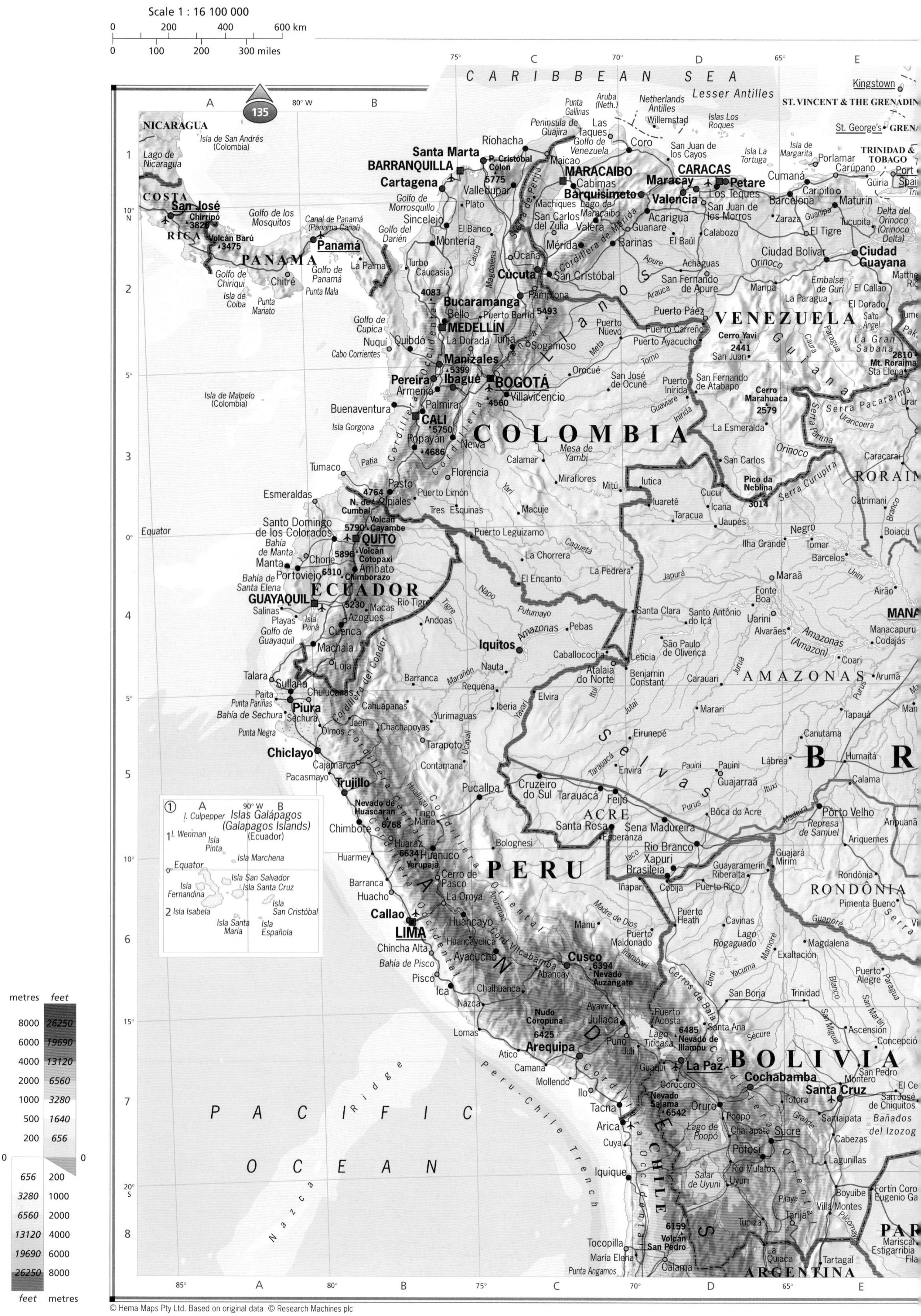
Scale 1 : 16 100 000
0 200 400 600 km
0 100 200 300 miles
CARIBBEAN SEA
Lesser Antilles
Kingstown
ST. VINCENT & THE GRENADINES
St. George's GRENADA
TRINIDAD & TOBAGO
Port of Spain
Aruba (Neth.)
Netherlands Antilles
Willemstad
Islas Los Roques
Punta Gallinas
Peninsula de Guajira
Golfo de Venezuela
NICARAGUA
Lago de Nicaragua
Isla de San Andrés (Colombia)
COSTA RICA
San José
Chirripó 3820
Volcán Barú 3475
PANAMA
Golfo de los Mosquitos
Canal de Panamá (Panama Canal)
Panamá
Golfo de Panamá
Golfo de Chiriquí
Isla de Coiba
Punta Mariato
Punta Mala
Chitré
La Palma
Golfo del Darién
Golfo de Morrosquillo
Santa Marta
BARRANQUILLA
Cartagena
Ríohacha
P. Cristóbal Colón 5775
Valledupar
Maicao
MARACAIBO
Cabimas
Lago de Maracaibo
Sierra de Perijá
Machiques
San Carlos del Zulia
Barquisimeto
Maracay
CARACAS
Petare
Valencia
Los Teques
San Juan de los Morros
San Juan de los Cayos
Coro
Las Taques
Isla La Tortuga
Isla de Margarita
Porlamar
Cumaná
Carúpano
Barcelona
Caripito
Maturín
Güiria
Delta del Orinoco (Orinoco Delta)
Tucupita
El Tigre
Zaraza
Guanipa
Calabozo
Valera
Acarigua
Guanare
Mérida
Barinas
El Baúl
Cordillera de Mérida
Sincelejo
Plato
El Banco
Montería
Turbo
Caucasia
Ocaña
Cúcuta
San Cristóbal
Pamplona
Apure
Achaguas
San Fernando de Apure
Arauca
Ciudad Bolívar
Ciudad Guayana
Orinoco
Embalse de Guri
El Callao
Matthews Ridge
Maripa
La Paragua
El Dorado
Salto Ángel
La Gran Sabana
2810 Mt. Roraima
Sta Elena
Bucaramanga
4083
Bello
Puerto Berrío
5493
MEDELLÍN
La Dorada
Tunja
Sogamoso
Golfo de Cupica
Nuquí
Quibdó
Cabo Corrientes
Manizales
5399
Pereira
Ibagué
Armenia
BOGOTÁ
Villavicencio
4560
Palmira
Buenaventura
CALI
5750
Popayán
4686
Neiva
Isla Gorgona
Isla de Malpelo (Colombia)
Cordillera Occidental
Cordillera Central
Cordillera Oriental
Llanos
Meta
Puerto Nuevo
Puerto Carreño
Puerto Páez
Puerto Ayacucho
Tomo
Orocué
San José de Ocuné
Puerto Inírida
San Fernando de Atabapo
Guaviare
Inírida
VENEZUELA
Cerro Yavi 2441
San Juan
Guiana
Caura
Paragua
Cerro Marahuaca 2579
Serra Pacaraima
Serra Parima
Uraricoera
La Esmeralda
COLOMBIA
Mesa de Yambi
Calamar
Miraflores
Mitú
Iutica
Iuaretê
Taracua
San Carlos
Cucuí
Içana
Uaupés
Pico da Neblina 3014
Serra Curupira
Caracaraí
RORAIMA
Catrimani
Branco
Boiaçu
Tumaco
Patia
Pasto
4764
Florencia
Puerto Limón
Esmeraldas
Ipiales
N. de Cumbal
Volcán Cayambe 5790
Tres Esquinas
Macuje
Yari
Santo Domingo de los Colorados
Equator
QUITO
Bahía de Manta
Manta
Chone
5896 Volcán Cotopaxi
Ambato
Portoviejo
6310 Chimborazo
Bahía de Santa Elena
ECUADOR
GUAYAQUIL
Salinas
Playas
Isla Puná
Golfo de Guayaquil
5230
Macas
Azogues
Cuenca
Machala
Loja
Río Tigre
Tigre
Andoas
Puerto Leguizamo
Caquetá
La Chorrera
La Pedrera
El Encanto
Napo
Putumayo
Japurá
Negro
Tomar
Ilha Grande
Barcelos
Unini
Maraã
Fonte Boa
Uarini
Alvarães
Airão
Manacapuru
Codajás
MANAUS
Santa Clara
Santo Antônio do Içá
São Paulo de Olivença
Amazonas
Iquitos
Pebas
Caballococha
Leticia
Atalaia do Norte
Benjamin Constant
Nauta
Coari
Amazonas (Amazon)
AMAZONAS
Juruá
Carauari
Arumã
Talara
Sullana
Paita
Punta Pariñas
Bahía de Sechura
Sechura
Piura
Chulucanas
Punta Negra
Olmos
Jaén
Cordillera del Cóndor
Barranca
Marañón
Requena
Cahuapanas
Yurimaguas
Iberia
Javari
Elvira
Itui
Jutai
Marari
Purus
Tapauá
Chachapoyas
Tarapoto
Ucayali
Chiclayo
Cajamarca
Eirunepé
Selvas
Canutama
Humaitá
Lábrea
Pauini
Envira
Tarauacá
Guajarrã
Ituxi
Calama
Contamana
Pacasmayo
Trujillo
Pucallpa
Cruzeiro do Sul
Tarauacá
Feijó
Sena Madureira
Bôca do Acre
Porto Velho
Represa de Samuel
Ariquemes
Aripuanã
Madeira
ACRE
Santa Rosa
Esperanza
Iaco
Rio Branco
Xapuri
Brasiléia
Guajará Mirim
Guayaramerín
Riberalta
Rondônia
RONDÔNIA
Pimenta Bueno
Serra
Guaporé
Nevado de Huascarán 6768
Chimbote
Tingo María
Huallaga
Cordillera Central
Cordillera Oriental
Bolognesi
Huarmey
Huaraz 6634
Huánuco
Yerupajá
Cerro de Pasco
PERU
Barranca
Huacho
La Oroya
Callao
LIMA
Chincha Alta
Bahía de Pisco
Pisco
Ica
Nazca
Huancayo
Huancavelica
Ayacucho
Apurímac
Cord. Vilcabamba
Cusco
Abancay
6394 Nevado Auzangate
Chalhuanca
Manú
Madre de Dios
Puerto Maldonado
Inambari
Iñapari
Cobija
Puerto Rico
Puerto Heath
Cavinas
Lago Rogaguado
Mamoré
Exaltación
Magdalena
Beni
Yacuma
San Borja
Trinidad
Puerto Alegre
Paraguá
Blanco
San Martín
San Miguel
Ascensión
Concepción
Cerros de Bala
Puerto Acosta
Ayaviri
Juliaca
Nudo Coropuna
6425
Arequipa
Puno
Lago Titicaca
Juli
6485 Nevado de Illampu
Santa Ana
Sécure
BOLIVIA
Lomas
Atico
Camaná
Mollendo
Ilo
Guaqui
La Paz
Corocoro
Cochabamba
Montero
Santa Cruz
San Pedro
San José de Chiquitos
El Cerro
Nevado Sajama 6542
Oruro
Tacna
Arica
Cuya
Lago de Poopó
Poopó
Challapata
Sucre
Potosí
Samaipata
Bañados del Izozog
Cabezas
Lagunillas
Cordillera Occidental
Cordillera Oriental
Iquique
Salar de Uyuni
Río Mulatos
Uyuni
Pilaya
Tarija
Tupiza
Villa Montes
Pilcomayo
Boyuibe
Fortín Coronel Eugenio Garay
CHILE
Tocopilla
María Elena
Punta Angamos
6159 Volcán San Pedro
Calama
La Quiaca
Tartagal
ARGENTINA
PARAGUAY
Mariscal Estigarribia
ANDES
Peru-Chile Trench
Nazca Ridge
PACIFIC OCEAN
Islas Galápagos (Galapagos Islands) (Ecuador)
I. Culpepper
I. Wenman
Isla Pinta
Isla Marchena
Equator
Isla San Salvador
Isla Fernandina
Isla Santa Cruz
Isla Isabela
Isla San Cristóbal
Isla Santa María
Isla Española
metres feet
8000 26250
6000 19690
4000 13120
2000 6560
1000 3280
500 1640
200 656
0 0
656 200
3280 1000
6560 2000
13120 4000
19690 6000
26250 8000
feet metres
135
85° 80° 75° 70° 65°
A B C D E
1 2 3 4 5 6 7 8

Northern South America

Bolivia • Brazil • Colombia • Ecuador • French Guiana
Galapagos Islands • Guyana • Peru • Suriname • Venezuela

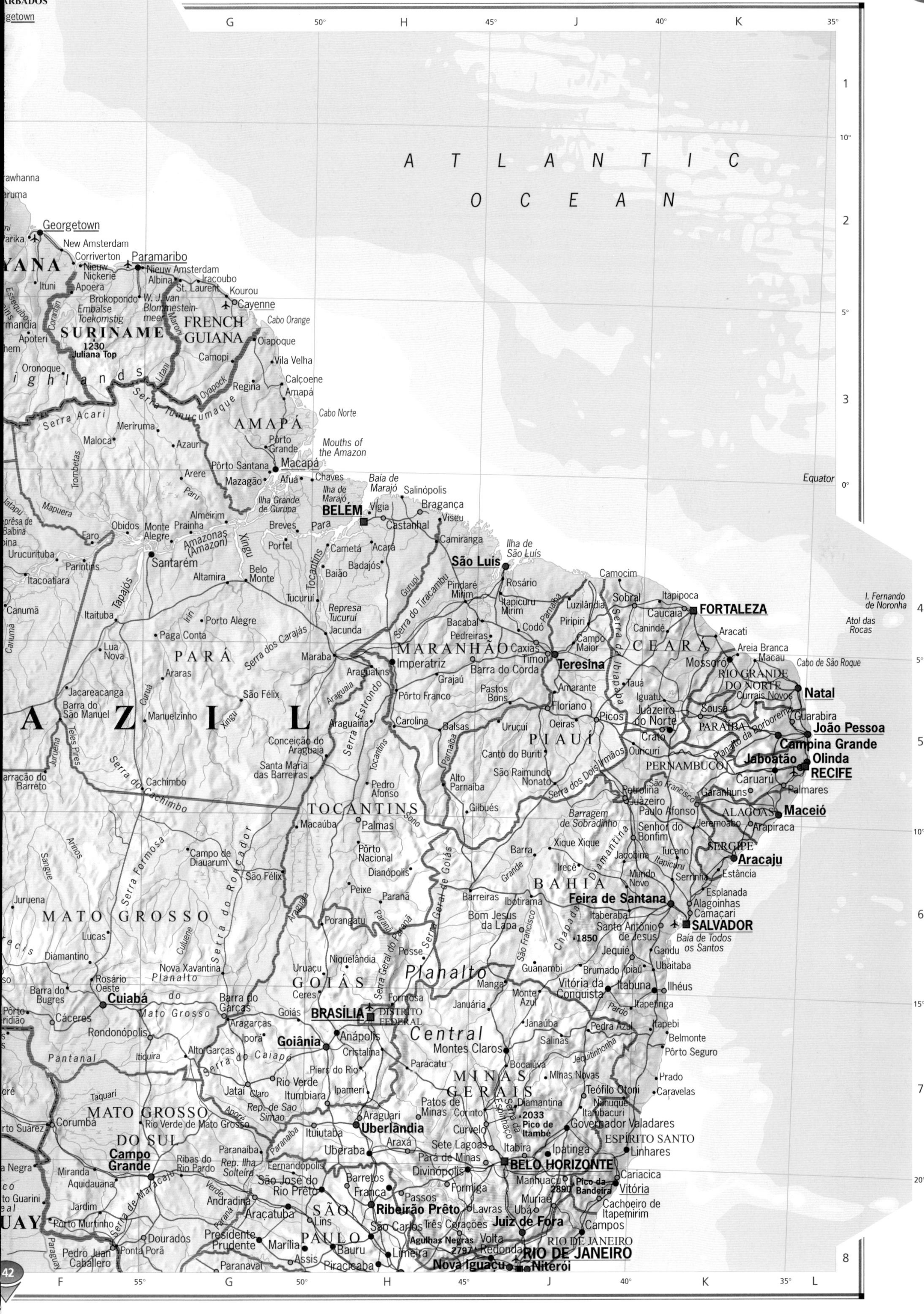

■	over 3 million	•	100 000 – 250 000	——	country capital underline
■	1 – 3 million	◦	25 000 – 100 000	——	state or province capital underline
●	250 000 – 1 million	•	under 25 000		

Scale 1 : 16 100 000

0 200 400 600 km

0 100 200 300 miles

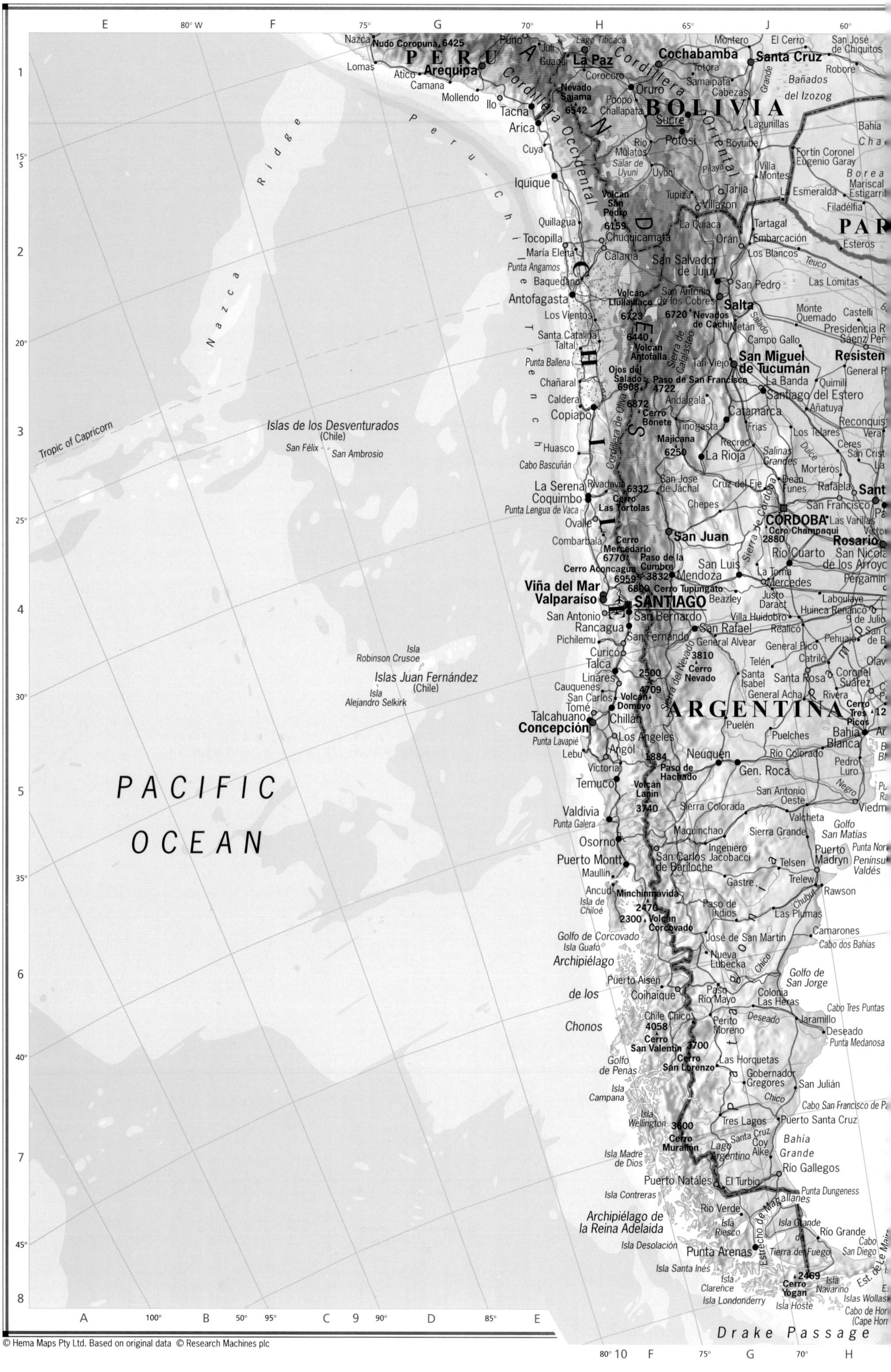

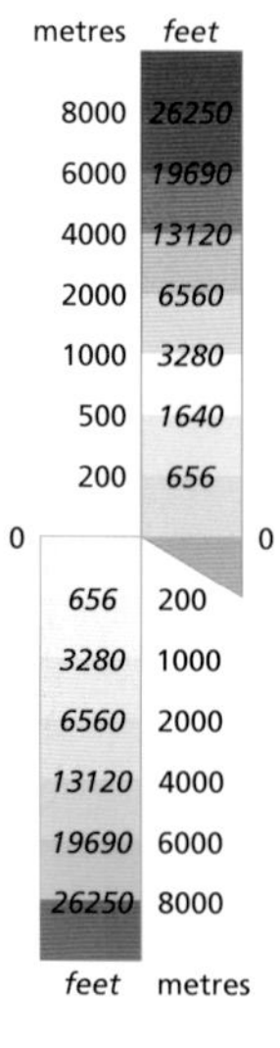

E 80° W F 75° G 70° H 65° J 60°

P E R U Nazca
Nudo Coropuna, 6425 Puno
Lomas Juli Guaqui Lago Titicaca **Cochabamba** Montero El Cerro San José de Chiquitos
Arequipa **La Paz** Cordillera Totora **Santa Cruz** Robore
1 Atico Corocoro Oruro Samaipata Bañados del Izozog
Camana Nevado Sajama Poopó Cabezas **B O L I V I A**
Mollendo 6542 Challapata Villa Montes Bahía
Ilo Tacna Rio Sucre Lagunillas Cha
Arica Mulatos Potosí Boyuibe Fortín Coronel Eugenio Garay
15° S Cuya Salar de Uyuni Uyuni Pilaya Villa Montes B o r e a
Tupiza Tarija La Esmeralda Mariscal Estigarri
Iquique Villazon La Quiaca Orán Filadélfia
Volcán San Pedro La Quiaca Tartagal Embarcación **PAR**
2 Quillagua 6159 Chuquicamata San Salvador de Jujuy Los Blancos Teuco Esteros
Tocopilla Calama San Pedro Las Lomitas
María Elena San Antonio **Salta** Monte
Punta Angamos Volcán de los Cobres Quemado Castelli
Baquedano Llullaillaco 6720 Nevados Metán Campo Gallo Presidencia R Sáenz Per
Antofagasta 6723 de Cachi Monte
Los Vientos 6440 Tafi Viejo **San Miguel** **Resisten**
Santa Catalina Volcán **de Tucumán** General F
Taltal Antofalla La Banda Quimili
20° Punta Ballena Ojos del Andalgalá Santiago Añatuya Reconquis
Salado Paso de San Francisco del Estero Vera
Chañaral 6908 4722 Catamarca Frias Los Telares San Crist
3 Caldera 6872 Cerro Tinogasta Recreo Salinas
Copiapó Bonete Majicena Grandes Ceres Morteros
Islas de los Desventurados Huasco 6250 La Rioja San Francisco
(Chile) Cabo Bascuñán Dean Funes **Sant**
San Félix San Ambrosio 6332 San Jose Cruz del Eje Rafaela
Rivadavia de Jáchal **CORDOBA** San Francisco
La Serena Las Tortolas Chepes Cerro Champaqui Las Varillas
25° Coquimbo Cerro San Juan 2880 **Rosario**
Punta Lengua de Vaca Mercedario San Luis Rio Cuarto San Nicolas
Ovalle 6770 Paso de la de los Arroyos
Combarbalá Cerro Aconcagua Cumbre La Toma Mercedes Pergamin
4 Cerro 6959 3832 Cerro Tupungato Mendoza Justo Labouaye
Viña del Mar 6800 Daract Huinca Renanco 9 de July
Valparaiso **SANTIAGO** San Rafael Villa Huidobro Realico San
San Antonio San Bernardo General Pico Pehuajó
Rancagua Beazley Pedro Catrilo
Pichilemu San Fernando General Alvear Luro
Curicó 3810 Santa Coronel Suárez
5 Talca Cerro Rosa
Linares 2500 Nevado Santa Isabel General Acha Rivera Viedm
Cauquenes 4709 Rio Ra
San Carlos Volcán **A R G E N T I N A** Cerro 12
Tomé Domuyo Tres Picos
Talcahuano Chillán Puelén Puelches Bahía Ar
Concepción Los Angeles Neuquén Blanca
Punta Lavapié Angol Río Colorado Pedro
Lebu 1884 Luro
6 Victoria Paso de Gen. Roca
Hachado San Antonio Negro
Temuco Volcán Oeste Va
Lanín Sierra Colorada
Valdivia 3740 Valcheta
Punta Galera Maquinchao Sierra Grande Golfo
San Matias
Osorno San Carlos Ingeniero Puerto Punta Norl
de Bariloche Jacobacci Madryn Peninsu
Puerto Montt Telsen Valdés
Maullín San Julián
Ancud Minchinmavida Paso de Gastre Rawson
Isla de 2470 Indios
Chiloé 2300 Volcán Las Plumas Trelew Chubut
Corcovado José de San Martin Camarones
Golfo de Corcovado Cabo dos Bahias
Isla Guafo Nueva
Archipiélago Lubecka Golfo de
Puerto Aisén San Jorge
de los Colonia Cabo Tres Puntas
Coihaique Paso Las Heras
Chonos Río Mayo Deseado Jaramillo
Chile Chico Perito Deseado
4058 Moreno Punta Medanosa
Cerro Las Horquetas
San Valentin 3700 Gobernador
Golfo Cerro Gregores San Julián
de Penas San Lorenzo Chico
Isla Cabo San Francisco de P
Campana Tres Lagos Puerto Santa Cruz
Isla Santa Cruz Bahía
7 Wellington 3600 Cruz Grande
Cerro Lago Puerto
Murallón Argentino Coyle Río Gallegos
Isla Madre Puerto Natáles El Turbio
de Dios Punta Dungeness
Isla Contreras Río Verde
Archipiélago de Punta Arenas Isla Grande
la Reina Adelaida Isla de
Riesco Isla Grande Río Grande
Isla Desolación Cabo
San Diego
45° Punta Arenas Tierra del Fuego
Isla Santa Inés 2469
Cerro Isla Est de Le Mair
8 Isla Yogan Navarino
Clarence Islas Wollas
Isla Londonderry Isla Hoste Cabo de Horn
(Cape Hori)

PACIFIC

OCEAN

Nazca Ridge

Tropic of Capricorn

Isla Robinson Crusoe

Islas Juan Fernández
(Chile)
Isla
Alejandro Selkirk

Peru-Ch

A 100° B 50° 95° C 9 90° D 85° E

80° 10 F 75° G 70° H

Drake Passage

metres	feet
8000	26250
6000	19690
4000	13120
2000	6560
1000	3280
500	1640
200	656
0	0

feet	metres
656	200
3280	1000
6560	2000
13120	4000
19690	6000
26250	8000
feet	metres

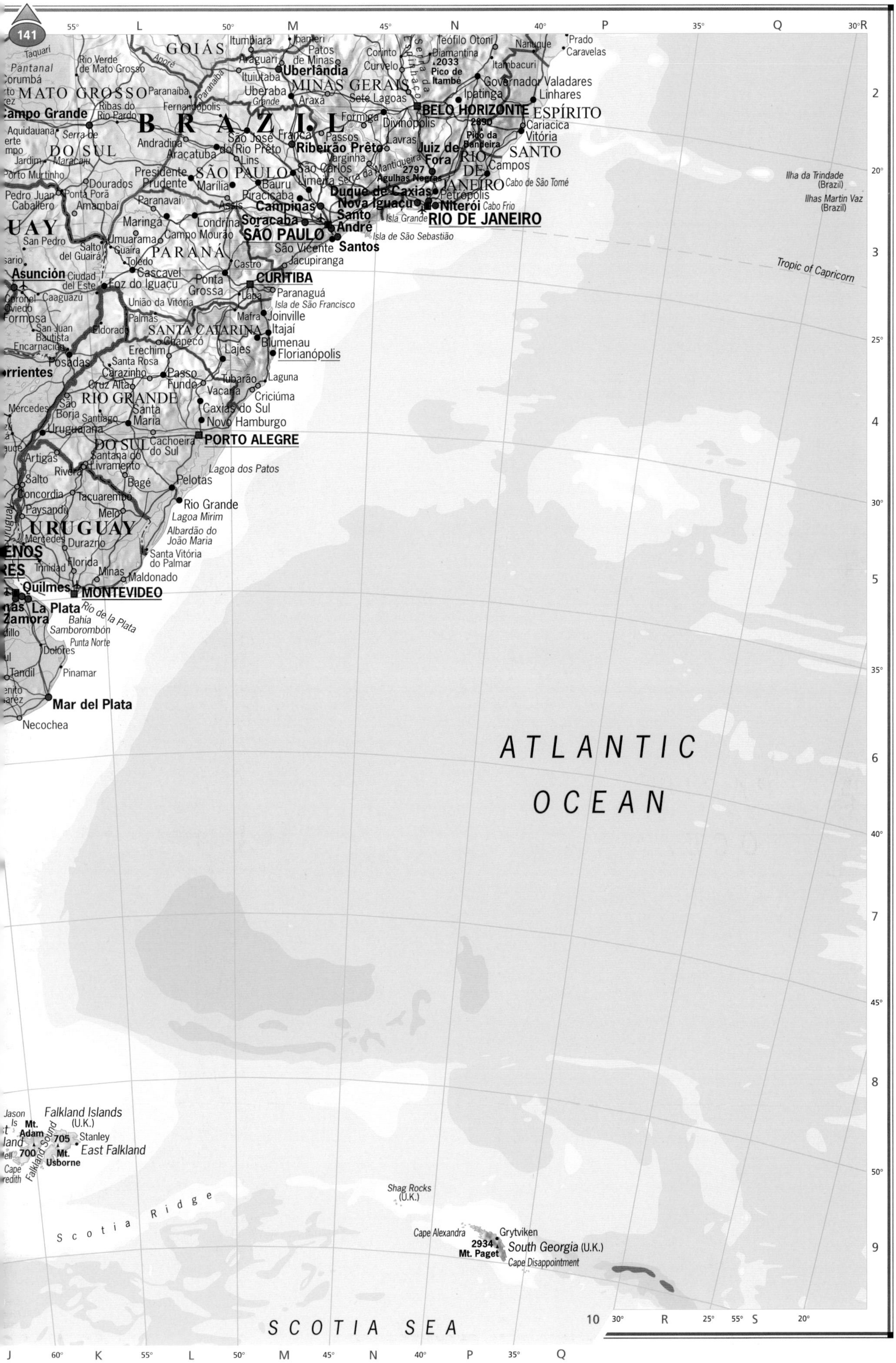

■ over 3 million
■ 1 – 3 million
● 250 000 – 1 million
● 100 000 – 250 000
◉ 25 000 – 100 000
• under 25 000
country capital underline
state or province capital underline

Polar Regions

Scale 1 : 50 700 000

0 500 1000 1500 2000 km

0 250 500 750 1000 miles

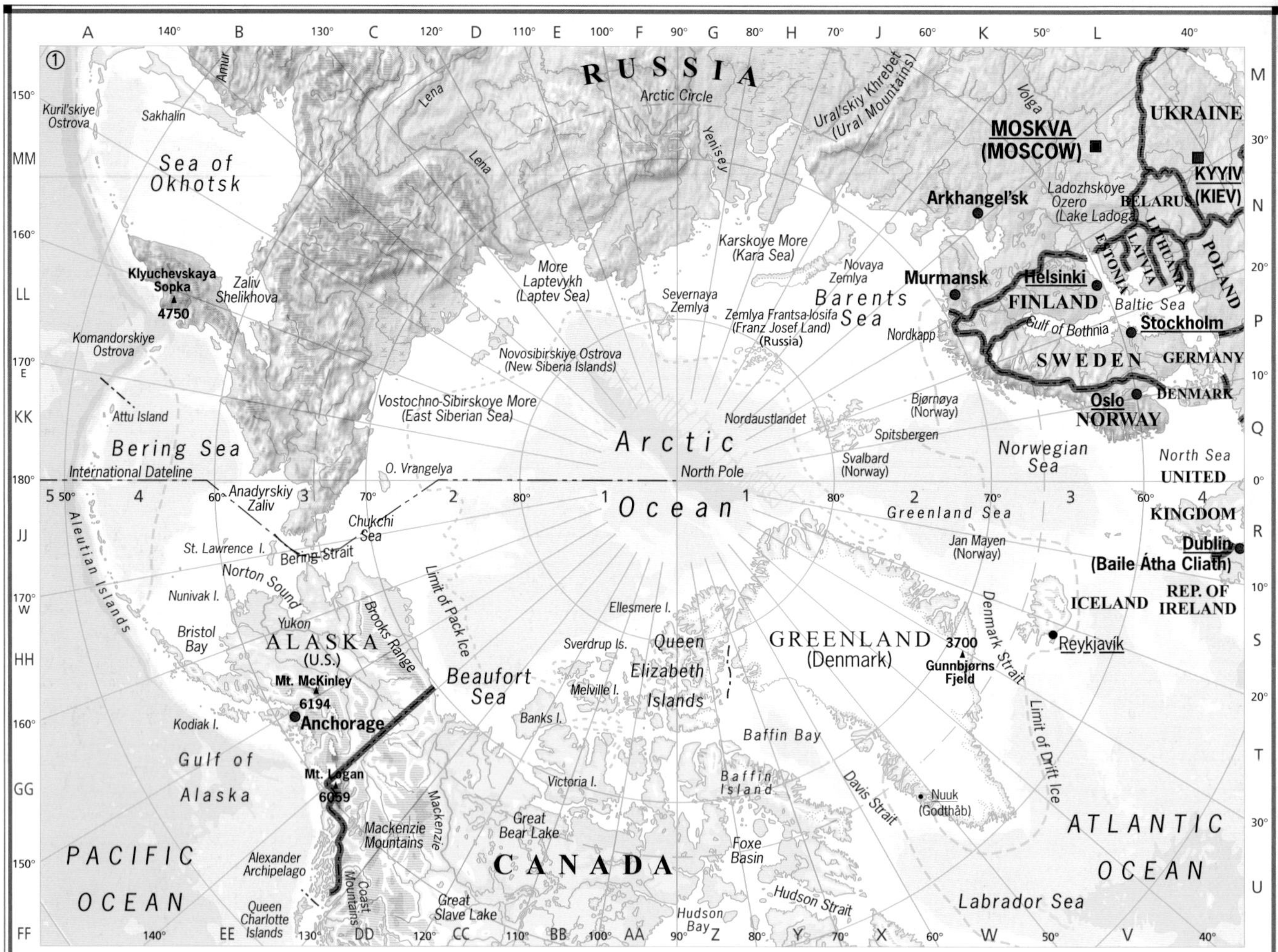
①
RUSSIA
Arctic Circle
Amur
Lena
Yenisey
Ural'skiy Khrebet (Ural Mountains)
Volga
MOSKVA (MOSCOW)
UKRAINE
KYYIV (KIEV)
Kuril'skiye Ostrova
Sakhalin
Sea of Okhotsk
Arkhangel'sk
Ladozhskoye Ozero (Lake Ladoga)
BELARUS
ESTONIA
LATVIA
LITHUANIA
POLAND
Klyuchevskaya Sopka
4750
Zaliv Shelikhova
More Laptevykh (Laptev Sea)
Karskoye More (Kara Sea)
Novaya Zemlya
Severnaya Zemlya
Murmansk
Helsinki
FINLAND
Baltic Sea
Barents Sea
Zemlya Frantsa-Iosifa (Franz Josef Land) (Russia)
Nordkapp
Gulf of Bothnia
Stockholm
SWEDEN
GERMANY
Komandorskiye Ostrova
Novosibirskiye Ostrova (New Siberia Islands)
DENMARK
Bjørnøya (Norway)
Vostochno-Sibirskoye More (East Siberian Sea)
Nordaustlandet
Oslo
NORWAY
Attu Island
Spitsbergen
Bering Sea
Arctic Ocean
Norwegian Sea
North Sea
International Dateline
O. Vrangelya
North Pole
Svalbard (Norway)
UNITED KINGDOM
Anadyrskiy Zaliv
Greenland Sea
Chukchi Sea
Aleutian Islands
St. Lawrence I.
Bering Strait
Jan Mayen (Norway)
Dublin (Baile Átha Cliath)
Norton Sound
Limit of Pack Ice
Nunivak I.
Ellesmere I.
REP. OF IRELAND
ICELAND
Denmark Strait
Brooks Range
Yukon
Bristol Bay
ALASKA (U.S.)
Sverdrup Is.
Queen Elizabeth Islands
GREENLAND (Denmark)
3700
Gunnbjørns Fjeld
Reykjavík
Mt. McKinley
6194
Beaufort Sea
Melville I.
Anchorage
Kodiak I.
Banks I.
Baffin Bay
Limit of Drift Ice
Gulf of Alaska
Mt. Logan
6059
Victoria I.
Baffin Island
Davis Strait
Nuuk (Godthåb)
Mackenzie
Great Bear Lake
Mackenzie Mountains
ATLANTIC OCEAN
PACIFIC OCEAN
Alexander Archipelago
CANADA
Foxe Basin
Coast Mountains
Queen Charlotte Islands
Great Slave Lake
Hudson Bay
Hudson Strait
Labrador Sea

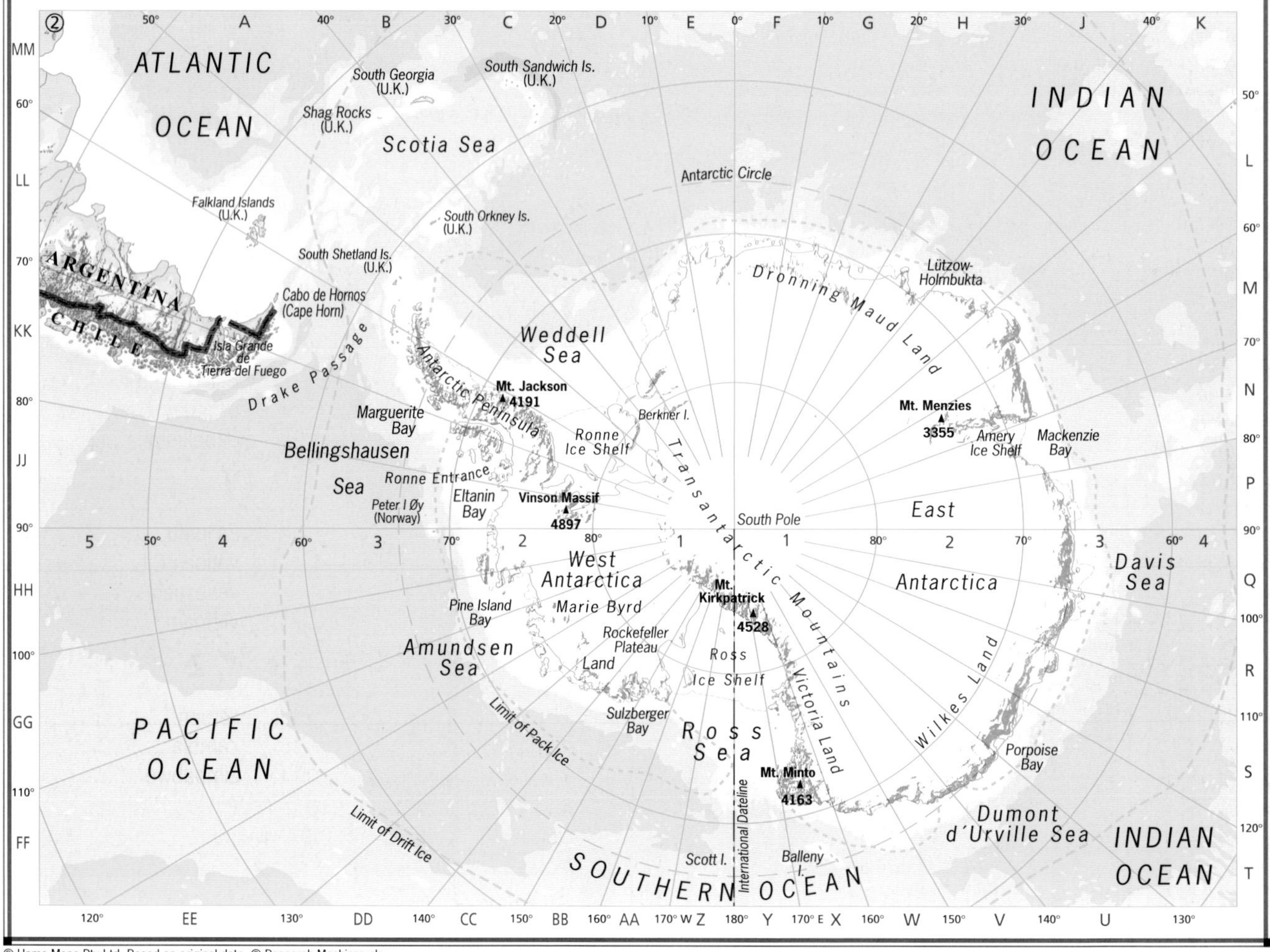
②
ATLANTIC OCEAN
South Georgia (U.K.)
South Sandwich Is. (U.K.)
Shag Rocks (U.K.)
Scotia Sea
INDIAN OCEAN
Antarctic Circle
Falkland Islands (U.K.)
South Orkney Is. (U.K.)
South Shetland Is. (U.K.)
Lützow-Holmbukta
ARGENTINA
Dronning Maud Land
Cabo de Hornos (Cape Horn)
CHILE
Isla Grande de Tierra del Fuego
Weddell Sea
Drake Passage
Antarctic Peninsula
Mt. Jackson
4191
Mt. Menzies
3355
Marguerite Bay
Berkner I.
Ronne Ice Shelf
Amery Ice Shelf
Mackenzie Bay
Bellingshausen Sea
Ronne Entrance
Transantarctic Mountains
Peter I Øy (Norway)
Eltanin Bay
Vinson Massif
4897
South Pole
East Antarctica
Davis Sea
West Antarctica
Mt. Kirkpatrick
4528
Pine Island Bay
Marie Byrd Land
Rockefeller Plateau
Amundsen Sea
Ross Ice Shelf
Victoria Land
Wilkes Land
Limit of Pack Ice
Sulzberger Bay
PACIFIC OCEAN
Ross Sea
Porpoise Bay
Mt. Minto
4163
Limit of Drift Ice
International Dateline
Dumont d'Urville Sea
Scott I.
Balleny I.
SOUTHERN OCEAN

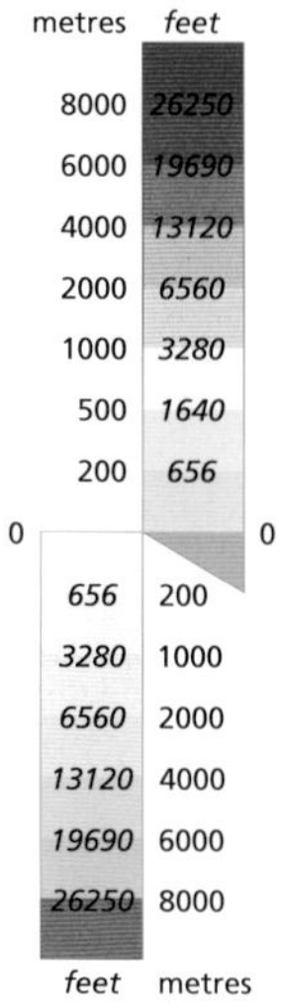
metres
feet
8000
26250
6000
19690
4000
13120
2000
6560
1000
3280
500
1640
200
656
0
0
656
200
3280
1000
6560
2000
13120
4000
19690
6000
26250
8000
feet
metres

- ■ over 3 million
- ■ 1 – 3 million
- ● 250 000 – 1 million
- ● 100 000 – 250 000
- ● 25 000 – 100 000
- • under 25 000
- —— country capital underline

INDEX TO COUNTRY MAPS

A

Afghanistan 91
Albania 68
Algeria 103
Andorra 61
Angola 98
Antigua & Barbuda 135
Argentina 142
Armenia 93
Australia 114
Austria 63
Azerbaijan 93

B

Bahamas, The 135
Bahrain 95
Bangladesh 88
Barbados 135
Belarus 70
Belgium 55
Belize 134
Benin 105
Bhutan 88
Bolivia 140
Bosnia and Herzegovina 66
Botswana 108
Brazil 141
Brunei 86
Bulgaria 67
Burkina 104
Burma (see Myanmar) 84
Burundi 106

C

Cambodia 84
Cameroon 105
Canada 122
Cape Verde 104
Central African Republic 106
Chad 100
Chile 142
China 80
Colombia 140
Comoros 109
Congo 105
Congo, Democratic Republic of the 106
Costa Rica 135
Côte d'Ivoire 104
Croatia 66
Cuba 135
Cyprus 92
Czech Republic 51

D

Denmark 49
Djibouti 101
Dominica 135
Dominican Republic 135

E

East Timor 87
Ecuador 140
Egypt 100
El Salvador 134
Equatorial Guinea 105
Eritrea 101
Estonia 49
Ethiopia 107

F

Fiji 112
Finland 48
France 58

G

Gabon 105
Gambia, The 104
Georgia 93
Germany 52
Ghana 104
Greece 68
Grenada 135
Guatemala 134
Guinea 104
Guinea-Bissau 104
Guyana 141

H

Haiti 135
Honduras 134
Hungary 66

I

Iceland 48
India 88
Indonesia 86
Iran 90
Iraq 90
Ireland 57
Israel 94
Italy 64

J

Jamaica 135
Japan 83
Jordan 94

K

Kazakhstan 77
Kenya 107
Kiribati 113
Kuwait 95
Kyrgyzstan 77

L

Laos 84
Latvia 49
Lebanon 94
Lesotho 108
Liberia 104
Libya 100
Liechtenstein 62
Lithuania 49
Luxembourg 55

M

Macedonia 68
Madagascar 109
Malawi 109
Malaysia 86
Maldives 89
Mali 102
Malta 65
Marshall Islands 112
Mauritania 102
Mauritius 109
Mexico 134
Micronesia, Federated States of 112
Moldova 67
Monaco 62
Mongolia 75
Montenegro 66
Morocco 102
Mozambique 109
Myanmar (Burma) 84

N

Namibia 108
Nauru 112
Nepal 88
Netherlands 55
New Zealand 116
Nicaragua 135
Niger 103
Nigeria 105
North Korea 82
Norway 48

O

Oman 91

P

Pakistan 91
Palau 112
Panama 135
Papua New Guinea 112
Paraguay 142
Peru 140
Philippines 85
Poland 50
Portugal 60

Q

Qatar 95

R

Romania 67
Russia 74
Rwanda 106

S

Saint Kitts and Nevis 135
Saint Lucia 135
Saint Vincent & the Grenadines 135
Samoa 113
San Marino 63
São Tomé and Príncipe 105
Saudi Arabia 90
Senegal 104
Serbia 66
Seychelles 109
Sierra Leone 104
Singapore 86
Slovakia 51
Slovenia 63
Solomon Islands 112
Somalia 107
South Africa 108
South Korea 82
Spain 60
Sri Lanka 89
Sudan 100
Suriname 141
Swaziland 109
Sweden 48
Switzerland 62
Syria 90

T

Taiwan 85
Tajikistan 91
Tanzania 107
Thailand 84
Togo 104
Tonga 113
Trinidad & Tobago 135
Tunisia 103
Turkey 92
Turkmenistan 91
Tuvalu 112

U

Uganda 106
Ukraine 70
United Arab Emirates 90
United Kingdom 56
United States 124
Uruguay 143
Uzbekistan 77

V

Vanuatu 112
Vatican City 64
Venezuela 140
Vietnam 84

Y, Z

Yemen 90
Zambia 108
Zimbabwe 108

GLOSSARY

This is an alphabetically arranged glossary of the geographical terms used on the maps and in this index. The first column shows the map form, the second the language of origin and the third the English translation.

A		
açude	Portuguese	reservoir
adası	Turkish	island
akra	Greek	peninsula
alpen	German	mountains
alpes	French	mountains
alpi	Italian	mountains
älven	Swedish	river
archipiélago	Spanish	archipelago
arquipélago	Portuguese	archipelago
B		
bab	Arabic	strait
bahía	Spanish	bay
bahir, bahr	Arabic	bay, lake, river
baía	Portuguese	bay
baie	French	bay
baja	Spanish	lower
bandar	Arabic, Somalian, Malay, Persian	harbour, port
baraji	Turkish	dam
barragem	Portuguese	reservoir
ben	Gaelic	mountain
Berg(e)	German	mountain(s)
boğazı	Turkish	strait
Bucht	German	bay
buḩayrat	Arabic	lake
burnu, burun	Turkish	cape
C		
cabo	Spanish	cape
canal	French, Spanish	canal, channel
canale	Italian	canal, channel
cerro	Spanish	mountain
chott	Arabic	marsh, salt lake
co	Tibetan	lake
collines	French	hills
cordillera	Spanish	range
D		
dağ(ı)	Turkish	mountain
dağlar(ı)	Turkish	mountains
danau	Indonesian	lake
daryacheh	Persian	lake
dasht	Persian	desert
djebel	Arabic	mountain(s)
-do	Korean	island
E		
embalse	Spanish	reservoir
erg	Arabic	sandy desert
estrecho	Spanish	strait
F		
feng	Chinese	mountain
-fjördur	Icelandic	fjord
-flói	Icelandic	bay
G		
Gebirge	German	range
golfe	French	bay, gulf
golfo	Italian, Portuguese, Spanish	bay, gulf
göl, gölü	Turkish	lake
gora	Russian	mountain
gory	Russian	mountains
gunong	Malay	mountain
gunung	Indonesian	mountain
H		
hai	Chinese	lake, sea
hāmūn	Persian	lake, marsh
hawr	Arabic	lake
hu	Chinese	lake, reservoir
I		
île(s)	French	island(s)
ilha(s)	Portuguese	island(s)
isla(s)	Spanish	island(s)
J		
jabal	Arabic	mountain(s)
-järvi	Finnish	lake
jaza'īr	Arabic	islands
jazīrat	Arabic	island
jbel	Arabic	mountain
jebel	Arabic	mountain
jezero	Serbo-Croatian	lake
jezioro	Polish	lake
jiang	Chinese	river
-jima	Japanese	island
-joki	Finnish	river
-jökull	Icelandic	glacier
K		
kepulauan	Indonesian	islands
khrebet	Russian	mountain range
-ko	Japanese	lake
kolpos	Greek	bay, gulf
körfezi	Turkish	bay, gulf
kryazh	Russian	ridge
kūh(ha)	Persian	mountain(s)
L		
lac	French	lake
lacul	Romanian	lake
lago	Italian, Portuguese, Spanish	lake
lagoa	Portuguese	lagoon
laguna	Spanish	lagoon, lake
limni	Greek	lake
ling	Chinese	mountain(s), peak
liqeni	Albanian	lake
loch, lough	Gaelic	lake
M		
massif	French	mountains
-meer	Dutch	lake, sea
mont	French	mount
monte	Italian, Portuguese, Spanish	mount
montes	Portuguese, Spanish	mountains
monts	French	mountains
muntii	Romanian	mountains
mys	Russian	cape
N		
nafud	Arabic	desert
nevado	Spanish	snow-capped mountain
nuruu	Mongolian	mountains
nuur	Mongolian	lake
O		
ostrov(a)	Russian	island(s)
ozero	Russian	lake
P		
pegunungan	Indonesian	mountains
pelagos	Greek	sea
pendi	Chinese	basin
pesky	Russian	sandy desert
pic	French	peak
pico	Portuguese, Spanish	peak
planalto	Portuguese	plateau
planina	Bulgarian	mountains
poluostrov	Russian	peninsula
puerto	Spanish	harbour, port
puncak	Indonesian	peak
punta	Italian, Spanish	point
puy	French	peak
Q		
qundao	Chinese	archipelago
R		
ras, rås, ra's	Arabic	cape
represa	Portuguese	dam, reservoir
-rettō	Japanese	archipelago
rio	Portuguese	river
río	Spanish	river
S		
sahra	Arabic	desert
salar	Spanish	salt flat
-san	Japanese, Korean	mountain
-sanmaek	Korean	mountains
sebkha	Arabic	salt flat
sebkhet	Arabic	salt marsh
See	German	lake
serra	Portuguese	range
severnaya, severo-	Russian	northern
shan	Chinese	mountain(s)
-shima	Japanese	island
-shotō	Japanese	islands
sierra	Spanish	range
T		
tanjona	Malagasy	cape
tanjung	Indonesian	cape
teluk	Indonesian	bay, gulf
ténéré	Berber	desert
-tō	Japanese	island
V		
vârful	Romanian	mountain
-vesi	Finnish	lake
vodokhranilishche	Russian	reservoir
volcán	Spanish	volcano
W		
wādī	Arabic	watercourse
Wald	German	forest
Z		
-zaki	Japanese	cape
zaliv	Russian	bay, gulf

Abbreviations

Ak.	Alaska
Al.	Alabama
Ariz.	Arizona
Ark.	Arkansas
B.C.	British Columbia
Calif.	California
Colo.	Colorado
Conn.	Connecticut
Del.	Delaware
Dem. Rep. of the Congo	Democratic Republic of the Congo
Eng.	England
Fla.	Florida
Ga.	Georgia
Ia.	Iowa
Id.	Idaho
Ill.	Illinois
Ind.	Indiana
Kans.	Kansas
Ky.	Kentucky
La.	Louisiana
Man.	Manitoba
Mass.	Massachusetts
Md.	Maryland
Me.	Maine
M.G.	Mato Grosso
Mich.	Michigan
Minn.	Minnesota
Miss.	Mississippi
Mo.	Missouri
Mont.	Montana
N.B.	New Brunswick
N.C.	North Carolina
N.D.	North Dakota
Nebr.	Nebraska
Nev.	Nevada
Nfld.	Newfoundland
N.H.	New Hampshire
N. Ire.	Northern Ireland
N.J.	New Jersey
N. Mex.	New Mexico
N.W.T.	Northwest Territories
N.Y.	New York
Oh.	Ohio
Okla.	Oklahoma
Ont.	Ontario
Oreg.	Oregon
Orkney Is.	Orkney Islands
Pa.	Pennsylvania
R.G.S.	Rio Grande do Sul
R.I.	Rhode Island
S.C.	South Carolina
Scot.	Scotland
S.D.	South Dakota
Shetland Is.	Shetland Islands
Tenn.	Tennessee
Tex.	Texas
UK	United Kingdom
US	United States
Ut.	Utah
Va.	Virginia
Vt.	Vermont
Wash.	Washington
Wis.	Wisconsin
W. Va.	West Virginia
Wyo.	Wyoming
Y.T.	Yukon Territory

How to use the index

This is an alphabetically arranged index of the places and features that can be found on the maps in this atlas. Each name is generally indexed to the largest scale map on which it appears. If that map covers a double page, the name will always be indexed by the left-hand page number.

Names composed of two or more words are alphabetised as if they were one word.

All names appear in full in the index, except for 'St.' and 'Ste.', which although abbreviated, are indexed as though spelled in full.

Where two or more places have the same name, they can be distinguished from each other by the country or province name which immediately follows the entry. These names are indexed in the alphabetical order of the country or province.

Alternative names, such as English translations, can also be found in the index and are cross-referenced to the map form by the '=' sign. In these cases the names also appear in brackets on the maps.

Settlements are indexed to the position of the symbol, all other features are indexed to the position of the name on the map.

Finding a name on the map

Each index entry contains the name, followed by a symbol indicating the feature type (for example, settlement, river), a page reference and a grid reference:

Name	Owosso	126	D2
	Owyhee	124	C2
	Owyhee	124	C2
Symbol	Oxford, *New Zealand*	112	D6
	Oxford, *United Kingdom*	40	A3
	Oxnard	130	C2
Page reference	Oyama	72	K5
	Oyapock	140	G3
	Oyem	98	G4
Grid reference	Oyen	122	D1

The grid reference locates a place or feature within a rectangle formed by the network of lines of longitude and latitude. A name can be found by referring to the red letters and numbers placed around the maps. First find the letter, which appears along the top and bottom of the map, and then the number, down the sides. The name will be found within the rectangle uniquely defined by that letter and number. A number in brackets preceding the grid reference indicates that the name is to be found within an inset map.

Symbols

- Continent name
- Country name
- State or province name
- Country capital
- State or province capital
- Settlement
- Mountain, volcano, peak
- Mountain range
- Physical region or feature
- River, canal
- Lake, salt lake
- Gulf, strait, bay
- Sea, ocean
- Cape, point
- Island or island group, rocky or coral reef
- Place of interest
- Historical or cultural region

A

Aachen	54	J4
Aalborg	48	E8
Aalen	52	F8
Aalst	54	G4
Aarau	62	D3
Aare	62	C3
Aarschot	54	G4
Aba	104	F3
Abādān	95	C1
Ābādeh	95	E1
Abadla	102	E2
Abaji	104	F3
Abakaliki	104	F3
Abakan	76	S7
Āb Anbar	95	E1
Abancay	140	C6
Abano Terme	62	G5
Abarqū	95	E1
Abashiri	82	N1
Abava	48	M8
Ābaya Hāyk'	106	F2
Abay Wenz	100	G5
Abbeville, *France*	54	D4
Abbeville, *US*	130	C4
Abd al Kūrī	90	F7
Abéché	100	D5
Abengourou	104	D3
Abenójar	60	F6
Åbenrå	52	E1
Abensberg	52	G8
Abeokuta	104	E3
Aberaeron	56	H9
Aberdeen, *South Africa*	108	C6
Aberdeen, *UK*	56	K4
Aberdeen, *Miss., US*	130	D3
Aberdeen, *S.D., US*	126	G1
Aberdeen, *Wash., US*	126	B1
Aberdeen Lake	122	M4
Aberystwyth	56	H9
Abez'	70	M1
Abhā	100	H4
Abhar	92	N5
Abidjan	104	D3
Abilene	132	G2
Abiline	120	M6
Abingdon, *UK*	54	A3
Abingdon, *US*	130	E2
Abnûb	100	F2
Aboisso	104	D3
Abomey	104	E3
Abong Mbang	104	G4
Abou Déia	100	C5
Abqaiq	95	C4
Abrantes	60	B5
Abrud	66	L3
Absaroka Range	126	E1
Abū al Abayḍ	95	E4
Abu Aweigîla	94	B6
Abu Ballâs	100	E3
Abu Dhabi = Abū Ẓabī	95	F4
Abu Hamed	100	F4
Abuja	104	F3
Abumombazi	106	C3
Ābune Yosēf	100	G5
Abū Nujaym	100	C1
Abu Qarin	100	C1
Aburo	106	E3
Abu Simbel	100	F3
Abut Head	116	B6
Abuye Meda	106	F1
Abū Ẓabī	95	F4
Abv Nujaym	102	J2
Acaponeta	124	E7
Acapulco	134	E5
Acará	140	H4
Acarigua	140	D2
Accra	104	D3
Achaguas	134	L7
Achayvayam	78	W4
Acheng	80	H1
Achenkirch	62	G3
Achen See	62	G3
Achill Island	56	B8
Achim	52	E3
Achinsk	76	S6
Achit	70	L3
Aci Göl	68	M7
A Cihanbeyli	68	Q6
Acireale	64	K11
Acklins Island	134	K4
Aconcagua	138	D7
Açores	102	(1)B2
A Coruña	60	B1
Acquarossa	62	D4
Acqui Terme	62	D6
Acre	140	C5
Acri	64	L9
Ada	50	K12
Ada	130	B3
Adak Island	132	(3)C1
Adam	90	G5
Adamas	68	G8
Adams Island	116	(2)B1
'Adan	90	E7
Adana	92	F5
Adda	62	E5
Ad Dafrah	95	E5
Ad Dahnā	95	B3
Ad Dakhla	102	B4
Ad Dammām	95	D3
Ad Dawādimī	90	D5
Ad Dawḥah	95	D4
Ad Dilam	95	B5
Ad Dir'īyah	95	B4
Addis Ababa = Ādīs Ābeba	106	F2
Ad Dīwānīyah	90	D3
Adel	128	B2
Adelaide	114	G6
Adelaide Peninsula	122	M3
Adelaide River	114	F2
Aden = Adan	90	E7
Aderbissinat	104	F1
Adh Dhayd	95	F4
Adi	87	D3
Adige	62	G5
Adīgrat	100	G5
Adilabad	88	C5
Adin	126	B2
Adīrī	100	B2
Ādīs Ābeba	106	F2
Adi Ugri	100	G5
Adıyaman	90	C2
Adjud	66	Q3
Adler	92	H2
Admiralty Island	122	E5
Admiralty Islands	112	E6
Adoni	88	C5
Adour	58	F10
Adra	60	H8
Adrano	64	J11
Adrar	102	E3
Adrar des Ifôghas	102	F5
Adrar Tamgak	102	G5
Adria	62	H5
Adriatic Sea	64	H4
Adycha	78	P3
Adygeya	92	J1
Adygeysk	92	H1
Adzopé	104	D3
Adz'vavom	70	L1
Aegean Sea	68	H5
A Estrada	60	B2
Afghanistan	90	H3
Afgooye	106	H3
'Afīf	100	H3
Afikpo	104	F3
Afmadow	106	G3
Afognak Island	132	(1)G4
A Fonsagrada	60	C1
Afragola	64	J8
'Afrīn	92	G5
Afuá	140	G4
'Afula	94	C4
Afyon	68	N6
Agadez	102	G5
Agadir	102	D2
Agadyr'	76	N8
Agalega Islands	98	J7
Agan	78	B4
Āgaro	106	F2
Agartala	88	F4
Agathonisi	68	J7
Agattu Island	78	W6
Ağcabädi	92	M3
Agde	58	J10
Agen	58	F9
Agia Triada	68	D7
Ağin	92	H4
Aginskoye	76	S6
Agiokampos	68	E5
Agios Efstratios	68	H5
Agios Georgios	68	F7
Agios Nikolaos	68	H9
Agnibilekrou	104	D3
Agnita	66	M4
Agra	88	C3
Agrakhanskiy Poluostrov	92	M2
Agri	64	L8
Ağri	92	K4
Agrigento	64	H11
Agrinio	68	D6
Agropoli	64	K8
Agryz	70	K3
Ağsu	92	N3
Agua Prieta	132	E2
Aguascalientes	134	D4
A Gudiña	60	C2
Aguelhok	102	F5
Águilas	60	J7
Agulhas Negras	140	H8
Ağva	68	M3
Ahar	92	M4
Ahaura	116	C6
Ahaus	54	K2
Ahititi	116	E4
Ahlen	54	K3
Ahmadabad	88	B4
Ahmadnagar	88	B5
Ahmadpur East	88	B3
Ahr	52	B6
Ahram	95	D2
Ahrensburg	52	F3
Ahvāz	90	E3
Aichach	52	G8
Aigialousa	92	F6
Aigina	68	F7
Aigina	68	F7
Aigio	68	E6
Aigosthena	68	F6
Aiguillon	58	F9
Aihui	78	M6
Aim	78	N5
Ain	58	L7
Aïn Beïda	102	G1
'Aîn Ben Tili	102	D3

Aïn Bessem 60 P8
Aïn el Hadjel 60 P9
Aïn Oussera 102 F1
Ainsa 60 L2
Aïn Sefra 102 E2
Aïn Taya 60 P8
Aïn-Tédélès 60 L8
Aïn Témouchent 60 J9
Airão 140 E4
Aire 56 L8
Air Force Island 122 S3
Airolo 62 D4
Airpanas 87 C4
Aisne 54 F5
Aitape 87 F3
Aitkin 128 B1
Aitutaki 112 K7
Aiud 66 L3
Aix-en-Provence 58 L10
Aix-les-Bains 58 L8
Aizawl 88 F4
Aizkraukle 48 N8
Aizpute 48 L8
Aizu-wakamatsu 82 K5
Ajaccio 64 C7
Aj Bogd Uul 80 B2
Ajdābiyā 100 D1
Ajigasawa 82 L3
Ajka 50 G10
Ajlun 94 C4
Ajmān 95 F4
Ajmer 88 B3
Ajo 132 D2
Akanthou 94 A1
Akaroa 116 D6
Akasha 100 F3
Akashi 82 H6
Akbalyk 76 P8
Akbasty 76 L8
Akçakale 92 H5
Akçakoca 68 P3
Akdağmadeni 92 F4
Aken 52 H5
Aketi 106 C3
Akhalk'alak'i 92 K3
Akhisar 68 K6
Akhmīm 100 F2
Akhty 92 M3
Akimiski Island 122 Q6
Akita 82 L4
Akjoujt 102 C5
Akka 102 D3
Akkajaure 48 J3
Akkeshi 82 N2
'Akko 94 C4
Akmeqit 90 L2
Aknanes 48 (1)B2
Akobo 106 E2
Akola 88 C4
Akonolinga 104 G4
Akordat 100 G4
Akpatok Island 122 T4
Akqi 76 P9
Akra Drepano 68 G5
Akra Sounio 68 F7
Akra Spatha 68 F9
Akra Trypiti 68 G9
Åkrehamn 48 C7
Akron 128 D2
Aksaray 92 E4
Aksarka 76 M4
Akşehir 68 P6
Akseki 68 P7
Aksha 78 J6
Akshiy 76 P9
Aksu 76 Q9
Aksuat 76 Q8
Āksum 100 G5
Aktau, *Kazakhstan* 46 K3
Aktau, *Kazakhstan* 76 N7
Aktobe 70 L4
Aktogay, *Kazakhstan* 76 N8
Aktogay, *Kazakhstan* 76 P8
Aktuma 76 M8
Akula 106 C3
Akulivik 122 R4
Akune 82 F8
Akure 104 F3
Akureyri 48 (1)E2
Akwanga 104 F3
Alabama 130 D3
Alaçam 92 F3
Alaejos 60 E3
Alagoas 140 K5
Alagoinhas 140 K6
Alagón 60 J3
Al Ahmadi 95 C2
Al 'Amārah 90 E3
Alaminos 84 F3
Alamo 126 C3
Alamogordo 132 E2
Alamo Lake 132 D2
Åland 48 K6
Alanya 92 E5
Alappuzha 88 C7
Al Argoub 102 B4
Al Arṭāwīyah 90 E4
Alaşehir 68 L6
Al 'Ashurīyah 100 H1
Alaska 132 (1)F2
Alaska Peninsula 132 (1)E4
Alaska Range 132 (1)G3
Alassio 62 D6
Alatri 64 H7
Alatyr' 70 J4
Alaverdi 92 L3
Alavus 48 M5
Alaykuu 76 N9
Al 'Ayn 95 F4
Alazeya 78 S2
Alba, *Italy* 62 D6
Alba, *Spain* 60 E4
Albacete 60 J5
Alba Iulia 66 L3
Albania 68 B3
Albany 122 Q6
Albany, *Australia* 114 C6
Albany, *Ga., US* 130 E3
Albany, *Ky., US* 130 E2
Albany, *N.Y., US* 128 F2
Albany, *Oreg., US* 126 B2
Albardão do João Maria 142 L4
Al Bardī 100 D1
Al Başrah 90 E3
Albatross Bay 114 H2
Albatross Point 116 E4
Al Bayḍā' 100 D1
Albenga 62 D6
Albert 54 E4
Alberta 122 H6
Albertirsa 50 J10
Albert Kanaal 54 G3
Albert Lea 128 B2
Albert Nile 106 E3
Albertville 58 M8
Albi 58 H10
Albina 140 G2
Albino 62 E5
Albion 126 F1
Ålborg Bugt 48 F8
Albox 60 H7
Albstadt 52 E8
Albufeira 60 B7
Āl Bū Kamāl 92 J6
Albuquerque 132 E1
Al Burayj 94 D2
Al Buraymī 90 G5
Alburquerque 60 D5
Albury 114 J7
Al Buşayyah 95 B1
Alcácer do Sal 60 B6
Alcala de Guadaira 60 E7
Alcala de Henares 60 G4
Alcalá la Real 60 G7
Alcamo 64 G11
Alcañiz 60 K3
Alcantarilla 60 J7
Alcaraz 60 H6
Alcaudete 60 F7
Alcazar de San Juan 60 G5
Alcobendas 60 G4
Alcoi 60 K6
Alcolea del Pinar 60 H3
Alcorcón 60 G4
Alcoutim 60 C7
Aldabra Group 108 (2)A2
Aldan 78 M5
Aldan 78 N5
Aldeburgh 54 D2
Alderney 58 C4
Aldershot 54 B3
Aleg 102 C5
Aleksandrov-Sakhalinskiy 78 Q6
Aleksandrovskiy Zavod 78 K6
Aleksandrovskoye 70 Q2
Alekseyevka 76 N7
Aleksinac 66 J6
Alençon 58 F5
Aleppo = Ḥalab 92 G5
Aléria 64 D6
Alès 58 K9
Aleşd 50 M10
Alessandria 62 D6
Ålesund 48 D5
Aleutian Islands 132 (3)B1
Aleutian Range 132 (1)F4
Aleutian Trench 74 W5
Alexander Archipelago 132 (1)K4
Alexander Bay 108 B5
Alexander City 130 D3
Alexandra 116 B7
Alexandreia 68 E4
Alexandria = El Iskandarîya, *Egypt* 100 E1
Alexandria, *Romania* 66 N6
Alexandria, *La., US* 130 C3
Alexandria, *Minn., US* 128 A1
Alexandria, *Va., US* 128 E3
Alexandroupoli 68 H4
Alexis Creek 122 G6
Aley 76 Q7
'Āley 94 C3
Aleysk 76 Q7
Al Farwānīyah 95 B2
Al Fāw 95 C2
Alfeld 52 E5
Alföld 66 H2
Alfonsine 62 H6
Alfreton 54 A1
Al Fuḥayḥil 95 C2
Al-Fujayrah 95 G4
Algeciras 60 E8
Algemes 60 K5
Algena 100 G4
Alger 102 F1
Algeria 102 E3
Al Ghāṭ 95 A3
Al Ghayḍah 90 F6
Alghero 64 C8
Algiers = Alger 102 F1
Algona 128 B2
Al Ḥadīthah 94 E5
Alhama de Murcia 60 J7
Al Ḥamar 95 B5
Al Ḥamīdīyah 94 C2
Al Ḥammādah al Ḥamrā' 102 G3
Al Harūj al Aswad 100 C2
Al Ḥasakah 92 J5
Alhaurmín el Grande 60 F8
Al Ḥijāz 100 G2
Al Ḥillah 90 D3
Al Ḥilwah 95 B5
Al Hoceima 102 E1
Al Ḥudaydah 100 H5
Al Hufūf 95 C4
Al Humayḍah 90 C4
Aliabad 95 F2
Aliağa 68 J6
Aliakmonas 68 E4
Äli Bayramlı 92 N4
Alicante 60 K6
Alice 130 B4
Alice Springs 114 F4
Alicudi 64 J10
Aligarh 88 C3
Alindao 106 C2
Alingås 48 G8
Alisos 132 D2
Aliwal North 108 D6
Al Jabal al Akhḍar 100 D1
Al Jaghbūb 100 D2
Al Jālamīd 100 G1
Al Jarah 95 B2
Al Jawf, *Libya* 100 D3
Al Jawf, *Saudi Arabia* 100 G2
Aljezur 60 B7
Al Jifārah 95 A5
Al Jubayl 95 C3
Aljustrel 60 B7
Al Kāmil 90 G5
Al Khābūrah 95 G5
Al Khālis 92 L7
Al Kharj 95 B4
Al Khaṣab 95 G3
Al Khawr 95 D4
Al Khubar 95 D3
Al Khufrah 100 D3
Al Khums 102 H2
Al Khuwayr 95 D3
Al Kir'ānah 95 D4
Alkmaar 54 G2
Al Kūt 90 E3
Al Kuwayt 95 C2
Al Lādhiqīyah 92 F6
Allahabad 88 D3
Allakh-Yun' 78 P4
Alldays 108 D4
Allen 84 G4
Allendale 130 E3
Allentown 128 E2
Aller 52 E4
Aller = Cabañaquinta 60 E1
Alliance 126 F2
Allier 58 J8
Allinge 50 D2
Al Līth 100 H3
Alma, *Canada* 128 F1
Alma, *Nebr., US* 126 G2
Alma, *Wis., US* 128 B2
Almada 60 A6
Almadén 60 F6
Al Madīnah 100 G3
Al Mahbas 102 D3
Al Majma'ah 90 E4
Almalyk 76 M9
Al Manāmah 95 D3
Almansa 60 J6
Al Ma'qil 95 B1
Al Marj 100 D1
Almaty 76 P9
Al Mawşil 92 K5
Al Mazāḥimīyah 95 B4
Almazán 60 H3
Almeirim 140 G4
Almelo 54 J2
Almendralejo 60 D6
Almería 60 H8
Al'met'yevsk 76 J7
Almiros 68 E5
Al Mish'āb 95 C2
Almonte 60 D7
Almora 88 C3
Almosa 126 E3
Al Mubarraz 95 C4
Al Mudawwara 94 D7
Al Mukallā 90 E7
Al Mukhā 100 H5
Almuñécar 60 G8
Al Muqdādīyah 92 L7
Al Nu'ayrīyah 95 C3
Alnwick 56 L6
Alonnisos 68 F5
Alor 87 B4
Alor Setar 84 C5
Alotau 114 K2
Alpena 128 D1
Alphen 54 G2
Alpi Lepontine 62 D4
Alpine 132 E2
Alpi Orobie 62 E4
Alps 62 B5
Al Qadmūs 94 D1
Al Qalībah 100 G2
Al Qāmishlī 92 J5
Al Qar'ah 95 B3
Al Qarqar 94 E5
Al Qaryāt 100 B1
Al Qaryatayn 94 E2
Al Qaṭīf 95 C3
Al Qaṭrūn 100 B3
Al Qunayṭirah 94 C3
Al Qunfudhah 100 H4
Al Qurayyāt 100 G1
Al Qurnah 95 B1
Al 'Quşayr, *Iraq* 95 A1
Al 'Quşayr, *Syria* 94 D2
Al Quṭayfah 94 D3
Als 52 E1
Alsask 122 K6
Alsasua 60 H2
Alsfeld 52 E6
Alta 48 M2
Altaelva 48 M2
Altai Mountains 80 A1
Al Tamīnī 100 D1
Altamira 140 G4
Altamura 64 L8
Altanbulag 78 H6
Altay 76 R7
Altay, *China* 76 R8
Altay, *Mongolia* 80 B1
Altdorf 62 D4
Alte Mellum 52 D3
Altenberg 52 J6
Altenburg 52 H6
Altenkirchen 52 J2
Altkirch 62 C3
Alto Garças 140 G7
Alto Molócuè 108 F3
Alton, *UK* 54 B3
Alton, *US* 128 B3
Altoona 128 E2
Alto Parnaiba 140 H5
Altötting 62 H2
Altun Shan 76 S10
Alturas 126 B2
Altus 130 B3
Al 'Ubaylah 90 F5
Alūksne 48 P8
Alupka 92 E1
Al 'Uqaylah 100 C1
Alushta 92 F1
Al 'Uthmānīyah 95 C4
Al 'Uwaynāt, *Libya* 100 B2
Al 'Uwaynāt, *Libya* 100 D3
Al 'Uwayqīlah 100 H1
Al 'Uzayr 95 B1
Alva 130 B2
Alvarães 140 E4
Älvdalen 48 H6
Älvsbyn 48 L4
Al Wafrā' 95 B2
Al Wajh 100 G2
Al Wannān 95 C3
Alwar 88 C3
Al Wari'ah 95 B3
Alxa Zouqi 80 D3
Alytus 50 P3
Alzey 52 D7
Alzira 60 K5
Amadi 106 E2
Amādīyah 92 K5
Amadjuak Lake 122 S4
Amadora 60 A6
Amahai 87 C3
Amakusa-Shimo-shima 82 E7
Amaliada 68 D7
Amalner 88 C4
Amamapare 87 E3
Amambaí 142 K3
Amami-Ōshima 74 S7
Amanab 87 F3
Amandola 64 H6
Amantea 64 L9
Amapá 140 G3
Amapá 140 G3
Amarante 140 J5
Amarapura 84 B2
Amareleja 60 C6
Amarillo 132 F1
Amasya 92 F3
Amay 54 H4
Amazar 78 L6
Amazon = Amazonas 138 F4
Amazonas 140 D4
Amazonas 140 E4
Ambala 88 C2
Ambanjā 108 H2
Ambarchik 78 U3
Ambato 140 B4
Ambato Boeny 108 H3
Ambatondrazaka 108 H3
Amberg 52 G7
Ambikapur 88 D4
Ambilobe 108 H2
Ambohimahasoa 108 H4
Amboise 58 G6
Ambon 87 C3
Ambositra 108 H4
Ambovombe 108 H5
Amchitka Island 132 (3)B1
Amderma 76 L4
Amdo 88 F2
Ameland 54 H1
Amengel'dy 76 M7
American Falls 126 D2
American Samoa 112 J7
Americus 130 E3
Amersfoort 54 H2
Amery 122 N5
Amery Ice Shelf 144 (2)M2
Ames 128 B2
Amfilochia 68 D6
Amfissa 68 E6
Amga 78 L5
Amga 78 N4
Amguid 102 G3
Amgun' 78 P6
Amherst 122 U7
Amiens 54 E5
Amirante Islands 108 (2)B2
Amistad Reservoir 132 F3
Amlekhganj 88 D3
Åmli 48 E7
'Amm Adam 100 G4
'Ammān 94 C5
Ammerland 54 K1
Ammersee 62 F2
Ammochostos 92 E6
Ammochostos Bay 94 A1
Amo 84 C2
Amol 90 F2
Amorgos 68 H8
Amos 128 E1
Amourj 102 D5
Ampana 87 B3
Ampanihy 108 G4
Amparai 88 D7

Ampezzo 62 H4
Amposta 60 L4
Amrān 90 D6
Amravati 88 C4
Amritsar 88 B2
Amroha 88 C3
Amrum 52 D2
Amsterdam, Netherlands 54 G2
Amsterdam, US 128 F2
Amstetten 62 K2
Am Timan 100 D5
Amudar'ya 76 L9
Amundsen Gulf 122 G2
Amundsen Sea 144 (2)GG3
Amungen 48 H6
Amuntai 86 F3
Amur 78 P6
Amursk 78 P6
Amvrakikos Kolpos 68 C6
Anabanua 87 B3
Anabar 78 J2
Anaconda 126 D1
Anacortes 126 B1
Anadarko 126 G3
Anadolu Dağları 92 H3
Anadyr' 78 X4
Anadyrskaya Nizmennost' 78 X3
Anadyrskiy Zaliv 78 Y3
Anafi 68 H8
'Ānah 92 J6
Anaheim 132 C2
Anáhuac 132 F3
Analalava 108 H2
Anamur 92 E5
Anan 82 H7
Anantapur 88 C6
Anan'yiv 66 T2
Anapa 92 G1
Anápolis 140 H7
Anār 95 F1
Anārak 90 F3
Anardara 90 H3
Anatolia 68 M6
Añatuya 142 J4
Anchorage 132 (1)H3
Ancona 64 H5
Ancud 142 G7
Anda 80 H1
Andalgalá 142 H4
Åndalsnes 48 D5
Andalusia 130 D3
Andaman Islands 84 A4
Andaman Sea 84 A4
Andapa 108 H2
Andarāb 90 J2
Andenne 54 H4
Andéramboukane 104 E1
Andermatt 62 D4
Andernach 54 K4
Anderson 122 F3
Anderson 130 E3
Andes 138 D5
Andfjorden 48 J2
Andijan 76 N9
Andilamena 108 H3
Andipsara 68 H6
Andkhvoy 90 J2
Andoas 140 B4
Andong 82 E5
Andorra 60 L2
Andorra la Vella 60 M2
Andover 54 A3
Andøya 48 H2
Andradina 142 L3
Andreanof Islands 132 (3)C1
Andrews 132 F2
Andria 64 L7
Andriamena 108 H3
Andros 68 G7
Andros, Greece 68 G7
Andros, The Bahamas 130 F5
Andros Town 130 F5
Andrott 88 B6
Andrychów 50 J8
Andújar 60 F6
Andulo 108 B2
Aneto 60 L2
Angara 78 G5
Angarsk 78 G6
Ånge 48 H5
Angel de la Guarda 132 D3
Angeles 84 G3
Ängelholm 48 G8
Angeln 52 E2
Angermünde 52 K4
Angern 62 M2
Angers 58 E6
Anglesey 56 H8
Angmagssalik = Tasiilaq 122 Z3
Ango 106 D3
Angoche 108 F3
Angohrān 95 G3
Angol 142 G6
Angola 98 E7
Angola 128 D2
Angostura Reservoir 126 F2
Angoulême 58 F8
Angren 76 M9
Anguilla 134 M5
Aniak 132 (1)F3
Anina 66 J4
Anıyaman 92 H5
Ankang 80 D4
Ankara 92 E4
Ankazoabo 108 G4
Anklam 52 J3
Ankpa 104 F3
Ånn 48 G5
Anna 70 H4
Annaba 102 G1
Annaberg-Buchholz 52 H6
An Nabk, Saudi Arabia 94 E5
An Nabk, Syria 94 D2
An Nafud 100 G2
An Nāirīyah 90 E3
An Najaf 90 D3
Annapolis 128 E3
Annapurna 88 D3
Ann Arbor 128 D2
An Nāşirīyah 100 J1
Annecy 62 B5
Annemasse 62 B4
Anniston 130 D3
Annobón 104 F5
Annonay 58 K8
An Nukhayb 90 D3
Anqing 80 F4
Ansbach 52 F7
Anshan 82 B3
Anshun 80 D5
Ansley 126 G2
Anson 130 B3
Ansongo 102 F5
Antakya 92 G5
Antalaha 108 J2
Antalya 68 N8
Antalya Körfezi 68 N8
Antananarivo 108 H3
Antarctic Peninsula 144 (2)LL3
Antequera 60 F7
Anti-Atlas 102 D3
Antibes 62 C7
Antigo 128 C1
Antigua 134 M5
Antigua and Barbuda 134 M5
Antikythira 68 F9
Antiparos 68 G7
Antipaxoi 68 C5
Antipayuta 76 P4
Antipodes Islands 116 (3)A1
Antlers 130 B3
Antofagasta 142 G3
Antonito 126 E3
Antrim 56 F7
Antropovo 70 H3
Antsalova 108 G3
Antsirabe 108 H3
Antsirañana 108 H2
Antu 82 E2
Antwerp = Antwerpen 54 G3
Antwerpen 54 G3
Anuradhapura 88 D7
Anveh 95 F3
Anxi 80 B2
Anyang, China 80 E3
Anyang, South Korea 82 D5
Anyuysk 78 U3
Anzhero-Sudzhensk 76 R6
Anzi 106 C4
Anzio 64 G7
Aoga-shima 82 K7
Aomori 82 L3
Aoraki (Mount Cook) 116 C6
Aosta 62 C5
Aoukâr 102 C5
Aoukoukar 104 C1
Apalachee Bay 130 E4
Apalachicola 130 D4
Aparri 84 G3
Apatin 66 F4
Apatity 70 F1
Ape 48 P8
Apeldoorn 54 H2
Api 88 D2
Apia 112 J7
Apoera 140 F2
Apolda 52 G5
Apollo Bay 114 H7
Aporé 140 G7
Apostle Islands 128 B1
Apoteri 140 F3
Appalachian Mountains 130 E3
Appennino 64 G5
Appennino Abruzzese 64 H6
Appennino Calabro 64 K10
Appennino Lucano 64 K8
Appennino Tosco-Emiliano 62 E6
Appennino Umbro-Marchigiano 64 H6
Appleton 128 C2
Aprilia 64 G7
Apure 140 D2
Apurimac 140 C6
Āqā 90 H3
'Aqaba 94 C7
Aquidauana 140 F8
Ara 88 D3
Arabian Sea 90 H6
Aracaju 140 K6
Aracati 140 K4
Araçatuba 140 G8
Aracuca 134 L7
Arad 66 J3
Arādah 90 F5
Arafura Sea 87 D5
Aragarças 140 G7
Araguaia 138 F4
Araguaína 140 H5
Araguari 140 H7
Araguatins 140 H5
Arāk 90 E3
Arak 102 F3
Aral Sea 76 K8
Aral'sk 70 M5
Aranda de Duero 60 G3
Arandjelovac 66 H5
Aran Island 56 D6
Aran Islands 56 B8
Aranjuez 60 G4
Aranos 108 B4
Aranyaprathet 84 C4
Araouane 102 E5
Arapahoe 126 G2
Arapiraca 140 K5
'Ar'ar 90 D3
Araras 140 G5
Ararat 92 L4
Arauca 140 D2
Araxá 140 H7
Araz 92 L4
Arbīl 92 K5
Arbon 62 E3
Arbre du Ténéré 102 G5
Arbroath 56 K5
Arcachon 58 D9
Arcadia 130 E4
Arcata 126 B2
Archidona 60 F7
Archipelago of the Recherche 114 D6
Archipel de la Société 112 L7
Archipel des Tuamotu 112 M7
Archipiélago de Camagüey 134 J4
Archipiélago de la Reina Adelaida 142 F9
Archipiélago de los Chonos 142 F7
Arco, Italy 62 F5
Arco, US 126 D2
Arcos de la Frontera 60 E8
Arctic Bay 122 P2
Arctic Ocean 144 (1)A1
Arctic Red River 122 E3
Arda 68 H3
Ardabīl 92 N4
Ardahan 92 K3
Årdalstangen 48 D6
Ardas 68 J3
Ardatov 70 J4
Ardennes 54 G4
Ardestān 90 F3
Ardila 60 C6
Ardmore 124 G5
Aredo 87 D3
Areia Branca 140 K5
Arendal 48 E7
Arenys de Mar 60 N3
Areopoli 68 E8
Arequipa 140 C7
Arere 140 G4
Arévalo 60 F3
Arezzo 64 F5
Argan 76 R9
Argenta 62 G6
Argentan 54 B6
Argentera 62 B6
Argentina 142 H6
Argenton-sur-Creuse 58 G7
Argeş 66 N5
Argolikos Kolpos 68 E7
Argos 68 E7
Argos Orestiko 68 D4
Argostoli 68 C6
Argun' 78 K6
Argungu 104 E2
Argunsk 78 L6
Argyll 56 G5
Ar Horqin Qi 80 G2
Århus 48 F8
Ariano Irpino 64 K7
Ari Atoll 88 B8
Arica 140 C7
Ariège 58 G11
Arihge 60 M2
Arinos 140 F6
Aripuanã 140 E5
Aripuanã 140 E5
Ariquemes 140 E5
Arizona 132 D2
Arjäng 48 G7
Arjasa 86 F4
Arka 78 Q5
Arkadak 70 H4
Arkadelphia 130 C3
Arkalyk 76 M7
Arkansas 130 C3
Arkansas 130 C3
Arkansas City 130 B2
Arkhalts'ikhe 92 K3
Arkhangel'sk 70 H2
Arkhipelag Nordenshel'da 76 R2
Arklow 56 F9
Arkoudi 68 C6
Arles 58 K10
Arlington, Oreg., US 126 B1
Arlington, Tex., US 130 B3
Arlington, Va., US 128 E3
Arlit 102 G5
Arlon 54 H4
Armagh 56 F7
Armavir 92 J1
Armenia 92 K3
Armenia 140 B3
Armentières 54 E4
Armidale 114 K6
Armstrong 122 P6
Armyans'k 70 F5
Arnedo 60 H2
Arnett 130 B2
Arnhem 54 H3
Arnhem Land 114 F2
Arno 62 F7
Arnøy 48 G3
Arnøya 48 L1
Arnprior 128 E1
Arnsberg 54 L3
Arnstadt 52 F6
Aroab 108 B5
Arolsen 52 E5
Aroma 100 G4
Arorae 112 H6
Arquipélago dos Bijagós 104 A2
Ar Ramādī 90 D3
Ar Ramlah 94 C7
Arran 56 G6
Ar Raqqah 92 H6
Arras 54 E4
Arrasate 60 H1
Ar Rastan 94 D2
Ar Rawdah 90 E7
Ar Rayn 95 A5
Arrecife 102 C3
Ar Riyād 90 E5
Arrow Lake 126 C1
Arroyo Grande 132 B1
Ar Ruşāfah 92 H6
Ar Rustāq 90 G5
Ar Rutba 90 D3
Ar Ruways 90 F5
Årsandøy 48 G4
Arta, Greece 68 C5
Arta, Mallorca 60 P5
Artem 82 G2
Artemovsk 76 S7
Artemovskiy 78 K5
Artesia 132 F2
Arthur 126 F2
Arthur's Town 130 F5
Artigas 142 K5
Artillery Lake 122 J4
Artsyz 66 S4
Artux 76 P10
Artvin 92 J3
Artyk 78 Q4
Aru 112 D6
Arua 106 E3
Aruba 134 K6
Arumã 140 E4
Arusha 106 F4
Arvayheer 80 C1
Arviat 122 N4
Arvidsjaur 48 K4
Arvika 48 G7
Ary 76 Y3
Aryta 78 M4
Arzamas 70 H3
Arzew 60 K9
Arzignano 62 G5
Asahi-dake 82 M2
Asahikawa 82 M2
Āsalē 100 G5
Asansol 88 E4
Asarum 50 D1
Asbest 70 M3
Ascea 64 K8
Ascension 98 B6
Ascensión 140 E7
Aschaffenburg 52 E7
Aschersleben 52 G5
Ascoli Piceno 64 H6
Āsela 106 F2
Åsele 48 J4
Asenovgrad 68 G3
Asha 70 L3
Ashburton 116 C6
Ashdod 94 B5
Asherton 130 B4
Asheville 128 D3
Ashford 54 C3
Ash Fork 132 D1
Ashgabat 90 G2
Ashington 56 L6
Ashizuri-misaki 82 G7
Ashkhabad = Ashgabat 90 G2
Ashland, Kans., US 126 G3
Ashland, Ky., US 128 D3
Ashland, Mont., US 126 E1
Ashland, Oreg., US 126 B2
Ashland, Wis., US 128 B1
Ashoro 82 M2
Ashqelon 94 B5
Ash Shadādah 92 J5
Ash Shāriqah 95 F4
Ash Sharqāt 92 K6
Ash Shihr 90 E7
Ash Shu'bah 95 A2
Ash Shuqayq 100 H4
Ash Shurayf 100 G2
Ash Shuwayrif 102 H3
Ashtabula 128 D2
Ashuanipi 122 T6
Ashuanipi Lake 122 T6
Asia 112 B2
Āsika 88 D5
Asilah 102 D1
Asinara 64 C7
Asino 76 R6
Asīr 100 H3
Aşkale 92 J4
Askim 48 F7
Askot 88 D3
Asmara 100 G4
Åsnen 48 H8
Āsosa 106 E1
Aspang Markt 62 M3
Aspe 60 K6
Aspermont 132 F2
As Pontes de Garcia Rodriguez 60 C1
As Sa'an 94 E1
Assab 100 H5
As Şalīf 90 D6
As Salmān 90 E3
As Salwā 95 D4
Assamakka 102 G5
As Samāwah 100 J1
Aş Şanamayn 94 D3
As Sarīr 100 D2
Asse 54 G4
Assemini 64 C9
Assen 54 J2
Assens 52 E1
As Sīb 95 H5
As Sidrah 100 C1
Assiniboia 122 K7
Assiniboine 122 M7
Assis 142 L3
Assisi 64 G5
As Sukhnah 92 H6
As Sulaymānīyah 92 L6

As Sulayyil 90 E5
Assumption Island 106 H5
As Suwaydā' 94 D4
As Suwayh 90 G5
Astakida 68 J9
Astana 76 N7
Astara 90 E2
Asti 62 D6
Astorga 60 D2
Astoria 126 B1
Astove Island 106 H6
Astrakhan' 70 J5
Astypalaia 68 J8
Asunción 142 K4
Aswân 100 F3
Aswân Dam 100 F3
Asyût 100 F2
As Zaydīyah 100 H4
Ata 112 J8
Atafu 112 J6
Atakpamé 104 E3
Atalaia do Norte 140 C4
Atâr 102 C4
Atasu 76 N8
Atbara 100 F4
Atbasar 70 N4
Atchison 130 B2
Aterno 64 H6
Ath 54 F4
Athabasca 122 J5
Athens = Athina 68 F7
Athens, *Al., US* 130 D3
Athens, *Ga., US* 130 E3
Athens, *Oh., US* 130 E2
Athens, *Tenn., US* 130 E2
Athens, *Tex., US* 130 B3
Athina 68 F7
Athlone 56 E8
Ath Thāyat 94 D7
Athy 56 F8
Ati 100 C5
Atiamuri 116 F4
Atico 140 C7
Atikokan 128 B1
Atka 78 S4
Atka Island 132 (3)C1
Atlanta 130 E3
Atlantic, *Ia., US* 130 B1
Atlantic, *N.C., US* 130 F3
Atlantic City 128 F3
Atlantic Ocean 46 C3
Atlas Bogd 80 B2
Atlas Mountains 60 N9
Atlasovo 78 T5
Atlas Saharien 102 E2
Atlin 122 E5
Atmakur 88 C5
Atmore 130 D3
Atoka 130 B3
Atokos 68 C6
Atol das Rocas 140 L4
Atri 64 H6
Aṭ Ṭā'if 90 D5
Attapu 84 D4
Attawapiskat 122 Q6
Attersee 62 J3
Attica 128 C2
Attu Island 132 (3)A1
Attu Island 144 (1)KK4
Attur 88 C6
At Turbah 100 H5
Atyrau 70 K5
Aubagne 58 L10
Aubange 54 H5
Aube 58 K5
Aubenas 58 K9
Aubry Lake 122 F3
Auburn, *Al., US* 130 D3
Auburn, *Calif., US* 126 B3
Auburn, *Nebr., US* 126 G2
Auburn, *Wash., US* 126 B1
Aubusson 58 H8
Auce 50 M1
Auch 58 F10
Auchi 104 F3
Auckland 116 E3
Auckland Island 116 (2)B1
Aude 58 H10
Aue 52 H6
Auerbach 52 H6
Augathella 114 J5
Augsburg 62 F2
Augusta, *Australia* 114 C6
Augusta, *Italy* 64 K11
Augusta, *Ga., US* 130 E3
Augusta, *Me., US* 128 G2
Augustów 50 M4
Aulla 62 E6
Aurangābād 88 C5
Auray 58 C6
Aurich 54 K1
Aurillac 58 H9
Aurora, *Colo., US* 126 F3
Aurora, *Ill., US* 128 C2
Aurora, *Mo., US* 130 C2
Aurukun 114 H2
Aus 108 B5
Auschwitz = Oświęcim 50 J7
Austin, *Minn., US* 128 B2
Austin, *Nev., US* 126 C3
Austin, *Tex., US* 130 B3
Australia 114 E4
Australian Alps 112 E9
Australian Capital Territory 114 J7
Austria 62 J3
Autun 58 K7
Auxerre 58 J6
Auxonne 58 L6
Avallon 58 J6
Avam 78 E2
Āvārsin 92 M4
Aveiro 60 B4
Avellino 64 J8
Averøya 48 D5
Avesnes-sur-Helpe 54 F4
Avesta 48 J6
Avezzano 64 H6
Aviemore 56 J4
Avignon 58 K10
Ávila 60 F4
Avilés 60 E1
Avion 54 E4
Avola 64 K12
Avon, *UK* 54 A2
Avon, *UK* 54 A3
Avranches 58 D5
Avrig 66 M4
Awaji-shima 82 H6
Awanui 116 D2
Awat 76 Q9
Awatere 116 D5
Awbārī 100 B2
Aweil 106 D2
Awjilah 100 D2
Awka 104 F3
Ax-les-Thermes 58 G11
Ayacucho 140 C6
Ayaguz 76 Q8
Ayakkuduk 76 M9
Ayamonte 60 C7
Ayan 78 E3
Ayan 78 P5
Aya Napa 94 A2
Ayancık 92 F3
Ayanka 78 V4
Ayaviri 140 C6
Aydin 92 B5
Aydıncık 68 R8
Ayers Rock = Uluru 114 F5
Aykhal 78 J3
Aykino 76 H5
Aylesbury 54 B3
Aylmer Lake 122 K4
'Ayn al Baida' 94 D5
Ayní 76 M10
Ayni 90 J2
Ayn 'Isá 92 H5
Ayoûn el 'Atroûs 102 D5
Ayr, *Australia* 114 J3
Ayr, *UK* 56 H6
Aytos 66 Q7
Ayutthaya 84 C4
Ayvalik 68 J5
Azaila 60 K3
Azaouâd 102 E5
Āzarān 92 M5
Azare 104 G2
Azauri 140 G3
A'zāz 92 G5
Azdavay 68 R3
Azerbaijan 92 M3
Aziza 60 H3
Azogues 140 B4
Azores = Açores 102 (1)B2
Azov 70 G5
Azpeitia 60 H1
Azrou 102 D2
Aztec 126 E3
Azuaga 60 E6
Azul 142 K6
Az Zabadānī 94 D3
Az Zahrān 95 D3
Az Zāwīyah 100 B1
Az Zubayr 95 B1

B

Ba'albek 94 D2
Baaqline 94 C3
Baardheere 106 G3
Babadag 66 R5
Babaeski 68 K3
Bāb al Mandab 90 D7
Babana 87 A3
Babanusa 106 D1
Babar 87 C4
Babayevo 70 G3
Babayurt 92 M2
Babo 87 D3
Bābol 90 F2
Babruysk 70 E4
Babura 104 F2
Babushkin 78 H6
Babuyan Islands 84 G3
Bacaadweyn 106 H2
Bacabal 140 J4
Bacan 87 C3
Bacău 66 P3
Baccarat 62 B2
Bachu 90 L2
Back 122 M3
Bačka Palanka 66 G4
Bačka Topola 66 G4
Backnang 62 E2
Bac Liêu 84 D5
Bacolod 84 G4
Badajós 140 H4
Badajoz 60 D6
Bad al Milh 92 K7
Badalona 60 N3
Bad Ausee 62 J3
Bad Bentheim 54 K2
Bad Berleburg 52 D5
Bad Doberan 52 G2
Bad Dürkheim 52 D7
Bad Ems 54 K4
Baden 50 F9
Baden-Baden 62 D2
Baderna 64 H3
Bad Freienwalde 52 K4
Badgastein 62 J3
Badgingarra 114 C6
Bad Harzburg 52 F5
Bad Hersfeld 52 E6
Bad Homburg 52 D6
Bad Honnef 54 K4
Badin 88 A4
Bad Ischl 62 J3
Bādiyat ash Shām 94 D4
Bad Kissingen 52 F6
Bad Kreuznach 54 K5
Bad Langensalza 52 F5
Bad Lauterberg 52 F5
Bad Liebenwerda 52 J5
Bad Mergentheim 52 E7
Bad Nauheim 52 D6
Bad Neuenahr-Ahrweiler 54 K4
Bad Neustadt 52 F6
Bad Oeynhausen 52 D4
Badong 80 E4
Bad Reichenhall 62 H3
Badr Ḥunayn 100 G3
Bad Säckingen 52 C9
Bad Salzuflen 52 D4
Bad Salzungen 52 F6
Bad Schwartau 52 F3
Bad Segeberg 52 F3
Bad Sobernheim 54 K5
Bad Urach 62 E2
Bad Vöslau 66 D2
Bad Waldsee 62 E3
Bad Wilbad 62 D2
Bad Wildungen 52 E5
Bad Windsheim 52 F7
Bad Wurzach 62 E3
Baena 60 F7
Bærum 48 F7
Baeza 60 G6
Baffin Bay 120 J2
Baffin Island 122 R2
Bafia 104 G4
Bafoulabé 104 B2
Bafoussam 104 G3
Bāfq 90 G3
Bafra 92 F3
Bafra Burun 92 G3
Bāft 95 G2
Bafwasende 106 D3
Baga 100 B5
Bagani 108 C3
Bagansiapiapi 86 C2
Bagaroua 104 E2
Bagdad 132 D2
Bagdarin 78 J6
Bagé 142 L5
Baggs 126 E2
Baghdād 90 D3
Bagheria 64 H10
Baghlān 90 J2
Bagnères-de-Bigorre 58 F10
Bagno di Romagna 62 G7
Bagnols-sur-Cèze 58 K9
Bago 84 G4
Baguio 84 G3
Bagun Datuk 86 C2
Baharampur 88 E4
Bahawalnagar 88 B3
Bahawalpur 88 B3
Bahçe 92 G5
Bahia 140 J6
Bahía Blanca 142 J6
Bahía Blanca 142 J6
Bahía de Banderas 134 C4
Bahía de Campeche 134 F4
Bahía de Manta 140 A4
Bahía de Petacalco 134 D5
Bahía de Pisco 140 B6
Bahía de Santa Elena 140 A4
Bahía de Sechura 140 A5
Bahía Grande 142 H9
Bahía Kino 124 D6
Bahía Negra 142 K3
Bahía Samborombón 142 K6
Bahır Dar 100 G5
Bahraich 88 D3
Bahrain 95 D4
Bahrat Ḥimṣ 94 D2
Bahr el Abiad 100 F5
Bahr el Azraq 100 F5
Bahr el Ghazal 100 C5
Bahr el Ghazal 106 D2
Bahr el Jebel 106 E2
Bahr el Nîl = Nile 100 F4
Baia 66 R5
Baía de Marajó 140 H4
Baía de Todos os Santos 140 K6
Baía do Bengo 104 G6
Baia Mare 66 L2
Baião 140 H4
Baia Sprie 66 L2
Baïbokoum 106 B2
Baicheng, *China* 76 Q9
Baicheng, *China* 80 G1
Baie Comeau 128 G1
Baie de la Seine 54 B5
Baie de la Somme 54 D4
Baie du Poste 122 S6
Baie St. Paul 128 F1
Baiji 92 K6
Baile Átha Cliath = Dublin 56 F8
Bailén 60 G6
Bailleul 54 E4
Bailundo 108 B2
Bainbridge 130 E3
Bairiki 112 H5
Bairin Youqi 80 F2
Bairin Zuoqi 80 F2
Bairnsdale 114 J7
Bais 84 G5
Baja 66 F3
Baja California 124 C5
Bajram Curri 68 B2
Bakchar 76 Q6
Bakel 104 B2
Baker 112 J5
Baker, *Calif., US* 126 C3
Baker, *Mont., US* 126 F1
Baker, *Oreg., US* 126 C2
Baker Lake 122 M4
Baker Lake 122 N4
Bakersfield 132 C1
Bakharden 76 K10
Bakhta 78 D4
Baki 90 E1
Bakkafjörður 48 (1)F1
Bakkaflói 48 (1)F1
Baku = Baki 90 E1
Balâ 92 E4
Balabac 84 F5
Balabac 84 F5
Balabac Strait 84 F5
Balagansk 78 G6
Balaghat 88 D4
Balaguer 60 L3
Balakhta 76 S6
Balaklava 92 E1
Balakovo 70 J4
Bālā Morghāb 76 L10
Bălan 66 N3
Balāngīr 88 D4
Balashov 70 H4
Balassagyarmat 66 G1
Balaton 66 E3
Balatonfüred 66 E3
Balatonlelle 66 E3
Balbina 140 F4
Balchik 92 C2
Balclutha 116 B8
Bald Knob 128 B3
Baldwin 130 E3
Balearic Islands = Islas Baleares 60 N5
Baler 84 G3
Bāleshwar 88 E4
Baley 78 K6
Baléyara 104 E2
Balguntay 76 R9
Bali 86 F4
Balige 86 B2
Balıkesir 68 K5
Balikpapan 86 F3
Balimo 87 F4
Balingen 62 D2
Balintang Channel 84 G3
Balkhash 76 N8
Balladonia 114 D6
Ballarat 114 H7
Balleny Island 144 (2)Y3
Ballina, *Australia* 114 K5
Ballina, *Ireland* 56 C7
Ballinasloe 56 D8
Ballinger 132 G2
Ball's Pyramid 114 L6
Ballum 54 H1
Ballymena 56 F7
Balmazújváros 66 J2
Balotra 88 B3
Balranald 114 H6
Balș 66 M5
Balsas 134 D5
Balsas 140 H5
Balta 66 S2
Bălți 66 Q2
Baltic Sea 48 J8
Baltijsk 50 J3
Baltimore 128 E3
Baltrum 52 C3
Balvi 48 P8
Balykchy 76 P9
Balykshi 70 K5
Bam 90 G4
Bamaga 114 H2
Bamako 104 C2
Bamba 102 E5
Bambari 106 C2
Bamberg 52 F7
Bambesa 106 D3
Bambouk 102 C6
Bambouk Kaarta 104 B2
Bamda 80 B4
Bamenda 104 G3
Bāmīān 90 J3
Banaba 112 G6
Bañados del Izozog 140 E7
Banalia 106 D3
Banana, *Australia* 114 K4
Banana, *Dem. Rep. of the Congo* 106 A5
Banaz 68 M6
Ban Ban 84 C3
Ban Betong 86 C1
Banbury 56 L9
Banda 88 D3
Banda Aceh 84 B5
Bandar Lampung 86 D4
Bandama 104 C3
Bandar-e 'Abbās 95 G3
Bandar-e Anzalī 90 E2
Bandar-e Deylam 95 D1
Bandar-e Ganāveh 95 D2
Bandar-e Khoemir 95 F3
Bandar-e Lengeh 95 F3
Bandar-e Ma'shur 95 C1
Bandar-e Torkeman 90 F2
Bandar Khomeynī 95 C1
Bandar Seri Begawan 86 E2
Band-e Chārak 95 F3
Band-e Moghūyeh 95 F3
Bandirma 68 K4
Bandundu 106 B4
Bandung 86 D4
Băneasa 66 Q5
Bāneh 92 L6
Banff, *Canada* 122 H6
Banff, *UK* 56 K4
Bangalore 88 C6
Bangangté 104 G3
Bangassou 106 C3
Bangbong 87 B3
Banggi 86 F1

Name	Page	Grid
Banghāzī	100	D1
Bangka	86	D3
Bangkalan	86	E4
Bangkok = Krung Thep	84	C4
Bangladesh	88	E4
Bangor, *N. Ire., UK*	56	G7
Bangor, *Wales, UK*	56	H8
Bangor, *US*	128	G2
Bang Saphan Yai	84	B4
Bangued	84	G3
Bangui, *Central African Republic*	106	B3
Bangui, *Philippines*	84	G3
Ban Hat Yai	84	C5
Ban Hua Hin	84	B4
Bani-Bangou	104	E1
Banī Walīd	102	H2
Bāniyās	92	F6
Banja Luka	66	E5
Banjarmasin	86	E3
Banjul	104	A2
Ban Khemmarat	84	D3
Banks Island = Moa, *Australia*	114	H2
Banks Island, *B.C., Canada*	122	E6
Banks Island, *N.W.T., Canada*	122	G2
Banks Lake	126	C1
Banks Peninsula	116	D6
Banks Strait	114	J8
Bannerman Town	130	F5
Bannu	88	B2
Bánovce	50	H9
Banská	50	J9
Banská Štiavnica	50	H9
Bansko	68	F3
Bantry	56	C10
Banyo	104	G3
Banyoles	60	N2
Banyuwangi	86	E4
Baode	80	E3
Baoding	80	F3
Baoji	80	D4
Bao Lôc	84	D4
Baoro	106	B2
Baoshan	84	B1
Baotou	80	E2
Baoying	80	F4
Bap	88	B3
Bapaume	54	E4
Ba'qūbah	90	D3
Baquedano	142	H3
Bar	66	G7
Barabai	86	F3
Baraboo	128	C2
Barakaldo	60	H1
Baramati	88	B5
Baramula	88	B2
Baran	88	C3
Baranavichy	70	E4
Baraolt	66	N3
Barbados	140	F1
Barbastro	60	L2
Barbate	60	E8
Barbuda	134	M5
Barcaldine	114	J4
Barcău	66	K2
Barcellona Pozzo di Gotto	64	K10
Barcelona, *Spain*	60	N3
Barcelona, *Venezuela*	134	M6
Barcelos, *Brazil*	140	E4
Barcelos, *Spain*	60	B3
Barclayville	104	C4
Barco de Valdeorras = O Barco	60	D2
Barcs	66	E4
Bärdä	92	M3
Bardai	100	C3
Barddhamān	88	E4
Bardejov	50	L8
Bardonecchia	62	B5
Bareilly	88	C3
Barentin	54	C5
Barents Sea	76	E3
Barentu	100	G4
Bareo	86	F2
Barga	88	D2
Bargaal	106	J1
Bargteheide	52	F3
Barguzin	78	H6
Bar Harbor	128	G2
Bari	64	L7
Barikot	88	B1
Barinas	140	C2
Bârîs	100	F3
Barisal	88	F4
Barito	87	A3
Barkam	80	C4
Barkava	48	P8
Barkly Tableland	114	F3
Barkol	76	S9
Bârlad	66	Q3
Bârlad	66	Q3
Bar-le-Duc	54	H6
Barletta	64	L7
Barmer	88	B3
Barmouth Bay	56	H9
Barnaul	76	Q7
Barnsley	56	L8
Barnstaple	56	H10
Barnstaple Bay	56	H10
Barpeta	88	F3
Barquisimeto	140	D1
Barr	62	C2
Barra, *Brazil*	140	J6
Barra, *UK*	56	E4
Barracão do Barreto	140	F5
Barracas	60	K5
Barra do Bugres	140	F7
Barra do Corda	140	H5
Barra do Cuanza	106	A5
Barra do Garças	140	G7
Barra do São Manuel	140	F5
Barragem de Santa Clara	60	B7
Barragem de Sobradinho	140	J5
Barragem do Castelo de Bode	60	B5
Barragem do Maranhão	60	C6
Barranca, *Peru*	140	B4
Barranca, *Peru*	140	B6
Barranquilla	134	K6
Barreiras	140	H6
Barreiro	60	A6
Barretos	140	H8
Barrie	128	E2
Barron	128	B1
Barrow	132	(1)F1
Barrow Creek	114	F4
Barrow-in-Furness	56	J7
Barrow Island	114	B4
Barrow Strait	122	N2
Barshatas	76	P8
Barsi	88	C5
Barstow	132	C2
Bar-sur-Aube	58	K5
Bar-sur-Seine	58	K5
Barth	52	H2
Bartın	92	E3
Bartle Frere	112	E7
Bartlesville	130	B2
Bartlett	126	G2
Bartoszyce	50	K3
Barus	86	B2
Baruun Urt	80	E1
Barwani	88	B4
Barysaw	70	E4
Basaidu	95	F3
Basankusu	106	B3
Basarabeasca	66	R3
Basarabi	66	R5
Basca	64	C2
Basco	84	G2
Basel	62	C3
Bashkiriya	70	K4
Băsht	95	D1
Basilan	87	B1
Basildon	54	C3
Basiluzzo	64	K10
Basingstoke	56	L10
Başkale	92	K4
Basoko	106	C3
Bassano	124	D1
Bassano del Grappa	62	G5
Bassar	104	E3
Bassas da India	108	F4
Basse Santa Su	102	C6
Basse Terre	134	M5
Bassett	126	G2
Bassikounou	102	D5
Bass Strait	114	H7
Bassum	52	D4
Bastak	95	F3
Bastānābād	92	M5
Basti	88	D3
Bastia	64	D6
Bastogne	54	H4
Bastrop, *La., US*	130	C3
Bastrop, *Tex., US*	130	B3
Bata	104	F4
Batagay	78	N3
Batagay-Alyta	78	N3
Batak	68	G3
Batamay	78	M4
Batang	80	B5
Batangas	84	G4
Batan Islands	84	G2
Batanta	87	C3
Batchelor	114	F2
Batemans Bay	114	K7
Batesville	130	D3
Bath, *UK*	56	K10
Bath, *US*	128	E2
Bathinda	88	B2
Bathurst, *Australia*	114	J6
Bathurst, *Canada*	122	T7
Bathurst Inlet	122	K3
Bathurst Island, *Australia*	114	E2
Bathurst Island, *Canada*	122	M1
Batman	90	D2
Batna	102	G1
Baton Rouge	130	C3
Bátonyterenye	66	G2
Batouri	104	G4
Batroûn	94	C2
Batticaloa	88	D7
Battipaglia	64	J8
Battle	122	J6
Battle Creek	128	C2
Battle Harbour	122	V6
Battle Mountain	126	C2
Batu	106	F2
Batui	87	B3
Bat'umi	92	J3
Batu Pahat	86	C2
Baturino	76	R6
Baubau	87	B4
Bauchi	104	F2
Baudette	128	B1
Baukau	87	C4
Baume-les-Dames	58	M6
Bauru	142	M3
Bauska	48	N8
Bautzen	50	D6
Bawean	86	E4
Bawiti	100	E2
Bawku	104	D2
Bayamo	134	J4
Bayanaul	76	P7
Bayandelger	78	H7
Bayan Har Shan	80	B4
Bayanhongor	80	C1
Bayan Mod	80	C2
Bayan Obo	80	D2
Bayansumküre	76	Q9
Bayburt	92	J3
Bay City, *Mich., US*	128	D2
Bay City, *Tex., US*	130	B4
Baydhabo	106	G3
Bayerische Alpen	62	G3
Bayeux	54	B5
Bayfield	128	B1
Bayindir	68	K6
Bāyir	94	D6
Baykit	76	T5
Baykonur	76	M8
Bay Minette	130	D3
Bay of Bengal	88	E5
Bay of Biscay	58	C9
Bay of Fundy	122	T8
Bay of Islands	116	E2
Bay of Plenty	116	F3
Bayonne	58	D10
Bayramaly	90	H2
Bayramiç	68	J5
Bayreuth	52	G7
Baysun	90	J2
Bayt al Faqīh	100	H5
Bay View	116	F4
Baza	60	H7
Bazas	58	E9
Bazdar	90	J4
Beach	126	F1
Beachy Head	54	C4
Beagle Gulf	114	E2
Bealanana	108	H2
Bear Island = Bjørnøya, *Norway*	76	B3
Bear Island, *Republic of Ireland*	56	B10
Bear Lake	126	D2
Beasain	60	H1
Beas de Segura	60	H6
Beatrice	130	B1
Beatty	132	C1
Beaufort, *Malaysia*	86	F1
Beaufort, *N.C., US*	130	F3
Beaufort, *S.C., US*	130	E3
Beaufort Sea	120	Q2
Beaufort West	108	C6
Beaumont, *New Zealand*	116	B7
Beaumont, *US*	130	C3
Beaune	58	K6
Beauvais	54	E5
Beaver	126	D3
Beaver Creek	132	(1)J3
Beaver Dam	128	C3
Beaver Falls	128	D2
Beawar	88	B3
Beazley	142	H5
Bebra	52	E6
Bečej	66	H4
Béchar	102	E2
Beckley	130	E2
Becks	116	B7
Beckum	54	L3
Beclean	66	M2
Bedelē	106	F2
Bedford, *UK*	56	M9
Bedford, *US*	130	D2
Bedworth	54	A2
Beenleigh	114	K5
Beer Menuha	94	C6
Beer Ora	94	C7
Be'ér Sheva'	94	B5
Beeville	130	B4
Behbehān	95	D1
Bei'an	78	M7
Beihai	84	D2
Beijing	80	F3
Beipan	80	D5
Beipiao	80	G2
Beira	108	E3
Beirut = Beyrouth	94	C3
Beiuş	66	K3
Beizhen	82	A3
Béja	102	G1
Bejaïa	102	G1
Béjar	60	E4
Bekdash	90	F1
Békés	50	L11
Békéscsaba	66	J3
Bekily	108	H4
Bekkai	82	N2
Bela	90	J4
Bela Crkva	66	J5
Belaga	86	E2
Belarus	46	G2
Bela Vista	108	E5
Belaya	70	K3
Belaya Gora	78	R3
Bełchatów	50	J6
Belcher Islands	122	Q5
Beledweyne	106	H3
Belek	76	J10
Belém	140	H4
Belen	134	C2
Belfast	56	G7
Belfield	126	F1
Belfort	62	B3
Belgazyn	76	T7
Belgium	54	G4
Belgorod	70	G4
Belgrade = Beograd	66	H5
Beli	104	G3
Belice	64	H11
Beli Manastir	66	F4
Belinyu	86	D3
Belitung	86	D3
Belize	134	G5
Belize	134	G5
Bellac	58	G7
Bella Coola	122	F6
Bellary	88	C5
Bellefontaine	128	D2
Belle Fourche	126	F2
Belle Glade	130	E4
Belle Île	58	B6
Belle Isle	122	V6
Bellême	58	F5
Belleterre	128	E1
Belleville, *Canada*	128	E2
Belleville, *US*	130	B2
Bellingham	126	B1
Bellingshausen Sea	144	(2)JJ4
Bellinzona	62	E4
Bello	140	B2
Belluno	62	H4
Bellyk	78	E6
Belmont	128	E2
Belmonte, *Brazil*	140	K7
Belmonte, *Spain*	60	H5
Belmopan	134	G5
Belmullet	56	B7
Belogorsk	78	M6
Belogradchik	66	K6
Beloha	108	H5
Belo Horizonte	140	J7
Beloit, *Kans., US*	130	B2
Beloit, *Wis., US*	128	C2
Belo Monte	140	G4
Belomorsk	70	F2
Belorechensk	92	H1
Beloretsk	70	L4
Belo Tsiribihina	108	G3
Belovo	76	R7
Beloyarskiy	76	M5
Beloye More	70	G1
Belozersk	70	G2
Belozerskoye	70	N3
Belye Vody	76	M9
Belyy Yar	76	Q6
Belzig	52	H4
Bembibre	60	D2
Bemidji	128	A1
Bena Dibele	106	C4
Benavente	60	E3
Benbecula	56	E4
Bend	126	B2
Bender-Bayla	106	J2
Bendigo	114	H7
Bendorf	54	K4
Bene	108	E3
Benešov	50	D8
Benevento	64	J7
Bengbu	80	F4
Bengkalis	86	C2
Bengkulu	86	C3
Benguela	108	A2
Benguerir	102	D2
Benha	100	F1
Beni	106	D3
Beni	140	D6
Beni Abbès	102	E2
Benicarló	60	L4
Benidorm	60	K6
Benī Mazâr	100	F2
Beni Mellal	102	D2
Benin	104	E2
Benin City	104	F3
Beni Saf	60	J9
Beni Slimane	60	P8
Beni Suef	100	F2
Benito Juaréz	142	K6
Benjamin Constant	140	D4
Benkelman	126	F2
Benkovac	62	L6
Ben More Assynt	56	H3
Ben Nevis	56	H5
Bennington	128	F2
Benoud	102	F2
Bensheim	52	D7
Benson, *Ariz., US*	132	D2
Benson, *Minn., US*	124	G2
Benteng	87	B4
Bentinck Island	114	G3
Bent Jbail	94	C3
Bentonville	130	C2
Bentung	86	C2
Benue	104	G3
Benxi	80	G2
Beo	84	H6
Beograd	66	H5
Bepazarı	92	D3
Berat	68	B4
Beravina	108	H3
Berber	100	F4
Berbera	100	H5
Berbérati	106	B3
Berchtesgaden	62	J3
Berck	54	D4
Berdigestyakh	78	M4
Berdyans'k	70	G5
Berdychiv	70	E5
Bereeda	106	J1
Berehove	66	K1
Bererreá	60	C2
Berettyóújfalu	66	J2
Berettys	50	L10
Bereznik	70	H2
Berezniki	70	L3
Berezovo	70	N2
Berezovyy	78	P6
Berga	60	M2
Bergama	68	K5
Bergamo	62	E5
Bergara	60	H1
Bergby	48	J6
Bergedorf	52	F3
Bergen, *Germany*	52	J2
Bergen, *Germany*	52	E4
Bergen, *Netherlands*	54	G2
Bergen, *Norway*	48	C6
Bergen op Zoom	54	G3
Bergerac	58	F9
Bergheim	54	J4
Bergisch Gladbach	52	C6
Bergsfjordhalvøya	48	L1
Beringen	54	H3
Beringovskiy	78	X4
Bering Sea	132	(1)C4
Bering Strait	132	(1)C2
Berīzak	95	G3

Berkeley 132 B1
Berkner Island 144 (2)A2
Berkovitsa 66 L6
Berlin, *Germany* 52 J4
Berlin, *US* 128 F2
Bermejillo 132 F3
Bermejo 142 K4
Bermeo 60 H1
Bermuda 120 H6
Bern 62 C4
Bernado 132 E2
Bernalda 64 L8
Bernau 52 J4
Bernay 54 C5
Bernburg 52 G5
Berner Alpen 62 C4
Beroun 50 D8
Berounka 52 J7
Berovo 68 E3
Berrouaghia 60 N8
Berry Islands 130 F4
Bertoua 104 G4
Bertram 128 D1
Beruni 76 L9
Berwick-upon-Tweed 56 L6
Besalampy 108 G3
Besançon 58 M6
Besbay 76 K8
Beshneh 95 F2
Bessemer 130 D3
Bestamak 76 P8
Bestuzhevo 70 H2
Bestyakh, *Russia* 78 L3
Bestyakh, *Russia* 78 M4
Betanzos 60 B1
Bětdâmbâng 84 C4
Bethany 128 B2
Bethel, *Ak., US* 132 (1)E3
Bethel, *Pa., US* 128 F2
Bethlehem, *Israel* 94 C5
Bethlehem, *South Africa* 108 D5
Béthune 54 E4
Betioky 108 G4
Betoota 114 H5
Betpak-Dala 76 M8
Betroka 108 H4
Bet-She'an 94 C4
Bettiah 88 D3
Betul 88 C4
Betzdorf 52 C6
Beulah 128 C2
Beverley 56 M8
Beverungen 52 E5
Bexhill 54 C4
Bey Dağlari 68 M8
Beykoz 68 M3
Beyla 104 C3
Beyneu 76 J8
Beypazarı 68 P4
Beyra 106 H2
Beyrouth 94 C3
Beyşehir 68 P7
Beyşehir Gölü 68 P7
Bezhetsk 70 G3
Béziers 58 J10
Bhadgaon 88 E3
Bhadrakh 88 E4
Bhadravati 88 C6
Bhagalpur 88 E3
Bhairab Bazar 88 F4
Bhakkar 88 B2
Bhamo 84 B2
Bharuch 88 B4
Bhatpara 88 E4
Bhavnagar 88 B4
Bhawanipatna 88 D5
Bhilai 88 D4
Bhilwara 88 B3
Bhīmavaram 88 D5
Bhind 88 C3
Bhiwandi 88 B5
Bhopal 88 C4
Bhubaneshwar 88 E4
Bhuj 88 A4
Bhusawal 88 C4
Bhutan 88 E3
Biak 87 E3
Biak 87 E3
Biała 50 K8
Biała Podlaska 50 N5
Białogard 50 F3
Białystok 50 N4
Biarritz 58 D10
Biasca 62 D4
Bibbiena 62 G7
Biberach 62 E2
Bicaz 66 P3
Bicester 54 A3
Bickerton Island 114 G2
Bicske 66 F2
Bida 104 F3
Bidar 88 C5
Bidbid 95 H5
Biddeford 128 F2
Bideford 56 H10
Bidyadanga (Lagrange) 114 D3
Biedenkopf 52 D6
Biel 62 C3
Bielefeld 52 D4
Biella 62 D5
Bielsko-Biała 50 J8
Bielsk Podlaski 50 N5
Biên Hoa 84 D4
Bietigheim-Bissingen 62 E2
Big 122 G2
Biga 68 K4
Bigadiç 68 L5
Big Desert 114 H7
Big Falls 128 B1
Bighorn 124 E2
Bighorn Lake 126 E1
Bighorn Mountains 126 E2
Bight of Bangkok 84 C4
Bight of Benin 104 E3
Bight of Biafra 104 F4
Big Lake 132 (1)H2
Bignona 102 B6
Big Pine 130 E5
Big Rapids 128 C2
Big River 122 K6
Big Sandy 126 D1
Big Sioux 126 G2
Big Spring 132 F2
Big Sur 132 B1
Big Trout Lake 122 P6
Bihać 62 L6
Bihoro 82 N2
Bijapur 88 C5
Bījār 92 M6
Bijeljina 66 G5
Bijelo Polje 66 G6
Bijie 80 D5
Bikanar 88 B3
Bikin 78 N7
Bikini 112 G4
Bilaspur 88 D4
Biläsuvar 92 N4
Bila Tserkva 70 F5
Bilbao 60 H1
Bileća 66 F7
Bilecik 68 M4
Bilećko Jezero 66 F7
Biled 66 H4
Biłgoraj 50 M7
Bilhorod-Dnistrovs'kyy 70 F5
Bilibino 78 V3
Bilina 52 J6
Billings 126 D1
Bill of Portland 56 K11
Bilma 100 B4
Biloela 114 K4
Biloxi 130 D3
Bimini Islands 130 F4
Bina-Etawa 88 C4
Binche 54 G4
Bindi Bindi 114 C6
Bindura 108 E3
Bingen 52 C7
Binghamton 128 E2
Bingöl 92 J4
Binongko 87 D4
Bintuhan 86 C3
Bintulu 86 E2
Bintuni 87 D3
Binyang 84 D2
Binzhou 80 F3
Biograd 62 L7
Birāk 102 H3
Birao 100 D5
Biratnagar 88 E3
Bi'r Bazīrī 94 E2
Birdsville 114 G5
Bireun 86 B1
Bir Gandouz 102 B4
Bir Gifgâfa 94 A6
Birhan 100 G5
Bîr Hasana 94 A6
Bīrjand 90 G3
Birkenfeld 54 K5
Birmingham, *UK* 56 L9
Birmingham, *US* 130 D3
Bir Mogrein 102 C3
Birnie 112 J6
Birnin-Gwari 104 F2
Birnin Kebbi 104 E2
Birnin Konni 104 F2
Birnin Kudu 104 F2
Birobidzhan 78 N7
Birsk 70 L3
Bir Tâba 94 B7
Biržai 50 P1
Bi'r Zalṭan 100 C2
Bisbee 132 E2
Bisceglie 64 L7
Bischofshofen 62 J3
Bischofswerda 50 D6
Biševo 64 L6
Bishkek 76 N9
Bishop 126 C3
Bishop Auckland 56 L7
Bishop's Stortford 54 C3
Biskra 102 G2
Bislig 84 H5
Bismarck 124 F2
Bismarck Sea 112 E6
Bissau 102 B6
Bistcho Lake 122 H5
Bistriţa 66 M2
Bistriţa 66 P3
Bitburg 54 J5
Bitche 52 C7
Bitkine 100 C5
Bitlis 92 K4
Bitola 68 D3
Bitonto 64 L7
Bitterfeld 52 H5
Bitterroot Range 126 C1
Bitti 64 D8
Bitung 87 C2
Biu 104 G2
Biwa-ko 82 H6
Bixby 128 B3
Biyāvra 88 C4
Biysk 76 R7
Bizerte 102 G1
Bjelovar 66 D4
Bjerkvik 48 J2
Bjørnøya 76 B3
B-Köpenick 52 J4
Bla 104 C2
Blackburn 56 K8
Blackfoot 126 D2
Blackfoot Reservoir 126 D2
Black Hills 126 F2
Blackpool 56 J8
Black Range 132 E2
Black River Falls 128 B2
Black Rock Desert 126 C2
Blacksburg 128 D3
Black Sea 92 D2
Blacks Harbour 128 G1
Black Sugarloaf 114 K6
Black Volta 104 D3
Blackwater 56 D9
Blackwater 114 J4
Blagodarnyy 92 K1
Blagoevgrad 68 F3
Blagoveshchenka 76 P7
Blagoveshchensk 78 M6
Blain 58 D6
Blair 128 A2
Blairsden 126 B3
Blairsville 130 E3
Blaj 66 L3
Blakely 130 E3
Blanco 140 E6
Blanding 132 E1
Blangy-sur-Bresle 54 D5
Blankenberge 54 F3
Blankenburg 52 F5
Blankenheim 54 J4
Blantyre 108 F3
Blasket Islands 56 B9
Blaubeuren 62 E2
Blaye-et-Sainte-Luce 58 E8
Bled 62 K4
Blenheim 116 D5
Blevands Huk 52 D1
Blida 102 F1
Blind River 124 K2
Bloemfontein 108 D5
Bloemhof 108 D5
Blois 58 G6
Blönduós 48 (1)C2
Błonie 50 K5
Bloomfield 130 D2
Bloomington, *Ill., US* 128 C2
Bloomington, *Ind., US* 128 C3
Bludenz 62 E3
Blue Earth 128 B2
Bluefield 128 D3
Bluefields 134 H6
Blue Mountain Lake 128 F2
Blue Mountains 126 C2
Blue Nile = Bahr el Azraq 100 F5
Bluenose Lake 122 H3
Bluff, *New Zealand* 116 B8
Bluff, *US* 132 E1
Blumenau 142 M4
Blythe 132 D2
Blytheville 130 D2
Bo 104 B3
Boac 84 G4
Boa Vista, *Brazil* 140 E3
Boa Vista, *Cape Verde Islands* 104 (1)B1
Bobbili 88 D5
Bobbio 62 E6
Bobigny 54 E6
Bobingen 62 F2
Böblingen 62 E2
Bobo Dioulasso 104 D2
Bobolice 50 F4
Bobr 50 E6
Bobrov 70 H4
Bôca do Acre 140 D5
Boca Grande 134 M7
Boca Grande 138 E3
Bocaiúva 140 J7
Bocaranga 106 B2
Bochart 128 F1
Bochnia 50 K8
Bocholt 52 B5
Bochum 52 C5
Bockenem 52 F4
Bodaybo 78 J5
Bode 52 G4
Bodélé 100 C4
Boden 48 L4
Bodham 88 C5
Bodmin 56 H11
Bodø 48 H3
Bodrog 50 L9
Bodrum 68 K7
Boe 126 D2
Boende 106 C4
Boffa 104 B2
Bogale 84 B3
Bogalusa 130 D3
Boggabilla 114 K5
Boghni 60 P8
Bognor Regis 54 B4
Bogo 84 G4
Bogor 86 D4
Bogorodskoye 78 Q6
Bogotá 140 C3
Bogotol 76 R6
Bogra 88 E4
Boguchany 78 F5
Bogué 102 C5
Bo Hai 80 F3
Bohmerwald 52 H7
Bohol 84 G5
Bohumin 50 H8
Boiaçu 140 E4
Boise 126 C2
Boise City 132 F1
Bojnūrd 76 K10
Bokatola 106 B4
Boké 104 B2
Bokoro 104 H2
Bokspits 108 C5
Bokungu 106 C4
Bolbec 54 C5
Boldu 66 Q4
Bole, *China* 76 Q9
Bole, *Ghana* 104 D3
Bolechiv 50 N8
Bolesławiec 50 E6
Bolgatanga 104 D2
Bolhrad 66 R4
Bolintin-Vale 66 N5
Bolivar 128 B3
Bolivia 140 D7
Bollène 58 K9
Bollnäs 48 J6
Bolmen 48 G8
Bolnisi 92 L3
Bolobo 104 H5
Bologna 62 G6
Bolognesi 140 C5
Bolomba 104 H4
Bolotnoye 76 Q6
Bol'shaya Pyssa 70 J2
Bol'sherech'ye 70 P3
Bol'shezemel'skaya Tundra 76 J4
Bol Shirta 78 C4
Bolshoy Atlym 70 N2
Bol'shoy Osinovaya 78 W3
Bol'shoy Vlas'evo 78 Q6
Bolshoy Yuga 70 P2
Bolsover 54 A1
Bolton 56 K8
Bolu 92 D3
Bolvadin 68 P6
Bolzano 62 G4
Boma 104 G6
Bombala 114 J7
Bombay = Mumbai 88 B5
Bomili 106 D3
Bom Jesus da Lapa 140 J6
Bømlo 48 C7
Bomnak 78 M6
Bomossa 104 H4
Bonāb 92 M5
Bonaparte Archipelago 114 B2
Bonavista Bay 122 W7
Bondeno 62 G6
Bondo 106 C3
Bondokodi 114 C1
Bondoukou 104 D3
Bondowoso 86 E4
Bonerate 87 B4
Bongaigaon 88 F3
Bongandanga 106 C3
Bongao 87 A1
Bongor 104 H2
Bonifacio 64 D7
Bonn 52 C6
Bonners Ferry 126 C1
Bonneville 62 B4
Bonnie Rock 114 C6
Bonorva 64 C8
Bonthe 104 B3
Bontoc 84 G3
Bontosunggu 87 A4
Bonyhád 66 F3
Boone 128 D3
Boonville 130 C2
Boorama 106 G2
Boosaaso 106 H1
Boothia Peninsula 122 M2
Booué 104 G5
Boppard 52 C6
Bor, *Russia* 78 D4
Bor, *Sudan* 106 E2
Bor, *Turkey* 68 S7
Bor, *Serbia* 66 K5
Borah Peak 126 C3
Borås 48 G8
Borāzjān 95 D2
Bordeaux 58 E9
Bordeira 60 B7
Borden Peninsula 122 Q2
Bordertown 114 H7
Bordj Bou Arréridj 102 F1
Bordj Bounaam 60 M9
Bordj Flye Sante Marie 102 E3
Bordj Messaouda 102 G2
Bordj Mokhtar 102 F4
Bordj Omar Driss 102 G3
Borgarnes 48 (1)C2
Borger 132 F1
Borgholm 48 J8
Borgomanero 62 D5
Borgo San Dalmazzo 62 C6
Borgo San Lorenzo 62 G7
Borgosesia 62 D5
Borgo Val di Taro 62 E6
Bori Jenein 102 H2
Borislav 50 N8
Borisoglebsk 70 H4
Borjomi 92 K3
Borken 54 J3
Borkou 100 C4
Borkum 54 J1
Borkum 54 J1
Borlänge 48 H6
Bormida 62 D6
Bormio 62 F4
Borna 52 H5
Borne 54 J2
Borneo 86 E3
Bornholm 48 H9
Borodino 76 R5
Borodinskoye 48 Q6
Boromo 104 D2
Borongan 84 H4
Borovichi 70 F3
Borovskoy 70 M4
Borriana 60 K5
Borroloola 114 G3
Borşa 66 M2
Borshchiv 66 P1
Borshchovochnyy Khrebet 78 J7
Borðeyri 48 (1)C2
Borūjerd 90 E3
Borzya 78 K6

Bosa 64 C8
Bosanska Dubica 66 D4
Bosanska Gradiška 66 E4
Bosanska Kostajnica 62 M5
Bosanska Krupa 66 D5
Bosanski Brod 66 F4
Bosanski Novi 66 D4
Bosanski Petrovac 66 D5
Bosansko Grahovo 62 M6
Boşca 66 J4
Bose 84 D2
Bosilegrad 66 K7
Boskovice 50 F8
Bosna 66 F5
Bosnia and Herzegovina 66 E5
Bosobolo 106 B3
Bosporus = İstanbul Boğazı 68 M3
Bosporus 90 A1
Bossambélé 106 B2
Bossangoa 106 B2
Bossier City 130 C3
Bosten Hu 76 R9
Boston, *UK* 56 M9
Boston, *US* 128 F2
Botevgrad 66 L7
Botlikh 90 E1
Botna 66 R3
Botoşani 66 P2
Botou 80 F3
Botrange 54 J4
Botswana 108 C4
Bottrop 54 J3
Bou Ahmed 60 F9
Bouaké 104 C3
Bouar 106 B2
Bouârfa 102 E2
Boufarik 60 N8
Bougainville Island 112 F6
Bougainville Reef 114 J3
Bougouni 104 C2
Bougzoul 60 N9
Bouira 102 F1
Bou Ismaïl 60 N8
Bou Izakarn 102 D3
Boujdour 102 C3
Bou Kadir 60 M8
Boukra 102 C3
Boulder 126 E2
Boulder City 132 D1
Boulia 114 G4
Boulogne-sur-Mer 54 D4
Bouna 104 D3
Boundiali 104 C3
Bounty Islands 112 H10
Bourem 102 E5
Bourg 58 E8
Bourg-de-Piage 58 L9
Bourg-en-Bresse 58 L7
Bourges 58 H6
Bourgoin-Jallieu 58 L8
Bourke 114 J6
Bournemouth 56 L11
Bou Saâda 102 F1
Bousso 100 C5
Boussu 54 F4
Boutilimit 102 C5
Bouzghaïa 60 M8
Bowbells 126 F1
Bowen 114 J4
Bowie, *Ariz., US* 132 E2
Bowie, *Tex., US* 132 G2
Bowkan 92 M5
Bowling Green, *Fla., US* 130 E4
Bowling Green, *Ky., US* 130 D2
Bowling Green, *Mo., US* 130 C2
Bowman 126 F1
Bowman Bay 122 R3
Bo Xian 80 F4
Boxwood Hill 114 C6
Boyabat 92 F3
Boyang 80 F5
Boyarka 78 F2
Boyle 56 D8
Boysen Reservoir 126 E2
Boyuibe 142 J3
Bozcaada 68 H5
Boz Dağ 68 M7
Bozeman 126 D1
Bozkır 68 Q7
Bozoum 106 B2
Bozova 92 H5
Bozüyük 68 N5
Bra 62 C6
Brač 66 D6
Bracciano 64 G6
Bräcke 48 H5
Bracknell 54 B3
Brad 66 K3
Bradano 64 L8
Bradford 56 L8
Brady 130 B3
Braga 60 B3
Bragança, *Brazil* 140 H4
Bragança, *Portugal* 60 D3
Brahmapur 88 D5
Brahmaputra 88 F3
Brăila 66 Q4
Brainerd 128 B1
Braintree 54 C3
Brake 52 D3
Bramming 52 D1
Brampton 128 E2
Bramsche 52 D4
Branco 140 E3
Brandberg 108 A4
Brandenburg 52 H4
Brandenton 130 E4
Brandon 122 M7
Brandvlei 108 C5
Brandýs 50 D7
Braniewo 50 J3
Brasileia 140 D6
Brasília 140 H7
Braslaw 48 P9
Braşov 66 N4
Bratislava 50 G9
Bratsk 78 G5
Bratskoye Vodokhranilishche 78 G5
Brattleboro 128 F2
Braţul 66 R4
Bratunac 66 G5
Braunau 62 J2
Braunschweig 52 F4
Brawley 132 C2
Bray 56 F8
Brazil 138 F4
Brazzaville 106 B4
Brčko 66 F5
Brda 50 G4
Bream Bay 116 E2
Breckenridge 132 G2
Břeclav 50 F9
Breda 54 G3
Bredasdorp 108 C6
Bredstedt 52 E2
Bredy 70 M4
Bree 54 H3
Bree 58 L2
Bregenz 62 E3
Breiðafjörður 48 (1)A2
Bremangerlandet 48 B6
Bremen, *Germany* 52 D3
Bremen, *US* 130 D3
Bremerhaven 52 D3
Bremerton 126 B1
Bremervörde 52 E3
Brenham 130 B3
Brennero 62 G4
Breno 62 F5
Brentwood 54 C3
Brescia 62 F5
Breslau = Wrocław 50 G6
Bressanone 62 G4
Bressay 56 M1
Bressuire 58 E7
Brest, *Belarus* 70 D4
Brest, *France* 58 A5
Breteuil 54 E5
Bretten 52 D7
Breves 140 G4
Brewarrina 114 J5
Brewton 130 D3
Brežice 66 C4
Brézina 102 F2
Brezno 50 J9
Bria 106 C2
Briançon 62 B6
Briceni 66 Q1
Bridgend 56 J10
Bridgeport, *Calif., US* 132 C1
Bridgeport, *Conn., US* 128 F2
Bridgeport, *Nebr., US* 126 F2
Bridgetown 140 F1
Bridgewater 122 U8
Bridgwater 56 J10
Bridlington 56 M7
Brienzer See 62 D4
Brig 62 C4
Brigham City 126 D2
Brighton, *UK* 54 B4
Brighton, *US* 126 F3
Brignoles 62 B7
Brikama 104 A2
Brilon 52 D5
Brindisi 64 M8
Brinkley 130 C3
Brisbane 114 K5
Bristol, *UK* 56 K10
Bristol, *US* 130 E2
Bristol Bay 132 (1)E4
Bristol Channel 56 H10
British Columbia 122 F5
Britstown 108 C6
Brive-la-Gaillarde 58 G8
Briviesca 60 G2
Brixham 56 J11
Brlik 76 N9
Brno 50 F8
Broad Sound 114 J4
Broadus 126 E1
Brockton 128 F2
Brockville 128 E2
Brod 66 J9
Brodeur Peninsula 122 P2
Brodick 56 G6
Brodnica 50 J4
Broken Arrow 134 E1
Broken Bow 130 C3
Broken Hill 114 H6
Brokopondo 140 F2
Bromölla 50 D1
Bromsgrove 56 K9
Brønderslev 48 E8
Broni 62 E5
Brooke's Point 84 F5
Brookhaven 124 H5
Brookhaven 130 C3
Brookhaven 134 F2
Brookings, *Oreg., US* 126 B2
Brookings, *S.D., US* 126 G2
Brooks 122 J6
Brooks Range 132 (1)F2
Brooksville 130 E4
Broome 114 D3
Brora 56 J3
Brösarp 48 H9
Broughton Island 122 U3
Brovary 70 F4
Brownfield 132 F2
Browning 126 D1
Brownsville, *Tenn., US* 130 D2
Brownsville, *Tex., US* 130 B4
Brownwood 130 B3
Bruchsal 52 D7
Bruck, *Austria* 62 L3
Bruck, *Austria* 62 M2
Bruck an der Mur 66 C2
Brugge 54 F3
Brühl 54 J4
Bruint 88 G3
Brumado 140 J6
Brumath 62 C2
Bruneau 126 C2
Brunei 86 E2
Brunflo 48 H5
Brunico 64 F2
Brunsbüttel 52 E3
Brunswick, *Ga., US* 130 E3
Brunswick, *Me., US* 128 G2
Bruntal 50 G8
Brush 126 F2
Brussels = Bruxelles 54 G4
Bruxelles 54 G4
Bryan 130 B3
Bryanka 76 S6
Bryansk 70 F4
Brzeg 50 G7
Brzeg Dolny 50 F6
Brzeziny 50 J6
B-Spandau 50 C5
Bubi 108 E4
Bucak 92 D5
Bucaramanga 140 C2
Buchanan 104 B3
Buchan Gulf 122 S2
Bucharest = Bucureşti 66 P5
Buchen 52 E7
Buchholz 52 E3
Buchy 58 M5
Bückeburg 52 E4
Bučovice 50 F8
Bucureşti 66 P5
Budapest 66 G2
Bude 56 H11
Budennovsk 92 L1
Büdingen 52 E6
Budoni 64 D8
Budrio 62 G6
Budva 66 F7
Buenaventura, *Colombia* 140 B3
Buenaventura, *Mexico* 132 E3
Buena Vista 126 E3
Buenos Aires 142 K5
Buffalo, *Okla., US.* 130 B2
Buffalo, *N.Y., US* 128 E2
Buffalo, *S.D., US* 126 F1
Buffalo, *Tex., US* 130 B3
Buffalo, *Wyo., US.* 126 E2
Buffalo Lake 122 J4
Buffalo Narrows 122 K5
Buftea 66 N5
Bug 50 L5
Bugojno 66 E5
Bugrino 76 H4
Bugsuk 84 F5
Bugul'ma 70 K4
Buguruslan 70 K4
Buḩayrat al Asad 92 H5
Buḩayrat ath Tharthār 92 K6
Buhuşi 66 P3
Builth Wells 56 J9
Buinsk 70 J3
Buir Nuur 80 F1
Bujanovac 66 J7
Buje 62 J5
Bujumbura 106 D4
Bukachacha 78 K6
Bukavu 106 D4
Bukhara 90 H2
Bukkittinggi 86 C3
Bukoba 106 E4
Bula, *Indonesia* 87 D3
Bula, *Papua New Guinea* 87 F4
Bülach 62 D3
Bulan 84 G4
Bûlâq 100 F2
Bulawayo 108 D4
Buldir Island 78 X6
Bulgan 78 G7
Bulgaria 66 M7
Buli 87 C2
Bulle 62 C4
Bullhead City 132 D1
Bulls 116 E5
Bulukumba 87 B4
Bulun 78 M2
Bumba 106 C3
Bumbeşti Jiu 66 L4
Buna 106 F3
Bunbury 114 C6
Buncrana 56 E6
Bunda 106 E4
Bundaberg 114 K4
Bünde 52 D4
Bungunya 114 J5
Bunia 106 E3
Bunkie 130 C3
Bunnell 130 E4
Bünyan 92 F4
Bu ol Kheyr 95 D2
Buôn Mê Thuột 84 D4
Buotama 78 M4
Bura 106 F4
Buran 76 R8
Buranj 88 D2
Burao 106 H2
Burāq 94 D3
Buraydah 90 D4
Burco 100 J6
Burdur 92 D5
Burdur Gölü 68 N7
Burē 100 G5
Büren 54 L3
Burg 52 G4
Burgas 66 Q7
Burgaski Zaliv 66 Q7
Burgdorf 62 C3
Burghausen 62 H2
Burglengenfeld 52 H7
Burgos 60 G2
Burgsvik 48 K8
Burhaniye 68 K5
Burhanpur 88 C4
Burjassot 60 K5
Burj Şāfitā 94 D2
Burketown 114 G3
Burkeville 128 E3
Bur-Khaybyt 78 P3
Burkina 104 D2
Burlin 70 K4
Burlington, *Colo., US* 132 F1
Burlington, *Ia., US* 128 B2
Burlington, *Vt., US* 128 F2
Burma = Myanmar 84 B2
Burnet 130 B3
Burney 126 B2
Burnie 114 J8
Burns 126 C2
Burns Junction 126 C2
Burns Lake 122 F6
Burqin 76 R8
Burra 114 G6
Burrel 68 C3
Bursa 68 M4
Bûr Safâga 100 F2
Bûr Sa'îd 100 F1
Bur Sudan 100 G4
Burtnieks 48 N8
Burton-upon-Trent 56 L9
Buru 87 C3
Burundi 106 D4
Bururi 106 D4
Burwell 126 G2
Buryatiya 78 J6
Bury St. Edmunds 54 C2
Būshehr 95 D2
Bushire = Būshehr 95 D2
Businga 106 C3
Busira 106 C4
Buşrá ash Shām 94 D4
Bussum 54 H2
Busto Arsizio 62 D5
Buta 106 C3
Butare 106 D4
Butaritari 112 H5
Bute 56 G6
Butembo 106 D3
Buðardalur 48 (1)C2
Buton 87 B3
Butte, *Mont., US* 126 D1
Butte, *Nebr., US* 126 G2
Butuan 84 H5
Butwal 88 D3
Butzbach 52 D6
Bützow 52 G3
Buulobarde 106 H3
Buur Gaabo 106 G4
Buurhabaka 106 G3
Buxtehude 52 E3
Buxton 54 A1
Buy 70 H3
Buynaksk 92 M2
Büyükada 68 L4
Büyükçekmece 68 L4
Buzai Gumbad 90 K2
Buzançais 58 G7
Buzău 66 P4
Buzău 66 Q4
Buzuluk 70 K4
Byala, *Bulgaria* 66 N6
Byala, *Bulgaria* 66 Q7
Byala Slatina 66 L6
Byam Martin Island 122 L2
Byaroza 48 N10
Bydgoszcz 50 H4
Bygdin 48 D6
Bygland 48 D7
Bykovskiy 78 M2
Bylot Island 122 R2
Byskeälven 48 L4
Bystřice 50 G8
Bystrzyca Kłodzka 50 F7
Bytatay 78 N3
Bytča 50 H8
Bytom 50 H7
Bytów 50 G3
Bzura 50 J5

C

Caaguazú 142 K4
Caballococha 140 C5
Caballo Reservoir 132 E2
Cabañaquinta 60 E1
Cabanatuan 84 G3
Cabano 128 G1
Cabdul Qaadir 100 H5
Cabeza del Buey 60 E6
Cabezas 140 E7
Cabimas 140 C1
Cabinda 104 G6
Cabinda 104 G6
Cabo Bascuñán 142 G4
Cabo Beata 134 K5
Cabo Camarón 134 G5
Cabo Carvoeiro 60 A5
Cabo Catoche 134 G4
Cabo Corrientes, *Colombia* 140 B2
Cabo Corrientes, *Mexico* 134 C4
Cabo Corrubedo 60 A2
Cabo Cruz 134 J5
Cabo de Espichel 60 A6
Cabo de Gata 60 H8
Cabo de Hornos 142 H10
Cabo de la Nao 60 L6
Cabo Delgado 108 G2
Cabo de Palos 60 K7

Cabo de São Roque	**140**	K5
Cabo de Sao Tomé	**142**	N3
Cabo de São Vicente	**60**	A7
Cabo de Trafalgar	**60**	D8
Cabo dos Bahias	**142**	H8
Cabo Fisterra	**60**	A2
Cabo Frio	**142**	N3
Cabo Gracias á Dios	**134**	H6
Cabo Mondego	**60**	A4
Cabo Norte	**140**	H3
Cabo Orange	**140**	G3
Cabo Ortegal	**60**	B1
Cabo Peñas	**60**	E1
Caborca	**132**	D2
Cabo Rojo	**134**	E4
Cabo Roxo	**104**	A2
Cabo San Diego	**142**	H9
Cabo San Francisco de Paula	**142**	H8
Cabo San Juan	**104**	F4
Cabo San Lucas	**124**	D7
Cabo Santa Elena	**134**	J7
Cabo Tortosa	**60**	L4
Cabo Tres Puntas	**142**	H8
Cabot Strait	**122**	U7
Cabrera	**60**	N5
Čačak	**66**	H6
Cáceres, *Brazil*	**140**	F7
Cáceres, *Spain*	**60**	D5
Cacheu	**104**	A2
Cachimbo	**140**	G5
Cachoeira do Sul	**142**	L4
Cachoeiro de Itapemirim	**140**	J8
Cacola	**108**	B2
Caconda	**108**	B2
Čadca	**50**	H8
Cadillac, *Mich., US*	**128**	C2
Cadillac, *Mont., US*	**124**	E2
Cádiz	**60**	D8
Caen	**54**	B5
Caernarfon	**56**	H8
Cagayan de Oro	**84**	G5
Cagli	**62**	H7
Cagliari	**64**	D9
Cagnes-sur-Mer	**62**	C7
Caguas	**134**	L5
Cahama	**108**	A3
Cahersiveen	**56**	B10
Cahir	**56**	E9
Cahors	**58**	G9
Cahuapanas	**140**	B5
Cahul	**66**	R4
Caia	**108**	F3
Caianda	**108**	C2
Caicos Islands	**134**	K4
Cairns	**114**	J3
Cairo = El Qâhira, *Egypt*	**100**	F1
Cairo, *US*	**130**	D2
Cairo Montenotte	**62**	D6
Caiundo	**108**	B3
Cajamarca	**140**	B5
Čakovec	**66**	D3
Calabar	**104**	F3
Calabozo	**140**	D2
Calabro	**64**	L9
Calafat	**66**	K6
Calagua Islands	**84**	G4
Calahorra	**60**	J2
Calais	**54**	D4
Calama, *Brazil*	**140**	E5
Calama, *Peru*	**142**	H3
Calamar	**140**	C3
Calamian Group	**84**	F4
Calamocha	**60**	J4
Călan	**66**	L4
Calanscio Sand Sea	**100**	D2
Calapan	**84**	G4
Călărași, *Moldova*	**66**	R2
Călărași, *Romania*	**66**	Q5
Calatafim	**64**	G11
Calatayud	**60**	J3
Calauag	**84**	G4
Calbayog	**84**	G4
Calçoene	**140**	G3
Calcutta = Kolkata	**88**	E4
Caldas da Rainha	**60**	A5
Caldera	**142**	G4
Caldwell, *Id., US*	**126**	C2
Caldwell, *Kans., US*	**130**	B2
Calf of Man	**56**	H7
Calgary	**122**	J6
Calhoun	**130**	E3
Calhoun City	**130**	D3
Calhoun Falls	**130**	E3
Cali	**140**	B3
Calicut = Kozhikode	**88**	C6
Caliente	**126**	D3
California	**124**	B4
Calilabad	**92**	N4
Callao	**140**	B6
Caloundra	**114**	K5
Caltagirone	**64**	J11
Caltanissetta	**64**	J11
Caluquembe	**108**	A2
Caluula	**106**	J1
Calvi	**64**	C6
Calvin	**130**	B3
Calvinia	**108**	B6
Calw	**62**	D2
Camaçari	**140**	K6
Camacupa	**108**	B2
Camagüey	**134**	J4
Camaiore	**62**	F7
Camana	**140**	C7
Camargue	**58**	K10
Camariñas	**60**	A1
Camarones	**142**	H7
Ca Mau	**84**	D5
Camberley	**56**	M10
Cambodia	**84**	C4
Cambrai	**54**	F4
Cambre	**60**	B1
Cambria	**126**	B3
Cambrian Mountains	**56**	H10
Cambridge, *New Zealand*	**116**	E3
Cambridge, *UK*	**56**	N9
Cambridge, *Md., US*	**128**	E3
Cambridge, *Mass., US*	**128**	F2
Cambridge, *Oh., US*	**128**	D3
Cambridge Bay	**122**	K3
Cambrils	**60**	M3
Camden, *Ark., US*	**130**	C3
Camden, *S.C., US*	**130**	E3
Cameron, *La., US*	**130**	C4
Cameron, *Mo., US*	**130**	C2
Cameron, *Tex., US*	**130**	B3
Cameroon	**104**	G3
Cametá	**140**	H4
Çamiçigölü	**68**	K7
Caminha	**60**	B3
Camiranga	**140**	H4
Camocim	**140**	J4
Camooweal	**114**	G3
Camopi	**140**	G3
Campbell Island	**116**	(2)C2
Campbell River	**122**	F7
Campbellsville	**128**	C3
Campbellton	**128**	G1
Campbeltown	**56**	G6
Campeche	**134**	F5
Câmpeni	**66**	L3
Câmpia Turzii	**66**	L3
Câmpina	**66**	N4
Campina Grande	**140**	L5
Campinas	**142**	M3
Campobasso	**64**	J7
Campo de Criptana	**60**	G5
Campo de Diauarum	**140**	G6
Campo Gallo	**142**	J4
Campo Grande	**142**	L3
Campo Maior	**140**	J4
Campo Mourão	**142**	L3
Campos	**142**	N3
Câmpulung	**66**	N4
Câmpulung Moldovenesc	**66**	N2
Cam Ranh	**84**	D4
Çan	**68**	K4
Canada	**120**	M4
Canadian	**132**	F1
Canadian	**132**	F1
Çanakkale	**68**	J4
Çanakkale Boğazı	**68**	J4
Canal de Panamá	**134**	J7
Cananea	**132**	D2
Canary Islands = Islas Canarias	**98**	A3
Canary Islands = Islas Canarias	**102**	B3
Cañaveras	**60**	H4
Canberra	**114**	J7
Cancún	**134**	G4
Çandarli Körfezi	**68**	J6
Candelaro	**66**	C8
Candlemas Island	**138**	J9
Cangamba	**108**	B2
Cangas	**60**	B2
Cangas de Narcea	**60**	D1
Cangyuan	**84**	B2
Cangzhou	**80**	F3
Canicatti	**64**	H11
Canindé	**140**	K4
Çankiri	**92**	E3
Canna	**56**	F4
Cannanore	**88**	B6
Cannanore	**88**	C6
Cannes	**62**	C7
Cannock	**54**	A2
Canon City	**132**	E1
Cantanduanes	**84**	G4
Canterbury	**54**	D3
Canterbury Bight	**116**	C7
Canterbury Plains	**116**	C6
Cân Tho	**84**	D5
Canto do Buriti	**140**	J5
Canton, *Miss., US*	**130**	D3
Canton, *Oh., US*	**130**	E1
Canton, *S.D., US*	**126**	G2
Canumã	**140**	F4
Canumã	**140**	F5
Canutama	**140**	E5
Canyon	**132**	F1
Canyon Ferry Lake	**126**	D1
Cao Băng	**84**	D2
Caorle	**62**	H5
Cap Blanc	**64**	D11
Cap Bon	**102**	H1
Cap Corse	**64**	D5
Cap d'Agde	**58**	J10
Cap d'Antifer	**54**	C5
Cap de Fer	**102**	G1
Cap de Formentor	**60**	P5
Cap de la Hague	**58**	D4
Cap-de-la-Madeleine	**128**	F1
Cap de Nouvelle-France	**122**	S4
Cap de ses Salines	**60**	P5
Cap des Trois Fourches	**60**	H9
Cape Agulhas	**108**	C6
Cape Alexandra	**142**	P9
Cape Andreas	**90**	B2
Cape Apostolos Andreas	**92**	F6
Cape Arid	**114**	D6
Cape Arnaoutis	**92**	D6
Cape Arnhem	**114**	G2
Cape Barren Island	**114**	J8
Cape Bauld	**122**	V6
Cape Blanco	**126**	B2
Cape Borda	**114**	G7
Cape Breton Island	**122**	U7
Cape Brett	**116**	E2
Cape Byron	**114**	K5
Cape Campbell	**116**	E5
Cape Canaveral	**130**	E4
Cape Canaveral	**130**	E4
Cape Carnot	**114**	F6
Cape Charles	**128**	E3
Cape Chidley	**122**	U4
Cape Christian	**122**	T2
Cape Churchill	**122**	N5
Cape Clear	**56**	C10
Cape Cleare	**132**	(1)H4
Cape Coast	**104**	D3
Cape Cod	**128**	G2
Cape Columbine	**108**	B6
Cape Colville	**116**	E3
Cape Comorin	**88**	C7
Cape Constantine	**132**	(1)E4
Cape Coral	**130**	E4
Cape Crawford	**114**	G3
Cape Croker	**114**	F2
Cape Dalhousie	**132**	(1)L1
Cape Direction	**114**	H2
Cape Disappointment	**142**	P9
Cape Dominion	**122**	R3
Cape Dorchester	**122**	Q3
Cape Dorset	**122**	R4
Cape Dyer	**122**	U3
Cape Egmont	**116**	D4
Cape Eleaia	**94**	B1
Cape Farewell, *Greenland*	**120**	F4
Cape Farewell, *New Zealand*	**116**	D5
Cape Fear	**130**	F3
Cape Finisterre = Cabo Fisterra	**60**	A2
Cape Flattery, *Australia*	**114**	J2
Cape Flattery *United States*	**126**	A1
Cape Forestier	**114**	J8
Cape Foulwind	**116**	C5
Cape Fria	**108**	A3
Cape Girardeau	**128**	C3
Cape Greko	**92**	F6
Cape Grenville	**114**	H2
Cape Grim	**114**	H8
Cape Harrison	**122**	V6
Cape Hatteras	**130**	F2
Cape Henrietta Maria	**122**	Q5
Cape Horn = Cabo de Hornos	**142**	H10
Cape Howe	**114**	K7
Cape Inscription	**114**	B5
Cape Jaffa	**114**	G7
Cape Karikari	**116**	D2
Cape Kellett	**122**	F2
Cape Kidnappers	**116**	F4
Cape Leeuwin	**114**	B6
Cape Lévêque	**114**	D3
Cape Londonderry	**114**	E2
Cape Lookout	**134**	J2
Cape May	**128**	F3
Cape Melville	**114**	H2
Cape Mendenhall	**132**	(1)D4
Cape Mendocino	**126**	A2
Cape Mercy	**122**	U4
Cape Meredith	**142**	J9
Cape Naturaliste	**114**	B6
Capenda-Camulemba	**108**	B1
Cape Negrais	**84**	A3
Cape Nelson	**114**	H7
Cape Newenham	**132**	(1)E4
Cape of Good Hope	**108**	B6
Cape Palliser	**116**	E5
Cape Palmas	**104**	C4
Cape Parry	**122**	G2
Cape Providence	**116**	A8
Cape Race	**120**	G5
Cape Ray	**122**	V7
Cape Reinga	**116**	D2
Cape Romanzof	**132**	(1)D3
Cape Runaway	**116**	G3
Cape Sable	**122**	T8
Cape St. Elias	**132**	(1)J4
Cape St. Francis	**108**	C6
Cape San Agustin	**84**	H5
Cape San Blas	**130**	D4
Cape Saunders	**116**	C7
Cape Scott	**114**	E1
Cape Stephens	**116**	D5
Cape Terawhiti	**116**	E5
Cape Three Points	**104**	D4
Cape Town	**108**	B6
Cape Turnagain	**116**	F5
Cape Verde	**104**	(1)B2
Cape Wessel	**114**	G2
Cape Wrangell	**78**	W6
Cape Wrath	**56**	G3
Cape York	**114**	H2
Cape York Peninsula	**114**	H2
Cap Figalo	**60**	J9
Cap Fréhel	**58**	C5
Cap Gris-Nez	**54**	D4
Cap-Haïtien	**134**	K5
Cap Juby	**102**	C3
Čapljina	**66**	E6
Cap Lopez	**104**	F5
Cap Negro	**60**	E9
Capo Carbonara	**64**	D10
Capo Colonna	**64**	M9
Capo Gallo	**64**	H10
Capo Granitola	**64**	G11
Capo Murro di Porco	**64**	K11
Capo Palinuro	**64**	J8
Capo Passero	**64**	K12
Capo Santa Maria di Leuca	**64**	N9
Capo San Vito	**64**	G10
Capo Spartivento, *Italy*	**64**	C10
Capo Spartivento, *Italy*	**64**	L11
Capo Vaticano	**64**	K10
Capraia	**64**	D5
Cap Rhir	**102**	C2
Capri	**64**	J8
Capri	**64**	J8
Capricorn Group	**114**	K4
Cap Rosa	**64**	C11
Cap Serrat	**64**	D11
Cap Spartel	**60**	E9
Cap Timiris	**102**	B5
Capua	**64**	J7
Cap Verga	**104**	B2
Cap Vert	**104**	A2
Caquetá	**140**	C4
Caracal	**66**	M5
Caracarai	**140**	E3
Caracas	**140**	D1
Caransebeș	**66**	K4
Carauari	**140**	D4
Caravaca de la Cruz	**60**	J6
Caravelas	**140**	K7
Carazinho	**142**	L4
Carballiño	**60**	B2
Carballo	**60**	B1
Carbondale, *Ill., US*	**130**	D2
Carbondale, *Pa., US*	**130**	F1
Carboneras	**60**	J7
Carbonia	**64**	C9
Carcar	**84**	G4
Carcassonne	**58**	H10
Cardiff	**56**	J10
Cardigan	**56**	H9
Cardigan Bay	**56**	H9
Cardston	**126**	D1
Carei	**66**	K2
Carentan	**58**	D4
Cariacica	**142**	N3
Cariati	**64**	L9
Caribbean Sea	**134**	J6
Caripito	**140**	E1
Carlet	**60**	K5
Carleton Place	**128**	E1
Carlisle, *UK*	**56**	K7
Carlisle, *US*	**128**	E2
Carlow	**56**	F9
Carlsbad	**132**	F2
Carlyle	**126**	F1
Carmacks	**122**	D4
Carmagnola	**62**	C6
Carmarthen	**56**	H10
Carmarthen Bay	**56**	G10
Carmaux	**58**	H9
Carmen	**134**	B3
Carmona	**60**	E7
Carnarvon, *Australia*	**114**	B4
Carnarvon, *South Africa*	**108**	C6
Car Nicobar	**88**	F7
Carnot	**106**	B2
Carnsore Point	**56**	F9
Carolina	**140**	H5
Carolina Beach	**130**	F3
Caroline Island	**112**	L6
Caroline Islands	**112**	E5
Carpathian Mountains	**50**	J8
Carpații Meridionali	**66**	K4
Carpentras	**58**	L9
Carpi	**62**	F6
Carrabelle	**130**	E4
Carrara	**62**	F6
Carrickfergus	**56**	G7
Carrick-on-Suir	**56**	E9
Carrington	**126**	G1
Carrizozo	**132**	E2
Carroll	**128**	B2
Carrollton, *Ky., US*	**128**	D3
Carrollton, *Mo., US*	**130**	C1
Çarşamba	**92**	G3
Carson City	**126**	C3
Cartagena, *Colombia*	**140**	B1
Cartagena, *Spain*	**60**	K7
Carthage	**130**	C3
Cartwright	**122**	V6
Caruarú	**140**	K5
Carúpano	**140**	E1
Casablanca	**102**	D2
Casa Grande	**132**	D2
Casale Monferrato	**62**	D5
Casalmaggiore	**62**	F6
Casamozza	**64**	D6
Casarano	**64**	N9
Cascade, *Id., US*	**126**	C2
Cascade, *Mont., US*	**126**	C1
Cascade Range	**126**	B2
Cascade Reservoir	**126**	C2
Cascais	**60**	A6
Cascavel	**142**	L3
Caserta	**64**	J7
Cashel, *Ireland*	**56**	E9
Cashel, *Zimbabwe*	**108**	E3
Casiguran	**84**	G3
Casino	**114**	K5
Čáslav	**62**	M5
Caspe	**60**	K3
Casper	**126**	E2
Caspian Sea	**46**	J3
Cassiar	**122**	F5
Cassino	**64**	H7
Castanhal	**140**	H4
Castelbuono	**64**	J11
Castèl di Sangro	**64**	J7
Castelfidardo	**64**	H5
Castellammare del Golfo	**64**	G10
Castellane	**62**	B7
Castellaneta	**64**	L8
Castelli	**142**	J4
Castelló de la Plana	**60**	K5
Castelnaudary	**58**	G10
Castelo Branco	**60**	C5
Castelsarrasin	**58**	G10
Castelvetrano	**64**	G11
Castets	**58**	D10
Castiglion Fiorentino	**62**	G7
Castlebar	**56**	C8
Castleford	**56**	L8
Castle Point	**116**	F5
Castres	**58**	H10
Castricum	**54**	G2
Castries	**134**	M6
Castro	**142**	M3
Castro Verde	**60**	B7
Castrovillari	**64**	L9
Castuera	**60**	E6
Çatak	**92**	K5
Catamarca	**142**	H4

Catandica	**108**	E3
Catania	**64**	K11
Catanzaro	**64**	L10
Catanzaro Marina	**64**	L10
Catarman	**84**	G4
Catbalogan	**84**	H4
Catió	**104**	A2
Cat Island	**130**	F5
Cat Lake	**122**	N6
Cato Island	**114**	L4
Catriló	**142**	J6
Catrimani	**140**	E3
Catskill Mountains	**124**	M3
Cattolica	**62**	H7
Cauayan	**84**	G5
Cauca	**140**	C2
Caucaia	**140**	K4
Caucasia	**140**	B2
Caucasus	**92**	K2
Caudry	**54**	F4
Cauquenes	**142**	G6
Caura	**140**	E2
Causapscal	**128**	G1
Căuşeni	**66**	S3
Cavaillon	**58**	L10
Cavalese	**62**	G4
Cavan	**56**	E8
Cavarzere	**62**	H5
Cavinas	**140**	D6
Cavtat	**66**	F7
Caxias	**140**	J4
Caxias do Sul	**142**	L4
Caxito	**104**	G6
Cay	**68**	P6
Cayce	**130**	E3
Çaycuma	**68**	Q3
Cayenne	**140**	G3
Cayman Islands	**134**	H5
Caynabo	**106**	H2
Cayos Miskitos	**134**	H6
Cay Sal Bank	**130**	E5
Cazorla	**60**	H7
Ceanannus Mor	**56**	F8
Ceará	**140**	J4
Cebu	**84**	G4
Cebu	**84**	G4
Cecina	**62**	F7
Cedar City	**126**	D3
Cedar Falls	**128**	B2
Cedar Lake	**122**	L6
Cedar Rapids	**128**	B2
Cedros	**124**	C6
Ceduna	**114**	F6
Ceerigaabo	**106**	H1
Cefalù	**64**	J10
Cegléd	**66**	G2
Celaya	**134**	D4
Celebes = Sulawesi	**87**	A3
Celebes Sea	**87**	B2
Celje	**66**	C3
Celldömölk	**66**	E2
Celle	**52**	F4
Celtic Sea	**56**	E10
Centerville	**128**	B2
Cento	**62**	G6
Central African Republic	**106**	C2
Central City	**126**	G2
Centralia, *Ill., US*	**128**	C3
Centralia, *Wash., US*	**126**	B1
Central Range	**87**	F3
Central Siberian Plateau = Srednesibirskoye Ploskogor'ye	**74**	N2
Cenxi	**84**	E2
Cerea	**62**	G5
Ceres, *Argentina*	**142**	J4
Ceres, *Brazil*	**140**	H7
Cerezo de Abajo	**60**	G3
Cerignola	**64**	K7
Çerikli	**92**	E4
Çerkes	**68**	Q4
Çerkezköy	**68**	K3
Cerknica	**62**	K5
Cernavodă	**66**	R5
Cero Champaqui	**142**	J5
Cerralvo	**124**	E7
Cërrik	**68**	C3
Cerritos	**132**	F4
Cerro Aconcagua	**142**	G5
Cerro Bonete	**142**	H4
Cerro de la Encantada	**124**	C5
Cerro de Pasco	**140**	B6
Cerro Huehuento	**134**	C4
Cerro Las Tórtolas	**142**	H5
Cerro Marahuaca	**140**	D3
Cerro Mercedario	**142**	G5
Cerro Murallón	**142**	G8
Cerro Nevado	**142**	H6
Cerro Pena Nevade	**134**	D4
Cerro San Lorenzo	**142**	G8
Cerro San Valentín	**142**	G8
Cerros de Bala	**140**	D6
Cerro Tres Picos	**142**	J6
Cerro Tupungato	**142**	H5
Cerro Yavi	**140**	D2
Cerro Yogan	**142**	H9
Certaldo	**62**	G7
Cervaro	**64**	K7
Cervia	**62**	H6
Cervionne	**64**	D6
Cervo	**60**	C1
Cesano	**62**	J7
Cesena	**62**	H6
Cesenatico	**62**	H6
Cēsis	**48**	N8
Česka Lípa	**52**	K6
České Budějovice	**62**	K2
Český Krumlov	**62**	K2
Çeşme	**68**	J6
Česna	**62**	M5
Cessnock	**114**	K6
Cestas	**58**	E9
Cetate	**66**	L5
Cetinje	**66**	F7
Cetraro	**64**	K9
Ceuta	**102**	D1
Cevizli	**68**	P7
Chachapoyas	**140**	B5
Chaco Boreal	**142**	K3
Chad	**100**	C5
Chadan	**76**	S7
Chadron	**126**	F2
Chagai	**90**	H4
Chagda	**78**	N5
Chaghcharān	**90**	J3
Chagyl	**90**	G1
Chāh Bahār	**90**	H4
Chāībāsa	**88**	E4
Chainat	**84**	C3
Chaiyaphum	**84**	C3
Chalais	**58**	F8
Chalhuanca	**140**	C6
Chalinze	**106**	F5
Chalki	**68**	K8
Chalkida	**68**	F6
Chalkidiki	**68**	F4
Challans	**58**	D7
Challapata	**140**	D7
Challenger Deep	**112**	E4
Challis	**126**	D2
Châlons-sur-Marne	**54**	G6
Chalon-sur-Saône	**58**	K7
Cham	**52**	H7
Chama	**108**	E2
Chamba	**88**	C2
Chambal	**88**	C3
Chamberlain	**126**	G2
Chambersburg	**128**	E3
Chambéry	**62**	A5
Chambly	**54**	E5
Chamonix	**62**	B5
Champagnole	**62**	A4
Champaign	**128**	C2
Champaubert	**54**	F6
Champlitte	**62**	A3
Chañaral	**142**	G4
Chandalar	**122**	B3
Chandeleur Islands	**134**	G3
Chandigarh	**88**	C2
Chandler	**132**	D2
Chandrapur	**88**	C5
Changane	**108**	E4
Changara	**108**	E3
Changchun	**82**	C2
Changde	**80**	E5
Chang-hua	**80**	G6
Chang Jiang	**80**	D4
Changsha	**80**	E5
Changshou	**80**	D5
Changshu	**80**	G4
Changting	**80**	F5
Changzhi	**80**	E3
Changzhou	**80**	F4
Chania	**68**	G9
Channel Islands, *UK*	**56**	K12
Channel Islands, *US*	**124**	C5
Channel-Port aux Basques	**122**	V7
Chanthaburi	**84**	C4
Chantilly	**54**	E5
Chanute	**130**	B2
Chao Phraya	**84**	C4
Chaouèn	**102**	D1
Chao Xian	**80**	F4
Chaoyang	**80**	G2
Chaozhou	**80**	F6
Chapada Diamantina	**140**	J6
Chapais	**128**	F1
Chapayev	**70**	K4
Chapayevo	**78**	K4
Chapayevskoye	**76**	N7
Chapecó	**142**	L4
Chapleau	**128**	D1
Chapra	**88**	D3
Chara	**78**	K5
Charcas	**132**	F4
Chard	**122**	J5
Chardara	**90**	J1
Chardzhev	**90**	H2
Chari	**100**	C5
Chārīkār	**90**	J2
Charleroi	**54**	G4
Charlesbourg	**128**	F1
Charleston, *New Zealand*	**116**	C5
Charleston, *S.C., US*	**130**	F3
Charleston, *W. Va., US*	**130**	E2
Charlestown	**130**	D2
Charleville	**114**	J5
Charleville-Mézières	**54**	G5
Charlevoix	**128**	C1
Charlotte, *Mich., US*	**128**	D2
Charlotte, *N.C., US*	**130**	E2
Charlottesville	**130**	F2
Charlottetown	**122**	U7
Charlton Island	**122**	Q6
Charrat	**62**	C4
Charsk	**76**	Q8
Charters Towers	**114**	J4
Chartres	**58**	G5
Charymovo	**70**	Q3
Chasel'ka	**78**	C3
Chastyye	**70**	K3
Châteaguay	**128**	F1
Châteaubriant	**58**	D6
Châteaudun	**58**	G5
Châteaulin	**58**	A5
Châteauneuf-sur-Loire	**58**	H6
Châteauroux	**58**	G7
Château-Thierry	**54**	F5
Châtellerault	**58**	F7
Châtenois	**62**	A2
Chatham	**128**	D2
Chatham Island	**116**	(1)B1
Chatham Islands	**116**	(1)B1
Châtillon-sur Seine	**58**	K6
Chattanooga	**124**	J4
Chauffayer	**62**	B6
Chauk	**88**	F4
Chaumont	**58**	L5
Chaunskaya Guba	**78**	V3
Chauny	**54**	F5
Chaves, *Brazil*	**140**	G4
Chaves, *Portugal*	**60**	C3
Chavuma	**108**	C2
Cheb	**52**	H6
Cheboksary	**70**	J3
Chechnya	**92**	L2
Cheduba Island	**88**	F5
Cheektowaga	**128**	E2
Chegdomyn	**78**	N6
Chegga	**102**	D3
Chegutu	**108**	E3
Chehalis	**126**	B1
Cheju	**82**	D7
Cheju do	**82**	D7
Chekhov	**78**	Q7
Chelan	**126**	C1
Cheleken	**90**	F2
Chélif	**60**	L8
Chelkar	**76**	K8
Chełm	**50**	N6
Chełmno	**50**	H4
Chelmsford	**54**	C3
Chełmza	**50**	H4
Cheltenham	**56**	L10
Chelyabinsk	**70**	M3
Chelyuskin	**76**	U2
Chemnitz	**52**	H6
Chenab	**88**	B2
Chenachane	**102**	E3
Cheney Reservoir	**130**	B2
Chengde	**80**	F2
Chengdu	**80**	C4
Chengshan Jiao	**82**	B5
Chennai	**88**	D6
Chenzhou	**80**	E5
Chepes	**142**	H5
Cher	**58**	G6
Cheraw	**130**	F3
Cherbaniani Reef	**88**	B6
Cherbourg	**58**	D4
Cherchell	**60**	N8
Cherdyn	**70**	L2
Cheremkhovo	**78**	G6
Cherepovets	**70**	G3
Cherkasy	**70**	F5
Cherkessk	**92**	K1
Chermoz	**70**	L3
Chernihiv	**70**	F4
Chernivtsi	**70**	E5
Chernushka	**70**	L3
Chernyakhovsk	**50**	L3
Chernyayevo	**78**	M6
Chernyshevsk	**78**	K6
Chernyshevskiy	**78**	J4
Chernyye Zemli	**70**	J5
Cherokee	**128**	A2
Cherskiy	**78**	U3
Cherven Bryag	**66**	M6
Červonohrad	**70**	D4
Chesapeake	**130**	F2
Cheshskaya Guba	**70**	J1
Cheshunt	**54**	C3
Chester, *UK*	**56**	K8
Chester, *Calif., US*	**126**	B2
Chester, *Mont., US*	**126**	D1
Chesterfield	**56**	L8
Chesterfield Inlet	**122**	N4
Chetumal	**134**	G5
Chetwynd	**122**	G5
Cheviot	**116**	D6
Cheviot Hills	**56**	K6
Ch'ew Bahir	**106**	F3
Cheyenne	**126**	F2
Cheyenne	**126**	F2
Cheyenne Wells	**132**	F1
Cheyne Bay	**114**	C6
Chhatarpur	**88**	C4
Chhindwara	**88**	C4
Chhuka	**88**	E3
Chia-i	**80**	G6
Chiang Khan	**84**	C3
Chiang-Mai	**84**	B3
Chiang Rai	**84**	B3
Chiavari	**62**	E6
Chiavenno	**62**	E4
Chiba	**82**	L6
Chibougamau	**122**	S6
Chibuto	**108**	E4
Chicago	**128**	C2
Chicapa	**106**	C5
Chichagof Island	**132**	(1)K4
Chichaoua	**102**	D2
Chichester	**54**	B4
Chickasha	**130**	B3
Chiclana de la Frontera	**60**	D8
Chiclayo	**140**	B5
Chico	**142**	H8
Chicopee	**128**	F2
Chicoutimi	**122**	S7
Chicualacuala	**108**	E4
Chiemsee	**62**	H3
Chieri	**62**	C5
Chiese	**62**	F5
Chieti	**64**	J6
Chifeng	**80**	F2
Chiganak	**76**	N8
Chigubo	**108**	E4
Chihuahua	**132**	E3
Chili	**76**	M9
Chikwa	**108**	E2
Chilas	**88**	B1
Childress	**132**	F2
Chile	**138**	D8
Chile Chico	**142**	G8
Chilik	**76**	P9
Chilika Lake	**88**	D4
Chillán	**142**	G6
Chillicothe, *Mo., US*	**128**	B3
Chillicothe, *Oh., US*	**128**	D3
Chilliwack	**126**	B1
Chiloquin	**126**	B2
Chilpancingo	**134**	E5
Chi-lung	**80**	G5
Chimbay	**76**	K9
Chimborazo	**140**	B4
Chimbote	**140**	B5
Chimchememel'	**78**	V3
Chimec	**66**	J1
Chimoio	**108**	E3
China	**74**	N6
Chincha Alta	**140**	B6
Chincilla de Monte-Aragón	**60**	J6
Chinde	**108**	F3
Chin do	**82**	C6
Chindwin	**84**	A2
Chingola	**108**	D2
Chinguetti	**102**	C4
Chinhoyi	**108**	E3
Chiniot	**88**	B2
Chinju	**82**	E6
Chinmen	**84**	F2
Chinnur	**88**	C5
Chino	**82**	K6
Chioggia	**62**	H5
Chios	**68**	H6
Chios	**68**	J6
Chipata	**108**	E2
Chippewa Falls	**128**	B2
Chipping Norton	**54**	A3
Chirala	**88**	D5
Chirchik	**76**	M9
Chirikof Island	**132**	(1)F5
Chiromo	**108**	F3
Chirpan	**68**	H2
Chirripo	**134**	H7
Chişinău	**66**	R2
Chişineu-Criş	**66**	J3
Chita	**78**	J6
Chitado	**108**	A3
Chitato	**106**	C5
Chitembo	**108**	B2
Chitipa	**106**	E5
Chitradurga	**88**	C6
Chitral	**88**	B1
Chitré	**134**	H7
Chittagong	**88**	F4
Chittaurgarh	**88**	B4
Chittoor	**88**	C6
Chitungwiza	**108**	E3
Chiume	**108**	C3
Chivasso	**62**	C5
Chizha	**70**	H1
Chodov	**52**	H6
Chodzież	**50**	F5
Choiseul	**112**	F6
Chojnice	**50**	G4
Chojnów	**50**	F6
Chokurdakh	**78**	R2
Chókwé	**108**	E4
Cholet	**58**	E6
Choma	**108**	D3
Chomutov	**50**	C7
Chona	**78**	H4
Chonan	**82**	D5
Chone	**140**	A4
Ch'ŏngjin	**82**	E3
Chŏngju	**82**	C4
Ch'ŏngju	**82**	D6
Chŏngp'yŏng	**82**	D4
Chongqing	**74**	P7
Chŏngŭp	**82**	D6
Ch'ŏnju	**82**	D5
Chonogol	**80**	F1
Chon Thanh	**84**	D4
Chop	**50**	M9
Chornobyl'	**70**	F4
Chornomors'ke	**70**	F5
Ch'osan	**82**	C3
Chōshi	**82**	L6
Choszczno	**50**	E4
Choteau	**126**	D1
Chott el Hodna	**102**	F1
Chott el Jerid	**102**	G2
Chott Melrhir	**102**	G2
Choûm	**102**	C4
Choybalsan	**78**	J7
Choyr	**80**	D1
Chre	**58**	H9
Christchurch	**116**	D6
Christiansburg	**128**	D3
Christiansø	**50**	E2
Christmas Island	**86**	D5
Chrudim	**50**	E8
Chrysi	**68**	H10
Chrysoupoli	**66**	M9
Chu	**76**	N9
Chubut	**142**	H7
Chugach Mountains	**122**	B4
Chūgoku-sanchi	**80**	J3
Chugwater	**126**	F2
Chukchi Sea	**132**	(1)C2
Chukotskiy Khrebet	**78**	W3
Chukotskiy Poluostrov	**78**	Z3
Chula Vista	**132**	C2
Chulucanas	**140**	A5
Chulym	**76**	R6
Chum	**70**	M1
Chumikan	**78**	P6
Chum Phae	**84**	C3
Chumphon	**84**	B4
Ch'unch'ŏn	**82**	D5
Chunchura	**88**	E4
Chundzha	**76**	P9
Ch'ungju	**82**	D5
Chuquicamata	**142**	H3
Chur	**62**	E4
Churapcha	**78**	N4
Churchill	**122**	N5

Name	Page	Grid
Churchill, *Man., Canada*	122	M5
Churchill, *Nfld., Canada*	122	U6
Churchill Falls	122	U6
Churchill Peak	122	F5
Churu	88	B3
Chuska Mountains	132	E1
Chusovoy	70	L3
Chute des Passes	122	S7
Chuuk	112	F5
Chuvashiya	70	J3
Chuxiong	84	C2
Chuya	78	J5
Ciadîr-Lunga	66	R3
Cide	92	E3
Ciechanów	50	K5
Ciechocinek	50	H5
Ciego de Avila	134	J4
Cienfuegos	134	H4
Cieza	60	J6
Cihanbeyli	92	E4
Cijulang	86	D4
Cilacap	86	D4
Cili	80	E5
Cimarron	130	B2
Cimişlia	66	R3
Cîmpeni	50	N11
Cinca	60	L3
Cincinnati	128	D3
Çine	68	L7
Ciney	54	H4
Cintalapa	134	F5
Circle, *Ak., US*	132	(1)J2
Circle, *Mont., US*	126	E1
Circleville	128	D3
Cirebon	86	D4
Cirò Marina	64	M9
Cisco	130	B3
Cistierna	60	E2
Čitluk	66	E6
Citronelle	130	D3
Cittadella	62	G5
Città di Castello	62	H7
Ciucea	66	K3
Ciudad Acuña	132	F3
Ciudad Bolívar	140	E2
Ciudad Camargo	132	E3
Ciudad del Carmen	134	F5
Ciudad del Este	142	L4
Ciudad Delicias	132	E3
Ciudad del Maíz	132	G4
Ciudad de Valles	134	E4
Ciudad Guayana	140	E2
Ciudad Juárez	132	E2
Ciudad Madero	132	G4
Ciudad Mante	134	E4
Ciudad Obregón	134	C3
Ciudad Real	60	G6
Ciudad-Rodrigo	60	D4
Ciudad Valles	132	G4
Ciudad Victoria	124	G7
Ciutadella	60	P4
Cividale del Friuli	62	J4
Civita Castellana	64	G6
Civitanova Marche	64	H5
Civitavecchia	64	F6
Cizre	92	K5
Clacton-on-Sea	54	D3
Clair Engle Lake	126	B2
Clairview	114	J4
Clamecy	58	J6
Clare Island	56	B8
Claremorris	56	D8
Clarence	116	D6
Clarence Strait	114	E2
Clarendon	132	F2
Clarkdale	132	D2
Clarksburg	130	E2
Clarksdale	130	C3
Clarks Junction	116	C7
Clarkston	126	C1
Clarksville, *Ark., US*	130	C2
Clarksville, *Tenn., US*	130	D2
Claro	140	G7
Clausthal-Zellerfeld	52	F5
Claveria	84	G3
Clayton	132	F1
Clear Island	56	C10
Clear Lake	128	B2
Clear Lake Reservoir	126	B2
Clearwater	126	C1
Clearwater	130	E4
Clearwater Mountains	126	C1
Cleburne	130	B3
Clermont, *Australia*	114	J4
Clermont, *France*	54	E5
Clermont-Ferrand	58	J8
Clervaux	54	J4
Cles	62	F4
Cleveland, *Oh., US*	128	D2
Cleveland, *Tenn., US*	130	E2
Cleveland, *Tex., US*	130	B3
Clifden	116	A7
Clifton	132	E2
Climax	126	E1
Clines Corners	132	E2
Clinton, *Canada*	122	G6
Clinton, *New Zealand*	116	B8
Clinton, *Ark., US*	128	B3
Clinton, *Ia., US*	124	H3
Clinton, *Miss., US*	130	C3
Clinton, *Mo., US*	128	B3
Clinton, *N.C., US*	130	F3
Clinton, *Okla., US*	130	B2
Clipperton Island	134	C6
Clonakilty	56	D10
Cloncurry	114	H4
Clonmel	56	E9
Cloppenburg	52	D4
Cloquet	128	B1
Cloud Peak	126	E2
Clovis, *Calif., US*	126	C3
Clovis, *N. Mex., US*	132	F2
Cluj-Napoca	66	L3
Cluny	58	K7
Cluses	62	B4
Clyde	56	H6
Clyde River	122	T2
Coaldale	126	C3
Coalville	126	C2
Coari	140	E4
Coast Mountains	122	E5
Coast Range	126	B3
Coatbridge	56	J6
Coats Island	122	Q4
Coatzacoalcos	134	F5
Cobalt	122	R7
Cobán	134	F5
Cobija	140	D6
Cobourg	124	L3
Cobourg Peninsula	114	F2
Cóbuè	108	E2
Coburg	52	F6
Cochabamba	140	D7
Cochin = Kochi	88	C7
Cochrane	128	D1
Cockburn Town	130	G5
Coco	134	H6
Cocoa	130	E4
Cocobeach	104	F4
Coco Channel	84	A4
Coco Island	84	A4
Codajás	140	E4
Codigoro	62	H6
Cod Island	122	U5
Codlea	66	N4
Codó	140	J4
Codogno	62	E5
Codroipo	62	J5
Cody	126	E2
Coen	114	H2
Coesfeld	52	C5
Coëtivy Island	98	J6
Coeur d'Alene	126	C1
Coeur d'Alene Lake	126	C1
Coevorden	54	J2
Coffs Harbour	114	K6
Cofrents	60	J5
Cognac	58	E8
Cogne	62	C5
Coiba	138	C3
Coihaique	142	G8
Coimbatore	88	C6
Coimbra	60	B4
Colchester	54	C3
Colebrook	128	F1
Coleman	130	B3
Coleraine	56	F6
Colesberg	108	D6
Colfax	126	C1
Colibaşi	66	M5
Colico	62	E4
Coll	56	F5
Collado-Villalba	60	F4
Collecchio	62	F6
College Station	130	B3
Collier Bay	114	D3
Collingwood	128	E2
Collins	130	D3
Collooney	56	D7
Colmar	62	C2
Colmenar Viejo	60	G4
Colombia	140	C3
Colombo	88	C7
Colomiers	58	G10
Colonia Las Heras	142	H8
Colonial Heights	128	E3
Colonsay	56	F5
Colorado	126	E3
Colorado, *Colo., US*	132	E1
Colorado, *Tex., US*	132	G2
Colorado Plateau	132	D1
Colorado Springs	126	F3
Columbia	126	C1
Columbia, *La., US*	130	C3
Columbia, *Md., US*	130	F2
Columbia, *Mo., US*	130	C2
Columbia, *S.C., US*	130	E3
Columbia, *Tenn., US*	130	D2
Columbia Mountains	122	G6
Columbus, *Ga., US*	130	E3
Columbus, *Ind., US*	130	D2
Columbus, *Miss., US*	130	D3
Columbus, *Mont., US*	126	E1
Columbus, *Nebr., US*	126	G2
Columbus, *N. Mex., US*	132	E2
Columbus, *Oh., US*	130	E1
Columbus, *Tex., US*	130	B4
Colville	116	E3
Colville	132	(1)G2
Colville Lake	132	(1)M2
Comacchio	62	H6
Comăneşti	66	P3
Comarnic	66	N4
Combarbalá	142	G5
Combeaufontaine	58	M6
Comilla	84	A2
Comino = Kemmuna	64	J12
Commentry	58	H7
Commercy	54	H6
Como	62	E5
Comoé	104	D3
Comondú	124	D6
Comoros	108	G2
Compiègne	54	E5
Comrat	66	R3
Comstock	132	F3
Conakry	104	B3
Concarneau	58	B6
Conceição do Araguaia	140	H5
Concepción, *Bolivia*	140	E7
Concepción, *Chile*	142	G6
Conches-en-Ouche	54	C6
Conchos	134	C3
Concord, *Calif., US*	132	B1
Concord, *N.H., US*	128	F2
Concord, *N.C., US*	130	E2
Concordia, *Argentina*	142	K5
Concordia, *US*	130	B2
Condé-sur-Noireau	54	B6
Condobolin	114	J6
Condom	58	F10
Conegliano	62	H5
Conggar	88	F3
Congo	98	E6
Congo	104	G5
Connecticut	128	F2
Connemara	56	C8
Conrad	126	D1
Côn Son	84	D5
Constanţa	92	C1
Constantina	60	E7
Constantine	102	G1
Consul	126	E1
Contact	126	D2
Contamana	140	B5
Contwoyto Lake	122	J3
Convay	130	F3
Conway	130	C2
Conwy	56	J8
Conwy Bay	56	H8
Coober Pedy	114	F5
Cookeville	128	C3
Cook Inlet	132	(1)G4
Cook Islands	112	K7
Cook Strait	116	E5
Cooktown	114	J3
Coolabah	114	J6
Coolgardie	114	D6
Cooma	114	J7
Coonabarabran	114	J6
Coon Rapids	128	B1
Coopers Town	130	F4
Coorabie	114	F6
Coos Bay	126	B2
Cootamundra	114	J6
Copenhagen = København	48	G9
Copertino	64	N8
Copiapó	142	G4
Copper Harbor	128	C1
Côqen	88	E2
Coquille	126	B2
Coquimbo	142	G4
Corabia	66	M6
Coral	124	K1
Coral Harbour	122	Q4
Coral Sea	114	K2
Coral Sea Islands Territory	112	F7
Coral Sea Islands Territory	114	J2
Coral Springs	130	E4
Corantijn	140	F3
Corbeil-Essonnes	58	H5
Corbigny	58	J6
Corbu	66	R5
Corby	54	B2
Cordele	130	E3
Cordillera Cantábrica	60	D2
Cordillera Central	138	E5
Cordillera del Condor	140	B5
Cordillera de Mérida	138	D3
Cordillera de Oliva	142	G4
Cordillera Isabella	134	G6
Cordillera Occidental	138	E5
Cordillera Oriental	138	D5
Cordillera Penibética	60	F8
Cordillera Vilcabamba	140	C6
Córdoba, *Argentina*	142	J5
Córdoba, *Spain*	60	F7
Corfu = Kerkyra	68	B5
Coria	60	D5
Corinth	130	D3
Corinto	140	H7
Cork	56	D10
Cork Harbour	56	D10
Corleone	64	H11
Çorlu	68	K3
Corn Islands	138	C2
Cornwall	124	M2
Cornwallis Island	122	M2
Coro	140	D1
Corocoro	140	D7
Coromandel	116	E3
Coromandel Coast	88	D6
Coromandel Peninsula	116	E3
Coron	84	G4
Coronation Gulf	122	J3
Coronel Oviedo	142	K4
Coronel Pringles	142	J6
Coronel Suárez	142	J6
Corpus Christi	130	B4
Corrientes	142	K4
Corrigan	130	C3
Corriverton	140	F2
Corse	64	D6
Corsica = Corse	64	D6
Corsicana	130	B3
Corte	64	D6
Cortegana	60	D7
Cortez	132	E1
Cortina d'Ampezzo	62	H4
Cortland	128	E2
Cortona	64	F5
Coruche	60	B6
Çorum	92	F3
Corumbá	140	F7
Corvallis	126	B2
Corvo	102	(1)A2
Cosenza	64	L9
Cosmoledo Group	108	(2)A2
Cosne-sur-Loire	58	H6
Cossato	62	D5
Costa Blanca	60	K7
Costa Brava	60	P3
Costa del Sol	60	F8
Costa de Mosquitos	134	H6
Costa Dorada	60	M4
Costa do Sol	60	A6
Costa Rica	134	G7
Costa Smeralda	64	D7
Costa Verde	60	D1
Costeşti	66	M5
Coswig	52	H5
Cotabato	84	G5
Côte d'Ivoire	104	C3
Cotonou	104	E3
Cottage Grove	126	B2
Cottbus	50	D6
Cotulla	130	B4
Couhe	58	F7
Coulommiers	54	F6
Council Bluffs	126	F2
Courland Lagoon	50	L2
Courtacon	54	F6
Courtenay	124	B2
Coushatta	130	C3
Coutances	58	D4
Couvin	54	G4
Covasna	66	P4
Coventry	56	L9
Covilhã	60	C4
Covington, *Ga., US*	130	E3
Covington, *Ky., US*	130	E2
Covington, *Va., US*	128	D3
Cowell	114	G6
Cowes	54	A4
Cowra	114	J6
Cox's Bazar	88	F4
Coy Aike	142	H9
Cradock	108	D6
Craig	126	E2
Crailsheim	52	F7
Craiova	66	L5
Cranbrook, *Australia*	114	C6
Cranbrook, *US*	124	C2
Crater Lake	126	B2
Crato	140	K5
Crawford	126	F2
Crawfordsville	128	C2
Crawley	54	B3
Cree Lake	122	K5
Creil	54	E5
Crema	62	E5
Cremona	62	F5
Crépy-en-Valois	54	E5
Cres	62	K6
Cres	62	K6
Crescent City	126	B2
Crest	58	L9
Creston	128	B2
Crestview	124	J5
Crestview	134	G2
Crete = Kriti	68	H10
Créteil	54	E6
Creuse	58	G7
Crevillent	60	K6
Crewe	56	K8
Crianlarich	56	H5
Criciúma	142	M4
Cristalina	140	H7
Cristóbal Colón	120	J8
Crna Gora	66	F7
Croatia	66	C4
Crockett	130	B3
Croker Island	114	F2
Cromer	56	P9
Cromwell	116	B7
Crooked Island	134	K4
Crookston	124	G2
Cross City	130	E3
Cross Lake	122	M6
Crossville	128	C3
Crotone	64	M9
Crowley	130	C3
Crownest Pass	124	D2
Crown Point	128	C2
Croydon	114	H3
Cruz Alta	142	L4
Cruz del Eje	142	J5
Cruzeiro do Sul	140	C5
Crvenka	66	G4
Crystal City	130	B4
Crystal Falls	128	C1
Crystal River	130	E4
Crystal Springs	130	C3
Csorna	66	E2
Csurgó	62	N4
Cuamba	108	F2
Cuando	108	C3
Cuangar	108	B3
Cuango	106	B5
Cuanza	106	B5
Cuatro Ciénegas	132	F3
Cuauhtémoc	132	E3
Cuba	126	E3
Cuba	134	H4
Cubal	106	A6
Cubali	108	A2
Cubango	108	B3
Çubuk	68	R4
Cucuí	140	D3
Cúcuta	140	C2
Cuddalore	88	C6
Cuddapah	88	C6
Cuemba	108	B2
Cuenca, *Ecuador*	140	B4
Cuenca, *Spain*	60	H4
Cuernavaca	134	E5
Cuero	130	B4
Cuiabá	140	F7
Cuilo	106	B5
Cuio	106	A6
Cuito	108	B3
Cuito Cuanavale	108	B3
Culbertson	126	E1
Culfa	92	L4
Culiacán	134	C4
Cullera	60	K5
Cullman	130	D3
Culpepper	140	(1)A1

Culuene 140 G6
Culverden 116 D6
Cumaná 140 E1
Cumberland 128 E3
Cumberland Peninsula 122 T3
Cumberland Sound 122 T3
Cummings 126 B3
Cumpas 132 E2
Çumra 68 Q7
Cunderdin 114 C6
Cunene 108 A3
Cuneo 62 C6
Cunnamulla 114 J5
Cuorgne 62 C5
Ćuprija 66 J6
Cure 58 J6
Curicó 142 G5
Curitiba 142 M4
Currais Novos 140 K5
Curral Velho 104 (1)B1
Currie 114 H7
Curtea de Argeş 66 M4
Curtici 66 J3
Curtis Island 114 K4
Curuá 140 G5
Curup 86 C3
Curuzú Cuatiá 142 K4
Curvelo 140 J7
Cusco 140 C6
Cuthbert 130 E3
Cutro 64 L9
Cuttack 88 E4
Cuvier Island 116 E3
Cuxhaven 52 D3
Cuya 140 C7
Cuyuni 140 F2
Cwmbran 56 J10
Cyclades = Kyklades 68 G7
Cypress Hills 124 D2
Cyprus 92 E6
Czarnków 50 F5
Czech Republic 50 C8
Częstochowa 50 J7
Człuchow 50 G4

D

Da'an 80 G1
Daaquam 128 F1
Dab'a 94 D5
Dabas 66 G2
Dabat 100 G5
Dabola 104 B2
Dabra 88 C3
Dąbrowa Górńicza 50 J7
Dąbrowa Tarnowska 50 K7
Dăbuleni 66 M6
Dachau 62 G2
Dadu 88 A3
Daet 84 G4
Dagana 102 B5
Dagestan 92 M2
Dagupan 84 G3
Dahabān 100 G3
Da Hinggan Ling 80 G1
Dahlak Archipelago 100 H4
Dahlonega 130 E3
Dahn 54 K5
Dahod 88 B4
Dahongliutan 90 L2
Dahūk 92 K5
Daimiel 60 G5
Dai Xian 80 E3
Dakar 104 A2
Dakoro 104 F2
Dakota City 126 G2
Dakovica 66 H7
Dakovo 66 F4
Dala 106 C6
Dalai Nur 80 F2
Dalälven 48 H6
Dalaman 92 C5
Dalandzadgad 80 C2
Dalap-Uliga-Darrit 112 H5
Da Lat 84 D4
Dalbandin 90 H4
Dalby 114 K5
Dalgān 90 G4
Dalhart 132 F1
Dalhousie 88 C2
Dali 84 C1
Dalian 80 G3
Dalizi 82 D3
Dallas 130 B3
Dalmā 95 E4
Daloa 104 C3
Dalry 56 H6
Dalrymple Lake 114 J4
Dāltenganj 88 D4
Dalton 130 E3
Dalvík 48 (1)D2
Daly Waters 114 F3
Daman 88 B4
Damanhûr 100 F1
Damar 87 C4
Damara 104 H3
Damasak 104 G2
Damascus = Dimashq 94 D3
Damaturu 104 G2
Dāmiya 94 C4
Damoh 88 C4
Damqawt 90 F6
Damxung 88 F2
Danau Poso 87 A3
Danau Toba 86 B2
Danau Towuti 87 B3
Danba 80 C4
Dandeldhura 88 D3
Dandong 82 C3
Da Nĕng 84 D3
Daneţi 66 M6
Dangara 90 J2
Danger Islands 112 K7
Danghe Nanshan 80 B3
Daniel 126 D1
Danilov 70 H3
Dank 95 G5
Dankov 70 G4
Dannenberg 52 G3
Dannevirke 116 F5
Dansville 128 E2
Danube 46 F3
Danville, *Ill., US* 130 D1
Danville, *Ky., US* 130 E2
Danville, *Va., US* 130 F2
Dan Xian 84 D3
Dao Phu Quôc 84 C4
Dapa 84 H5
Dapaong 104 E2
Da Qaidam 80 B3
Daqing 78 M7
Dar'ā 94 D4
Dārāb 95 F2
Darabani 66 P1
Daraj 100 B1
Dārākūyeh 95 F2
Darazo 104 G2
Dar Ben Karricha el Behri 60 E9
Darbhanga 88 E3
Dardanelles = Çanakkale Boğazı 68 J4
Darende 92 G4
Dar es Salaam 106 F5
Darfo Boario Terme 62 F5
Dargan-Ata 76 L9
Dargaville 116 D2
Darham 78 H7
Darjeeling 88 E3
Darling 114 H6
Darlington 56 L7
Darłowo 48 J9
Dărmăneşti 66 P3
Dar Mazār 95 G2
Darmstadt 52 D7
Darnah 100 D1
Darnley Bay 122 G3
Daroca 60 J3
Darß 52 H2
Dartmouth 122 U8
Daru 87 F4
Daruba 87 C2
Daruvar 62 N5
Darvaza 76 K9
Darwin 114 F2
Daryācheh-ye Bakhtegan 95 E2
Daryācheh-ye Orūmīyeh 92 L5
Daryācheh-ye Tashk 95 E2
Dārzīn 95 H2
Dashizhai 80 G1
Dashkhovuz 76 K9
Dasht-e Kavir 90 F3
Dasht-e Lut 95 H1
Datça 68 K8
Datça 92 B5
Date 82 L2
Datong 80 C3
Datong 80 E2
Daugava 70 E3
Daugavpils 70 E3
Daun 54 J4
Dauphin 122 M6
Daura 104 F2
Dausa 88 C3
Dăvăci 92 N3
Davangere 88 C6
Davao 84 H5
Davenport 128 B2
Daventry 54 A2
David 134 H7
Davis Sea 144 (2)Q3
Davis Strait 122 V3
Davlekanovo 76 J7
Davos 62 E4
Dawa 80 G2
Dawqah, *Oman* 90 F6
Dawqah, *Saudi Arabia* 100 H4
Dawson 132 (1)K3
Dawson Creek, *B.C., Canada* 122 G5
Dawson Creek, *Y.T., Canada* 122 D4
Dawu 80 C4
Dax 58 D10
Daxian 80 D4
Dayong 80 E5
Dayr az Zawr 92 J6
Dayton, *Oh., US* 128 D3
Dayton, *Tenn., US* 128 C3
Dayton, *Tex., US* 130 C4
Dayton, *Wash., US* 126 C1
Daytona Beach 130 E4
Dayu 80 E5
Dazhu 80 D4
De Aar 108 C6
Dead Sea 94 C5
Deakin 114 E6
Deal 54 D3
De'an 80 F5
Deán Funes 142 J5
Dease Lake 132 (1)M4
Dease Strait 122 J3
Death Valley 126 C3
Deba Habe 104 G2
Debar 68 C3
Dębica 50 L7
Debin 78 S4
Dęblin 50 L6
Dębno 50 D5
Debre Birhan 106 F2
Debrecen 66 J2
Debre Markos 100 G5
Debrešte 68 D3
Debre Tabor 100 G5
Decatur, *Al., US* 128 C4
Decatur, *Ill., US* 128 C3
Decazeville 58 H9
Deccan 88 C5
Děčín 50 D7
Decize 58 J7
De Cocksdorp 54 G1
Decorah 128 B2
Dedoplis 92 M3
Dédougou 104 D2
Dedza 108 E2
Dee, *Scot., UK* 56 K4
Dee, *Wales, UK* 56 J9
Deering 132 (1)E2
Deer Lake 122 V7
Deer Lodge 126 D1
Deer Park 126 C1
De Funiak Springs 130 D3
Dêgê 80 B4
Degeh Bur 106 G2
Degema 104 F4
Deggendorf 62 J2
Dehaj 95 F1
Dehalak Desēt 90 D6
Deh Bid 95 E1
Deh-Dasht 95 D1
Dehiba 102 H2
Dehkūyeh 95 F3
Dehlonān 90 E3
Dehra 90 L3
Dehra Dun 88 C2
Dehri 88 D4
Deh Shū 90 H3
Deinze 54 F4
Dej 66 L2
De Kalb 130 C3
De-Kastri 78 Q6
Dekese 106 C4
Delano 132 C1
Delaware 128 D2
Delaware 130 F2
Delbrück 52 D5
Delémont 62 C3
Delfoi 68 E6
Delft 54 G2
Delfzijl 54 J1
Delgo 100 F3
Delhi, *India* 88 C3
Delhi, *US* 128 F2
Delingha 80 B3
Delitzsch 52 H5
Dellys 60 P8
Delmenhorst 52 D3
Delnice 62 K5
Delray Beach 130 E4
Del Rio 132 F3
Delta, *Colo., US* 126 E3
Delta, *Ut., US* 126 D3
Delta del Orinoco 140 E2
Delta Junction 132 (1)H3
Deming 132 E2
Demirci 68 L5
Demmin 52 J3
Dem. Rep. of the Congo 106 C4
Demopolis 130 D3
Demyanka 70 P3
Dem'yanskoye 70 N3
Denain 54 F4
Denau 90 J2
Denbigh 128 E1
Den Burg 54 G1
Dendang 86 D3
Dender 54 F4
Dendi 106 F2
Dengkou 80 D2
Denham 114 B5
Den Helder 54 G2
Dénia 60 L6
Deniliquin 114 H7
Denio 126 C2
Denison, *Ia., US* 128 A2
Denison, *Tex., US* 130 B3
Denizli 92 C5
Denmark 46 E2
Denmark 114 C6
Denmark Strait 120 D3
Denpasar 86 E4
Denton 132 G2
D'Entrecasteaux Islands 114 K1
Denver 126 F3
Deogarh, *India* 88 B3
Deogarh, *India* 88 D4
Deoghar 88 E4
Déols 58 G7
De Panne 54 E3
Depok 86 D4
Dépression du Mourdi 100 D4
Deputatskiy 78 P3
Dêqên 84 B1
Dera Ghazi Khan 90 K3
Dera Ismail Khan 90 K3
Derbent 90 E1
Derby, *Australia* 114 D3
Derby, *UK* 56 L9
De Ridder 130 C3
Dermott 130 C3
Derudeb 100 G4
Derventa 66 E5
Desē 100 G5
Deseado 142 H8
Deseado 142 H8
Desert Center 132 C2
Des Moines, *Ia., US* 124 H3
Des Moines, *N. Mex., US* 132 F1
Desna 70 F4
Dessau 52 H5
Desvres 54 D4
Deta 66 J4
Detmold 52 D5
Detroit 124 K3
Detroit Lakes 128 A1
Det Udom 84 C4
Detva 50 J9
Deurne 54 H3
Deva 66 K4
Deventer 54 J2
Devikot 88 B3
Devil's Lake 122 L7
Devils Lake 126 G1
Devil's Point 130 F5
Devnya 66 Q6
Devon Island 122 P1
Devonport 114 J8
Dewangiri 88 F3
Dewas 88 C4
Deyang 80 C4
Deyhuk 90 G3
Deyyer 95 E3
Dezfūl 90 E3
Dezhou 80 F3
Dhahran = Az Zahrān 95 D3
Dhaka 88 F4
Dhamār 100 H5
Dhamtri 88 D4
Dhanbad 88 E4
Dhar 88 C4
Dhārwād 88 B5
Dhaulagiri 88 D3
Dhekelia 94 A2
Dhībān 94 C5
Dhoraji 88 B4
Dhule 88 B4
Dhulian 88 E4
Dhuudo 106 J2
Dhuusa Marreeb 106 H2
Dia 68 H9
Diaca 106 G6
Diamantina 140 H7
Diamantino 140 F6
Diamond Islets 114 K3
Diane Bank 114 J3
Dianópolis 140 H6
Dibā al Ḩişn 95 G4
Dibbiena 64 F5
Dibrugarh 88 F3
Dickens 132 F2
Dickinson 126 F1
Dickson 130 D2
Didcot 54 A3
Didiéni 104 C2
Didymoteicho 68 J3
Die 58 L9
Diébougou 104 D2
Dieburg 52 D7
Diéma 104 C2
Diemel 52 E5
Diemeringen 52 C8
Diepholz 52 D4
Dieppe 54 D5
Diest 54 H4
Diffa 104 G2
Digne-les-Bains 62 B6
Digoin 58 J7
Dijon 58 L6
Dikhil 100 H5
Dikili 68 J5
Diklosmta 92 L2
Diksmuide 54 E3
Dikson 76 Q3
Dikwa 104 G2
Dīla 106 F2
Dili 87 C4
Dilijan 92 L3
Dillenburg 52 D6
Dilling 100 E5
Dillingen, *Germany* 52 F8
Dillingen, *Germany* 52 B7
Dillingham 132 (1)F4
Dillion 124 D2
Dillon 126 D1
Dillon Cone 116 D6
Dilolo 108 C2
Dimapur 88 F3
Dimashq 94 D3
Dimitrovgrad, *Bulgaria* 66 N7
Dimitrovgrad, *Russia* 70 J4
Dimitrovgrad, *Serbia* 66 K7
Dīmona 94 C5
Dinagat 84 H4
Dinajpur 88 E3
Dinan 58 C5
Dinant 54 G4
Dinar 92 D4
Dinard 58 C5
Dinaric Alps 62 L6
Dindigul 88 C6
Dindori 88 D4
Dingle Bay 56 B9
Dingolfing 62 H2
Dinguiraye 104 B2
Dingwall 56 H4
Dingxi 80 C3
Dinkelsbühl 52 F7
Dinosaur 126 E2
Diomede Islands 78 AA3
Dioriga Kointhou 68 F7
Diourbel 102 B6
Dipolog 84 G5
Dir 88 B1
Dirē Dawa 106 G2
Dirk Hartog Island 114 B5
Dirranbandi 114 J5
Disko = Qeqertarsuatsiaq 122 V2
Disko Bugt = Qeqertarsuup Tunua 122 V3
Diss 54 D2
Distrito Federal 140 H7
Dithmarschen 52 D2
Dīvāndarreh 92 M6
Divinópolis 142 N3
Divo 104 C3
Divriği 92 H4
Dixon 128 C2
Dixon Entrance 132 (1)L5
Diyarbakır 92 J5
Dja 104 G4

Djado 102 H4
Djamâa 102 G2
Djambala 104 G5
Djanet 102 G4
Djelfa 102 F2
Djéma 106 D2
Djenné 102 E6
Djibo 104 D2
Djibouti 100 H5
Djibouti 100 H5
Djolu 106 C3
Djougou 104 E3
Djúpivogur 48 (1)F2
Dnestrovsc 66 S3
Dnieper 70 F5
Dniester 66 Q1
Dnipro 46 H3
Dniprodzerzhyns'k 70 F5
Dnipropetrovs'k 70 F5
Dnister 46 G3
Dno 70 E3
Doba, *Chad* 106 B2
Doba, *China* 88 E2
Dobbiaco 62 H4
Döbeln 52 J5
Döbern 52 K5
Doboj 66 F5
Dobre Miasto 50 K4
Dobrich 66 Q6
Dobryanka 70 L3
Doctor Arroyo 132 F4
Dodecanese = Dodekanisos 68 J8
Dodge City 126 F3
Dodoma 106 F5
Doetinchem 54 J3
Dofa 87 C3
Doğanşehir 92 G4
Dōgo 82 G5
Dogondoutchi 104 E2
Dogubeyazıt 92 L4
Doha = Ad Dawḩah 95 D4
Doka 87 D4
Dokkum 52 B3
Dolak 87 E4
Dolbeau 128 F1
Dole 62 A3
Dolgany 78 E2
Dolinsk 78 Q7
Dullard 52 C3
Dolný Kubrín 50 J8
Dolomiti 62 G4
Dolo Odo 106 G3
Dolores 142 K6
Dolphin and Union Strait 122 H3
Domar 88 D2
Domažlice 52 H7
Dombås 48 E5
Dombóvár 66 F3
Domfront 58 E5
Dominica 138 E2
Dominican Republic 138 D1
Domodossola 62 D4
Domokos 68 E5
Dompu 87 A4
Domžale 62 K4
Don 46 H2
Donau = Danube 62 H2
Donaueschingen 62 D3
Donauwörth 52 F8
Don Benito 60 E6
Doncaster 56 L8
Dondra Head 88 D7
Donegal 56 D7
Donegal Bay 56 D7
Donets 46 H3
Donets'k 70 G5
Dongara 114 B5
Dongco 88 D2
Dongfang 84 D3
Donggala 87 A3
Donggou 82 C4
Dongguan 84 E2
Dông Hôi 84 D3
Dongjingcheng 82 E1
Donglük 76 R10
Dongning 82 F2
Dongo 104 H4
Dongola 100 F4
Dongou 104 H4
Dongsha Qundao 84 F2
Dongsheng 80 E3
Dong Ujimqin Qi 80 F1
Dongying 80 F3
Doniphan 130 C2
Donji Vakuf 62 N6
Donner Pass 126 B3
Donostia 60 J1
Donousa 68 H7
Dora 62 C5
Dorchester 56 K11
Dordrecht 54 G3
Dorfen 62 H2
Dori 104 D2
Doring 108 B6
Dorion 128 C1
Dormagen 54 J3
Dornbirn 62 E3
Doro 104 D1
Dorog 50 H10
Dorohoi 66 P2
Döröö Nuur 76 S8
Dorotea 48 J4
Dorsten 54 J3
Dortmund 52 C5
Doruma 106 D3
Dos Hermanas 60 E7
Dosse 52 H4
Dosso 104 E2
Dothan 130 D3
Douai 54 F4
Douala 104 F4
Douarnenez 58 A5
Doubs 62 B3
Douentza 104 C2
Douglas, *South Africa* 108 C5
Douglas, *UK* 56 H7
Douglas, *Ariz., US* 132 E2
Douglas, *Ga., US* 130 E3
Douglas, *Wyo., US* 126 E2
Doullens 54 E4
Dourados 142 L3
Douro 60 B3
Dover, *UK* 54 D3
Dover, *US* 130 F2
Dover, *Australia* 114 J8
Dover-Foxcroft 128 G1
Dowlatābād, *Iran* 95 E2
Dowlatābād, *Iran* 95 G2
Downpatrick 56 G7
Dowshī 90 J2
Drac 62 B6
Drachten 54 J1
Dragan 48 H4
Drăgănești-Olt 66 M5
Drăgășani 66 M5
Draguignan 62 B7
Drakensberg 108 D6
Drake Passage 142 G10
Drama 68 G3
Drammen 48 F7
Drasenhofen 62 M2
Drau 62 J4
Drava 66 E4
Dravograd 64 K2
Drawsko Pomorskie 50 E4
Dresden 52 J5
Dreux 54 D6
Drezdenko 50 E5
Drina 66 G5
Driva 48 E5
Drniš 66 D6
Drobeta-Turnu Severin 66 K5
Drochia 66 Q1
Drogheda 56 F8
Drohobych 50 N8
Drôme 58 K9
Dronne 58 F8
Dronning Maud Land 144 (2)F2
Dronten 54 H2
Drummondville 128 F1
Druskininkai 48 M9
Druzhina 78 Q3
Drvar 66 D5
Dryanovo 66 N7
Dryden 124 H2
Drysdale River 114 E3
Dschang 104 G3
Dubā 100 G2
Dubai = Dubayy 95 F4
Dubăsari 66 S2
Dubawnt Lake 122 L4
Dubayy 95 F4
Dubbo 114 J6
Dübendorf 62 D3
Dublin, *Ireland* 56 F8
Dublin, *US* 130 E3
Dublin Bay 56 F8
Dubna 70 G3
Dubnica 50 H9
Du Bois 128 E2
Dubois, *Id., US* 126 D2
Dubois, *Wyo., US* 126 E2
Dubovskoye 70 H5
Dubreka 104 B3
Dubrovnik 66 F7
Dubuque 128 B2
Duchesne 126 D2
Ducie Island 112 P8
Dudelange 54 J5
Duderstadt 52 F5
Dudinka 76 R4
Dudley 56 K9
Duero 60 F3
Dugi Otok 66 B6
Duifken Point 114 H2
Duisburg 54 J3
Duiveland 54 F3
Dukat 78 T4
Duk Faiwil 106 E2
Dukhān 95 D4
Dukla 50 L8
Dukou 80 C5
Dulan 80 B3
Dulce 132 E1
Dulce 142 J4
Dul'Durga 78 J6
Dullewala 88 B2
Dülmen 52 C5
Dulovo 66 Q6
Duluth 128 B1
Dūmā 94 D3
Dumaguete 84 G5
Dumai 86 C2
Dumas, *Ark., US* 130 C3
Dumas, *Tex., US* 126 F3
Dumayr 94 D3
Dumbarton 56 H5
Ďumbier 50 J9
Dumboa 104 G2
Dumfries 56 J6
Dümmer 52 D4
Dumont d'Urville Sea 144 (2)U3
Dumyât 100 F1
Duna = Danube 66 E2
Dunaj = Danube 50 G10
Dunajská Streda 66 E2
Dunakeszi 66 G2
Dunărea = Danube 66 K5
Dunaújváros 66 F3
Dunav = Danube 66 J5
Dunayivtsi 70 E5
Dunbar, *UK* 56 K6
Duncan 126 B1
Duncan Passage 84 A4
Dundaga 48 M8
Dundalk 56 F7
Dundalk Bay 56 F8
Dundee, *South Africa* 108 E5
Dundee, *UK* 56 K5
Dunedin 116 C7
Dunfermline 56 J5
Dungarvan 56 E9
Dungeness 54 C4
Dungu 106 D3
Dungun 84 C6
Dungunab 100 G3
Dunhua 82 E2
Dunhuang 80 A2
Dunkerque 54 E3
Dunkirk 128 E2
Dunkwa 104 D3
Dun Laoghaire 56 F8
Dunnet Head 56 J3
Dunseith 126 G1
Dunsmuir 126 B2
Duque de Caxias 142 N3
Du Quoin 130 D2
Durance 58 L10
Durango, *Mexico* 132 F4
Durango, *Spain* 60 H1
Durango, *US* 126 E3
Durankurak 66 R6
Durant 130 B3
Durazno 142 K5
Durban 108 E5
Durban-Corbières 58 H10
Düren 54 J4
Durgapur 88 E4
Durham, *Canada* 128 D2
Durham, *UK* 56 L7
Durham, *US* 130 F2
Duri 86 C2
Durmā 95 B4
Durmanec 66 C3
Durmitor 66 G6
Durness 56 H3
Durrës 68 B3
Dursey 56 B10
Dursunbey 68 L5
D'Urville Island 116 D5
Dushanbe 90 J2
Düsseldorf 54 J3
Duvno 62 N7
Duyun 80 D5
Düzce 68 P4
Dvina 46 H2
Dvinskaya Guba 70 G1
Dwarka 88 A4
Dworshak Reservoir 126 C1
Dyat'kovo 70 F4
Dyersburg 130 D2
Dyje 62 M2
Dzamin Üüd 78 J8
Dzavhan 76 S8
Dzerzhinsk 70 H3
Dzhalinda 78 L6
Dzhambeyty 70 K4
Dzhankoy 70 F5
Dzhardzhan 78 L3
Dzharkurgan 90 J2
Dzhetygara 70 M4
Dzhezkazgan 70 N5
Dzhigudzhak 78 T4
Dzhizak 76 M9
Dzhusaly 70 M5
Działdowo 50 K4
Dzüünbulag 80 F1
Dzuunmod 80 D1

E

Eads 126 F3
Eagle 132 (1)J3
Eagle Lake 126 B2
Eagle Pass 132 F3
East Antarctica 144 (2)P2
Eastbourne 54 C4
East Cape 116 G3
East China Sea 80 H4
East Dereham 54 C2
Easter Island 112 Q8
Eastern Cape 108 D6
Eastern Ghats 88 C6
Eastern Ross 56 H4
East Falkland 142 K9
East Grinstead 54 C3
East Kilbride 56 H6
Eastleigh 54 A4
East Liverpool 130 E1
East London 108 D6
Eastmain 122 R6
Eastmain 122 S6
East Point 130 E3
East Retford 54 B1
East St. Louis 128 B3
East Sea = Sea of Japan 82 G3
East Siberian Sea = Vostochno-Sibirskoye More 78 U2
East Timor 87 C4
Eatonton 130 E3
Eau Claire 128 B2
Ebbw Vale 56 J10
Ebensee 62 J3
Eberbach 52 D7
Ebersbach 50 D6
Ebersberg 62 G2
Eberswalde 52 J4
Ebinur Hu 76 Q9
Eboli 64 K8
Ebolowa 104 G4
Ebro 60 K3
Eceabat 68 J4
Ech Chélif 102 F1
Echinos 68 G3
Echo Bay 122 H3
Écija 60 E7
Eckernförde 52 E2
Ecuador 140 B4
Ed 100 H5
Edam 54 H2
Eday 56 K2
Ed Da'ein 100 E5
Ed Damazin 100 F5
Ed Debba 100 F4
Ed Dueim 100 F5
Ede, *Netherlands* 54 H2
Ede, *Nigeria* 104 E3
Edéa 104 G4
Edelény 50 K9
Eden, *Australia* 114 J7
Eden, *US* 132 G2
Edendale 116 B8
Eder 52 D5
Edersee 52 E5
Edessa 68 E4
Edgecumbe 116 F3
Edinburgh 56 J6
Edineț 66 Q1
Edirne 68 J3
Edmonds 126 B1
Edmonton 122 J6
Edmundson 124 N2
Edmundston 128 G1
Edolo 62 F4
Edremit 68 J5
Edremit Körfezi 68 H5
Edwards 132 C2
Edwards Plateau 132 F2
Eeklo 54 F3
Eemshaven 54 J1
Éfaté 112 G7
Eferding 50 D9
Effingham 130 D2
Eganville 128 E1
Eger 52 G6
Eger 66 H2
Egersund 48 D7
Eggenfelden 62 H2
Egilsstaðir 48 (1)F2
Eğridir 68 N7
Eğridir Gölü 68 N6
Egvekinot 78 Y3
Egypt 100 E2
Ehingen 62 E2
Eibar 60 H1
Eichstätt 62 G2
Eider 52 D2
Eidfjord 48 D6
Eidsvold 114 K5
Eidsvoll 48 F6
Eifel 54 J4
Eigg 56 F5
Eight Degree Channel 88 B7
Eilenburg 52 H5
Einbeck 52 E5
Eindhoven 54 H3
Eirunepé 140 D5
Eiseb 108 C4
Eisenach 52 F6
Eisenerz 62 K3
Eisenhüttenstadt 50 D5
Eisenstadt 62 M3
Eisleben 52 G5
Eivissa 60 M5
Eivissa 60 M6
Ejea de los Caballeros 60 J2
Ejido Insurgentes 124 D6
Ejin Horo Qi 80 D3
Ejin Qi 80 C2
Ejmiadzin 92 L3
Ekalaka 126 F1
Ekenäs 48 M7
Eketahuna 116 E5
Ekibastuz 76 P7
Ekimchan 78 N6
Ekonda 76 V4
Eksjo 48 H8
Ekwan 122 Q6
El Aaiún 102 C3
Elafonisos 68 E8
El 'Alamein 100 E1
El Amria 60 J9
El 'Arîsh 94 A5
Elat 94 B7
Elazığ 92 H4
El Azraq 94 D5
Elba 64 E6
El Banco 140 C2
Elbasan 68 C3
El Baúl 140 D2
Elbe 52 F3
Elbeuf 54 D5
Elbistan 92 G4
Elbląg 50 J3
El Borj 60 E9
Elbow 124 E1
Elbrus 92 K2
El Burgo de Ebro 60 K3
El Burgo de Osma 60 G3
El Cajon 132 C2
El Callao 140 E2
El Campo 130 B4
El Centro 132 C2
El Cerro 140 E7
Elch 60 K6
Elda 60 K6
El'dikan 78 P4
Eldorado 142 L4
El Dorado, *Mexico* 124 E7
El Dorado, *Ark., US* 130 C3
El Dorado, *Kans., US* 130 B2
El Dorado, *Venezuela* 140 E2
Eldoret 106 F3
Elefsina 68 F6
Elektrėnai 50 P3
El Encanto 140 C4
Elephant Butte Reservoir 132 E2

Eleuthera	**124**	L6
El Fahs	**64**	D12
El Faiyûm	**100**	F2
El Fasher	**100**	E5
El Geneina	**100**	D5
Elgin, *UK*	**56**	J4
Elgin, *Ill., US*	**128**	C2
Elgin, *N.D., US*	**126**	F1
El'ginskiy	**78**	Q4
El Gîza	**100**	F1
El Goléa	**102**	F2
El Homr	**102**	F3
El Iskandarîya	**100**	E1
Elista	**70**	H5
Elizabeth	**128**	F2
Elizabeth City	**130**	F2
Elizabethton	**130**	E2
El Jadida	**102**	D2
El Jafr	**94**	D6
El Jafr	**94**	D6
Ełk	**50**	M4
Ełk	**50**	M4
El Kala	**64**	C12
Elk City	**132**	G1
El Kef	**64**	C12
El Kelaâ des Srarhna	**102**	D2
El Khandaq	**100**	F4
El Khârga	**100**	F2
Elkhart, *Ind., US*	**128**	C2
Elkhart, *Kans., US*	**130**	A2
El Khartum	**100**	F4
El Khartum Bahri	**100**	F4
Elkhorn	**126**	G2
Elkhorn	**128**	C2
Elkhovo	**68**	J2
Elkins	**128**	E3
Elko, *Canada*	**126**	C1
Elko, *US*	**126**	C2
Elk River	**128**	B1
El Kuntilla	**94**	B7
Ellendale	**124**	G2
Ellensburg	**126**	B1
Ellesmere Island	**120**	K1
Ellice Islands	**112**	H6
Elliot	**108**	D6
Ellis	**122**	J8
Ellisras	**108**	D4
Elliston	**114**	F6
Ellsworth	**128**	G2
Ellwangen	**62**	F2
Elmadağ	**68**	R5
Elmali	**68**	M8
El Mansûra	**100**	F1
El Mazâr	**94**	A5
El Minya	**100**	F2
Elmira	**128**	E2
Elmshorn	**52**	E3
El Muglad	**100**	E5
El Nido	**84**	F4
El Obeid	**100**	F5
El Odaiya	**100**	E5
El Oued	**102**	G2
El Paso	**132**	E2
El Portal	**132**	C1
El Potosi	**132**	F4
El Prat de Llobregat	**60**	N3
El Puerto de Santa Maria	**60**	D8
El Qâhira	**100**	F1
El Qasr	**100**	E2
El Quseima	**94**	B6
El Quweira	**94**	C7
El Reno	**130**	B2
El Sahuaro	**132**	D2
El Salvador	**134**	F6
Elster	**52**	H5
Elsterwerda	**52**	J5
El Sueco	**132**	E3
El Suweis	**100**	F2
Eltanin Bay	**144**	(2)JJ2
El Tarf	**64**	C12
El Thamad	**94**	B7
El Tigre	**140**	E2
El Turbio	**142**	G9
Eluru	**88**	D5
Elvas	**60**	C6
Elverum	**48**	F6
Elvira	**140**	C5
El Wak	**106**	G3
Ely, *UK*	**56**	N9
Ely, *US*	**126**	D3
Emajõgi	**48**	P7
Emāmrūd	**90**	F2
Emba	**70**	L5
Emba	**70**	L5
Embalse de Alarcon	**60**	H5
Embalse de Alcántara Uno	**60**	D5
Embalse de Almendra	**60**	D3
Embalse de Contreras	**60**	J5
Embalse de Gabriel y Galán	**60**	D4
Embalse de Garcia Sola	**60**	E5
Embalse de Guadalhorce	**60**	F8
Embalse de Guadalmena	**60**	G6
Embalse de Guri	**140**	E2
Embalse de la Serena	**60**	E6
Embalse de la Sotonera	**60**	K2
Embalse del Bembézar	**60**	E6
Embalse del Ebro	**60**	G1
Embalse del Río Negro	**138**	F7
Embalse de Negratin	**60**	G7
Embalse de Ricobayo	**60**	E3
Embalse de Santa Teresa	**60**	E4
Embalse de Yesa	**60**	J2
Embalse Toekomstig	**140**	F3
Embarcación	**142**	J3
Emden	**52**	C3
Emerald	**114**	J4
Emi Koussi	**100**	C4
Emin	**76**	Q8
Emirdağ	**68**	P5
Emmeloord	**54**	H2
Emmen	**54**	J2
Emmendingen	**62**	C2
Emmerich	**54**	J3
Emory Peak	**132**	F3
Empalme	**132**	D3
Empangeni	**108**	E5
Empoli	**62**	F7
Emporia	**130**	B2
Empty Quarter = Rub' al Khālī	**90**	E6
Ems	**54**	J1
Ems-Jade-Kanal	**52**	C3
Enafors	**70**	B2
Encarnación	**142**	K4
Encs	**66**	J1
Ende	**87**	B4
Enderby Island	**116**	(2)B1
Energetik	**70**	L4
Enewetak	**112**	F4
Enez	**68**	J4
Enfida	**64**	E12
Enfield	**54**	B3
Engel's	**70**	J4
Enggano	**86**	C4
Enghien	**54**	G4
England	**56**	L9
English Channel	**56**	J12
Engozero	**48**	S4
'En Hazeva	**94**	C6
Enid	**130**	B2
Enkhuizen	**54**	H2
Enköping	**48**	J7
Enna	**64**	J11
En Nahud	**100**	E5
Enngonia	**114**	J5
Ennis, *Ireland*	**56**	D9
Ennis, *US*	**126**	D1
Enniscorthy	**56**	F9
Enniskillen	**56**	E7
Enn Nâqoûra	**94**	C3
Enns	**62**	K2
Enns	**62**	K3
Enschede	**54**	J2
Ensenada	**132**	C2
Enshi	**80**	D4
Entebbe	**106**	E3
Enterprise	**126**	C1
Entrevaux	**62**	B7
Entroncamento	**60**	B5
Enugu	**104**	F3
Enurmino	**78**	Z3
Envira	**140**	C5
Enz	**62**	D2
Enza	**62**	F6
Epanomi	**68**	E4
Epéna	**106**	B3
Épernay	**58**	J4
Épinal	**62**	B2
Episkopi	**68**	Q10
Epsom	**54**	B3
Eqlīd	**95**	E1
Equatorial Guinea	**104**	F4
Erbach	**52**	D7
Erçek	**92**	K4
Erciş	**92**	K4
Ercolano	**64**	J8
Érd	**66**	F2
Erdek	**68**	K4
Erdemli	**68**	S8
Erdenet	**78**	G7
Erding	**62**	G2
Erechim	**142**	L4
Ereğli, *Turkey*	**92**	D3
Ereğli, *Turkey*	**92**	F5
Ereikoussa	**68**	B5
Erenhot	**80**	E2
Erfurt	**52**	G6
Ergani	**92**	H4
Erg Chech	**102**	D4
Erg du Ténéré	**102**	H5
Ergel	**80**	D2
Erg Iguidi	**102**	D3
Er Hai	**80**	C5
Erie	**128**	D2
Erimo	**82**	M2
Erimo-misaki	**82**	M3
Eriskay	**56**	E4
Eritrea	**100**	G4
Erlangen	**52**	G7
Ermenek	**92**	E5
Ermoupoli	**68**	G7
Erode	**88**	C6
Er Rachidia	**102**	E2
Er Rahad	**100**	F5
Er Renk	**106**	E1
Errol	**128**	F2
Er Ruseifa	**94**	D4
Ersekë	**68**	C4
Erskine	**128**	A1
Ertai	**76**	S8
Ertix	**76**	R8
Erzgebirge	**52**	H6
Erzin	**76**	S7
Erzincan	**92**	H4
Erzurum	**92**	J4
Esan-misaki	**82**	L3
Esashi, *Japan*	**82**	L3
Esashi, *Japan*	**82**	M1
Esbjerg	**48**	E9
Escanaba	**128**	C1
Escárcega	**134**	F5
Esch	**54**	J5
Eschwege	**52**	F5
Eschweiler	**54**	J4
Escondido	**132**	C2
Eséka	**104**	G4
Eşfahān	**90**	F3
Eskifjörður	**48**	(1)G2
Eskilstuna	**48**	J7
Eskimo Lakes	**132**	(1)L2
Eskişehir	**92**	D4
Esla	**60**	E3
Eslāmābād e Gharb	**92**	M6
Eslamshahr	**90**	F2
Esler Dağ	**68**	M7
Eslö	**50**	C2
Esmeraldas	**140**	B3
Esneux	**54**	H4
Espalion	**58**	H9
Espanola, *Canada*	**128**	D1
Espanola, *US*	**126**	E3
Espelkamp	**52**	D4
Esperance	**114**	D6
Esperance Bay	**114**	D6
Esperanza	**140**	C5
Espinho	**60**	B4
Espírito Santo	**140**	J7
Espíritu Santo	**112**	G7
Esplanada	**140**	K6
Espoo	**48**	N6
Espungebera	**108**	E4
Es Samrā	**94**	D4
Essaouira	**102**	D2
Es Semara	**102**	C3
Essen, *Belgium*	**54**	G3
Essen, *Germany*	**54**	K3
Essequibo	**140**	F2
Esslingen	**62**	E2
Eşţahbānāt	**95**	F2
Este	**62**	G5
Estella	**60**	H2
Estepona	**60**	E8
Esteros	**142**	J3
Estevan	**124**	F2
Estonia	**48**	M7
Estoril	**60**	A6
Estrecho de Le Maire	**142**	H10
Estrecho de Magallanes	**142**	G9
Estrela	**60**	C4
Estremoz	**60**	C6
Estuário do Rio Amazonaz	**140**	H3
Esztergom	**66**	F2
Étain	**54**	H5
Étampes	**58**	H5
Étang de Berre	**58**	L10
Étaples	**54**	D4
Etawah	**88**	C3
Ethiopia	**98**	G5
Etolin Strait	**132**	(1)D3
Etosha Pan	**108**	B3
Étretat	**54**	C5
Ettelbruck	**52**	B7
Ettlingen	**52**	D8
Eucla	**114**	E6
Euclid	**128**	D2
Eufala	**130**	D3
Eufaula Lake	**130**	B2
Eugene	**126**	B2
Eupen	**52**	B6
Euphrates = Firat	**92**	H4
Eure	**54**	D6
Eureka, *Calif., US*	**126**	B2
Eureka, *Mont., US*	**126**	C1
Eureka, *Nev., US*	**132**	C1
Eureka, *Ut., US*	**126**	D3
Europoort	**54**	F3
Euskirchen	**52**	B6
Eutin	**52**	F2
Eutsuk Lake	**122**	F6
Evans Strait	**122**	Q4
Evanston, *Ill., US*	**128**	C2
Evanston, *Wyo., US*	**126**	D2
Evansville	**130**	D2
Evaz	**95**	F3
Everett	**126**	B1
Everglades City	**130**	E4
Evergreen	**130**	D3
Evesham	**54**	A2
Évora	**60**	C6
Évreux	**54**	D5
Evron	**58**	E5
Evros	**68**	J3
Evvoia	**68**	F6
Ewo	**104**	G5
Exaltación	**140**	D6
Exe	**56**	J11
Exeter	**56**	J11
Exmouth, *Australia*	**114**	B4
Exmouth, *UK*	**56**	J11
Exuma Sound	**124**	L7
Eyl	**106**	H2
Eyre Peninsula	**114**	G2
Ezine	**68**	J5

F

Faadippolu Atoll	**88**	B8
Fåborg	**52**	F1
Fabriano	**62**	H7
Fachi	**102**	H5
Fada	**100**	D4
Fada Ngourma	**104**	E2
Faenza	**62**	G6
Færingehavn = Kangerluarsoruseq	**122**	W4
Faeroes	**46**	D1
Fafanlap	**87**	D3
Făgăraş	**66**	M4
Fagernes	**48**	E6
Fagersta	**48**	H6
Făget	**66**	K4
Fagurhólsmýri	**48**	(1)E3
Fahraj	**95**	H2
Faial	**102**	(1)B2
Fairbanks	**132**	(1)H3
Fair Isle	**56**	L2
Fairlie	**116**	C7
Fairmont	**128**	B2
Faisalabad	**88**	B2
Faith	**126**	F1
Faizabad	**88**	D3
Fakfak	**87**	D3
Fakse	**52**	H1
Fakse Bugt	**48**	G9
Faku	**80**	G2
Falaise	**54**	B6
Falaise de Tiguidit	**102**	G5
Falconara Marittima	**62**	J7
Falcon Lake	**130**	B4
Fălesţi	**66**	Q2
Falfurrias	**130**	B4
Falkenberg	**48**	G8
Falkensee	**52**	J4
Falkland Islands	**142**	K9
Falkland Sound	**142**	J9
Falköping	**48**	G7
Fallingbostel	**52**	E4
Fallon	**126**	C3
Fall River	**128**	F2
Falls City	**124**	G3
Falmouth, *UK*	**56**	G11
Falmouth, *US*	**128**	F2
Falster	**52**	H2
Fălticeni	**66**	P2
Falun	**48**	H6
Famagusta = Ammochostos	**94**	A1
Fanchang	**80**	F4
Fandriana	**108**	H4
Fangzheng	**80**	H1
Fannūj	**90**	G4
Fanø	**52**	D1
Fano	**62**	J7
Fanø Bugt	**52**	D1
Faradje	**106**	D3
Farafangana	**108**	H4
Farāh	**90**	H3
Farah Rud	**90**	H3
Faranah	**104**	B2
Fareham	**54**	A4
Farewell Spit	**116**	D5
Fargo	**124**	G2
Faribault	**128**	B2
Faridabad	**88**	C3
Farihy Alaotra	**108**	H3
Färjestaden	**50**	F1
Farmington, *Me., US*	**128**	F2
Farmington, *N. Mex., US*	**132**	E1
Farnborough	**54**	B3
Farne Islands	**56**	L6
Fårö	**48**	K8
Faro, *Brazil*	**140**	F4
Faro, *Portugal*	**60**	C7
Fårösund	**48**	K8
Farquhar Group	**108**	(2)B3
Farrāshband	**95**	E2
Farson	**126**	E2
Fasā	**95**	E2
Fasano	**64**	M8
Fategarh	**88**	C3
Fatehpur	**88**	D3
Făurei	**66**	Q4
Fauske	**48**	H3
Fauville-en-Caux	**54**	C5
Favara	**64**	H11
Faversham	**54**	C3
Favignana	**64**	G11
Faxaflói	**48**	(1)B2
Faya	**100**	C4
Fayette	**130**	D3
Fayetteville, *Ark., US*	**130**	C2
Fayetteville, *N.C., US*	**128**	E3
Fayetteville, *Tenn., US*	**130**	D2
Faylakah	**95**	C2
Fažana	**64**	H4
Fdérik	**102**	C4
Featherston	**116**	E5
Fécamp	**54**	C5
Federated States of Micronesia	**112**	E5
Fedorovka	**70**	M4
Fehmarn	**52**	G2
Feijó	**140**	C5
Feilding	**116**	E5
Feira de Santana	**140**	K6
Feistritz	**62**	L3
Fejø	**52**	G2
Feldbach	**62**	L4
Feldkirch	**62**	E3
Feldkirchen	**62**	K4
Felidu Atoll	**88**	B8
Felixstowe	**54**	D3
Feltre	**62**	G4
Femø	**52**	G2
Femund	**48**	F5
Fengcheng	**82**	C3
Fenghua	**80**	G5
Fengning	**80**	F2
Feng Xian	**80**	D4
Feni	**88**	F4
Fenyang	**80**	E3
Feodosiya	**92**	F1
Feres	**68**	J4
Fergana	**90**	K1
Fergus Falls	**124**	G2
Ferkessédougou	**104**	C3
Ferlach	**62**	K4
Fermo	**64**	H5
Fernandina Beach	**130**	E3
Fernandópolis	**142**	L3
Ferrara	**62**	G6
Ferreira do Alentejo	**60**	B7
Ferrol	**60**	B1
Ferry Lake	**130**	C2
Fès	**102**	E2
Festus	**128**	B3
Feteşti	**66**	Q5
Fethiye	**68**	M8
Fetisovo	**90**	F1
Fetlar	**56**	M1
Feucht	**52**	G7
Feuchtwangen	**52**	F7
Feyzābād	**90**	K2
Fianarantsoa	**108**	H4
Fianga	**106**	B2
Fichē	**106**	F2
Fidenza	**62**	F6
Fieni	**66**	N4
Fier	**68**	B4

Figari	**64**	D7
Figeac	**58**	G9
Figline Valdarno	**62**	G7
Figueira da Foz	**60**	B4
Figueres	**60**	N2
Figuig	**102**	E2
Figuil	**104**	G3
Fiji	**112**	H8
Filadélfia	**142**	J3
Fil'akovo	**50**	J9
Filiaşi	**66**	L5
Filicudi	**64**	J10
Filtu	**106**	G2
Finale Ligure	**62**	D6
Findlay	**128**	D2
Fingoè	**108**	E3
Finike	**68**	N8
Finland	**48**	P3
Finlay	**122**	F5
Finley	**114**	J7
Finnsnes	**48**	K2
Finsterwalde	**52**	J5
Fırat	**92**	H4
Firenze	**62**	G7
Firminy	**58**	K8
Firozabad	**88**	C3
Firozpur	**88**	B2
Firth of Clyde	**56**	G6
Firth of Forth	**56**	K5
Firth of Lorn	**56**	G5
Firth of Thames	**116**	E3
Fish	**108**	B5
Fisher Strait	**122**	Q4
Fishguard	**56**	H9
Fiskenæsset = Qeqertarsuatsiaat	**122**	W4
Fismes	**54**	F5
Fitzroy Crossing	**114**	E3
Fivizzano	**62**	F6
Fizi	**106**	D4
Flå	**48**	E6
Flaming Gorge Reservoir	**126**	E2
Flamingo	**130**	E4
Flannan Islands	**56**	E3
Flåsjön	**48**	H4
Flateyri	**48**	(1)B1
Flathead Lake	**126**	D1
Flat Point	**116**	E5
Flekkefjord	**48**	D7
Flensburg	**52**	E2
Flensburg Fjorde	**52**	E2
Flers	**54**	B6
Flinders Island	**114**	J7
Flinders Ranges	**114**	G6
Flinders Reefs	**114**	J3
Flin Flon	**122**	L6
Flint	**128**	D2
Flint Island	**112**	L7
Flirey	**62**	A2
Flöha	**52**	J6
Florac	**58**	J9
Florence = Firenze, *Italy*	**62**	G7
Florence, *Al., US*	**130**	D3
Florence, *S.C., US*	**130**	F3
Florencia	**140**	B3
Florennes	**54**	G4
Florenville	**54**	H5
Flores, *Azores*	**102**	(1)A2
Flores, *Indonesia*	**87**	B4
Floreşti	**66**	R2
Floriano	**140**	J5
Florianópolis	**142**	M4
Florida	**130**	E4
Florida	**142**	K5
Florida Keys	**120**	K7
Florina	**68**	D4
Florissant	**128**	B3
Florø	**48**	C6
Floydada	**132**	F2
Flumendosa	**64**	D9
Fly	**87**	F4
Foča	**66**	F6
Foça	**68**	J6
Focşani	**66**	Q4
Foggia	**64**	K7
Fogo	**104**	(1)B1
Fogo Island	**122**	W7
Fohnsdorf	**62**	K3
Föhr	**52**	D2
Foix	**58**	G11
Folegandros	**68**	G8
Foleyet	**128**	D1
Foligno	**64**	G6
Folkestone	**54**	D3
Folkston	**130**	E3
Follonica	**64**	E6
Fomboni	**108**	G2
Fond du Lac	**128**	C2
Fondi	**64**	H7
Fongafale	**112**	H6
Fontainebleau	**58**	H5
Fontana	**64**	M8
Fonte Boa	**140**	D4
Fontenay-le-Comte	**58**	E7
Fontur	**48**	(1)F1
Fonyód	**64**	M2
Forbach, *France*	**54**	J5
Forbach, *Germany*	**54**	L6
Forchheim	**52**	G7
Førde	**48**	C6
Fordyce	**130**	C3
Forest, *Canada*	**128**	D2
Forest, *US*	**130**	D3
Forestville	**128**	G1
Forfar	**56**	K5
Forges-les-Eaux	**54**	D5
Forks	**126**	B1
Forlì	**62**	H6
Formazza	**62**	D4
Formentera	**60**	M6
Formia	**64**	H7
Formiga	**142**	M3
Formosa, *Brazil*	**140**	H7
Formosa, *Paraguay*	**142**	K4
Fornovo di Taro	**62**	F6
Forsayth	**114**	H3
Forssa	**48**	M6
Forst	**52**	K5
Forsyth	**126**	E1
Fort Abbas	**88**	B3
Fortaleza	**140**	K4
Fort Augustus	**56**	H4
Fort Bayne	**128**	C4
Fort Beaufort	**108**	D6
Fort Benton	**126**	D1
Fort Bragg	**132**	B1
Fort Chipewyan	**122**	J5
Fort Cobb Reservoir	**130**	B2
Fort Collins	**126**	E2
Fort-de-France	**134**	M6
Fort Dodge	**128**	B2
Forte dei Marmi	**62**	F7
Fortezza	**62**	G4
Fort Frances	**128**	B1
Fort George	**122**	R6
Fort Gibson Lake	**130**	B2
Fort Good Hope	**122**	F3
Forth	**56**	H5
Fort Hope	**122**	P6
Fortín Coronel Eugenio Garay	**142**	J3
Fort Kent	**128**	G1
Fort Lauderdale	**130**	E4
Fort Liard	**122**	G4
Fort Mackay	**122**	J5
Fort Macleod	**126**	D1
Fort McMurray	**122**	J5
Fort McPherson	**132**	(1)L2
Fort Munro	**90**	J4
Fort Myers	**130**	E4
Fort Nelson	**122**	G5
Fort Norman	**132**	(1)M3
Fort Payne	**130**	D3
Fort Peck Reservoir	**126**	E1
Fort Pierce	**130**	E4
Fort Pierre	**126**	F2
Fort Portal	**106**	E3
Fort Providence	**122**	H4
Fortrose	**116**	B8
Fort Rupert	**122**	R6
Fort St. John	**122**	G5
Fort Saint Lucie	**130**	E4
Fort Scott	**130**	C2
Fort Severn	**122**	P5
Fort Shevchenko	**76**	J9
Fort Simpson	**122**	G4
Fort Smith, *Canada*	**122**	J4
Fort Smith, *US*	**130**	C2
Fort Stockton	**132**	F2
Fort Summer	**132**	F2
Fortuna	**126**	F1
Fortune Bay	**122**	V7
Fort Vermilion	**122**	H5
Fort Wayne	**130**	D1
Fort William	**56**	G5
Fort Worth	**130**	B3
Fort Yates	**126**	F1
Foshan	**84**	E2
Fosna	**48**	F5
Fossano	**62**	C6
Fossombrone	**62**	H7
Fougamou	**104**	G5
Fougères	**58**	D5
Foula	**56**	K1
Foulness	**54**	C3
Foumban	**104**	G3
Fourmies	**54**	G4
Fournoi	**68**	J7
Fouta Djallon	**104**	B2
Foveaux Strait	**116**	A8
Foxe Basin	**122**	R3
Foxe Channel	**122**	R4
Foxe Peninsula	**122**	R4
Fox Glacier	**116**	B6
Fox Islands	**132**	(1)D5
Foz	**60**	C1
Foz do Cunene	**108**	A3
Foz do Iguaçu	**142**	L4
Fraga	**60**	L3
Franca	**142**	M3
Francavilla al Mare	**64**	J6
France	**58**	G7
Franceville	**104**	G5
Francisco I. Madero	**132**	F4
Francistown	**108**	D4
Francs Peak	**126**	E2
Franeker	**54**	H1
Frankenberg	**52**	D5
Frankenthal	**52**	D7
Frankfort, *Ind., US*	**130**	D1
Frankfort, *Ky., US*	**130**	E2
Frankfurt, *Germany*	**52**	K4
Frankfurt, *Germany*	**52**	D6
Franklin, *N.C., US*	**128**	D3
Franklin, *Tenn., US*	**128**	C3
Franklin Bay	**122**	F2
Franklin D. Roosevelt Lake	**126**	C1
Franklin Mountains	**122**	F3
Franklin Strait	**122**	M2
Franz Josef Glacier	**116**	C6
Franz Josef Land = Zemlya Frantsa-Iosifa	**76**	J2
Fraser	**122**	G6
Fraserburg	**108**	C6
Fraserburgh	**56**	L4
Fraser Island	**114**	K5
Frasertown	**116**	F4
Frater	**128**	D1
Frauenfeld	**62**	D3
Fredensborg	**50**	B2
Frederick, *Md., US*	**128**	E3
Frederick, *Okla., US*	**130**	B3
Fredericksburg, *Tex., US*	**130**	B3
Fredericksburg, *Va., US*	**128**	E3
Fredericktown	**128**	B3
Fredericton	**122**	T7
Frederikshåb = Paamiut	**122**	X4
Frederikshavn	**48**	F8
Frederikssund	**50**	B2
Frederiksværk	**48**	G9
Fredrikstad	**48**	F7
Freeport, *Ill., US*	**128**	C2
Freeport, *Tex., US*	**130**	B4
Freeport City	**130**	F4
Freer	**130**	B4
Free State	**108**	D5
Freetown	**104**	B3
Fregenal de la Sierre	**60**	D6
Freiberg	**52**	J6
Freiburg	**62**	C3
Freilassing	**62**	H3
Freising	**62**	G2
Freistadt	**62**	K2
Fréjus	**58**	M10
Fremantle	**114**	C6
Fremont, *Calif., US*	**132**	B1
Fremont, *Nebr., US*	**124**	G3
Frenchglen	**126**	C2
French Guiana	**140**	G3
French Pass	**116**	D5
French Polynesia	**112**	L7
Frenda	**102**	F1
Fresnes-sur-Apances	**62**	A3
Fresnillo	**134**	D4
Fresno	**132**	C1
Fresno Reservoir	**126**	E1
Freudenstadt	**62**	D2
Freyung	**52**	J8
Frias	**142**	H4
Fribourg	**62**	C4
Friedburg	**62**	G2
Friedrichshafen	**62**	E3
Friesach	**62**	K4
Friesoythe	**52**	C3
Frisian Islands	**54**	H1
Fritzlar	**52**	E5
Frobisher Bay	**122**	T4
Frolovo	**70**	H5
Frome	**56**	K10
Frontera	**134**	F5
Frontignan	**58**	J10
Frosinone	**64**	H7
Frøya	**48**	D5
Fruges	**54**	E4
Frýdek Místek	**50**	H8
Fudai	**82**	L4
Fuding	**80**	G5
Fuengirola	**60**	F8
Fuentesauco	**60**	E3
Fuerte Olimpo	**142**	K3
Fuerteventura	**102**	C3
Fugu	**80**	E3
Fuhai	**76**	R8
Fujieda	**82**	K6
Fujin	**78**	N7
Fuji-san	**82**	K6
Fukuchiyama	**82**	H6
Fukue	**82**	E7
Fukue-jima	**82**	E7
Fukui	**82**	J5
Fukuoka	**82**	F7
Fukushima	**82**	L5
Fukuyama	**82**	G6
Fulda	**52**	E6
Fulda	**52**	E6
Fuling	**80**	D5
Fulton	**130**	D2
Funabashi	**82**	L6
Funafuti	**112**	H6
Funchal	**102**	B2
Fundão	**60**	C4
Funing	**84**	D2
Funtua	**104**	F2
Furano	**82**	M2
Fürg	**95**	F2
Furmanovka	**76**	N9
Furmanovo	**70**	J5
Furneaux Group	**114**	J8
Furqlus	**94**	E2
Fürstenberg	**52**	J3
Fürstenfeldbruck	**62**	G2
Fürstenwalde	**52**	K4
Fürth	**52**	F7
Furukawa	**82**	L4
Fushun	**82**	B3
Fusong	**82**	D2
Füssen	**62**	F3
Futog	**66**	G4
Fuxhou	**80**	F5
Fu Xian	**80**	D3
Fuxin	**80**	G2
Fuyang	**80**	F4
Fuyu	**80**	G1
Fuyun	**76**	R8
Fuzhou	**84**	F1
Fyn	**52**	F1
Fynshav	**52**	F2
G		
Gaalkacyo	**106**	H2
Gabès	**102**	H2
Gabon	**104**	G5
Gaborone	**108**	D4
Gābrik	**95**	H4
Gabrovo	**66**	N7
Gacé	**54**	C6
Gacko	**66**	F6
Gäddede	**48**	H4
Gadsden	**130**	D3
Găeşti	**66**	N5
Gaeta	**64**	H7
Gafsa	**102**	G2
Gaggenau	**62**	D2
Gagnoa	**104**	C3
Gagra	**92**	J2
Gaildorf	**62**	E2
Gaillac	**58**	G10
Gainesville, *Fla., US*	**130**	E4
Gainesville, *Ga., US*	**130**	E3
Gainesville, *Mo., US*	**130**	C2
Gainesville, *Tex., US*	**130**	B3
Gai Xian	**82**	B3
Gala	**88**	E3
Galana	**106**	F4
Galanta	**62**	N2
Galapagos Islands = Islas Galápagos	**140**	(1)B1
Galashiels	**56**	K6
Galatas	**68**	F7
Galaţi	**66**	R4
Galdhøpiggen	**48**	D6
Galena	**132**	(1)F3
Galesburg	**128**	B2
Galich	**70**	H3
Gallabat	**100**	G5
Galle	**88**	D7
Gallipoli	**64**	N8
Gallipolis	**130**	E2
Gällivare	**48**	L3
Gallup	**132**	E1
Galtat Zemmour	**102**	C3
Galveston Bay	**124**	G6
Galway	**56**	C8
Galway Bay	**56**	C8
Gamalakhe	**108**	E6
Gambēla	**106**	E2
Gambell	**78**	Z4
Gambier Islands	**112**	N8
Gamboma	**106**	B4
Gamboula	**106**	B3
Gan	**78**	L7
Ganado	**132**	E1
Gäncä	**92**	M3
Gandajika	**106**	C5
Gander	**122**	W7
Ganderkesee	**52**	D3
Gandesa	**60**	L3
Gāndhīdhām	**88**	B4
Gandhinagar	**88**	B4
Gandia	**60**	K6
Gandu	**140**	K6
Ganganagar	**88**	B3
Gangara	**104**	F2
Gangdise Shan	**88**	D2
Ganges	**58**	J10
Ganges	**88**	E3
Gangi	**64**	J11
Gangtok	**88**	E3
Gannett Peak	**126**	E2
Ganta	**104**	C3
Ganye	**104**	G3
Ganzhou	**80**	E5
Gao	**102**	E5
Gaoual	**102**	C6
Gap	**62**	B6
Gapan	**84**	G3
Garanhuns	**140**	K5
Garba	**104**	J3
Garbsen	**52**	E4
Gardelegen	**52**	G4
Garden City	**126**	F3
Gardēz	**90**	J3
Gardone Val Trompia	**62**	F5
Gargždai	**50**	L2
Gariau	**87**	D3
Garies	**108**	B6
Garissa	**106**	F4
Garland	**130**	B3
Garlasco	**62**	D5
Garliava	**50**	N3
Garmisch-Partenkirchen	**62**	G3
Garnett	**130**	B2
Garonne	**58**	E9
Garoowe	**106**	H2
Garoua	**104**	G3
Garoua Boulaï	**104**	G3
Garry Lake	**122**	L3
Garsen	**106**	G4
Garut	**86**	D4
Garwa	**88**	D4
Garwolin	**50**	L6
Gary	**124**	J3
Garyarsa	**88**	D2
Garzê	**80**	B4
Gasan Kuli	**90**	F2
Gasht	**90**	H4
Gashua	**104**	G2
Gastonia	**130**	E2
Gastre	**142**	H7
Gatchina	**70**	F3
Gateshead	**56**	L7
Gatesville	**130**	B3
Gatineau	**128**	E1
Gatrūyeh	**95**	F2
Gauja	**48**	N8
Gaula	**48**	F5
Gaurella	**88**	D4
Gauteng	**108**	D5
Gava	**60**	N3
Gāvbandī	**95**	E3
Gavdos	**68**	G10
Gävle	**48**	J6
Gawler	**114**	G6
Gawler Ranges	**114**	G6
Gaxun Nur	**80**	C2
Gaya, *India*	**88**	E4
Gaya, *Niger*	**104**	E2
Gaylord	**128**	D1
Gayndah	**114**	K5
Gayny	**70**	K2
Gaza	**94**	B5
Gaz-Achak	**76**	L9
Gazandzhyk	**76**	K10
Gaza Strip	**94**	B5
Gaziantep	**92**	G5
Gazipaşa	**68**	Q8
Gazli	**76**	L9
Gaz Şāleh	**95**	G2

Name	Page	Grid
Gbaaka	104	C3
Gbarnga	104	C3
Gdańsk	50	H3
Gdov	48	P7
Gdyel	60	K9
Gdynia	50	H3
Gebel el Tīh	94	A7
Gebel Halâl	94	A6
Gebel Katherina	100	F2
Gebel Yi'allaq	94	A6
Gebze	68	M4
Gedaref	100	G5
Gediz	68	K6
Gediz	68	M6
Gedser	52	G2
Geel	54	H3
Geelong	114	H7
Geesthacht	52	F3
Gê'gvai	88	D2
Geidam	104	G2
Geilenkirchen	54	J4
Geilo	48	E6
Geinhausen	52	E6
Geislingen	62	E2
Geita	106	E4
Gejiu	84	C2
Gela	64	J11
Geladī	106	H2
Geldern	54	J3
Geleen	54	H4
Gelendzhik	92	H1
Gelibolu	68	J4
Gelibolu Yarimadasi	68	J4
Gelsenkirchen	54	K3
Gembloux	54	G4
Gembu	104	G3
Gemena	106	B3
Gemlik	68	M4
Gemlik Körfezi	68	L4
Gemona del Friuli	62	J4
Genalē Wenz	106	G2
General Acha	142	J6
General Alvear	142	H6
General Pico	142	J6
General Pinedo	142	J4
General Roca	142	H6
General Santos	84	H5
Geneva	128	E2
Genève	62	B4
Gengma	84	B2
Genil	60	F7
Genk	54	H4
Genoa = Genova	62	D6
Genova	62	D6
Gent	54	F3
Genteng	86	D4
Genthin	52	H4
Geographe Bay	114	B6
George	108	C6
George	122	T5
George Town, *Australia*	114	J8
George Town, *Malaysia*	86	C1
George Town, *US*	130	F5
Georgetown, *Australia*	114	H3
Georgetown, *Gambia*	104	B2
Georgetown, *Guyana*	140	F2
Georgetown, *Ky., US*	130	E2
Georgetown, *S.C., US*	130	F3
Georgetown, *Tex., US*	130	B3
George West	130	B4
Georgia	92	K2
Georgia	130	E3
Georgian Bay	128	D1
Gera	52	H6
Geraldine	116	C7
Geraldton, *Australia*	114	B5
Geraldton, *Canada*	124	J2
Gérardmer	62	B2
Gerāsh	95	F3
Gerede	92	E3
Gerefsried	62	G3
Gereshk	90	H3
Gérgal	60	H7
Gerik	84	C5
Gerlach	126	C2
Germantown	128	C3
Germany	52	E6
Germencik	68	K7
Germering	62	G2
Germersheim	54	L5
Gernika	60	H1
Gerolzhofen	52	F7
Gêrzê	88	D2
Geser	87	D3
Getafe	60	G4
Gettysburg	126	F2
Getxo	60	H1
Geugnon	58	K7
Gevaş	92	K4
Gevgelija	68	E3
Gewanē	100	H5
Geyik Dağ	68	Q8
Geyser	126	D1
Geyve	68	N4
Ghabāghib	94	D3
Ghadāmis	102	G2
Ghadīr Minqār	94	E3
Ghana	104	D3
Ghanzi	108	C4
Gharandal	94	C6
Ghardaïa	102	F2
Gharo	90	J5
Gharyān	102	H2
Ghāt	100	B2
Ghazaouet	102	E1
Ghaziabad	88	C3
Ghazipur	88	D3
Ghazn	90	J3
Gheorgheni	66	N3
Gherla	66	L2
Ghizar	88	B1
Ghotāru	88	B3
Ghōwrī	95	F2
Ghunthur	94	E2
Giannitsa	68	E4
Giannutri	64	F6
Giarre	64	K11
Gibraleón	60	D7
Gibraltar	60	E8
Gibson Desert	114	D4
Gideån	48	K5
Gien	58	H6
Gießen	52	D6
Gifhorn	52	F4
Gifu	82	J6
Gigha	56	G6
Giglio	64	E6
Giglio Castello	64	E6
Gijón	60	E1
Gila	132	E2
Gila Bend	132	D2
Gilan Garb	92	L6
Gilău	66	L3
Gilazi	92	N3
Gilbert Islands	112	H5
Gilbués	140	H5
Gilching	62	G2
Gilf Kebir Plateau	100	E3
Gilgandra	114	J6
Gilgit	88	B1
Gilgit	90	K2
Gilimanuk	86	E4
Gillam	122	N5
Gillette	126	E2
Gillingham	54	C3
Gills Rock	128	C1
Gilroy	126	B3
Gīmbī	106	F2
Gimli	122	M6
Gimol'skoe Ozero	48	R5
Gīnīr	106	G2
Gioia del Colle	64	L8
Gioia Tauro	64	K10
Gioura	68	F5
Giresun	92	H3
Girga	100	F2
Girona	60	N3
Gironde	58	E8
Girvan	56	H6
Gisborne	116	G4
Gisenyi	106	D4
Gitega	106	D4
Giurgiu	66	N6
Givet	54	G4
Givors	58	K8
Giyon	106	F2
Gizhiga	78	U4
Gizhiginskaya Guba	78	T4
Giżycko	50	L3
Gjiri i Vlorës	68	B4
Gjirokaster	68	C4
Gjoa Haven	122	M3
Gjøvik	48	F6
Glacier Peak	126	B1
Gladstone	114	K4
Glamoč	66	D5
Glan	52	C7
Glan	87	C1
Glarner Alpen	62	D4
Glasgow, *UK*	56	H6
Glasgow, *Ky., US*	128	C3
Glasgow, *Mont., US*	126	E1
Glauchau	52	H6
Glazov	76	J6
Gleisdorf	62	L3
Glendale, *Ariz., US*	132	D2
Glendale, *Calif., US*	132	C2
Glendambo	114	G6
Glendive	126	F1
Glenmorgan	114	J5
Glennallen	132	(1)H3
Glenn Innes	114	K5
Glenrothes	56	J5
Glens Falls	128	F2
Glenwood, *Ark., US*	128	B4
Glenwood, *Minn., US*	128	A1
Glenwood, *N. Mex., US*	132	E2
Glenwood Springs	126	E3
Glidden	128	B1
Glina	62	M5
Gliwice	50	H7
Glodeni	66	Q2
Głogów	50	F6
Glomfjord	48	H3
Glomma	48	F5
Glorieuses	98	H7
Gloucester, *UK*	56	K10
Gloucester, *US*	128	F2
Głowno	50	J6
Głuchołazy	50	G7
Glückstadt	52	E3
Gmünd, *Austria*	62	J4
Gmünd, *Austria*	62	L2
Gmunden	62	J3
Gniezno	50	G5
Gnjilane	68	D2
Gnoien	52	H3
Goalpara	88	F3
Goba	106	F2
Gobabis	108	B4
Gobernador Gregores	142	G8
Gobi Desert	80	C2
Gobo	82	H7
Gobustan	90	E1
Goch	54	J3
Gochas	108	B4
Godbout	128	G1
Godé	106	G2
Goderich	128	D2
Godhra	88	B4
Gödöllő	66	G2
Gods Lake	122	N6
Godthåb = Nuuk	122	W4
Goeree	54	F3
Goes	54	F3
Gogama	128	D1
Goiânia	140	H7
Goiás	140	G6
Goiás	140	G7
Gökçeada	68	H4
Gökova Körfezi	68	K8
Göksun	92	G5
Golaghat	88	F3
Golan Heights	94	C3
Golbāf	95	G2
Gölbasi	92	G5
Gol'chikha	76	Q3
Gölcük	68	K5
Gołdap	50	M3
Gold Coast	114	K5
Golden Bay	116	D5
Goldendale	126	B1
Golden Gate	132	B1
Goldfield	126	C3
Goldsboro	128	E3
Göle	92	K3
Goleniów	50	D4
Golestānak	95	F1
Golfe d'Ajaccio	64	C7
Golfe de Gabès	102	H2
Golfe de Hammamet	102	H1
Golfe de Porto	64	C6
Golfe de Sagone	64	C6
Golfe de Saint-Malo	58	C5
Golfe de Tunis	64	E11
Golfe de Valinco	64	C7
Golfe du Lion	58	J10
Golfo de Almería	60	H8
Golfo de Batabanó	134	H4
Golfo de Cádiz	60	C7
Golfo de California	134	B3
Golfo de Chiriquí	134	H7
Golfo de Corcovado	142	F7
Golfo de Cupica	140	B2
Golfo de Fonseca	134	G6
Golfo de Guayaquil	140	A4
Golfo de Honduras	134	G5
Golfo del Darién	140	B2
Golfo dell' Asinara	64	C7
Golfo de los Mosquitos	140	A2
Golfo de Mazarrón	60	J7
Golfo de Morrosquillo	140	B1
Golfo de Panamá	134	J7
Golfo de Penas	142	F8
Golfo de San Jorge	142	H8
Golfo de Santa Clara	132	D2
Golfo de Tehuantepec	134	E5
Golfo de València	60	L5
Golfo de Venezuela	140	C1
Golfo di Augusta	64	K11
Golfo di Catania	64	K11
Golfo di Gaeta	64	H7
Golfo di Gela	64	J11
Golfo di Genova	64	C4
Golfo di Manfredonia	64	L7
Golfo di Olbia	64	D8
Golfo di Oristano	64	C9
Golfo di Orosei	64	D8
Golfo di Palmas	64	C10
Golfo di Policastro	64	K9
Golfo di Salerno	64	J8
Golfo di Santa Eufemia	64	K10
Golfo di Squillace	64	L10
Golfo di Taranto	64	L8
Golfo di Trieste	62	J5
Golfo di Venezia	62	H5
Golfo San Matías	142	J6
Gölhisar	68	M8
Golin Baixing	82	A1
Gölköy	92	G3
Gölmarmara	68	K6
Golyshmanovo	76	M6
Goma	106	D4
Gombe	104	G2
Gombi	104	G2
Gomera	102	B3
Gómez Palacio	132	F3
Gonam	78	M5
Gonbad-e Kavus	90	G2
Gonda	88	D3
Gonder	100	G5
Gondia	88	D4
Gondomar	60	B3
Gönen	68	K4
Gonfreville-Orcher	54	C5
Gongga Shan	80	C5
Gonghe	80	C3
Gongliu	76	Q9
Gongpoquan	80	B2
Gongshan	84	B1
Gonzáles	124	G7
Gonzales	130	B4
González	132	G4
Goodland	126	F3
Goolgowi	114	J6
Goomalling	114	C6
Goondiwindi	114	K5
Goose Lake	126	B2
Göppingen	62	E2
Góra	50	F6
Gora Bazardyuzi	92	M3
Gora Kamen	76	S4
Gorakhpur	88	D3
Gora Ledyanaya	78	W4
Gora Pobeda	78	R4
Gora Yenashimskiy Polkan	76	S6
Goražde	66	F6
Gorbitsa	78	K6
Goré	104	H3
Gorē	106	F2
Gore	116	B8
Gorgān	90	F2
Gorgona	62	E7
Gori	92	L2
Gorinchem	54	H3
Goris	92	M4
Gorizia	62	J5
Gorki	70	N1
Gorlice	50	L8
Görlitz	50	D6
Gorna Oryakhovitsa	66	N6
Gornji Milanovac	66	H5
Gorno-Altaysk	76	R7
Gorno Oryakhovitsa	68	H1
Gorodets	70	H3
Gorontalo	87	B2
Goryachiy Klyuch	92	H1
Gory Belukha	76	R8
Gory Ulutau	70	N5
Gorzów Wielkopolski	50	E5
Goslar	52	F5
Gospić	64	K4
Gosport	58	D3
Gossau	62	E3
Gossi	104	D1
Gostivar	68	C3
Gostyń	50	G6
Gostynin	50	J5
Göteborg	48	F8
Gotha	52	F6
Gothèye	104	E2
Gotland	48	K8
Gotō-rettō	82	E7
Gotse Delchev	68	F3
Gotska Sandön	48	K7
Göttingen	52	E5
Gouda	54	G2
Gough Island	98	B10
Goundam	102	E5
Gouraya	60	M8
Gourcy	104	D2
Gourdon	58	G9
Gournay-en-Bray	54	D5
Governador Valadares	140	J7
Governor's Harbour	130	F4
Govorovo	78	M3
Gowārān	90	J4
Goya	142	K4
Gozha Co	88	D1
Gozo = Gwardex	64	J12
Graaff-Reinet	108	C6
Grabovica	66	K5
Gračac	62	L6
Gračanica	66	F5
Gradačac	66	F5
Gräfenhainichen	52	H5
Grafton, *Australia*	114	K5
Grafton, *US*	126	G1
Graham Island	132	(1)L5
Grajaú	140	H5
Grajewo	50	M4
Gram	52	E1
Gramat	58	G9
Grampian Mountains	56	H5
Granada, *Nicaragua*	134	G6
Granada, *Spain*	60	G7
Granby	128	F1
Gran Canaria	102	B3
Grand Bahama	130	F4
Grand Ballon	58	N6
Grand Bank	122	V7
Grand Canyon	126	D3
Grande, *Bolivia*	140	E7
Grande, *Brazil*	140	J6
Grande Cache	122	H6
Grande Prairie	122	H5
Grand Erg de Bilma	102	H5
Grand Erg Occidental	102	E3
Grand Erg Oriental	102	F3
Grand Falls, *N.B., Canada*	128	G1
Grand Falls, *Nfld., Canada*	122	V7
Grand Forks, *Canada*	124	C2
Grand Forks, *US*	126	G1
Grand Haven	128	C2
Grand Island	126	G2
Grand Junction	126	E3
Grand Marais, *Mich., US*	128	C1
Grand Marais, *Minn., US*	128	B1
Grand-Mère	128	F1
Grândola	60	B6
Grand Portage	128	C1
Grand Rapids, *Canada*	122	M6
Grand Rapids, *Mich., US*	128	C2
Grand Rapids, *Minn., US*	128	B1
Grand Teton	126	D2
Grangeville	126	C1
Granite Falls	128	A2
Granollers	60	N3
Gran Paradiso	62	C5
Grantham	56	M9
Grants	132	E1
Grants Pass	126	B2
Granville	58	D5
Granville Lake	122	M5
Gräsö	48	K6
Grasse	62	B7
Grassrange	126	E1
Grass Valley	126	B3
Graulhet	58	G10
Graus	60	L2
Gravelines	54	E3
Gravenhurst	128	E2
Gravesend	54	C3
Gravina in Puglia	64	L8
Gray	58	L6
Grayling	128	D2
Grays	54	C3
Grays Lake	126	D2
Grayville	128	C3
Graz	62	L3
Great Abaco	130	F4
Great Artesian Basin	114	H4
Great Australian Bight	114	E6
Great Bahama Bank	134	J4
Great Barrier Island	116	E3
Great Barrier Reef	114	J2
Great Basin	126	C3
Great Bear Lake	132	(1)M2

Great Bend 132 G1
Great Dividing Range 114 J4
Greater Antilles 134 J5
Greater Sunda Islands 112 B6
Great Exhibition Bay 116 D2
Great Exuma 124 L7
Great Falls 126 D1
Great Inagua 134 K4
Great Karoo 108 C6
Great Malvern 56 K9
Great Nicobar 88 F7
Great Ouse 56 N9
Great Plains 126 F2
Great Rift Valley 106 E5
Great Salt Lake 126 D2
Great Salt Lake Desert 126 D2
Great Sand Sea 100 D2
Great Sandy Desert 114 D4
Great Slave Lake 120 N3
Great Victoria Desert 114 E5
Great Wall 80 C3
Great Yarmouth 56 P9
Greece 68 D5
Greeley 126 F2
Green 126 D3
Green Bay 128 C2
Greenfield 130 D2
Greenland 120 G2
Greenland Sea 120 B2
Greenock 56 H6
Green River, *Wyo., US* 126 E2
Green River, *Ut., US* 126 D3
Greensboro 130 F2
Greensburg, *Ind., US* 130 D2
Greensburg, *Pa., US* 128 E2
Greenvale 114 J3
Green Valley 134 B2
Greenville, *Liberia* 104 C3
Greenville, *Al., US* 130 D3
Greenville, *Fla., US* 130 E3
Greenville, *Miss., US* 130 C3
Greenville, *N.C., US* 128 E3
Greenville, *S.C., US* 130 E3
Greenwood, *Miss., US* 130 C3
Greenwood, *S.C., US* 130 E3
Gregory 126 G2
Gregory Lake 114 E4
Greifswald 52 J2
Greifswalder Bodden 52 J2
Greiz 52 H6
Grenada 124 J5
Grenada 140 E1
Grenchen 62 C3
Grenoble 58 L8
Gretna 130 C4
Greve in Chianti 62 G7
Greven 54 K2
Grevena 68 D4
Grevenbroich 54 J3
Grevesmühlen 52 G3
Greybull 126 E2
Greymouth 116 C6
Grey Range 114 H5
Griesheim 52 D7
Grieskirchen 62 J2
Grigoriopol 66 S2
Grimma 52 H5
Grimmen 52 J2
Grimsby 56 M8
Grimsey 48 (1)D1
Grimsstaðir 48 (1)E2
Grimsvötn 48 (1)E2
Grindsted 48 E9
Grobina 50 L1
Gröbming 62 J3
Grodekovo 80 J2
Grodzisk Wielkopolski 50 F5
Grójec 50 K6
Gronau 52 C4
Groningen 52 B3
Groote Eylandt 114 G2
Grootfontein 108 B3
Großenhain 52 J5
Großer Arber 52 J7
Grosser Beerberg 52 F6
Grosseto 64 F6
Groß-Gerau 52 D7
Großglockner 62 H3
Groß Mohrdorf 52 H2
Groswater Bay 122 V6
Grottaglie 64 M8
Groupe Actéon 112 N8
Grove Hill 130 D3
Groznyy 92 L2
Grubišno Polje 66 E4
Grudovo 68 K2
Grudziądz 50 H4
Grünau 108 B5
Grünberg 52 D6
Gryazi 70 G4
Gryazovets 70 H3
Gryfice 50 E4
Gryfino 52 K3
Grytøya 48 J2
Grytviken 142 P9
Gstaad 62 C4
Guadalajara, *Mexico* 134 D4
Guadalajara, *Spain* 60 G4
Guadalcanal 112 F7
Guadalope 60 K4
Guadalquivir 60 E7
Guadalupe 134 A3
Guadalupe 134 E3
Guadeloupe 138 E2
Guadiana 60 C7
Guadix 60 G7
Guaíra 142 L3
Guajará Mirim 140 D6
Guajarraã 140 D5
Guam 112 E4
Guanambi 140 J6
Guanare 140 D2
Guane 134 H4
Guangshui 80 E4
Guangyuan 80 D4
Guangzhou 84 E2
Guanipa 140 E2
Guanling 80 D5
Guantánamo 134 J4
Guanyun 80 F4
Guaporé 140 E6
Guaqui 140 D7
Guarabira 140 K5
Guarda 60 C4
Guardo 60 F2
Guasave 124 E6
Guastalla 62 F6
Guatemala 134 F5
Guatemala 134 F6
Guaviare 140 D3
Guayaquil 140 B4
Guayaramerín 140 D6
Guaymas 132 D3
Guba, *Dem. Rep. of the Congo* 106 D6
Guba, *Ethiopia* 100 G5
Guba Buorkhaya 78 N2
Gubakha 70 L3
Guban 106 G2
Gubbi 88 C6
Gubbio 62 H7
Guben 52 K5
Gubin 50 D6
Gudaut'a 92 J2
Gudbransdalen 48 E6
Gudermes 92 M2
Gudvangen 48 D6
Guebwiller 52 C9
Guéckédou 104 B3
Guelma 102 G1
Guelph 128 D2
Guérande 58 C6
Guéret 58 B7
Guernsey 58 C4
Guernsey 126 F2
Guérou 102 C5
Guerrero Negro 132 D3
Gugē 106 F2
Gūh Kūh 90 G4
Guiana 134 L7
Guiana Highlands 140 F3
Guider 104 G3
Guiglo 104 C3
Guijuelo 60 E4
Guildford 56 M10
Guilianova 64 H6
Guilin 84 E1
Guillaumes 62 B6
Guillestre 62 B6
Guimarães 60 B3
Guinea 104 B2
Guinea-Bissau 104 A2
Güines 134 H4
Guingamp 58 B5
Guiria 140 E1
Guise 54 F5
Guitiriz 60 C1
Guiyang 80 D5
Gujranwala 88 B2
Gujrat 88 B2
Gulang 80 C3
Gulbarga 88 C5
Gulbene 48 P8
Gulf of Aden 90 E7
Gulf of Alaska 132 (1)H4
Gulf of Aqaba 90 B4
Gulf of Boothia 122 N2
Gulf of Bothnia 48 K6
Gulf of Carpentaria 114 G2
Gulf of Finland 48 M7
Gulf of Gdansk 50 J3
Gulf of Guinea 104 D4
Gulf of Mannar 88 C7
Gulf of Martaban 84 B3
Gulf of Mexico 134 F3
Gulf of Oman 95 G4
Gulf of Riga 48 M8
Gulf of St. Lawrence 122 U7
Gulf of Santa Catalina 132 C2
Gulf of Thailand 84 C4
Gulf of Tongking 84 D3
Gulfport 130 D3
Gulistan 76 M9
Gülşehir 68 S6
Gulu 106 E3
Gülübovo 68 H2
Gumdag 90 F2
Gumel 104 F2
Gumla 88 D4
Gummersbach 54 K3
Gummi 104 F2
Gümüşhane 92 H3
Guna 88 C4
Guna Terara 100 G5
Gungu 106 B5
Gunib 92 M2
Gunnbjørns Fjeld 144 (1)U2
Gunnedah 114 K6
Gunnison, *Colo., US* 126 E3
Gunnison, *Ut., US* 126 D3
Gunong Kinabalu 86 F1
Guntakal 88 C5
Guntur 88 D5
Gunung Kerinci 86 C3
Gunung Korbu 86 C2
Gunung Kwoka 87 D3
Gunung Leuser 86 B2
Gunung Mekongga 87 B3
Gunung Mulu 86 E2
Gunung Pangrango 86 D4
Gunungsitoli 86 B2
Gunung Togwomeri 87 D3
Günzburg 62 F2
Gunzenhausen 52 F7
Guoyang 80 F4
Gura Humorului 66 N2
Gurk 62 K4
Gurskoye 78 P6
Gürün 92 G4
Gurupi 140 H4
Gusau 104 F2
Gusev 50 M3
Gushgy 90 H2
Gusinoozersk 78 H6
Guspini 64 C9
Güssing 62 M3
Güstrow 50 B4
Gütersloh 52 D5
Guthrie, *Okla., US* 126 G3
Guthrie, *Tex., US* 132 F2
Gutsuo 88 E3
Guttenberg 128 B2
Guwahati 88 F3
Guyana 140 F2
Guyang 80 E2
Guymon 132 F1
Guyuan 80 D3
Guzar 90 J2
Gvardejsk 50 L3
Gwadar 90 H4
Gwalior 88 C3
Gwanda 108 D4
Gwardex 64 J12
Gwda 50 F4
Gweebarra Bay 56 C7
Gweru 108 D3
Gyangzê 88 E3
Gyaring Hu 80 B4
Gyaros 68 G7
Gyda 76 P3
Gydanskiy Poluostrov 76 P3
Gyirong 88 E3
Gyldenløues Fjord 122 Y4
Gympie 114 K5
Gyomaendrőd 66 H3
Gyöngyös 66 G2
Győr 66 E2
Gypsumville 122 M6
Gytheio 68 E8
Gyula 66 J3
Gyumri 92 K3
Gyzylarbat 90 G2

H

Haapajärvi 48 N5
Haapsalu 48 M7
Haar 62 G2
Haarlem 54 G2
Haast 116 B6
Habahe 76 R8
Habarūt 90 F6
Habaswein 106 F3
Habbān 90 E7
Habbānīyah 92 K7
Habirag 80 F2
Habomai-Shoto 78 R8
Haboro 82 L1
Hachijō-jima 82 K7
Hachinohe 82 L3
Hachiōji 82 K6
Hadadong 76 Q9
Haddunmahti Atoll 88 B8
Hadejia 104 F2
Hadejia 104 G2
Hadera 94 B4
Haderslev 52 E1
Haḍhramaut 90 E6
Hadilik 76 R10
Hadjout 60 N8
Haeju 82 C4
Haenam 82 D6
Hafar al Bāṭin 95 A2
Hafik 92 G4
Hafnarfjördur 48 (1)C2
Haft Gel 95 C1
Hagen 54 K3
Hagenow 52 G3
Hägere Hiywet 106 F2
Hagerstown 128 E3
Ha Giang 80 C6
Haguenau 54 K6
Haicheng 82 B3
Haifa = Ḥefa 94 B4
Haikou 84 E3
Hā'il 90 D4
Hailar 78 K7
Hailey 126 D2
Hailong 82 C2
Hailuoto 48 N4
Hainan 84 D3
Haines Junction 132 (1)K3
Haining 80 G4
Hai Phong 84 D2
Haiti 134 K5
Haiya 100 G4
Hajdúböszörmény 66 J2
Hajdúhadház 50 L10
Hajdúnánás 50 L10
Hajdúszoboszló 50 L10
Hajipur 88 E3
Hājjīābād 95 F2
Hajmah 90 G6
Hajnówka 50 N5
Haka 88 F4
Hakkâri 92 K5
Hakodate 82 L3
Ḥalab 92 G5
Halabān 100 H3
Halabja 92 L6
Halaib 100 G3
Halba 94 D2
Halberstadt 52 G5
Halden 48 F7
Haldensleben 52 G4
Halifax 122 U8
Halifax Bay 114 J3
Hall 62 G3
Hall Beach 122 Q3
Halle 54 G4
Hallein 62 J3
Halligen 52 D2
Hallock 126 G1
Hall Peninsula 122 T4
Halls Creek 114 E3
Halmahera 87 C2
Halmahera Sea 87 C3
Halmstad 50 B1
Haltern 54 K3
Hamada 82 G6
Hamadān 90 E3
Hamaguir 102 E2
Hamāh 92 G6
Hamamatsu 82 J6
Hamar 48 F6
Hamarøy 48 H2
Hamatonbetsu 82 M1
Hambantota 88 D7
Hamburg, *Germany* 52 E3
Hamburg, *Ark., US* 130 C3
Hamburg, *N.Y., US* 128 E2
Hämeenlinna 48 N6
Hameln 52 E4
Hamersley Range 114 C4
Hamhŭng 82 D3
Hami 76 S9
Hamīd 100 F3
Hamilton, *Australia* 114 H7
Hamilton, *Bermuda* 134 M2
Hamilton, *Canada* 128 E2
Hamilton, *New Zealand* 116 E3
Hamilton, *Al., US* 130 D3
Hamilton, *Mont., US* 126 D1
Hamilton, *Oh., US* 128 D3
Hamina 48 P6
Hamirpur 88 D3
Hamm 52 C5
Hammada du Drâa 102 D3
Hammam Bou Hadjar 60 K9
Hammamet 64 E12
Hammam Lif 102 H1
Hammelburg 52 E6
Hammerfest 48 M1
Hammer Springs 116 D6
Hampden 116 C7
Hāmūn-e Jaz Mūrīān 95 H3
Hanalc 100 G2
Hanamaki 82 L4
Hanau 52 D6
Hâncești 66 R3
Hancheng 80 E3
Hancock 128 C1
Handan 80 E3
Handeni 106 F5
Handerslev 48 E9
Handlová 50 H9
Hanford 132 C1
Hangayn Nuruu 76 T8
Hangu 80 F3
Hangzhou 80 F4
Hanīdh 95 C3
Hanko 48 M7
Hanksville 126 D3
Hanna 122 K6
Hannibal 130 C2
Hannover 52 E4
Hanö 50 D2
Hanöbukten 50 D2
Ha Nôi 84 D2
Hanoi = Ha Nôi 84 D2
Hanover 128 F2
Han Shui 80 D4
Hanson Bay 116 (1)B1
Hanumangarh 88 B3
Hanzhong 80 D4
Hao 112 M7
Hāora 88 E4
Haouza 102 C3
Haparanda 48 N4
Hāpoli 88 F3
Hapur 88 C3
Haraḍ, *Saudi Arabia* 90 E5
Haraḍ, *Yemen* 100 H4
Haramachi 82 L5
Harare 108 E3
Harbin 80 H1
Harbour Breton 122 V7
Harburg 52 F3
Hardangerfjorden 48 C7
Hardangervidda 48 D6
Hardenberg 54 J2
Harderwijk 54 H2
Hardin 126 E1
Hardy 130 C2
Haren 54 K2
Hārer 106 G2
Hargeysa 106 G2
Har Hu 80 B3
Haridwar 88 C3
Harihari 116 C6
Harima-nada 82 H6
Hari Rud 90 H3
Harlan 128 A2
Hârlău 66 P2
Harlem 126 E1
Harlingen, *Netherlands* 54 H1
Harlingen, *US* 130 B4
Harlow 56 N10
Harlowtown 126 E1
Harney Basin 124 B3
Harney Lake 126 C2
Härnösand 48 J5
Har Nur 78 K7
Har Nuur 76 S8
Haro 60 H2
Harricanaw 122 R6
Harrisburg, *Ill., US* 128 C3
Harrisburg, *Pa., US* 130 F1
Harrison 128 B3

Harrison Bay 132 (1)G1
Harrisville 128 D2
Harrogate 56 L8
Har Saggi 94 B6
Harsin 92 M6
Hârşova 66 Q5
Harstad 48 J2
Hartberg 62 L3
Hartford 128 F2
Hartland Point 56 H10
Hartlepool 56 L7
Har Us Nuur 76 S8
Harvey 126 G1
Harwich 54 D3
Harz 52 F5
Hāsā 94 C6
Haselünne 52 C4
Hashtpar 92 N5
Hāsik 90 G6
Haskell 130 B3
Haslemere 54 B3
Hassan 88 C6
Hasselfelde 52 F5
Hasselt 54 H4
Haßfurt 52 F6
Hassi Bel Guebbour 102 G3
Hassi Messaoud 102 G2
Hässleholm 48 G8
Hastings, *New Zealand* 116 F4
Hastings, *UK* 54 C4
Hastings, *Minn., US* 128 B2
Hastings, *Nebr., US* 126 G2
Haţeg 66 K4
Hatgal 78 G6
Ha Tinh 84 D3
Hatteras 130 F2
Hattiesburg 130 D3
Hatvan 66 G2
Haud 100 H6
Haud Ogadēn 106 G2/H2
Haugesund 48 C7
Hauraki Gulf 116 E3
Haut Atlas 102 D2
Hauts Plateaux 102 E2
Havana 130 C1
Havana = La Habana 134 H4
Havant 56 M11
Havel 50 C5
Havelock, *New Zealand* 116 D5
Havelock, *US* 130 F3
Havelock North 116 F4
Havenby 52 D1
Haverfordwest 56 H10
Havlíčkův Brod 50 E8
Havre 126 E1
Havre-St-Pierre 122 U6
Havrylivtsi 66 P1
Havza 92 F3
Hawaii 132 (2)E2
Hawaii 132 (2)E4
Hawaiian Islands 112 J3
Hawera 116 E4
Hawi 132 (2)F3
Hawick 56 K6
Hawke Bay 116 F4
Hawker 114 G6
Hawr al'Awdah 95 B1
Hawr al Hammar 95 B1
Hawthorne 126 C3
Hay 114 H6
Hay 122 H5
Hayange 54 J5
Haydarābad 92 L5
Hayden 132 D2
Hayrabolu 68 K3
Hay River 122 H4
Hays 130 B2
Hazard 128 D3
Hazāribāg 88 E4
Hazebrouck 54 E4
Hazelton, *Canada* 122 F5
Hazelton, *US* 128 E2
Head of Bight 114 F6
Hearne 130 B3
Hearst 128 D1
Hebbronville 132 G3
Hebgen Lake 126 D2
Hebi 80 E3
Hebron, *Canada* 122 U5
Hebron, *Israel* 94 C5
Hebron, *Nebr., US* 126 G2
Hebron, *N.D., US* 126 F1
Hecate Strait 122 E6
Hechi 84 D2
Hechingen 62 D2
Hede 48 G5
Heerenveen 54 H2
Heerlen 54 J4
Ḩefa 94 B4
Hefei 80 F4
Hegang 80 J1
Hegura-jima 82 J5
Hegyfalu 62 M3
Heide 52 E2
Heidelberg 52 D7
Heidenheim 62 F2
Heilbad Heiligenstadt 52 F5
Heilbronn 52 E7
Heiligenhafen 52 F2
Heimaey 48 (1)C3
Heinola 48 N6
Hejing 76 R9
Hekla 48 (1)D3
Helagsfjället 48 G5
Helena, *Ark., US* 130 C3
Helena, *Mont., US* 126 D1
Helen Reef 87 D2
Helensville 116 E3
Helgea 50 D1
Helgoland 52 C2
Helgoländer Bucht 52 D2
Hellin 60 J6
Helmand 90 H3
Helmond 54 H3
Helmsdale 56 J3
Helmstedt 52 G4
Helodrano Antongila 108 H3
Helong 82 E2
Helsingborg 48 G8
Helsinge 50 B1
Helsingør 48 G8
Helsinki 48 N6
Helston 56 G11
Helwan 100 F2
Hemel Hempstead 56 M10
Henashi-zaki 82 K3
Hendek 68 N4
Henderson, *Ky., US* 128 C3
Henderson, *Nev., US* 126 D3
Henderson, *N.C. US* 130 F2
Henderson Island 112 P8
Hendersonville 128 C3
Hendījarn 95 C1
Hengelo 54 J2
Hengyang 80 E5
Henichesk 70 F5
Hénin-Beaumont 54 E4
Hennebont 58 B6
Hennigsdorf 52 J4
Henryetta 128 A3
Henzada 84 B3
Heppenheim 52 D7
Heppner 126 C1
Hepu 84 D2
Héradsflói 48 (1)F2
Herald Cays 114 J3
Herāt 90 H3
Herbert 116 C7
Herborn 52 D6
Herceg-Novi 66 F7
Hereford, *UK* 56 K9
Hereford, *US* 134 D2
Herekino 116 D2
Herentals 54 G3
Herford 52 D4
Herisau 62 E3
Herlen Gol 80 E1
Hermagor 62 J4
Herma Ness 56 M1
Hermel 94 D2
Hermiston 126 C1
Hermosillo 124 D6
Hernád 50 L9
Herne 52 C5
Herne Bay 54 D3
Herning 48 E8
Hérouville-St-Clair 54 B5
Herrenberg 62 D2
Hersbruck 52 G7
Herstat 54 H4
Hertlay 54 E6
Hervey Bay 114 K5
Herzberg 52 F5
Herzliyya 94 B4
Hesdin 54 E4
Heshan 84 D2
Hesselø 50 A1
Hessisch-Lichtenau 52 E5
Hettstedt Lutherstadt 52 G5
Heves 50 K10
He Xian 84 E2
Hexigten Qi 80 F2
Heze 80 F3
Hezuozhen 80 C3
Hialeah 130 E4
Hiawatha 130 B2
Hibbing 128 B1
Hickory 128 D3
Hidaka-sammyaku 82 M2
Hidalgo del Parral 134 C3
Hiddensee 52 H2
Hierro 102 B3
Higashi-suidō 82 E7
High Point 128 E3
High Wycombe 54 B3
Hiiumaa 48 M7
Hikurangi 116 E2
Hikurangi 116 G3
Hikutaia 116 E3
Hildburghausen 52 F6
Hildesheim 52 E4
Hillsboro, *Oh., US* 130 E2
Hillsboro, *Oreg., US* 126 B1
Hillsboro, *Tex., US* 132 G2
Hillsville 128 D3
Hillswick 56 L1
Hilo 132 (2)F4
Hilton Head Island 130 E3
Hilva 92 H5
Hilversum 54 H2
Himalayas 74 L6
Himarë 68 B4
Himatnagar 88 B4
Himeji 82 H6
Himi 82 J5
Himora 100 G5
Ḩimş 94 D2
Hindu Kush 88 A1
Hindupur 88 C6
Hinesville 130 E3
Hingoli 88 C5
Hinnøya 48 H2
Hiroo 82 M2
Hirosaki 82 L3
Hiroshima 82 G6
Hirschaid 52 F7
Hirson 54 G5
Hirtshals 48 E8
Hisar 88 C3
Hischberg 52 G6
Hisdal 48 C6
Hispaniola 138 D2
Hisyah 94 D2
Hīt 92 K7
Hitachi 82 L5
Hitoyoshi 82 F7
Hitra 48 D5
Hiuchi-nada 82 G6
Hiva Oa 112 M6
Hjälmaren 48 H7
Hjalmar Lake 122 K4
Hjelmsøya 48 M1
Hlinsko 50 E8
Hlohovec 62 N2
Hlyboka 66 N1
Hlybokaye 70 E3
Ho 104 E3
Hobart, *Australia* 114 J8
Hobart, *US* 132 G1
Hobbs 132 F2
Hobro 48 E8
Hobyo 106 H3
Hô Chi Minh 84 D4
Höchstadt 52 F7
Hockenheim 52 D7
Hódmezővásárhely 66 H3
Hodonin 50 G9
Hoek van Holland 54 G3
Hoeryŏng 82 E2
Hoeyang 82 D4
Hof 52 G6
Hofgeismar 52 E5
Höfn 48 (1)F2
Hofsjökull 48 (1)D2
Hofsos 48 (1)D2
Hōfu 82 F6
Hohe 62 H3
Hohe Dachstein 50 C10
Hohe Tauern 64 G1
Hohhot 80 E2
Hoh Xil Shan 88 E1
Hôi An 84 D3
Hoima 106 E3
Hokitika 116 C6
Hokkaidō 82 N2
Holbæk 50 A2
Holbrook 132 D2
Holdrege 126 G2
Holguín 134 J4
Holíč 62 N2
Hollabrunn 62 M2
Holland 128 C2
Hollis 132 G2
Hollywood 130 E4
Holman 122 H2
Hólmavík 48 (1)C2
Holmes Reefs 114 J3
Holstebro 48 E8
Holsteinische Schweiz 52 F2
Holsteinsborg = Sisimiut 122 W3
Holton 130 B2
Holyhead 56 H8
Holy Island, *Eng., UK* 56 L6
Holy Island, *Wales, UK* 56 H8
Holyoke 126 F2
Holzkirchen 62 G3
Holzminden 52 E5
Homa Bay 106 E4
Homberg 52 E5
Hombori 102 E5
Home Bay 122 T3
Homestead 130 E4
Homewood 130 D3
Homs = Ḩimş 94 D2
Homyel' 70 F4
Hondo, *N. Mex., US* 132 E2
Hondo, *Tex., US* 132 G3
Honduras 134 G6
Hønefoss 48 F6
Honey Lake 126 B2
Honfleur 54 C5
Hon Gai 84 D2
Hong Kong 84 E2
Hongliuyuan 80 B2
Hongor 80 E1
Honiara 112 F6
Honjō 82 K4
Honokaa 132 (2)F3
Honolulu 132 (2)D2
Honshū 82 L5
Hooge 52 D2
Hoogeveen 54 J2
Hoogezand-Sappemeer 54 J1
Hooper Bay 132 (1)D3
Hoorn 54 H2
Hoorn Islands 112 H7
Hopa 92 J3
Hope, *Canada* 126 B1
Hope, *Ak., US* 122 B4
Hope, *Ark., US* 130 C3
Hopedale 122 U5
Hopetoun 114 H7
Hopin 88 G4
Hopkinsville 128 C3
Hoquiam 126 B1
Horadiz 92 M4
Horasan 92 K3
Horgo 78 F7
Horizon Depth 112 D8
Hormak 90 H4
Hormoz 95 F3
Horn 62 L2
Hornavan 48 J3
Horncastle 54 B1
Horodenka 66 N1
Horodok 50 N8
Horqin Youyi Qianqi 78 L7
Horsens 48 E9
Horsham, *Australia* 114 H7
Horsham, *UK* 54 B3
Horten 48 F7
Hortiguela 60 G2
Horton 132 (1)N2
Hoseynābād 95 E1
Hoshab 90 H4
Hoshangabad 88 C4
Hospet 88 C5
Hosséré Vokre 104 G3
Hotan 76 Q10
Hotan 76 Q10
Hot Springs, *Ark., US* 128 B4
Hot Springs, *N.C., US* 128 D3
Hottah Lake 122 H3
Houdan 54 D6
Houdelaincourt 62 A2
Houghton 128 C1
Houlton 128 G1
Houma, *China* 80 E3
Houma, *US* 124 H6
Houmt Souk 102 H2
Houston 124 G6
Hovd 76 S8
Hövsgöl Nuur 78 F6
Hövüün 80 C2
Howard Junction 116 D5
Howland 112 J5
Ḩowz-e Panj 95 G1
Hoxie 130 C2
Höxter 52 E5
Hoxud 76 R9
Hoy 56 J3
Høyanger 48 D6
Hoyerswerda 52 K5
Hradeç Králové 50 E7
Hranice 50 G8
Hrazdan 92 L3
Hrodna 50 N4
Hron 50 H9
Hrubieszów 50 N7
Hsin-chu 84 G2
Hsueh-Shan 84 G2
Hsweni 84 B2
Huacho 140 B6
Huade 80 E2
Huadian 82 D2
Huaibei 80 F4
Huaibin 80 F4
Huaihua 80 D5
Huainan 80 F4
Huaiyin 80 F4
Huaki 87 C4
Huallaga 140 B5
Huambo 108 B2
Huancayelica 140 B6
Huancayo 140 B6
Huang 80 F3
Huangchuan 80 F4
Huangshan 80 F5
Huangshi 80 F4
Huang Xian 80 G3
Huangyan, *China* 80 C3
Huangyan, *China* 80 G5
Huanren 82 C3
Huanuco 140 B5
Huaráz 140 B5
Huarmey 140 B6
Huasco 142 G4
Huashixia 80 B3
Huatabampo 124 E6
Hubli 88 C5
Huch'ang 82 D3
Huddersfield 56 L8
Huddinge 48 K7
Hudiksvall 48 J6
Hudson 128 F2
Hudson 128 F2
Hudson Bay 122 L6
Hudson Bay 122 P5
Hudson Strait 122 S4
Huê 84 D3
Huelva 60 D7
Huercal Overa 60 J7
Huesca 60 K2
Huéscar 60 H7
Huftaroy 48 C6
Hughenden 114 H4
Hugo 130 B3
Hugo Lake 130 B3
Huia 116 E3
Huich'ŏn 82 D3
Huila Plateau 108 A3
Huinan 82 C2
Huinca Renancó 142 J5
Huizhou 84 E2
Hulin 78 N7
Hull 128 E1
Hulst 54 G3
Hulun Nur 78 K7
Huma 78 M6
Huma 78 M6
Humaitá 140 E5
Humbe 108 A3
Humble 52 F2
Humboldt 122 L6
Humboldt 126 C2
Hūmedān 90 G4
Humenné 50 L9
Humphrey 126 D2
Humpolec 50 E8
Hūn 100 C2
Húnaflói 48 (1)C2
Hunchun 82 F2
Hunedoara 66 K4
Hünfeld 52 E6
Hungary 66 F3
Hungen 52 D6
Hungerford, *Australia* 114 H5
Hungerford, *UK* 54 A3
Hŭngnam 82 D4
Hunjiang 82 D3
Hunsrück 52 B7
Hunstanton 54 C2
Hunte 52 D4
Hunter Island 112 H8
Huntingburg 130 D2
Huntingdon, *UK* 54 B2
Huntingdon, *US* 130 E2
Huntington 130 D1

Huntington Beach 132 C2
Huntly 116 E3
Huntsville, *Canada* 128 E1
Huntsville, *Al., US* 130 D3
Huntsville, *Tex., US* 134 E2
Hunyuan 80 E3
Hūr 95 G1
Hurdiyo 106 J1
Hurghada 100 F2
Huron 126 G2
Hürth 54 J4
Húsavík 48 (1)E1
Huşi 66 R3
Huslia 132 (1)F2
Husn 94 C4
Husum 52 E2
Hutag 78 G7
Hutanopan 86 B2
Hutchinson 132 G1
Hūth 100 H4
Huttwil 62 C3
Huvadu Atoll 88 B8
Huy 54 H4
Huzou 80 G4
Hvannadalshnúkur 48 (1)E2
Hvar 66 D6
Hvar 66 D6
Hvolsvöllur 48 (1)C3
Hwange 108 D3
Hyak 126 B1
Hyannis 126 F2
Hyargas Nuur 76 S8
Hyden 114 C6
Hyderabad, *India* 88 C5
Hyderabad, *Pakistan* 90 J4
Hyères 58 M10
Hyesan 82 E3
Hyndam Peak 126 D2
Hyūga 82 F7
Hyvinkää 48 N6

I

Iaco 140 D6
Ialomiţa 66 P5
Ianca 66 Q4
Iaşi 66 Q2
Ibadan 104 F3
Ibagué 140 B3
Ibar 66 H6
Ibb 100 H5
Ibbenbüren 52 C4
Iberia 140 C5
Ibiza = Eivissa 60 M5
Ibiza = Eivissa 60 M6
Ibotirama 140 J6
Ibrā' 90 G5
'Ibrī 95 G5
Ica 140 B6
Içana 140 D3
Içel 92 F5
Iceland 46 C1
Ichalkaranji 88 B5
Ichinoseki 82 L4
Idabel 130 C3
Ida Grove 128 A2
Idah 104 F3
Idaho 126 D2
Idaho Falls 126 D2
Idar-Oberstein 52 C7
Idfu 100 F3
Idhān Awbārī 102 H3
Idhan Murzūq 102 H4
Idiofa 106 C4
Idlib 92 G6
Idstein 52 D6
Ieper 54 E4
Ierapetra 68 H9
Ifakara 106 F5
Ifanadiana 108 H4
Ife 104 E3
Ifjord 48 P1
Igarka 76 R4
Iggesund 48 J6
Igizyar 90 L2
Iglesias 64 C9
Igli 102 E2
Igloolik 122 Q3
Ignace 128 B1
İğneada 68 K3
Igoumenitsa 68 C5
Igra 70 K3
Igrim 70 M2
Igualada 60 M3
Iguatu 140 K5
Iharaña 108 H2
Ihosy 108 H4
Ihtiman 68 F2
Iida 82 J6
Iim 62 G2
Iisalmi 48 P5
Iiulissat 122 W3
Ijebu Ode 104 E3
IJmuiden 54 G2
IJssel 54 J2
IJsselmeer 54 H2
Ikaria 68 J7
Ikeda 82 M2
Ikela 106 C4
Ikhtiman 66 L7
Iki 82 E7
Ikire 104 E3
Ikom 104 F3
Ikopa 108 H3
Ikorodu 104 E3
Ilagan 84 G3
Īlām 90 E3
Iława 50 J4
Ilbenge 78 L4
Ilebo 106 C4
Île d'Anticosti 122 U7
Île de Jerba 102 H2
Île de la Gonâve 134 K5
Île de Noirmoutier 58 C7
Île de Ré 58 D7
Île d'Oléron 58 D8
Île d'Yeu 58 C7
Île Europa 108 G4
Ilek 70 K4
Ilek 70 K4
Île Plane 64 E11
Îles Cani 64 D11
Îles Chesterfield 112 F7
Îles Crozet 98 J10
Îles de la Madeleine 122 U7
Îles Désappointement 112 M7
Îles d'Hyères 58 M11
Îles Duc de Gloucester 112 M7
Îles Glorieuses 108 H2
Ilesha 104 E3
Îles Kerkenah 102 H2
Îles Maria 112 L8
Îles Palliser 112 M7
Île Tidra 102 B5
Île Zembra 64 E11
Ilfracombe 56 H10
Ilgın 92 D4
Ilha da Trindade 138 H6
Ilha de Marajó 140 H4
Ilha de São Luís 140 J4
Ilha do Bazaruto 108 F4
Ilha Fernando de Noronha 140 L4
Ilha Grande 140 E4
Ilha Grande de Gurupa 140 G4
Ilhas Martin Vaz 142 Q3
Ilhéus 140 K6
Iliamna Volcano 132 (1)G4
Iligan 84 G5
Ilkal 88 C5
Iller 62 F3
Illertissen 62 F2
Illichivs'k 66 T3
Illinois 124 H3
Illinois 128 C2
Illizi 102 G3
Ilmenau 52 F6
Ilo 140 C7
Iloilo 84 G4
Ilorin 104 E3
Ilovlya 70 H5
Il'pyrskiy 78 U4
Ilwaco 126 B1
Ilych 70 L2
Imabari 82 G6
Imatra 48 Q6
Imeni-Babushkina 76 G6
Imeni Polinyosipenko 78 P6
Imese 106 B3
Īmī 106 G2
İmişli 92 N4
Immeln 50 D1
Immenstadt 62 F3
Imola 62 G6
Imotski 66 E6
Imperatriz 140 H5
Imperia 62 D7
Imperial 126 F2
Impfondo 106 B3
Imphal 88 F4
Imrali Adası 68 L4
Imroz 68 H4
Ina 82 J6
Inambari 140 C6
In Aménas 102 G3
Inangahua 116 C5
Inanwatan 87 D3
Iñapari 140 D6
Inarijärvi 48 P2
Inca 60 N5
İnce Burun 92 F2
Inch'ŏn 82 D5
Incirliova 68 K7
Indalsälven 48 H5
Independence, *Kans., US* 130 B2
Independence, *Mo., US* 128 B3
India 88 C4
Indiana 124 J3
Indiana 128 E2
Indianapolis 130 D2
Indian Ocean 88 D8
Indianola 128 B2
Indian Springs 126 C3
Indiga 70 J1
Indio 132 C2
Indonesia 86 D3
Indore 88 C4
Indramayu 86 D4
Indre 58 G6
Indre Sula 48 C6
Indus 90 K3
İnebolu 92 E3
İnecik 68 K4
İnegöl 92 C3
In Ekker 102 G4
Ineu 66 J3
Ingelheim 54 L5
Ingeniero Jacobacci 142 H7
Ingham 114 J3
Ingoda 78 J6
Ingolstadt 62 G2
Ingrāj Bāzār 88 E3
I-n-Guezzam 102 G5
Ingushetiya 92 L2
Inhambane 108 F4
Inhaminga 108 E3
Inirida 140 D3
Inishmore 56 B8
Inkisi-Kisantu 104 H6
Inn 62 H2
Inner Hebrides 56 F5
Inner Mongolia =
Nei Monggol 80 E2
Innisfail 114 J3
Innsbruck 62 G3
Inongo 106 B4
Inowrocław 50 H5
In Salah 102 F3
Insein 84 B3
Inta 76 K4
Interlaken 62 C4
International Falls 128 B1
Intsy 70 H1
Inubō-zaki 82 L6
Inukjuak 122 R5
Inuvik 132 (1)L2
Inveraray 56 G5
Invercargill 116 B8
Inverness 56 H4
Investigator Group 114 F6
Investigator Strait 114 G7
Inya 76 R7
Inya 78 R4
Ioannina 68 C5
Iokanga 76 F4
Iola 130 B2
Iona 56 F5
Ioneşti 66 M5
Ionian Sea 68 B6
Ionioi Nisoi 68 B5
Ios 68 H8
Ios 68 H8
Iowa 124 H3
Iowa City 128 B2
Iowa Falls 128 B2
Ipameri 140 H7
Ipatinga 142 N2
Ipatovo 70 H5
Ipiales 140 B3
Ipiaú 140 K6
Ipoh 86 C2
Iporá 140 G7
Ippy 106 C2
Ipsala 68 J4
Ipswich 56 P9
Iqaluit 122 T4
Iquique 142 G3
Iquitos 140 C4
Iracoubo 140 G2
Irakleia 68 F3
Irakleia 68 H8
Irakleio 68 H9
Iraklion = Irakleio 46 G4
Iran 90 F3
Irānshahr 90 H4
Irapuato 134 D4
Iraq 90 D3
Irbid 94 C4
Irbit 70 M3
Irecê 140 J6
Ireland 56 D8
Irgiz 70 M5
Irgiz 70 M5
Irhil M'Goun 102 D2
Iringa 106 F5
Iriri 140 G4
Irish Sea 56 G8
Irkutsk 78 G6
Iron Mountain 128 C1
Ironton 130 E2
Ironwood 128 B1
Irrawaddy 88 F5
Irshava 66 L1
Irta 70 J2
Irtysh 70 P3
Irtyshsk 76 P7
Irumu 106 D3
Irún 60 J1
Irvine 56 H6
Irving 132 G2
Isabela 87 B1
Isabella 128 B1
Isabella Lake 132 C1
Ísafjarðardjúp 48 (1)A1
Ísafjörður 48 (1)B1
Isahaya 82 F7
Isar 62 G3
Ischia 64 H8
Ischia 64 H8
Ise 82 J6
Isel 62 H4
Isère 62 B5
Iserlohn 54 K3
Isernia 64 J7
Isetskoye 70 N3
Iseyin 104 E3
Isfana 90 J2
Ishikari-wan 82 L2
Ishim 70 N3
Ishim 70 N4
Ishinomaki 82 L4
Ishkoshim 90 K2
Isigny-sur-Mer 54 A5
Isiolo 106 F3
Isiro 106 D3
Iskăr 66 M6
İskenderun 92 G5
Iskitim 76 Q7
Isla Alejandro Selkirk 142 E5
Isla Campana 142 F8
Isla Clarence 142 G9
Isla Clarión 134 B5
Isla Coiba 134 H7
Isla Contreras 142 F9
Isla de Alborán 60 G9
Isla de Bioco 104 F4
Isla de Chiloé 142 G7
Isla de Coco 134 G7
Isla de Cozumel 134 G4
Isla de la Juventud 134 H4
Isla de los Estados 142 J9
Isla de Malpelo 140 A3
Isla de Margarita 140 E1
Isla de Providencia 134 H6
Isla de San Andrés 134 H6
Isla de São Francisco 142 M4
Isla de São Sebastião 142 M3
Isla Desolación 142 F9
Isla Española 140 (1)B2
Isla Fernandina 140 (1)A2
Isla Gorgona 140 B3
Isla Grande 142 N3
Isla Grande de Tierra del Fuego 142 H9
Isla Guafo 142 F7
Isla Hoste 142 G10
Isla Isabela 140 (1)A2
Isla La Tortuga 140 D1
Isla Londonderry 142 G9
Islamabad 88 B2
Isla Madre de Dios 142 F8/9
Isla Marchena 140 (1)A1
Islamgarh 88 B3
Islamorada 130 E5
Isla Navarino 142 H10
Island Lake 122 M6
Islands of the Four Mountains 132 (1)C5
Isla Pinta 140 (1)A1
Isla Puná 140 A4
Isla Riesco 142 G9
Isla Robinson Crusoe 142 E5
Isla San Benedicto 134 B5
Isla San Cristóbal 140 (1)B2
Isla San Salvador 140 (1)A2
Isla Santa Cruz 140 (1)A2
Isla Santa Inés 142 F9
Isla Santa María 140 (1)A2
Islas Baleares 60 N5
Islas Canarias 98 A3
Islas Canarias 102 B3
Islas Columbretes 60 L5
Islas de la Bahía 134 G5
Islas de los Desventurados 142 E4
Islas Galápagos 140 (1)B1
Islas Juan Fernández 142 E5
Islas Los Roques 140 D1
Islas Marías 134 C4
Islas Socorro 134 B5
Islas Revillagigedo 134 B5
Islas Wollaston 142 H10
Isla Wellington 142 F8
Islay 56 F6
Isle 58 F8
Isle of Man 56 H7
Isle of Wight 56 L11
Isle Royale 128 C1
Isles of Scilly 56 F12
Ismâ'ilîya 100 F1
İsmayıllı 92 N3
Isna 100 F2
Isoka 108 E2
Isola delle Correnti 64 J12
Isola di Capo Rizzuto 64 M10
Isola di Pantelleria 64 G12
Isole Égadi 64 F11
Isole Lipari 64 J10
Isole Ponziane 64 H8
Isole Tremiti 64 K6
Iso-Vietonen 48 N3
Isparta 68 N7
Ispica 64 J12
Israel 94 B5
Israelite Bay 114 D6
Issia 104 C3
Issimu 87 B2
Issoire 58 J8
Issoudun 58 H7
İstanbul 92 C3
İstanbul Boğazı 92 C3
Istiaia 68 F6
Istmo de Tehauntepec 134 F5
Istra 62 J5
Istres 58 K10
Itaberaba 140 J6
Itabira 140 J7
Itabuna 140 K6
Itacoatiara 140 F4
Itaituba 140 F4
Itajaí 142 M4
Italy 64 E4
Itambacuri 140 J7
Itanagar 88 F3
Itapebi 140 K7
Itapetinga 140 J7
Itapicuru 140 K6
Itapicuru Mirim 140 J4
Itapipoca 140 K4
Itarsi 88 C4
Ithaca 128 E2
Ithaki 68 C6
Ithaki 68 C6
Itiquira 140 F/G7
Ituí 140 C5
Ituiutaba 140 H7
Itumbiara 140 H7
Ituni 140 F2
Ituri 106 D3
Ituxi 140 D5
Itzehoe 52 E3
Iuaretê 140 D3
Iutica 140 D3
Ivalo 48 P2
Ivanava 48 N10
Ivangrad 66 G7
Ivanhoe, *Australia* 114 H6
Ivanhoe, *US* 128 A2
Ivano-Frankivs'k 70 D5
Ivanovo 70 H3
Ivatsevichy 48 N10
Ivdel' 70 M2
Ivittuut 122 X4
Ivohibe 108 H4
Ivosjön 50 D1
Ivrea 62 C5
Ivujivik 122 R4
Iwaki 82 L5
Iwamizawa 82 L2
Iwo 104 E3
Iyo-nadā 82 G7
Izberbash 92 M2

Izegern 54 F4
Izhevsk 70 K3
Izhma 70 K1
Izhma 70 K2
Izk 90 G5
Izkī 95 G5
Izmayil 66 R4
Izmir 92 B4
Izmir Körfezi 68 J6
Izmit 92 C3
Iznik 92 C3
Iznik Gölü 92 C3
Izola 62 J5
Izra' 94 D4
Izuhara 82 E6
Izumo 82 G6
Izu-shotō 82 K6

J

Jabal ad Durūz 94 D4
Jabal Akhḍar 95 G5
Jabal al Nuṣayrīyah 94 D1
Jabal an Nabī Shu'ayb 100 H4
Jabal Ash Sham 95 G5
Jabal aẓ Ẓannah 95 E4
Jabalpur 88 C4
Jabal Shammar 100 G2
Jabal Thamar 100 J5
Jabiru 114 F2
Jablah 94 C1
Jablonec 50 E7
Jablunkov 50 H8
Jaboatão 140 K5
Jaca 60 K2
Jacareacanga 140 F5
Jackman 128 F1
Jacksboro 130 B3
Jackson, Calif., US 126 B3
Jackson, Minn., US 128 B2
Jackson, Miss., US 130 C3
Jackson, Oh., US 130 E2
Jackson, Tenn., US 130 D2
Jackson Head 116 B6
Jackson Lake 126 D2
Jacksonville, Fla., US 130 E3
Jacksonville, Ill., US 128 B3
Jacksonville, N.C., US 130 F3
Jacksonville, Tex., US 130 B3
Jacmel 134 K5
Jacobabad 88 A3
Jacobina 140 J6
Jacunda 140 H4
Jacupiranga 142 M3
Jade 52 D3
Jadebusen 52 D3
Jādū 102 H2
Jaén 60 G7
Jaen 140 B5
Jaffna 88 D7
Jagdalpur 88 D5
Jagersfontein 108 D5
Jaggang 88 C2
Jagst 52 E7
Jahrom 95 E2
Jaipur 88 C3
Jaisalmer 88 B3
Jajce 66 E5
Jakarta 86 D4
Jäkkvik 48 J3
Jakobshavn = Ilulissat 122 W3
Jakobstad 48 M5
Jalālābād 88 B2
Jalandhar 88 C2
Jalapa Enriquez 134 E5
Jalgaon 88 C4
Jalībah 95 B1
Jalingo 104 G3
Jalna 88 C5
Jalón 60 J3
Jalpaiguri 88 E3
Jālū 100 D2
Jalūlā 92 L6
Jamaica 134 H5
Jamalpur 88 E3
Jambi 86 C3
James 126 G2
James Bay 122 Q6
Jamestown, N.Y., US 128 E2
Jamestown, N.D., US 126 G1
Jammerbugten 48 E8
Jammu 88 B2
Jammu and Kashmir 88 C2
Jamnagar 88 B4
Jämsä 48 N6
Jamshedpur 88 E4
Janakpur 88 E3
Janaúba 140 J7
Jandaq 90 F3
Jandongi 106 C3
Jane Peak 116 B7
Janesville 128 C2
Jan Mayen 120 C2
Jannatabad 76 L10
Janos 132 E2
Jánossomorja 62 N3
Janów Lubelski 50 M7
Jantarnyj 50 J3
Januária 140 J7
Jaora 88 C4
Japan 82 L5
Japan Trench 112 E2
Japurá 140 D4
Jarābulus 92 H5
Jaramillo 142 H8
Jarash 94 C4
Jardim 142 K3
Jarosław 50 M7
Järpen 48 G5
Jarud Qi 80 G2
Järvenpää 48 N6
Jarvis 112 K6
Jasel'da 48 N10
Jāsk 95 G4
Jason Islands 142 J9
Jasper, Al., US 130 D3
Jasper, Fla., US 130 E3
Jasper, Tex., US 130 C3
Jastrebarsko 62 L5
Jászberény 66 G2
Jataí 140 G7
Jatapu 140 F4
Jaunpur 88 D3
Java = Jawa 86 E4
Javarthushuu 78 J7
Javoriv 50 N8
Jawa 86 E4
Jawhar 106 H3
Jayapura 87 F3
Jayrūd 94 D3
Jazā'ir Farasān 100 H4
Jazīrat Būbīyān 95 C2
Jazīrat-ye Khārk 95 D2
Jbail 94 C2
Jbel Ayachi 102 E2
Jbel Bou Naceur 102 E2
Jbel Toubkal 102 D2
Jean 126 C3
Jebba 104 E3
Jebel Bāqir 94 C7
Jebel el Atā'ita 94 C6
Jebel el Batrā 94 C7
Jebel-esh Sharqi 94 C3
Jebel Gimbala 100 D5
Jebel Ithrīyat 94 D6
Jebel Liban 94 C3
Jebel Mubrak 94 C6
Jebel Ram 94 C7
Jebel Uweinat 100 E3
Jedburgh 56 K6
Jedda = Jiddah 90 C5
Jedeida 64 D12
Jędrzejów 50 K7
Jefferson 128 B2
Jefferson City, Mo., US 128 B3
Jefferson City, Tenn., US 130 E2
Jeffersonville 128 C3
Jega 104 E2
Jēkabpils 48 N8
Jelgava 48 M8
Jemaja 86 D2
Jena 52 G6
Jendouba 102 G1
Jenin 94 C4
Jenkins 128 D3
Jequié 140 J6
Jequitinhonha 140 J7
Jerada 102 E2
Jeremoabo 140 K6
Jerez 132 F4
Jerez de la Frontera 60 D8
Jerez de los Caballeros 60 D6
Jericho, Australia 114 J4
Jericho, Israel 94 C5
Jerramungup 114 C6
Jersey 58 C4
Jersey City 130 G1
Jerusalem = Yerushalayim 94 C5
Jesenice 66 B3
Jesenik 50 G7
Jesi 62 J7
Jessore 88 E4
Jesup 130 E3
Jeumont 54 G4
Jever 52 C3
Jeypore 88 D5
Jezioro 50 D4
Jezioro Gardno 48 J9
Jezioro Jeziorsko 50 H6
Jezioro Łebsko 50 F3
Jezioro Śniardwy 50 L4
Jezioro Wigry 50 N2
Jezzine 94 C3
Jhang Maghiana 88 B2
Jhansi 88 C3
Jharsuguda 88 D4
Jhelum 88 B2
Jialing Jiang 80 D4
Jiamusi 80 J1
Ji'an 80 E5
Jiangle 80 F5
Jiangling 80 E4
Jiangmen 80 E6
Jiangyou 80 C4
Jianyang 80 F5
Jiaonan 80 F3
Jiaozou 80 E3
Jiaxing 80 G4
Jiayuguan 80 B3
Jibou 66 L2
Jičín 50 E7
Jiddah 90 C5
Jiesjavrre 48 N2
Jiexiu 80 E3
Jihlava 50 E8
Jijia 66 Q2
Jijiga 106 G2
Jilib 106 G3
Jilin 82 D2
Jima 106 F2
Jimbolia 66 H4
Jiménez 132 F3
Jimsar 76 R9
Jinan 80 F3
Jinapo Hu 82 E2
Jinchang 80 C3
Jincheng 80 E3
Jindřichův Hradec 50 E8
Jingdezhen 80 F5
Jinggu 80 C6
Jinghe 76 Q9
Jinghong 80 C6
Jingmen 80 E4
Jingning 80 D3
Jingxi 80 D6
Jingyuan 80 C3
Jinhua 80 F5
Jining, China 80 E2
Jining, China 80 F3
Jinja 106 E3
Jinka 106 F2
Jinsha 80 C5
Jinshi 80 E5
Jinta 80 B2
Jinxi 80 G2
Jinzhou 80 G2
Jirgatol 90 K2
Jirin Gol 80 F2
Jirkov 52 J6
Jīroft 95 G2
Jirriiban 106 H2
Jishou 80 D5
Jisr ash Shughūr 92 G6
Jiu 66 L4
Jiujiang 80 F5
Jiwani 90 H4
Jixi 82 F1
Jīzān 100 H4
Jizera 50 D7
J. J. Castelli 140 D4
Joal-Fadiout 102 B6
João Pessoa 140 L5
Jódar 60 G7
Jodhpur 88 B3
Joensuu 70 E2
Jōetsu 82 K5
Jõgeva 48 P7
Johannesburg, South Africa 108 D5
Johannesburg, US 132 C1
John Day 126 C2
John o' Groats 56 J3
John Redmond Reservoir 130 B2
Johnson 130 A2
Johnson City 128 D3
Johnson's Crossing 132 (1)L3
Johnston Island 112 J4
Johnstown 128 E2
Johor Bahru 86 C2
Joigny 58 J5
Joinville, Brazil 142 M4
Joinville, France 58 L5
Jokkmokk 48 K3
Jökulsa á Fjöllum 48 (1)E1
Jolfa 92 L4
Joliet 124 J3
Joliette 128 F1
Jolo 87 B1
Jolo 87 B1
Jonava 50 P2
Jonesboro 128 B3
Jones Sound 122 P1
Jonesville 130 C3
Jonglei Canal 106 E2
Jongunjärvi 48 P4
Joniškis 50 N1
Jönköping 48 H8
Jonquière 128 F1
Joplin 130 C2
Jordan 94 D5
Jordan 126 E1
Jordan Valley 126 C2
Jorhat 88 F3
Jörn 48 L4
Jos 104 F3
José de San Martin 142 G7
Joseph Bonaparte Gulf 114 E2
Joûnié 94 C2
Joure 54 H2
Juan de Nova 108 G3
Juàzeiro 140 J5
Juàzeiro do Norte 140 K5
Juba 106 E3
Jubba 106 G3
Júcar 60 J5
Juchitán 134 F5
Judenburg 62 K3
Juhre 78 L8
Juist 52 B3
Juiz de Fora 142 N3
Julesburg 126 F2
Juli 140 C7
Juliaca 140 C7
Juliana Top 140 F3
Jülich 54 J4
Jullouville 54 A6
Jumilla 60 J6
Jumla 88 D3
Junagadh 88 B4
Junction 130 B3
Junction City 130 B2
Jundah 114 H4
Juneau 132 (1)L4
Jungfrau 62 C4
Junggar Pendi 76 R8
Junsele 48 J5
Jun Xian 80 E4
Jūra 50 M2
Jura 56 G5
Jura 62 B4
Jurbarkas 50 M2
Jurf ed Darāwīsh 94 C6
Jurhe 80 G2
Jurilovca 66 R5
Jūrmala 48 M8
Jūrmala 70 D3
Juruá 140 D4
Juruena 140 F5
Juruena 140 F6
Justo Daract 142 H5
Jutaí 140 D5
Jüterbog 52 J5
Juwain 90 H3
Ju Xian 80 F3
Jūymand 90 G3
Jūyom 95 F2
Juzur al Halaniyat 90 G6
Jylland 48 E8
Jyvädskylä 70 E2
Jyväskylä 48 N5

K

K2 88 C1
Kaakhka 90 G2
Kaamanen 48 P2
Kaaresuvanto 48 M2
Kaarta 102 C6
Kabaena 87 B4
Kabakly 90 H2
Kabala 104 B3
Kabale 106 E4
Kabalo 106 D5
Kabardino-Balkariya 92 K2
Kåbdalis 48 L3
Kabompo 108 C2
Kabongo 106 D5
Kabugao 84 G3
Kābul 90 J3
Kabwe 108 D2
Kachikattsy 78 M4
Kachug 78 H6
Kadama 88 B6
Kadañ 50 C7
Kadınhanı 68 Q6
Kadirli 92 G5
Kadoka 126 F2
Kadoma 108 D3
Kadugli 100 E5
Kaduna 104 F2
Kadzherom 70 L2
Kaédi 102 C5
Kaeo 116 D2
Kaesŏng 82 D5
Kāf 94 E5
Kafanchan 104 F3
Kaffrine 104 A2
Kafiau 87 C3
Kåfjord 48 N1
Kafr Buhum 94 D1
Kafr el Sheikh 100 F1
Kafue 108 D3
Kaga 82 J5
Kaga Bandoro 106 B2
Kagoshima 82 F8
Kahemba 106 B5
Kahnūj 95 G3
Kahraman Maraş 92 G5
Kahta 92 H5
Kahurangi Point 116 C5
Kaiama 104 E3
Kai Besar 87 D4
Kaifeng 80 E4
Kaihu 116 D2
Kaihua 80 F5
Kai Kecil 87 D4
Kaikohe 116 D2
Kaikoura 116 D6
Kaili 80 D5
Kailua 132 (2)D2
Kailua Kona 132 (2)E4
Kaimana 87 D3
Käina 48 M7
Kainji Reservoir 104 E2
Kaipara Harbour 116 D3
Kairouan 102 H1
Kaiserslautern 52 C7
Kaišiadorys 50 P3
Kaitaia 116 D2
Kaiwatu 87 C4
Kaiyuan 84 C2
Kajaani 48 P4
Kakamega 106 E3
Kakata 104 B3
Kakhovs'ke Vodoskhovyshche 70 F5
Kākī 95 D2
Kākināda 88 D5
Kaktovik 132 (1)J1
Kalabagh 88 B2
Kalabahi 87 B4
Kalabakan 86 F2
Kalach 70 H4
Kalachinsk 70 P3
Kalach-na-Donu 70 H5
Kaladar 128 E2
Ka Lae 132 (2)F5
Kalahari Desert 108 C4
Kalajoki 48 M4
Kalakan 78 K5
Kalam 88 B1
Kalamata 68 E7
Kalamazoo 128 C2
Kalampaka 68 D5
Kalana 104 C2
Kalaotoa 87 B4
Kalapana 132 (2)G4
Kalaupapa 132 (2)E2
Kalavryta 68 E6
Kalbarri 114 B5
Kale 68 L7
Kalecik 92 E3
Kaledupa 87 B4
Kalemie 106 D5
Kalemyo 88 F4
Kalevala 48 R4
Kalewa 88 F4
Kalgoorlie 114 D6
Kalianda 86 D4
Kalibo 84 G4
Kalima 106 D4
Kalimantan 86 E2
Kaliningrad 50 K3
Kaliningradskij Zaliv 50 J3
Kalispell 126 D1
Kalisz 50 H6
Kalixälven 48 M3

Kalkan	68	M8
Kalkarindji	114	F3
Kalkaska	128	C2
Kallavesi	48	P5
Kallsjön	48	G5
Kalmar	48	J8
Kalmykiya	92	M1
Kalmykovo	70	K5
Kalocsa	66	F3
Kalol	88	B4
Kalpakio	68	C5
Kalpeni	88	B6
Kaltag	132	(1)F3
Kaltenkirchen	52	E3
Kaluga	70	G4
Kalyan	88	B5
Kalymnos	68	J7
Kalymnos	68	J8
Kama	46	K1
Kama	106	D4
Kamaishi	82	L4
Kaman	92	E4
Kamande	106	D4
Kamango	76	U6
Kamares	68	G8
Kambarka	70	K3
Kambo Ho	82	E3
Kamchatka	78	U6
Kamchatskiy Zaliv	78	U5
Kamenica	68	E2
Kamenka, *Russia*	70	H1
Kamenka, *Russia*	70	H4
Kamen'-na-Obi	76	Q7
Kamen'-Rybolov	82	F1
Kamensk-Shakhtinskiy	70	H5
Kamensk-Ural'skiy	70	M3
Kamenz	50	D6
Kamet	88	C2
Kamiiso	82	L3
Kamina	106	C5
Kamitsushima	82	E6
Kamituga	106	D4
Kamiyaku	82	F8
Kamloops	122	G6
Kamoenai	82	L2
Kampala	106	E3
Kampen	54	H2
Kampong Cham	84	D4
Kâmpóng Chhnăng	84	C4
Kâmpot	84	C4
Kamsuuma	106	G3
Kam"yanets'-Podil's'kyy	70	E5
Kamyanyets	48	M10
Kāmyārān	92	M6
Kamyshin	70	J4
Kamyzyak	70	J5
Kan	100	F6
Kanab	132	D1
Kananga	106	C5
Kanazawa	82	J5
Kanbalu	88	G4
Kanchipuram	88	C6
Kandahār	90	J3
Kandalaksha	48	S3
Kandalakshskiy Zaliv	70	F1
Kandi	104	E2
Kandira	68	N3
Kandy	88	D7
Kane	128	E2
Kaneohe	132	(2)D2
Kang	108	C4
Kangaatsiaq	122	W3
Kangal	92	G4
Kangān, *Iran*	95	E3
Kangān, *Iran*	95	G4
Kangar	86	C1
Kangaroo Island	114	G7
Kangchenjunga	88	E3
Kangding	80	C4
Kangeq	122	Y4
Kangerluarsoruseq	122	W4
Kangersuatsiaq	122	W2
Kangetet	106	F3
Kanggye	82	D3
Kangiqsualujjuaq	122	T5
Kangiqsujuaq	122	S4
Kangirsuk	122	S4
Kangmar	88	E3
Kangnŭng	82	E5
Kango	104	G4
Kangping	80	G2
Kaniama	106	C5
Kanin Nos	76	G4
Kanji Reservoir	98	D4
Kanjiža	66	H3
Kankaanpää	48	M6
Kankakee	128	C2
Kankan	104	C2
Kankossa	102	C5
Kannapolis	130	E2
Kano	104	F2
Kanoya	82	F8
Kanpur	88	D3
Kansas	130	A2
Kansas	130	B2
Kansas City, *Kans., US*	130	C2
Kansas City, *Mo., US*	130	C2
Kansk	76	T6
Kanta	106	F2
Kantchari	104	E2
Kantemirovka	70	G5
Kanye	108	C4
Kao-Hsiung	80	G6
Kaolack	102	B6
Kaoma	108	C2
Kapanga	106	C5
Kap Arkona	50	C3
Kapchagay	76	P9
Kap Cort Adelaer = Kangeq	122	Y4
Kap Farvel = Uummannarsuaq	122	Y5
Kapfenberg	62	L3
Kapıdağı Yarimadası	68	K4
Kapiri Mposhi	108	D2
Kapit	86	E2
Kapiti Island	116	E5
Kaplice	62	K2
Kapoeta	106	E3
Kaposvár	66	E3
Kappel	52	C6
Kappeln	52	E2
Kappl	62	F3
Kapsan	82	E3
Kapuskasing	124	K2
Kapuvár	66	E2
Kara	76	M4
Kara, *Russia*	76	M4
Kara, *Togo*	104	E3
Kara Ada	68	K8
Kara-Balta	76	N9
Karabekaul	90	H2
Kara-Bogaz-Gol	90	F1
Karabutak	70	M5
Karacabey	68	L4
Karacaköy	68	L3
Karacal Tepe	68	Q8
Karachayevo-Cherkesiya	92	J2
Karachayevsk	92	J2
Karachi	90	J5
Karaganda	76	N8
Karaginskiy Zaliv	78	V5
Karaj	90	F2
Karak	94	C5
Kara-Kala	90	G2
Karakalpakiya	76	K9
Karakoçan	92	J4
Kara-Köl	76	N9
Karakol	76	P9
Karakoram	74	L6
Karaksar	78	K6
Karam	78	H5
Karaman	92	E5
Karamay	76	R8
Karamea	116	D5
Karamea Bight	116	C5
Karamürsel	68	M4
Karand	92	M6
Karaoy	76	N8
Karapınar	68	R7
Kara-Say	76	P9
Karasburg	108	B5
Kara Sea = Karskoye More	76	L3
Karasu	92	D3
Karasuk	76	P7
Karasuk	76	P7
Karatal	76	P8
Karataş	92	F5
Karatobe	70	K5
Karaton	70	K5
Karatsu	82	E7
Karazhal	70	P5
Karbalā'	90	D3
Karcag	66	H2
Karditsa	68	D5
Kärdla	48	M7
Kareliya	48	R4
Karepino	70	L2
Karesuando	48	M2
Kargalinskaya	92	M2
Kargasok	76	Q6
Kargat	76	P6
Kargil	88	C2
Kargopol'	70	G2
Kariba	108	D3
Kariba Dam	108	D3
Karibib	108	B4
Karimata	86	D3
Karimnagar	88	C5
Karkaralinsk	76	P8
Karkinits'ka Zatoka	70	F5
Karlik Shan	80	A2
Karlovac	66	C4
Karlovasi	68	J7
Karlovo	68	G2
Karlovy Vary	52	H6
Karlshamn	50	D1
Karlskoga	48	H7
Karlskrona	48	H8
Karlsruhe	52	D8
Karlstad, *Norway*	48	G7
Karlstad, *US*	128	A1
Karlstadt	52	E7
Karmala	88	C5
Karmi'el	94	C4
Karmøy	48	C7
Karnafuli Reservoir	88	F4
Karnal	88	C3
Karnische Alpen	62	H4
Karnobat	68	J2
Karodi	90	J4
Karonga	106	E5
Karpathos	68	K9
Karpathos	68	K9
Karpenisi	68	D6
Karpogory	70	H2
Karrabük	92	E3
Karratha	114	C4
Kars	92	K3
Karsakpay	70	N5
Kärsava	48	P8
Karshi	90	J2
Karskoye More	76	L3
Karslyaka	68	K6
Karstula	48	N5
Kartal	68	M4
Kartaly	70	M4
Kartayel'	70	K2
Kartuzy	50	H3
Karufa	87	D3
Karumba	114	H3
Karur	88	C6
Karvina	50	H8
Karwar	88	B6
Karystos	68	G6
Kasai	106	B4
Kasaji	108	C2
Kasama	108	E2
Kasansay	76	N9
Kasba Lake	122	L4
Kasempa	108	D2
Kasenga	108	D2
Kāshān	90	F3
Kashi	90	L2
Kashima	80	L3
Kashiwazaki	82	K5
Kāshmar	90	G2
Kashmor	90	J4
Kasimov	70	H4
Kasli	70	M3
Kasongo	106	D4
Kasos	68	K9
Kaspi	92	L3
Kaspiysk	92	M2
Kassala	100	G4
Kassandreia	68	F4
Kassel	52	E5
Kasserine	102	G1
Kastamonu	92	E3
Kastelli	68	F9
Kastoria	68	D4
Kasulu	106	E4
Kasumkent	92	N3
Kasur	88	B2
Kata	78	G5
Katchall	88	F7
Katerini	68	E4
Katete	108	E2
Katha	88	G4
Katherine	114	F2
Kathiawar	90	K5
Kathmandu	88	E3
Kati	104	C2
Katihar	88	E3
Katiola	104	C3
Kato Nevrokopi	68	F3
Katonga	106	E3
Katoomba	114	K6
Katowice	50	J7
Katrineholm	48	J7
Katsina	104	F2
Katsina-Ala	104	F3
Katsuta	82	L5
Katsuura	82	L6
Kattakurgan	90	J2
Kattavia	68	K9
Kattegat	48	F8
Katun'	76	R7
Katwijkaan Zee	54	G2
Kauai	132	(2)B1
Kaufbeuren	62	F3
Kauhajoki	48	M5
Kaunas	50	N3
Kauno	50	P3
Kaunus	46	G2
Kaura Namoda	104	F2
Kavadarci	68	D3
Kavajë	68	B3
Kavala	68	G4
Kavali	88	C5
Kavār	95	E2
Kavaratti	88	B6
Kavarna	66	R6
Kawabe	82	L4
Kawagoe	82	K6
Kawakawa	116	E2
Kawambwa	106	D5
Kawasaki	82	K6
Kawau Island	116	E3
Kaweka	116	F4
Kawhia	116	E4
Kawkareik	84	B3
Kawthaung	84	B4
Kaya	104	D2
Kayak	76	U3
Kaycee	126	E2
Kayenta	132	D1
Kayes	104	B2
Kaymaz	68	P5
Kaynar	76	P8
Kayseri	92	F4
Kayyerkan	76	R4
Kazachinskoye	78	E5
Kazach'ye	78	P2
Kazakdar'ya	76	K9
Kazakhstan	76	L8
Kazan'	70	J3
Kazan	122	M4
Kazanlŭk	68	H2
Kazan-rettō	112	E3
Kazbek	92	L2
Käzerūn	95	D2
Kazincbarcika	66	H1
Kazungula	108	D3
Kazuno	82	L3
Kazymskiy Mys	76	M5
Kea	68	G7
Kea	68	G7
Kearney	124	G3
Keban Barajı	92	H4
Kébémèr	102	B5
Kebkabiya	100	D5
Kebnekajse	48	K3
K'ebrī Dehar	106	G2
K'ech'a Terara	106	F2
Keçiborlu	68	N7
Kecskemet	66	G3
Kėdainiai	50	N2
Kedgwick	128	G1
Kediri	86	E4
Kédougou	104	B2
Kędzierzyn-Koźle	50	H7
Keele	132	(1)M3
Keene	128	F2
Keetmanshoop	108	B5
Keewatin	128	B1
Kefallonia	68	C6
Kefamenanu	87	B4
Keflavík	48	(1)B2
Kegen'	76	P9
Keg River	122	H5
Keheili	100	F4
Kehl	62	C2
Keila	48	N7
Keitele	48	N5
Kekerengu	116	D5
Kékes	66	H2
Kelai Thiladhunmathee Atoll	88	B7
Kelheim	62	G2
Kelibia	64	F12
Kelkit	92	G3
Kelmë	50	M2
Kélo	104	H3
Kelowna	122	H7
Kelso	126	B1
Keluang	86	C2
Kem'	70	F2
Kemaliye	92	H4
Kemalpaşa	68	K6
Kemasik	86	C2
Kemer, *Turkey*	68	M8
Kemer, *Turkey*	68	N8
Kemerovo	76	R6
Kemi	48	N4
Kemijärvi	48	P3
Kemijärvi	48	P3
Kemijoki	48	P3
Kemmerer	126	D3
Kemmuna	64	J12
Kemnath	52	G7
Kemp's Bay	130	F5
Kempten	62	F3
Kendal	56	K7
Kendall	130	E4
Kendari	87	B3
Kendawangan	86	E3
Kendégué	104	H2
Kendujhargarh	88	E4
Kenedy	130	B4
Kenema	104	B3
Keneurgench	90	G1
Kenge	106	B4
Kengtung	84	B2
Kenhardt	108	C5
Kénitra	102	D2
Kenmare	56	C10
Kennett	130	D2
Kennewick	126	C1
Keno Hill	132	(1)K3
Kenora	124	H2
Kenosha	128	C2
Kentau	76	M9
Kentucky	124	J4
Kentwood	130	C3
Kenya	98	G5
Keokuk	128	B2
Kępno	50	H6
Kepulauan Anambas	86	D2
Kepulauan Aru	87	E4
Kepulauan Ayu	87	D2
Kepulauan Balabalangan	86	F3
Kepulauan Banggai	87	B3
Kepulauan Barat Daya	87	C4
Kepulauan Batu	86	B3
Kepulauan Bonerate	87	A4
Kepulauan Kai	87	D4
Kepulauan Kangean	86	F4
Kepulauan Karimunjawa	86	D4
Kepulauan Karkaralong	87	B2
Kepulauan Laut Kecil	86	F3
Kepulauan Leti	87	C4
Kepulauan Lingga	86	C2
Kepulauan Lucipara	87	C4
Kepulauan Mentawai	86	B3
Kepulauan Nanusa	87	C2
Kepulauan Natuna	86	D2
Kepulauan Riau	86	C2
Kepulauan Sabalana	86	F4
Kepulauan Sangir	87	C2
Kepulauan Solor	87	B4
Kepulauan Sula	87	B3
Kepulauan Talaud	87	C2
Kepulauan Tanimbar	87	D4
Kepulauan Tengah	86	F4
Kepulauan Togian	87	B3
Kepulauan Tukangbesi	87	B4
Kepulauan Watubela	87	D3
Kerch	92	G1
Kerchevskiy	70	L3
Kerempe Burnu	68	R2
Keren	100	G4
Kericho	106	F4
Kerikeri	116	D2
Kerio	106	F3
Kerki	90	J2
Kerkrade	54	J4
Kerkyra	68	B5
Kerkyra	68	B5
Kerma	100	F4
Kermadec Islands	112	H8
Kermadec Trench	112	J9
Kermān	95	G1
Kermānshāh	90	E3
Kermānshāhān	95	F1
Keros	68	H8
Kerpen	54	J4
Kerrville	130	B3
Kerulen	78	J7
Keryneia	92	E6
Keşan	68	J4
Kesennuma	82	L4
Keşiş Dağları	90	C2
Keszthely	66	E3
Keta	104	E3
Ketapang	86	D3
Ketchikan	132	(1)L4
Kêtou	104	E3
Kętrzyn	50	L3
Kettering	56	M9

Kettle Falls	124	C2
Kewanee	128	C2
Keweenaw Peninsula	128	C1
Key Largo	130	E4
Keystone Lake	130	B2
Key West	130	E5
Kezhma	78	G5
Kežmarok	50	K8
Khabarovsk	78	P7
Khadyzhensk	92	H1
Khakasiya	76	R7
Khairwāra	88	B4
Khalafabād	95	C1
Khalīg el Suweis	100	F2
Khalīj Surt	100	C1
Khalūf	90	G5
Khambhat	88	B4
Khamis Mushay	90	D6
Khamis Mushayt	100	H4
Khamkkeut	84	C3
Khampa	78	L4
Khamrà	78	J4
Khān al Baghdādī	92	K7
Khān az Zabīb	94	D5
Khandagayty	76	S7
Khandwa	88	C4
Khanewal	88	B2
Khannya	76	X4
Khanpur	88	B3
Khān Shaykhūn	94	D1
Khantau	76	N9
Khantayka	78	D3
Khanty-Mansiysk	70	N2
Khān Yūnis	94	B5
Khapalu	88	C1
Kharabali	70	J5
Kharagpur	88	E4
Kharampur	78	B4
Kharan	90	J4
Khargon	88	C4
Kharkiv	70	G5
Kharlu	48	R6
Kharmanli	68	H3
Kharnmam	88	D5
Kharovsk	70	H3
Khartoum = El Khartum	100	F4
Khasavyurt	92	M2
Khāsh	90	H4
Khashgort	70	N1
Khashm el Girba	100	G4
Khashuri	92	K3
Khaskovo	68	H3
Khatanga	78	G2
Khātūnābād	95	F1
Khatyrka	78	X4
Khavda	90	J5
Khawr Fakkān	95	G4
Khaydarken	90	K2
Khayelitsha	108	B6
Khemis Miliana	102	F1
Khemisset	102	D2
Khenchela	102	G1
Kherāmeh	95	E2
Kherson	70	F5
Kheta	76	T3
Kheta	76	T3
Kheygiyakha	70	P2
Khilok	78	J6
Khirbat Isrīyah	94	E1
Khīyāv	92	M4
Khmel'nyts'kyy	70	E5
Khodā Afarīn	92	M4
Kholmsk	78	Q7
Khonj	95	E3
Khon Kaen	84	C3
Khonuu	78	Q3
Khoper	70	H4
Khor	78	P7
Khor	78	P7
Khoreyver	70	L1
Khorinsk	78	H6
Khorramābād	90	E3
Khorramshahr	95	C1
Khorugh	90	K2
Khoseda Khard	70	L1
Khouribga	102	D2
Khrebet Cherskogo	78	P3
Khrebet Dzhagdy	78	N6
Khrebet Dzhugdzhur	78	N5
Khrebet Khamar Daban	78	G6
Khrebet Kolymskiy	74	U3
Khrebet Kopet Dag	90	G2
Khrebet Suntar Khayata	78	P4
Khrebet Tarbagatay	76	Q8
Khroma	78	Q2
Khudoseya	78	C3
Khudzhakh	78	R4
Khujand	90	J1
Khulna	88	E4
Khurays	95	B4
Khushab	88	B2
Khust	66	L1
Khuwei	100	E5
Khuzdar	90	J4
Khvormūj	95	D2
Khvoy	92	L4
Khyber Pass	90	K3
Kibaya	106	F4
Kibombo	106	D4
Kibondo	106	E4
Kibre Mengist	106	F2
Kičevo	68	C3
Kichmengskiy Gorodok	70	J3
Kicking Horse Pass	122	H6
Kidal	102	F5
Kidderminster	56	K9
Kidira	104	B2
Kiel	52	F2
Kielce	50	K7
Kieler Bucht	52	F2
Kiev = Kyyiv	70	F4
Kiffa	102	C5
Kigali	106	E4
Kigoma	106	D4
Kihnu	48	M7
Kıkıköy	68	L3
Kikinda	66	H4
Kikonai	82	L3
Kikori	87	F4
Kikwit	106	B5
Kilchu	82	E3
Kilifi	106	F4
Kilindoni	106	F5
Kilingi-Nõmme	48	N7
Kilis	92	G5
Kiliya	66	S4
Kilkenny	56	E9
Kilkis	68	E4
Killarney, *Canada*	128	D1
Killarney, *Ireland*	56	C9
Kilmarnock	56	H6
Kil'mez	70	K3
Kilosa	106	F5
Kilrush	56	C9
Kilttan	88	B6
Kilwa	106	D5
Kilwa Masoko	106	F5
Kimberley	108	C5
Kimberley Plateau	114	E3
Kimch'aek	82	E3
Kimolos	68	G8
Kimongo	104	G5
Kimry	70	G3
Kinango	106	F4
Kincardine	128	D2
Kinda	106	C5
Kinder	130	C3
Kindia	104	B2
Kindu	106	D4
Kineshma	70	H3
Kingaroy	114	K5
King City	126	B3
King George Islands	122	R5
Kingisepp	48	Q7
King Island, *Australia*	114	H7
King Island, *Canada*	78	AA3
Kingman	132	D1
Kingri	90	J3
Kingscote	114	G7
Kingsland	130	E3
King's Lynn	56	N9
King Sound	114	D3
Kings Peak	126	D2
Kingsport	130	E2
Kingston, *Canada*	128	E2
Kingston, *Jamaica*	134	J5
Kingston, *US*	128	F2
Kingston-upon-Hull	56	M8
Kingston upon Thames	54	B3
Kingstown	140	E1
Kingsville	130	B4
Kingville	134	E3
King William Island	122	M3
King William's Town	108	D6
Kinik	68	K5
Kinka-san	82	L4
Kinna	48	G8
Kinsale	56	D10
Kinshasa	106	B4
Kinsley	130	B2
Kinston	128	E3
Kintampo	104	D3
Kintyre	56	G6
Kinyeti	106	E3
Kinzig	52	E6
Kipini	106	G4
Kipnuk	132	(1)E3
Kirchheim	62	E2
Kirchheimbolanden	54	L5
Kirenga	78	H5
Kirensk	78	H5
Kiribati	112	J6
Kırıkhan	92	G5
Kırıkkale	92	E4
Kirillov	70	G3
Kirinyaga	106	F4
Kirishi	70	F3
Kiritimati	112	L5
Kirkağaç	68	K5
Kirk Bulāg Dāgh	90	E2
Kirkcaldy	56	J5
Kirkcudbright	56	H7
Kirkjubæjarklaustur	48	(1)E3
Kirkland Lake	128	D1
Kırklareli	68	K3
Kirkūk	92	L6
Kirkwall	56	K3
Kirov, *Kyrgyzstan*	76	N9
Kirov, *Russia*	70	F4
Kirov, *Russia*	70	J3
Kirovohrad	70	F5
Kiroyo-Chepetsk	70	K3
Kirriemuir	56	K5
Kirs	70	K3
Kirsanov	70	H4
Kırşehir	92	F4
Kiruna	48	L3
Kiryū	82	K5
Kisangani	106	D3
Kisbér	66	E2
Kiselevsk	76	R7
Kishanganj	88	E3
Kishangarh, *India*	88	B3
Kishangarh, *India*	88	B3
Kishi	104	E3
Kishiwada	82	H6
Kishtwar	88	C2
Kisii	106	E4
Kiska Island	132	(3)B1
Kiskőrös	66	G3
Kiskunfélegyháza	66	G3
Kiskunhalas	66	G3
Kiskunmajsa	66	G3
Kislovodsk	92	K2
Kismaayo	106	G4
Kissidougou	104	B3
Kisumu	106	E4
Kisvárda	66	K1
Kita	104	C2
Kitakami	82	L4
Kita-Kyūshū	80	H4
Kita-Kyūshū	82	F7
Kitami	82	M2
Kitchener	128	D2
Kitgum	106	E3
Kitimat	122	F6
Kittilä	48	N3
Kitunda	106	E5
Kitwe	108	D2
Kitzingen	52	F7
Kiuruvesi	48	P5
Kivijärvi	48	N5
Kivik	50	D2
Kiya	78	D5
Kıyıköy	92	C3
Kizel	70	L3
Kizilalan	68	R8
Kızılcahamam	92	E3
Kızılırmak	92	F3
Kızılkaya	68	N7
Kizil'skoye	70	L4
Kızıltepe	92	J5
Kizlyar	92	M2
Kizlyarskiy Zaliv	92	M1
Kizyl-Atrek	76	J10
Kladanj	66	F5
Kladno	50	D7
Klagenfurt	62	K4
Klaipėda	48	L9
Klamath	126	B2
Klamath	126	B2
Klamath Falls	126	B2
Klarälven	48	G6
Klatovy	52	J7
Klaus	62	K3
Klerksdorp	108	D5
Kleve	52	B5
Klin	70	G3
Klingenthal	52	H6
Klínovec	52	H6
Klintsy	70	F4
Ključ	62	M6
Kłobuck	50	H7
Kłodzko	50	F7
Kløfta	48	F6
Klosterneuburg	62	M2
Klosters	62	E4
Kluane	122	D4
Kluane Lake	132	(1)J3
Kluczbork	50	H7
Klyuchevskaya Sopka	78	U5
Klyuchi	78	U5
Knezha	66	M6
Knin	66	D5
Knittelfeld	66	B2
Knjaževac	66	K6
Knokke-Heist	54	F3
Knoxville	128	D3
Knysna	108	C6
Koba	86	D3
Kōbe	82	H6
Kobe	87	C2
København	48	G9
Kobenni	102	D5
Koblenz	52	C6
Kobo	88	G3
Kobroör	87	E4
Kobryn	50	P5
Kobuk	132	(1)F2
Kobuk	132	(1)F2
Kočani	68	E3
Koçarli	68	K7
Kočevje	66	B4
Koch'ang	82	E6
Ko Chang	84	C4
Kochechum	78	F3
Kōchi	82	G7
Kochi	88	C7
Kochkor	76	P9
Kochki	76	Q7
Kochubey	92	M1
Kodiak	132	(1)G4
Kodiak Island	132	(1)G4
Kodino	70	G2
Kodinsk	78	F5
Kodomari-misaki	82	L3
Kodyma	66	S1
Köflach	66	C2
Kōfu	82	K6
Køge	50	B2
Køge Bugt	50	B2
Kohat	88	B2
Kohima	88	F3
Koh-i-Qaisir	90	H3
Koh-i-Sangan	90	J3
Kohtla-Järve	48	P7
Koidu	104	B3
Koi Sanjaq	92	L6
Koitere	48	R5
Kokenau	87	E3
Kokkola	48	M5
Kokomo	130	D1
Kokpekty	76	Q8
Kokshetau	70	N4
Kokstad	108	D6
Kolaka	87	B3
Kolar	88	C6
Kolari	48	M3
Kolašin	66	G7
Kolda	104	B2
Kolding	48	E9
Kole	106	C4
Kolhapur	88	B5
Kolín	50	E7
Kolkata	88	E6
Kollam	88	C7
Köln	52	B6
Kolno	50	L4
Koło	50	H5
Kołobrzeg	50	E3
Kologriv	70	H3
Kolomna	70	G3
Kolomyya	66	N1
Kolonedale	87	B3
Kolosovka	70	P3
Kolpashevo	76	Q6
Kolpos Agiou Orous	68	F4
Kolpos Kassandras	68	F4
Kolpos Murampelou	68	H9
Kolskijzaliv	48	S2
Kolskiy Poluostrov	70	G1
Kolumadulu Atoll	88	B8
Koluton	70	N4
Kolva	70	L2
Kolwezi	108	D2
Kolyma	78	R4
Kolymskaya Nizmennost'	78	S3
Kolymskaye	78	T3
Komandorskiye Ostrova	78	V5
Komárno	66	F2
Komárom	66	F2
Komatsu	82	J5
Kombe	106	D4
Komi	70	K2
Komló	66	F3
Kom Ombo	100	F3
Komotini	68	H3
Komsa	76	R5
Komsomol'skiy	70	J5
Komsomol'sk-na-Amure	78	P6
Konārka	88	E5
Konda	70	N3
Kondagaon	88	D5
Kondinskoye	70	N3
Kondoa	106	F4
Kondopoga	70	F2
Kondrat'yeva	76	V5
Kondūz	90	J2
Kong Frederick VI Kyst	122	Y4
Kongi	76	R9
Kongola	108	C3
Kongolo	106	D5
Kongsberg	48	E7
Kongur Shan	76	N10
Königsberg = Kaliningrad	50	K3
Königswinter	52	C6
Königs-Wusterhausen	52	J4
Konin	50	H5
Konispol	68	C5
Konitsa	68	C4
Köniz	62	C4
Konjic	66	E6
Konosha	70	H2
Konotop	70	F4
Konstanz	62	E3
Konstinbrod	66	L7
Kontagora	104	F2
Kon Tum	84	D4
Konya	92	E5
Konz	52	B7
Kookynie	114	D5
Kootenai	126	C1
Kootenay Lake	124	C2
Kópasker	48	(1)E1
Kópavogur	48	(1)C2
Koper	62	J5
Kopeysk	70	M3
Köping	48	J7
Koplik	66	G7
Koprivnica	66	D3
Korba, *India*	88	D4
Korba, *Tunisia*	64	E12
Korbach	52	D5
Korçë	68	C4
Korčula	66	D7
Kord Sheykh	95	E2
Korea Bay	82	B4
Korea Strait	82	E6
Korf	78	V4
Korhogo	104	C3
Korinthiakos Kolpos	68	E6
Korinthos	68	F7
Kōriyama	82	L5
Korkino	70	M4
Korkuteli	92	D5
Korla	76	R9
Korliki	78	C4
Körmend	66	D2
Kornat	66	C6
Koroba	87	F4
Köroğlu Dağları	68	Q4
Köroğlu Tepesi	68	P4
Korogwe	106	F5
Koronowo	50	G4
Koror	112	D5
Korosten'	70	E4
Koro Toro	100	C4
Korsakov	78	Q7
Korsør	52	G1
Korti	100	F4
Kortrijk	54	F4
Korumburra	114	J7
Koryakskiy Khrebet	78	V4
Koryazhma	76	H5
Kos	68	K8
Kos	68	K8
Kosa	70	L3
Ko Samui	84	C5
Kościan	50	F5
Kościerzyna	50	H3
Kosciusko	130	D3
Kosh Agach	76	R8
Koshoba	90	F1
Košice	50	L9
Koslan	70	J2
Kosŏng	82	E4
Kosovo	68	C2
Kosovska Mitrovica	68	C2

Kosrae	112	G5
Kostajnica	62	M5
Kostenets	68	F2
Kosti	100	F5
Kostino	78	D3
Kostomuksha	48	R4
Kostroma	70	H3
Kostrzyn	50	D5
Kos'yu	70	L1
Koszalin	50	F3
Kőszeg	66	D2
Kota	88	C3
Kotaagung	86	C4
Kotabaru	86	F3
Kota Belud	86	F1
Kota Bharu	86	C1
Kotabumi	86	C3
Kota Kinabalu	86	F1
Kotamubagu	87	B2
Kotapinang	86	B2
Kotel'nich	70	J3
Kotel'nikovo	70	H5
Köthen	52	G5
Kotido	106	E3
Kotka	48	P6
Kotlas	70	J2
Kotlik	132	(1)E3
Kotor Varoš	66	E5
Kotov'sk	70	E5
Kottagudem	88	D5
Kotte	88	D7
Kotto	106	C2
Kotuy	78	G3
Kotzebue	132	(1)E2
Kotzebue Sound	132	(1)D2
Kouango	104	H3
Koudougou	104	D2
Koufey	104	G2
Koulamoutou	104	G5
Koum	104	G3
Koumra	104	H3
Koundâra	104	B2
Koupéla	102	C6
Kourou	140	G2
Koutiala	104	C2
Kouvola	70	E2
Kovdor	48	R3
Kovel'	70	D4
Kovin	66	H5
Kovrov	70	H3
Kowanyama	114	H3
Köyceğiz	68	L8
Koygorodok	70	K2
Koykuk	132	(1)E3
Koynas	70	J2
Koyukuk	132	(1)F2
Kozan	92	F5
Kozani	68	D4
Kozheynikovo	76	W3
Kozhikode	88	C6
Kozienice	50	L6
Kozloduy	66	L6
Kozlu	68	P3
Kōzu-shima	82	K6
Kpalimé	104	E3
Kraai	108	D6
Krabi	84	B5
Kradeljevo	64	M5
Kragujevac	66	H5
Kraków	50	J7
Kraljeviča	62	K5
Kraljevo	66	H6
Kralovice	50	C8
Kramators'k	70	G5
Kramfors	48	J5
Kranj	66	B3
Krapina	64	K2
Krapinske Toplice	62	L4
Krasino	76	J3
Krāslava	48	P9
Kraśnik	50	M7
Krasnoarmeysk	70	N4
Krasnoborsk	70	J2
Krasnodar	70	G5
Krasnohrad	70	G5
Krasnokamensk	78	K6
Krasnosel'kup	78	C3
Krasnotur'insk	70	M3
Krasnoufimsk	70	L3
Krasnovishersk	70	L2
Krasnoyarsk	78	E5
Krasnoyarskoye Vodokhranilishche	76	S6
Krasnoznamensk	50	M3
Krasnystaw	50	N7
Krasnyy Chikoy	78	H6
Krasnyy Kut	70	J4
Krasnyy Yar	70	J5
Kratovo	68	E2
Kraynovka	92	M2
Krefeld	54	J3
Kremenchuk	70	F5
Kremmling	126	E2
Krems	62	L2
Kremsmünster	62	K2
Krestovka	70	K1
Krestyakh	78	K4
Kretinga	50	L2
Kribi	104	F4
Krichim	68	G2
Krieglach	62	L3
Krishna	88	C5
Krishnagiri	88	C6
Kristiansand	48	E7
Kristianstad	48	H8
Kristiansund	48	D5
Kristinehamn	48	H7
Kristinestad	48	L5
Kriti	68	H10
Kriva Palanka	68	E2
Križevci	66	D3
Krk	62	K5
Krk	62	K5
Kroměříž	50	G8
Kronach	52	G6
Krŏng Kaôh Kŏng	84	C4
Kronotskiy Zaliv	78	U6
Kroonstadt	108	D5
Kroper	64	H3
Kropotkin	70	H5
Krosno	50	L8
Krško	62	L5
Krugë	68	B3
Krui	86	C4
Krumbach	62	F2
Krung Thep	84	C4
Kruså	52	E2
Kruševac	66	J6
Krychaw	70	F4
Krym'	92	E1
Krymsk	92	H1
Krynica	50	L8
Krytiko Pelagos	68	G9
Kryve Ozero	66	T2
Kryvyy Rih	70	F5
Krzna	50	N5
Ksar el Boukhari	60	N9
Ksen'yevka	78	K6
Ksour Essaf	102	H1
Kuala Kerai	86	C1
Kuala Lipis	86	C2
Kuala Lumpur	86	C2
Kuala Terengganu	86	C1
Kuandian	82	C3
Kuantan	86	C2
Kuçadasi	68	K7
Kučevo	66	J5
Kuching	86	E2
Kucovë	68	B4
Kudat	86	F1
Kudus	86	E4
Kudymkar	70	K3
Kufstein	62	H3
Kugmallit Bay	122	E2
Kūhbonān	95	G1
Kūhdasht	92	M7
Kūh-e Alījuq	95	D1
Kūh-e Bābā	90	J3
Kūh-e Būl	95	E1
Kūh-e Dīnār	95	D1
Kūh-e Fūrgun	95	G3
Kūh-e Hazārān	95	G2
Kūh-e Hormoz	95	F3
Kūh-e Kalat	90	G3
Kūh-e Kūhrān	95	H3
Kūh-e Lāleh Zār	95	G2
Kūh-e Masāhūn	95	F1
Kūh-e Safidār	95	E2
Kuh-e Sahand	92	M5
Kūhestak	95	G3
Kūh-e Taftān	90	H4
Kūhhā-ye Bashākerd	95	G3
Kūhhā-ye Zāgros	95	D1
Kuhmo	48	Q4
Kūhpāyeh	95	G1
Kuito	108	B2
Kuji	82	L3
Kukës	66	H7
Kukhtuy	78	Q4
Kukinaga	82	F8
Kula	66	K6
Kulagino	70	K5
Kulandy	76	K8
Kuldīga	48	L8
Kulgera	114	F5
Kulmbach	52	G6
Kŭlob	90	J2
Kul'sary	70	K5
Kultsjön	48	H4
Kulu	92	E4
Kulunda	76	P7
Kulynigol	78	C4
Kuma	70	N3
Kumamoto	82	F7
Kumanovo	66	J7
Kumara, *New Zealand*	116	C6
Kumara, *Russia*	78	M6
Kumasi	104	D3
Kumba	104	F4
Kumbağ	68	K4
Kumbakonam	88	C6
Kumeny	70	K3
Kumertau	70	L4
Kumla	48	H7
Kumluca	68	N8
Kummerower See	52	H3
Kumo	104	G3
Kumta	88	B6
Kumukh	92	M2
Kunene	108	A3
Kungälv	48	F8
Kungrad	76	K9
Kungu	106	B3
Kungur	70	L3
Kunhing	84	B2
Kunlun Shan	88	D1
Kunming	80	C6
Kunsan	82	D6
Kunszetmarton	50	K11
Kununurra	114	E3
Künzelsau	52	E7
Kuolayarvi	48	Q3
Kuopio	70	E2
Kupang	114	B2
Kupino	76	P7
Kupreanof Point	132	(1)F4
Kup"yans'k	70	G5
Kuqa	76	Q9
Kür	92	M3
Kura	90	E2
Kuragino	78	E6
Kurashiki	82	G6
Kurasia	88	D4
Kurchum	76	Q8
Kürdämir	92	N3
Kurduvadi	88	C5
Kŭrdzhali	68	H3
Kure	82	G6
Kure Island	112	J3
Kuressaare	48	M7
Kureyka	78	D3
Kureyka	78	E3
Kurgal'dzhinskiy	76	N7
Kurgan	70	N3
Kurikka	48	M5
Kuril Islands = Kuril'skiye Ostrova	78	S7
Kuril'sk	78	R7
Kuril'skiye Ostrova	78	S7
Kuril Trench	74	V5
Kuripapango	116	F4
Kurmuk	100	F5
Kurnool	88	C5
Kuroiso	82	K5
Kurow	116	C7
Kuršėnai	50	M1
Kursk	70	G4
Kuršumlija	66	J6
Kurşunlu	92	E3
Kuruman	108	C5
Kurume	82	F7
Kurumkan	78	J6
Kurunegala	88	D7
Kushikino	82	F8
Kushimoto	82	H7
Kushir	78	H6
Kushiro	82	N2
Kushmurun	70	M4
Kushum	70	K4
Kuskokwim Bay	132	(1)E4
Kuskokwim Mountains	132	(1)F3
Kussharo-ko	82	N2
Kustanay	70	M4
Kütahya	92	C4
K'ut'aisi	92	K2
Kutan	92	M1
Kutchan	82	L2
Kutina	66	D4
Kutno	50	J5
Kutu	104	H5
Kutum	100	D5
Kuujjua	122	J2
Kuujjuaq	122	T5
Kuujjuarapik	122	R5
Kuusamo	70	E1
Kuvango	108	B2
Kuwait	95	B2
Kuwait = Al Kuwayt	95	C2
Kuya	70	H1
Kuybyshev	76	P6
Kuygan	76	N8
Kuytun	76	R9
Kuyumba	78	F4
Kuznetsk	70	J4
Kuzomen'	70	G1
Kvaløya, *Norway*	48	M1
Kvaløya, *Norway*	48	J2
Kvalynsk	76	H7
Kwale	106	F4
Kwangju	82	D6
Kwango	106	B5
Kwazulu Natal	108	E5
Kwekwe	108	D3
Kwidzyn	48	K10
Kwilu	104	H5
Kyakhta	78	H6
Kyancutta	114	G6
Kyaukpyu	84	A3
Kyaukse	88	G4
Kyeburn	116	C7
Kyeintali	88	F5
Kyjov	62	N2
Kyklades	68	G7
Kyle of Lochalsh	56	G4
Kyll	54	J4
Kyllini	68	D7
Kymi	68	G6
Kyŏngju	82	E6
Kyōto	82	H6
Kyparissia	68	D7
Kyperissiakos Kolpos	68	C7
Kyra Panagia	68	G5
Kyren	78	G6
Kyrgyzstan	76	N9
Kyritz	52	H4
Kyrta	70	L2
Kyshtovka	76	P6
Kystatyam	78	L3
Kytalyktakh	78	N3
Kythira	68	E8
Kythira	68	F8
Kythnos	68	G7
Kyushe	76	K8
Kyūshū	82	F7
Kyūshū-sanchi	82	F7
Kyustendil	68	E2
Kyusyur	78	M2
Kyyiv	70	F4
Kyzyl	76	S7
Kyzyl-Dzhar	70	N5
Kyzyl-Orda	70	N6
Kzyltu	76	N7

L

Laascaanood	106	H2
Laatzen	52	E4
Laba	104	F2
La Banda	142	J4
La Bañeza	60	E2
La Baule	58	C6
La Bazoge	58	F5
Labbezenga	102	F5
Labe	50	E7
Labé	104	B2
Labin	62	K5
Labinsk	92	J1
Laboulaye	142	J5
Labrador	122	U6
Labrador City	122	T6
Labrador Sea	122	V4
Lábrea	140	E5
Labrieville	128	G1
Labuha	87	C3
Labuhan	86	D4
Labuhanbajo	87	A4
Labutta	84	A3
Labytnangi	76	M4
Laç	66	G8
Lac à l'Eau Claire	122	R5
Lacanau	58	D8
La Carlota	60	F7
La Carolina	60	G6
Lac Bienville	122	S5
Lac Brochet	122	L5
Laccadive Islands	88	B6
Lac d'Annecy	62	B5
Lac de Bizerte	64	D11
Lac Débo	102	E5
Lac de Kossou	104	C3
Lac de Lagdo	104	G3
Lac de Manantali	104	C2
Lac de Mbakaou	104	G3
Lac de Neuchâtel	62	B4
Lac de Retenue de la Lufira	106	D6
Lac de St-Croix	62	B7
Lac des Bois	122	G3
Lac de Sélingue	104	C2
Lac Do	102	E5
Lac du Bourget	62	A5
Lacedonia	64	K7
Lacepede Bay	114	G7
Lac Evans	122	R6
Lac Faguibine	102	E5
Lac Fitri	100	C5
La Charité-sur-Loire	58	J6
La Chaux-de-Fonds	62	B3
La Chorrera	140	C4
Lac Ichkeul	64	D11
La Ciotat	58	L10
Lac La Biche	122	J6
Lac La Martre	122	H4
Lac Léman = Lake Geneva	62	B4
Lac Mai-Ndombe	106	B4
Lac-Megantic	128	F1
Lac Minto	122	R5
Lac Nzilo	106	D6
Lac Onangué	104	F5
Laconi	64	D9
Laconia	128	F2
Lac Payne	122	S5
La Crosse	128	B2
La Cruz	124	E7
Lac St-Jean	128	F1
Lac St. Joseph	122	N6
Lac Seul	122	N6
Lac Tumba	106	B4
Lacul Brateş	66	Q4
Lacul Razim	66	R5
Lacul Sinoie	66	R5
Lac Upemba	106	D5
La Dorada	140	C2
Ladozhskoye Ozero	70	F2
Ladysmith, *South Africa*	108	D5
Ladysmith, *US*	128	B1
Ladyzhenka	70	N4
La Esmeralda, *Bolivia*	142	J3
La Esmeralda, *Venezuela*	140	D3
Læsø	48	F8
Lafayette, *Ind., US*	128	C2
Lafayette, *La., US*	130	C3
La Ferté-St-Aubin	58	G6
Lafia	104	F3
Lafiagi	104	F3
La Flèche	58	E6
Lafnitz	62	M3
Laft	95	F3
Lagan	48	G8
Lagan'	70	J5
Lage	54	L3
Lågen	48	E6
Lage's	126	D2
Laghouat	102	F2
Lagkadas	68	F4
Lagoa dos Patos	142	L5
Lagoa Mirim	142	L5
Lago Argentino	142	G9
Lago de Cahora Bassa	108	E3
Lago del Coghinas	64	C8
Lago del Flumendosa	64	D9
Lago de Maracaibo	140	C2
Lago de Nicaragua	134	G6
Lago de Poopó	140	D7
Lago di Bolsena	64	F6
Lago di Caine	62	D5
Lago di Como	62	E4
Lago di Garda	62	F5
Lago di Lecco	62	E5
Lago di Lugano	62	E5
Lago d'Iseo	62	E5
Lago di Varano	64	K7
Lago Maggiore	62	D5
Lago Omodeo	64	C8
Lago Rogaguado	140	D6
Lagos, *Nigeria*	104	E3
Lagos, *Portugal*	60	B7
Lago Titicaca	140	D7
Lago Trasimeno	64	G5
La Goulette	64	E12
La Grand-Combe	58	K9
La Grande	126	C1
La Grange	130	E3
La Gran Sabana	140	E2
Laguna	142	M4
Laguna de Caratasca	134	H5
Laguna Madre	130	B4
Laguna Mar Chiquita	138	E7
Lagunillas	140	E7

La Habana	**134**	H4
Lahad Datu	**84**	F5
Lahat	**86**	C3
La Haye-du-Puits	**54**	A5
Lāhījān	**90**	F2
Lahn	**54**	L4
Lahnstein	**54**	K4
Laholmsbukten	**50**	B1
Lahore	**88**	B2
Lahr	**62**	C2
Lahti	**48**	N6
Laï	**106**	B2
Laiagam	**87**	F4
Lai Chau	**84**	C2
L'Aigle	**54**	C6
Laihia	**48**	M5
Laingsburg	**108**	C6
Laiwu	**80**	F3
Laiyuan	**80**	E3
Lajanurpekhi	**92**	K2
Lajes	**142**	L4
Lajosmizse	**50**	J10
La Junta	**126**	F3
Lake Abbe	**106**	G1
Lake Abitibi	**128**	E1
Lake Albert, *Dem. Rep. of the Congo/Uganda*	**106**	D3
Lake Albert, *US*	**126**	B2
Lake Almanor	**126**	B2
Lake Amadeus	**114**	F4
Lake Andes	**126**	G2
Lake Argyle	**114**	E3
Lake Athabasca	**122**	K5
Lake Austin	**114**	C5
Lake Balkhash = Ozero Balkhash	**74**	L5
Lake Bangweulu	**108**	E2
Lake Barlee	**114**	C5
Lake Benmore	**116**	C7
Lake Blanche	**114**	H5
Lake Buchanan	**132**	G2
Lake Callabonna	**114**	H5
Lake Carey	**114**	D5
Lake Carnegie	**114**	D5
Lake Chad	**100**	B5
Lake Charles	**130**	C3
Lake Chelan	**126**	B1
Lake Chilwa	**108**	F3
Lake City	**130**	E3
Lake Claire	**122**	J5
Lake Coleridge	**116**	C6
Lake Constance	**62**	E3
Lake Crowley	**126**	C3
Lake C. W. McConaughy	**126**	F2
Lake Diefenbaker	**122**	K6
Lake Disappointment	**114**	D4
Lake District	**56**	J7
Lake Dojran	**68**	E3
Lake Dora	**114**	D4
Lake Dundas	**114**	B6
Lake Edward	**106**	D4
Lake Elwall	**126**	D1
Lake Erie	**128**	D2
Lake Eyasi	**106**	E4
Lake Eyre	**112**	D8
Lake Eyre Basin	**114**	G5
Lake Eyre North	**114**	G5
Lake Eyre South	**114**	G5
Lake Francis Case	**126**	G2
Lake Frome	**114**	H6
Lake Gairdner	**114**	G6
Lake Geneva	**62**	B4
Lake Gordon	**114**	H8
Lake Grace	**114**	C6
Lake Harbour	**122**	T4
Lake Hauroko	**116**	A7
Lake Havasu	**132**	C2
Lake Havasu City	**132**	D2
Lake Hopkins	**114**	E4
Lake Hudson	**130**	B2
Lake Huron	**128**	D1
Lake Jackson	**130**	B4
Lake Kariba	**108**	D3
Lake Kemp	**130**	B2
Lake Kerkinitis	**66**	L8
Lake Kivu	**106**	D4
Lake Kyoga	**106**	E3
Lake Ladoga = Ladozhskoye Ozero	**70**	F2
Lakeland	**130**	E4
Lake Lefroy	**114**	D6
Lake Louis	**122**	H6
Lake Macdonald	**114**	E4
Lake Mackay	**114**	E4
Lake Macleod	**114**	B4
Lake Manapouri	**116**	A7
Lake Manitoba	**122**	M6
Lake Manyara	**106**	F4
Lake Maurice	**114**	F5
Lake McDonald	**126**	D1
Lake McMillan	**132**	F2
Lake Mead	**126**	D3
Lake Melville	**122**	U6
Lake Michigan	**128**	C2
Lake Moore	**114**	C5
Lake Murray	**87**	F4
Lake Mweru	**106**	D5
Lake Mweru Wantipa	**106**	E5
Lake Nasser	**100**	F3
Lake Natron	**106**	F4
Lake Neale	**114**	E4
Lake Nipigon	**122**	P6/7
Lake Nipissing	**128**	E1
Lake Nyasa	**108**	E2
Lake Oahe	**126**	F2
Lake of the Woods	**128**	B1
Lake Ohau	**116**	B7
Lake Ohrid	**68**	C4
Lake Okeechobee	**130**	E4
Lake Onega = Onezhskoye Ozero	**46**	H1
Lake Ontario	**128**	E2
Lake O' The Cherokees	**128**	B3
Lake O' The Pines	**130**	C3
Lake Paringa	**116**	B6
Lake Peipus	**48**	P7
Lake Placid	**130**	E4
Lakeport	**126**	B3
Lake Poteriteri	**116**	A8
Lake Powell	**126**	D3
Lake Prespa	**68**	D4
Lake Providence	**130**	C3
Lake Pskov	**48**	P7
Lake Pukaki	**116**	C7
Lake Rotorua	**116**	F4
Lake Rukwa	**106**	E5
Lake St. Lucia	**108**	E5
Lake Sakakawea	**126**	F1
Lake Scutari	**66**	G7
Lake Simcoe	**128**	E2
Lake Superior	**128**	C1
Lake Tahoe	**126**	B3
Lake Tanganyika	**106**	D5
Lake Taupo	**116**	E4
Lake Te Anau	**116**	A7
Lake Tekapo	**116**	C6
Lake Tekapo	**116**	C6
Lake Texoma	**130**	B3
Lake Torrens	**114**	G6
Lake Travis	**132**	G2
Lake Tschida	**126**	F1
Lake Turkana	**106**	F3
Lake Victoria	**106**	E4
Lakeview	**126**	B2
Lake Volta	**104**	D3
Lake Waikare	**116**	E3
Lake Waikaremoana	**116**	F4
Lake Wakatipu	**116**	B7
Lake Wanaka	**116**	B7
Lake White	**114**	E4
Lake Wills	**114**	E4
Lake Winnipeg	**122**	M6
Lake Winnipegosis	**122**	L6
Lakewood	**126**	E3
Lake Woods	**114**	F3
Lake Xau	**108**	C4
Lake Yamma Yamma	**114**	H5
Lakhdaria	**60**	P8
Lakhimpur	**88**	D3
Lakhnadon	**88**	C4
Lakhpat	**88**	A4
Lakin	**130**	A2
Lakki	**88**	B2
Lakonikos Kolpos	**68**	E8
Lakota	**126**	G1
Lakselv	**48**	N1
Lalín	**60**	B2
La Línea	**60**	E8
Lalitpur	**88**	C4
Lal-Lo	**84**	G3
La Loche	**122**	K5
La Louvière	**54**	G4
La Maddalena	**64**	D7
Lamar, *Colo., US*	**132**	F1
Lamar, *Mo., US*	**130**	C2
Lamard	**95**	E3
La Marsa	**64**	E12
Lamballe	**58**	C5
Lambaréné	**104**	G5
Lambay Island	**56**	G8
Lambert's Bay	**108**	B6
Lam Chi	**84**	C3
Lamesa	**132**	F2
Lamia	**68**	E6
Lamone	**62**	G6
Lampang	**84**	B3
Lampasas	**132**	G2
Lampedusa	**102**	H1
Lamu	**106**	G4
Lanai	**132**	(2)D3
Lanai City	**132**	(2)E3
Lancang	**84**	B2
Lancaster, *UK*	**56**	K7
Lancaster, *Mo., US*	**128**	B2
Lancaster, *N.H., US*	**128**	F2
Lancaster, *Oh., US*	**128**	D3
Lancaster, *Pa., US*	**128**	E2
Lancaster, *S.C., US*	**130**	E3
Lancaster Sound	**122**	Q2
Lanciano	**64**	J6
Landau, *Germany*	**54**	L5
Landau, *Germany*	**62**	H2
Landeck	**62**	F3
Lander	**126**	E2
Landerneau	**58**	A5
Landsberg	**62**	F2
Land's End	**56**	F11
Landshut	**62**	H2
Landskrona	**50**	B2
Landstuhl	**54**	K5
Land Wursten	**52**	D3
La'nga Co	**88**	D2
Langarūd	**92**	N5
Langdon	**126**	G1
Langebæk	**52**	H1
Langeland	**52**	F2
Langen, *Germany*	**52**	D3
Langen, *Germany*	**54**	L5
Langenau	**62**	F2
Langenhagen	**52**	E4
Langeoog	**52**	C3
Langeoog	**52**	C3
Langfang	**80**	F3
Langjökull	**48**	(1)C2
Langkawi	**84**	B5
Langkon	**84**	F5
Langogne	**58**	J9
Langon	**58**	E9
Langøya	**48**	H2
Langreo	**60**	E1
Langres	**62**	A3
Langsa	**84**	B6
Langtry	**132**	F3
Langvatnet	**48**	G3
Länkäran	**92**	N4
Lannion	**58**	B5
L'Anse	**128**	C1
Lansing	**128**	D2
Lanxi	**80**	H1
Lanya	**106**	E2
Lanzarote	**102**	C3
Lanzhou	**80**	C3
Laoag	**84**	G3
Lao Cai	**84**	C2
Laohekou	**80**	E4
Laon	**54**	F5
La Oroya	**140**	B6
Laos	**84**	C3
Laotougou	**82**	E2
Lapa	**142**	M4
La Palma	**102**	B3
La Palma	**134**	J7
La Paragua	**140**	E2
La Paz, *Argentina*	**142**	K5
La Paz, *Bolivia*	**140**	D7
La Paz, *Mexico*	**134**	B4
La Pedrera	**140**	D4
La Perla	**132**	F3
La Pérouse Strait	**80**	L1
La Pesca	**130**	B5
La Pine	**126**	B2
Lapithos	**94**	A1
La Plant	**126**	F1
La Plata	**142**	K5
Lappajärvi	**48**	M5
Lappeenranta	**48**	Q6
Lappland	**48**	M2
Laptev Sea = More Laptevykh	**78**	L1
Lapua	**48**	M5
Łapy	**50**	M5
La Quiaca	**142**	H3
L'Aquila	**64**	H6
Lār	**95**	F3
Larache	**102**	D1
Laramie	**126**	E2
Laramie Range	**126**	E2
Larantuka	**87**	B4
Larat	**87**	D4
Larba	**60**	P8
Laredo, *Spain*	**60**	G1
Laredo, *US*	**132**	G3
Largo	**130**	E4
L'Ariana	**64**	E12
Lariang	**87**	A3
La Rioja	**142**	H4
Larisa	**68**	E5
Larkana	**90**	J4
Larnaka	**94**	A2
Larne	**56**	G7
La Rochelle	**58**	D7
La Roche-sur-Yon	**58**	D7
La Roda	**60**	H5
La Romana	**134**	L5
La Ronge	**122**	K5
Larrimah	**114**	F3
Lar'yak	**76**	Q5
La Sarre	**128**	E1
Las Cabezas de San Juan	**60**	E7
Las Cruces	**132**	E2
La Serena	**142**	G4
La Seu d'Urgell	**60**	M2
La Seyne-sur-Mer	**58**	L10
Lashio	**84**	B2
Lashkar Gāh	**90**	H3
Las Horquetas	**142**	G8
Łask	**50**	J6
Las Lomitas	**142**	J3
La Solana	**60**	G6
Las Palmas	**102**	B3
Las Petas	**140**	F7
La Spezia	**62**	E6
Las Plumas	**142**	H7
Las Taques	**140**	C1
Last Chance	**126**	F3
Lastoursville	**104**	G5
Lastovo	**66**	D7
Las Varas	**124**	E7
Las Varillas	**142**	J5
Las Vegas, *Nev., US*	**126**	C3
Las Vegas, *N. Mex., US*	**132**	E1
La Teste	**58**	D9
Latina	**64**	G7
Latisana	**62**	J5
La Toma	**142**	H5
La Tuque	**128**	F1
Latur	**88**	C5
Latvia	**48**	M8
Lauchhammer	**52**	J5
Lauenburg	**52**	F3
Lauf	**52**	G7
Lau Group	**112**	J7
Launceston, *Australia*	**114**	J8
Launceston, *UK*	**56**	H11
La Union	**60**	K7
Laupheim	**62**	E2
Laura	**114**	H3
Laurel	**130**	D3
Lauria	**64**	K8
Laurinburg	**130**	F3
Lausanne	**62**	B4
Laut Banda	**87**	C3
Laut, *Indonesia*	**86**	F3
Laut, *Malaysia*	**86**	D2
Lauter	**54**	K5
Lauterbach	**52**	E6
Laut Flores	**87**	A4
Laut Java	**86**	E4
Laut Molucca	**87**	C2
Laut Sawu	**87**	B4
Laut Seram	**87**	C3
Lava	**50**	L3
Laval, *Canada*	**128**	F1
Laval, *France*	**58**	E5
La Vall d'Uixo	**60**	K5
Lavant	**62**	K4
Lāvar Kabkān	**95**	D2
La Vega	**134**	K5
Laviana	**60**	E1
La Vila Joiosa	**60**	K6
Lavras	**142**	N3
Lavrentiya	**78**	Z3
Lavrio	**68**	G7
Lawdar	**100**	J5
Lawra	**104**	D2
Lawrence, *New Zealand*	**116**	B7
Lawrence, *Kans., US*	**128**	A3
Lawrence, *Mass., US*	**128**	F2
Lawrenceville	**130**	D2
Lawton	**130**	B3
Laya	**70**	L1
Laylā	**100**	J3
Laysan Island	**112**	J3
Layton	**126**	D2
Lazarev	**78**	Q6
Lázaro Cárdenas	**134**	D5
Lazdijai	**50**	N3
Lāzeh	**95**	E3
Lazo	**78**	P3
Leadville	**126**	E3
Leamington	**128**	D2
Leavenworth, *Kans., US*	**128**	A3
Leavenworth, *Wash., US*	**126**	B1
Lebach	**54**	J5
Lebanon	**94**	C3
Lebanon, *Mo., US*	**128**	B3
Lebanon, *N.H., US*	**128**	F2
Lebanon, *Pa., US*	**128**	E2
Lebanon, *Tenn., US*	**128**	C3
Lebel-sur-Quévillon	**128**	E1
Lebork	**50**	G3
Lebrija	**60**	D8
Lebu	**142**	G6
Lecce	**64**	N8
Lecco	**62**	E5
Lech	**62**	F3
Leck	**52**	D2
Le Creusot	**58**	K7
Le Crotoy	**54**	D4
Łeczna	**50**	M6
Łęczyca	**50**	J5
Ledmozero	**48**	R4
Lee	**56**	D10
Leech Lake	**128**	B1
Leeds	**56**	L8
Leek, *Netherlands*	**54**	J1
Leek, *UK*	**54**	A1
Leer	**54**	K1
Leesburg	**130**	E4
Leeston	**116**	D6
Leesville	**130**	C3
Leeuwarden	**54**	H1
Leeward Islands	**134**	M5
Lefkada	**68**	C6
Lefkada	**68**	C6
Lefkimmi	**68**	C5
Lefkonikon	**94**	A1
Lefkosia	**68**	R9
Legaspi	**84**	G4
Legionowo	**50**	K5
Legnago	**62**	G5
Legnica	**50**	F6
Leh	**88**	C2
Le Havre	**54**	C5
Lehre	**52**	F4
Lehrte	**52**	F4
Leiah	**88**	B2
Leibnitz	**62**	L4
Leicester	**54**	A2
Leiden	**54**	G2
Leie	**54**	F4
Leigh Creek	**114**	G6
Leighton Buzzard	**54**	B3
Leine	**52**	E4
Leinster	**114**	D5
Leipzig	**52**	H5
Leiria	**60**	B5
Leiyang	**80**	E5
Lek	**54**	G3
Lelystad	**54**	H2
Le Mans	**58**	F6
Le Mars	**128**	A2
Lemberg	**52**	D8
Lemesos	**68**	Q10
Lemgo	**54**	L2
Lemieux Islands	**122**	U4
Lemmer	**54**	H2
Lemmon	**126**	F1
Le Muret	**58**	E9
Lena	**60**	E1
Lena	**78**	L4
Lendava	**62**	M4
Lendinare	**62**	G5
Lengerich	**54**	K2
Lengshuijiang	**80**	E5
Lengshuitan	**80**	E5
Lenininsk-Kuznetskiy	**76**	R7
Leninskoye	**70**	J3
Lenmalu	**87**	D3
Lenne	**54**	K3
Lennestadt	**54**	L3
Lens	**54**	E4
Lensk	**78**	K4
Lenti	**62**	M4
Lentini	**64**	J11
Léo	**104**	D2
Leoben	**62**	L3
León, *Mexico*	**134**	D4
León, *Nicaragua*	**134**	G6
León, *Spain*	**60**	E2
Leonardville	**108**	B4
Leonberg	**62**	E2
Leonforte	**64**	J11
Leonidi	**68**	E7
Leonora	**114**	D5
Leova	**66**	R3
Le Palais	**58**	B6
Lepe	**60**	C7

Le Perthus 58 H11
Lepoura 68 G6
Lepsy 76 P8
Le Puy 58 J8
Léré 104 G3
Lerici 62 E6
Lerik 92 N4
Lerma 60 G2
Leros 68 J7
Lerwick 56 L1
Lešak 66 H6
Les Andelys 54 D5
Lesatima 106 F4
Lesbos = Lesvos 68 H5
Les Escaldes 58 G11
Les Escoumins 122 T7
Leshan 80 C5
Les Herbiers 58 D7
Leshukonskoye 70 J2
Leskovac 66 J7
Lesosibirsk 76 S6
Lesotho 108 D5
Lesozavodsk 82 G1
Lesparre-Médoc 58 E8
Les Sables-d'Olonne 58 D7
Les Sept Îles 58 B5
Lesser Antilles 134 L6
Lesser Slave Lake 122 J5
Lesvos 68 H5
Leszno 50 F6
Letaba 108 E4
Letchworth 54 B3
Letenye 62 M4
Lethbridge 126 D1
Lethem 140 F3
Leticia 140 D4
Letpadan 84 B3
Le Tréport 54 D4
Letterkenny 56 E7
Leutkirch 62 F3
Leuven 54 G4
Leuze 54 F4
Levadeia 68 E6
Levanzo 64 G10
Levashi 92 M2
Levaya Khetta 70 P2
Leverano 64 N8
Leverkusen 54 J3
Levice 50 H9
Levico Terme 62 G4
Levin 116 E5
Lévis 128 F1
Levitha 68 J7
Levoča 50 K9
Levski 66 N6
Lewe 84 B3
Lewes 54 C4
Lewis 56 F3
Lewis and Clark Lake 126 G2
Lewis Range 122 J7
Lewiston, *Id., US* 126 C1
Lewiston, *Me., US* 128 F2
Lewistown, *Mont., US* 126 E1
Lewistown, *Pa., US* 128 E2
Lexington, *Ky., US* 128 D3
Lexington, *Nebr., US* 126 G2
Lexington, *Va., US* 128 E3
Lexington Park 130 F2
Leyte 84 G4
Lezhë 66 G8
Lhari 88 F2
Lhasa 88 F3
Lhazê 88 E3
Lhokseumawe 84 B5
Lian Xian 84 E2
Lianyuan 84 E1
Lianyungang 80 F4
Liaocheng 80 F3
Liao He 82 B3
Liaoyang 82 B3
Liaoyuan 82 C2
Liard 122 F5
Liard River 122 F5
Libby 126 C1
Libenge 106 B3
Liberal 130 A2
Liberec 50 E7
Liberia 104 B3
Liberia 134 G6
Liberty 130 C1
Libjo 84 H4
Libourne 58 E9
Libreville 104 F4
Libya 100 C2
Libyan Desert 100 D2
Libyan Plateau 100 E1
Licata 64 H11
Lich 52 D6
Lichinga 108 F2
Lichtenfels 52 G6
Lida 48 N10
Lidköping 48 G7
Lidodi Jesolo 62 H5
Lido di Ostia 64 G7
Lidzbark Warmiński 50 K3
Liebenwalde 52 J4
Liechtenstein 62 E3
Liège 54 H4
Lieksa 48 R5
Lienz 62 H4
Liepāja 50 L1
Lier 54 G3
Liezen 62 K3
Lifford 56 E7
Lignières 58 H7
Ligueil 58 F6
Ligurian Sea 62 D7
Lihue 132 B2
Lijiang 84 C1
Likasi 106 D6
Lilienfeld 62 L2
Lille 54 F4
Lillebonne 54 C5
Lillehammer 48 F6
Lillerto 62 G3
Lilongwe 108 E2
Liloy 84 G5
Lima, *Peru* 140 B6
Lima, *Mont., US* 126 D2
Lima, *Oh., US* 128 D2
Limanowa 50 K8
Limassol = Lemesos 68 Q10
Limbaži 48 N8
Limburg 54 L4
Limeira 142 M3
Limerick 56 D9
Limingen 48 G4
Limni Kastorias 68 C4
Limni Kerkinitis 68 E3
Limni Koronia 68 F4
Limni Trichonida 68 D6
Limni Vegoritis 68 D4
Limni Volvi 68 F4
Limnos 68 H5
Limoges 58 G8
Limon 126 F3
Limón 134 H7
Limoux 58 H10
Limpopo 108 D4
Limpopo 108 D4
Linares, *Chile* 142 G6
Linares, *Mexico* 132 G4
Linares, *Spain* 60 G6
Linaria 68 G6
Lincang 84 C2
Linchuan 80 F5
Lincoln, *UK* 54 B1
Lincoln, *Ill., US* 128 C2
Lincoln, *Me., US* 128 G1
Lincoln, *Nebr., US* 126 G2
Lincoln, *N.H., US* 128 F2
Lindenow Fjord 122 Y4
Lindesnes 48 D8
Lindi 106 D3
Lindi 106 F6
Lindos 68 L8
Line Islands 112 L5
Linfen 80 E3
Lingayen 84 G3
Lingen 54 K2
Lingga 86 C3
Lingshui 84 D3
Linguère 104 A1
Lingyuan 80 F2
Linhal 80 G5
Linhares 140 J7
Linhe 80 D2
Linjiang 82 D3
Linköping 48 H7
Linkou 82 F1
Linosa 64 G13
Lins 142 M3
Linton 126 F1
Linxi 80 F2
Linxia 80 C3
Lin Xian 80 E3
Linyi 80 F3
Linz 62 K2
Liobomil' 50 P6
Lipari 64 J10
Lipari 64 J10
Lipcani 66 P1
Lipetsk 70 G4
Lipin Bor 70 G2
Lipno 50 J5
Lipova 66 J3
Lippe 54 L3
Lippstadt 54 L3
Lipsoi 68 J7
Liptovský-Mikuláš 50 J8
Lipu 84 E2
Liqeni i Fierzës 66 H7
Liqeni Komanit 66 G7
Lira 106 E3
Liri 64 H7
Lisala 106 C3
Lisboa 60 A6
Lisbon = Lisboa 60 A6
Lisburn 56 G7
Liscannor Bay 56 C9
Lishi 80 E3
Lishui 80 F5
Lisieux 54 C5
Liski 70 G4
L'Isle-sur-la-Sorgue 58 L10
Lisse 54 G2
Lištica 64 M5
Listowel 56 C9
Listvyanka 78 H6
Litang 80 C5
Litani 140 G3
Litava 50 F8
Litchfield, *Ill., US* 128 C3
Litchfield, *Minn., US* 128 B1
Lithgow 114 K6
Lithuania 48 L9
Litke 78 Q6
Litomerice 52 K6
Litomyši 50 F8
Litovel 50 G8
Litovko 78 P7
Little Abaco 130 F4
Little Andaman 88 F6
Little Barrier Island 116 E3
Little Current 128 D1
Little Desert 114 H7
Little Falls 128 B1
Littlefield 132 F2
Little Inagua 134 K4
Little Karoo 108 C6
Little Minch 56 E4
Little Nicobar 88 F7
Little Ouse 54 C2
Little Rock 130 C3
Littleton 126 E3
Litvinov 52 J6
Liupanshui 80 C5
Liuzhou 80 D6
Live Oak 130 E3
Liverpool, *Canada* 122 U8
Liverpool, *UK* 56 K8
Liverpool Bay 122 F2
Livingston, *UK* 56 J6
Livingston, *US* 126 D1
Livingstone 108 D3
Livingstonia 108 E2
Livno 66 E6
Livny 70 G4
Livonia 128 D2
Livorno 62 F7
Liwale 106 F5
Lizard Point 56 G12
Ljubljana 62 K4
Ljugarn 48 K8
Ljungan 48 J5
Ljungby 48 G8
Ljusdal 48 J6
Ljusnan 70 C2
Llandovery 56 J9
Llandudno 56 J8
Llanelli 56 H10
Llanes 60 F1
Llanos 140 C2
Lleida 60 L3
Llerena 60 E6
Lli 76 P9
Lloret de Mar 60 N3
Llucmajor 60 N5
Loano 62 D6
Lobamba 108 E5
Lobatse 108 D5
Löbau 52 K5
Łobez 50 E4
Lobito 108 A2
Locarno 62 D4
Lochboisdale 56 E4
Lochem 54 J2
Lochinver 56 G3
Loch Linnhe 56 G5
Loch Lomond 56 H5
Lochmaddy 56 E4
Loch Ness 56 H4
Lockhart 130 B4
Lock Haven 128 E2
Lockport 128 E2
Locri 64 L10
Lodève 58 J10
Lodeynoye 70 F2
Lodge Grass 126 E1
Lodi, *Italy* 62 E5
Lodi, *US* 126 B3
Lodja 106 C4
Lodwar 106 F3
Łódź 50 J6
Loei 84 C3
Lofoten 48 G3
Logan, *Ia., US* 128 A2
Logan, *N. Mex., US* 132 F1
Logan, *Ut., US* 126 D2
Logansport 128 C2
Logatec 62 K5
Logroño 60 H2
Lohiniva 48 N3
Lohr 52 E7
Loikaw 84 B3
Loir 58 F6
Loire 58 D6
Loja, *Ecuador* 140 B4
Loja, *Spain* 60 F7
Lokan tekojärvi 48 P3
Lokeren 54 F3
Lokichar 106 F3
Lokichokio 106 E3
Lokoja 104 F3
Lokosovo 70 P2
Loks Land 122 U4
Lolland 52 G2
Lollondo 106 F4
Lolo 126 D1
Lom 66 L6
Lomami 106 C4
Lomas 140 C7
Lomas de Zamora 142 K5
Lombadina 114 D3
Lomblen 87 B4
Lombok 86 F4
Lombok 86 F4
Lomé 104 E3
Lomela 106 C4
Lomela 106 C4
Lommel 54 H3
Lomonosovka 70 N4
Lompoc 132 B2
Łomża 50 M4
London, *Canada* 128 D2
London, *UK* 54 B3
London, *US* 130 E2
Londonderry 56 E6
Londrina 142 L3
Longarone 62 H4
Long Bay 134 J2
Long Beach 132 C2
Long Branch 128 F2
Long Eaton 54 A2
Longford 56 E8
Long Island, *Canada* 122 Q5
Long Island, *US* 128 F2
Longlac 122 P7
Long Lake 126 F1
Longmont 126 E2
Long Prairie 128 B1
Long Range Mountains 122 V6
Longreach 114 H4
Longueuil 128 F1
Longview, *Tex., US* 130 C3
Longview, *Wash., US* 126 B1
Longwy 54 H5
Long Xuyên 84 D4
Longyan 84 F1
Löningen 54 K2
Lönsdalen 48 H3
Lons-le-Saunier 62 A4
Lookout Pass 126 C1
Loop Head 56 B9
Lopez 84 G4
Lop Nur 76 S9
Lopphavet 48 L1
Loptyuga 70 J2
Lora del Rio 60 E7
Lorain 128 D2
Loralai 88 A2
Lorca 60 J7
Lordegān 95 D1
Lord Howe Island 114 L6
Lordsburg 132 E2
Loreto 134 B3
Lorient 58 B6
Lörrach 62 C3
Los Alamos 132 E1
Los Angeles, *Chile* 142 G6
Los Angeles, *US* 132 C2
Los Banos 126 B3
Los Blancos 142 J3
Losheim 54 J5
Losice 50 M5
Lošinj 62 K6
Los Mochis 134 C3
Lospalos 87 C4
Los Telares 142 J4
Los Teques 140 D1
Lost Trail Pass 126 D1
Los'va 70 M2
Los Vientos 142 H3
Lotta 48 Q2
Lotte 54 K2
Louang Namtha 84 C2
Louangphrabang 84 C3
Loubomo 104 G5
Loudéac 58 C5
Louga 104 A1
Loughborough 54 A2
Lough Conn 56 C7
Lough Corrib 56 C8
Lough Derg 56 D8
Lough Foyle 56 E6
Lough Leane 56 C9
Lough Mask 56 C8
Lough Neagh 56 F7
Lough Ree 56 E8
Louhans 58 L7
Louisa 128 D3
Louisiade Archipelago 114 K2
Louisiana 130 C3
Louis Trichardt 108 D4
Louisville, *Ga., US* 130 E3
Louisville, *Ky., US* 130 D2
Louisville, *Miss., US* 130 D3
Loukhi 48 S3
Loulé 60 C7
Louny 52 J6
Loup 126 G2
Lourdes 58 E10
Louros 68 C5
Louth, *Australia* 114 J6
Louth, *UK* 54 C1
Loutra Aidipsou 68 F6
Louviers 54 D5
Lovech 66 M6
Lovell 126 E2
Lovelock 126 C2
Lovosice 52 K6
Lovran 62 K5
Lôvua 108 C2
Lowa 106 D4
Lowell 128 F2
Lower Hutt 116 E5
Lower Lake 126 B2
Lower Lough Erne 56 E7
Lower Post 122 F5
Lowestoft 54 D2
Lowicz 50 J5
Lowville 128 F2
Loxstedt 52 D3
Loyalty Islands 112 G8
Loyno 70 K3
Loznica 66 G5
L-Travemünde 52 F3
Luama 106 D4
Luampa 108 C3
Lu'an 80 F4
Luanda 106 A5
Luangwa 108 E2
Luangwa 108 E3
Lua Nova 140 F5
Luanping 80 F2
Luanshya 108 D2
Luarca 60 D1
Luau 108 C2
Lubaczów 50 N7
Lubań 50 E6
Lubango 108 A2
Lubāns 48 P8
Lubao 106 D5
Lubartów 50 M6
Lübbecke 54 L2
Lübben 52 J5
Lübbenau 52 J5
Lubbock 132 F2
Lübeck 52 F3
Lubefu 106 C4
Lubero 106 D4
Lubilash 106 C5
Lubin 50 F6
Lublin 50 M6
Lubliniec 50 H7
Lubny 70 F4
Luboń 50 F5
Lubsko 50 D6

Lubudi 106 D5
Lubuklinggau 86 C3
Lubumbashi 106 D6
Lubutu 106 D4
Lucala 106 B5
Lucas 140 F6
Lucca 62 F7
Luce Bay 56 H7
Lucedale 130 D3
Lucena, *Philippines* 84 G4
Lucena, *Spain* 60 F7
Lučenec 50 J9
Lucera 64 K7
Lucero 132 E2
Lucira 108 A2
Luckau 52 J5
Luckenwalde 52 J4
Lucknow 88 D3
Luçon 58 D7
Lucusse 108 C2
Ludden 126 G1
Lüdenscheid 54 K3
Lüderitz 108 B5
Ludhiana 88 C2
Ludington 128 C2
Ludlow 132 C2
Ludogori 66 P6
Luduș 66 M3
Ludvika 48 H6
Ludwigsburg 62 E2
Ludwigsfelde 52 J4
Ludwigshafen 54 L5
Ludwigslust 52 G3
Ludza 48 P8
Luebo 106 C5
Luena 108 B2
Lufeng 84 F2
Lufira 106 D6
Lufkin 130 C3
Luga 48 Q7
Luga 70 E3
Lugano 62 D4
Lugela 108 F3
Lugenda 108 F2
Luggate 116 B7
Lugo 62 G6
Lugoj 66 J4
Lugovoy 76 N9
Lugu 88 D2
Luhans'k 70 G5
Luhuo 80 C4
Lui 84 E2
Luilaka 106 B4
Luino 62 D4
Luis Moya 132 F4
Luiza 106 C5
Lukavac 66 F5
Lukovit 66 M6
Łuków 50 M6
Lukulu 108 C2
Lukumburu 106 F5
Lukuni 106 B5
Luleå 48 M4
Lüleburgaz 68 K3
Lulua 106 D5
Lumbala Kaquengue 108 C2
Lumberton 130 F3
Lumbrales 60 D4
Lumimba 108 E2
Lumsden 116 B7
Lund 50 C2
Lundazi 108 E2
Lundy 56 H10
Lüneburg 52 F3
Lüneburger Heide 52 F4
Lunel 58 K10
Lünen 54 K3
Lunéville 62 B2
Lungau 62 J3
Luntai 76 Q9
Luohe 80 E4
Luoyang 80 E4
Luozi 106 A4
Lupeni 66 L4
Lūrā Shīrīn 92 L5
Lure 62 B3
Luremo 106 B5
Lurgan 56 F7
Lurio 108 F2
Lusaka 108 D3
Lusambo 106 C5
Lushnjë 68 B4
Lushui 80 B5
Lüshun 80 G3
Lusk 126 F2
Lutembo 108 C2
Lutherstadt Wittenberg 52 H5
Luton 54 B3
Luts'k 70 E4
Lutto 48 P2
Lützow-Holmbukta 144 (2)J3
Luuq 106 G3
Luverne 128 A2
Luvua 106 D5
Luwuk 87 B3
Luxembourg 54 H5
Luxembourg 54 J5
Luxeuil-les-Bains 62 B3
Luxor 100 F2
Luza 70 J2
Luza 70 J2
Luzern 62 D3
Luzhou 80 D5
Luziânia 140 J4
Luznice 62 K1
Luzon 84 G3
Luzon Strait 84 G2
Luzy 58 J7
Luzzi 64 L9
L'viv 50 N8
Lyady 48 Q7
Lyapin 70 M2
Lycksele 70 C2
Lydenburg 108 E5
Lyme Bay 56 K11
Lymington 54 A4
Lynchburg 128 E3
Lynn 128 F2
Lynn Lake 122 L5
Lynx Lake 122 K4
Lyon 58 K8
Lys 54 E4
Lys'va 70 L3
Lysychans'k 70 G5
Lyttelton 116 D6

M

Maalosmadulu Atoll 88 B7
Ma'ān 94 C6
Maardu 48 N7
Ma'arrat an Nu'mān 92 G6
Maas 54 J3
Maasin 84 G4
Maastricht 54 H4
Mabalane 108 E4
Mabanza-Ngungu 104 G6
Mabaruma 140 F2
Mabein 84 B2
Mablethorpe 54 C1
Macapá 140 G3
Macas 140 B4
Macassar Strait 112 B6
Macau, *Brazil* 140 K5
Macau, *China* 84 E2
Macaúba 140 G6
Macclesfield 56 K8
Macdonnell Ranges 114 F4
Macedonia 68 C3
Maceió 140 K5
Macerata 62 J7
Machakos 106 F4
Machala 140 B4
Macheng 80 F4
Machilipatnam 88 D5
Machiques 140 C1
Macia 108 E4
Măcin 66 R4
Mack 132 E1
Mackay 114 J4
Mackay Lake 122 J4
Mackenzie 122 G4
Mackenzie Bay 122 D3
Mackenzie Mountains 122 E3
Mackinaw City 128 D1
Macmillan 122 E4
Macmillan Pass 122 F4
Macomb 128 B2
Macomer 64 C8
Macon, *Ga., US* 130 E3
Macon, *Mo., US* 130 C2
Mâcon 58 K7
Macuje 140 C3
Mādabā 94 C5
Madagascar 108 H3
Madan 66 M8
Madanapalle 88 C6
Madaoua 104 F2
Madeira 102 B2
Madeira 140 E5
Maden 92 H4
Madera 132 E3
Madikeri 88 C6
Madison 128 C2
Madison, *Ind., US* 128 C3
Madison, *Minn., US* 128 A1
Madison, *S.D., US* 126 G2
Madisonville 128 C3
Madiun 86 E4
Mado Gashi 106 F3
Madoi 80 B4
Madona 48 P8
Madras = Chennai, *India* 88 D6
Madras, *US* 126 B2
Madre de Dios 140 C6
Madrid, *Philippines* 84 H5
Madrid, *Spain* 60 G4
Madridejos 60 G5
Madura 86 E4
Madurai 88 C6
Maebashi 82 K5
Mae Hong Son 84 B3
Mae Nam Mun 84 C3
Mae Sariang 84 B3
Maevatanana 108 H3
Mafeteng 108 D5
Maffighofen 62 J2
Mafia Island 106 G5
Mafinga 106 F5
Mafra 142 M4
Mafraq 94 D4
Magadan 78 S5
Magadi 106 F4
Magdagachi 78 M6
Magdalena 140 C2
Magdalena, *Bolivia* 140 E6
Magdalena, *Mexico* 132 D2
Magdalena, *US* 132 E2
Magdeburg 52 G4
Magdelaine Cays 114 K3
Magelang 86 E4
Magenta 62 D5
Magerøya 48 N1
Maglaj 66 F5
Maglie 64 N8
Magnitogorsk 70 L4
Magnolia 130 C3
Mago 78 P6
Magog 128 F1
Magta Lahjar 102 C5
Magu 106 E4
Magwe 84 A2
Mahābād 92 L5
Mahaboboka 108 G4
Mahagi 106 E3
Mahajamba 108 H3
Mahajanga 108 H3
Mahalapye 108 D4
Mahān 95 G1
Mahanadi 88 D4
Mahanoro 108 H3
Mahasamund 88 D4
Mahavavy 108 H3
Mahbubnagar 88 D5
Maḥḍah 95 G4
Mahé Island 108 (2)C1
Mahenge 106 F5
Mahesāna 88 B4
Mahia Peninsula 116 F4
Mahilyow 70 F4
Mahnomen 128 A1
Mahón 60 Q5
Mahuva 90 K5
Maicao 140 C1
Maidenhead 54 B3
Maidstone 54 C3
Maiduguri 104 G2
Mai Gudo 106 F2
Maímédy 52 B6
Main 52 E7
Mainburg 62 G2
Main-Donau-Kanal 52 G7
Maine 128 G1
Maïné Soroa 104 G2
Maingkwan 84 B1
Mainland, *Orkney Is., UK* 56 J2
Mainland, *Shetland Is., UK* 56 L1
Maintirano 108 G3
Mainz 52 D6
Maio 104 (1)B1
Majene 87 A3
Majicana 142 H4
Majuro 112 H5
Makale 87 A3
Makamba 106 D4
Makanza 106 B3
Makarora 116 B7
Makarov 78 Q7
Makarska 66 E6
Makar'yev 70 H3
Makassa 87 A4
Makat 70 K5
Makeni 104 B3
Makgadikgadi 108 C4
Makhachkala 92 M2
Makhorovka 76 M7
Makindu 106 F4
Makinsk 70 P4
Makiyivka 70 G5
Makkah 100 G3
Makó 66 H3
Makokou 104 G4
Makongolosi 106 E5
Makorako 116 F4
Makoua 104 H4
Maków Mazowiecka 50 L5
Makran 90 G4
Makronisi 68 G7
Mākū 92 L4
Makumbako 106 E5
Makurazaki 82 F8
Makurdi 104 F3
Makūyeh 95 E2
Makuyuni 106 F4
Malabar Coast 88 B6
Malabo 104 F4
Malack 50 F9
Malacky 62 M2
Malad City 126 D2
Maladzyechna 70 E4
Málaga 60 F8
Malaimbandy 108 H4
Malaita 112 G6
Malakal 106 E2
Malakanagiri 88 D5
Malakula 112 G7
Malamala 87 B3
Malang 86 E4
Malanje 106 B5
Malanville 104 E2
Malaryta 50 P6
Malatya 92 H4
Malaut 88 B2
Mālavi 92 M7
Malawi 108 E2
Malaya Baranikha 78 V3
Malaya Vishera 70 F3
Malaybalay 84 H5
Malāyer 90 E3
Malay Peninsula 84 C6
Malay Reef 114 J3
Malaysia 86 C2
Malbork 50 J3
Malchin, *Germany* 52 H3
Malchin, *Mongolia* 76 S8
Malden Island 112 L6
Maldives 88 B8
Maldonado 142 L5
Malé 62 F4
Male 88 B8
Male Atoll 88 B8
Malegaon 88 B4
Malé Karpaty 62 N2
Maleme 68 F9
Malesherbes 58 H5
Maleta 78 H6
Malheur 126 C2
Malheur Lake 126 C2
Mali 102 E5
Malindi 106 G4
Malin Head 56 E6
Malkara 68 J4
Malko Tŭrnovo 66 Q8
Mallaig 56 G4
Mallawi 100 F2
Mallorca 60 P5
Mallow 56 D9
Malmédy 54 J4
Malmesbury 108 B6
Malmö 50 C2
Malmyzh 70 K3
Maloca 140 F3
Malone 128 F2
Måløy 48 C6
Malozemel'skaya Tundra 70 K1
Målselv 48 K2
Malta 64 J13
Malta 126 E1
Malta Channel 64 J12
Maltahöhe 108 B4
Malvern 128 B4
Malý Dunaj 62 N2
Malyy Uzen' 70 J4
Mama 78 J5
Mamadysh 70 K3
Mambasa 106 D3
Mamburao 84 G4
Mamelodi 108 D5
Mammoth Hot Springs 126 D2
Mamonovo 50 J3
Mamoré 140 D6
Mamou 104 B2
Mamoudzou 108 H2
Mamuju 87 A3
Ma'mūl 90 G6
Mamuno 108 C4
Man 104 C3
Mana 132 (2)A1
Manacapuru 140 E4
Manacor 60 P5
Manado 87 B2
Managua 134 G6
Manakara 108 H4
Manali 88 C2
Mananara 108 H4
Mananara Avaratra 108 H3
Mananjary 108 H4
Manankoro 104 C2
Manantenina 108 H4
Manassas 128 E3
Manaus 140 E4
Manavgat 68 P8
Manbij 92 G5
Manchester, *UK* 56 K8
Manchester, *Ia., US* 128 B2
Manchester, *Ky., US* 128 D3
Manchester, *Tenn., US* 128 C3
Manchester, *Vt., US* 128 F2
Mand 90 H4
Mandabe 108 G4
Mandal 48 D7
Mandalay 84 B2
Mandalgovĭ 80 D1
Mandan 126 F1
Mandera 106 G3
Mandi 88 C2
Mandi Burewala 88 B2
Mandimba 108 F2
Manding 102 D6
Mandla 88 D4
Mandø 52 D1
Mandritsara 108 H3
Mandsaur 88 C4
Mandurah 114 C6
Manduria 64 M8
Mandvi 88 A4
Mandya 88 C6
Manfredonia 64 K7
Manga 104 G2
Manga 140 J6
Mangaia 112 K8
Mangalia 66 R6
Mangalore 88 B6
Mangareva 112 N8
Mangatupopo 116 E4
Mangaweka 116 F4
Manggar 86 D3
Mangit 90 H1
Mangnai 76 S10
Mango 104 E2
Mangoky 108 G4
Mangole 87 C3
Mangonui 116 D2
Mangrove Cay 130 F5
Manhad 88 B5
Manhattan 130 B2
Manhuaçu 140 J8
Mania 108 H3
Maniamba 108 F2
Manicoré 140 E5
Manicouagan 122 T6
Manīfah 95 C3
Manihiki 112 K7
Maniitsoq 122 W3
Manila 84 G4
Manisa 68 K6
Manistee 128 C2
Manistique 128 C1
Manitoba 122 M6
Manitou 126 G1
Manitoulin Island 128 D1
Manitouwadge 128 C1
Manitowoc 128 C2
Maniwaki 128 E1
Manizales 140 B2
Manja 108 G4
Manjimup 114 C6
Mankato 128 B2
Manley Hot Springs 122 A4
Manlleu 60 N3
Manna 86 C3
Mannar 88 D7
Mannheim 54 L5
Manning, *Canada* 122 H5
Manning, *US* 130 E3
Manokwari 87 D3
Manono 106 D5

Mano River	104	B3
Manosque	58	L10
Manouane	128	F1
Manouane Lake	122	S6
Manp'o	82	D3
Manra	112	J6
Manresa	60	M3
Mansa	108	D2
Mansel Island	122	Q4
Mansfield, *UK*	54	A1
Mansfield, *La., US*	130	C3
Mansfield, *Oh., US*	128	D2
Manta	140	A4
Manteo	130	F2
Mantes-la-Jolie	54	D5
Mantova	62	F5
Manturovo	70	H3
Manú	140	C6
Manuelzinho	140	G5
Manūjān	95	G3
Manukan	84	G5
Manukau	116	E3
Manukau Harbour	116	E3
Manyberries	126	D1
Manyinga	108	C2
Manyoni	106	E5
Manzanares	60	G5
Manzanillo	134	J4
Manzhouli	78	K7
Manzil	94	D5
Manzini	108	E5
Mao	100	C5
Maoming	84	E2
Mapam Yumco	88	D2
Mapi	87	E4
Mapinhane	108	F4
Maple Creek	124	E2
Mapuera	140	E4
Maputo	108	E5
Maqueda	60	F4
Maquela do Zombo	106	B5
Maquinchao	142	H7
Maquoketa	128	B2
Māra	88	D4
Maraã	140	D4
Maraba	140	H5
Maracaibo	140	C1
Maracay	140	D1
Marādah	100	C2
Maradi	104	F2
Marāgheh	92	M5
Maralal	106	F3
Marand	92	L4
Maranhão	140	H5
Marañón	140	B4
Marans	58	E7
Marari	140	D5
Mărășești	66	Q4
Marathon, *Canada*	128	C1
Marathon, *US*	132	F2
Marbella	60	F8
Marble Bar	114	C4
Marburg	54	L4
Marcal	62	N3
Marcali	62	N4
March	54	C2
Marche	54	H4
Marchena	60	E7
Mardan	88	B2
Mar del Plata	142	K6
Mardin	92	J5
Maré	112	G8
Mareeba	114	J3
Marettimo	64	F11
Marfa	132	F2
Margate	54	D3
Margherita di Savoia	64	L7
Marghita	66	K2
Margilan	90	K1
Marguerite Bay	144	(2)KK3
María Elena	142	H3
Marianas Trench	112	E4
Marianna	130	D3
Mariánské Lázně	52	H7
Mariazell	62	L3
Mar'ib	100	J4
Maribo	52	G2
Maribor	62	L4
Maridi	106	D2
Marie Byrd Land	144	(2)F F2
Marie Galante	134	M5
Mariehamn	48	K6
Marienberg	52	J6
Mariental	108	B4
Mariestad	48	G7
Marietta	130	E2
Marietta, *Oh., US*	128	D3
Marietta, *Okla., US*	130	B3
Mariinsk	76	R6
Marijampolė	50	N3
Marília	142	M3
Marín	60	B2
Marinette	128	C1
Maringá	142	L3
Marino	64	G7
Marion, *Ill., US*	128	C3
Marion, *Ind., US*	128	C2
Marion, *Oh., US*	128	D2
Maripa	140	D2
Mariscal Estigarribia	142	J3
Maritime Alps	62	C6
Mariupol'	70	G5
Marīvān	92	M6
Mariy El	70	J3
Marjayoûn	94	C3
Marka	106	G3
Markam	80	B5
Markaryd	50	C1
Marked Tree	130	C2
Marken	54	H2
Markermeer	54	H2
Market Harborough	54	B2
Markham	128	E2
Marki	50	L5
Markit	76	P10
Markkleeberg	52	H5
Markovo	78	W4
Marktoberdorf	62	F3
Marktredwitz	52	H7
Marla	114	F5
Marle	54	F5
Marmande	58	F9
Marmara Adası	68	K4
Marmara Denizi	68	L4
Marmaris	68	L8
Marmolada	62	G4
Marne	54	F5
Marne-la-Vallée	54	E6
Maro	104	H3
Maroansetra	108	H3
Marolambo	108	H4
Maroni	140	G3
Maros	87	A3
Marotiri	112	M8
Maroua	104	G2
Marquesas Islands	112	M6
Marquette	128	C1
Marradi	62	G6
Marrakech	102	D2
Marra Plateau	100	D5
Marree	114	G5
Marrupa	108	F2
Marsa Alam	100	F2
Marsabit	106	F3
Marsala	64	G11
Marsberg	54	L3
Marsden	114	J6
Marseille	58	L10
Marseille-en-Beauvaisis	54	D5
Marshall, *Ill., US*	130	D2
Marshall, *Tex., US*	130	C3
Marshall Islands	112	G4
Marshalltown	128	B2
Marsh Harbour	130	F4
Marsh Island	130	C4
Martapura, *Indonesia*	86	C3
Martapura, *Indonesia*	86	E3
Martigny	62	C4
Martigues	58	L10
Martin, *Slovakia*	50	H8
Martin, *US*	126	F2
Martina Franca	64	M8
Martinborough	116	E5
Martinique	134	M6
Martinsburg	128	E3
Martinsville, *Ind., US*	128	C3
Martinsville, *Va., US*	128	E3
Marton	116	E5
Martos	60	G7
Maruchak	90	H2
Mårvatn	48	E6
Mary	90	H2
Maryborough	114	K5
Maryland	128	E3
Marysville, *Canada*	128	G1
Marysville, *Calif., US*	132	B1
Marysville, *Kans., US*	130	B2
Maryville	128	B2
Masai Steppe	106	F4
Masaka	106	E4
Masalembu Besar	86	E4
Masallı	92	N4
Masamba	87	B3
Masan	82	E6
Masasi	106	F6
Masbate	84	G4
Masbate	84	G4
Mascara	102	F1
Maseru	108	D5
Mashhad	90	G2
Masi-Manimba	106	B4
Masindi	106	E3
Maşīrah	90	G5
Masjed Soleymān	90	E3
Maskanah	92	H5
Mason	130	B3
Mason Bay	116	A8
Mason City	128	B2
Masqaţ	95	H5
Massa	62	F6
Massachusetts	128	F2
Massachusetts Bay	128	G2
Massafra	64	M8
Massa Marittimo	64	E5
Massawa	100	G4
Massena	128	F2
Masset	122	E6
Massif Central	58	H8
Massif de Guéra	100	C5
Massif de l'Aïr	102	G5
Massif des Écrins	62	B5
Massif du Chaillu	104	G5
Massif du Tsaratanana	108	H2
Massif Ennedi	100	D4
Massillon	128	D2
Massinga	108	F4
Masteksay	70	K5
Masterton	116	E5
Mastung	90	J4
Masty	48	N10
Masuda	82	F6
Masuguru	108	F2
Masvingo	108	E4
Maşyāf	94	D1
Matadi	106	A5
Matagami	128	E1
Matagorda Island	130	B4
Matakana Island	116	F3
Matakawau	116	E3
Matale	88	D7
Matam	104	B1
Matamoros, *Mexico*	132	F3
Matamoros, *Mexico*	132	G3
Matane	128	G1
Matanzas	124	K7
Matara	88	D7
Mataram	86	F4
Mataranka	114	F3
Mataró	60	N3
Mataura	116	B8
Matawai	116	F4
Matehuala	132	F4
Matera	64	L8
Mátészalka	66	K2
Mateur	64	D11
Matheson	128	D1
Mathraki	68	B5
Mathura	88	C3
Mati	84	H5
Matlock	54	A1
Matmata	102	G2
Mato Grosso	140	F6
Mato Grosso	140	F6
Mato Grosso do Sul	140	F7
Matosinhos	60	B3
Maţraḥ	95	H5
Matrel	62	H4
Matrûh	100	E1
Matsiatra	108	H4
Matsu	80	G5
Matsue	82	G6
Matsumae	82	L3
Matsumoto	82	J5
Matsusaka	82	J6
Matsuyama	82	G7
Mattawa	128	E1
Matterhorn	62	C5
Matthews Ridge	140	E2
Mattighofen	52	J8
Mattoon	128	C3
Maturín	140	E2
Maubeuge	54	F4
Mauganj	88	D4
Maui	132	(2)F3
Maullín	142	G7
Maun	62	K6
Maun	108	C3
Mauna Kea	132	(2)F4
Mauna Loa	132	(2)F4
Mauritania	102	C5
Mauritius	108	(1)B2
Mauron	58	C5
Mauthen	62	H4
Mavinga	108	C3
Mawlaik	84	A2
Max	126	F1
Maya	78	P5
Maya	86	D3
Mayādīn	92	J6
Mayaguana	134	K4
Mayagüez	134	L5
Mayamba	106	B4
Maych'ew	100	G5
Maydh	106	H1
Mayenne	58	E5
Mayenne	58	E5
Mayer	132	D2
Maykamys	76	P8
Maykop	92	J1
Mayly-Say	90	K1
Maymecha	78	G3
Mayn	78	W4
Mayo	122	D4
Mayor Island	116	F3
Mayotte	108	H2
Mayrhofen	62	G3
Mayskiy	78	M6
Mayumba	104	G5
Mayya	78	N4
Mazagão	140	G4
Mazagran	58	K4
Mazama	126	B1
Mazamet	58	H10
Mazar	76	P10
Mazār	94	C5
Mazara del Vallo	64	G11
Mazār-e Sharīf	90	J2
Mazatlán	134	C4
Mažeikiai	50	M1
Mazocahui	132	D3
Mazomora	106	F5
Mazra	94	C5
Mazyr	70	E4
Mazzarino	64	J11
Mbabane	108	E5
Mbaïki	104	H4
Mbala	106	E5
Mbale	106	E3
Mbalmayo	104	G4
Mbamba Bay	108	E2
Mbandaka	106	B3
Mbanga	104	F4
M'banza Congo	106	A5
Mbarara	106	E4
Mbeya	106	E5
Mbomou	106	C3
Mbour	104	A2
Mbout	102	C5
Mbuji-Mayi	106	C5
Mbuyuni	106	F5
McAlester	130	B3
McBride	122	G6
McCamey	132	F2
McCammon	126	D2
McClintock	122	N5
McClintock Channel	122	L2
McComb	130	C3
McCook	126	F2
McDermitt	126	C2
McGehee	130	C3
McGrath	132	(1)F3
Mchinga	106	F5
McKinlay	114	H4
McKinney	130	B3
McLaughlin	126	F1
McLennan	122	H5
McMinnville	128	C3
McPherson	130	B2
McRae	130	E3
Meadow Lake	122	K6
Meadville	128	D2
Meander River	122	H5
Meaux	54	E6
Mecca = Makkah	100	G3
Mechelen	54	G3
Mechernich	54	J4
Mecidiye	68	J4
Mecklenburger Bucht	52	G2
Mecula	108	F2
Meda	60	C4
Medak	88	C5
Medan	86	B2
Médéa	60	N8
Medellín	140	B2
Medenine	102	H2
Mederdra	102	B5
Medford	126	B2
Medgidia	66	R5
Mediaş	66	M3
Medicine Bow	126	E2
Medicine Hat	122	J7
Medicine Lodge	130	B2
Medina = Al Madīnah	100	G3
Medinaceli	60	H3
Medina de Campo	60	F3
Medina Sidonia	60	E8
Mediterranean Sea	46	E4
Mednogorsk	70	L4
Medveditsa	70	H4
Medvezh'yegorsk	70	F2
Meekatharra	114	C5
Meeker	126	E2
Meerane	52	H6
Meerut	88	C3
Mega	87	D3
Mēga	106	F3
Megalopoli	68	E7
Meganisi	68	C6
Megara	68	F6
Megisti	68	M8
Mehrān	92	M7
Mehriz	90	F3
Meiktila	84	B2
Meiningen	52	F6
Meiringen	62	D4
Meißen	52	J5
Meizhou	84	F2
Mejez El Bab	64	D12
Mékambo	104	G4
Mek'elē	100	G5
Meknès	102	D2
Mekong	84	D4
Melaka	86	C2
Melanesia	112	F5
Melbourne, *Australia*	114	H7
Melbourne, *US*	130	E4
Melchor de Mencos	134	G5
Meldorf	52	D2
Meldrum Bay	128	D1
Meleuz	70	L4
Mélfi	100	C5
Melfi	64	K8
Melfort	122	L6
Melide	60	B2
Melilla	60	H9
Melita	126	F1
Melitopol'	70	G5
Melk	62	L2
Melkosopochnik	76	N8
Mělník	52	K6
Melo	142	L5
Melton Mowbray	54	B2
Melun	58	H5
Melut	100	F5
Melvern Lake	130	B2
Melville	122	L6
Melville Island, *Australia*	114	F2
Melville Island, *Canada*	120	N2
Melville Peninsula	122	P3
Memba	108	G2
Memberamo	87	E3
Memboro	87	A4
Memmert	54	J1
Memmingen	62	F3
Mempawah	86	D2
Memphis, *Mo., US*	128	B2
Memphis, *Tenn., US*	128	C3
Mena	130	C3
Menai Strait	56	H8
Ménaka	102	F5
Mendawai	86	E3
Mende	58	J9
Menden	54	K3
Mendī	106	F2
Mendoza	142	H5
Menemen	68	K6
Menen	54	F4
Menfi	64	G11
Menggala	86	D3
Meniet	102	F4
Menindee	114	H6
Menkere	78	L3
Menominee	128	C1
Menomonee Falls	128	C2
Menongue	108	B2
Menorca	60	Q4
Mentok	86	D3
Menunu	87	B2
Menyuan	80	C3
Menzel Bourguiba	64	D11
Menzel Bouzelfa	64	E12
Menzel Temime	64	E12
Menzies	114	D5
Meppel	54	J2
Meppen	54	K2
Merano	62	G4
Merauke	87	F4
Mercato Saraceno	62	H7

Merced 126 B3
Mercedes, *Argentina* 142 H5
Mercedes, *Argentina* 142 K4
Mercedes, *US* 130 B4
Mercedes, *Uruguay* 142 K5
Mercury Islands 116 E3
Mere 54 F4
Mergenevo 70 K5
Mergui 84 B4
Mergui Archipelago 84 B4
Merichas 68 G7
Mérida, *Mexico* 134 G4
Mérida, *Spain* 60 D6
Mérida, *Venezuela* 134 K7
Meridian 130 D3
Mérignac 58 E9
Merinha Grande 60 B5
Meriruma 140 G3
Merke 76 N9
Merkys 48 N9
Merowe 100 F4
Merredin 114 C6
Merrill 128 C1
Merriman 126 F2
Merritt 122 G6
Mersch 54 J5
Merseburg 52 H5
Mers el Kébir 60 K9
Mersey 56 J8
Mersin = Icel 68 S8
Mersing 86 C2
Mērsrags 48 M8
Merthyr Tydfil 56 J10
Méru 54 E5
Meru 106 F3
Merzifon 92 F3
Merzig 54 J5
Mesa 132 D2
Mesa de Yambi 140 C3
Mesagne 64 M8
Meschede 54 L3
Mesöaria Plain 94 A1
Mesolongi 68 D6
Mesopotamia 92 K6
Messaad 102 F2
Messina, *Italy* 64 K10
Messina, *South Africa* 108 D4
Messini 68 E7
Messiniakos Kolpos 68 D8
Mestre 62 H5
Meta 140 C2
Metairie 130 C4
Metaline Falls 126 C1
Metán 142 J4
Metangula 108 E2
Metema 100 G5
Meteor Depth 138 J9
Metković 66 E6
Metlika 62 L5
Metro 86 D4
Metsovo 68 D5
Mettet 54 G4
Mettlach 54 J5
Metz 54 J5
Metzingen 62 E2
Meulaboh 84 B6
Meuse 54 G4
Mexia 130 B3
Mexicali 132 C2
Mexican Hat 132 E1
Mexico 128 B3
Mexico 134 D4
México 134 E5
Meymaneh 90 H2
Meynypil'gyno 78 X4
Mezdra 66 L6
Mezen' 70 H1
Mezenskaya Guba 70 H1
Mezhdurechensk 76 R7
Mezőberény 66 J3
Mezőkövesd 66 H2
Mezőtúr 66 H2
Mfuwe 108 E2
Miajadas 60 E5
Miami, *Fla., US* 130 E4
Miami, *Okla., US* 130 C2
Miandowāb 92 M5
Miandrivazo 108 H3
Mīāneh 92 M5
Miangyang 80 E4
Mianning 80 C5
Mianwali 88 B2
Mianyang 80 C4
Miaodao Qundao 80 G3
Miao'ergou 76 Q8
Miass 70 M4
Miastko 50 G4
Michalovce 50 L9
Michigan 128 C1
Michipicoten Island 128 C1
Michurin 66 Q7
Michurinsk 70 H4
Micronesia 112 F4
Mid-Atlantic Ridge 138 G1
Middelburg, *Netherlands* 54 F3
Middelburg, *South Africa* 108 D6
Middelfart 52 E1
Middelkerke 54 E3
Middle America Trench 120 L8
Middle Andaman 84 A4
Middlebury 128 F2
Middle Lake 126 C2
Middlesboro 128 D3
Middlesbrough 56 L7
Middletown, *N.Y., US* 128 F2
Middletown, *Oh., US* 128 D3
Mīdī 100 H4
Midland, *Canada* 128 E2
Midland, *Mich., US* 128 D2
Midland, *Tex., US* 132 F2
Midway Islands 112 J3
Midwest City 130 B2
Midzor 66 K6
Miechów 50 K7
Międzyrzec Podlaski 50 M5
Miedzyrzecz 50 E5
Mielan 58 F10
Mielec 50 L7
Miembwe 106 F5
Mien 50 D1
Miercurea-Ciuc 66 N3
Mieres 60 E1
Miesbach 62 G3
Mī'ēso 106 G2
Miging 88 F3
Miguel Auza 132 F4
Mikhaylovka 70 H4
Mikhaylovskiy 76 P7
Mikino 78 U4
Mikkeli 48 P6
Mikulov 62 M2
Mikun' 70 K2
Mikuni-sammyaku 82 K5
Mikura-jima 82 K7
Mila 102 G1
Milaca 128 B1
Miladhunmadulu Atoll 88 B7
Milan = Milano, *Italy* 62 E5
Milan, *US* 130 D2
Milano 62 E5
Milas 68 K7
Milazzo 64 K10
Mildura 114 H6
Miles 114 K5
Miles City 126 E1
Milford, *Del., US* 128 E3
Milford, *Ut., US* 126 D3
Milford Haven 56 G10
Milford Sound 116 A7
Milford Sound 116 A7
Miliana 60 N8
Milicz 50 G6
Milk 122 J7
Mil'kovo 78 T6
Millau 58 J9
Millbank 126 G1
Milledgeville 130 E3
Miller 126 G2
Millerovo 70 H5
Millington 128 C3
Millinocket 128 G1
Miloro 106 E5
Milos 68 G8
Milton, *New Zealand* 116 B8
Milton, *US* 130 D3
Milton Keynes 54 B2
Miluo 80 E5
Milwaukee 128 C2
Mily 76 L8
Mimizan-Plage 58 D9
Mīnāb 95 G3
Mina Jebel Ali 95 F4
Minas, *Indonesia* 86 C3
Minas, *Uruguay* 142 K5
Mīnā' Sa'ūd 95 C2
Minas Gerais 140 H7
Minas Novas 140 J7
Minatitlán 134 F5
Minbu 84 A2
Minchinmávida 142 G7
Mincivan 92 M4
Mindanao 84 G5
Mindelheim 62 F2
Mindelo 104 (1)B1
Minden 54 L2
Mindoro 84 G4
Mindoro Strait 84 G4
Minehead 56 J10
Mineola 130 B3
Mineral'nyye Vody 92 K1
Minerva Reefs 112 J8
Minfeng 76 Q10
Minga 106 D6
Mingäçevir 92 M3
Mingäçevir Su Anbarı 92 M3
Mingulay 56 D5
Minhe 80 C3
Minicoy 88 B7
Minilya Roadhouse 114 B4
Minna 104 F3
Minneapolis 128 B2
Minnesota 128 A1
Minnesota 128 A2
Miño 60 C2
Minot 126 F1
Minsk 70 E4
Minturn 126 E3
Minusinsk 76 S7
Min Xian 80 C4
Min'yar 70 L3
Miquelon 128 E1
Miraflores 140 C3
Miramas 58 K10
Mirambeau 58 E8
Miranda 140 F8
Miranda de Ebro 60 H2
Miranda do Douro 60 D3
Mirandela 60 C3
Mirbāt 90 F6
Mīrjāveh 90 H4
Mirnyy 78 J4
Mirow 52 H3
Mirpur Khas 88 A3
Mirtoö Pelagos 68 F7
Mirzapur 88 D3
Miskolc 66 H1
Misoöl 87 D3
Misrātah 100 C1
Missinaibi 122 Q6
Missinipe 122 L5
Mission 126 F2
Mississippi 130 C3
Mississippi 130 D2
Mississippi River Delta 130 D4
Missoula 126 D1
Missouri 126 F1
Missouri 128 B3
Missouri City 130 B4
Mistassibi 122 S7
Mistelbach 62 M2
Mitchell 126 G2
Mithankot 90 K4
Mithaylov 70 G4
Mithymna 68 J5
Mito 82 L5
Mitsamiouli 108 G2
Mitsinjo 108 H3
Mits'iwa 90 C6
Mittellandkanal 54 K2
Mittersill 62 H3
Mittweida 52 H6
Mitú 140 C3
Mitzic 104 G4
Miyake-jima 82 K6
Miyako 82 L4
Miyakonojō 82 F8
Miyazaki 82 F8
Miyoshi 82 G6
Mīzan Teferī 106 F2
Mizdah 102 H2
Mizen Head 56 B10
Mizhhir"ya 66 L1
Mizil 66 P4
Mizpe Ramon 94 B6
Mjölby 48 H7
Mjøsa 48 F6
Mkuze 108 E5
Mladá Boleslav 50 D7
Mladenovac 66 H5
Mława 50 K4
Mljet 66 E7
Mmabatho 108 D5
Moa 114 H2
Moanda 104 G5
Moapa 126 D3
Moba 106 D5
Mobaye 106 C3
Mobayi-Mbongo 106 C3
Moberly 128 B3
Mobile 130 D3
Moçambique 108 G3
Môc Châu 84 C2
Mochudi 108 D4
Mocimboa da Praia 108 G2
Mocuba 108 F3
Modane 62 B5
Modena 62 F6
Modesto 126 B3
Modica 64 J12
Mödling 62 M2
Modowi 87 D3
Modriča 66 F5
Moenkopi 132 D1
Moers 54 J3
Moffat 56 J6
Moffat Peak 116 B7
Mogadishu = Muqdisho 106 H3
Mogaung 84 B1
Mogilno 50 G5
Mogocha 78 K6
Mogochin 76 Q6
Mogok 84 B2
Mohács 66 F4
Mohammadia 60 L9
Mohe 78 L6
Mohembo 108 C3
Mohoro 106 F5
Mohyliv-Podil's'kyy 66 Q1
Moi 48 D7
Moincêr 88 D2
Moinești 66 P3
Mo i Rana 48 H3
Moissac 58 G9
Mojave 132 C1
Mojave Desert 132 C2
Mokau 116 E4
Mokohinau Island 116 E2
Mokolo 104 G2
Mokoreta 116 B8
Mokp'o 82 D6
Mol 54 H3
Mola di Bari 64 M7
Molat 62 K6
Molde 48 D5
Moldova 66 P2
Moldova 66 R2
Moldova Nouă 66 J5
Molepolole 108 C4
Molfetta 64 L7
Molina de Aragón 60 J4
Molina de Segura 60 J6
Moline 128 B2
Möll 62 J4
Mollendo 140 C7
Molokai 132 (2)D2
Molopo 108 C5
Molsheim 62 C2
Moma 108 F3
Mombasa 106 G4
Momchilgrad 66 N8
Møn 52 H2
Monach Islands 56 E4
Monaco 62 C7
Monaco 62 C7
Monahans 132 F2
Mona Passage 134 L5
Monbetsu, *Japan* 82 M1
Monbetsu, *Japan* 82 M2
Moncalieri 62 C5
Monchegorsk 48 S3
Mönchengladbach 54 J3
Monchique 60 B7
Monclova 132 F3
Moncton 122 U7
Mondovi 62 C6
Mondragone 64 H7
Mondy 78 G6
Monemvasia 68 F8
Monfalcone 62 J5
Monforte 60 C5
Monforte de Lemos 60 C2
Monfredónia 64 K7
Monga 106 C3
Mongkung 84 B2
Mongo 100 C5
Mongolia 80 B2
Mongonu 104 G2
Mongora 88 B2
Mongu 108 C3
Mong Yai 84 B2
Mong Yu 84 B2
Monkoto 106 C4
Monmouth 128 B2
Mono 104 E3
Mono Lake 126 C3
Monopoli 64 M8
Monor 50 J10
Monowai 116 A7
Monreal del Campo 60 J4
Monreale 64 H10
Monroe, *La., US* 130 C3
Monroe, *Mich., US* 128 D2
Monroe, *N.C., US* 130 E3
Monroe, *Wash., US* 126 B1
Monroe City 130 C2
Monrovia 104 B3
Mons 54 F4
Monschau 54 J4
Monselice 62 G5
Montabaur 54 K4
Montague Island 138 J9
Montalbán 60 K4
Montalto Uffugo 64 L9
Montana 66 L6
Montana 126 E1
Montargis 58 H6
Montauban 58 G10
Montauk 128 F2
Mont aux Sources 108 D5
Montbard 58 K6
Montbéliard 62 B3
Montblanc 60 M3
Mont Blanc 62 B5
Montbrison 58 K8
Mont Cameroun 104 F4
Montceau-les-Mines 58 K7
Mont-de-Marsan 58 E10
Montdidier 54 E5
Monte Alegre 140 G4
Monte Azul 140 J7
Montebello 128 F1
Montebello Islands 114 B4
Montebelluna 62 H5
Monte Calvo 64 K7
Monte Cinto 64 C6
Montecristo 64 E6
Monte Etna 64 J11
Montefiascone 64 G6
Montego Bay 134 J5
Montélimar 58 K9
Monte Limbara 64 D8
Monte Lindo 142 K4
Montemorelos 130 B4
Monte Namuli 108 F3
Monte Perdino 60 L2
Monte Pollino 64 L9
Montepuez 108 F2
Montepulciano 64 F5
Monte Quemado 142 J4
Montereau-faut-Yonne 58 H5
Monterey 128 E3
Monterey Bay 126 B3
Montería 140 B2
Montero 140 E7
Monte Rosa 62 C5
Monterotondo 64 G6
Monterrey 132 F3
Monte Sant'Angelo 64 K7
Montes Claros 140 J7
Montesilvano 64 J6
Montevarchi 62 G7
Montevideo, *US* 128 A1
Montevideo, *Uruguay* 142 K5
Monte Viso 62 C6
Monte Vista 132 E1
Montgomery 130 D3
Monthey 62 B4
Monticello 126 E3
Montijo 60 D6
Montilla 60 F7
Mont Joli 128 G1
Mont-Laurier 128 E1
Montluçon 58 H7
Montmagny 128 F1
Montmedy 54 H5
Mont Mézenc 58 K9
Montone 62 G6
Montoro 60 F6
Mont Pelat 58 M9
Montpelier, *Id., US* 126 D2
Montpelier, *Vt., US* 128 F2
Montpellier 58 J10
Montréal 128 F1
Montreul 54 D4
Montreux 62 B4
Montrose, *UK* 56 K5
Montrose, *US* 126 E3
Monts Bagzane 102 G5
Mont Serkout 102 G4
Montserrat 134 M5
Monts Nimba 104 C3
Monts Otish 122 S6
Mont Tahat 102 G4
Monywa 84 A2
Monza 62 E5
Monzón 60 L3
Moonie 114 K5
Moorcroft 126 F2

Moorhead	128	A1
Moosburg	62	G1
Moose Jaw	122	K6
Moose Lake	122	M6
Moosomin	122	L6
Moosonee	122	Q6
Mopeia	108	F3
Mopti	102	E6
Moqor	90	J3
Mór	66	F2
Mora	48	H6
Móra	60	B6
Moradabad	88	C3
Morafenobe	108	G3
Morag	50	J4
Moramanga	108	H3
Moran	126	D2
Morane	112	N8
Moratuwa	88	D7
Morava	50	G8
Moravské Budějovice	62	L1
Morawhanna	140	F2
Moray Firth	56	J4
Morbach	54	K5
Morbegno	62	E4
Morbi	88	B4
Morcenx	58	E9
Mordaga	78	L6
Mordoviya	70	H4
Moreau	126	F1
Morecambe	56	K7
Moree	114	J5
Morehead, *Papua New Guinea*	87	F4
Morehead, *US*	128	D3
More Laptevykh	78	L1
Morelia	134	D5
Morella	60	K4
Moresby Island	132	(1)L5
Moreton Island	114	K5
Morez	58	M7
Morfou	68	Q9
Morgan	114	G6
Morgan City	130	C4
Morgantown	128	D3
Morges	62	B4
Mori	82	L2
Morioka	82	L4
Morkoka	78	J4
Morlaix	58	B5
Mornington Island	114	G3
Morocco	98	C2
Morogoro	106	F5
Moro Gulf	84	G5
Morombe	108	G4
Mörön	78	G7
Morondava	108	G4
Morón de la Frontera	60	E7
Moroni	108	G2
Moron Us He	88	F2
Morotai	87	C2
Moroto	106	E3
Morpeth	56	L6
Morris	126	G1
Morristown	130	E2
Mors	48	E8
Morshansk	70	H4
Mortain	54	B6
Morteros	142	J5
Morvern	56	G5
Morwell	114	J7
Mosbach	52	E7
Mosby	126	D1
Moscow = Moskva	70	G3
Mosel	54	K4
Moselle	54	G6
Moses Lake	126	C1
Mosgiel	116	C7
Moshi	106	F4
Mosjøen	48	G4
Moskenesøy	48	F3
Moskva	70	G3
Mosonmagyaróvár	62	N3
Mosquero	132	F1
Moss	48	F7
Mossburn	116	B7
Mosselbaai	108	C6
Mossoró	140	K5
Most	52	J6
Mostaganem	60	L9
Mostar	66	E6
Mostoles	60	G4
Møsvatn	48	E7
Mot'a	100	G5
Motala	48	H7
Motherwell	56	J6
Motihari	88	D3
Motilla del Palancar	60	J5
Motiti Island	116	F3
Motril	60	G8
Motru	66	K5
Motu One	112	L7
Motygino	76	S6
Mouchard	62	A4
Moudjéria	102	C5
Moudros	68	H5
Mouila	104	G5
Moulins	58	J7
Moulmein	84	B3
Moultrie	130	E3
Moundou	100	C6
Mount Adam	142	J9
Mount Adams	126	B1
Mountain Grove	128	B3
Mountain Home	128	B3
Mountain Nile = Bahr el Jebel	106	E2
Mount Alba	116	B7
Mount Aloysius	114	E5
Mount Anglem	116	A8
Mount Apo	84	H5
Mount Ararat	92	L4
Mount Arrowsmith	116	C6
Mount Aspiring	116	B7
Mount Assiniboine	122	H6
Mount Augustus	114	C4
Mount Baco	84	G3
Mount Baker	126	B1
Mount Bartle Frere	114	J3
Mount Bogong	114	J7
Mount Brewster	116	B7
Mount Bruce	114	C4
Mount Cameroun	98	D5
Mount Carmel	126	D3
Mount Columbia	122	H6
Mount Cook = Aoraki	116	C6
Mount Cook	116	C6
Mount Donald	116	A7
Mount Douglas	114	J4
Mount Egmont	116	E4
Mount Elbert	126	E3
Mount Elgon	106	E3
Mount Essendon	114	D4
Mount Evelyn	114	F2
Mount Everest	88	E3
Mount Fairweather	122	D5
Mount Gambier	114	H7
Mount Garnet	114	J3
Mount Hermon	94	C3
Mount Hood	126	B1
Mount Hutt	116	C6
Mount Huxley	116	B7
Mount Isa	114	G4
Mount Jackson	144	(2)MM2
Mount Karisimbi	106	D4
Mount Kendall	116	D5
Mount Kenya = Kirinyaga	106	F4
Mount Kilimanjaro	106	F4
Mount Kirkpatrick	144	(2)AA1
Mount Kosciuszko	114	J7
Mount Liebig	114	F4
Mount Lloyd George	122	G5
Mount Logan	122	C4
Mount Magnet	114	C5
Mount Maunganui	116	F3
Mount McKinley	132	(1)G3
Mount Meharry	114	C4
Mount Menzies	144	(2)L2
Mount Minto	144	(2)Y2
Mount Mulanje	108	F3
Mount Murchison	116	C6
Mount Nyiru	106	F3
Mount Olympus	126	B1
Mount Ord	114	E3
Mount Ossa	114	J8
Mount Owen	116	D5
Mount Paget	142	P9
Mount Pleasant, *Ia., US*	128	B2
Mount Pleasant, *Mich., US*	128	D2
Mount Pleasant, *S.C., US*	130	F3
Mount Pleasant, *Tex., US*	130	B3
Mount Pleasant, *Ut., US*	126	D3
Mount Pulog	84	G3
Mount Rainier	126	B1
Mount Ratz	122	E5
Mount Richmond	116	D5
Mount Roberts	114	K5
Mount Robson	122	H6
Mount Roosevelt	122	F5
Mount Roraima	140	E2
Mount Ross	116	E5
Mount Shasta	126	B2
Mount Somers	116	C6
Mount Stanley	106	D3
Mount Tahat	98	D3
Mount Travers	116	D6
Mount Tuun	82	D3
Mount Usborne	142	K9
Mount Vernon, *Al., US*	130	D3
Mount Vernon, *Ill., US*	128	C3
Mount Vernon, *Oh., US*	128	D2
Mount Vernon, *Wash., US*	126	B1
Mount Victoria, *Myanmar*	84	A2
Mount Victoria, *Papua New Guinea*	112	E6
Mount Waddington	122	F6
Mount Washington	122	S8
Mount Whitney	126	C3
Mount Wilson	126	E3
Mount Woodroffe	114	F5
Mount Ziel	114	F4
Moura	60	C6
Mousa	56	L2
Moussoro	100	C5
Moutamba	104	G5
Mouth of the Shannon	56	B9
Mouths of the Amazon	138	G3
Mouths of the Danube	66	S4
Mouths of the Ganges	88	E4
Mouths of the Indus	90	J5
Mouths of the Irrawaddy	84	A3
Mouths of the Krishna	88	D5
Mouths of the Mekong	84	D5
Mouths of the Niger	104	F4
Moûtiers	62	B5
Moutong	87	B2
Mouzarak	104	H2
Moyale	106	F3
Moyen Atlas	102	D2
Moyenvic	54	J6
Moyeroo	76	U4
Moyynty	76	N8
Mozambique	108	E3
Mozambique Channel	108	F4
Mozdok	92	L2
Mozhga	70	K3
Mozirje	62	K4
Mpanda	106	E5
Mpika	108	E2
Mporokoso	106	E5
Mpumalanga	108	D5
Mragowo	50	L4
Mrkonjić-Grad	62	N6
M'Sila	102	F1
Mtsensk	70	G4
Mtwara	106	G6
Muang Khammouan	84	C3
Muang Không	84	D4
Muang Khôngxédôn	84	D3
Muang Khoua	84	C2
Muang Pakxan	84	C3
Muang Phin	84	D3
Muang Sing	84	C2
Muang Xai	84	C2
Muar	86	C2
Muarabungo	86	C3
Muaradua	86	C3
Muarasiberut	86	B3
Muaratewen	86	E3
Muarawahau	86	F2
Mubarek	76	M10
Mubende	106	E3
Mubrani	87	D3
Muck	56	F5
Muckadilla	114	J5
Muconda	106	C6
Mucur	68	S5
Mudanjiang	82	E1
Mudanya	68	L4
Muddy Gap	126	E2
Mudurnu	68	P4
Mufulira	108	D2
Mughshin	90	F6
Muğla	68	L7
Mugodzhary	70	L5
Muhammad Qol	100	G3
Mühldorf	62	H2
Mühlhausen	52	F5
Muhos	48	N4
Muhu	48	M7
Muhulu	106	D4
Mukacheve	50	M9
Mukdahan	84	C3
Mukomuko	86	C3
Mukry	90	J2
Mukuku	108	D2
Mulaku Atoll	88	B8
Mulde	52	H5
Muleshoe	132	F2
Mulgrave Island	114	H2
Mulhacén	60	G7
Mülheim	54	J3
Mulhouse	62	C3
Muling	82	G1
Mull	56	G5
Mullaittivu	88	D7
Mullewa	114	C5
Müllheim	62	C3
Mullingar	56	E8
Mulobezi	108	D3
Multan	90	K3
Mumbai	88	B5
Mumbwa	108	D2
Muna	87	B4
Münchberg	52	G6
München	62	G2
Münden	52	E5
Mundo Novo	140	J6
Mundrabilla	114	E6
Muneðarnes	48	(1)C1
Munera	60	H5
Mungbere	106	D3
Munger	88	E3
Munich = München	62	G2
Munster, *France*	62	C2
Munster, *Germany*	52	F4
Münster, *Germany*	54	K3
Munte	87	A2
Muojärvi	48	Q4
Muonio	48	M3
Muqdisho	106	H3
Mur	62	L4
Muradiye	92	K4
Murang'a	106	F4
Murashi	70	J3
Murat	92	K4
Muratlı	68	K3
Murchison	116	D5
Murcia	60	J7
Murdo	126	F2
Mureş	66	J3
Muret	58	G10
Murfreesboro, *N.C., US*	130	F2
Murfreesboro, *Tenn., US*	130	D2
Murghob	90	K2
Muriaé	140	J8
Müritz	52	H3
Muriwai	116	F4
Murmansk	48	S2
Murnau	62	G3
Murom	70	H3
Muroran	82	L2
Muros	60	A2
Muroto	82	H7
Murphy	130	E2
Murray	114	H6
Murray	128	C3
Murray Bridge	114	G7
Murray River Basin	114	H6
Murska Sobota	62	M4
Murter	62	L7
Murtosa	60	B4
Murud	88	B5
Murupara	116	F4
Mururoa	112	M8
Murwara	88	D4
Murzūq	102	H3
Mürzzuschlag	62	L3
Muş	92	J4
Mūša	50	N1
Musala	68	F2
Musandam Peninsula	95	G3
Musay'īd	95	D4
Muscat = Masqaţ	95	H5
Musgrave Ranges	114	E5
Mushin	104	E3
Muskegon	128	C2
Muskogee	130	B2
Musmar	100	G4
Musoma	106	E4
Mussende	106	B6
Mustafakemalpaşa	68	L4
Mut, *Egypt*	100	E2
Mut, *Turkey*	68	R8
Mutare	108	E3
Mutarnee	114	J3
Mutnyy Materik	70	L1
Mutoray	76	U5
Mutsamudu	108	G2
Mutsu	82	L3
Mutsu-wan	82	L3
Muttaburra	114	H4
Mutur	88	D7
Muyezerskiy	48	R5
Muyinga	106	E4
Muynak	76	K9
Muzaffarnagar	88	C3
Muzaffarpur	88	E3
Muzillac	58	C6
Múzquiz	132	F3
Muztagata	76	N10
Mwali	108	G2
Mwanza	106	E4
Mweka	106	C4
Mwenda	106	D6
Mwene-Ditu	106	C5
Mwenezi	108	E4
Mwenezi	108	E4
Mwinilunga	108	C2
Myanmar	84	B2
Myaungmya	84	A3
Myingyan	84	B2
Myitkyina	84	B1
Myjava	62	N2
Myjava	62	N2
Mykolayiv	50	N8
Mykonos	68	H7
Mymensingh	88	F4
Mynbulak	76	L9
Myndagayy	78	N4
Myŏjin	80	K4
Myonggan	82	E3
Myrdalsjökull	48	(1)D3
Myrina	68	H5
Myrtle Beach	130	F3
Mys Alevina	78	S5
Mys Aniva	80	L1
Mys Buorkhaya	78	N2
Mys Dezhneva	78	Z3
Mys Elizavety	78	Q6
Mys Enkan	78	P5
Mys Govena	78	V5
Mys Kanin Nos	70	H1
Mys Kekurskij	48	S2
Mys Kril'on	80	L1
Myślenice	50	J8
Myślibórz	50	D5
Mys Lopatka, *Russia*	78	T6
Mys Lopatka, *Russia*	78	S2
Mys Navarin	78	X4
Mys Olyutorskiy	78	W5
Mysore	88	C6
Mys Peschanyy	76	J9
Mys Povorotnyy	82	G2
Mys Prubiynyy	70	F5
Mys Shelagskiy	78	V2
Mys Sivuchiy	78	U5
Mys Terpeniya	78	Q7
Mys Tolstoy	78	T5
Mys Yuzhnyy	78	T5
Mys Zhelaniya	76	M2
Myszksw	50	J7
My Tho	84	D4
Mytilini	68	J5
Mývatn	48	(1)E2
Mže	52	H7
Mzimba	108	E2
Mzuzu	108	E2

N

Naalehu	132	(2)F4
Naas	56	F8
Nabas	84	G4
Naberezhnyye Chelny	70	K3
Nabeul	64	E12
Nabīd	95	G2
Nabire	87	E3
Nablus	94	C4
Nacala	108	G2
Nacaroa	108	F2
Náchod	50	F7
Nacogdoches	130	C3
Nadiad	88	B4
Nador	102	E2
Nadvirna	66	M1
Nadym	70	P1
Nadym	70	P2
Næstved	52	G1
Nafpaktos	68	D6
Nafplio	68	E7
Naga	84	G4
Nagano	82	K5
Nagaoka	82	K5
Nagaon	88	F3
Nagarzê	88	F3
Nagasaki	82	E7
Nagaur	88	B3
Nagercoil	88	C7
Nago	80	H5
Nagold	52	D8
Nagorsk	70	K3
Nagoya	82	J6
Nagpur	88	C4
Nagqu	88	F2
Nagyatád	62	N4
Nagykálló	66	J2
Nagykanizsa	62	N4
Nagykáta	50	J10
Nagykőrös	66	G2

Naha 80 H5
Nahanni 122 G4
Nahanni Butte 122 G4
Nahr en Nile = Nile 100 F2
Naiman Qi 80 G2
Nain 122 U5
Nairn 56 J4
Nairobi 106 F4
Naivasha 106 F4
Naizishan 82 D2
Najafābād 90 F3
Nájera 60 H2
Najibabad 88 C3
Najin 82 F2
Najrān 100 H4
Naju 82 D6
Nakamura 82 G7
Nakatsu 82 F7
Nakhl 94 A7
Nakhodka, *Russia* 76 P4
Nakhodka, *Russia* 82 G2
Nakhon Ratchasima 84 C3
Nakhon Sawan 84 B3
Nakhon Si Thammarat 84 B5
Nakina 122 P6
Nakło nad Notecią 50 G4
Naknek 132 (1)F4
Nakonde 106 E5
Nakskov 52 G2
Nakten 48 H5
Nakuru 106 F4
Nal'chik 92 K2
Nallihan 68 P4
Nālūt 102 H2
Namagan 76 N9
Namakzar-e Shadad 95 G1
Namanga 106 F4
Namapa 108 F2
Namasagali 106 E3
Nam Can 84 C5
Nam Co 88 F2
Namdalen 48 G4
Nam Dinh 84 D2
Namib Desert 108 A4
Namibe 108 A3
Namibia 108 B4
Namidobe 108 F3
Namlea 87 C3
Namo 87 A3
Nampa 126 C2
Nampala 104 C1
Nam Ping 84 B3
Namp'o 82 C4
Nampula 108 F3
Namsos 48 F4
Namtsy 78 M4
Namur 54 G4
Namwala 108 D3
Namwŏn 82 D6
Nan 84 C3
Nanaimo 126 B1
Nanao 82 J5
Nanchang 80 F5
Nanchong 80 D4
Nancy 62 B2
Nanda Devi 88 C2
Nānded 88 C5
Nandurbar 88 B4
Nandyal 88 C5
Nanfeng 80 F5
Nangalala 114 G2
Nangapinoh 86 E3
Nangatayap 86 E3
Nangis 58 J5
Nangong 80 F3
Nang Xian 88 F3
Nanjing 80 F4
Nankoku 82 G7
Nannine 114 C5
Nanning 84 D2
Nanortalik 122 X4
Nanpan 84 D2
Nanping 80 F5
Nansei-shotō 80 H5
Nantes 58 D6
Nanton 124 D1
Nantong 80 G4
Nanumea 112 H6
Nanuque 140 J7
Nanutarra Roadhouse 114 C4
Nanyang 80 E4
Napa 126 B3
Napalkovo 76 N3
Napamute 132 (1)F3
Napas 78 C4
Napasoq 122 W3
Napier 116 F4
Naples = Napoli 64 J8
Naples 130 E4
Napo 140 C4
Napoli 64 J8
Naqb Ashtar 94 C6
Nara, *Japan* 82 H6
Nara, *Mali* 102 D5
Narathiwat 84 C5
Narbonne 58 H10
Nardò 64 N8
Nares Strait 120 J2
Narev 50 N5
Narew 50 L5
Narib 108 B4
Narmada 88 C4
Narnaul 88 C3
Narni 64 G6
Narok 106 F4
Närpes 48 L5
Narrabi 114 J6
Narrandera 114 J6
Narsimhapur 88 C4
Nart 80 F2
Narva 48 P7
Narva 48 Q7
Narva Bay 48 P7
Narvik 48 J2
Nar'yan Mar 70 K1
Naryn 78 F6
Năsăud 66 M2
Nashua 128 F2
Nashville 130 D2
Našice 66 F4
Nasik 88 B4
Nasir 106 E2
Nassarawa 104 F3
Nassau 130 F4
Nässjö 48 H8
Nastapoka Islands 122 R5
Nasugbu 84 G4
Naswá 95 G5
Nata 108 D4
Natal 140 K5
Natara 78 L3
Natashquan 122 U6
Natchez 130 C3
Natchitoches 130 C3
National Park 116 E4
Natitingou 104 E2
Natori 82 L4
Natuna Besar 86 D2
Naucelle 58 H9
Nauchas 108 B4
Nauders 62 F4
Naujoji Akmenė 50 M1
Naumburg 52 G5
Na'ūr 94 C5
Nauru 112 G6
Nauta 140 C4
Nautonwa 88 D3
Navahermosa 60 F5
Navahrudak 48 N10
Navajo Reservoir 126 E3
Navalero 60 H3
Navalmoral de la Mata 60 E5
Navalvillar de Pela 60 E5
Navapolatsk 70 E3
Navlya 70 F4
Navoi 76 M9
Navojoa 124 E6
Navrongo 104 D2
Navsari 88 B4
Nawá 94 D4
Nawabshah 90 J4
Nāwah 90 J3
Naxçıvan 92 L4
Naxos 68 H7
Naxos 68 H7
Nayakhan 78 T4
Nāy Band, *Iran* 90 G3
Nāy Band, *Iran* 95 E3
Nayoro 82 M1
Naypyidaw 84 B3
Nazaré 60 A5
Nazareth 94 C4
Nazarovo 76 S6
Nazca 140 C6
Nazca Ridge 142 E3
Naze 80 H5
Nazilli 68 L7
Nazino 76 P6
Nazran' 92 L2
Nazrēt 106 F2
Nazwá 90 G5
Nazyvayevsk 70 P3
Ncojane 108 C4
Ndélé 106 C2
Ndjamena 100 B5
Ndjolé 104 G5
Ndola 108 D2
Nea Ionia 68 E5
Neale Junction 114 E5
Neapoli 68 F8
Nea Roda 68 F4
Nea Zichni 68 F3
Nebbi 106 E3
Nebitdag 90 F2
Nebo 114 J4
Nebraska 126 G2
Neckar 52 D7
Neckar 52 D8
Neckarsulm 52 E7
Necker Island 112 K3
Necochea 142 K6
Nédély 100 C4
Nedre Soppero 48 L3
Needles 132 D2
Nefedovo 70 P3
Nefta 102 G2
Neftçala 92 N4
Neftekamsk 70 K3
Neftekumsk 92 L1
Nefteyugansk 70 P2
Nefza 64 D12
Negage 106 B5
Negār 95 G2
Negēlē 106 F2
Negele 106 F2
Negev 94 B6
Negomane 108 F2
Negombo 88 C7
Negotin 66 K5
Negotino 68 E3
Négrine 102 G2
Negro, *Argentina* 142 J7
Negro, *Brazil* 140 E4
Negros 84 G5
Negru Vodă 66 R6
Nehbandān 90 G3
Nehe 78 M7
Nehoiu 66 P4
Neijiang 80 C5
Nei Monggol 80 E2
Neiva 140 B3
Neixiang 80 E4
Nejanilini Lake 122 M5
Nek'emtē 106 F2
Nelidovo 70 F3
Neligh 126 G2
Nellore 88 C6
Nel'ma 78 P7
Nelson 122 N5
Nelson, *Canada* 126 C1
Nelson, *New Zealand* 116 D5
Nelspruit 108 E5
Nëma 102 D5
Nëman 48 N10
Neman 50 M2
Nemours 58 H5
Nemperola 87 B5
Nemunas 50 P3
Nemuro 82 N2
Nen 78 L7
Nenagh 56 D9
Nenana 132 (1)H3
Nene 54 B2
Nenjiang 78 M7
Neosho 128 B3
Nepa 78 H5
Nepal 88 D3
Nepalganj 88 D3
Nepean 128 E1
Nepomuk 52 J7
Ner 50 H5
Nera 64 G6
Neratovice 52 K6
Neris 50 P2
Nerja 60 G8
Neryungri 78 L5
Nesebŭr 66 Q7
Ness City 130 B2
Netanya 94 B4
Netherlands 54 H2
Netherlands Antilles 134 L6
Nettilling Lake 122 S3
Neubrandenburg 52 J3
Neuburg 52 G8
Neuchâtel 62 B3
Neuenhagen 52 J4
Neufchâteau, *Belgium* 54 H5
Neufchâteau, *France* 58 L5
Neufchâtel-en-Bray 54 D5
Neuhof 52 E6
Neukirchen 52 D2
Neumarkt 52 G7
Neumünster 52 F2
Neunkirchen, *Austria* 62 M3
Neunkirchen, *Germany* 52 C7
Neuquén 142 H6
Neuruppin 52 H4
Neusiedler 50 F10
Neusiedler See 62 M3
Neuss 54 J3
Neustadt, *Germany* 52 F2
Neustadt, *Germany* 52 F7
Neustadt, *Germany* 52 G6
Neustadt, *Germany* 52 G8
Neustadt, *Germany* 52 H7
Neustadt, *Germany* 54 L5
Neustrelitz 52 J3
Neu-Ulm 52 F8
Neuwerk 52 D3
Neuwied 54 K4
Nevada 126 C3
Nevada 128 B3
Nevado Auzangate 140 C6
Nevado de Colima 134 D5
Nevado de Cumbal 140 B3
Nevado de Huascaran 140 B5
Nevado de Illampu 140 D7
Nevado Sajama 140 D7
Nevados de Cachi 142 H4
Never 78 L6
Nevers 58 J7
Nevesinje 66 F6
Nevėžis 48 M9
Nevinnomyssk 92 J1
Nevşehir 68 S6
Newala 106 F6
New Albany, *Ind., US* 128 C3
New Albany, *Miss., US* 130 D3
New Amsterdam 140 F2
Newark, *N.J., US* 128 F2
Newark, *Oh., US* 128 D3
Newark-on-Trent 54 B1
New Bedford 128 F2
Newberg 126 B1
New Bern 130 F2
Newberry 130 E3
New Braunfels 130 B4
New Britain 112 F6
New Brunswick 122 T7
Newburgh 128 F2
Newbury 54 A3
New Bussa 104 E3
Newcastle, *Australia* 114 K6
Newcastle, *US* 126 F2
Newcastle-under-Lyme 56 K8
Newcastle-upon-Tyne 56 L6
Newcastle Waters 114 F3
New Delhi 88 C3
New England 126 F1
Newe Zohars 94 C5
Newfoundland 122 V7
Newfoundland and Labrador 122 V5
New Georgia Island 112 F6
New Glasgow 122 U7
New Guinea 74 S10
New Hampshire 128 F2
New Hampton 128 B2
New Hanover 112 F6
Newhaven 54 C4
New Haven 128 F2
New Iberia 130 C3
New Ireland 112 F6
New Jersey 128 F2
New Liskeard 128 E1
New London 128 F2
Newman 114 C4
Newmarket 54 C2
New Meadows 126 C2
New Mexico 132 E2
Newnan 130 E3
New Orleans 130 D4
New Plymouth 116 E4
Newport, *Eng., UK* 54 A4
Newport, *Wales, UK* 56 K10
Newport, *Ark., US* 130 C2
Newport, *Oreg., US* 126 B2
Newport, *R.I., US* 128 F2
Newport, *Vt., US* 128 F2
Newport, *Wash., US* 126 C1
New Providence 130 F5
Newquay 56 G11
Newry 56 F7
New Siberia Islands = Novosibirskiye Ostrova 78 P1
New Smyrna Beach 130 E4
New South Wales 114 H6
Newton, *Ia., US* 128 B2
Newton, *Kans., US* 130 B2
Newtownards 56 G7
New Ulm 128 B2
New York 128 E2
New York 128 F2
New Zealand 116 B5
Neya 70 H3
Neyrīz 95 F2
Neyshābūr 90 G2
Ngabang 86 D2
Ngalu 87 B5
Ngamring 88 E3
Ngaoundéré 104 G3
Ngara 106 E4
Ngawihi 116 E5
Ngo 104 H5
Ngoura 100 C5
Ngozi 106 D4
Nguigmi 104 G2
Nguru 104 G2
Nhachengue 108 F4
Nha Trang 84 D4
Nhulunbuy 114 G2
Niafounké 102 E5
Niagara Falls 128 E2
Niakaramandougou 104 C3
Niamey 104 E2
Niangara 106 D3
Nia-Nia 106 D3
Nias 86 B2
Nicaragua 134 G6
Nicastro 64 L10
Nice 62 C7
Nicholls Town 130 F4
Nicobar Islands 84 A5
Nicosia = Lefkosia 68 R9
Nida 50 K7
Nidym 78 F4
Nidzica 50 K4
Niebüll 52 D2
Niedere Tauern 62 J3
Niefang 104 G4
Niemegk 52 H4
Nienburg 52 E4
Niesky 52 K5
Nieuw Amsterdam 140 F2
Nieuw Nickerie 140 F2
Nieuwpoort 54 E3
Niğde 68 S7
Niger 102 G5
Niger 104 E2
Nigeria 104 F2
Nigoring Hu 80 B3
Niigata 82 K5
Niihau 132 (2)A2
Nii-jima 82 K6
Nijar 60 H8
Nijmegen 54 H3
Nikel' 48 R2
Nikolayevsk-na-Amure 78 Q6
Nikol'sk 70 J3
Nikol'skoye 78 V5
Nikopol' 70 F5
Nik Pey 92 N5
Nikšić 66 F7
Nilande Atoll 88 B8
Nile 100 F3
Niles 128 C2
Nimach 88 B4
Nîmes 58 K10
Nimule 106 E3
Nin 62 L6
Nine Degree Channel 88 B7
9 de Julio 142 J6
Ning'an 82 E1
Ningbo 80 G5
Ningde 80 F5
Ninghai 80 G5
Ninh Binh 84 D2
Ninh Hoa 84 D4
Ninohoe 82 L3
Niobrara 126 F2
Niobrara 126 G2
Nioro 102 D5
Nioro du Sahel 104 C1
Niort 58 E7
Nipigon 128 C1
Niquelândia 140 H6
Nirmal 88 C5
Niš 66 J6
Nisa 60 C5
Niscemi 64 J11
Nishinoomote 82 F8
Nisporeni 66 R2
Nisyros 68 K8
Niţă 95 C3
Niterói 142 N3
Nitra 50 H9
Nitra 50 H9
Nitsa 70 M3
Niue 112 K7

Nivelles 54 G4
Nizamabad 88 C5
Nizhnekamsk 70 K3
Nizhnekamskoye
Vodokhranilishche 70 K3
Nizhneudinsk 78 F5
Nizhnevartovsk 70 Q2
Nizhneyansk 78 P2
Nizhniy Lomov 70 H4
Nizhniy Novgorod 70 H3
Nizhniy Tagil 70 M3
Nizhnyaya Tunguska 78 H4
Nizhyn 70 F4
Nizip 92 G5
Nizza Monferrato 62 D6
Njazidja 108 G2
Njombe 106 E5
Njombe 106 E5
Nkambe 104 G3
Nkhotakota 108 E2
Nkongsamba 104 F4
Nkurenkuru 108 B3
Noatak 132 (1)F2
Nobeoka 82 F7
Noboribetsu 82 L2
Noci 64 M8
Nogales, *Mexico* 132 D2
Nogales, *US* 132 D2
Nogat 50 J3
Nogent-le-Rotrou 58 F5
Noginsk 70 G3
Noginskiy 76 S5
Nogliki 78 Q6
Noheji 82 L3
Noia 60 B2
Noire 84 C2
Noirmoutier-en-l'Île 58 C6
Nojima-zaki 82 K6
Nok Kundi 90 H4
Nokou 102 H6
Nola, *Central African Republic* 106 B3
Nola, *Italy* 64 J8
Nolinsk 70 J3
Noma-misaki 82 F8
Nome 132 (1)D3
Nomoi Islands 112 F5
Nomo-saki 82 E7
Nong'an 82 C1
Nong Khai 84 C3
Noord-Beveland 54 F3
Noord-Oost-Polder 54 H2
Noordwijk aan Zee 54 G2
Norak 90 J2
Noranda 128 E1
Nordaustlandet 144 (1)L1
Nordborg 52 E1
Norden 52 C3
Nordenham 52 D3
Norderney 52 C3
Norderney 52 C3
Norderstedt 52 F3
Nordfjordeid 48 D6
Nordfriesische Inseln 52 D2
Nordhausen 52 F5
Nordhorn 54 K2
Nordkapp 48 N1
Nordkinn 48 P1
Nordkinnhalvøya 48 P1
Nordkvaløya 48 J1
Nordli 48 G4
Nördlingen 52 F8
Nord-Ostsee-Kanal 52 E2
Nordstrand 52 D2
Nordvik 76 W3
Nore 56 E9
Norfolk, *Nebr., US* 126 G2
Norfolk, *Va., US* 128 E3
Norfolk Island 112 G8
Noril'sk 76 R4
Norman 130 B2
Normandia 140 F3
Normanton 114 H3
Norman Wells 122 F3
Nørre Åby 52 E1
Nørre Alslev 52 G2
Norristown 128 E2
Norrköping 48 J7
Norrtälje 48 K7
Norseman 114 D6
Norsk 78 N6
Northallerton 56 L7
Northam 114 C6
North America 112 P2
Northampton, *Australia* 114 B5
Northampton, *UK* 54 B2
North Andaman 84 A4
North Battleford 122 K6
North Bay 128 E1
North Cape 116 D2
North Carolina 130 F2
North Channel 56 G6
North Charleston 130 F3
North Dakota 126 F1
Northeast Providence Channel 130 F4
Northeim 52 F5
Northern Cape 108 C5
Northern Ireland 56 E7
Northern Mariana Islands 112 E4
Northern Territory 114 F4
North Foreland 54 D3
North Horr 106 F3
North Iberia 134 F2
North Island 116 D3
North Korea 82 C4
North Little Rock 130 C3
North Platte 124 F3
North Platte 126 F2
North Ronaldsay 56 K2
North Sea 56 N4
North Stradbroke Island 114 K5
North Taranaki Bight 116 D4
North Uist 56 E4
Northumberland Strait 122 U7
North Vancouver 126 B1
North West 108 C5
North West Basin 114 C4
North West Cape 114 B4
North West Christmas
Island Ridge 112 K4
North West Highlands 56 G4
Northwest Territories 122 G4
Norton 130 B2
Norton Sound 132 (1)E3
Nortorf 52 E2
Norway 48 F5
Norwegian Sea 48 B4
Norwich, *UK* 54 D2
Norwich, *US* 128 F2
Nos 70 H1
Nos Emine 66 Q7
Nosevaya 70 K1
Noshiro 82 K3
Nos Kaliakra 66 R6
Noşratābād 90 G4
Nossen 52 J5
Nos Shabla 66 R6
Nosy Barren 108 G3
Nosy Bé 108 H2
Nosy Boraha 108 J3
Nosy Mitsio 108 H2
Nosy Radama 108 H2
Nosy-Varika 108 H4
Notec 50 G4
Notia Pindos 68 D5
Notios Evvoïkos Kolpos 68 F6
Notre Dame Bay 122 V7
Notsé 104 E3
Nottingham 54 A2
Nottingham Island 122 R4
Nouâdhibou 102 B4
Nouakchott 102 B5
Nouâmghar 102 B5
Nouméa 112 G8
Nouvelle Calédonie 112 G8
Nova Gorica 62 J5
Nova Gradiška 66 E4
Nova Iguaçu 142 N3
Nova Mambone 108 F4
Nova Pazova 66 H5
Novara 62 D5
Nova Scotia 122 T8
Nova Xavantina 140 G6
Novaya Igirma 78 G5
Novaya Karymkary 70 N2
Novaya Kasanka 70 J5
Novaya Lyalya 70 M3
Novaya Zemlya 76 J3
Nova Zagora 66 P7
Novelda 60 K6
Nové Město 50 F8
Nové Mesto 50 G9
Nové Zámky 50 H10
Novgorod 70 F3
Novi Bečej 66 H4
Novigrad 64 H3
Novi Iskŭr 66 L7
Novi Ligure 62 D6
Novi Marof 62 M4
Novi Pazar, *Bulgaria* 66 Q6
Novi Pazar, *Serbia* 66 H6
Novi Sad 66 G4
Novi Vinodolski 62 K5
Novoaleksandrovsk 70 H5
Novoalekseyevka 70 L4
Novoanninsky 70 H4
Novocheboksarsk 70 J3
Novocherkassk 70 H5
Novodvinsk 70 H2
Novo Hamburgo 142 L4
Novohrad-Volyns'kyy 70 E4
Novokazalinsk 70 M5
Novokutznetsk 76 R7
Novokuybyshevsk 70 J4
Novoletov'ye 76 U3
Novo Mesto 62 L5
Novomikhaylovskiy 92 H1
Novomoskovsk 70 G4
Novonazimovo 78 E5
Novorossiysk 92 G1
Novorybnoye 78 H2
Novoselivka 66 S2
Novosergiyevka 70 K4
Novosibirsk 76 Q6
Novosibirskiye Ostrova 78 P1
Novosil' 70 G4
Novotroitsk 70 L4
Novouzensk 70 J4
Novozybkov 70 F4
Novvy 76 V3
Nový Bor 52 K6
Nový Jičín 50 H8
Novyy Port 76 N4
Novyy Uoyan 78 J5
Novyy Urengoy 76 P4
Novyy Urgal 78 N6
Novyy Uzen' 76 J9
Nowa Dęba 50 L7
Nowa Ruda 50 F7
Nowata 130 B2
Nowogard 50 E4
Nowo Warpno 52 K3
Nowra 114 K6
Now Shahr 90 F2
Nowy Dwór Mazowiecki 50 K5
Nowy Sącz 50 K8
Nowy Targ 50 K8
Nowy Tomyśl 50 F5
Noyabr'sk 76 P5
Noyon 54 E5
Nsombo 108 D2
Ntem 104 G4
Ntwetwe Pan 108 C4
Nu 88 G2
Nuasjärvi 48 Q4
Nubian Desert 100 F3
Nudo Coropuna 140 C7
Nueltin Lake 122 M4
Nueva Lubecka 142 G7
Nueva Rosita 132 F3
Nueva San Salvador 134 G6
Nuevo Casas Grandes 132 E2
Nuevo Laredo 132 G3
Nugget Point 116 B8
Nuhaka 116 F4
Nuku'alofa 112 J8
Nuku Hiva 112 M6
Nukumanu Islands 112 F6
Nukunonu 112 J6
Nukus 76 K9
Nullagine 114 D4
Nullarbor Plain 114 E6
Numan 104 G3
Numata 82 K5
Numazu 82 K6
Numbulwar 114 G2
Numfor 87 E3
Numto 70 P2
Nunarsuit 122 X4
Nunavut 122 M3
Nuneaton 54 A2
Nungnain Sum 80 F1
Nunivak Island 132 (1)D3
Nunligram 78 Y3
Nuoro 64 D8
Nuquí 140 B2
Nura 70 P4
Nurābād 95 D1
Nurata 90 J1
Nurmes 48 Q5
Nürnberg 52 G7
Nürtingen 62 E2
Nurzec 50 M5
Nusaybin 92 J5
Nushki 90 J4
Nutak 122 U5
Nuuk 122 W4
Nuussuaq 122 W2
Nyagan' 70 N2
Nyahururu 106 F3
Nyala 100 D5
Nyalam 88 E3
Nyamlell 106 D2
Nyamtumbo 106 F6
Nyandoma 70 H2
Nyantakara 106 E4
Nyborg 52 F1
Nybro 48 H8
Nyda 76 N4
Nyima 88 E2
Nyingchi 88 F3
Nyírbátor 66 K2
Nyíregyháza 50 L10
Nykarleby 48 M5
Nykøbing 52 G2
Nyköping 48 J7
Nylstroom 108 D4
Nymburk 50 E7
Nynäshamn 48 J7
Nyngan 114 J6
Nyon 62 B4
Nysa 50 D6
Nysa 50 G7
Nysted 52 G2
Nyukhcha 70 J2
Nyunzu 106 D5
Nyurba 78 K4
Nyuya 78 K4
Nzega 106 E4
Nzérékoré 104 C3
N'zeto 106 A5
Nzwami 108 G2

O

Oaho 132 (2)D2
Oahu 112 L3
Oakdale 130 C3
Oakham 54 B2
Oak Lake 126 F1
Oakland 126 B3
Oak Lawn 128 C2
Oakley 130 A2
Oak Ridge 128 D3
Oamaru 116 C7
Oaxaca 134 E5
Ob' 70 N2
Obama 82 H6
Oban 56 G5
O Barco 60 D2
Oberdrauburg 62 H4
Oberhausen 54 J3
Oberkirch 52 D8
Oberlin 130 A2
Oberndorf 62 H3
Oberstdorf 62 F3
Oberursel 52 D6
Obervellach 50 C11
Oberwart 62 M3
Obi 87 C3
Óbidos 140 F4
Obigarm 90 K2
Obihiro 82 M2
Obluch'ye 78 N7
Obninsk 70 G3
Obo, *Central African Republic* 106 D2
Obo, *China* 80 C3
Oborniki 50 F5
Obouya 104 H5
Oboyan' 70 G4
Obskaya Guba 76 N4
Obuasi 104 D3
Ob'yachevo 70 J2
Ocala 130 E4
Ocaña, *Colombia* 140 C2
Ocaña, *Spain* 60 G5
Ocean City 128 E3
Ocean Falls 122 F6
Oceanside 132 C2
Och'amch'ire 92 J2
Ochsenfurt 52 E7
Oconto 128 C2
Oda 104 D3
Ōda 82 G6
Ōdate 82 L3
Odda 48 D6
Odemira 60 B7
Ödemiş 68 L6
Odense 52 F1
Oder = Odra 50 F6
Oderzo 62 H5
Odesa 70 F5
Odessa = Odesa, *Ukraine* 70 F5
Odessa, *US* 132 F2
Odienné 104 C3
Odorheiu Secuiesc 66 N3
Odra 50 F6
Odžaci 66 G4
Oeh 80 C2
Oeiras 140 J5
Oelrichs 126 F2
Oelsnitz 52 H6
Oeno 112 N8
Oestev 142 H7
Ofaqim 94 B5
Offenbach 52 D6
Offenburg 62 C2
Ōgaki 82 J6
Ogasawara-shotō 74 T7
Ogbomosho 104 E3
Ogden 126 D2
Ogdensburg 122 R8
Ogilvie Mountains 122 C4
Oglio 62 E5
Ogosta 66 L6
Ogre 48 N8
Ogre 48 N8
O Grove 60 B2
Ogulin 62 L5
Ohai 116 A7
Ohanet 102 G3
Ohio 128 C3
Ohio 128 D2
Ohre 52 J6
Ohrid 68 C3
Ohura 116 E4
Oia 68 H8
Oiapoque 140 G3
Oil City 128 E2
Oise 54 E5
Ōita 82 F7
Ojinaga 132 F3
Ojiya 82 K5
Ojos del Salado 142 H4
Oka 78 G6
Okaba 87 E4
Okahandja 108 B4
Okanagan Lake 124 C2
Okano 104 G4
Okanogan 126 C1
Okara 88 B2
Okarem 90 F2
Okato 116 D4
Okavango Delta 108 C3
Okaya 82 K5
Okayama 82 G6
Okene 104 F3
Oker 52 F4
Okha, *India* 90 J5
Okha, *Russia* 78 Q6
Okhansk 70 L3
Okhotsk 78 Q5
Okhtyrka 70 F4
Okinawa 80 H5
Okinawa 80 H5
Oki-shotō 82 G5
Okitipupa 104 E3
Oklahoma 130 B2
Oklahoma City 130 B2
Okoppe 82 M1
Okoyo 104 H5
Okranger 48 E5
Oksino 70 K1
Oktinden 48 H4
Oktyabr'sk 70 L5
Oktyabr'skiy 70 K4
Okurchan 78 S5
Okushiri-tō 82 K2
Ólafsvík 48 (1)B2
Olancha 126 C3
Öland 48 J8
Olanga 48 Q3
Olathe 130 C2
Olava 52 J7
Olavarría 142 J6
Oława 50 G7
Olbia 64 D8
Olching 62 G2
Old Crow 132 (1)K2
Oldenburg, *Germany* 52 D3
Oldenburg, *Germany* 52 F2
Oldenzaal 54 J2
Oldham 56 L8
Old Head of Kinsale 56 D10
Olean 128 E2
Olecko 50 M3
Olekma 78 L5
Olekminsk 78 L4
Oleksandriya 70 F5
Olenegorsk 48 S2
Olenek 78 J3
Olenëk 78 L2
Olenëkskiy Zaliv 78 L2
Oleśnica 50 G6
Olesno 50 H7
Olhão 60 C7
Olib 62 K6
Olinda 140 L5
Oliva 60 K6

Olivet, *France* 58 G6
Olivet, *US* 126 G2
Olivia 128 B2
Olmos 140 B5
Olney 130 B3
Olochi 78 K6
Olonets 70 F2
Olongapo 84 G4
Oloron-Ste-Marie 58 E10
Olot 60 N2
Olovyannaya 78 K6
Olpe 54 K3
Olsztyn 50 K4
Olt 66 M4
Olten 62 C3
Oltenița 66 P5
Oltu 92 K3
Oluan-pi 84 G2
Olvera 60 E8
Olympia 126 B1
Olympos 68 E4
Olympus 68 Q10
Olyutorskiy 78 W4
Olyutorskiy Zaliv 78 V4
Om' 76 N6
Oma 88 D2
Omae-saki 82 K6
Omagh 56 E7
Omaha 126 G2
Omak 126 C1
Omakau 116 B7
Oman 90 G5
Omapere 116 D2
Omarama 116 B7
Omaruru 108 B4
Omba, *China* 88 E2
Omba, *Russia* 76 E4
Omboué 104 F5
Ombrone 64 F6
Omdurman = Umm Durman 100 F4
Omegna 62 D5
Omeo 114 J7
Om Hajer 100 G5
Omīdeyeh 95 C1
Omis 62 M7
Ommen 54 J2
Omolon 78 T3
Omoloy 78 N3
Omo Wenz 106 F2
Omsk 76 N6
Omsukchan 78 S4
Ōmū 82 M1
Omulew 50 L4
Ōmura 82 F7
Ōmuta 82 F7
Onang 87 A3
Onda 60 K5
Ondangwa 108 B3
Ondjiva 108 B3
Ondo 104 E3
Ondörhaan 80 E1
One and a Half Degree Channel 88 B8
Onega 70 G2
O'Neill 126 G2
Oneonta 128 F2
Onești 66 P3
Onezhskoye Ozero 70 F2
Ongjin 82 C5
Ongole 88 D5
Onguday 76 R7
Oni 92 K2
Onilahy 108 G4
Onitsha 104 F3
Ono 82 J6
Onon 78 J7
Onon 78 J7
Onslow Bay 134 J2
Onsong 82 E2
Ontario 122 N6
Ontinyent 60 K6
Ontonagon 128 C1
Onyx 132 C1
Oodnadatta 114 G5
Oologah Lake 130 B2
Oostburg 54 F3
Oostelijk-Flevoland 54 H2
Oostende 54 E3
Oosterhout 54 G3
Oosterschelde 54 F3
Oost-Vlieland 54 H1
Ootsa Lake 122 F6
Opala 106 C4
Oparino 70 J3
Opava 50 G8
Opelika 130 D3
Opelousas 130 C3
Opheim 126 E1
Opochka 70 E3
Opoczno 50 K6
Opole 50 G7
Opornyy 76 J8
Opotiki 116 F4
Opp 130 D3
Opunake 116 D4
Opuwo 108 A3
Oradea 66 J2
Orahovac 66 H7
Orai 88 C3
Oran 60 K9
Orán 142 J3
Orange 108 C5
Orange, *Australia* 114 J6
Orange, *France* 58 K9
Orange, *US* 130 C3
Orangeburg 130 E3
Orangemund 108 B5
Orangeville 128 D2
Orango 104 A2
Oranienburg 52 J4
Orapa 108 D4
Orăștie 66 L4
Oravița 66 J4
Orbec 58 F4
Orbetello 64 F6
Orco 62 C5
Ordes 60 B1
Ordes Santa Comba 60 B1
Ordu 92 G3
Ordway 126 F3
Öreälven 48 K4
Örebro 48 H7
Oregon 126 B2
Oregon 128 A3
Orekhovo-Zuyevo 70 G3
Orel 70 G4
Orem 126 D2
Ören 68 K7
Orenburg 70 L4
Orestiada 68 J3
Orewa 116 E3
Orford Ness 54 D2
Orhei 66 R2
Orihuela 60 K6
Orillia 128 E2
Orinoco 140 D2
Orinoco Delta = Delta del Orinoco 140 E2
Orissaare 48 M7
Oristano 64 C9
Orivesi 48 Q5
Orkla 48 F5
Orkney Islands 56 K3
Orlando 130 E4
Orléans 58 G6
Orlik 78 F6
Orly 54 E6
Ormara 90 H4
Ormoc 84 G4
Ormos Almyrou 68 G9
Ormos Mesara 68 G9
Ornans 58 M6
Ornö 48 K7
Örnsköldsvik 48 K5
Orocué 140 C3
Orofino 126 C1
Oromocto 128 G1
Orona 112 J6
Oronoque 140 F3
Oroqen Zizhiqi 78 L6
Orosei 64 D8
Orosháza 66 H3
Oroszlany 50 H10
Orotukan 78 S4
Oroville 126 B3
Orroroo 114 G6
Orsa 48 H6
Orsay 58 H5
Orsha 70 F4
Orsk 70 L4
Orșova 66 K5
Ørsta 48 D5
Ortaklar 68 K7
Orthez 58 E10
Ortigueira 60 C1
Ortisei 62 G4
Ortles 62 F4
Ortona 64 J6
Ortonville 128 A1
Orūmīyeh 92 L5
Oruro 140 D7
Orvieto 64 G6
Orville 58 L6
Ōsaka 82 H6
Osăm 66 M6
Osceola 128 B2
Oschatz 52 J5
Oschersleben 52 G4
O Seixo 60 B3
Osh 76 N9
Oshamambe 82 L2
Oshawa 128 E2
Oshkosh, *Nebr., US* 126 F2
Oshkosh, *Wis., US* 128 C2
Oshogbo 104 E3
Osijek 66 F4
Osimo 62 J7
Oskaloosa 128 B2
Oskarshamn 48 J8
Oslo 48 F7
Oslofjorden 48 F7
Osmancık 92 F3
Osmaniye 92 G5
Osnabrück 54 L2
Osor 62 K6
Osorno 142 G7
Osprey Reef 114 J2
Oss 54 H3
Ossa de Montiel 60 H6
Osseo 128 B2
Ossora 78 U5
Ostashkov 70 F3
Oste 52 E3
Osterburg 52 G4
Østerdalen 48 F6
Osterholz-Scharmbeck 52 D3
Osterode 52 F5
Östersund 48 H5
Ostfriesische Inseln 52 C3
Ostiglia 62 G5
Ostrava 50 H8
Ostróda 50 K4
Ostrołęka 50 L4
Ostrov, *Czech Republic* 52 H6
Ostrov, *Russia* 70 E3
Ostrova Arkticheskogo Instituta 76 P2
Ostrova Medvezh'l 78 T2
Ostrov Atlasova 78 S6
Ostrova Vrangelya 120 V4
Ostrov Ayon 78 V2
Ostrov Belyy 76 N3
Ostrov Beringa 78 V6
Ostrov Bol'shevik 76 V2
Ostrov Bol'shoy Begichev 78 J2
Ostrov Bol'shoy Lyakhovskiy 78 Q2
Ostrov Bol'shoy Shantar 78 P6
Ostrov Chechen' 92 M2
Ostrov Iturup 82 P1
Ostrov Karaginskiy 78 U5
Ostrov Kil'din 48 T2
Ostrov Kolguyev 76 H4
Ostrov Komsomolets 76 T1
Ostrov Kotel'nyy 78 P1
Ostrov Kunashir 82 P1
Ostrov Mednyy 78 V6
Ostrov Mezhdusharskiy 76 H3
Ostrov Novaya Sibir' 78 S2
Ostrov Ogurchinskiy 90 F2
Ostrov Oktyabr'skoy 76 S2
Ostrov Onekotan 78 S7
Ostrov Paramushir 78 T6
Ostrov Rasshua 78 S7
Ostrov Shiashkotan 78 S7
Ostrov Shumshu 78 T6
Ostrov Simushir 78 S7
Ostrov Urup 78 S7
Ostrov Ushakova 76 Q1
Ostrov Vaygach 76 K3
Ostrov Vise 76 P2
Ostrov Vosrozhdeniya 76 K9
Ostrov Vrangelya 78 W2
Ostrowiec Świętokrzyski 50 L7
Ostrów Mazowiecka 50 L5
Ostrów Wielkopolski 50 G6
Ostuni 64 M8
Osum 68 C4
Ōsumi-shotō 82 F8
Osuna 60 E7
Oswego 128 E2
Oświęcim 50 J7
Otago Peninsula 116 C7
Otaki 116 E5
Otaru 82 L2
Oțelu Roșu 66 K4
Othonoi 68 B5
Oti 104 E3
Otira 116 C6
Otjiwarongo 108 B4
Otočac 62 L6
Otog Qi 80 D3
Otoineppu 82 M1
Otorohanga 116 E4
Otranto 64 N8
Otrøy 48 D5
Otrozhnyy 78 W3
Ōtsu 82 H6
Otta 48 E6
Ottawa 128 E1
Ottawa, *Canada* 128 E1
Ottawa, *Ill., US* 128 C2
Ottawa, *Kans., US* 130 B2
Ottawa Islands 122 Q5
Otterøy 48 F4
Ottobrunn 62 G2
Ottumwa 128 B2
Otukpo 104 F3
Ouachita Mountains 130 C3
Ouadâne 102 C4
Ouadda 106 C2
Ouagadougou 104 D2
Oualâta 102 D5
Ouallam 104 E2
Ouanda-Djalle 106 C2
Ouargla 102 G2
Ouarzazate 102 D2
Oudenaarde 54 F4
Oudenbosch 54 G3
Oudtshoorn 108 C6
Oued Laou 60 E9
Oued Medjerda 64 D12
Oued Meliane 64 D12
Oued Tiélat 60 K9
Oued Zem 102 D2
Ouéléssébougou 104 C2
Ouésso 104 H4
Ouezzane 102 D2
Oujda 102 E2
Oujeft 102 C4
Oulainen 48 N4
Ould Yenjé 102 C5
Oulu 48 N4
Oulujärvi 48 P4
Oulujoki 48 P4
Oulx 62 B5
Oum-Chalouba 100 D4
Oum-Hadjer 100 C5
Ounarjoki 48 N3
Our 54 J4
Ouray 126 E3
Ourense 60 C2
Ouricuri 140 J5
Ourthe 54 H4
Oustreham 54 B5
Outer Hebrides 56 D4
Outjo 108 B4
Outokumpu 48 Q5
Out Skerries 56 M1
Ouyen 114 H7
Ovacık 68 R8
Ovada 62 D6
Ovalle 142 G5
Ovareli 92 L3
Overflakkee 54 G3
Overlander Roadhouse 114 B5
Overland Park 130 C2
Overton 126 D3
Övertorneå 48 M3
Ovidiopol' 66 T3
Oviedo 60 E1
Owaka 116 B8
Owando 104 H5
Owase 82 J6
Owatonna 128 B2
Owen River 116 D5
Owensboro 128 C3
Owens Lake 126 C3
Owen Sound 128 D2
Owerri 104 F3
Owo 104 F3
Owosso 128 D2
Owyhee 126 C2
Owyhee 126 C2
Oxford, *New Zealand* 116 D6
Oxford, *UK* 54 A3
Oxnard 132 C2
Oyama 82 K5
Oyapock 140 G3
Oyem 104 G4
Oyen 124 D1
Oyonnax 62 A4
Ózd 50 K9
Ozernovskiy 78 T6
Ozero Alakol' 76 Q8
Ozero Aralsor 70 J5
Ozero Aydarkul' 76 M9
Ozero Balkhash 76 N8
Ozero Baykal 78 H6
Ozero Beloye 70 G2
Ozero Chany 76 P7
Ozero Chernoye 70 N3
Ozero Il'men' 70 F3
Ozero-Imandra 48 R2
Ozero Inder 76 J8
Ozero Janis'jarvi 48 R5
Ozero Kamennoje 48 R4
Ozero Kanozero 48 T3
Ozero Khanka 82 G1
Ozero Kolvitskoye 48 S3
Ozero Kovdozero 48 S3
Ozero Kulundinskoye 76 P7
Ozero Kushmurun 70 N4
Ozero Lama 78 D2
Ozero Leksozero 48 R5
Ozero Lovozero 48 T2
Ozero Morzhovets 70 H1
Ozero Njuk 48 R4
Ozero Ozhogino 78 R3
Ozero Pirenga 48 R3
Ozero Pyaozero 48 R3
Ozero Saltaim 70 P3
Ozero Sarpa 70 J5
Ozero Segozeroskoye 70 F2
Ozero Seletyteniz 76 N7
Ozero Sredneye Kuyto 48 R4
Ozero Taymyr 76 U3
Ozero Teletskoye 76 R7
Ozero Tengiz 70 N4
Ozero Topozero 48 R4
Ozero Umbozero 48 T3
Ozero Vygozero 70 G2
Ozero Yalpug 66 R4
Ozero Zaysan 76 Q8
Ozero Zhaltyr 70 K5
Ozero Zhamanakkol' 70 M5
Ozersk 50 M3
Ozhogina 78 R3
Ozhogino 78 R3
Ozieri 64 C8
Ozinki 70 J4
Ozona 132 F2
Ozurget'i 92 J3

P

Paamiut 122 X4
Paar 52 G8
Paarl 108 B6
Pabbay 56 E4
Pabianice 50 J6
Pabna 88 E4
Pacasmayo 140 B5
Pachino 64 K12
Pachuca 134 E4
Pacific Ocean 112 M3
Pacitan 86 E4
Packwood 126 B1
Padalere 87 B3
Padang 86 C3
Padangpanjang 86 C3
Padangsidempuan 86 B2
Padborg 52 E2
Paderborn 52 D5
Padova 62 G5
Padre Island 130 B4
Padrón 60 B2
Paducah, *Ky., US* 128 C3
Paducah, *Tex., US* 132 F2
Padum 88 C2
Paekdu San 82 D3
Paeroa 116 E3
Pafos 68 Q10
Pag 62 K6
Pag 62 L6
Paga Conta 140 G4
Pagadian 84 G5
Pagai Selatan 86 B3
Pagai Utara 86 B3
Pagalu = Annobón 104 F5
Pagan 112 E4
Pagatan 86 F3
Page, *Ariz., US* 132 D1
Page, *Okla., US* 130 C3
Pagosa Springs 126 E3
Pagri 88 E3
Pahiatua 116 E5
Paia 132 (2)E3
Paide 48 N7
Päijänne 48 N6
Painan 86 C3
Painesville 128 D2
Paisley 56 H6
Paita 140 A5
Pakaraima Mountains 140 E2
Pakch'ŏn 82 C4
Pakhachi 78 V4
Paki 104 F2

Pakistan **90** J4
Pakokku **84** A2
Pakotai **116** D2
Pakrac **62** N5
Paks **66** F3
Pakxé **84** D3
Pala **100** B6
Palafrugell **60** P3
Palagonia **64** J11
Palagruža **64** L6
Palaiochora **68** F9
Palamós **60** P3
Palana **78** U5
Palanan **84** G3
Palanga **50** L2
Palangkaraya **86** E3
Palanpur **88** B4
Palantak **90** H4
Palapye **108** D4
Palatka, *Russia* **78** S4
Palatka, *US* **130** E4
Palau **64** D7
Palau **112** D5
Palau **112** D5
Palaw **84** B4
Palawan **84** F5
Palazzolo Arceide **64** J11
Palembang **86** C3
Palencia **60** F2
Paleokastritsa **68** B5
Palermo **64** H10
Palestine **130** B3
Palestrina **64** G7
Paletwa **84** A2
Palghat **88** C6
Pali **88** B3
Palikir **112** F5
Palimbang **84** G5
Pālkohda **88** D5
Palk Strait **88** C7
Palma **60** N5
Palma del Rio **60** E7
Palma di Montechiaro **64** H11
Palmanova **62** J5
Palmares **140** K5
Palmarola **64** G8
Palmas **140** H6
Palmas **142** L4
Palm Bay **130** E4
Palmdale **132** C2
Palmerston **116** C7
Palmerston Island **112** K7
Palmerston North **116** E5
Palm Harbor **130** E4
Palmi **64** K10
Palmira **140** B3
Palmyra Island **112** K5
Palojärvi **48** M2
Palopo **87** B3
Palu, *Indonesia* **87** A3
Palu, *Turkey* **92** J4
Palyavaam **78** W3
Pama **104** E2
Pamekasan **86** E4
Pamhagen **62** M3
Pamiers **58** G10
Pamlico Sound **130** F2
Pampa **132** F1
Pampas **142** J6
Pamplona, *Colombia* **134** K7
Pamplona, *Spain* **60** J2
Pana **128** C3
Panagyurishte **66** M7
Panaji **88** B5
Panama **134** H7
Panamá **140** B2
Panama Canal = Canal de Panamá **134** J7
Panama City **130** D3
Panarea **64** K10
Panarik **86** D2
Panaro **62** G6
Panay **84** G4
Pančevo **66** H5
Panciu **66** Q4
Pandan **84** G4
Pandharpur **88** C5
Panevėžys **50** P2
Pangani **106** F5
Pangin **88** F3
Pangkajene **87** A3
Pangkalanbuun **86** E3
Pangkalpinang **86** D3
Pangnirtung **122** T3
Panguitch **126** D3
Pangutaran Group **84** G5
Panhandle **132** F1
Panipat **88** C3
Panjāb **90** J3
Panjgur **90** H4
Pankshin **104** F3
Pantanal **140** F7
Pantar **87** B4
Pantelleria **102** H1
Pantemakassar **87** B4
Paola **64** L9
Paoua **106** B2
Pápa **66** E2
Papa **132** (2)F4
Papakura **116** E3
Papantla **134** E4
Paparoa **116** E3
Papa Stour **56** L1
Papatowi **116** B8
Papa Westray **56** K2
Papenburg **52** C3
Papey **48** (1)F2
papua **87** E3
Papua New Guinea **112** E6
Papun **84** B3
Pará **140** G5
Para **140** H4
Parabel' **76** Q6
Paracatu **140** H7
Paracel Islands **84** E3
Paraćin **66** J6
Pará de Minas **140** J7
Paragould **130** C2
Paragua, *Bolivia* **140** E6
Paragua, *Venezuela* **140** E2
Paraguay **138** F6
Paraguay **142** J3
Paraíba **140** K5
Parakou **104** E3
Paralia **68** E8
Paralimni **94** A1
Paramaribo **140** F2
Paranã **140** H6
Paranã **140** H6
Paraná **142** J5
Paraná **142** K4
Paraná **142** L3
Paranaguá **142** M4
Paranaíba **140** G7
Paranaíba **140** G7
Paranavaí **142** L3
Paranestio **68** G3
Paraparaumu **116** E5
Paray-le Monial **58** K7
Parbhani **88** C5
Parchim **52** G3
Pardo **140** J7
Pardubice **50** E7
Pareh **92** L4
Parepare **87** A3
Parga **68** C5
Parigi **87** B3
Parika **140** F2
Parintins **140** F4
Paris, *France* **58** H5
Paris, *Tenn., US* **130** D2
Paris, *Tex., US* **130** B3
Parkersburg **128** D3
Park Rapids **128** A1
Parla **60** G4
Parma **62** F6
Parma, *Italy* **62** F6
Parma, *US* **128** D2
Parnaíba **140** J4
Parnassus **116** D6
Pärnu **48** N7
Pärnu **48** N7
Paros **68** H7
Paros **68** H7
Parry Bay **122** Q3
Parry Islands **122** L1
Parry Sound **128** D2
Parsons **130** B2
Parthenay **58** E7
Partinico **64** H10
Partizansk **82** G2
Paru **140** G4
Parvatipuram **88** D5
Paryang **88** D2
Pasadena, *Calif., US* **132** C2
Pasadena, *Tex., US* **130** B4
Paşalimani Adası **68** K4
Pasawng **84** B3
Paşcani **66** P2
Pasco **126** C1
Pascual **84** G4
Pasewalk **52** K3
Pasig **84** G4
Pasinler **92** J3
Pasłęk **50** J3
Pasłek **50** J3
Pasleka **48** L9
Pašman **62** L7
Pasni **90** H4
Paso de Hachado **142** G6
Paso de Indios **142** H7
Paso de la Cumbre **142** H5
Paso de San Francisco **142** H4
Paso Río Mayo **142** G8
Paso Robles **132** B1
Passau **52** J8
Passo Fundo **142** L4
Passos **140** H8
Pastavy **48** P9
Pasto **140** B3
Pastos Bons **140** J5
Pasvalys **50** P1
Pásztó **66** G2
Patagonia **142** G8
Patan, *India* **88** B4
Patan, *Nepal* **88** E3
Patea **116** E4
Pate Island **106** G4
Paterna **60** K5
Paternò **64** J11
Paterson **128** F2
Pathankot **88** C2
Pathein **84** A3
Pathfinder Reservoir **126** E2
Patia **140** B3
Patiala **88** C2
Patmos **68** J7
Patna **88** E3
Patnos **92** K4
Patos de Minas **140** H7
Patra **68** D6
Patraikis Kolpos **68** D6
Patreksfjörður **48** (1)B2
Pattani **84** C5
Pattaya **84** C4
Patti **64** J10
Paturau River **116** D5
Pau **60** K1
Pauini **140** D5
Pauini **140** D5
Paulatuk **132** (1)N2
Paulo Afonso **140** K5
Paul's Valley **130** B3
Päveh **92** M6
Pavia **62** E5
Pāvilosta **48** L8
Pavlikeni **66** N6
Pavlodar **76** P7
Pavlohrad **70** G5
Pavlovsk **70** H4
Pavlovskaya **70** G5
Pavullo nel Frignano **62** F6
Paxoi **68** C5
Paxson **132** (1)H3
Payerne **62** B4
Payette **126** C2
Paynes Find **114** C5
Paysandu **142** K5
Payson **132** D2
Payturma **76** S3
Pazar **92** J3
Pazardzhik **66** M7
Pazin **62** J5
Peace **122** H5
Peace River **122** H5
Peach Springs **132** D1
Pearsall **130** B4
Pebane **108** F3
Pebas **140** C5
Peć **66** H7
Pecan Island **130** C4
Pechora **70** K1
Pechora **70** L1
Pechorskoye More **76** J4
Pechory **48** P8
Pecos **132** F2
Pecos **132** F2
Pécs **66** F3
Pedja **48** P7
Pedra Azul **140** J7
Pedra Lume **104** (1)B1
Pedreiras **140** J4
Pedro Afonso **140** H5
Pedro Juan Caballero **142** K3
Pedro Luro **142** J6
Peel Sound **122** M2
Peene **52** J3
Peenemünde **52** J2
Pegasus Bay **116** D6
Pegnitz **52** G7
Pegu **84** B3
Pegunungan Barisan **86** B2
Pegunungan Iban **86** F2
Pegunungan Maoke **87** E3
Pegunungan Meratus **86** F3
Pegunungan Schwaner **86** E3
Pegunungan Van Rees **87** E3
Pehuajó **142** J6
Peine **52** F4
Peißenberg **62** G3
Peixe **140** H6
Pekalongan **86** D4
Pekanbaru **86** C2
Peking = Beijing **80** F3
Pelaihari **86** E3
Peleduy **78** J5
Peleng **87** B3
Pelhřimov **50** E8
Pelješac **64** M6
Pello **48** N3
Pellworm **52** D2
Pelly Bay **122** P3
Peloponnisos **68** D7
Pelotas **142** L5
Pelym **70** M2
Pemangkat **86** D2
Pematangsiantar **86** B2
Pemba **108** G2
Pemba Island **106** F5
Pembina **126** G1
Pembine **128** C1
Pembroke, *Canada* **128** E1
Pembroke, *UK* **56** H10
Pembroke, *US* **130** E3
Peñafiel **60** F3
Peñaranda de Bracamonte **60** E4
Peñarroya-Pueblonuevo **60** E6
Pendik **68** M4
Pendleton **126** C1
Pendolo **86** G3
Pend Oreille Lake **126** C1
Pen Hills **128** E2
Peniche **60** A5
Península de Azuero **134** H7
Península de Guajira **134** K6
Península Valdés **142** J7
Péninsule de Gaspé **122** T7
Péninsule d'Ungava **122** R4
Penmarch **58** A6
Penne **64** H6
Pennines **56** K7
Pennsylvania **128** E2
Penrith **56** K7
Pensacola **134** G2
Penticton **126** C1
Penza **70** J4
Penzance **56** G11
Penzhina **78** V4
Penzhinskaya Guba **78** U4
Penzhinskiy Khrebet **78** V4
Peoria, *Ariz., US* **132** D2
Peoria, *Ill., US* **128** C2
Percival Lakes **114** D4
Peregrebnoye **70** N2
Pereira **140** B3
Pergamino **142** J5
Périers **58** D4
Périgueux **58** F8
Peristera **68** G5
Perito Moreno **142** G8
Perleberg **52** G3
Perm' **70** L3
Përmet **68** C4
Pernambuco **140** K5
Pernik **66** L7
Péronne **54** E5
Perpignan **58** H11
Perrine **130** E4
Perry, *Fla., US* **130** E3
Perry, *Ga., US* **130** E3
Persepolis **95** E2
Persian Gulf **95** C2
Perth, *Australia* **114** C6
Perth, *UK* **56** J5
Pertuis Breton **58** D7
Peru **128** C2
Peru **140** C6
Peru-Chile Trench **138** D5
Perugia **64** G5
Pervomays'k **70** F5
Pervoural'sk **70** L3
Pesaro **62** H7
Pescara **64** J6
Pescia **62** F7
Peshawar **88** B2
Peshkopi **68** C3
Peshtera **68** G2
Peski Karakumy **90** G2
Peski Kzyylkum **76** L9
Peski Priaral'skiye Karakumy **76** L8
Pesnica **62** L4
Pessac **58** E9
Petah Tiqwa **94** B4
Petalioi **68** G7
Petaluma **126** B3
Pétange **54** H5
Petare **134** L6
Petauke **108** E2
Peterborough, *Canada* **128** E2
Peterborough, *UK* **56** M9
Peterhead **56** L4
Peter I Øy **144** (2)JJ3
Petersburg **128** E3
Petersfield **54** B3
Petershagen **52** D4
Petit Mécatina **122** U6
Peto **134** G4
Petre Bay **116** (1)B1
Petrich **68** F3
Petrila **66** L4
Petrinja **62** M5
Petrolina **140** J5
Petropavlovka **78** H6
Petropavlovsk **70** N4
Petropavlovsk-Kamchatskiy **78** T6
Petrópolis **142** N3
Petroşani **66** L4
Petrovac **66** J5
Petrovsk-Zabaykal'skiy **78** H6
Petrozavodsk **70** F2
Petrun **70** M1
Petukhovo **70** N3
Pevek **78** W3
Pezinok **50** G9
Pfaffenhofen **52** G8
Pfarrkirchen **52** H8
Pflach **62** F3
Pforzheim **52** D8
Pfunds **62** F4
Pfungstadt **52** D7
Phalaborwa **108** E4
Phalodi **88** B3
Phan Rang **84** D4
Phan Thiêt **84** D4
Phatthalung **84** C5
Phet Buri **84** B4
Phichit **84** C3
Philadelphia, *Miss., US* **130** D3
Philadelphia, *Pa., US* **130** F2
Philippeville **54** G4
Philippines **84** G5
Philippine Trench **74** R8
Philips **122** K7
Phillipsburg **126** G3
Phitsanulok **84** C3
Phnum Penh **84** C4
Phoenix **108** (1)B2
Phoenix **132** D2
Phoenix Islands **112** J6
Phôngsali **84** C2
Phuket **84** B5
Phumĭ Sâmraông **84** C4
Piacenza **62** E5
Piadena **62** F5
Pianoro **62** G6
Pianosa **64** E6
Piatra-Neamţ **66** P3
Piauí **140** J5
Piazza Armerina **64** J11
Pibor Post **106** E2
Picacho del Centinela **132** F3
Picayune **130** D3
Pichilemu **142** G5
Pico **102** (1)B2
Pico Almanzor **60** E4
Pico Cristóbal Colón **134** K6
Pico da Bandeira **142** N3
Pico da Neblina **140** D3
Pico de Itambé **142** N2
Pico de Teide **102** B3
Pico Duarte **134** K5
Picos **140** J5
Picton, *New Zealand* **116** D5
Picton, *US* **128** E2
Pic Tousside **100** C3
Piedras Negras **132** F3
Pieksämäki **48** P5
Pielinen **48** Q5
Pierre **126** F2
Pierrelatte **58** K9
Piers do Rio **140** H7
Piešťany **50** G9
Pietermaritzburg **108** E5
Pietersburg **108** D4
Pietrasanta **62** F6
Piet Retief **108** E5
Pieve di Cadore **62** H4
Pihlajavesi **48** P6

Pik Aborigen	**78**	R4
Piketberg	**108**	B6
Pik Kommunizma	**90**	K2
Pik Pobedy	**76**	P9
Piła	**50**	F4
Pilaya	**142**	H3
Pilcomayo	**140**	E8
Pilibhit	**88**	C3
Pilica	**50**	J7
Pimba	**114**	G6
Pimenta Bueno	**140**	E6
Pinamalayan	**84**	G4
Pinamar	**142**	K6
Pinang	**84**	B5
Pınarbaşı	**92**	G4
Pinar del Río	**134**	H4
Pinarhisar	**68**	K3
Pińczów	**50**	K7
Pindaré Mirim	**140**	H4
Pine Bluff	**128**	B4
Pine Bluffs	**126**	F2
Pine City	**128**	B1
Pine Creek	**114**	F2
Pine Creek Reservoir	**128**	A4
Pinega	**70**	H2
Pineios	**68**	E5
Pine Island Bay	**144**	(2)GG3
Pineland	**130**	C3
Pinerolo	**62**	C6
Pineville, *Ky., US*	**128**	D3
Pineville, *La., US*	**130**	C3
Pingdingshan	**80**	E4
Pingguo	**84**	D2
Pingle	**84**	E2
Pingliang	**80**	D3
Pingshi	**80**	E5
P'ing-tung	**84**	G2
Pingxiang, *China*	**84**	D2
Pingxiang, *China*	**84**	E1
Pinhel	**60**	C4
Pini	**86**	B2
Pinka	**62**	M3
Pink Mountain	**122**	G5
Pinneberg	**52**	E3
Pinsk	**70**	E4
Pioche	**126**	D3
Piombino	**64**	E6
Pioneer	**132**	D2
Pioneer Mountains	**126**	D1
Pionerskii	**50**	K3
Pionerskiy	**70**	M2
Piopio	**116**	E4
Piotrków Trybunalski	**50**	J6
Piove di Sacco	**62**	H5
Piperi	**68**	G5
Pipestone	**128**	A2
Pipiriki	**116**	E4
Piqua	**128**	D2
Piracicaba	**142**	M3
Pireas	**68**	F7
Pirin	**68**	F3
Piripiri	**140**	J4
Pirmasens	**52**	C7
Pirna	**52**	J6
Pirot	**66**	K6
Piru	**87**	C3
Pisa	**50**	L4
Pisa	**62**	F7
Pisco	**140**	B6
Písek	**50**	D8
Pīshīn	**90**	H4
Pishin	**90**	J3
Piska	**50**	L4
Pisticci	**64**	L8
Pistoia	**62**	F7
Pisz	**50**	L4
Pitcairn Islands	**112**	P8
Piteå	**48**	L4
Piteälven	**70**	C1
Pitești	**66**	M5
Pithara	**114**	C6
Pithiviers	**58**	H5
Pitkyaranta	**70**	F2
Pitlochry	**56**	J5
Pitlyar	**70**	N1
Pitt Island	**116**	(1)B2
Pittsburg	**130**	C2
Pittsburgh	**128**	D2
Pitt Strait	**116**	(1)B2
Piura	**140**	A5
Pivka	**62**	K5
Placer	**84**	G4
Placerville	**132**	B1
Plaiamonas	**68**	E5
Plains	**132**	F2
Plainview	**132**	F2
Plampang	**86**	F4
Planalto Central	**140**	H6
Planalto da Borborema	**140**	K5
Planalto do Mato Grosso	**140**	G6
Plankinton	**126**	G2
Plano	**130**	B3
Plasencia	**60**	D5
Plast	**70**	M4
Plateau du Djado	**102**	H4
Plateau du Limousin	**58**	F8
Plateau du Tademaït	**102**	F3
Plateau of Tibet = Xizang Gaoyuan	**88**	D2
Plateaux Batéké	**104**	G5
Platinum	**132**	(1)E4
Plato	**134**	K7
Plato Ustyurt	**76**	J9
Platte	**130**	B1
Platteville	**128**	B2
Plattling	**52**	H8
Plattsburgh	**128**	F2
Plattsmouth	**130**	B1
Plau	**52**	H3
Plauen	**52**	H6
Plavnik	**62**	K6
Plavsk	**70**	G4
Playa de Castilla	**60**	D7
Playas	**140**	A4
Plây Cu	**84**	D4
Pleasanton	**132**	G3
Pleiße	**52**	H5
Plentywood	**126**	F1
Plesetsk	**70**	H2
Pleven	**66**	M6
Pljevlja	**66**	G6
Płock	**50**	J5
Pločno	**66**	E6
Ploërmel	**58**	C6
Ploiești	**66**	P5
Plomari	**68**	J6
Plön	**52**	F2
Płońsk	**50**	K5
Plovdiv	**66**	M7
Plumtree	**108**	D4
Plungė	**50**	L2
Plymouth, *UK*	**56**	H11
Plymouth, *US*	**128**	C2
Plyussa	**48**	Q7
Plyussa	**70**	E3
Plzeň	**50**	C8
Po	**62**	E5
Pocahontas	**134**	F1
Pocatello	**126**	D2
Pochet	**78**	F5
Pochinok	**70**	F4
Pocking	**62**	J2
Pocomoke City	**128**	E3
Podgorica	**66**	G7
Podkamennaya Tunguska	**78**	F4
Podol'sk	**70**	G3
Podravska Slatina	**66**	E4
Poel	**52**	G2
Pofadder	**108**	B5
Poggibonsi	**62**	G7
Pogradec	**68**	C4
P'ohang	**82**	E5
Pohnpei	**112**	F5
Pohokura	**116**	F4
Pohořelice	**62**	M2
Point Arena	**124**	B4
Point Barrow	**132**	(1)F1
Point Conception	**132**	B2
Point Culver	**114**	D6
Point d'Entrecasteaux	**114**	B6
Pointe-Noire	**104**	G5
Point Hope	**132**	(1)D2
Point Hope	**132**	(1)D2
Point Pedro	**88**	D7
Point Sur	**126**	B3
Poitiers	**58**	F7
Pokaran	**88**	B3
Pokhara	**88**	D3
Poko	**106**	D3
Pokrovsk	**78**	M4
Pola de Siero	**60**	E1
Poland	**50**	G6
Polar Bluff	**134**	F1
Polatlı	**68**	Q5
Polatsk	**70**	E3
Police	**52**	K3
Polichnitos	**68**	J5
Policoro	**64**	L8
Poligny	**58**	L7
Poligus	**76**	S5
Polillo Islands	**84**	G4
Poliocastro	**64**	L9
Polis	**68**	Q9
Polistena	**64**	L10
Pollachi	**88**	C6
Pollença	**60**	P5
Polohy	**70**	G5
Polomoloc	**84**	H5
Polonnaruwa	**88**	D7
Poltava	**70**	F5
Poltavka	**82**	F1
Põltsamaa	**48**	N7
Poluostrov Shmidta	**78**	Q6
Poluostrov Taymyr	**76**	R3
Poluostrov Yamal	**76**	M3
Poluy	**76**	M4
Põlva	**48**	P7
Polyaigos	**68**	G8
Polyarnye Zori	**48**	S3
Polyarnyy	**78**	X3
Polykastro	**68**	E4
Polynesia	**112**	J6
Pombal	**60**	B5
Pomeranian Bay	**50**	D3
Pomeroy	**126**	C1
Pomorie	**66**	Q7
Pompano Beach	**130**	E4
Pompei	**64**	J8
Ponca City	**130**	B2
Ponce	**134**	L5
Pondicherry	**88**	C6
Pond Inlet	**122**	R2
Ponferrada	**60**	D2
Poniatowa	**50**	M6
Ponoy	**70**	H1
Pons	**58**	E8
Ponta Delgada	**102**	(1)B2
Ponta do Podrão	**104**	G6
Ponta do Sol	**104**	(1)B1
Ponta Grossa	**142**	L4
Ponta Khehuene	**108**	E5
Pont-à-Mousson	**58**	M5
Ponta Porã	**142**	K3
Pontarlier	**58**	M7
Pontassieve	**62**	G7
Ponta Zavora	**108**	F4
Pont-d'Alin	**58**	L7
Ponteareas	**60**	B2
Ponte da Barca	**60**	B3
Pontedera	**62**	F7
Ponte de Sor	**60**	C5
Pontevedra	**60**	B2
Pontiac	**128**	C2
Pontianak	**86**	D3
Pontivy	**58**	C5
Pontoise	**54**	E5
Pontorson	**58**	D5
Pontremoli	**62**	E6
Ponza	**64**	G8
Poogau	**62**	J3
Poole	**56**	L11
Poole Bay	**56**	L11
Pooncarie	**114**	H6
Poopó	**140**	D7
Poopó Challapata	**142**	H2
Poor Knights Islands	**116**	E2
Popayán	**134**	J8
Poperinge	**54**	E4
Popigay	**76**	W3
Poplar Bluff	**128**	B3
Poplarville	**130**	D3
Popocatépetl	**134**	E5
Popoh	**86**	E4
Popokabaka	**104**	H6
Popovača	**62**	M5
Popovo	**66**	P6
Poprad	**50**	K8
Poprad	**50**	K8
Porangatu	**140**	H6
Porbandar	**90**	J5
Porcupine	**132**	(1)K2
Pordenone	**62**	H5
Poreč	**62**	J5
Poret	**64**	H3
Pori	**48**	L6
Porirua	**116**	E5
Porlamar	**134**	M6
Poronaysk	**78**	Q7
Poros	**68**	F7
Porosozero	**70**	F2
Porozina	**62**	K5
Porpoise Bay	**144**	(2)T3
Porriño	**60**	B2
Porsangen	**48**	N1
Porsgrunn	**48**	E7
Portadown	**56**	F7
Portage	**128**	C2
Portage la Prairie	**126**	G1
Port Alberni	**126**	B1
Port Albert	**114**	J7
Portalegre	**60**	C5
Portales	**132**	F2
Port Arthur, *Australia*	**114**	J8
Port Arthur, *US*	**130**	C4
Port Augusta	**114**	G6
Port-au-Prince	**134**	K5
Port Austin	**128**	D2
Port Blair	**84**	A4
Port Burwell	**122**	U4
Port Charlotte	**130**	E4
Port Douglas	**114**	J3
Portel, *Brazil*	**140**	G4
Portel, *Portugal*	**60**	C6
Port Elizabeth	**108**	D6
Port Ellen	**56**	F6
Porterville	**132**	C1
Port Fitzroy	**116**	E3
Port-Gentil	**104**	F5
Port Harcourt	**104**	F4
Port Hardy	**122**	F6
Port Hawkesbury	**122**	U7
Port Hedland	**114**	C4
Port Hope Simpson	**122**	V6
Port Huron	**128**	D2
Portimão	**60**	B7
Port Jefferson	**128**	F2
Portland, *Australia*	**114**	H7
Portland, *New Zealand*	**116**	E2
Portland, *Ind., US.*	**128**	D2
Portland, *Me., US.*	**128**	F2
Portland, *Oreg., US*	**126**	B1
Portland Island	**116**	F4
Port Laoise	**56**	E8
Port Lavaca	**130**	B4
Port Lincoln	**114**	G6
Port Loko	**104**	B3
Port Louis	**108**	(1)B2
Port Macquarie	**114**	K6
Port-Menier	**122**	U7
Port Moresby	**114**	J1
Port Nolloth	**108**	B5
Porto, *Corsica*	**64**	C6
Porto, *Portugal*	**60**	B3
Porto Alegre, *R.G.S., Brazil*	**142**	L5
Porto Alegre, *Pará, Brazil*	**140**	G4
Porto Amboim	**108**	A2
Portocheli	**68**	F7
Porto do Son	**60**	A2
Pôrto Esperidião	**140**	F7
Portoferraio	**64**	E6
Pôrto Franco	**140**	H5
Port of Spain	**140**	E1
Pôrto Grande	**140**	G3
Portogruaro	**62**	H5
Porto Inglês	**104**	(1)B1
Portomaggiore	**62**	G6
Pôrto Murtinho	**142**	K3
Pôrto Nacional	**140**	H6
Porto-Novo	**104**	E3
Port Orford	**126**	B2
Porto San Giorgio	**64**	H5
Pôrto Santana	**140**	G3
Porto Santo	**102**	B2
Pôrto Seguro	**140**	K7
Porto Tolle	**62**	H6
Porto Torres	**64**	C8
Porto-Vecchio	**64**	D7
Pôrto Velho	**140**	E5
Portoviejo	**140**	A4
Port Pire	**114**	G6
Portree	**56**	F4
Port Renfrew	**126**	B1
Port Said = Bûr Sa'îd	**100**	F1
Port St. Johns	**108**	D6
Port Shepstone	**108**	E6
Portsmouth, *UK*	**54**	A4
Portsmouth, *N.H., US*	**128**	F2
Portsmouth, *Oh., US*	**128**	D3
Portsmouth, *Va., US*	**128**	E3
Port Sudan = Bur Sudan	**100**	G4
Port Sulphur	**130**	D4
Port Talbot	**56**	J10
Portugal	**60**	B5
Portugalete	**60**	G1
Port-Vendres	**58**	J11
Port-Vila	**112**	G7
Posadas	**142**	K4
Poschiavo	**62**	F4
Poshekhon'ye	**70**	G3
Poso	**87**	B3
Posŏng	**82**	D6
Posse	**140**	H6
Pößneck	**52**	G6
Post	**132**	F2
Postmasburg	**108**	C5
Postojna	**62**	K5
Post Weygand	**102**	F4
Posušje	**66**	E6
Pota	**86**	G4
Potapovo	**76**	R4
Poteau	**130**	C2
Potenza	**62**	J7
Potenza	**64**	K8
Potgietersrus	**108**	D4
P'ot'i	**92**	J2
Potiskum	**104**	G2
Potlatch	**126**	C1
Potosí	**140**	D7
Potsdam, *Germany*	**52**	J4
Potsdam, *US*	**128**	F2
Pottuvil	**88**	D7
Poughkeepsie	**128**	F2
Pourerere	**116**	F5
Pouto	**116**	E3
Póvoa de Varzim	**60**	B3
Povorino	**70**	H4
Powder	**126**	E1
Powder River	**126**	E2
Powell River	**122**	G7
Poyang Hu	**80**	F5
Požarevac	**66**	J5
Poza Rica	**134**	E4
Požega	**66**	H6
Poznań	**50**	F5
Pozoblanco	**60**	F6
Pozzuoli	**64**	J8
Prabumulih	**86**	C3
Prachatice	**50**	D8
Prachuap Khiri Khan	**84**	B4
Prado	**140**	K7
Præstø	**52**	H1
Prague = Praha	**50**	D7
Praha	**50**	D7
Praia	**104**	(1)B2
Prainha	**140**	G4
Prairie du Chien	**128**	B2
Prapat	**86**	B2
Praslin Island	**108**	(2)B1
Pratas = Dongsha Qundao	**84**	F2
Prato	**62**	G7
Pratt	**126**	G3
Prattville	**130**	D3
Praya	**86**	F4
Preetz	**52**	F2
Preganziòl	**62**	H5
Preiļi	**48**	P8
Premnitz	**52**	H4
Premuda	**62**	K6
Prentice	**128**	B1
Prenzlau	**50**	C4
Preobrazhenka	**78**	H4
Preparis Island	**84**	A4
Preparis North Channel	**84**	A3
Preparis South Channel	**84**	A4
Přerov	**50**	G8
Presa de la Boquilla	**132**	E3
Presa de las Adjuntas	**132**	G4
Presa Obregón	**132**	E3
Prescott	**126**	D4
Preševo	**66**	J7
Presho	**126**	G2
Presidencia Roque Sáenz Peña	**142**	J4
Presidente Prudente	**142**	L3
Presidio	**132**	F3
Preslav	**66**	P6
Presnogorkovka	**70**	N4
Prešov	**50**	L9
Presque Isle	**128**	G1
Přeštice	**52**	J7
Preston, *UK*	**56**	K8
Preston, *Minn., US*	**128**	B2
Preston, *Mo., US*	**128**	B3
Pretoria	**108**	D5
Preveza	**68**	C6
Priargunsk	**78**	K6
Pribilof Islands	**132**	(1)D4
Priboj	**66**	G6
Příbram	**50**	D8
Price	**126**	D3
Prichard	**130**	D3
Priego de Córdoba	**60**	F7
Priekule	**48**	L8
Prienai	**50**	N3
Prieska	**108**	C5
Priest Lake	**126**	C1
Prievidza	**50**	H9
Prijedor	**66**	D5
Prijepolje	**66**	G6
Prikaspiyskaya Nizmennost'	**70**	K5
Prilep	**68**	D3
Primolano	**62**	G5
Primorsk	**48**	Q6
Primorsko Akhtarsk	**70**	G5
Prince Albert	**122**	K6
Prince Albert Peninsula	**122**	H2
Prince Albert Sound	**122**	H2
Prince Charles Island	**122**	R3
Prince Edward Island	**98**	G10

Prince Edward Island 122 U7
Prince George 122 G6
Prince of Wales Island, *Australia* 114 H2
Prince of Wales Island, *Canada* 122 L2
Prince of Wales Island, *US* 122 E5
Prince of Wales Strait 122 H2
Prince Patrick Island 120 Q2
Prince Regent Inlet 122 N2
Prince Rupert 122 E6
Princess Charlotte Bay 114 H2
Princeton, *Canada* 126 B1
Princeton, *Ill., US* 128 C2
Princeton, *Ky., US* 128 C3
Princeton, *Mo., US* 128 B2
Prince William Sound 122 B4
Príncipe 104 F4
Prineville 126 B2
Priozersk 48 R6
Priština 66 J7
Pritzwalk 52 H3
Privas 58 K9
Privolzhskaya Vozvyshennost 70 H4
Prizren 66 H7
Probolinggo 86 E4
Proddatur 88 C6
Progreso 134 G4
Prokhladnyy 92 L2
Prokop'yevsk 76 R7
Prokuplje 66 J6
Proletarsk 70 H5
Proliv Longa 78 X2
Proliv Matochkin Shar 76 K3
Proliv Vil'kitskogo 76 U2
Prophet 122 G5
Propriano 64 C7
Prorer Wiek 52 J2
Proserpine 114 J4
Prosna 50 G6
Prosperidad 84 H5
Prostojov 50 G8
Proti 68 D7
Provadiya 66 Q6
Prøven = Kangersuatsiaq 122 W2
Providence 128 F2
Providence Island 108 (2)B2
Provideniya 78 Z4
Provincetown 128 F2
Provins 58 J5
Provo 126 D2
Provost 122 J6
Prudhoe Bay 132 (1)H1
Prudnik 50 G7
Prüm 54 J4
Pruszków 50 K5
Prut 66 R4
Pružany 50 P5
Prvić 62 K6
Pryluky 70 F4
Prypyats' 46 G2
Przasnysz 50 K4
Przemyśl 50 M8
Przeworsk 50 M7
Psara 68 H6
Psebay 92 J1
Pskov 70 E3
Ptolemaïda 68 D4
Ptuj 62 L4
Pucallpa 140 C5
Pucheng 80 F5
Puch'ŏn 82 D5
Púchov 50 H8
Pucioasa 66 N4
Puck 50 H3
Pudasjärvi 48 P4
Pudozh 70 G2
Puebla 134 E5
Puebla de Don Rodrigo 60 F5
Pueblo 126 F3
Puelches 142 H6
Puelén 142 H6
Puente-Genil 60 F7
Puerto Acosta 140 D7
Puerto Aisén 142 G8
Puerto Alegre 140 E6
Puerto Angel 134 E5
Puerto Ayacucho 134 L7
Puerto Barrios 134 G5
Puerto Berrío 140 C2
Puerto Cabezas 134 H6
Puerto Carreño 134 L7
Puerto del Rosario 102 C3
Puerto de Navacerrada 60 G4
Puerto Guarini 140 F8
Puerto Heath 140 D6
Puerto Inírida 140 D3
Puerto Leguizamo 140 C4
Puerto Libertad 132 D3
Puerto Limón 140 B3
Puertollano 60 F6
Puerto Madryn 142 J7
Puerto Maldonado 140 D6
Puerto Montt 142 G7
Puerto Natáles 142 G9
Puerto Nuevo 134 K7
Puerto Páez 140 D2
Puerto Peñasco 132 D2
Puerto Princesa 84 F5
Puerto Real 60 D8
Puerto Rico 134 L5
Puerto Rico 140 D6
Puerto Rico Trench 138 E1
Puerto Santa Cruz 142 H9
Puerto Suárez 140 F7
Pukapuka 112 N7
Pukatawagen 122 L5
Pukch'ŏng 82 E3
Pukë 66 G7
Pukeuri Junction 116 C7
Pula 62 J6
Pulaski 128 E2
Puławy 50 M6
Pullman 126 C1
Pułtusk 48 L10
Pultusk 50 L5
Pulu 76 Q10
Pülümür 92 H4
Puncak Jaya 87 E3
Puncak Mandala 87 F3
Pune 88 B5
P'ungsan 82 E3
Punia 106 D4
Puno 140 C7
Punta Albina 108 A3
Punta Alice 64 M9
Punta Angamos 142 G3
Punta Arena 126 B3
Punta Arenas 142 G9
Punta Ballena 142 G4
Punta da Estaca de Bares 60 C1
Punta Dungeness 142 H9
Punta Eugenia 134 A3
Punta Galera 142 G6
Punta Gallinas 134 K6
Punta Gorda 130 E4
Punta La Marmora 64 D8
Punta Lavapié 142 G6
Punta Lengua de Vaca 142 G5
Punta Mala 140 B2
Punta Mariato 134 H7
Punta Medanosa 142 H8
Punta Negra 140 A5
Punta Norte, *Argentina* 142 J7
Punta Norte, *Argentina* 142 K6
Punta Pariñas 140 A5
Punta Rasa 142 J7
Puntarenas 134 H6
Punta San Gabriel 132 D3
Punta San Telmo 134 D5
Punta Sarga 102 B4
Puponga 116 D5
Puqi 80 E5
Pur 76 P4
Puri 88 E5
Purmerend 54 G2
Purpe 78 B4
Purukcahu 86 E3
Purus 140 E5
Puruvesi 48 Q6
Pusan 82 E6
Pushkin 70 F3
Püspökladany 50 L10
Putao 84 B1
Putaruru 116 E3
Putian 80 F5
Putna 66 P4
Putrajaya 86 C2
Puttalami 88 C7
Putten 54 G3
Puttgarden 52 G2
Putumayo 140 C4
Putusibau 86 E2
Puuwai 132 (2)A2
Puvurnituq 122 R5
Puy de Dôme 58 H8
Puy de Sancy 58 H8
Puysegur Point 116 A8
Pweto 106 D5
Pwllheli 56 H9
Pyal'ma 70 G2
Pyasina 76 R3
Pyatigorsk 92 K1
Pyè 84 B3
Pyhäjärvi 48 M6
Pylos 68 D8
Pyŏktong 82 C3
P'yŏnggang 82 D4
P'yŏngyang 82 C4
Pyramid Island 116 (1)B2
Pyramid Lake 126 C2/3
Pyrenees 58 E11
Pyrgos 68 D7
Pyrzyce 50 D4
Pyshchug 70 J3
Pytalovo 48 P8

Q

Qā 'Azamān 94 E5
Qadīmah 90 C5
Qādub 90 F7
Qagan Nur 80 F2
Qal'aikhum 90 K2
Qalamat Nadqān 95 D5
Qalāt 90 J3
Qal'at Bīshah 90 D5
Qal'eh-ye Now 90 H3
Qamdo 80 B4
Qamīnīs 100 C1
Qandala 106 H1
Qaraaoun 92 F7
Qardho 106 H2
Qartaba 94 C2
Qasr el Azraq 94 D5
Qasr el Kharana 94 D5
Qasr Farafra 100 E2
Qaṭanā 94 D3
Qatar 95 D4
Qatrāna 94 D5
Qattâra Depression 100 E2
Qax 92 M3
Qāyen 90 G3
Qazangöldag 92 M4
Qazax 92 L3
Qazımämmäd 92 N3
Qazvīn 90 E2
Qena 100 F2
Qeqertarsuatsiaat 122 W4
Qeqertarsuatsiaq 122 V2
Qeqertarsuup Tunua 122 V3
Qeshm 95 F3
Qeshm 95 G3
Qeys 95 E3
Qezel Owzan 92 N5
Qeẓi'ot 94 B6
Qianshanlaoba 76 Q8
Qiaowan 80 B2
Qidukou 88 G2
Qiemo 76 R10
Qijiang 80 D5
Qijiaojing 76 S9
Qila Saifullah 90 J3
Qilian 80 C3
Qilian Shan 80 B3
Qingdao 80 G3
Qinghai Hu 80 B3
Qinghai Nanshan 80 B3
Qingjiang 80 F4
Qingshuihe 80 E3
Qingyang 80 D3
Qingyuan, *China* 80 E6
Qingyuan, *China* 80 G2
Qinhuangdao 80 F3
Qinzhou 84 D2
Qionghai 84 E3
Qiqian 78 L6
Qiqihar 78 L7
Qīr 95 E2
Qira 76 Q10
Qiryat Ata 94 C4
Qiryat Motzkin 94 C4
Qiryat Shemona 94 C3
Qishn 90 F6
Qolleh-ye Damāvand 90 F2
Qom 90 F3
Qornet es Saouda 94 D2
Qorveh 92 M6
Qotbābād 95 G3
Qotūr 92 L4
Quang Ngai' 84 D3
Quangolodougou 104 C3
Quang Tri 84 D3
Quanzhou 84 F2
Quaqtaq 122 T4
Quarto Sant'Elena 64 D9
Quba 92 N3
Quchan 90 G2
Québec 128 F1
Quedlinburg 52 G5
Queen Charlotte 122 E6
Queen Charlotte Islands 122 E6
Queen Charlotte Sound 122 E6
Queen Charlotte Strait 122 F6
Queen Elizabeth Islands 120 M2
Queen Maud Gulf 122 L3
Queensland 114 G4
Queenstown, *Australia* 114 J8
Queenstown, *New Zealand* 116 B7
Queenstown, *South Africa* 108 D6
Queets 126 B1
Quelimane 108 F3
Quemado 132 E2
Querétaro 134 D4
Quesnel 122 G6
Quetta 90 J3
Quezaltenango 134 F6
Quezon 84 F5
Quezon City 84 G4
Qufu 80 F3
Quibala 108 A2
Quibdó 134 J7
Quiberon 58 B6
Quijotoa 132 D2
Quillagua 142 H3
Quilmes 142 K5
Quilpie 114 H5
Quimbele 106 B5
Quimili 142 J4
Quimper 58 A5
Quimperlé 58 B6
Quincy 128 B3
Qui Nhon 84 D4
Quionga 106 G6
Quirindi 114 K6
Quito 140 B4
Qujing 84 C1
Qumar He 88 F1
Qumaryan 88 F1
Qurayyāt 90 G5
Qurghonteppa 90 J2
Qurlurtuuq 122 H3
Qus 100 F2
Qusar 92 N3
Quseir 100 F2
Quzhou 80 F5

R

Raab 62 L3
Raahe 48 N4
Raalte 54 J2
Raasay 56 G4
Raas Caseyr 90 F7
Rab 62 K6
Rab 62 K6
Rába 66 E2
Raba 87 A4
Răbăgani 66 K3
Rabak 100 F5
Rabat, *Malta* 64 J13
Rabat, *Morocco* 102 D2
Rabca 62 N3
Rābigh 90 C5
Rabka 50 K8
Rach Gia 84 D5
Racine 128 C2
Ráckeve 66 F2
Rădăuţi 66 N2
Radbuza 52 H7
Radeberg 52 J5
Radebeul 52 J5
Radhanpur 88 B4
Radnevo 66 N7
Radom 50 L6
Radomir 66 K7
Radomsko 50 J6
Radoviš 68 E3
Radstadt 50 C10
Raduzhny 76 P5
Radviliškis 50 N2
Radzyń Podlaski 50 M6
Rae-Edzo 122 H4
Raevavae 112 M8
Rafaela 142 J4
Rafah 94 B5
Rafai 106 C3
Rafḥā 90 D4
Rafsanjān 95 G1
Raglan 116 E3
Ragusa 64 J12
Raha 87 B3
Rahad el Berdi 100 D5
Rahimyar Khan 90 K4
Raichur 88 C5
Raiganj 88 E3
Raigarh 88 D4
Rainach 62 L4
Rainbow Lake 122 H5
Rainier 126 B1
Rainy Lake 128 B1
Rainy River 128 B1
Raipur 88 D4
Rai Valley 116 D5
Rajahmundry 88 D5
Raja-Jooseppi 48 Q2
Rajapalaiyam 88 C7
Rajgarh 88 C3
Rajkot 90 K5
Rajnandgaon 88 D4
Rajsamand 88 B3
Rajshahi 88 E4
Rakhiv 66 M1
Rakovica 62 L6
Rakovník 50 C7
Rakovski 66 M7
Rakvere 48 P7
Raleigh 130 F2
Ralik Chain 112 G5
Ram 94 C7
Rama 134 H6
Ramallah 94 C5
Rambouillet 58 G5
Rameswaram 88 C7
Rāmhormoz 95 C1
Ramla 94 B5
Ramlat Rabyānah 100 C3
Râmnicu Sărat 66 Q4
Râmnicu Vâlcea 66 M4
Ramonville-St-Agne 58 G10
Rampur, *India* 88 C2
Rampur, *India* 88 C3
Ramree Island 84 A3
Ramsgate 56 P10
Ramtha 94 D4
Ranau 86 F1
Rancagua 142 G5
Ranchi 88 E4
Randazzo 64 J11
Randers 48 F8
Randijaure 48 K3
Randolph 126 G2
Rânes 54 B6
Rangamati 88 F4
Rangiora 116 D6
Rangoon = Yangon 84 B3
Rankin 132 F2
Rankin Inlet 122 N4
Ranong 84 B5
Ransiki 87 D3
Rānya 92 L5
Rapa 112 M8
Rapalla 64 D4
Rapallo 62 E6
Rapar 90 K5
Raperswil 62 D3
Rapid City 126 F2
Rapid River 128 C1
Rapla 48 N7
Rapur 90 J5
Raroia 112 N7
Rarotonga 112 K8
Râs Abu Shagara 100 G3
Ra's al Ḥadd 90 G5
Ra's al Ḥazrah 95 D4
Ra's al Hilāl 100 D1
Ra's al Khajī 95 C2
Ra's al Khaymah 95 F4
Ra's al Kūh 95 G4
Ra's al Muraysah 100 E1
Ra's al 'Udayd 95 D4
Ra's az Zawr 95 C3
Râs Banâs 100 G3
Ras Beddouza 102 C1
Ras Bir 100 H5
Ras Dashen Terara 100 G5
Ra's-e Barkan 95 C2
Raseiniai 48 M9
Râs el Nafas 94 B7
Ra's Fartak 90 F6
Râs Ghârib 100 F2
Rasht 92 N5
Rāsk 90 H4
Raška 66 H6
Ras Kasar 100 G4
Ra's Madrakah 90 G6
Râs Nouâdhibou 102 B4
Rason Lake 114 D5
Rass Ajdir 102 H2
Rass Jebel 64 E11
Rass Mostefa 64 F12
Rassokha 78 H2
Rast 66 L6
Ras Tannūrah 95 D3
Rastatt 54 L6
Rastede 52 D3
Ratak Chain 112 H4
Ratangarh 90 K4

Rat Buri 84 B4
Rath 88 C3
Rathenow 52 H4
Rathlin Island 56 F6
Rathluirc 56 D9
Ratlam 88 C4
Ratnagiri 90 K6
Raton 126 F3
Ratta 78 C4
Ratten 62 D4
Ratzeburg 52 F3
Rauđamýri 48 (1)B2
Raudhatain 95 B1
Raukumara Range 116 F4
Rauma 48 L6
Raurimu 116 E4
Rausu 82 N1
Răut 66 R2
Ravalli 126 D1
Ravānsar 92 M6
Rāvar 95 G1
Ravenna 62 H6
Ravensburg 62 E3
Ravensthorpe 114 D6
Ravnina 90 H2
Rāwah 92 J6
Rawaki 112 J6
Rawalpindi 90 K3
Rawa Mazowiecka 50 K6
Rawāndiz 92 L5
Rawicz 50 F6
Rawlinna 114 E6
Rawlins 126 E2
Rawson 142 J7
Rawu 88 G3
Raychikhinsk 78 M7
Raymond 126 B1
Raymondville 132 G3
Rayong 84 C4
Razdol'noye 82 F2
Razgrad 66 P6
Razlog 66 L8
Reading, *UK* 56 M10
Reading, *US* 128 E2
Realicó 142 J6
Rebaa 102 G2
Rebbenesøya 48 J1
Rebun-tō 80 L1
Rechytsa 70 F4
Recife 140 L5
Recklinghausen 54 K3
Recknitz 52 H3
Reconquista 142 K4
Recreo 142 H4
Red, *Canada/US* 126 G1
Red, *US* 130 B3
Reda 50 H3
Red Bluff 132 B1
Red Cloud 130 B1
Red Deer 122 J6
Redding 126 B2
Redditch 54 A2
Redfield 126 G2
Red Lake 122 N6
Red Lakes 124 H2
Red Lodge 126 E1
Red Oak 128 A2
Redon 58 C6
Redondela 60 B2
Red River = Song Hông 84 C2
Red Sea 100 G3
Redwater 122 J6
Red Wing 128 B2
Redwood City 126 B3
Redwood Falls 128 A2
Reed City 128 C2
Reedsport 126 B2
Reefton 116 C6
Rega 50 E4
Regen 52 H7
Regen 52 J8
Regensburg 52 H7
Regenstauf 52 H7
Reggane 102 F3
Reggio di Calabria 64 K10
Reggio nell'Emilia 62 F6
Reghin 66 M3
Regina, *Brazil* 140 G3
Regina, *Canada* 124 F1
Rehau 52 H6
Rehoboth 108 B4
Rehovot 94 B5
Reichenbach 52 H6
Reigate 56 M10
Reims 54 G5
Reinach Bad 62 C3
Reindeer Lake 122 L5
Reinosa 60 F1
Reisi 64 J11
Reliance 122 K4
Relizane 102 F1
Remada 102 H2
Remagen 54 K4
Rembang 86 E4
Remeshk 95 H3
Remiremont 58 M6
Remscheid 54 K3
Rena 48 F6
Rendina 68 F4
Rendsburg 52 E2
Rengat 86 C3
Reni 66 R4
Renmark 114 H6
Rennes 58 D5
Reno 62 G6
Reno 126 C3
Rentería 60 J1
Renton 126 B1
Renukut 88 D4
Reo 87 B4
Replot 48 L5
Represa de Balbina 140 F4
Represa de Samuel 140 E5
Represa de Sao Simao 140 G7
Represa Ilha Solteira 140 G7
Represa Tucuruí 140 H4
Republic 126 C1
Repulse Bay 114 J4
Repulse Bay 122 P3
Requena, *Peru* 140 C5
Requena, *Spain* 60 J5
Reşadiye 92 G3
Resen 66 J8
Réservoir Cabonga 128 E1
Réservoir Caniapiscau 122 T6
Réservoir de La Grande 2 122 R6
Réservoir de La Grande 3 122 R6
Réservoir de La Grande 4 122 S6
Réservoir Gouin 128 F1
Réservoir Manicouagan 122 T6
Réservoir Opinaca 122 R6
Réservoir Pipmuacan 128 G1
Reshteh-ye Kūhhā-ye Alborz 90 F2
Resistencia 142 K4
Reşiţa 66 J4
Resolute 122 N2
Resolution Island, *Canada* 122 U4
Resolution Island, *New Zealand* 116 A7
Resovo 68 K3
Rethel 54 G5
Rethymno 68 G9
Réunion 108 (1)B2
Reus 60 M3
Reutlingen 52 E8
Revda 70 L3
Revillagigedo Island 132 (1)L4
Revin 54 G5
Revivim 94 B5
Revúca 50 K9
Rewa 88 D4
Rexburg 126 D2
Reykjanes 48 (1)B3
Reykjavík 48 (1)C2
Reynosa 130 B4
Rezat 52 F7
Rezé 58 D6
Rēzekne 48 P8
Rezina 66 R2
Rezovo 66 R8
Rezzato 62 F5
Rheda-Wiedenbrück 52 D5
Rhein = Rhine 62 C2
Rheinbach 54 K4
Rheine 54 K2
Rheinfelden 62 C3
Rhin = Rhine 62 C2
Rhine 62 C2
Rhinelander 128 C1
Rho 62 E5
Rhode Island 128 F2
Rhodes = Rodos 68 L8
Rhondda 56 J10
Rhône 58 K9
Rhyl 56 J8
Ribadeo 60 C1
Ribas do Rio Pardo 142 L3
Ribe 48 E9
Ribeauville 58 N5
Ribeirão Prêto 142 M3
Ribeira = Santa Eugenia 60 A2
Ribera 64 H11
Riberalta 140 D6
Ribnica 64 J3
Rîbniţa 66 S2
Ribnitz-Damgarten 52 H2
Říčany 52 K6
Riccione 62 H7
Richardson Mountains 132 (1)K2
Richfield 126 D3
Richland 126 C1
Richlands 128 D3
Richmond, *Australia* 114 H4
Richmond, *New Zealand* 116 D5
Richmond, *Ky., US* 128 D3
Richmond, *Va., US* 128 E3
Ridgecrest 132 C1
Ridgway 128 E2
Ried 62 J2
Riesa 52 J5
Rieti 64 G6
Rifle 126 E3
Rīga 48 N8
Rīgān 95 H2
Riggins 126 C1
Rigolet 122 V6
Rijeka 62 K5
Riley 126 C2
Rimava 50 J9
Rimavská Sobota 50 K9
Rimini 62 H6
Rimouski 128 G1
Rineia 68 H7
Ringe 52 F1
Ringkøbing 48 E8
Ringkøbing Fjord 48 D9
Ringsted 52 G1
Ringvassøya 48 J1
Rinteln 52 E4
Rio Branco 140 D5
Rio Colorado 142 J6
Rio Cuarto 142 J5
Rio de Janeiro 142 N3
Rio de Janeiro 142 N3
Rio de la Plata 142 K6
Rio Gallegos 142 H9
Rio Grande 132 E2
Rio Grande, *Argentina* 142 H9
Rio Grande, *Mexico* 132 F4
Rio Grande 142 L5
Rio Grande City 130 B4
Rio Grande do Norte 140 K5
Rio Grande do Sul 142 L4
Riohacha 134 K6
Río Largartos 134 G4
Riom 58 J8
Río Mulatos 140 D7
Rionero in Vulture 64 K8
Río Tigre 140 B4
Rio Verde, *Brazil* 140 G7
Río Verde, *Chile* 142 G9
Rio Verde de Mato Grosso 140 G7
Ripley, *Oh., US* 128 D3
Ripley, *Tenn., US* 128 C3
Ripley, *W.Va., US* 128 D3
Ripoll 60 N2
Ripon 56 L7
Rishiri-tō 78 Q7
Rishon le Ẓiyyon 94 B5
Risør 48 E7
Ritchie's Archipelago 84 A4
Ritzville 126 C1
Rivadavia 142 G4
Riva del Garda 62 F5
Rivarolo Canavese 62 C5
Rivas 134 G6
Rivera, *Argentina* 142 J6
Rivera, *Uruguay* 142 K5
River Cess 104 C3
Riversdale 108 C6
Riversdale Beach 116 E5
Riverton, *Canada* 122 M6
Riverton, *New Zealand* 116 A8
Rivesaltes 58 H11
Rivière-du-Loup 128 G1
Rivne 70 E4
Rivoli 62 C5
Riwoqê 88 G2
Riyadh = Ar Riyāḑ 95 B4
Rıze 92 J3
Rizhao 80 F3
Roanne 58 K7
Roanoke 128 D3
Roanoke Rapids 130 F2
Robāţ 95 G1
Robe 114 G7
Robertsfors 48 L4
Robertval 128 F1
Roboré 140 F7
Robstown 130 B4
Roccastrada 64 F6
Rochefort, *Belgium* 54 H4
Rochefort, *France* 58 E8
Rochelle 128 C2
Rocher River 122 J4
Rochester, *UK* 54 C3
Rochester, *Minn., US* 128 B2
Rochester, *N.H., US* 128 F2
Rochester, *N.Y., US* 128 E2
Rockall 46 C2
Rockefeller Plateau 144 (2)EE2
Rockford 128 C2
Rockhampton 114 K4
Rock Hill 128 D4
Rock Island 128 B2
Rocklake 126 G1
Rockport 126 B1
Rock Rapids 128 A2
Rock Springs 126 E2
Rocksprings 132 F3
Rocky Mount 128 E3
Rocky Mountains 122 F5
Rødby Havn 52 G2
Roddickton 122 V6
Roden 54 J1
Rodez 58 H9
Rodi Garganico 64 K7
Roding 52 H7
Rodney 128 D2
Rodopi Planina 66 M7
Rodos 68 L8
Rodos 68 L8
Roebourne 114 C4
Roermond 54 J3
Roeselare 54 F4
Roes Welcome Sound 122 P4
Rogers City 128 D1
Rogerson 126 D2
Rogliano 64 D6
Rogozno 50 G5
Rogue 126 B2
Rohrbach 62 K2
Rohtak 88 C3
Roi Et 84 C3
Roja 48 M8
Rokiškis 48 N9
Rokycany 50 C8
Rolla 128 B3
Rolleston 116 D6
Rolvsøya 48 M1
Roma 87 C4
Roma, *Australia* 114 J5
Roma, *Italy* 64 G7
Roman 66 P3
Romania 66 L4
Romans-sur-Isère 58 L8
Rombas 54 J5
Rome = Roma 64 G7
Rome, *Ga., US* 130 D3
Rome, *N.Y., US* 128 E2
Romney 128 E3
Romny 70 F4
Rømø 52 D1
Romorantin-Lanthenay 58 G6
Romsey 54 A3
Rona 56 G2
Ronan 124 D2
Roncesvalles 60 J2
Ronda 60 E8
Rondônia 140 E6
Rondônia 140 E6
Rondonópolis 140 G7
Rondu 90 L2
Rongcheng 80 G3
Rønne 50 D2
Ronneby 48 H8
Ronne Entrance 144 (2)JJ3
Ronne Ice Shelf 144 (2)MM2
Ronse 54 F4
Roosendaal 54 G3
Roper Bar 114 F2
Roquetas de Mar 60 H8
Roraima 140 E3
Røros 48 F5
Rosário 140 J4
Rosario, *Argentina* 142 J5
Rosario, *Mexico* 124 D6
Rosario, *Mexico* 124 E7
Rosario, *Paraguay* 142 K3
Rosário Oeste 140 F6
Rosarito 124 C6
Rosarno 64 K10
Roscommon 56 D8
Roscrea 56 E9
Roseau 134 M5
Roseburg 126 B2
Roseires Reservoir 100 F5
Rose Island 112 K7
Rosenburg 132 G3
Rosenheim 62 H3
Roses 60 P2
Rosetown 122 K6
Rosica 66 N6
Rosignano Marittimo 62 F7
Roşiori de Vede 66 N5
Rosita 66 Q6
Roskilde 48 G9
Roslavl' 70 F4
Rossano 64 L9
Ross Ice Shelf 144 (2)Z1
Ross Lake 126 B1
Rosslare 56 F9
Roßlau 52 H5
Rosso 102 B5
Rossosh' 70 G4
Ross River 122 E4
Ross Sea 144 (2)AA2
Røssvatnet 48 G4
Røst 48 G3
Rostāq 95 E3
Rosthern 122 K6
Rostock 52 H2
Rostov 70 G3
Rostov-na-Donu 70 G5
Rostrenen 58 B5
Roswell 132 F2
Rota 112 E4
Rote 87 B5
Rotenburg, *Germany* 52 E3
Rotenburg, *Germany* 52 E5
Roth 52 G7
Rothenburg 52 F7
Roto 114 J6
Rotorua 116 F4
Rott 62 H2
Rottenmann 62 K3
Rotterdam 58 K2
Rottnen 50 E1
Rottumeroog 54 J1
Rottumerplaat 54 J1
Rottweil 62 D2
Rotuma 112 H7
Roubaix 54 F4
Rouen 54 D5
Rouiba 60 P8
Round Mountain 114 K6
Round Rock 130 B3
Roundup 126 E1
Rousay 56 J2
Rouyn 128 E1
Rovaniemi 48 N3
Rovato 62 E5
Rovereto 62 G5
Rovigo 62 G5
Rovinari 66 L5
Rovinj 62 J5
Rovuma 106 F6
Rowley Island 122 R3
Rowley Shoals 114 C3
Roxas 84 G4
Roxburgh 116 B7
Royal Leamington Spa 54 A2
Royal Tunbridge Wells 54 C3
Royan 58 D8
Roye 54 E5
Royston 54 C2
Rozdil'na 66 T3
Rožňava 50 K9
Rozzano 62 E5
Rrëshen 68 B3
Rtishchevo 70 H4
Ruacana 108 A3
Ruahine Range 116 E5
Ruapehu 116 F4
Ruapuke Island 116 B8
Ruarkela 88 D4
Ruatahuna 116 F4
Ruatoria 116 G3
Ruawai 116 D3
Rub' al Khālī 90 E6
Rubeshibe 82 M2
Rubi 106 C3
Rubtsovsk 76 Q7
Ruby 132 (1)F3
Rudan 95 G3
Ruda Śląska 50 H7
Rudbar 90 H3
Rüdersdorf 52 J4
Rudkøbing 52 F2
Rudnaya Pristan' 82 H2
Rudnyy 70 M4
Rudolstadt 52 G6
Rue 54 D4
Ruffec 58 F7
Rufiji 106 F5
Rugby, *UK* 54 A2
Rugby, *US* 124 G2
Rügen 50 C3
Ruhnu 48 M8

Ruhr 54 L3
Rui'an 80 G5
Rum 56 F5
Ruma 66 G4
Rumāh 95 B4
Rumaylah 95 B1
Rumbek 106 D2
Rum Cay 134 K4
Rumigny 54 G5
Rum Jungle 114 F2
Rumoi 82 L2
Runanaga 116 C6
Rundu 108 B3
Rundvik 48 K5
Ruoqiang 76 R10
Ruo Shui 80 C2
Rupa 62 K5
Rupat 86 C2
Rupert 122 R6
Rupert 126 D2
Rurutu 112 L8
Ruse 66 N6
Rushon 88 G3
Rushville, *Ill., US* 128 B2
Rushville, *Ind., US* 128 C3
Rushville, *Nebr., US* 126 F2
Russell 126 G3
Russellville, *Ark., US* 130 C2
Russellville, *Ky., US* 130 D2
Rüsselsheim 52 D7
Russia 48 L9
Russia 74 M3
Russoye Ust'ye 78 R2
Rust'avi 92 L3
Ruston 130 C3
Rutana 106 D4
Rute 60 F7
Ruteng 87 B4
Rutland 128 F2
Rutog 88 C2
Ruvo di Puglia 64 L7
Ruvuma 106 F6
Ruzayevka 70 H4
Ružomberok 50 J8
Rwanda 106 D4
R-Warnemünde 52 H2
Ryazan' 70 G4
Ryazhsk 70 H4
Rybinsk 70 G3
Rybinskoye Vodokhranilishche 70 G3
Rybnik 50 H7
Rychnov 50 F7
Ryde 54 A4
Rye 54 C4
Rye Patch Reservoir 126 C2
Ryki 50 L6
Ryl'sk 70 F4
Ryn-Peski 70 J5
Ryōtsu 82 K4
Rypin 50 J4
Ryukyu Islands = Nansei-shotō 80 H5
Rzeszów 50 M7
Rzhev 70 F3

S

Sa'ādatābād, *Iran* 95 E1
Sa'ādatābād, *Iran* 95 F2
Saale 52 G6
Saalfeld 52 G6
Saalfelden 62 H3
Saanen 64 B2
Saar 54 J5
Saarbrücken 54 J5
Saarburg 54 J5
Saaremaa 48 L7
Saarlouis 54 J5
Saatli 92 N4
Saatly 90 E2
Saba 134 M5
Sab' Ābār 94 E3
Šabac 66 G5
Sabadell 60 N3
Sabah 86 F1
Sabang 84 B5
Sabhā 102 H3
Sabiñánigo 60 K2
Sabinas 132 F3
Sabinas Hidalgo 132 F3
Sabine 130 B3
Sabine Lake 130 C3
Sabinov 50 L8
Sabkhet el Bardawîl 94 A5
Sable Island 122 V8
Sablé-sur-Sarthe 58 E6
Sabôr 60 D3
Sabres 58 E9
Sabun 76 Q5
Sabzevār 90 G2
Săcele 66 N4
Sachanga 108 B2
Sachs Harbour 122 G2
Sacile 62 H5
Säckingen 62 C3
Sacramento 126 B3
Sacramento 126 B3
Şad'ah 90 D6
Sadiqabad 90 K4
Sadiya 88 G3
Sado 60 B6
Sadoga-shima 82 K4
Sadon 92 K2
Sado-shima 80 K3
Sa Dragonera 60 N5
Sadūt 94 B5
Säffle 48 G7
Safford 132 E2
Safi, *Jordan* 94 C5
Safi, *Morocco* 102 D2
Safonovo, *Russia* 70 F3
Safonovo, *Russia* 70 J1
Safranbolu 68 Q3
Saga, *China* 88 E3
Saga, *Japan* 82 F7
Sagami-nada 82 K6
Sagar 88 C4
Sagastyr 76 Z3
Sage 126 D2
Saginaw 128 D2
Sagiz 70 K5
Sagiz 70 K5
Sagres 60 B7
Saguache 126 E3
Sagua la Grande 134 H4
Sagunt 60 K5
Sahāb 94 D5
Sahagún 60 E2
Sahara 98 C3
Saharah el Gharbîya 100 E2
Saharanpur 88 C3
Saharsa 88 E3
Sahbuz 92 L4
Sahel 98 C4
Sahiwal 90 K3
Sahuaripa 132 E3
Šahy 66 F1
Saïda, *Algeria* 102 F2
Saïda, *Lebanon* 94 C3
Sa'īdābād 95 F2
Saidpur 88 E3
Saigo 82 G5
Saigon = Hô Chi Minh 84 D4
Saiha 88 F4
Saihan Toroi 80 C2
Saiki 82 F7
Saimaa 48 P6
Saimbeyli 92 G4
Sā'īn 95 F1
Saindak 90 H4
St. Albans 54 B3
St-Amand-Montrond 58 H7
St. Andrä 62 K4
St. Andrews 56 K5
St. Anthony 122 V6
St. Arnaud 116 D5
St. Augustin 54 K4
St-Augustin 122 V6
St. Augustine 130 E4
St. Austell 56 H11
St-Avertin 58 F6
St-Avold 54 J5
St. Barthélémy 134 M5
St-Brieuc 58 C5
St. Catharines 124 L3
St-Chamond 58 K8
St-Claude 58 L7
St. Cloud 128 B1
St. David's 56 G10
St-Denis, *France* 54 E6
St-Denis, *Réunion* 108 (1)B2
St-Dié 62 B2
St-Dizier 58 K5
Ste-Anne-de-Beaupré 128 F1
Ste-Maxime 58 M10
Ste-Menehould 54 G5
Saintes 58 E8
Stes-Maries-de-la-Mer 58 K10
St-Étienne 58 K8
St-Étienne-du-Rouvray 54 D5
St-Félicien 128 F1
St-Florent 64 D6
St-Florentin 58 J5
St-Flour 58 J8
St. Francis 126 F3
St. Gallen 62 E3
St-Gaudens 58 F10
St. George, *Australia* 114 J5
St. George, *US* 126 D3
St. Georgen 62 D2
St. Georges 128 F1
St. George's 134 M6
St. George's Channel 56 F10
St-Germain-en-Laye 54 E6
St-Girons 58 G11
St. Helena 98 C7
St. Helena Bay 108 B6
St. Helens, *UK* 56 K8
St. Helens, *US* 126 B1
St. Helier 58 C4
St-Hubert 54 H4
St. Ignace 128 D1
St. Ives 56 G11
St-Jean-d'Angely 58 E8
St-Jean-de-Luz 58 D10
St-Jean-de-Maurienne 62 B5
St-Jean-sur-Richelieu 128 F1
St. John 122 T7
St. John's 122 W7
St. Johnsbury 128 F2
St. Joseph 128 B3
St-Jovité 128 F1
St-Junien 58 F8
St. Kilda 56 D4
St. Kitts-Nevis 134 M5
St. Laurent 140 G2
St-Laurent-en-Grandvaux 62 A4
St. Lawrence 128 G1
St. Lawrence Island 132 (1)C3
St-Léonard 128 G1
St-Lô 54 A5
St. Louis, *Senegal* 102 B5
St. Louis, *US* 128 B3
St. Lucia 134 M6
St. Maarten 134 M5
St-Malo 58 D5
St. Marys 128 D2
St. Matthew Island 132 (1)C3
St-Mihiel 54 H6
St. Moritz 62 E4
St-Nazaire 58 C6
St-Nicolas-de-Port 62 B2
St. Niklaas 54 G3
St-Omer 54 E4
St-Palais 58 D10
St-Pamphile 128 G1
St-Paul 62 B6
St. Paul, *Minn., US* 128 B2
St. Paul, *Nebr., US* 126 G2
St. Peter 128 B2
St. Peter Ording 52 D2
St. Peter-Port 58 C4
St. Petersburg = Sankt-Peterburg 70 F3
St. Petersburg 130 E4
St-Pierre 108 (1)B2
St-Pierre-et-Miquelon 122 V7
St. Pierre Island 108 (2)A2
St-Pol-de-Léon 58 A5
St-Pol-sur-Ternoise 54 E4
St. Pölten 62 L2
St-Quentin 54 F5
St-Raphaël 62 B7
St. Siméon 128 G1
St. Stephen 128 G1
St. Thomas 128 D2
St-Tropez 62 B7
St. Truiden 54 H4
St-Valéry-sur-Somme 54 D4
St. Veit 62 K4
St. Veit an der Glan 66 B3
St. Vincent and the Grenadines 134 M6
St-Vincent-les-Forts 62 B6
St-Vith 54 J4
Saipan 112 E4
Sajószentpéter 50 K9
Sākākah 90 D4
Sakaraha 108 G4
Sakarya 68 N4
Sakarya 68 N4
Sakata 82 K4
Sakchu 82 C3
Sakha 78 N3
Sakhalin 78 Q6
Sakhalinskiy Zaliv 78 Q6
Sakhon Nakhon 84 C3
Şäki 92 M3
Sakishima-shotō 80 H6
Sakskøbing 52 G2
Sal 70 H5
Sal 104 (1)B1
Šal'a 48 J7
Šal'a 50 G9
Salacgrīva 48 N8
Sala Consilina 64 K8
Saladillo 142 K6
Salado 142 J4
Salālah 90 F6
Salamanca, *Mexico* 134 D4
Salamanca, *Spain* 60 E4
Salamanca, *US* 128 E2
Salamina 68 F7
Salamīyah 94 E1
Salar de Uyuni 142 H3
Salawati 87 D3
Salayar 87 B4
Salbris 58 H6
Saldus 48 M8
Sale 114 J7
Salekhard 76 M4
Salem 126 B2
Salem, *India* 88 C6
Salem, *US* 128 C3
Salerno 64 J8
Salgótarján 50 J9
Salida 126 E3
Salihli 68 L6
Salihorsk 70 E4
Salima 108 E2
Salina 64 J10
Salina, *Kans., US* 126 G3
Salina, *Ut., US* 126 D3
Salinas, *Brazil* 140 J7
Salinas, *Ecuador* 140 A4
Salinas, *Mexico* 132 F4
Salinas, *US* 132 B1
Salinas Grandes 142 J4
Salinópolis 140 H4
Salisbury, *UK* 54 A3
Salisbury, *Md., US* 128 E3
Salisbury, *N.C., US* 128 D3
Salisbury Island 122 R4
Salkhad 94 D4
Salla 48 Q3
Salluit 122 R4
Salmās 92 L4
Salmon 126 C1/D1
Salmon 126 D1
Salmon Arm 122 H6
Salmon River Mountains 126 C1
Salo 48 M6
Salò 62 F5
Salon-de-Provence 58 L10
Salonta 66 J3
Sal'sk 70 H5
Salsomaggiore Terme 62 E6
Salt 94 C4
Salta 142 H3
Saltee Islands 56 F9
Saltillo 132 F3
Salt Lake City 126 D2
Salto 142 K5
Salto del Guairá 142 K3
Salton Sea 132 C2
Saluda 130 E3
Salūm 100 E1
Saluzzo 62 C6
Salvador 140 K6
Salvadore 138 H5
Salween 84 B2
Salyan 92 N4
Salyersville 128 D3
Salym 70 P3
Salzach 62 H2
Salzburg 62 J3
Salzgitter 52 F4
Salzwedel 52 G4
Samaipata 140 E7
Samar 84 H4
Samara 70 K4
Samarinda 86 F3
Samarkand 90 J2
Sāmarrā' 92 K6
Şamaxı 92 N3
Sambalpur 88 D4
Sambas 86 D2
Sambava 108 J2
Sambhal 88 C3
Sambir 50 N8
Sambo 87 A3
Samboja 86 F3
Sambre 54 F4
Samch'onp'o 82 E6
Same 106 F4
Sami 68 C6
Sämkir 92 M3
Samoa 112 J7
Samobor 62 L5
Samoded 70 H2
Samokov 66 L7
Šamorín 50 G9
Samos 68 J7
Samos 68 J7
Samothraki 68 H4
Samothraki 68 H4
Sampit 86 E3
Sam Rayburn Reservoir 130 C3
Samsang 88 D2
Samsø 48 F9
Samsun 92 G3
Samtredia 92 K2
Samut Songkhram 84 B4
San 50 L7
San 104 D2
Şan'ā 100 H4
Sanaga 104 G4
San Ambrosio 142 F4
Sanana 87 C3
Sanana 87 C3
Sanandaj 92 M6
San Angelo 132 F2
San Antonia Abad 60 M6
San Antonio, *Chile* 142 G5
San Antonio, *US* 134 E3
San Antonio de los Cobres 142 H3
San Antonio-Oeste 142 H7
Sanāw 90 F6
San Benedetto del Tronto 64 H6
San Bernardino 132 C2
San Bernardo 142 H5
San Borja 140 D6
San Carlos, *Chile* 142 G6
San Carlos, *Philippines* 84 G3
San Carlos, *Venezuela* 140 D3
San Carlos de Bariloche 142 G7
San Carlos de Bolivár 142 J6
San Carlos del Zulia 140 C2
San Carlos Lake 132 D2
San Cataldo 64 H11
Sanchahe 82 C1
Sanchakou 76 P10
Sanchor 88 B4
Sanchursk 70 J3
San Clemente Island 132 C2
San Cristóbal 112 G7
San Cristóbal, *Argentina* 142 J5
San Cristóbal, *Venezuela* 140 C2
San Cristóbal de las Casas 134 F5
Sancti Spíritus 134 J4
Sandakan 86 F1
Sandane 48 D6
Sandanski 68 F3
Sanday 56 K2
Sandby 52 G2
Sandefjord 48 F7
Sanders 132 E1
Sanderson 132 F2
Sandfire Roadhouse 114 D3
San Diego 132 C2
Sandıklı 68 N6
Sandnes 48 C7
Sandnessjøen 48 G4
Sandoa 106 C5
Sandomierz 50 L7
San Donà di Piave 62 H5
Sandoway 88 F5
Sandpoint 126 C1
Sandray 56 E5
Sandviken 48 J6
Sandy 126 D2
Sandy Cape 114 K4
Sandy Island 114 D2
Sandy Lake 122 N6
Sandy Lake 122 N6
Sandy Springs 130 E3
San Felipe 124 D5
San Félix 142 E4
San Fernando, *Chile* 142 G5
San Fernando, *Mexico* 130 B5
San Fernando, *Philippines* 84 G3
San Fernando, *Spain* 60 D8
San Fernando de Apure 140 D2
San Fernando de Atabapo 140 D3
Sanford, *Fla., US* 130 E4
Sanford, *N.C., US* 130 F2
San Francis 130 A2
San Francisco, *Argentina* 142 J5
San Francisco, *US* 126 B3
Sangamner 88 B5
Sangān 90 H3
Sangar 78 M4
Sangāreddi 88 C5
Sangasanga 86 F3
Sângeorz-Băi 66 M2
Sangerhausen 52 G5
Sanggau 86 E2
Sangha 104 H4

Sanghar	90	J4
San Gimignano	62	G7
San Giovanni in Fiore	64	L9
San Giovanni Valdarno	62	G7
Sangir	87	C2
Sangkhla Buri	84	B3
Sangkulirang	86	F2
Sangli	88	B5
Sangmélima	104	G4
Sangre de Cristo Range	132	E1
Sangsang	88	E3
Sangue	140	F6
Sangüesa	60	J2
Sanjō	82	K5
San Joaquin Valley	126	B3
San Jose	126	B3
San José	134	H7
San Jose de Buenavista	84	G4
San José de Chiquitos	140	E7
San Jose de Jáchal	142	H5
San José del Cabo	134	C4
San José de Ocuné	140	C3
San Juan	134	H4
San Juan, *Argentina*	142	H5
San Juan, *Costa Rica*	134	H6
San Juan, *Puerto Rico*	134	L5
San Juan, *US*	132	E1
San Juan, *Venezuela*	140	D2
San Juan Bautista, *Paraguay*	142	K4
San Juan Bautista, *Spain*	60	M5
San Juan de los Cayos	140	D1
San Juan de los Morros	140	D2
San Juan Mountains	126	E3
San Julián	142	H8
Sankt-Peterburg	70	F3
Sankuru	106	C4
Sanlıurfa	92	H5
San Lorenzo	132	D3
Sanlúcar de Barrameda	60	D8
San Lucas	134	C4
San Luis	142	H5
San Luis Obispo	132	B1
San Luis Potosí	134	D4
San Luis Rio Colorado	132	D2
San Marcos	130	B4
San Marino	62	H7
San Marino	62	H7
San Martín	140	E6
Sanmenxia	80	E4
San Miguel	134	G6
San Miguel	140	E7
San Miguel de Tucumán	142	H4
San Miguel Island	132	B2
San Miniato	62	F7
San Nicolas de los Arroyos	142	J5
San Nicolás de los Garzas	130	A4
San Nicolas Island	132	C2
Sânnicolau Mare	66	H3
Sanok	50	M8
San Pablo	84	G4
San-Pédro	104	C4
San Pedro, *Argentina*	142	J3
San Pedro, *Bolivia*	140	E7
San Pedro, *Paraguay*	142	K3
San Pedro, *Philippines*	84	G4
San Pedro de las Colonias	132	F3
San Pedro Sula	134	G5
San Pellegrino Terme	62	E5
San Pietro	64	C9
Sanqaçal	92	N3
San Rafael	142	H5
San Remo	62	C7
San Roque	60	E8
Sansalé	104	B2
San Salvador	130	G5
San Salvador	134	G6
San Salvador de Jujuy	142	H3
Sansar	88	C4
San Sebastián = Donostia	60	J1
San Sebastian de los Reyes	60	G4
Sansepolcro	62	H7
San Severo	64	K7
Sanski Most	62	M6
Santa Ana, *Bolivia*	140	D7
Santa Ana, *El Salvador*	134	G6
Santa Ana, *Mexico*	132	D2
Santa Ana, *US*	132	C2
Santa Bárbara	124	E6
Santa Barbara	132	C2
Santa Barbara Island	132	C2
Santa Catalina	142	H4
Santa Catalina Island	132	C2
Santa Catarina	142	L4
Santa Clara, *Columbia*	140	D4
Santa Clara, *Cuba*	124	K7
Santa Clarita	132	C2
Santa Comba Dão	60	B4
Santa Cruz	142	G9
Santa Cruz, *Bolivia*	140	E7
Santa Cruz, *Philippines*	84	G3
Santa Cruz, *US*	132	B1
Santa Cruz de Tenerife	102	B3
Santa Cruz Island	132	B2
Santa Cruz Islands	112	G7
Santa Elena	140	E3
Santa Eugenia	60	A2
Santa Fe	126	E3
Santa Fé	142	J5
Sant'Agata di Militello	64	J10
Santa Isabel	112	F6
Santa Isabel	142	H6
Santa la Grande	124	K7
Santa Margarita	124	D7
Santa Margherita Ligure	62	E6
Santa Maria	102	(1)B2
Santa Maria, *Brazil*	142	L4
Santa Maria, *US*	132	B2
Santa Maria das Barreiras	140	H5
Santa Marinella	64	F6
Santa Marta, *Colombia*	134	K6
Santa Marta, *Spain*	60	D6
Santana do Livramento	142	K5
Santander	60	G1
Sant'Antioco	64	C9
Sant'Antioco	64	C9
Santanyí	60	P5
Santa Pola	60	K6
Santarém, *Brazil*	140	G4
Santarém, *Spain*	60	B5
Santa Rosa, *Argentina*	142	J6
Santa Rosa, *R.G.S., Brazil*	142	L4
Santa Rosa, *Acre, Brazil*	140	C5
Santa Rosa, *Calif., US*	126	B3
Santa Rosa, *N. Mex., US*	132	F2
Santa Rosa Island	132	B2
Santa Vitória do Palmar	142	L5
Sant Boi	60	N3
Sant Carlos de la Ràpita	60	L4
Sant Celoni	60	N3
Sant Feliu de Guixols	60	P3
Santiago	142	G5
Santiago, *Brazil*	142	L4
Santiago, *Dominican Republic*	134	K5
Santiago, *Philippines*	84	G3
Santiago, *Spain*	60	B2
Santiago de Cuba	134	J5
Santiago del Estero	142	J4
Santo André	142	M3
Santo Antão	104	(1)A1
Santo Antônio de Jesus	140	K6
Santo Antônio do Içá	140	D4
Santo Domingo	134	L5
Santo Domingo de los Colorados	140	B4
Santoña	60	G1
Santos	142	M3
San Vicente	84	G3
San Vincenzo	64	E5
Sanya	84	D3
Sao Bernardo do Campo	140	E4
São Borja	142	K4
São Carlos	142	M3
São Félix, *M.G., Brazil*	140	G6
São Félix, *Pará, Brazil*	140	G5
São Filipe	104	(1)B2
São Francisco	140	J6
São João de Madeira	60	B4
São Jorge	102	(1)B2
São José do Rio Prêto	142	L3
São Luís	140	J4
São Miguel	102	(1)B2
Saône	58	K7
São Nicolau	104	(1)B1
São Paulo	142	L3
São Paulo	142	M3
São Paulo de Olivença	140	D4
São Raimundo Nonato	140	J5
São Tiago	104	(1)B1
São Tomé	104	F4
São Tomé	104	F4
São Tomé and Príncipe	104	F4
São Vicente	104	(1)A1
São Vicente	142	M3
Sapanca	68	M4
Saparua	87	C3
Sapele	104	F3
Sapes	68	H4
Sapientza	68	D8
Sa Pobla	60	P5
Sapporo	82	L2
Sapri	64	K8
Sapudi	86	E4
Sapulpa	130	B2
Saqqez	92	M5
Sarāb	92	M5
Sara Buri	84	C4
Sarajevo	66	F6
Sarakhs	90	H2
Saraktash	70	L4
Saramati	88	G3
Saran	76	N8
Saranac Lake	128	F2
Sarandë	68	C5
Sarangani Islands	87	C1
Saranpul	70	M2
Saransk	70	J4
Sarapul	70	K3
Sarapul'skoye	78	P7
Sarasota	130	E4
Sarata	66	S3
Saratoga	126	E2
Saratoga Springs	128	F2
Saratov	70	J4
Saravan	90	H4
Sarawak	86	E2
Saray	68	K3
Sarayköy	68	L7
Sarayönü	68	Q6
Sarbāz	90	H4
Sarbīsheh	90	G3
Sárbogárd	66	F3
Sar Dasht	92	L5
Sardegna	64	E8
Sardinia = Sardegna	64	E8
Sardis Lake	130	B3
Sar-e Pol	90	J2
Sargodha	90	K3
Sarh	104	H3
Sārī	90	F2
Saria	68	K9
Sarıkamış	92	K3
Sarıkaya	92	F4
Sarikei	86	E2
Sarina	114	J4
Sariñena	60	K3
Sarīr Tibesti	100	C3
Sariwŏn	82	C4
Sar'yer	68	M3
Sark	58	C4
Sarkad	66	J3
Sarkand	76	P8
Şarkikaraağaç	68	P6
Şarkişla	92	G4
Şarköy	68	K4
Sarmi	87	E3
Särna	48	G6
Sarnia	128	D2
Sarny	70	E4
Sarolangun	86	C3
Saronno	62	E5
Saros Körfezi	68	J4
Sárospatak	50	L9
Sarre	58	M5
Sarrebourg	58	N5
Sarreguemines	58	N4
Sarria	60	C2
Sartène	64	C7
Sartyn'ya	70	M2
Saruhanli	68	K6
Sărur	92	L4
Sárvár	62	M3
Sarvestān	95	E2
Sarviz	66	F2
Sarykamyshkoye Ozero	76	K9
Saryozek	76	P9
Saryshagan	76	N8
Sarysu	76	M8
Sary-Tash	90	K2
Sarzana	62	E6
Sasaram	88	D4
Sasebo	82	E7
Saskatchewan	122	K6
Saskatchewan	122	L6
Saskatoon	122	K6
Saskylakh	76	W3
Sassandra	104	C4
Sassari	64	C8
Sassnitz	52	J2
Sasso Marconi	62	G6
Sassuolo	62	F6
Satadougou	104	B2
Satara	88	B5
Satna	88	D4
Sátoraljaújhely	50	L9
Satti	88	C2
Sättna	48	J5
Satu Mare	66	K2
Satun	86	B1
Sauce	142	K5
Saudi Arabia	90	D4
Sauk Center	128	B1
Saulgau	62	E2
Saulieu	58	K6
Sault Ste. Marie, *Canada*	128	D1
Sault Ste. Marie, *US*	128	D1
Saumlakki	87	D4
Saumur	58	E6
Saunders Island	138	J9
Saura	76	J9
Saurimo	106	C5
Sauðarkrókur	48	(1)D2
Sava	62	L5
Savaii	112	J7
Savalou	104	E3
Savannah	120	K6
Savannah, *Ga., US*	130	E3
Savannah, *Tenn., US*	130	D2
Savannakhet	84	C3
Savaştepe	68	K5
Savè	104	E3
Save	108	E4
Sāveh	90	F2
Saverne	52	C8
Savigliano	62	C6
Savona	62	D6
Savonlinna	48	Q6
Savu	87	B5
Sawahlunto	86	C3
Sawai Madhopur	88	C3
Sawqirah	90	G6
Sayanogorsk	76	S7
Sayansk	78	G6
Sayhūt	90	F6
Sāylac	100	H5
Saynshand	80	E2
Sayram Hu	76	Q9
Say'ūn	90	E6
Say-Utes	76	J9
Sazan	68	B4
Sazin	90	K2
Sbaa	102	E3
Scafell Pike	56	J7
Scalea	64	K9
Scarborough	56	M7
Scargill	116	D6
Scarp	56	E3
Schaalsee	52	F3
Schaffhausen	62	D3
Schagen	54	G2
Scharbeutz	52	F2
Schärding	62	J2
Scharhörn	52	D3
Scheeßel	52	E3
Schefferville	122	T6
Scheibbs	62	L3
Schelde	54	F3
Schenectady	128	F2
Scheveningen	54	G2
Schiedam	54	G3
Schiermonnikoog	54	H1
Schiermonnikoog	54	J1
Schio	62	G5
Schiza	68	D8
Schkeuditz	52	H5
Schlei	52	E2
Schleiden	54	J4
Schleswig	52	E2
Schlieben	52	J5
Schlüchtern	52	E6
Schneeberg	52	G6
Schneeberg	52	H6
Schönebeck	52	G4
Schongau	62	F3
Schöningen	52	F4
Schouwen	54	F3
Schramberg	62	D2
Schreiber	128	C1
Schrems	62	L2
Schull	56	C10
Schwabach	52	G7
Schwäbische Alb	62	E2
Schwäbisch-Gmünd	62	E2
Schwäbisch-Hall	52	E7
Schwalmstadt	52	E6
Schwandorf	52	H7
Schwarzenbek	52	F3
Schwarzenberg	52	H6
Schwarzwald	62	D3
Schwaz	62	G3
Schwechat	50	F9
Schwedt	50	D4
Schweich	54	J5
Schweinfurt	52	F6
Schwenningen	62	D2
Schwerin	52	G3
Schweriner See	52	G3
Schwetzingen	52	D7
Schwyz	62	D3
Sciacca	64	H11
Scicli	64	J12
Scobey	126	E1
Scotia Ridge	142	K9
Scotia Sea	144	(2)A4
Scotland	56	H5
Scott City	126	F3
Scott Inlet	122	T2
Scott Island	144	(2)Z3
Scott Reef	114	D2
Scottsbluff	126	F2
Scottsboro	128	C4
Scotty's Junction	132	C1
Scranton	128	E2
Scunthorpe	56	M8
Seal	122	M5
Sea of Azov	70	G5
Sea of Galilee	94	C4
Sea of Japan	82	G3
Sea of Marmara = Marmara Denizi	68	L4
Sea of Okhotsk	78	Q5
Sea of the Hebrides	56	E4
Searchlight	132	D1
Searcy	128	B3
Seaside	126	B1
Seattle	126	B1
Sebeş	66	L4
Sebkha Azzel Matti	102	F3
Sebkha de Timimoun	102	E3
Sebkha de Tindouf	102	D3
Sebkha Mekerrhane	102	F3
Sebkha Oum el Drouss Telli	102	C4
Sebkhet de Chemchâm	102	C4
Sebnitz	52	K6
Sebring	130	E4
Secchia	62	F6
Sechura	140	A5
Secretary Island	116	A7
Secunderabad	88	C5
Sécure	140	D7
Sedalia	128	B3
Sedan	54	G5
Sedano	60	G2
Seddon	116	D5
Sede Boqer	94	B6
Sedeh	90	G3
Sederot	94	B5
Sedico	62	H4
Sedom	94	C5
Seeheim	108	B5
Seelow	52	K4
Sées	58	F5
Seesen	52	F5
Seevetal	52	E3
Séez	62	B5
Seferihisar	68	J6
Segamat	86	C2
Segezha	70	F2
Seghnān	90	K2
Ségou	104	C2
Segovia	60	F4
Segré	58	E6
Séguédine	102	H4
Seguin	130	B4
Segura	60	H6
Sehithwa	108	C4
Sehnde	52	E4
Seiland	48	M1
Seiling	130	B2
Seinäjoki	48	M5
Seine	58	F4
Sekayu	86	C3
Sekondi	104	D3
Selassi	87	D3
Selat Bangka	86	D3
Selat Berhala	86	C3
Selat Dampir	87	D3
Selat Karimata	86	D3
Selat Makassar	86	F3
Selat Mentawai	86	B3
Selat Sunda	86	D4
Selawik	132	(1)F2
Selb	52	H6
Selby	126	G1
Selçuk	68	K7
Selebi-Phikwe	108	D4
Sélestat	62	C2
Selfoss	48	(1)C3
Sélibabi	102	C5
Seligman	132	D1
Seljord	48	E7
Selkirk	124	G1
Selkirk Mountains	124	C1
Sells	132	D2
Selm	54	K3
Selmer	128	C3
Selpele	87	D3
Selvas	140	C5
Selwyn Lake	122	L5

Name	Page	Grid
Selwyn Mountains	132	(1)L3
Semanit	68	B4
Semarang	86	E4
Sematan	86	D2
Sembé	104	G4
Seminoe Reservoir	126	E2
Seminole, *Okla., US*	126	G3
Seminole, *Tex., US*	132	F2
Semiozernoye	76	L7
Semipalatinsk	76	Q7
Semiyarka	76	P7
Semois	54	H5
Semporna	86	F2
Sena Madureira	140	D5
Senanga	108	C3
Senatobia	130	D3
Sendai	82	L4
Senec	62	N2
Seneca	130	E3
Senegal	104	A2
Sénégal	104	B1
Senftenberg	52	J5
Sengerema	106	E4
Senhor do Bonfim	140	J6
Senica	50	G9
Senigallia	62	J7
Senj	62	K6
Senja	48	J2
Senlis	54	E5
Sennar	90	B7
Senneterre	128	E1
Sens	58	J5
Senta	66	H4
Seoni	88	C4
Seoul = Sŏul	82	D5
Separation Point	116	D5
Sepinang	86	F2
Sept-Îles	122	T6
Seraing	54	H4
Serakhs	90	H2
Seram	87	D3
Serang	86	D4
Serbia = Srbija	66	H6
Serbia	66	H6
Serdobsk	70	H4
Serebryansk	76	Q8
Sered'	66	E1
Şereflikoçhisar	68	R6
Seregno	62	E5
Serein	58	J6
Seremban	86	C2
Serenje	108	E2
Sergelen	80	E1
Sergeyevka	70	N4
Sergipe	140	K6
Sergiyev Posad	70	G3
Seria	86	E2
Serifos	68	G7
Serifos	68	G7
Serik	68	P8
Seringapatam Reef	114	D2
Sermata	87	C4
Seronga	108	C3
Serov	70	M3
Serowe	108	D4
Serpa	60	C7
Serpneve	66	S3
Serpukhov	70	G4
Serra Acari	140	F3
Serra Curupira	140	E3
Serra da Chela	108	A3
Serra da Espinhaço	140	J7
Serra da Ibiapaba	140	J4
Serra da Mantiqueira	142	M3
Serra de Maracaju	142	K3
Serra do Cachimbo	140	F5
Serra do Caiapó	140	G7
Serra do Roncador	140	G6
Serra dos Carajás	140	G5
Serra dos Dois Irmãos	140	J5
Serra dos Parecis	140	E6
Serra do Tiracambu	140	H4
Serra Estrondo	140	H5
Serra Formosa	140	F6
Serra Geral de Goiás	140	H6
Serra Geral do Paranã	140	H7
Serra Lombarda	140	G3
Serra Pacaraima	140	E3
Serra Parima	140	E3
Serra Tumucumaque	140	F3
Serre da Estrela	60	C4
Serres, *France*	58	L9
Serres, *Greece*	68	F3
Serrinha	140	K6
Sertã	60	B5
Serui	87	E3
Servia	68	D4
Sêrxü	80	B4
Sese Islands	106	E4
Sesfontein	108	A3
Sesheke	108	C3
Sessa Aurunca	64	H7
Sestri Levante	62	E6
Sestroretsk	48	Q6
Sestrunj	62	K6
Sestu	64	D9
Sesvete	62	M5
Setana	82	K2
Sète	58	J10
Sete Lagoas	140	J7
Setesdal	48	D7
Sétif	102	G1
Settat	102	D2
Setúbal	60	B6
Sŏul	112	C2
Seurre	58	L7
Sevana Lich	92	L3
Sevastopol'	92	E1
Seven Lakes	132	E1
Sevenoaks	54	C3
Sévérac-le-Château	58	J9
Severn, *Canada*	122	P5
Severn, *UK*	56	K10
Severnaya Dvina	70	H2
Severnaya Osetiya	92	L2
Severnaya Zemlya	76	U1
Severn Estuary	56	J10
Severnoye	70	K4
Severnyy	76	L4
Severobaykal'sk	78	H5
Severodvinsk	70	G2
Severo-Kuril'sk	78	T6
Severomorsk	48	S2
Severoural'sk	70	M2
Severo-Yeniseyskiy	76	S5
Sevier Lake	126	D3
Sevilla	60	E7
Sevlievo	66	N7
Seward Peninsula	132	(1)E2
Seyakha	76	N3
Seychelles	108	(2)B2
Seychelles Islands	98	J6
Seydişehir	68	P7
Seydisfjöður	48	(1)G2
Seyhan	92	F5
Seymchan	78	S4
Seymour, *Ind., US*	130	D2
Seymour, *Tex., US*	130	B3
Sézanne	58	J5
Sezze	64	H7
Sfakia	68	G9
Sfântu Gheorghe, *Romania*	66	N4
Sfântu Gheorghe, *Romania*	66	S5
Sfax	102	H2
's-Gravenhage	54	G2
Sha'am	95	G3
Shabla	66	R6
Shabunda	106	D4
Shabwah	90	E6
Shache	76	P10
Shādegān	95	C1
Shadehill Reservoir	126	F1
Shagamu	104	E3
Shagonar	76	S7
Shag Rocks	142	N9
Shahbā'	94	D4
Shahdāb	95	G1
Shahdol	88	D4
Shah Fuladi	90	J3
Shahjahanpur	88	C3
Shahrak	90	H3
Shahr-e Bābāk	95	F1
Shahreza	90	F3
Shahrtuz	90	J2
Shakhrisabz	90	J2
Shakhtërsk	78	Q7
Shakhty	70	H5
Shakhun'ya	70	J3
Shaki	104	E3
Shakotan-misaki	82	L2
Shama	106	E5
Shamattawa	122	N5
Shamis	95	E5
Shamrock	132	F1
Shand	90	H3
Shandan	80	C3
Shandong Bandao	80	G3
Shangani	108	D3
Shangdu	80	E2
Shanghai	80	G4
Shanghang	80	F6
Shangqui	80	F4
Shangrao	80	F5
Shangzhi	80	H1
Shangzhou	80	D4
Shantarskiye Ostrova	78	P5
Shantou	80	F6
Shanwei	84	F2
Shanyin	80	E3
Shaoguan	80	E6
Shaoxing	80	G5
Shaoyang	80	E5
Shapkina	70	K1
Shaqrā'	95	A4
Sharga	76	T8
Sharjah = Ash Shāriqah	95	F4
Shark Bay	112	B8
Shark Reef	114	J2
Sharmah	100	G2
Sharm el Sheikh	100	F2
Sharūrah	90	E6
Shashe	108	D4
Shashi	80	E4
Shasta Lake	126	B2
Shats'k	50	N6
Shatsk	70	H4
Shaubak	94	C6
Shawano	128	C2
Shaykh Miskīn	94	D4
Shcherbakove	78	U3
Shchigry	70	G4
Shchuch'ye	76	L6
Shchuchyn	48	N10
Sheberghān	90	J2
Sheboygan	128	C2
Sheffield, *New Zealand*	116	D6
Sheffield, *UK*	56	L8
Sheffield, *Al., US*	128	C4
Sheffield, *Tex., US*	132	F2
Shegmas	70	J2
Shelburne	122	T8
Shelby	126	D1
Shelbyville	128	C3
Shelikof Strait	132	(1)F4
Shenandoah	128	A2
Shendam	104	F3
Shendi	100	F4
Shenkursk	70	H2
Shenyang	82	B3
Shenzhen	80	E6
Shepetivka	70	E4
Shepparton	114	J7
Sherbro Island	104	B3
Sherbrooke	128	F1
Sheridan	126	E2
Sherkaly	70	N2
Sherlovaya Gora	78	K6
Sherman	130	B3
's-Hertogenbosch	54	H3
Shetland Islands	56	M1
Shetpe	76	J9
Sheyenne	126	G1
Sheykh Sho'eyb	95	E3
Shiant Islands	56	F4
Shibata	82	K5
Shibetsu, *Japan*	82	M1
Shibetsu, *Japan*	82	N2
Shibotsu-jima	82	P2
Shiderty	76	N7
Shihezi	76	R9
Shijiazhuang	80	E3
Shikarpur	90	J4
Shikoku	82	G7
Shikoku-sanchi	82	G7
Shikotan-tō	82	P2
Shikotsu-ko	82	L2
Shiliguri	88	E3
Shilka	78	K6
Shilka	78	K6
Shillong	88	F3
Shilovo	70	H4
Shimabara	82	F7
Shimla	88	C2
Shimoda	82	K6
Shimoga	88	C6
Shimo-Koshiki-jima	82	E8
Shimoni	106	F4
Shimonoseki	82	F7
Shināş	95	G4
Shīndan	90	H3
Shingū	82	H7
Shinjō	82	L4
Shinyanga	106	E4
Shiono-misaki	82	H7
Shiprock	126	E3
Shiquan	80	D4
Shirakawa	82	L5
Shīrāz	95	E2
Shire	108	E3
Shiretoko-misaki	82	N1
Shiriya-zaki	82	L3
Shır Kūh	90	F3
Shiv	88	B3
Shivpuri	88	C3
Shiyan	80	E4
Shizuishan	80	D3
Shizuoka	82	K6
Shkodër	66	G7
Shomishko	76	K8
Shorap	90	J4
Shoreham	54	B4
Shoshone, *Calif., US*	126	C3
Shoshone, *Id., US*	126	D2
Shoshoni	126	E2
Shostka	70	F4
Show Low	132	E2
Shoyna	70	H1
Shreveport	130	C3
Shrewsbury	56	K9
Shuangliao	82	B2
Shuangyashan	78	N7
Shubarkuduk	76	K8
Shulan	82	D1
Shumagin Islands	132	(1)E5
Shumen	66	P6
Shumikha	70	M3
Shuqrah	90	E7
Shurchi	90	J2
Shūr Gaz	95	H2
Shurinda	78	J5
Shuryshkary	70	N1
Shuya	70	H3
Shuyang	80	F4
Shwebo	84	B2
Shymkent	76	M9
Sia	87	D4
Sialkot	90	K3
Siatista	68	D4
Šiauliai	50	N2
Sibay	70	L4
Šibenik	66	C6
Siberia = Sibir	74	N3
Siberut	86	B3
Sibi	90	J4
Sibigo	86	B2
Sibir	74	N3
Sibiu	66	M4
Sibolga	86	B2
Sibu	86	E2
Sibuco	84	G5
Sibut	106	B2
Sicilia	64	G11
Sicilian Channel	64	F11
Sicily = Sicilia	64	G11
Šid	66	G4
Siddipet	88	C5
Siderno	64	L10
Sidi Barrani	100	E1
Sidi Bel Abbès	102	E1
Sidi Kacem	102	D2
Sidirokastro	68	F3
Sidney	126	F2
Sidoan	87	B2
Sidorovsk	76	Q4
Sieburg	54	K4
Siedlce	50	M5
Sieg	54	K4
Siegen	54	L4
Siemiatycze	50	M5
Siĕmréab	84	C4
Siena	62	G7
Sieradz	50	H6
Sierpc	50	J5
Sierra Blanca	132	E2
Sierra Colorada	142	H7
Sierra de Calalasteo	142	H4
Sierra de Córdoba	142	H5
Sierra de Gata	60	D4
Sierra de Gúdar	60	K4
Sierra del Nevado	142	H6
Sierra de Perija	134	K7
Sierra Grande	142	H7
Sierra Leone	104	B3
Sierra Madre	134	F5
Sierra Madre del Sur	134	E5
Sierra Madre Occidental	124	E6
Sierra Madre Oriental	132	F3
Sierra Morena	60	E6
Sierra Nevada, *Spain*	60	G7
Sierra Nevada, *US*	132	B1
Sierra Vizcaino	124	D6
Sierre	62	C4
Sifnos	68	G8
Sig	60	K9
Sigean	58	H10
Sighetu Marmaţiei	66	L2
Sighişoara	66	M3
Siglufjörður	48	(1)D1
Sigmaringen	62	E2
Signal Mountain	128	C3
Siguiri	104	C2
Sihanoukville	84	C4
Siilinjärvi	48	P5
Siirt	92	J5
Sikar	88	C3
Sikasso	104	C2
Sikea	68	F4
Sikeston	128	C3
Sikhote Alin	82	H1
Sikinos	68	G8
Siklós	66	F4
Siktyakh	78	L3
Şil	60	C2
Šilalė	50	M2
Silandro	62	F4
Silba	62	K6
Silchar	88	F4
Şile	68	M3
Silhouette Island	108	(2)B1
Siliana	64	D12
Silifke	92	E5
Siling Co	88	E2
Silistra	66	Q5
Silivri	68	L3
Siljan	48	H6
Sillamäe	48	P7
Silsbee	130	C3
Šiluas	86	D2
Šilutė	50	L2
Silvan	92	J4
Silver Bay	128	B1
Silver City	132	E2
Silver Lake	126	B2
Silver Plains	114	H2
Simanggang	86	E2
Simao	80	C6
Simav	92	C4
Simcoe	128	D2
Simeonovgrad	66	N7
Simeria	50	N12
Simeuluë	86	A2
Simferopol'	92	F1
Şimleu Silvaniei	66	K2
Simmerath	54	J4
Simojärvi	48	P3
Simpang	86	C3
Simpson Desert	114	G4
Sinabang	86	B2
Sinai	100	F2
Sinaia	66	N4
Şinak	92	K5
Sinalunga	64	F5
Sinanju	82	C4
Sinbaungwe	84	B3
Sincelejo	140	B2
Sinclair's Bay	56	J3
Sindangbarang	86	D4
Sindelfingen	52	E8
Sines	60	B7
Singa	100	F5
Singapore	86	C2
Singapore	86	C2
Singaraja	86	E4
Singen	62	D3
Sîngerei	66	R2
Singida	106	E4
Singkawang	86	D2
Singkep	86	C3
Singkilbaru	86	B2
Singleton	114	K6
Siniscola	64	D8
Sinj	66	D6
Sinjai	87	B4
Sinjār	92	J5
Sinkat	100	G4
Sinni	64	L8
Sinop	92	F2
Sinsheim	52	D7
Sintang	86	E2
Sinton	130	B4
Sinŭiju	82	C3
Sinyaya	78	L4
Sió	66	F3
Siófok	66	F3
Sion	62	C4
Sioux City	128	A2
Sioux Falls	128	A2
Sioux Lookout	124	H2
Siping	82	C2
Sipiwesk	122	M5
Sipura	86	B3
Sira	48	D7
Siracusa	64	K11
Sir Banī 'Yās	95	E4
Sir Edward Pellew Group	114	G3
Siret	66	P2
Siret	66	Q4
Sîrgān	90	H4

Şiria	50	L11
Şiri Kit Dam	84	B3
Sirk	95	G3
Sirohi	88	B4
Sirsa	88	C3
Sirsi	88	B6
Sisak	66	D4
Sisian	92	L4
Sisimiut	122	W3
Sisŏphŏn	84	C4
Sisseton	126	G1
Sistema Central	60	E4
Sistema Iberico	60	H3
Sisteron	62	A6
Sitapur	88	D3
Sitasjaure	48	J3
Siteia	68	J9
Sitges	60	M3
Sithonia	68	F4
Sitka	122	D5
Sittard	54	H4
Sittwe	88	F4
Sivand	95	E1
Sivas	92	G4
Siverek	92	H5
Sivrihisar	68	P5
Siwa	100	E1
Siyäzän	92	N3
Sjælland	48	F9
Sjenica	66	H6
Sjenica Jezero	66	G6
Sjöbo	50	C2
Skädlderviken	50	B1
Skaerbaek	52	D1
Skagen	48	F8
Skagerrak	48	D8
Skala	68	E8
Skantzoura	68	G5
Skardu	90	L2
Skarżysko-Kamienna	50	K6
Skaulo	48	L3
Skawina	50	J8
Skaymat	102	B4
Skegness	54	C1
Skellefteå	48	L4
Ski	48	F7
Skiathos	68	F5
Skibotn	48	L2
Skidal'	50	P4
Skien	48	E7
Skikda	102	G1
Skipton	56	L8
Skjern	48	E9
Škofja Loka	62	K4
Skopelos	68	F5
Skopje	66	J7
Skövde	48	G7
Skovorodino	78	L6
Skowhegan	128	G2
Skuodas	48	L8
Skye	56	F4
Skyros	68	G6
Skyros	68	G6
Slagelse	52	G1
Slagnäs	48	K4
Slaney	56	F9
Slano	66	E7
Slantsy	48	Q7
Slaný	52	K6
Slatina	66	M5
Slave	120	N3
Slave Lake	122	J5
Slavonska Požega	66	E4
Slavonski Brod	66	F4
Slavyanka	82	F2
Slavyansk-na-Kubani	92	H1
Sławno	50	F3
Sleaford	54	B1
Sleeper Islands	122	Q5
Slidell	130	D3
Sligo	56	D7
Sligo Bay	56	D7
Slite	48	K8
Sliven	66	P7
Slobozia, *Moldova*	66	S3
Slobozia, *Romania*	66	Q5
Slonim	48	N10
Slough	54	B3
Slovakia	50	H9
Slovenia	62	K4
Slovenj Gradec	62	L4
Slovenska Bistrica	62	L4
Slov"yans'k	70	G5
Słubice	50	D5
Slunj	62	L5
Słupca	50	G5
Słupsk	50	G3
Slussfors	48	J4
Slutsk	70	E4
Slyudyanka	78	G6
Smålandsfarvandet	52	G1
Smallwood Reservoir	122	U6
Smargon'	48	P9
Smederevo	66	H5
Smila	70	F5
Smirnykh	78	Q7
Smiths Falls	128	E2
Smokey Hills	130	B2
Smoky	122	H6
Smøla	48	D5
Smolensk	70	F4
Smolyan	68	G3
Smooth Rock Falls	128	D1
Smyrna	130	E3
Snæfell	48	(1)F2
Snake	126	C1
Snake River Plain	126	D2
Snåsavatnet	48	F4
Sneek	54	H1
Sneem	56	C10
Snezhnogorsk	76	R4
Snežnik	62	K5
Snina	50	M9
Snøhetta	48	E5
Snøtinden	48	G3
Snowdon	56	H8
Snowdrift	122	J4
Snowville	126	D2
Snyder	132	F2
Soalala	108	H3
Soanierana-Ivongo	108	H3
Soa-Siu	87	C2
Sobral	140	J4
Sochaczew	50	K5
Sochaux	62	B3
Sochi	92	H2
Socorro	132	E2
Socotra = Suquṭrā	90	F7
Socuéllamos	60	H5
Sodankylä	48	P3
Söderhamn	48	J6
Södertälje	48	J7
Sodo	106	F2
Soe	87	B4
Soest	54	L3
Sofia = Sofiya	66	L7
Sofiya	66	L7
Sofiysk, *Russia*	78	N6
Sofiysk, *Russia*	78	P6
Sofporog	48	R4
Sōfu-gan	80	L5
Sogamoso	140	C2
Sognefjorden	48	C6
Sogod	84	G4
Sog Xian	88	F2
Soḥâg	100	F2
Soignies	54	G4
Soissons	54	F5
Sokch'o	82	E4
Söke	68	K7
Sokhumi	92	J2
Sokode	104	E3
Sokol	70	H3
Sokółka	48	M10
Sokolo	104	C2
Sokolov	52	H6
Sokołów Podlaski	50	M5
Sokoto	104	F2
Sokoto	104	F2
Sokyryany	66	Q1
Solander Island	116	A8
Solapur	88	C5
Sölden	62	F4
Solenzara	64	D7
Solhan	92	J4
Solikamsk	70	L3
Sol'-Iletsk	70	L4
Soliman	64	E12
Solingen	54	K3
Sollefteå	48	J5
Soller	60	N5
Solna	48	J7
Solomon Islands	112	F6
Solothurn	62	C3
Solov'yevsk	78	K6
Šolta	66	D6
Soltau	52	E4
Sol'tsy	70	F3
Solway Firth	56	J7
Solwezi	108	D2
Soma	68	K5
Sōma	82	L5
Somalia	106	H2
Sombor	66	G4
Sombrerete	132	F4
Somerset, *Australia*	114	H2
Somerset, *Ky., US*	128	C3
Somerset, *Pa., US*	128	E2
Somerset Island	122	N2
Someș	66	K2
Somme	54	E4
Sommen	48	H8
Sömmerda	52	G5
Sømna	48	F4
Sondags	108	D6
Sønderborg Ærø	52	E2
Sondershausen	52	F5
Sondrio	62	E4
Songavatn	48	D7
Songea	106	F6
Song Hông	84	C2
Songhua	80	H1
Songhua Hu	82	D2
Songhua Jiang	82	D1
Songkan	80	D5
Songkhla	84	C5
Songnam	82	D5
Songnim	82	C4
Songo	108	E3
Songololo	104	G6
Songpan	80	C4
Sonid Yuoqi	80	E2
Sonid Zuoqi	80	E2
Son La	84	C2
Sonneberg	52	G6
Sono	140	H6
Sonora	132	B1
Sonora	132	D3
Sonoyta	132	D2
Sonsorol Islands	87	D1
Sonthofen	62	F3
Sopot	48	K9
Sopron	62	M3
Sora	64	H7
Soracaba	142	M3
Sorel	128	F1
Sorgun	92	F4
Soria	60	H3
Sorø	52	G1
Soroca	66	R1
Sorochinsk	70	K4
Sorong	87	D3
Soroti	106	E3
Sørøya	48	L1
Sorrento	64	J8
Sorsele	48	J4
Sorso	64	C8
Sorsogon	84	G4
Sort	60	M2
Sortavala	48	R6
Sørvagen	48	G3
Sŏsan	82	D5
Sosnogorsk	76	J5
Sosnovka	76	G4
Sosnovo	48	R6
Sosnowiec	50	J7
Sos'va	70	M3
Sos'vinskaya	70	M2
Soto la Marina	132	G4
Soubré	104	C3
Soufli	68	J3
Souilly	54	H5
Souk Ahras	64	B12
Sŏul	82	D5
Soulac-sur-Mer	58	D8
Soumussalmi	48	Q4
Soûr	94	C3
Soure	60	B5
Sour el Ghozlane	60	P8
Souris	124	F2
Souris	124	G2
Sousa	140	K5
Sousse	102	H1
South Africa	108	C6
South America	120	J9
Southampton, *Canada*	128	D2
Southampton, *UK*	54	A4
Southampton Island	122	Q4
South Andaman	88	F6
South Atlantic Ocean	142	P6
South Australia	114	F5
South Baymouth	128	D1
South Bend	128	C2
South Boston	128	E3
South Carolina	130	E3
South Charleston	130	E2
South China Sea	84	E4
South Dakota	126	F2
South Downs	54	B4
South East Cape	114	J8
South East Point	114	J7
Southend-on-Sea	54	C3
Southern Alps	116	B6
Southern Cross	114	C6
Southern Indian Lake	122	M5
Southern Uplands	56	H6
South Georgia	142	P9
South Harris	56	F4
South Haven	128	C2
South Hill	128	E3
South Island	116	B6
South Korea	82	D5
South Lake Tahoe	126	B3
South Orkney Islands	144	(2)A3
South Pacific Ocean	142	P6
South Platte	126	F2
Southport	56	J8
South Ronaldsay	56	K3
South Sandwich Islands	144	(2)C4
South Sandwich Trench	138	H9
South Saskatchewan	124	D1
South Shetland Islands	144	(2)MM4
South Shields	56	L7
South Taranaki Bight	116	D4
South Uist	56	E4
South West Cape, *Auckland Island*	116	(2)A1
South West Cape, *Australia*	114	H8
Southwest Cape	116	A8
South West Pacific Basin	112	L9
Southwold	54	D2
Sovata	66	N3
Soverato	64	L10
Sovetsk, *Russia*	48	L9
Sovetsk, *Russia*	70	J3
Soweto	108	D5
Sōya-misaki	82	L1
Sozopol	66	Q7
Spa	54	H4
Spain	60	F5
Spalding	54	B2
Sparks	132	C1
Spartanburg	130	E3
Sparti	68	E7
Sparwood	126	D1
Spassk-Dal'niy	82	G1
Spearfish	126	F2
Spencer	128	A2
Spencer Gulf	114	G6
Spetses	68	F7
Spey	56	J4
Speyer	54	L5
Spiekeroog	52	C3
Spiez	62	C4
Spilimbergo	62	H4
Spišska Nová Ves	50	K9
Spitsbergen	144	(1)P2
Spittal	62	J4
Split	66	D6
Spokane	126	C1
Spoleto	64	G6
Spooner	128	B1
Sprague	126	C1
Spratly Islands	84	E4
Spray	126	C2
Spree	52	K4
Spremberg	52	K5
Sprimont	54	H4
Spring	130	B3
Springbok	108	B5
Springe	52	E4
Springer	132	F1
Springerville	132	E2
Springfield, *Colo., US*	132	F1
Springfield, *Ill., US*	128	C3
Springfield, *Mass., US*	128	F2
Springfield, *Mo., US*	128	B3
Springfield, *Oh., US*	128	D3
Springfield, *Oreg., US*	126	B2
Springfield, *Vt., US*	128	F2
Spring Hill	130	E4
Springs	108	D5
Springs Junction	116	D6
Springsure	114	J4
Springville, *Al., US*	130	D3
Springville, *N.Y., US*	128	E2
Spulico	64	L9
Squamish	126	B1
Squinzano	64	N8
Srbija	66	H6
Srbobran	66	G4
Srebrenica	66	G5
Sredenekolymsk	78	S3
Sredinnyy Khrebet	78	T6
Srednesibirskoye Ploskogor'ye	78	F3
Srednogorie	68	G2
Šrem	50	G5
Sretensk	78	K6
Sri Jayewardenepura-Kotte	88	D7
Srikakulam	88	D5
Sri Lanka	88	D7
Srinagar	88	B2
Stack Skerry	56	H2
Stade	48	E10
Stadlandet	48	C5
Stadskanaal	54	J2
Stadtallendorf	52	E6
Stadthagen	52	E4
Staffa	56	F5
Staffelstien	52	F6
Stafford	56	K9
Staines	54	B3
Stainz	62	L4
Stakhanov	70	G5
Stalowa Wola	50	M7
Stambolijski	68	G2
Stamford, *UK*	54	B2
Stamford, *US*	128	F2
Standish	128	D2
Stanford	128	D3
Stanke Dimitrov	68	F2
Stanley, *Australia*	114	J8
Stanley, *Falkland Islands*	142	K9
Stanley, *US*	126	F1
Stanovaya	78	T3
Stanovoye Nagor'ye	78	J5
Stanovoy Khrebet	78	L5
Staphorst	54	J2
Stapleton	126	F2
Starachowice	50	L6
Stara L'ubovňa	50	K8
Stara Pazova	66	H5
Stara Planina	68	F1
Staraya Russa	70	F3
Stara Zagora	66	N7
Starbuck Island	112	L6
Stargard Szczeciński	48	H10
Starkville	130	D3
Starnberg	62	G2
Starnberger See	62	G3
Starogard Gdański	50	H4
Staro Oryakhovo	66	Q7
Start Point	58	B3
Staryy Oskol	70	G4
Staszów	50	L7
Statesboro	130	E3
Statesville	130	E2
Staunton	130	F2
Stavanger	48	C7
Stavoron	54	H2
Stavropol'	92	J1
Stavropol'skaya Vovyshennost'	70	H5
Steamboat Springs	126	E2
Steens Mountains	126	C2
Steenwijk	54	J2
Stefansson Island	122	L2
Stege	52	H1
Ştei	66	K3
Stein	52	G7
Steinach am Brenner	62	G3
Steinfurt	54	K2
Steinhausen	108	B4
Steinjker	48	F4
Stenay	54	H5
Stendal	52	G4
Steno Antikythiro	68	F9
Stephenville	130	B3
Sterling	126	F2
Sterling City	132	F2
Sterling Heights	128	D2
Sterlitamak	70	L4
Sternberk	50	G8
Stettiner Haff	48	G10
Stevenage	54	B3
Stevens Point	128	C2
Stevens Village	132	(1)H2
Stewart	122	F5
Stewart	132	(1)K3
Stewart Island	116	A8
Steyr	62	K2
Stillwater	130	B2
Stinnett	132	F1
Štip	68	E3
Stirling	56	J5
Stjørdal	48	F5
Stockach	62	E3
Stockerau	62	M2
Stockholm	48	K7
Stockport	56	K8
Stockton, *Calif., US*	132	B1
Stockton, *Kans., US*	132	G1
Stockton-on-Tees	56	L7
Stœng Trêng	84	D4
Stoke-on-Trent	56	K8
Stokksnes	48	(1)F2
Stolac	66	F6
Stolberg	54	J4

Stolin 70 E4
Stollberg 52 H6
Stomio 68 E5
Stonehaven 56 K5
Stony Rapids 122 K5
Stör 52 E2
Stora Lulevatten 48 K3
Stord 48 C7
Store Bælt 52 F1
Støren 48 F5
Store Sotra 48 B6
Storjord 48 H3
Storlien 48 G5
Storm Bay 114 J8
Storm Lake 128 A2
Stornoway 56 F3
Storozhevsk 70 K2
Storozhynets' 66 N1
Storsjøen 48 F6
Storsjön, *Sweden* 48 G5
Storsjön, *Sweden* 48 J6
Storuman 48 J4
Storuman 48 J4
Stour 54 C2
Stowmarket 54 D2
Strabane 56 E7
Stradella 62 E5
Strait of Belle Isle 122 V6
Strait of Bonifacio 64 D7
Strait of Dover 54 D4
Strait of Georgia 126 B1
Strait of Gibraltar 60 E9
Strait of Hormuz 95 G3
Strait of Juan de Fuca 126 B1
Strait of Malacca 86 C2
Straits of Florida 130 E5
Strakonice 52 J7
Stralsund 48 G9
Strand 108 B6
Stranda 48 D5
Strandavatn 48 D6
Stranraer 56 H7
Strasbourg 62 C2
Strasburg 132 F1
Străşeni 66 R2
Stratford, *Canada* 128 D2
Stratford, *New Zealand* 116 E4
Stratford, *US* 126 F3
Stratford-upon-Avon 54 A2
Strathroy 128 D2
Stratoni 68 F4
Stratton 128 F1
Straubing 62 H2
Straumnes 48 (1)B1
Strausberg 52 J4
Streaky Bay 114 F6
Streator 128 C2
Strehaia 66 L5
Strelka, *Russia* 78 E5
Strelka, *Russia* 78 S4
Strezhevoy 70 Q2
Strimonas 68 F4
Strofades 68 C7
Stromboli 64 K10
Strömsund 48 H5
Stronsay 56 K2
Stroud 56 K10
Struga 68 C3
Strugi-Krasnyye 48 Q7
Strumica 68 E3
Stryjama 66 M7
Stryy 50 N8
Stryy 50 N8
Strzegom 50 F7
Strzelce Opolskie 50 H7
Strzelin 50 G7
Strzelno 50 H5
Studholme Junction 116 C7
Sturgeon Bay 128 C2
Sturgeon Falls 128 E1
Sturgis, *Ky., US* 128 C3
Sturgis, *S.D., US* 126 F2
Sturkö 50 E1
Štúrovo 50 H10
Sturt Stony Desert 114 G5
Stuttgart, *Germany* 62 E2
Stuttgart, *US* 130 C3
Stykkishólmur 48 (1)B2
Suai 87 C4
Suakin 100 G4
Subcule 100 H5
Subi Besar 86 D2
Sublette 132 F1
Subotica 66 G3
Suceava 66 P2
Suck 56 D8
Suckow 52 G3
Sucre 140 D7
Sudak 92 F1
Sudan 100 E5
Sudan 104 D2
Suday 70 H3
Sudbury, *Canada* 128 D1
Sudbury, *UK* 54 C2
Sudd 106 E2
Sudová Vyshnya 50 N8
Suez = El Suweis 100 F2
Suez Canal 100 F1
Suffolk 130 F2
Sugun 90 L2
Suhār 95 G4
Suhl 52 F6
Suide 80 E3
Suifenhe 82 F1
Suigam 88 B4
Suihua 78 M7
Suippes 54 G5
Suir 56 E9
Suixi 80 E6
Suizhong 80 G2
Suizhou 80 E4
Sukabumi 86 D4
Sukadana 86 D3
Sukhinichi 70 G4
Sukhona 70 H3
Sukkertoppen = Maniitsoq 122 W3
Sukkur 90 J4
Sula 70 K1
Sula 70 K1
Sula Sgeir 56 F2
Sulawesi 87 A3
Sulejówek 50 L5
Sule Skerry 56 H2
Sulgachi 78 N4
Sulina 66 S4
Sulingen 54 L2
Sullana 140 A4
Sullivan 130 C2
Sulmona 64 H6
Sulphur Springs 130 B3
Sultan 100 D1
Sultanhanı 68 R6
Sultanpur 88 D3
Sulu Archipelago 84 G5
Sulu Sea 84 F5
Sulzbach 54 K5
Sulzbach-Rosenberg 52 G7
Sulzberger Bay 144 (2)CC2
Sumatera 86 C2
Sumatra = Sumatera 86 C2
Sumba 87 A5
Sumbawa 87 A4
Sumbawabesar 87 A4
Sumbawanga 106 E5
Sumbe 108 A2
Sumeih 106 D2
Šumen 92 B2
Sumenep 86 E4
Sumisu-jima 82 L8
Sumkino 70 N3
Summer Lake 126 B2
Summerville 130 E3
Summit 122 B4
Šumperk 50 G8
Sumqayıt 92 N3
Sumter 130 E3
Sumy 70 F4
Sunbury 128 E2
Sunch'ŏn 82 D6
Sun City 108 D5
Sundance 126 F2
Sundarbans 88 E4
Sunday Strait 114 D3
Sunderland 56 L7
Sundridge 128 E1
Sundsvall 48 J5
Sundsvallsbukten 48 J5
Sungaipenuh 86 C3
Sungei Petani 84 C5
Sungurlu 92 F3
Sunnyvale 126 B3
Sun Prairie 128 C2
Suntar 78 K4
Suntsar 90 H4
Sunwu 78 M7
Sunyani 104 D3
Suomussalmi 70 E2
Suō-nada 82 F7
Suonenjoki 48 P5
Suordakh 78 P3
Suoyarvi 70 F2
Superior 124 H2
Supetar 66 D6
Süphan Daği 92 K4
Sūqash Shuyūkh 95 B1
Suqian 80 F4
Suquṭrā 90 F7
Şūr 90 G5
Sura 70 J4
Surab 90 J4
Surabaya 86 E4
Sūrak 95 H4
Surakarta 86 E4
Šurany 66 F1
Surat 88 B4
Surat Thani 84 B5
Surdulica 66 K7
Sûre 54 H5
Surfers Paradise 114 K5
Surgut 76 N5
Surgutikha 76 R5
Surigao 84 H5
Surin 84 C4
Surinam 140 F3
Surkhet 88 D3
Sūrmaq 95 E1
Surovikino 70 H5
Surskoye 70 J4
Surt 102 J2
Surtsey 48 (1)C3
Susa 62 C5
Suşa 92 M4
Sušac 66 D7
Susak 62 K6
Susanville 126 B2
Suşehri 92 H3
Sušice 52 J7
Susitma 132 (1)G3
Susuman 78 R4
Susurluk 68 L5
Sutak 88 C2
Sutherland 108 C6
Sutlej 88 B3
Suusamyr 76 N9
Suva 112 H7
Suvorov Island 112 K7
Suwałki 50 M3
Suwannaphum 84 C3
Suweilih 94 C4
Suweima 94 C5
Suwŏn 82 D5
Suzak 70 N6
Suzhou, *China* 80 F4
Suzhou, *China* 80 G4
Suzuka 82 J6
Suzu-misaki 82 J5
Svalbard 144 (1)Q2
Svalyaya 66 L1
Svappavaara 48 L3
Svartenhuk Halvø 122 V2
Svatove 70 G5
Sveg 48 H5
Svendborg 48 F9
Šventoji 48 N9
Sverdrup Islands 144 (1)DD2
Svetac 66 C6
Sveti Nikole 68 D3
Svetlaya 78 P7
Svetlogorsk 50 K3
Svetlograd 92 K1
Svetlyy, *Russia* 50 K3
Svetlyy, *Russia* 76 L7
Svidník 50 L8
Svilengrad 68 J3
Svishtov 66 N6
Svitava 50 F8
Svitavy 50 F8
Svobodnyy 78 M6
Svratka 50 F8
Svyetlahorsk 70 E4
Swain Reefs 114 K4
Swains Island 112 J7
Swakopmund 108 A4
Swale 56 K7
Swan 138 C2
SwanHill 114 H7
Swan Islands 134 H5
Swan River 122 L6
Swansea, *Australia* 114 J8
Swansea, *UK* 56 J10
Swaziland 108 E5
Sweden 48 H6
Sweetwater 132 F2
Swider 50 L5
Swidnica 50 F7
Świdnik 50 M6
Świdwin 50 E4
Świebodzin 50 E5
Świecie 50 H4
Swift Current 124 E1
Swindon 54 A3
Świnoujście 48 H10
Switzerland 62 C4
Syalakh 78 L3
Syamzha 70 H2
Syców 50 G6
Sydney, *Australia* 114 K6
Sydney, *Canada* 122 U7
Syke 54 L2
Syktyvkar 70 K2
Sylacauga 130 D3
Sylhet 88 F4
Sylt 48 E9
Sylvania 128 D2
Sym 76 R5
Sym 76 R5
Symi 68 K8
Synya 70 L1
Syracuse, *Kans., US* 132 F1
Syracuse, *N.Y., US* 128 E2
Syrdar'ya 76 L8
Syrdar'ya 90 J1
Syria 90 C3
Syrian Desert = Bādiyat ash Shām 94 D4
Syrna 68 J8
Syros 68 G7
Sytomino 70 P2
Syzran' 70 J4
Szamos 66 K1
Szamotuły 50 F5
Szarvas 50 K11
Szczecin 50 D4
Szczecinek 50 F4
Szczytno 50 K4
Szeged 66 H3
Szeghalom 66 J2
Székesfehérvár 66 F2
Szekszárd 66 F3
Szentendre 66 G2
Szentes 66 H3
Szerencs 50 L9
Szigetvár 66 E3
Szolnok 66 H2
Szombathely 66 D2
Szprotawa 50 E6
Sztum 50 J4
Szydlowiec 50 K6

T

Tab 66 F3
Tabarka 64 C12
Tabas 90 G3
Tabāsin 95 G1
Taber 126 D1
Table Cape 116 G4
Tabong 88 G3
Tábor 50 D8
Tabor 78 R2
Tabora 106 E5
Tabou 104 C4
Tabrīz 92 M4
Tabuaeran 112 K5
Tabūk 90 C4
Tacheng 76 Q8
Tachov 52 H7
Tacloban 84 H4
Tacna 140 C7
Tacoma 124 B2
Tacuarembó 142 K5
Tacurong 87 B1
Tadjoura 100 H5
Tadmur 92 H6
Tadoussac 128 G1
Taech'ŏn 82 D5
Taegu 82 E6
Taejŏn 80 H3
Tafahi 112 J7
Tafalla 60 J2
Tafila 94 C6
Tafi Viejo 142 H4
Tagab 100 F4
Taganrog 70 G5
Taganrogskiy Zaliv 70 G5
Tagbilaran 84 G5
Tagul 78 F6
Tagum 84 H5
Tagus 60 B5
Taharoa 116 E4
Taheke 116 D2
Tahiti 112 M7
Tahoe Lake 122 K2
Tahoka 132 F2
Tahoua 104 F2
Tahrūd 95 G2
Tahuna 84 H6
Tai'an 80 F3
T'ai-chung 80 G6
Taihape 116 E4
Taihe 80 E5
Taikeng 80 E4
Tailem Bend 114 G7
Tain 56 H4
T'ai-nan 80 G6
T'ai-Pei 80 G6
Taiping 86 C1
Taipingchuan 82 B1
T'ai-tung 84 G2
Taivalkoski 48 Q4
Taiwan 84 G2
Taiwan Strait 84 F2
Taiyuan 80 E3
Taizhou 80 F4
Ta'izz 90 D7
Tajikistan 90 J2
Tajima 82 K5
Tajo 46 D3
Tak 84 B3
Takaka 116 D5
Takamatsu 82 H6
Takaoka 82 J5
Takapuna 116 E3
Takasaki 82 K5
Takayama 82 J5
Takefu 82 J6
Takengon 86 B2
Takestān 90 E2
Ta Khmau 84 D4
Takht 78 P6
Takhta-Bazar 90 H2
Takhtabrod 76 M7
Takhtakupyr 76 L9
Takijuq Lake 122 J3
Takikawa 82 L2
Takoradi 104 D4
Taksimo 78 J5
Takua Pa 84 B5
Takum 104 G3
Talak 102 F5
Talara 140 A4
Talas 76 N9
Tal'at Mūsá 92 G6
Talavera de la Reina 60 F5
Talaya 78 S4
Talbotton 130 E3
Talca 142 G6
Talcahuano 142 G6
Taldykorgan 76 P9
Tālesh 90 E2
Taliabu 87 B3
Talibon 84 G4
Talitsa 70 M3
Tall 'Afar 92 K5
Tallahassee 130 E3
Tallaimannar 88 C7
Tall al Lahm 95 B1
Tallinn 48 N7
Tall Kalakh 94 D2
Tallulah 124 H5
Tall 'Uwaynāt 92 K5
Tălmaciu 66 M4
Tal'menka 76 Q7
Talon 78 R5
Tāloqān 76 N10
Taloyoak 122 N3
Talsi 48 M8
Taltal 142 G4
Tama 128 B2
Tamale 104 D3
Tamanrasset 102 G4
Tamanthi 88 G3
Tamási 66 F3
Tamazunchale 124 G7
Tambacounda 104 B2
Tambey 76 N3
Tambo 114 J4
Tambov 70 H4
Tambu 87 A3
Tambura 106 D2
Tampa 130 E4
Tamp-e Gīrān 95 H3
Tampere 48 M6
Tampico 134 E4
Tamsagbulag 80 F1
Tamsweg 62 J3
Tamworth, *Australia* 114 K6
Tamworth, *UK* 54 A2
Tana, *Kenya* 106 G4
Tana, *Norway* 48 P2
Tanabe 82 H7
Tana bru 48 P1
Tanacross 132 (1)J3
Tanafjorden 48 Q1
Tanaga Island 132 (3)C1
T'ana Hāyk' 100 G5
Tanahgrogot 86 F3

Tanahjampea 87 A4
Tanahmerah 87 F4
Tanami Mine 114 E4
Tanami Desert 114 F3
Tanaro 62 C6
Tanch'ŏn 82 E3
Tanda 104 D3
Tandag 84 H5
Țăndărei 66 Q5
Tandil 142 K6
Tanega-shima 82 F8
Tanew 50 M7
Tanezrouft 102 E4
Tanga, *Russia* 78 J6
Tanga, *Tanzania* 106 F5
Tanger 102 D1
Tangermünde 52 G4
Tanggu 80 F3
Tangmai 88 G2
Tangra Yumco 88 E2
Tangshan 80 F3
Tanimbar 112 D6
Tanjona Ankaboa 108 G4
Tanjona Bobaomby 108 H2
Tanjona Masoala 108 J3
Tanjona Vilanandro 108 G3
Tanjona Vohimena 108 H5
Tanjung 86 F3
Tanjungbalai 86 B2
Tanjung Cangkuang 86 C4
Tanjung Datu 86 D2
Tanjung d'Urville 87 E3
Tanjung Libobo 87 C3
Tanjung Lumut 86 D3
Tanjung Mengkalihat 86 F2
Tanjungpandan 86 D3
Tanjung Puting 86 E3
Tanjungredeb 86 F2
Tanjung Selatan 86 E3
Tanjungselor 86 F2
Tanjung Vals 87 E4
Tankovo 76 R5
Tankse 88 C2
Tanlovo 70 P1
Tanney 54 G5
Tanout 104 F2
Tanta 100 F1
Tan-Tan 102 C3
Tanzania 106 E5
Tao'an 80 G1
Taomasina 108 H3
Taongi 112 J4
Taormina 64 K11
Taos 132 E1
Taoudenni 102 E5
Taourirt 102 E2
T'ao-yuan 84 G2
Tapa 48 N7
Tapachula 134 F6
Tapajós 140 F4
Tapauá 140 E5
Tapolca 66 E3
Tappahannock 130 F2
Tapsuy 70 M2
Tapuaenuku 116 D6
Taquari 140 F7
Tara 70 Q3
Tara 76 N6
Tarābulus 102 H2
Taraclia 66 R4
Taracua 140 D3
Tarāghin 102 H3
Tarakan 84 F6
Taran 76 N3
Taranaki = Mount Egmont 116 E4
Tarancón 60 H5
Taranto 64 M8
Tarapoto 140 B5
Tarare 58 K8
Tarascon 58 K10
Tarauacá 140 C5
Tarauacá 140 C5
Tarawa 112 H5
Tarawera Lake 116 F4
Tarazona 60 J3
Tarbert, *UK* 56 G6
Tarbes 58 F10
Tarbet, *UK* 56 F4
Tarcoola 114 F6
Taree 114 K6
Tareya 76 S3
Tarfaya 102 C3
Târgoviște 66 N5
Târgu Frumos 66 Q2
Târgu Jiu 66 L4
Târgu Lăpuș 66 L2
Târgu Mureș 66 M3
Târgu-Neamț 66 P2
Târgu Ocna 66 P3
Târgu Secuiesc 66 P3
Tarhunah 102 H2
Tarif 95 E4
Tarifa 60 E8
Tarija 142 J3
Tarim 76 Q9
Tarīm 90 E6
Tarim Pendi 76 Q10
Tarīn Kowt 90 J3
Tariskay Shan 76 Q9
Taritatu 87 E3
Tarkio 130 B1
Tarko Sale 76 P5
Tarlac 84 G3
Tarn 58 H10
Tarna 50 K10
Tärnaby 48 H4
Târnăveni 66 M3
Tarnogskiy Gorodok 70 H2
Tărnovo 68 K2
Tarnów 50 K7
Tarnowskie Góry 50 H7
Taro 62 E6
Tārom 95 F2
Taroom 114 J5
Taroudannt 102 D2
Tarquinia 64 F6
Tarragona 60 M3
Tarras 116 B7
Tàrrega 60 M3
Tarso Emissi 100 C3
Tarsus 92 F5
Tartagal 142 J3
Tartu 48 P7
Țarțūs 94 C2
Tarutyne 66 S3
Tarvisio 62 J4
Tasbuget 76 M9
Tashigang 88 F3
Tashir 92 L3
Tashkent = Toshkent 76 M9
Tash-Kömür 76 N9
Tashtagol 76 R7
Tasiilaq 122 Z3
Tasikmalaya 86 D4
Taskesken 76 Q8
Taşköprü 92 F3
Tasman Bay 116 D5
Tasmania 112 E10
Tasmania 114 H8
Tasman Mountains 116 D5
Tasman Sea 116 B3
Tășnad 66 K2
Taşova 92 G3
Tassili du Hoggar 102 F4
Tassili-n'-Ajjer 102 G3
Tasty 76 M9
Tasūj 92 L4
Tata, *Hungary* 66 F2
Tata, *Morocco* 102 D3
Tataba 87 B3
Tatabánya 66 F2
Tataouine 102 H2
Tatarbunary 66 S4
Tatariya 70 J3
Tatarsk 76 P6
Tatarskiy Proliv 78 P7
Tateyama 82 K6
Tathlina Lake 122 H4
Tatta 90 J5
Tatvan 92 K4
Tauá 140 J5
Tauberbischofsheim 52 E7
Tauern 62 J4
Taumarunui 116 E4
Taungdwingyi 84 B2
Taung-gyi 88 G4
Taungup 88 F5
Taunsa 88 B2
Taunton, *UK* 56 J10
Taunton, *US* 128 F2
Taunus 54 L4
Taunusstein 54 L4
Taupo 116 F4
Tauragė 50 M2
Tauranga 116 F3
Tauroa Point 116 D2
Tavda 70 N3
Tavda 70 N3
Tavira 60 C7
Tavoy 84 B4
Tavşanli 92 C4
Taw 56 J11
Tawas City 128 D2
Tawau 86 F2
Tawitawi 86 F1
Taxkorgan 76 P10
Tay 56 J5
Tayga 76 R6
Taylorville 130 D2
Taym 90 C4
Taymā' 100 G2
Taymura 78 F4
Taymylyr 78 L2
Tay Ninh 84 D4
Tayshet 78 F5
Tayuan 78 L6
Tayyebād 90 H3
Taza 102 E2
Tazeh Kand 92 M4
Tazenakht 102 D2
Tāzirbū 100 D2
Tazovskaya Guba 76 N4
Tazovskiy 76 P4
Tazovskiy Poluostrov 76 N4
Tazungdam 84 B1
T'bilisi 92 L3
Tchamba 104 G3
Tchibanga 104 G5
Tchin Tabaradene 102 G5
Tczew 50 H3
Te Anau 116 A7
Te Araroa 116 G3
Te Aroha 116 E3
Te Awamutu 116 E4
Teberda 92 J2
Tébessa 102 G1
Tebingtinggi 86 B2
Téboursouk 64 D12
Techa 70 M3
Techiman 104 D3
Tecuala 132 D4
Tecuci 66 Q4
Tedzhen 90 H2
Tees 56 L7
Tegal 86 D4
Tegernsee 62 G3
Tegina 104 F2
Teglio 62 F4
Tegucigalpa 134 G6
Tegul'det 76 R6
Te Hapua 116 D2
Te Haroto 116 F4
Tehek Lake 122 M3
Teheran = Tehrān 90 F2
Tehrān 90 F2
Teignmouth 56 J11
Tejo = Tagus 60 B5
Te Kaha 116 F3
Te Kao 116 D2
Tekirdağ 68 K4
Tekirdağ 92 B3
Teknaf 88 F4
Teku 87 B3
Te Kuiti 116 E4
T'elavi 92 L3
Tel Aviv-Yafo 94 B4
Telegraph Creek 132 (1)L4
Telén 142 H6
Teles Pires 140 F5
Telford 56 K9
Telfs 62 G3
Teller 132 (1)D2
Telsen 142 H7
Telšiai 50 M2
Teltow 52 J4
Teluk Berau 87 D3
Teluk Bone 87 B3
Teluk Cenderawasih 87 E3
Telukdalem 86 B2
Teluk Kumai 86 E3
Telukpakedai 86 D3
Teluk Sampit 86 E3
Teluk Sukadana 86 D3
Teluk Tomini 87 B2
Tema 104 D3
Tembenchi 76 T4
Temerin 66 G4
Temerloh 84 C6
Teminabuan 87 D3
Temochic 132 E3
Tempe 132 D2
Tempio Pausaria 64 D8
Temple 132 G2
Temryuk 92 G1
Temuco 142 G6
Tenali 88 D5
Tendaho 100 H5
Ten Degree Channel 88 F7
Tendo 82 L4
Tendrara 102 E2
Ténéré 102 G5
Ténéré du Tafassasset 102 G4
Tenerife 102 B3
Ténès 102 F1
Tenggarong 86 F3
Tenke 108 D2
Tenkodogo 104 D2
Tennant Creek 114 F3
Tennessee 120 K6
Tennessee 124 J4
Tenojoki 48 P2
Tenteno 87 B3
Tenterfield 114 K5
Teo 60 B2
Teófilo Otoni 140 J7
Tepa 87 C4
Tepehuanes 124 E6
Tepic 124 F7
Teplice 50 C7
Ter 60 N2
Terceira 102 (1)B2
Terek 92 L2
Teresina 140 J5
Tergnier 54 F5
Terme 92 G3
Termez 90 J2
Termini Imerese 64 H11
Termirtau 76 N7
Termoli 66 C8
Ternate 87 C2
Terneuzen 54 F3
Terni 64 G6
Ternitz 62 M3
Ternopil' 70 E5
Ternuka 116 C7
Terracina 64 H7
Terrassa 60 N3
Terre Haute 130 D2
Terry 126 E1
Tersa 70 H4
Terschelling 54 H1
Teruel 60 J4
Tervel 92 B2
Tervola 48 N3
Teseney 100 G4
Teshekpuk Lake 132 (1)F1
Teshikaga 82 N2
Teshio 82 L1
Teslin 132 (1)L3
Teslin 132 (1)L3
Tessalit 102 F4
Têt 58 H11
Tete 108 E3
Teterow 52 H3
Teteven 68 G2
Tétouan 102 D1
Tetovo 66 H8
Teuco 142 J3
Teulada 64 C10
Tevere 64 G6
Teverya 94 C4
Tevriz 70 P3
Te Waewae Bay 116 A8
Texarkana 130 C3
Texas 124 F5
Texel 54 G1
Teya 76 S5
Teykovo 70 H3
Tfarity 102 C3
Thaba Putsoa 108 D5
Thabazimbi 108 D4
Thailand 84 C4
Thai Nguyên 84 D2
Thal 88 B2
Thale Luang 84 C5
Thamarīt 90 F6
Thames 56 L10
Thamūd 90 E6
Thane 88 B5
Thanh Hoa 84 D3
Thanjavur 88 C6
Thann 62 C3
Tharad 88 B4
Thar Desert 88 B3
Thargomindah 114 H5
Tharwāniyyah 95 E5
Thasos 68 G4
Thasos 68 G4
Thaton 84 B3
Thaya 50 E9
The Bahamas 130 F4
The Bluff 130 F4
The Dalles 126 B1
Thedford 126 F2
The Fens 54 B2
The Gambia 104 A2
The Granites 114 E4
The Hague = 's-Gravenhage 54 G2
Thelon 122 L4
The Minch 56 F3
The Naze 54 D3
Thenia 60 P8
Theniet el Had 60 N9
Theodore Roosevelt 140 E5
Theodore Roosevelt Lake 132 D2
The Pas 122 L6
Thermaikos Kolpos 68 E4
Thermopolis 126 E2
The Sisters 116 (1)B1
The Solent 54 A4
Thessalon 128 D1
Thessaloniki 68 E4
Thetford 56 N9
Thetford Mines 128 F1
The Twins 116 D5
The Wash 56 N9
The Weald 54 B3
The Whitsundays 114 J4
Thief River Falls 128 A1
Thiers 58 J8
Thiès 104 A2
Thika 106 F4
Thimphu 88 E3
Þhingvallavatn 48 (1)C2
Thionville 54 J5
Thira 68 H8
Thira 68 H8
Thirasia 68 H8
Thirsk 56 L7
Thiruvananthapuram 88 C7
Thisted 48 E8
Þhistilfjöður 48 (1)F1
Thiva 68 F6
Thiviers 58 F8
Þhjórsá 48 (1)D2
Tholen 54 G3
Thomasville 130 E3
Thompson 122 H6
Thompson 122 M5
Thompson Falls 126 C1
Thomson 130 E3
Thonon-les-Bains 62 B4
Þhórisvatn 48 (1)D2
Þhorlákshöfn 48 (1)C3
Þhorshöfn 48 (1)F1
Thouars 58 E7
Thrakiko Pelagos 68 H4
Three Forks 126 D1
Three Kings Island 116 C2
Three Rivers 128 C2
Throckmorton 130 B3
Thuin 54 G4
Thun 62 C4
Thunder Bay 128 C1
Thuner See 62 C4
Thung Song 84 B5
Thüringer Wald 52 F6
Thurso 56 J3
Thusis 62 E4
Tīāb 95 G3
Tianjin 80 F3
Tianmen 80 E4
Tianqiaoling 82 E2
Tianshifu 82 C3
Tianshui 80 D4
Tianshuihai 90 L2
Tianyang 80 D6
Tiaret 102 F1
Tibati 104 G3
Tibesti 100 C3
Tibet = Xizang 88 E2
Tibooburra 114 H5
Tiburón 134 B3
Tîchît 102 D5
Tichla 102 C4
Ticino 62 D4
Ticul 134 G4
Tidjikdja 102 C5
Tieling 82 B2
Tielongtan 88 C1
Tielt 54 F3
Tienen 54 G4
Tien Shan 76 Q9
Tien Yen 84 D2
Tierra Amarilla 126 E3
Tiétar 60 E4
Tiflis = T'bilisi 98 H1
Tifton 130 E3
Tifu 87 C3
Tighina 66 S3
Tignère 104 G3
Tigre 140 B4
Tigris 92 K6
Tijuana 124 C5
Tikanlik 76 R9
Tikhoretsk 70 H5
Tikhvin 70 F3
Tikrīt 92 K6

Tiksi 78 M2
Tilburg 54 H3
Tilichiki 78 V4
Tillabéri 104 E2
Tillamook 126 B1
Tilos 68 K8
Timanskiy Kryazh 70 K2
Timaru 116 C7
Timashevsk 70 G5
Timber Creek 114 F3
Timerloh 86 C2
Timimoun 102 F3
Timişoara 66 J4
Timmins 128 D1
Timon 140 J5
Timor 87 C4
Timor Sea 114 E2
Tinaca Point 112 C5
Tin Alkoum 102 H4
Tinchebray 54 B6
Tindivanam 88 C6
Tindouf 102 D3
Tineo 60 D1
Tinfouchy 102 D3
Tinglev 52 E2
Tingo Maria 140 B5
Tingri 88 E3
Tingsryd 50 E1
Tiniroto 116 F4
Tinnsjø 48 E7
Tinogasta 142 H4
Tinos 68 H7
Tinos 68 H7
Tinsukia 88 G3
Tintâne 102 C5
T'i'o 100 H5
Tipperary 56 D9
Tirana = Tiranë 68 B3
Tiranë 68 B3
Tirari Desert 114 G5
Tiraspol 66 S3
Tire 68 K6
Tiree 56 F5
Tiroungoulou 106 C2
Tirschenreuth 52 H7
Tirso 64 C9
Tiruchchirāppalli 88 C6
Tirunelveli 88 C7
Tirupati 88 C6
Tiruppur 88 C6
Tiruvannamalai 88 C6
Tisa 66 H4
Tisīyah 94 D4
Tišnov 50 F8
Tisza 50 M9
Tiszaföldvár 66 H3
Tiszafüred 66 H2
Tiszaújváros 50 L10
Tit-Ary 76 Z3
Titel 66 H4
Titlagarh 88 D4
Titova Korenica 62 L6
Titovo Velenje 64 K2
Titu 66 N5
Titusville 130 E4
Tivaouane 102 B6
Tiverton 56 J11
Tivoli 64 G7
Tiyās 94 E2
Tizi Ouzou 102 F1
Tiznit 102 D3
Tjeldøya 48 H2
Tjørkolm 48 D7
Tlemcen 102 E2
Tmassah 100 C2
Toad River 122 F5
Tobago 134 M6
Tobelo 87 C2
Tobermory, *UK* 56 F5
Tobermory, *US* 128 D1
Tobi 87 D2
Toboali 86 D3
Tobol 70 M4
Tobol 70 M4
Tobol'sk 70 N3
Tobseda 70 K1
Tocantins 140 H5
Tocantins 140 H5
Toce 62 D4
Tocopilla 142 G3
Todeli 87 B3
Todi 64 G6
Tofino 126 A1
Togo 104 E3
Toimin 64 H2
Toi-misaki 82 F8
Tōjō 82 G6
Tok 132 (1)J3
Tokar 100 G4
Tokat, *Sudan* 90 C6
Tokat, *Turkey* 90 C1
Tokelau 112 J6
Tokmak 76 P9
Tokoroa 116 E4
Tokounou 104 C3
Toksun 76 R9
Tok-tō 80 J3
Toktogul 76 N9
Tokushima 82 H6
Tokuyama 82 F6
Tōkyō 82 K6
Tolaga Bay 116 G4
Tōlañaro 108 H4
Tolbo 76 S8
Toledo, *Brazil* 142 L3
Toledo, *Spain* 60 F5
Toledo, *US* 128 D2
Toliara 108 G4
Tolitoli 87 B2
Tol'ka 76 Q5
Tol'ka 76 Q5
Tollense 52 J3
Tolmezzo 62 J4
Tolmin 62 J4
Tolna 66 F3
Tolosa 60 H1
Tol'yatti 70 J4
Tolybay 76 L7
Tom' 76 R6
Tomah 128 B2
Tomakomai 82 L2
Tomamae 82 L1
Tomar, *Brazil* 140 E4
Tomar, *Portugal* 60 B5
Tomari 78 Q7
Tomaszów Lubelski 50 N7
Tomaszów Mazowiecki 50 K6
Tombouctou 102 E5
Tombua 108 A3
Tomé 142 G6
Tomelloso 60 H5
Tomini 87 B2
Tommot 78 M5
Tomo 140 D2
Tompo 78 P4
Tom Price 114 C4
Tomra 88 E2
Tomsk 76 Q6
Tomtor 78 Q4
Tomu 87 D3
Tonalá 134 F5
Tondano 87 B2
Tønder 52 D2
Tonga 106 E2
Tonga 112 J7
Tonga Islands 112 J8
Tongareva 112 K6
Tonga Trench 112 J8
Tongbai 80 E4
Tongchuan 80 D4
Tongduch'ŏn 82 D5
Tongeren 54 H4
Tonghae 82 E5
Tonghua 82 C3
Tongliao 80 G2
Tongling 80 F4
Tongshan 80 F4
Tongshi 84 D3
Tongue 126 E1
Tongyu 80 G2
Tōnichi 124 E6
Tonj 106 D2
Tonk 88 C3
Tonkābon 90 F2
Tônlé Sab 84 C4
Tonnay-Charente 58 E8
Tönning 52 D2
Tonopah 126 C3
Tooele 126 D2
Toora-Khem 76 T7
Toowoomba 114 K5
Topeka 124 G4
Topki 76 R6
Topliţa 66 N3
Topock 132 D2
Topol'čany 50 H9
Topolobampo 124 E6
Torbali 68 K6
Torbat-e Heydarīyeh 90 G2
Torbat-e Jām 90 H2
Tordesillas 60 F3
Töre 48 M4
Torells 60 N2
Torgau 52 H5
Torgelow 50 C4
Torhout 54 F3
Torino 62 C5
Tori-shima 82 L8
Torneälven 48 L3
Torneträsk 48 K2
Tornio 48 N4
Toro 60 E3
Toronto 128 E2
Tororo 106 E3
Toros Dağları 92 E5
Torquay 56 J11
Torrance 132 C2
Torreblanca 60 L4
Torre de Moncorvo 60 C3
Torrejón de Ardoz 60 G4
Torrelapaja 60 J3
Torrelavega 60 F1
Torremolinos 60 F8
Torrent 60 K5
Torreón 132 F3
Torre-Pacheco 60 K7
Torres Strait 114 H2
Torres Vedras 60 A5
Torrevieja 60 K6
Torrington 126 F2
Tortoli 64 D9
Tortona 62 D6
Tortosa 60 L4
Tortum 92 J3
Torūd 90 G2
Toruń 50 H4
Tory Island 56 D6
Torzhok 70 G3
Tosa-wan 82 G7
Toshkent 76 M9
Tostedt 52 E3
Tosya 68 S3
Totaranui 116 D5
Tôtes 54 D5
Tot'ma 70 H3
Totora 140 D7
Tottori 82 H6
Touba, *Côte d'Ivoire* 104 C3
Touba, *Senegal* 104 A2
Tougan 104 D2
Touggourt 102 G2
Tougouri 104 D2
Touil 102 C5
Toul 58 L5
Toulépleu 104 C3
Toulon 58 L10
Toulouse 58 G10
Toummo 102 H4
Toungoo 84 B3
Tourcoing 54 F4
Tournai 54 F4
Tournon-sur-Rhône 58 K8
Tours 58 F6
Touws River 108 C6
Tovuz 92 L3
Towanda 128 E2
Towari 87 B3
Towcester 54 B2
Towner 126 F1
Townsend 126 D1
Townshend Island 114 K4
Townsville 114 J3
Toxkan 76 P9
Toyama 82 J5
Toyohashi 82 J6
Toyooka 82 H6
Toyota 82 J6
Tozeur 102 G2
Tqvarch'eli 92 J2
Trâblous 94 C2
Trabzon 92 H3
Tracy 128 A2
Trail 126 C1
Traiskirchen 62 M2
Trakai 48 N9
Tralee 56 C9
Tralee Bay 56 B9
Tramán Tepuí 140 E2
Tranås 48 H7
Trancoso 60 C4
Trang 84 B5
Trangan 87 D4
Transantarctic Mountains 144 (2)B1
Trapani 64 G11
Trappes 54 E6
Traun 62 K2
Traunreut 62 H3
Traunsee 62 J3
Traversay Islands 138 H9
Traverse City 128 C2
Travnik 66 E5
Trbovlje 62 L4
Trebbia 62 E6
Třebíč 50 E8
Trebinje 66 F7
Trebišov 66 J1
Trebnje 62 L5
Trebon 62 K1
Tregosse Islets 114 K3
Trélazé 58 E6
Trelew 142 H7
Trelleborg 48 G9
Tremonton 126 D2
Tremp 60 L2
Trenčín 50 H9
Trent 56 M8
Trento 62 G4
Trenton, *Canada* 128 E2
Trenton, *US* 128 F2
Trepassey 122 W7
Tres Arroyos 142 J6
Três Corações 140 H8
Tres Esquinas 140 B3
Tres Lagos 142 G8
Trespaderne 60 G2
Treuchtlingen 62 F2
Treviglio 62 E5
Treviso 62 H5
Triangle 108 E4
Tricase 64 N9
Trichur 88 C6
Trier 54 J5
Trieste 62 J5
Triglav 62 J4
Trikala 68 D5
Trikomon 94 A1
Trilj 62 M7
Trincomalee 88 D7
Trinidad 140 E1
Trinidad, *Bolivia* 140 E6
Trinidad, *US* 132 F1
Trinidad, *Uruguay* 142 K5
Trinidad and Tobago 140 E1
Trinity Islands 132 (1)G4
Trino 62 D5
Trion 130 D3
Tripoli, *Greece* 68 E7
Tripoli = Trâblous, *Lebanon* 94 C2
Tripoli = Tarābulus, *Libya* 102 H2
Trischen 52 D2
Tristan da Cunha 98 B9
Trivandrum = Thiruvananthapuram 88 C7
Trjavna 92 A2
Trnava 66 E1
Trogir 66 D6
Troina 64 J11
Troisdorf 52 C6
Trois Rivières 128 F1
Troitsk 70 M4
Troitsko-Pechorsk 70 L2
Trojan 68 G2
Trollhättan 48 G7
Trombetas 140 F4
Tromsø 48 K2
Trona 126 C3
Trondheim 48 F5
Trondheimsfjorden 48 E5
Troodos 92 E6
Trotuş 66 P3
Trout Lake, *N.W.T., Canada* 122 G4
Trout Lake, *Ont., Canada* 122 N6
Troy, *Al., US* 130 D3
Troy, *N.Y., US* 128 F2
Troyan 66 M7
Troyes 58 K5
Trstenik 66 J6
Trudovoye 82 G2
Trujillo, *Peru* 140 B5
Trujillo, *Spain* 60 E5
Truro, *Canada* 122 U7
Truro, *UK* 56 G11
Trusovo 76 J4
Truth or Consequences 132 E2
Trutnov 50 E7
Tryavana 68 H2
Trzcianka 50 F4
Trzebnica 50 G6
Tržič 62 K4
Tsetserleg 78 G7
Tshabong 108 C5
Tshane 108 C4
Tshikapa 106 C5
Tshuapa 106 C4
Tsiafajavona 108 H3
Tsimlyanskoy Vodokhranilishche 70 H5
Tsiroanomandidy 108 H3
Ts'khinvali 92 K2
Tsuchiura 82 L5
Tsugaru-kaikyō 82 L3
Tsumeb 108 B3
Tsumkwe 108 C3
Tsuruga 82 J6
Tsuruoka 82 K4
Tsushima 82 E6
Tsuyama 82 H6
Tua 60 C3
Tual 87 D4
Tuân Giao 84 C2
Tuapse 92 H1
Tubarão 142 M4
Tubas 94 C4
Tübingen 62 E2
Tubize 54 G4
Tubruq 100 D1
Tubuai 112 M8
Tubuai Islands 112 L8
Tucano 140 K6
Tuchola 50 G4
Tucson 132 D2
Tucumcari 132 F1
Tucupita 140 E2
Tucuruí 140 H4
Tudela 60 J2
Tufayh 95 C3
Tuguegarao 84 G3
Tugur 78 P6
Tui 60 B2
Tuktoyaktuk 132 (1)L2
Tula, *Mexico* 132 G4
Tula, *Russia* 70 G4
Tulare 126 C3
Tulcea 66 R4
Tulkarm 94 B4
Tullamore 56 E8
Tulle 58 G8
Tulln 62 M2
Tuloma 48 S2
Tulsa 124 G4
Tulsequah 132 (1)L4
Tulun 78 G6
Tulung La 88 F3
Tulu Weiel 106 E2
Tumaco 140 B3
Tumān 90 H2
Tumen 82 E2
Tumereng 140 E2
Tumkur 88 C6
Tumut 114 J7
Tunca 68 J3
Tunceli 92 H4
Tunduru 108 F2
Tundzha 66 P8
Tungir 78 L5
Tungku 86 F1
Tungsten 132 (1)M3
Tungusk 76 S5
Tunis 102 H1
Tunisia 102 E2
Tunja 140 C2
Tupelo 130 D3
Tupik 78 L6
Tupiza 142 H3
Tupper Lake 128 F2
Tuquan 80 G1
Tura, *India* 88 F3
Tura, *Russia* 78 G4
Turan 76 S7
Turangi 116 E4
Turayf 100 G1
Turbat 90 H4
Turbo 140 B2
Turda 66 L3
Turek 50 H5
Turgay 76 L8
Turgay 76 L8
Turgayskaya Stolovaya Strana 76 L7
Türgovishte 66 P6
Turgutlu 68 K6
Turhal 92 G3
Turin = Torino 62 C5
Turinsk 70 M3
Turiy Rog 82 F1
Turka 78 H6
Türkeli Adası 68 K4
Turkestan 76 M9
Turkey 92 D4
Turkmenbashi 90 F1
Turkmenistan 90 G2
Turks and Caicos Islands 134 K4
Turks Islands 134 K4
Turku 48 M6
Turma 78 N6
Turnhout 54 G3
Turnov 50 E7
Turnu Măgurele 66 M6
Turpan 76 R9

Turpan Pendi 76 S9
Turquino 138 D2
Turtas 70 N3
Turtkul' 90 H1
Turtle Island 114 K3
Turu 76 U5
Turugart Pass 76 P9
Turukhan 78 C3
Turukhansk 76 R4
Turukta 78 K4
Tuscaloosa 130 D3
Tuscola 130 D2
Tuticorin 88 C7
Tutonchany 78 E4
Tutrakan 66 P5
Tuttle Creek Reservoir 130 B2
Tuttlingen 62 D3
Tutuila 112 K7
Tuvalu 112 H6
Tuxpan, *Mexico* 124 E7
Tuxpan, *Mexico* 124 G7
Tuxtla Gutiérrez 134 F5
Tuyên Quang 84 D2
Tuy Hoa 84 D4
Tuymazy 70 K4
Tuz Gölü 92 E4
Tuz Khurmātū 92 L6
Tuzla 66 F5
Tver' 70 G3
Tweed 56 K6
Twentynine Palms 132 C2
Twilight Cove 114 E6
Twin Buttes Reservoir 132 F2
Twin Falls 126 D2
Twizel 116 C7
Two Harbors 128 B1
Tyachiv 66 L1
Tygda 78 M6
Tyler 124 G5
Tylkhoy 78 U4
Tym 76 Q6
Tynda 78 L5
Tyne 56 K6
Tynemouth 56 L6
Tynset 48 F5
Tyra 76 S7
Tyrifjorden 48 F6
Tyrnavos 68 E5
Tyrrhenian Sea 64 F8
Tyry 78 P4
Tysa 50 N9
Tyukyan 78 K4
Tyumen' 76 M6
Tyung 78 K3
Tyva 78 F6

U

Uarini 140 D4
Uaupés 140 D3
Ubá 140 J8
Ubaitaba 140 K6
Ubangi 106 B3
Ube 82 F7
Úbeda 60 G6
Uberaba 140 H7
Uberlândia 140 H7
Überlingen 62 E3
Ubon Ratchathani 84 C3
Ubrique 60 E8
Ucayali 140 B5
Uchami 76 T5
Ucharal 76 Q8
Uchiura-wan 82 L2
Uchkuduk 76 L9
Uckermark 52 J3
Ucluelet 126 A1
Uda, *Russia* 78 F5
Uda, *Russia* 78 N6
Udachnyy 78 J3
Udagamandalam 88 C6
Udaipur 88 B4
Uddevalla 48 F7
Uddjaure 70 C1
Uddjaure Storavan 48 K4
Udine 62 J4
Udmurtiya 70 K3
Udon Thani 84 C3
Udupi 88 B6
Uecker 52 J3
Ueckermünde 52 J3
Ueda 82 K5
Uele 106 C3
Uelen 78 AA3
Uel'kal 78 Y3
Uelzen 52 F4
Ufa 70 L3
Ufa 70 L4
Uganda 106 E3
Ugep 104 F3
Ugine 62 B5
Uglegorsk 78 Q7
Uglich 70 G3
Ugljan 62 L6
Ugol'naya Zyryanka 78 R3
Ugol'nyye Kopi 78 X4
Ugulan 78 S4
Uh 66 K1
Uherské Hradiště 50 G8
Uherský Brod 50 G8
Uiju 82 C3
Uil 70 K5
Uil 70 K5
Uinta Mountains 126 D2
Uitenhage 108 D6
Újfehértó 66 J2
Ujiji 106 D4
Ujjain 88 C4
Ukerewe Island 106 E4
Ukhta 76 J5
Ukiah 126 B3
Ukkusissat 122 W2
Ukmergė 50 P2
Ukraine 46 G3
Ulaanbaatar 78 H7
Ulaangom 76 S8
Ulan 80 B3
Ulan Bator = Ulaanbaatar 80 D1
Ulan-Ude 78 H6
Ulaş 92 G4
Ulchin 82 E5
Ulcinj 66 G8
Uldz 78 J7
Ulety 78 J6
Ulhasnagar 88 B5
Uliastay 76 T8
Ulindi 106 D4
Ullapool 56 G4
Ullŭng do 82 F5
Ulm 62 F2
Ulog 66 F6
Ulongue 108 E2
Ulsan 82 E6
Ulu 78 M4
Ulubat Gölü 68 L4
Uluqqat 90 K2
Ulukışla 92 F5
Ulungur Hu 76 R8
Ulunkhan 78 J5
Uluru 114 F5
Ulu-Yul 78 D5
Ulva 56 F5
Ulverston 56 J7
Ulya 78 Q5
Ul'yanovsk 70 J4
Ulytau 76 M8
Umag 64 H3
Uman' 70 F5
Umarkot 90 J4
Umba 70 F1
Umeå 48 L5
Umeälven 48 J4
Umfolozi 108 E5
Ummal Arānib 102 H3
Umm al Jamājim 95 A3
Umm Durman 100 F4
Umm Keddada 100 E5
Umm Lajj 100 G3
Umm Qaṣr 95 B1
Umm Ruwaba 100 F5
Umnak Island 132 (1)E5
Umtata 108 D6
Umuarama 142 L3
Unalakleet 132 (1)E3
Unalaska Island 132 (1)E5
'Unayzah 94 C6
Underberg 108 D5
Ungava Bay 122 T5
Ungheni 66 Q2
Ungwana Bay 106 G4
União da Vitória 142 L4
Unije 62 K6
Unimak Island 132 (1)D5
Unim Bāb 95 D4
Unini 140 E4
Union 128 B3
Union City 134 G1
Union Springs 130 D3
United Arab Emirates 90 F5
United Kingdom 56 G6
United States 120 M5
Unna 54 K3
Unraven 132 E1
Unst 56 M1
Unstrut 52 G5
Unzha 70 H3
Upernavik 122 W2
Upernavik Kujalleq 122 V2
Upington 108 C5
Upolu 112 J7
Upper Hutt 116 E5
Upper Klamath Lake 126 B2
Upper Lake 126 C2
Upper Lough Erne 56 E7
Upper Sandusky 128 D2
Uppsala 48 J7
Upsala 128 B1
'Uqlat al 'Udhaybah 95 B2
Urad Houqi 80 D2
Urakawa 82 M2
Ural 70 K5
Ural Mountains = Ural'skiy Khrebet 46 L1
Ural'sk 70 K4
Ural'skiy Khrebet 46 L1
Urambo 106 E5
Uranium City 122 K5
Uraricoera 140 E3
Uraricoera 140 E3
Uray 70 M2
Urbana, *Ill., US* 128 C2
Urbana, *Oh., US* 128 D2
Urbania 62 H7
Urbino 62 H7
Urdzhar 76 Q8
Uren' 70 J3
Urengoy 76 P4
Urgench 90 H1
Urho 76 R8
Uritskiy 70 N4
Urla 68 J6
Urlaţi 66 P5
Uroševac 66 J7
Uro-teppa 90 J2
Urt 80 C2
Uruaçu 140 H6
Uruapan 134 D5
Urucurituba 140 F4
Uruguaiana 142 K4
Uruguay 142 K5
Uruguay 142 K5
Ürümqi 76 R9
Urus Martan 92 L2
Uruti 116 E4
Uryupino 78 L6
Uryupinsk 70 H4
Urzhum 70 K3
Urziceni 66 P5
Usa 76 L4
Usa 82 F7
Uşak 92 C4
Usedom 52 J3
Useless Loop 114 B5
Usfān 90 C5
Ushtobe 76 P8
Usingen 52 D6
Usk 56 J10
Usman' 70 G4
Usol'ye Sibirskoye 78 G6
Ussel 58 H8
Ussuri 82 G1
Ussuriysk 80 J2
Usta 70 J3
Ust'-Alekseyevo 70 J2
Ust'-Barguzin 78 H6
Ust' Chaun 78 W3
Ústí 50 F8
Ustica 64 H10
Ust'-Ilimsk 78 G5
Ústí nad Labem 50 D7
Ust'-Ishim 76 N6
Ustka 50 F3
Ust'-Kamchatsk 78 U5
Ust'-Kamenogorsk 76 Q8
Ust'-Kamo 76 T5
Ust'-Karenga 78 K6
Ust'-Khayryuzovo 78 T5
Ust'-Kulom 70 K2
Ust'-Kut 78 G5
Ust'-Kuyga 78 P3
Ust'-Labinsk 92 H1
Ust'-Maya 78 N4
Ust'-Mukduyka 76 R4
Ust'-Muya 78 K5
Ust' Nem 70 K2
Ust'-Nera 78 Q4
Ust'-Nyukzha 78 L5
Ust'-Olenek 78 K2
Ust'-Omchug 78 R4
Ust' Ozernoye 78 D5
Ust' Penzhino 78 V4
Ust'-Pit 78 E5
Ustrem 70 N2
Ust'-Sopochnoye 78 T5
Ust' Tapsuy 70 M2
Ust'-Tarka 76 P6
Ust'-Tatta 78 N4
Ust'-Tsil'ma 76 J4
Ust' Un'ya 70 L2
Ust'-Urkima 78 L5
Ust' Usa 70 L1
Ust'-Uyskoye 76 L7
Usu 76 Q9
Usuki 82 F7
Utah 124 D4
Utah Lake 126 D2
Utata 78 G6
Utena 48 N9
Uthal 90 J4
Utica 128 E2
Utiel 60 J5
Utrecht 54 H2
Utrera 60 E7
Utsjoki 48 P2
Utsunomiya 82 K5
Uttaradit 84 C3
Utva 70 K4
Uummannaq Fjord 122 V2
Uummannarsuaq 122 Y5
Uusikaupunki 48 L6
Uvalde 134 E3
Uvargin 78 X3
Uvat 70 N3
Uvinza 106 E5
Uvira 106 D4
Uvs Nuur 76 S7
Uwajima 82 G7
Uy 70 M4
Uyar 76 S6
Uyuk 76 N9
Uyuni 142 H3
Uzbekistan 76 L9
Uzhhorod 66 K1
Užice 66 G6
Uzunköprü 66 P8

V

Vaal 108 D5
Vaasa 48 L5
Vác 66 G2
Vacaria 142 M4
Vachi 90 E1
Vadodara 88 B4
Vado Ligure 62 D6
Vadsø 48 Q1
Vaduz 62 E3
Værøy 48 G3
Vaganski Vhr 62 L6
Vagay 70 N3
Váh 50 H8
Vakh 70 Q2
Valbonnais 62 A6
Valcheta 142 H7
Valdagno 62 G5
Valday 70 F3
Val-de-Meuse 62 A2
Valdemoro 60 G4
Valdepeñas 60 G6
Valdez 122 B4
Valdivia 142 G6
Val-d'Or 128 E1
Valdosta 124 K5
Valdres 48 E6
Valea lui Mihai 66 K2
Valence 58 K9
Valencia, *Spain* 60 K5
Valencia, *Venezuela* 140 D1
Valencia de Alcántara 60 C5
Valenciennes 54 F4
Vălenii de Munte 66 P4
Valentia Island 56 B10
Valentine 126 F2
Valenza 62 D5
Valera 140 C2
Valga 70 E3
Val Horn 124 F5
Valjevo 66 G5
Valka 48 N8
Val'karay 78 X3
Valkeakoski 48 N6
Valkenswaard 54 H3
Valladolid, *Mexico* 134 G4
Valladolid, *Spain* 60 F3
Valle 48 D7
Valledupar 140 C1
Vallée de Azaouagh 102 F5
Vallée du Tîlemsi 102 F5
Vallée-Jonction 128 F1
Vallejo 126 B3
Vallentuna 48 K7
Valletta 64 J13
Valley City 126 G1
Valley Falls 126 B2
Valley of the Kings 100 F2
Valli di Comacchio 62 H6
Vallorbe 62 B4
Valls 60 M3
Valmiera 48 N8
Valognes 54 A5
Val-Paradis 128 E1
Valparai 88 C6
Valparaíso, *Chile* 142 G5
Valparaíso, *Mexico* 132 F4
Valsad 88 B4
Val'tevo 70 H2
Valuyki 70 G4
Valverde del Camino 60 D7
Vammala 48 M6
Van 92 K4
Vanadzor 92 L3
Vanavara 78 G4
Van Buren 128 G1
Vancouver, *Canada* 126 B1
Vancouver, *US* 126 B1
Vancouver Island 122 F7
Vandalia 130 D2
Vanderbijlpark 108 D5
Vanderhoof 122 G6
Van Diemen Gulf 114 F2
Vänern 48 G7
Vangaindrano 108 H4
Van Gölü 92 K4
Van Horn 132 F2
Vanimo 87 F3
Vanino 78 Q7
Vankarem 78 Y3
Vanna 48 K1
Vännäs 48 K5
Vannes 58 C6
Vanrhynsdorp 108 B6
Vantaa 48 N6
Vanua Levu 112 H7
Vanuatu 112 G7
Van Wert 128 D2
Vanzevat 70 N2
Vanzhil'kynak 78 C4
Varāmīn 90 F2
Varanasi 88 D3
Varangerfjorden 48 R2
Varaždin 66 D3
Varazze 62 D6
Varberg 48 G8
Varda 68 D6
Vardar 68 E3
Varde 48 E9
Vardenis 92 L3
Vardø 48 R1
Varel 52 D3
Varėna 50 P3
Varese 62 D5
Vârful Moldoveanu 66 M4
Vârfurile 66 K3
Varginha 142 M3
Varkaus 48 P5
Varna 92 B2
Värnamo 48 H8
Varnsdorf 52 K6
Várpalota 66 F2
Varto 92 J4
Varzi 62 E6
Varzy 58 J6
Vásárosnamény 66 K1
Vasilikos 94 A2
Vaslui 66 Q3
Västerås 48 J7
Västervik 48 J8
Vasto 64 J6
Vasvár 62 M3
Vatan 58 G6
Vathia 68 E8
Vatican City 64 F7
Vatnajökull 48 (1)E2
Vatomandry 108 H3
Vatra Dornei 66 N2
Vättern 48 H7
Vaughn 132 E2
Vawkavysk 50 P4
Växjö 48 H8
Vayuniya 88 D7
Vazhgort 70 J2
Vecht 54 J2
Vechta 54 L2
Vecsés 66 G2
Vedaranniyam 88 C6

Vedea 66 N6
Vedi 92 L4
Veendam 54 J1
Veenendaal 54 H2
Vega 48 F4
Vega 132 F1
Vegreville 122 J6
Vejen 52 E1
Vejer de la Frontera 60 E8
Vejle 48 E9
Vel' 76 G5
Vela Luka 66 D7
Velenje 62 L4
Veles 68 D3
Vélez-Málaga 60 F8
Velika Gorica 62 M5
Velika Plana 66 J5
Velikaya 78 W4
Velikiye Luki 70 F3
Velikiy Ustyug 70 J2
Veliko Tŭrnovo 66 N6
Vélingara 104 B2
Velingrad 66 L7
Velita Kladuša 62 L5
Velké Meziříčí 50 F8
Velký Krtíš 50 J9
Velletri 64 G7
Vellinge 50 C2
Vellore 88 C6
Velopoula 68 F8
Vel'sk 70 H2
Velten 52 J4
Velva 126 F1
Venaria 62 C5
Vence 62 C7
Venda Nova 60 C3
Vendôme 58 G6
Venev 70 G4
Venezia 62 H5
Venezuela 140 D2
Vengurla 88 B5
Veniaminof Volcano 132 (1)F4
Venice = Venezia 62 H5
Venice 130 D4
Venlo 54 J3
Venray 54 H3
Venta 70 D3
Venta de Baños 60 F3
Ventimiglia 62 C7
Ventotene 64 H8
Ventspils 48 L8
Vera, *Argentina* 142 J4
Vera, *Spain* 60 J7
Veracruz 134 E5
Veraval 88 B4
Verbania 62 D5
Vercelli 62 D5
Verdalsøra 48 F5
Verde 140 G8
Verden 52 E4
Verdun 54 H5
Vereeniging 108 D5
Vereshchagino 78 D4
Verín 60 C3
Verkhneimbatsk 78 D4
Verkhne-Imbatskoye 76 R5
Verkhnetulomskoe Vodokhranilishche 48 R2
Verkhneural'sk 70 L4
Verkhniy Baskunchak 70 J5
Verkhnyaya Amga 78 M5
Verkhnyaya Toyma 70 J2
Verkhnyaya Tura 70 L3
Verkhovyna 66 M1
Verkhoyansk 78 N3
Verkhoyanskiy Khrebet 78 M3
Vermillion 126 G2
Vermont 124 M3
Vernal 126 E2
Verneuil 54 C6
Vernon, *France* 54 D5
Vernon, *US* 130 B3
Vero Beach 130 E4
Veroia 68 E4
Verona 62 F5
Versailles 54 E6
Verviers 54 H4
Veselí 62 N2
Vesijarvi 48 N6
Vesoul 52 B9
Vesterålen 48 G2
Vestfjorden 48 G3
Vestmannaeyjar 48 (1)C3
Vestvagøy 48 G2
Vesuvio 64 J8
Veszprém 66 E2
Vet 108 D5
Vetluga 70 J3
Vetluga 70 J3
Veurne 54 E3
Vevey 62 B4
Vezirköprü 92 F3
Viana do Castelo 60 B3
Vianden 54 J5
Viangchan 84 C3
Viareggio 62 F7
Viborg 48 E8
Vibo Valentia 64 L10
Vibraye 58 F5
Vic 60 N3
Vicenza 62 G5
Vichuga 70 H3
Vichy 58 J7
Vicksburg 130 C3
Victor Harbor 114 G7
Victoria 114 H7
Victoria, *Argentina* 142 J5
Victoria, *Canada* 126 B1
Victoria, *Chile* 142 G6
Victoria, *Malta* 64 J12
Victoria, *Romania* 66 M4
Victoria, *Seychelles* 108 (2)C1
Victoria, *US* 130 B4
Victoria de las Tunas 134 J4
Victoria Falls 108 D3
Victoria Island 122 J2
Victoria Land 144 (2)W2
Victoria River 114 F3
Victoria Strait 122 M3
Victoriaville 128 F1
Victoria West 108 C6
Vidalia 124 K5
Vidamlja 50 N5
Videle 66 N5
Vidin 66 K6
Viedma 142 J7
Vienenburg 52 F5
Vienna = Wien 62 M2
Vienna 128 C3
Vienne 58 F7
Vienne 58 K8
Vientiane = Viangchan 84 C3
Vierzon 58 H6
Vieste 64 L7
Vietnam 84 D3
Việt Tri 84 D2
Vigan 84 G3
Vigevano 62 D5
Vigia 140 H4
Vigo 60 B2
Vigo di Cadore 62 H4
Viho Valentia 64 L10
Vijaywada 88 D5
Vik 48 (1)D3
Vikna 48 E4
Vila de Conde 60 B3
Vilafranca del Penedàs 60 M3
Vila Franca de Xira 60 A6
Vila Nova de Gaia 60 B3
Vilanova y la Geltru 60 M3
Vila Real 60 C3
Vila-real 60 K5
Vilar Formoso 60 D4
Vila Velha 140 G3
Vilhelmina 48 J4
Vilhena 140 E6
Vilija 48 N9
Viljandi 48 N7
Vilkaviškis 50 N3
Villa Ahumada 134 C2
Villablino 60 D2
Villacarrillo 60 G6
Villach 62 J4
Villacidro 64 C9
Villa Constitución 124 D7
Villa de Cos 134 D4
Villafranca de los Barros 60 D6
Villafranca di Verona 62 F5
Villagarcia 60 B2
Villagrán 132 G4
Villahermosa 134 F5
Villa Huidobro 142 J5
Villalba 60 C1
Villaldama 132 F3
Villalpando 60 E3
Villamartin 60 E8
Villa Montes 142 J3
Villanueva 132 F4
Villanueva de Cordoba 60 F6
Villa Ocampo 132 E3
Villaputzu 64 D9
Villarrobledo 60 H5
Villa San Giovanni 64 K10
Villavelayo 60 H2
Villavicencio 140 C3
Villaviciosa 60 E1
Villazon 142 H3
Villedieu-les-Poêles 54 A6
Villefranche-de-Rouergue 58 H9
Villefranche-sur-Saône 58 K8
Villena 60 K6
Villeneuve-sur-Lot 58 F9
Villers-Bocage 54 B5
Villers-Cotterêts 54 F5
Villerupt 54 H5
Villeurbanne 58 K8
Villingen 62 D2
Vilnius 48 N9
Vilsbiburg 62 H2
Vilshofen 62 J2
Vilvoorde 54 G4
Vilyuy 78 L4
Vilyuysk 78 L4
Vilyuyskoye Vodokhranilishche 78 J4
Vimoutiers 54 C6
Vimperk 62 J1
Viña del Mar 142 G5
Vinarós 60 L4
Vincennes 130 D2
Vineland 128 F3
Vinh 84 D3
Vinkovci 66 F4
Vinnytsya 70 E5
Vinson Massif 144 (2)JJ2
Vinstri 48 E6
Vinzili 70 N3
Viöl 52 E2
Vioolsdrift 108 B5
Vipava 62 J5
Vipiteno 62 G4
Vir 62 L6
Virac 84 G4
Viranşehir 92 H5
Virawah 88 B4
Virden 126 F1
Vire 54 B6
Virginia 124 L4
Virginia 128 B1
Virginia Beach 128 E3
Virgin Islands, *UK* 138 E2
Virgin Islands, *US* 138 E2
Virihaure 48 J3
Virôchey 84 D4
Virovitica 66 E4
Virton 54 H5
Virtsu 48 M7
Virudunagar 88 C7
Vis 66 D6
Visalia 126 C3
Visby 48 K8
Viscount Melville Sound 122 J2
Viseu, *Brazil* 140 H4
Viseu, *Portugal* 60 C4
Vişeu de Sus 66 M2
Vishakhapatnam 88 D5
Vishera 76 K5
Vishnevka 76 N7
Visoko 66 F6
Visp 62 C4
Visšegrad 66 G6
Visselhövede 52 E4
Vistula = Wisła 46 F2
Viterbo 64 G6
Vitez 66 E5
Viti Levu 112 H7
Vitim 78 J5
Vitolište 68 D3
Vitória 142 N3
Vitória da Conquista 140 J6
Vitoria-Gasteiz 60 H2
Vitré 58 D5
Vitry-le-François 54 G6
Vitsyebsk 70 F3
Vitteaux 58 K6
Vittel 62 A2
Vittoria 64 J12
Vittorio Veneto 62 H5
Viveiro 60 C1
Vivi 76 T4
Vivonne 58 F7
Vize 68 K3
Vizhas 70 J1
Vizianagaram 88 D5
Vizinga 76 H5
Vizzini 64 J11
Vjosë 68 C4
Vladikavkaz 92 L2
Vladimir 70 H3
Vladivostok 82 F2
Vlasotince 66 K7
Vlasovo 78 N2
Vlieland 54 G1
Vlissingen 54 F3
Vlorë 68 B4
Vltava 50 D8
Vöcklabruck 62 J2
Vodice 62 L7
Vodnjan 62 J6
Vogelsberg 52 E6
Voghera 62 D6
Vohipeno 108 H4
Vöhringen 62 F2
Voi 106 F4
Voinjama 104 C3
Voiron 58 L8
Voitsberg 62 L3
Vojens 52 E1
Vojmsjön 48 J4
Vojvodina 66 G4
Volary 52 J8
Volcán Antofalla 142 H4
Volcán Barú 134 H7
Volcán Cayambe 140 B3
Volcán Citlaltépetl 120 L7
Volcán Corcovado 142 G7
Volcán Cotopaxi 140 B4
Volcán Domuyo 142 G6
Volcán Lanin 142 G6
Volcán Llullaillaco 142 H3
Volcán San Pedro 142 H3
Volcán Tajumulco 134 F5
Volga 70 J5
Volgodonsk 70 H5
Volgograd 70 H5
Völkermarkt 62 K4
Volkhov 70 F3
Völklingen 54 J5
Volksrust 108 D5
Volochanka 76 S3
Volodarskoye 70 N4
Vologda 70 H3
Volonga 70 J1
Volos 68 E5
Volosovo 48 Q7
Volta Redonda 140 J8
Volterra 62 F7
Voltri 62 D6
Volzhskiy 70 H5
Voorne 54 F3
Voranava 48 N9
Vorderrhein 62 E4
Vordingborg 52 G1
Voreios Evvoikos Kolpos 68 E6
Voreria Pindos 68 C4
Vorkuta 70 M1
Vormsi 48 M7
Vorona 70 H4
Voronezh 70 G4
Vorstershoop 108 C5
Võru 48 P8
Vosges 62 C2
Voss 48 D6
Vostochno-Sibirskoye More 78 U2
Vostochnyy Sayan 76 T7
Vostok Island 112 L6
Votkinsk 76 J6
Vozhgora 70 J2
Vranje 66 J7
Vranov 50 L9
Vranov nad Toplau 66 J1
Vratsa 66 L6
Vrbas 66 E5
Vrbas 66 G4
Vrbovsko 62 L5
Vrendenburg 108 B6
Vriddhachalam 88 C6
Vršac 66 J4
Vryburg 108 C5
Vryheid 108 E5
Vsetín 50 G8
Vstrechnyy 78 V3
Vučitrn 66 J7
Vukovar 66 G4
Vuktyl' 70 L2
Vulcăneşti 66 R4
Vulcano 64 J10
Vung Tau 84 D4
Vuollerim 48 L3
Vuotso 48 P2
Vyatka 70 K3
Vyazemskiy 78 N7
Vyaz'ma 70 F3
Vyborg 48 Q6
Vychegda 70 K2
Vyksa 70 H3
Vylkove 66 S4
Vynohradiv 50 N9
Vyshniy Volochek 70 F3
Vyškov 50 G8
Vytegra 70 G2

W

Wa 104 D3
Waal 54 H3
Waalwijk 54 H3
Wabē Shebelē Wenz 106 G2
Wabush 122 T6
Waco 130 B3
Wad Banda 100 E5
Waddān 100 C2
Waddeneilanden 54 G1
Waddenzee 54 H1
Wadena 128 A1
Wādī al Fārigh 100 C1
Wādī al Hamīm 100 D1
Wadi Halfa 100 F3
Wādī Mūsā 94 C6
Wad Medani 100 F5
Wadsworth 132 C1
Wafangdian 80 G3
Wafangdian 82 A4
Wager Bay 122 P3
Wagga Wagga 114 J7
Wahai 87 C3
Wahiawa 132 (2)C2
Wahpeton 126 G1
Waiau 116 D6
Waiblingen 62 E2
Waidhofen 62 K3
Waidhofen an der Ybbs 66 B2
Waigeo 87 D3
Waiheke Island 116 E3
Waihi 116 E3
Waikabubak 87 A4
Waikaia 116 B7
Waikaremoana 116 F4
Waikato 116 E4
Waikawa 116 B8
Wailuku 132 (2)E3
Waimana 116 F4
Waimate 116 C7
Waingapu 114 B1
Wainwright 132 (1)F1
Waiouru 116 E4
Waipara 116 D6
Waipawa 116 F4
Waipiro 116 G4
Waipu 116 E2
Waipukurau 116 F5
Wairoa 116 F4
Waitakaruru 116 E3
Waitaki 116 C7
Waitangi 116 (1)B1
Waitara 116 E4
Waitotara 116 E4
Waiuku 116 E3
Wajima 82 J5
Wajir 106 G3
Wakasa-wan 82 H6
Wakayama 82 H6
Wakeeney 132 G1
Wakefield 56 L8
Wake Island 112 G4
Wakkanai 82 L1
Waku-Kungo 108 B2
Wałbrzych 50 F7
Walcheren 54 F3
Wałcz 50 F4
Waldmünchen 52 H7
Waldshut-Tiengen 62 D3
Walen See 62 E3
Wales 56 J9
Wales Island 122 P3
Walgett 114 J6
Walker Lake 132 C1
Walkerville 114 J7
Wall 126 F2
Wallaceburg 128 D2
Walla Walla 126 C1
Wallis et Futuna 112 J7
Walpole 114 C6
Walsall 56 L9
Walsenburg 126 F3
Walsrode 52 E4
Waltershausen 52 F6
Walvis Bay 108 A4
Wamba 106 D3
Wana 90 J3
Wanaaring 114 H5
Wanaka 116 B7
Wandel Sea 120 A1
Wandingzhen 84 B2
Wando 82 D6
Wanganui 116 E4
Wanganui 116 E4
Wangen 62 E3

Wangerooge 52 D3
Wangiwangi 87 B4
Wan Hsa-la 84 B2
Wanxian 80 D4
Wanyuan 80 D4
Warangal 88 C5
Warburg 52 D5
Ward 116 E5
Wardha 88 C4
Waregem 54 F4
Waremme 54 H4
Waren 52 H3
Warendorf 54 K3
Warka 50 L6
Warla 50 H6
Warmandi 87 D3
Warminster 56 K10
Warm Springs 126 C3
Warren, *Mich., US* 128 D2
Warren, *Oh., US* 128 D2
Warren, *Pa., US* 128 E2
Warrensburg 128 B3
Warrenton 108 C5
Warri 104 F3
Warrington, *UK* 56 K8
Warrington, *US* 130 D3
Warrnambool 114 H7
Warroad 128 A1
Warsaw = Warszawa 50 K5
Warstein 52 D5
Warszawa 50 K5
Warta 50 F5
Warwick 56 L9
Wasatch Range 132 D1
Wasco 132 C1
Washap 90 H4
Washburn Lake 122 K2
Washington 126 B1
Washington, *N.C., US* 128 E3
Washington, *Pa., US* 128 D2
Washington, *Ut., US* 126 D3
Washington D.C. 120 J6
Wassenaar 54 G2
Wasserburg 62 H2
Watampone 87 B3
Watansoppeng 87 A3
Waterbury 128 F2
Waterford 56 E9
Waterloo, *Belgium* 54 G4
Waterloo, *US* 128 B2
Watersmeet 128 C1
Watertown, *N.Y., US* 128 E2
Watertown, *S.D., US* 126 G1
Watertown, *Wis., US* 128 C2
Waterville 128 G2
Watford 54 B3
Watford City 126 F1
Watmuri 87 D4
Watrous 122 K6
Watsa 106 D3
Watseka 130 D1
Watson Lake 132 (1)M3
Wau 106 D2
Waubay Lake 126 G1
Waukegan 128 C2
Waukesha 128 C2
Waurika 130 B3
Wausau 124 J3
Waverley 116 E4
Waverly 128 C3
Wavre 54 G4
Wawa 128 D1
Wāw al Kabīr 100 C2
Waxxari 76 R10
Waycross 130 E3
Waynesboro, *Ga., US* 130 E3
Waynesboro, *Miss., US* 130 D3
Waynesville 128 D3
Weaverville 126 B2
Weber 116 F5
Webi Shaabeelle 106 G3
Webster 126 G1
Weddell Island 142 J9
Weddell Sea 144 (2)A2
Wedel 52 E3
Weed 126 B2
Weert 54 H3
Węgorzewo 50 L3
Wei 80 D4
Weichang 80 F2
Weida 52 H6
Weiden 52 H7
Weifang 80 F3
Weihai 80 G3
Weilburg 52 D6
Weilheim 62 G3
Weimar 52 G6
Weinan 80 D4
Weinheim 52 D7
Weining 80 C5
Weipa 114 H2
Weiser 126 C2
Weißenburg 52 F7
Weißenfels 52 G5
Weißwasser 52 K5
Weixi 84 B1
Wejherowo 50 H3
Welkom 108 D5
Welland 54 B2
Wellawaya 88 D7
Wellesley Islands 114 G3
Wellingborough 58 E1
Wellington, *New Zealand* 116 E5
Wellington, *Colo., US* 126 F2
Wellington, *Kans., US* 130 B2
Wells 126 C2
Wellsboro 128 E2
Wellsford 116 E3
Wellton 132 D2
Wels 62 K2
Welshpool 56 J9
Welwyn Garden City 54 B3
Wenatchee 126 B1
Wenchang 84 E3
Wenga 106 B3
Wenman 140 (1)A1
Wen Xian 80 C4
Wenzhou 80 G5
Werder 52 H4
Werdēr 106 H2
Werl 54 K3
Werneck 52 F7
Wernigerode 52 F5
Werra 52 F6
Wertheim 52 E7
Wesel 54 J3
Wesel Dorsten 52 B5
Weser 52 E4
Wessel Islands 114 G2
West Antarctica 144 (2)GG2
West Bank 94 C4
West Branch 128 D2
West Cape 112 G10
West End 130 F4
Westerland 52 D2
Western Australia 114 D5
Western Cape 108 B6
Western Ghats 88 B5
Western Reef 116 (1)B1
Western Sahara 102 C4
Wester Ross 56 G4
Westerschelde 54 F3
Westerstede 54 K1
Westervoort 54 J3
Westerwald 54 K4
West Falkland 142 J9
West Frankfort 130 D2
West Glacier 126 D1
West Lunga 108 C2
West Memphis 130 C2
Weston 128 D3
Weston-super-Mare 56 K10
West Palm Beach 130 E4
West Plains 128 B3
Westport, *New Zealand* 116 C5
Westport, *Ireland* 56 C8
Westray 56 J2
West Siberian Plain = Zapadno-Sibirskaya Ravnina 74 L3
West-Terschelling 54 H1
West Virginia 128 D3
West Wendover 126 D2
West Yellowstone 126 D2
Wetar 87 C4
Wetaskiwin 122 J6
Wete 106 F5
Wetumpka 130 D3
Wetzlar 52 D6
Wewak 87 F3
Wexford 56 F9
Wexford Harbour 56 F9
Weyburn 124 F2
Weymouth 56 K11
Whakatane 116 F3
Whale Cove 122 N4
Whalsay 56 M1
Whangamata 116 E3
Whangamomona 116 E4
Whangarei 116 E2
Wharfe 56 L7
Wheeler Peak 132 E1
Wheeler Ridge 132 C2
Wheeling 130 E1
Whitby 56 M7
White, *Nev., US* 126 C3
White, *S.D., US* 122 L8
White Bay 122 V6
White Cliffs 114 H6
Whitecourt 122 H6
Whitefish Point 128 C1
Whitehaven 56 J7
Whitehorse 132 (1)L3
White Island 116 F3
Whitemark 114 J8
White Mountain Peak 126 C3
White Mountains 122 S8
Whitemouth 126 G1
White Nile = Bahr el Abiad 100 F5
White River, *Canada* 128 C1
White River, *US* 126 F2
White Sea = Beloye More 70 G1
White Sulphur Springs 126 D1
Whiteville 130 F3
White Volta 104 D3
Whitney 128 E1
Whitstable 54 D3
Whyalla 114 G6
Wichita 130 B2
Wichita Falls 130 B3
Wick 56 J3
Wickenburg 132 D2
Wicklow 56 F9
Wicklow Mountains 56 F8
Widawka 50 J6
Wieluń 50 H6
Wien 62 M2
Wiener Neustadt 62 M3
Wieringermeer Polder 54 G2
Wiesbaden 52 D6
Wiesloch 52 D7
Wiesmoor 52 C3
Wigan 56 K8
Wiggins 126 F2
Wil 62 E3
Wilbur 126 C1
Wilcannia 114 H6
Wildeshausen 52 D4
Wilhelmshaven 52 D3
Wilkes-Barre 128 E2
Wilkes Land 144 (2)U2
Willapa Bay 126 B1
Willemstad 140 D1
Williams, *Australia* 114 C6
Williams, *Ariz., US* 126 D3
Williams, *Calif., US* 126 B3
Williamsburg 128 E3
Williams Lake 122 G6
Williamson 130 E2
Williamsport 128 E2
Willis Group 114 K3
Williston, *South Africa* 108 C6
Williston, *Fla., US* 130 E4
Williston, *N.D., US* 126 F1
Williston Lake 122 G5
Willmar 128 A1
Willow 132 (1)H3
Willowmore 108 C6
Willow River 128 B1
Willow Springs 128 B3
Wilmington, *Del., US* 128 E3
Wilmington, *N.C., US* 130 F3
Wilson 128 E3
Wilson Reservoir 130 B2
Wilson's Promontory 114 J7
Wiluna 114 D5
Winamac 128 C2
Winchester, *UK* 56 L10
Winchester, *Ky., US* 128 D3
Winchester, *Va., US* 128 E3
Windhoek 108 B4
Windischgarsten 62 K3
Windom 128 A2
Windorah 114 H5
Windsor, *Canada* 128 D2
Windsor, *UK* 54 B3
Windsor, *US* 130 F2
Windward Islands 134 N6
Windward Passage 138 D2
Winfield, *Al., US* 130 D3
Winfield, *Kans., US* 132 G1
Wingate Mountains 114 E2
Winisk 122 P5
Winisk 122 P6
Winisk Lake 122 P6
Winnemucca 126 C2
Winner 126 G2
Winnfield 124 H5
Winnipeg 122 M7
Winona, *Minn., US* 128 B2
Winona, *Miss., US* 130 D3
Winschoten 54 K1
Winsen 52 F3
Winslow 132 D1
Winston-Salem 128 D3
Winterberg 52 D5
Winter Harbour 122 J2
Winterswijk 54 J3
Winterthur 62 D3
Winton, *Australia* 114 H4
Winton, *New Zealand* 116 B8
Wisbech 54 C2
Wisconsin 124 H2
Wisconsin 128 B2
Wisconsin Dells 128 C2
Wisconsin Rapids 128 C2
Wisil Dabarow 106 H2
Wisła 50 H4
Wisła 50 H8
Wisłoka 50 L8
Wismar 52 G3
Wissembourg 52 C7
Witney 54 A3
Witten 54 K3
Wittenberge 52 G3
Wittenoom 114 C4
Wittingen 52 F4
Wittlich 54 J5
Wittmund 52 C3
Wittstock 52 H3
Witzenhausen 52 E5
W. J. van Blommesteinmeer 140 G2
Wkra 50 K5
Władysławowo 50 H3
Włocławek 50 J5
Włodawa 50 N6
Wodzisław Śląski 50 H7
Wohlen 62 D3
Wokam 87 D4
Woking 56 M10
Wolf Creek 126 D1
Wolfen 52 H5
Wolfenbüttel 52 F4
Wolf Point 126 E1
Wolfratshausen 62 G3
Wolfsberg 62 K4
Wolfsburg 52 F4
Wolgast 52 J2
Wollaston Lake 122 K5
Wollaston Peninsula 122 H3
Wollongong 114 K6
Wołomin 50 L5
Wolsztyn 50 F5
Wolvega 54 J2
Wolverhampton 56 K9
Wŏnju 82 D5
Wŏnsan 82 D4
Woodbridge 54 D2
Woodburn 126 B1
Woodland 126 B3
Woodstock, *Canada* 128 G1
Woodstock, *UK* 54 A3
Woodstock, *US* 128 C2
Woodville, *New Zealand* 116 E5
Woodville, *Miss., US* 130 C3
Woodville, *Tex., US* 130 C3
Woodward 126 G3
Woody Head 116 E3
Woonsocket, *R.I., US* 128 F2
Woonsocket, *S.D., US* 126 G2
Worcester, *South Africa* 108 B6
Worcester, *UK* 56 K9
Worcester, *US* 124 M3
Wörgl 62 H3
Workington 56 J7
Worksop 54 A1
Worland 126 E2
Worms 52 D7
Wörth 52 D7
Worthing 56 M11
Worthington 124 G3
Wosu 87 B3
Wotu 87 B3
Wowoni 87 B3
Wrangell 122 E5
Wrangell Mountains 122 C4
Wray 124 F3
Wrexham 56 K8
Wrigley 122 G4
Wrocław 50 G6
Września 50 G5
Wu 80 D5
Wubin 114 C6
Wubu 80 E3
Wuchang 80 H2
Wuchuan 80 E2
Wuday'ah 90 E6
Wudu 80 C4
Wuhai 80 D3
Wuhan 80 E4
Wuhu 80 F4
Wüjang 88 C2
Wukari 104 F3
Wuli 88 F2
Wunsiedel 52 G6
Wunstorf 52 E4
Wuppertal 52 C5
Würzburg 52 E7
Wurzen 52 H5
Wushi 76 P9
Wusuli 80 J1
Wutach 62 D3
Wuwei 80 C3
Wuxi 80 G4
Wuxu 84 D2
Wuyuan 80 D2
Wuzhong 80 D3
Wuzhou 84 E2
Wye 56 J9
Wyndham 114 E3
Wynniatt Bay 122 J2
Wyoming 124 E3
Wyszków 50 L5
Wytheville 130 E2

X

Xaafuun 106 J1
Xàbia 60 L6
Xaçmaz 92 N3
Xaidulla 76 P10
Xainza 88 E2
Xai-Xai 108 E4
Xam Nua 84 C2
Xankändi 92 M4
Xanten 54 J3
Xanthi 68 G3
Xapuri 140 D6
Xar Moron 78 K8
Xàtiva 60 K6
Xiahe 80 C3
Xiamen 84 F2
Xi'an 80 D4
Xiangcheng 80 E4
Xiangfan 80 E4
Xianghoang 84 C3
Xianghuang Qi 80 E2
Xiangtan 80 E5
Xianning 80 E5
Xianyang 80 D4
Xiaogan 80 E4
Xiao Hinggan Ling 78 M7
Xiaonanchuan 88 F1
Xichang 84 C1
Xigazê 88 E3
Xi Jiang 80 E6
Xilinhot 80 F2
Xincai 80 E4
Xingcheng 80 G2
Xinghe 80 E2
Xinghua 80 F4
Xingtai 80 F3
Xingu 140 G5
Xingyi 84 C1
Xinhe 76 Q9
Xining 80 C3
Xinjie 80 D3
Xinjin 80 G3
Xinmin 82 B2
Xintai 80 E3
Xinxiang 80 E3
Xinyang 80 E4
Xinyu 80 F5
Xinyuan 76 Q9
Xinzhou 80 E3
Xinzo de Limia 60 C2
Xique Xique 140 J6
Xi Ujimqin Qi 80 F2
Xiushu 80 E5
Xiwu 88 G2
Xixia 80 E4
Xi Xiang 80 D4
Xizang 88 E2
Xizang Gaoyuan 88 D2
Xuanhua 80 E2
Xuchang 80 E4
Xuddur 106 G3
Xuwen 84 E2

Y

Ya'an 80 D3
Yabassi 104 F4
Yabēlo 106 F3
Yablonovyy Khrebet 78 J6
Yabrūd 94 D3
Yabuli 82 E1

Yacuma 140 D6
Yadgir 88 D5
Yagel'naya 76 P4
Yagodnyy 70 N3
Yahk 122 I17
Yakima 126 B1
Yako 104 D2
Yakoma 106 C3
Yaksha 70 L2
Yakumo 82 L2
Yaku-shima 82 F8
Yakutat 132 (1)K4
Yakutsk 78 M4
Yala 84 C5
Yalova 68 M4
Yalta 92 F1
Yalu 82 D3
Yalutorovsk 70 N3
Yamagata 82 L4
Yamaguchi 82 F6
Yamarovka 78 J6
Yambio 106 D3
Yambol 66 P7
Yamburg 76 P4
Yamdena 87 D4
Yammit 94 B5
Yamoussoukro 104 C3
Yampa 126 E2
Yampil' 66 R1
Yamsk 78 S5
Yan'an 80 D3
Yanbu'al Bahr 90 C5
Yancheng 80 G4
Yandun 80 A2
Yangambi 106 C3
Yangbajain 88 F2
Yangdok 82 D4
Yangi Kand 92 N5
Yangjiang 84 E2
Yangon 84 B3
Yangquan 80 E3
Yangshuo 84 E2
Yangtze = Chang Jiang 80 D4
Yangzhou 80 F4
Yanhuqu 88 D2
Yani-Kurgan 76 M9
Yanji 82 E2
Yankton 126 G2
Yano-Indigirskaya Nizmennost' 78 N2
Yanqi 76 R9
Yanqing 80 F2
Yanshan 84 C2
Yanskiy Zaliv 78 N2
Yantai 80 G3
Yaoundé 104 G4
Yap 112 D5
Yapen 87 E3
Yaqui 124 E6
Yaraka 114 H4
Yaransk 70 J3
Yardımcı Burnu 68 E8
Yare 54 D2
Yaren 112 G6
Yarensk 70 J2
Yari 140 C3
Yarkant 90 L2
Yarkovo 70 N3
Yarlung Zangbo 88 F3
Yarmouth 122 T8
Yaroslavl' 70 G3
Yar Sale 70 P1
Yartsevo 70 F3
Yashkul' 70 J5
Yasnyy 70 L4
Yāsūj 95 D1
Yatağan 68 L7
Yathkyed Lake 122 M4
Yatsushiro 82 F7
Yatta 94 C5
Yavari 140 C5
Yawatongguzlangar 76 Q10
Yaya 76 R6
Yayladaği 92 F6
Yazd 90 F3
Yazdān 90 H3
Yazd-e Khvāst 95 E1
Yazoo City 130 C3
Ydra 68 F7
Ye 84 B3
Yea 114 J7
Yecheng 90 L2
Yecla 60 J6
Yefremov 70 G4
Yegendybulak 76 P8
Yei 106 E3
Yekaterinburg 70 M3
Yelets 70 G4
Yelizovo 78 T6
Yell 56 L1
Yellowknife 122 J4
Yellow River = Huang He 80 C3
Yellow Sea 80 G3
Yellowstone 126 E1
Yellowstone Lake 126 D2
Yeloten 90 H2
Yelva 76 J5
Yelwa 104 E2
Yemen 90 D7
Yemetsk 70 H2
Yenakiyeve 70 G5
Yengisar 90 L2
Yenihisar 68 K7
Yenisey 76 S6
Yeniseysk 76 S6
Yeniseyskiy Kryazh 76 S5
Yeo Lake 114 D5
Yeovil 56 K11
Yeppoon 114 K4
Yeraliyev 76 J9
Yerbogachen 78 H4
Yerevan 92 L3
Yerington 126 C3
Yerkov 68 S5
Yerkoy 92 F4
Yermak 76 P7
Yermitsa 70 K1
Yernva 76 J5
Yershov 70 J4
Yerupaja 140 B6
Yerushalayim 94 C5
Yesil' 70 N4
Yeşilhisar 92 F4
Yeşilköy 68 L4
Yessey 76 U4
Yevlax 92 M3
Yevpatoriya 70 F5
Yeyik 76 Q10
Yeysk 70 G5
Yibin 80 C5
Yichang 80 E4
Yichun, *China* 80 E5
Yichun, *China* 80 H1
Yilan 80 H1
Yıldız Dağları 68 K2
Yıldızeli 92 G4
Yinchuan 80 D3
Yingcheng 80 E4
Yingkou 80 G2
Yingtan 80 F5
Yining 76 Q9
Yirga Alem 106 F2
Yitomio 48 M3
Yitulihe 78 L6
Yiyang 80 E5
Yli-Kitka 48 Q3
Ylivieska 48 N4
Ylöjärvi 48 M6
Yoakum 130 B4
Yoboki 100 H5
Yogyakarta 86 E4
Yohuma 106 C3
Yokadouma 104 G4
Yoko 104 G3
Yokohama, *Japan* 82 K6
Yokohama, *Japan* 82 L3
Yokosuka 82 K6
Yokote 82 L4
Yola 104 G3
Yonago 82 G6
Yonezawa 82 L5
Yong'an 84 F1
Yongdeng 80 C3
Yŏnghŭng 82 D4
Yongren 84 C1
Yongxiu 80 F5
Yonkers 128 F2
York, *UK* 56 L8
York, *Nebr., US* 126 G2
York, *Pa., US* 128 E3
Yorkton 122 L6
Yoshkar Ola 70 J3
Yŏsu 82 D6
Yotvata 94 C7
You 84 D2
Youghal 56 E10
Youghal Bay 56 E10
Youngstown 128 D2
Youvarou 104 D1
Yozgat 92 F4
Yreka 126 B2
Ystad 50 C2
Ysyk-Köl 76 P9
Ytre Sula 48 B6
Ytyk-Kyuyel' 78 N4
Yu 84 D2
Yuan 84 C2
Yuanjiang 84 C2
Yuanmou 84 C1
Yuanping 80 E3
Yucatán 134 F5
Yucatan Channel 134 G4
Yuci 80 E3
Yudoma 78 Q4
Yuendumu 114 F4
Yueyang 80 E5
Yugorenok 78 P5
Yugo-Tala 78 S3
Yukagirskoye Ploskogor'ye 78 S3
Yukon 132 (1)E3
Yukon Territory 132 (1)K2
Yukorskiy Poluostrov 76 L4
Yüksekova 92 L5
Yukta 78 H4
Yuli 76 R9
Yulin, *China* 80 D3
Yulin, *China* 84 E2
Yuma 132 C2
Yumen 80 B3
Yumin 76 Q8
Yunak 92 D4
Yuncheng 80 E3
Yun Xian 84 C2
Yuogi Feng 76 R8
Yurga 76 Q6
Yurimaguas 140 B5
Yurla 70 K3
Yuroma 70 J1
Yur'yevets 70 H3
Yu Shan 84 G2
Yushkozero 48 S4
Yushu, *China* 80 B4
Yushu, *China* 80 H2
Yusufeli 92 J3
Yutian 76 Q10
Yuxi 80 C6
Yuyao 80 G4
Yuzawa 82 L4
Yuzhno Kuril'sk 82 N1
Yuzhno-Sakhalinsk 78 Q7
Yuzhno-Sukhokumsk 92 L1
Yuzhnoural'sk 70 M4
Yverdon-les-Bains 62 B4
Yvetot 54 C5

Z

Zaanstad 54 G2
Ząbkowice Śląskie 50 F7
Zabok 62 L4
Zābol 90 H3
Zabrze 50 H7
Zacatecas 132 F4
Zadar 62 L6
Zadonsk 70 G4
Zafora 68 J8
Zafra 60 D6
Zāgheh-ye-Bālā 92 M6
Zagora 102 D2
Zagreb 62 L5
Zagyva 50 K10
Zāhedān 90 H4
Zahirabad 88 C5
Zahlé 94 C3
Zahrān 90 D6
Zaječar 66 K6
Zakamensk 78 G6
Zākhō 92 K5
Zakopane 50 J8
Zakynthos 68 C7
Zakynthos 68 C7
Zala 62 M4
Zalaegerszeg 62 M4
Zalakomár 66 E3
Zalari 78 G6
Zalaszentgrót 62 N4
Zalău 66 L2
Zalim 90 D5
Zalingei 100 D5
Zaliv Aniva 78 Q7
Zaliv Kara-Bogaz Gol 90 F1
Zaliv Kresta 78 Y3
Zaliv Paskevicha 70 L5
Zaliv Shelikhova 78 T5
Zaliv Terpeniya 78 Q7
Zamakh 90 E6
Zambezi 108 C2
Zambezi 108 E3
Zambia 108 D2
Zamboanga 84 G5
Zambrów 50 M5
Zamora 60 E3
Zamość 50 N7
Zanda 88 C2
Zandvoort 54 G2
Zanesville 130 E2
Zangguy 90 L2
Zanjān 92 N5
Zannone 64 H8
Zanzibar 106 F5
Zanzibar Island 106 F5
Zaouatallaz 102 G4
Zaozernyy 76 S6
Zapadnaya Dvina 70 E3
Zapadno-Sibirskaya Ravnina 76 L5
Zapadnyy Sayan 76 S7
Zapata 132 G3
Zapolyarnyy 48 R2
Zaporizhzhya 70 G5
Zaprešić 62 L5
Zaqatala 92 M3
Zara 92 G4
Zarafshan 76 L9
Zaragoza 60 K3
Zarand 95 G1
Zaranj 90 H3
Zarasai 48 P9
Zaraza 140 D2
Zarechensk 48 R3
Zaria 104 F2
Zărneşti 66 N4
Zarqā' 94 D4
Zarqān 95 E2
Żary 50 E6
Zarzadilla de Totana 60 J7
Žatec 50 C7
Zavetnoye 70 H5
Zavidoviči 66 F5
Zavitinsk 78 M6
Zayarsk 76 U6
Zaysan 76 Q8
Zayü 84 B1
Zazafotsy 108 H4
Zbraslav 50 D8
Zēbāk 90 K2
Zēbār 92 L5
Zeebrugge 54 F3
Zefat 94 C4
Zehdenick 52 J4
Zeilona Góra 50 E6
Zeist 54 H2
Zeitz 52 H5
Zelenoborskiy 48 S3
Zelenograd 70 G3
Zelenogradsk 50 K3
Zelenokumsk 92 K1
Zelina 66 D4
Zella-Mehlis 52 F6
Zell am See 62 H3
Zémio 106 D2
Zemlya Alexsandry 76 G1
Zemlya Frantsa-Iosifa 76 J2
Zemlya Vil'cheka 76 L1
Zempoalteptl 134 E5
Zenica 66 E5
Zerbst 52 H5
Zermatt 62 C4
Zeta Lake 122 K2
Zeulenroda 52 G6
Zeven 52 E3
Zevenaar 54 J3
Zeya 78 M6
Zeya 78 M6
Zeydābād 95 F2
Zeyskoye Vodokhranilishche 78 M5
Zgharta 94 C2
Zgierz 50 J6
Zgorzelec 50 E6
Zhailma 70 M4
Zhaksy 70 N4
Zhaksykon 70 N5
Zhaltyr 70 N4
Zhambyl 76 N9
Zhanatas 76 M9
Zhangbei 80 E2
Zhangguangcai Ling 80 H2
Zhangjiakou 80 E2
Zhangling 78 L6
Zhangwu 80 G2
Zhangye 80 B3
Zhangzhou 84 F2
Zhanjiang 84 E2
Zhaodong 78 M7
Zhaoqing 84 E2
Zhaosu 76 Q9
Zhaotong 80 C5
Zhaoyuan 80 H1
Zharkamys 76 K8
Zharkent 76 P9
Zharma 76 Q8
Zharyk 76 N8
Zhaxigang 88 C2
Zheleznogorsk 70 G4
Zhengzhou 80 E4
Zhenjiang 80 F4
Zherdevka 70 H4
Zhetybay 76 J9
Zhezkazgan 76 M8
Zhigalovo 78 H5
Zhigansk 78 L3
Zhilinda 78 J2
Zhob 90 J3
Zholymbet 76 N7
Zhongba 88 D3
Zhongdian 80 B5
Zhongning 80 D3
Zhongshan 84 E2
Zhongze 80 G5
Zhoukou 80 E4
Zhuanghe 80 G3
Zhucheng 80 F3
Zhumadian 80 E4
Zhuo Xian 80 F3
Zhytomyr 70 E4
Žiar 50 H9
Zibo 80 F3
Zichang 80 D3
Zieriksee 54 F3
Ziesar 52 H4
Zighan 100 D2
Zigon 84 B3
Zigong 80 C5
Ziguinchor 102 B6
Zikhron Ya'aqov 94 B4
Žilina 50 H8
Zillah 100 C2
Zima 78 G6
Zimbabwe 108 D3
Zimmi 104 B3
Zimnicea 66 N6
Zinder 104 F2
Zinjibār 100 J5
Zinnowitz 52 J2
Zirc 50 G10
Žirje 64 K5
Zistersdorf 62 M2
Zitava 50 H9
Zittau 52 K6
Ziway Hāyk' 106 F2
Zixing 84 E1
Zlaté Moravce 50 H9
Zlatoust 70 L3
Zlín 50 G8
Zlīţan 102 H2
Zlocieniec 50 F4
Zloczew 50 H6
Złotów 50 G4
Zmeinogorsk 76 Q7
Znamenskoye 76 N6
Żnin 50 G5
Znojmo 62 M2
Zoigê 80 C4
Zolotinka 78 M5
Zomba 108 F3
Zongo 106 B3
Zonguldak 68 P3
Zouar 100 C3
Zouérat 102 C4
Žovka 50 N7
Zrenjanin 66 H4
Zschopau 52 J6
Zug 62 D3
Zugdidi 92 J2
Zuger See 62 D3
Zugspitze 52 F9
Zuid-Beveland 54 F3
Zuni 132 E1
Zunyi 80 D5
Županja 66 F4
Zürich 62 D3
Zuru 104 F2
Žut 64 K5
Zutphen 54 J2
Zuwārah 100 B1
Zuyevka 76 J6
Zvishavane 108 E4
Zvolen 50 J9
Zvornik 66 G5
Zwedru 104 C3
Zweibrücken 54 K5
Zwettl 62 L2
Zwickau 52 H6
Zwiesel 52 J7
Zwoleń 50 L6
Zwolle 54 J2
Zyryanka 78 S3
Zyryanovsk 76 Q8
Żywiec 50 J8